GCSE/KEY STAGE 4
CHEMISTRY

REVISE GUIDES

Mark McElroy and John Sadler

Longman

LONGMAN REVISE GUIDES

SERIES EDITORS:
Geoff Black and Stuart Wall

TITLES AVAILABLE:
Art and Design
Biology*
Business Studies
Chemistry*
Computer Studies
Economics
English*
English Literature*
French
Geography
German
Home Economics
Information Systems*
Mathematics*
Mathematics: Higher Level*
Music
Physics*
Religious Studies
Science*
Sociology
Spanish
Technology*
World History

* new editions for Key Stage 4

Longman Group Ltd,
Longman House, Burnt Mill, Harlow,
Essex CM20 2JE, England
and Associated Companies throughout the world.

© Longman Group UK Ltd 1988
This edition © Longman Group Ltd 1994

All rights reserved; no part of this publication may be reproduced, stored in a retrieval system, or transmitted in any form or by any means, electronic, mechanical, photocopying, recording, or otherwise without either the prior written permission of the Publishers or a licence permitting restricted copying in the United Kingdom issued by the Copyright Licensing Agency Ltd, 90 Tottenham Court Road, London W1P 9HE.

First Published 1988
Second Edition 1994

ISBN 0 582 23773 4

British Library Cataloguing-in-Publication Data

A catalogue record for this book is
available from the British Library

Set by 19QQ in 10/12pt Century Old Style
Printed in Great Britain by William Clowes Ltd., Beccles and London

CONTENTS

Editors' Preface		iv
Acknowledgements		iv
CHAPTER 1	Chemistry: Key Stage 4	1
2	The chemical industry and its place in society	19
3	Elements, compounds and mixtures	31
4	Particles and their behaviour	47
5	Atomic structure and bonding	61
6	The periodic table	79
7	Electrochemistry	99
8	Calculations in chemistry – the mole	121
9	Chemical reactions	137
10	Acids, bases and salts	159
11	Metals and other strong materials	179
12	Chemistry of the non-metals and important compounds	
	12.1 Hydrogen and Water	209
	12.2 Oxygen	218
	12.3 Nitrogen and Sulphur	227
	12.4 Hydrogen chloride, chlorides and chlorine	249
	12.5 Carbon and carbon compounds	259
13	Making a start in organic chemistry: the building blocks	279
14	The organic chemistry of large molecules	295
15	Radioactivity – nuclear chemistry	317
16	The Earth and its atmosphere	325
17	Data	349
Index		361

EDITORS' PREFACE

Longman Revise Guides are written by experienced examiners and teachers, and aim to give you the best possible foundation for success in examinations and other modes of assessment. Much has been said in recent years about declining standards and disappointing examination results. While this may be somewhat exaggerated, examiners are well aware that the performance of many candidates falls well short of their true potential. The books encourage thorough study and a full understanding of the concepts involved and should be seen as course companions and study guides to be used throughout the year. Examiners are in no doubt that a structured approach in preparing for examinations and in presenting course work can, together with hard work and diligent application, substantially improve performance.

Geoff Black and Stuart Wall

ACKNOWLEDGEMENTS

This book has been prepared as a complete guide for all students studying for GCSE: Key Stage 4 and to help those wanting more information on chemistry aspects of Double Science or preparing for a separate GCSE in Science: Chemistry. It can be used either as a revision guide or as a text book to supplement the work you do at school, college or home. The book does not contain experiments for you to do; these will be supplied by your teacher. This book will not replace your teacher, but we hope that it will provide a valuable aid.

The authors are Chief Examiners in GCSE Chemistry and this enables them to pass on useful advice and tips which should be directly beneficial to the student. There is a background chapter on GCSE and this should be helpful, not only to students, but also to parents and to teachers starting out on their careers in Chemistry.

This book contains a contents page and an index. You should make full use of both of these to identify the sections you require. We have supplied answers to all the questions set in the book. Only look at the answers *after* you have attempted your own answer to each question. You should compare your answers with the supplied answers and, if need be, learn from any mistakes you may have made.

The authors' aims are to ensure that you get the best possible grade from your work; their experience in teaching, setting examination papers and marking question papers, together with your own hard work, should help to improve your chances of success.

We are indebted to the following Examination Groups for permission to reproduce questions which have appeared in their examination papers. Whilst permission has been granted to reproduce their questions, the answers, or hints on answers, are solely the responsibility of the authors and have not been provided or approved by a Group.

- Midland Examining Group (MEG)
- Northern Examinations and Assessment Board (NEAB)
- Southern Examining Group (SEG)
- University of London Examinations and Assessment Council (ULEAC)
- University of Cambridge Local Examinations Syndicate (UCLES)
- Welsh Joint Education Committee (WJEC)
- Northern Ireland Schools Examinations and Assessment Council (NISEAC)

We would like to record our thanks to Stuart Wall and Geoff Black from whom we have received a great deal of help and guidance and whose comments have led to improvements on the original manuscript.

Finally, we must thank our families for their patience and their encouragement during the preparation of this book.

Mark McElroy and John Sadler

CHAPTER 1

CHEMISTRY: KEY STAGE 4

ATTAINMENT TARGETS
LEVELS OF ATTAINMENT
CERTIFICATES
DIFFERENT SYLLABUSES
NATURE OF THE ASSESSMENT
TYPES OF QUESTION
COURSEWORK
USING YOUR PRACTICAL SKILLS

GETTING STARTED

The National Curriculum

Under the Education Reform Act (ERA) passed in 1988, every pupil in a state maintained school in England and Wales must study Science to the age of 16.

Key Stages (KS)

The National Curriculum is divided into four **Key Stages** (KS) which are related to age and levels of attainments. KS1 is designed for ages 4 to 7; KS2 for ages 8 to 11; KS3 for ages 12 to 14 and KS4 for ages 15 and 16.

If you choose to take **Chemistry** and you are at a maintained school then you **MUST** also take Biology and Physics in order to fulfil the requirements of the National Curriculum for Science. However, independent schools, overseas centres and post 16 students may take any or all the separate sciences. Every pupil in a state maintained school will be assessed in Science at every key stage.

Programmes of Study (PoS)

The **programmes of studies** state the matter, skills and processes which you must be taught in order for you to meet the objectives set out in the attainment targets during each of your two years leading up to key stage 4 assessment. The syllabuses in individual **chemistry** cover more subject matter and have more details than that required by the Programme of Study for the National Curriculum in Science. An example of part of a Chemistry Programme of Study is:

Pupils should carry out a more detailed* study of selected elements and their compounds, covering metals and non-metals, in order to understand the limitations and different ways in which elements can be classified and ordered in the Periodic Table.

* i.e. more detailed than if chemistry was only being studied as part of 'Science' GCSE.

ESSENTIAL PRINCIPLES

1 ATTAINMENT TARGETS (ATs)

These are objectives setting out the knowledge, skills and understandings that you are expected to develop. There are four **attainment targets** for *Science*:

AT1 Science Investigation
AT2 Life and living processes
AT3 Materials and their properties
AT4 Physical processes

Each attainment target is further sub-divided into ten levels of attainment. **Chemistry** is included in AT3 and a small amount in AT4. Attainment targets are further divided into **Strands** or **Themes**. The four strands for Chemistry are:

(i) The properties, classifications and structure of materials;
(ii) Explanation of the properties of materials;
(iii) Chemical changes;
(iv) The Earth and its atmosphere.

Examination groups have added other strands in order to make a broad and balanced syllabus for Chemistry.

Each strand is divided into levels (see below).

2 LEVELS OF ATTAINMENT

These are the ten levels of attainment defined within EACH attainment target and in most strands within the attainment target. Each level of attainment begins with either the verb description 'know' or 'be able to' or 'understand'.

- *'Know'* means that you must know this as a fact: e.g. you must know that group I of the periodic table contains lithium, sodium and potassium and that these metals have similar properties.

- *'Be able to'* means that you can perform some intellectual task at the 'knowledge level': e.g. you would be able to classify an aqueous solution as acidic if litmus paper turned from blue to red when placed in it.

- *'Understand'* means that you have such an understanding of a concept or theory that you are able to apply the idea to situations outside the range within which the concept was developed: e.g. understand how the formation of chalk helps to decrease the amount of carbon dioxide in the atmosphere.

All **Chemistry syllabuses** will contain the following strands at each of the following levels.

STRAND (i)
The properties, classification and structure of materials

Level 4 be able to classify materials as solids, liquids and gases on the basis of simple properties which relate to their everyday use

Level 5 know how to separate and purify the components of the mixture using physical processes

be able to classify aqueous solutions as acids, alkaline or neutral using indicators

Level 6 be able to distinguish between metallic and non-metallic elements, mixtures and compounds using simple chemical and physical properties

Level 7 be able to relate the properties of a variety of classes of materials to their everyday use

know that the periodic table groups contain elements with similar properties, which depend on their electron structure

Level 8 know the major characteristics of metals and non-metals as reflected in the properties of a range of compounds *(See above to see how this statement relates to the Programme of Study.)*

understand the structure of the atom in terms of protons, neutrons and electrons and how this can explain the existence of isotopes

Level 9 understand how the properties of elements depend on their electronic structure and their position in the periodic table

Level 10 be able to use data on the properties of different materials in order to make evaluative judgments about their use

STRAND (ii)
Explanation of the properties of materials

There are no statements of attainment for levels 4 and 5 in this strand.

Level 6 understand the physical differences between solids, liquid and gases in simple particle terms

Level 7 understand changes of state, including the associated energy changes, mixing and diffusion in terms of the proximity and motion of particles

understand the relationship between volume, pressure and temperature of a gas

understand the difference between elements, compounds and mixtures in terms of atoms, ions and molecules

Level 8 understand radioactivity and nuclear fission and the harmful and beneficial effects of ionising radiations

be able to relate the properties of molecular and giant structures to the arrangement of atoms and ions

Level 9 understand the nature of radioactive decay, relating half-life to the use of radioactive materials

Level 10 understand chemical reactions in terms of energy transfer associated with making and breaking chemical bonds

be able to relate the bulk properties of metals, ceramics, glass, plastics and fibres to simple models and their structure

STRAND (iii)
Chemical changes

Level 4 know that materials from a variety of sources can be converted into new and useful products by chemical reactions

know that the combustion of fuel releases energy and produces waste gases

Level 5 understand that burning and rusting involve a reaction with oxygen

Level 6 understand oxidation processes, including combustion, as reactions with oxygen to form oxides

be able to recognise variations in the properties of metals and make predictions based on the reactivity series

know that some chemical reactions are exothermic and others are endothermic

know about the readily observable effects of electrolysis

Level 7 understand the factors which influence the rate of a chemical reaction

be able to relate knowledge and understanding of chemical principles to manufacturing processes and everyday effects

Level 8 be able to explain the physical and chemical process by which different chemicals are made from oil be able to use symbolic equations to describe and explain a range of reactions including ionic interactions and those occurring in electrolytic cells

Level 9 be able to interpret chemical equations quantitatively

be able to use scientific information from a range of sources to evaluate the social, economic, health and safety and environmental factors associated with a major manufacturing process

Level 10 be able to interpret electrolytic processes quantitatively

STRAND (iv)
The Earth and its atmosphere

Level 4 know how measurements of temperature, rainfall, windspeed and direction describe the weather

know that weathering, erosion and transport lead to the formation of sediments and different types of soil

Level 5 understand the water cycle in terms of the physical processes involved

Level 6 understand how different airstreams give different weather related to their recent path over land and sea

understand the scientific processes involved in the formation of igneous, sedimentary and metamorphic rocks including the timescale over which these processes operate

Level 7 understand how some weather phenomena are driven by energy transfer processes

Level 8 understand how the atmosphere has evolved and how its composition remains broadly constant

be able to interpret evidence of models of formation and deformation of rocks

Level 9 be able to use appropriate scientific ideas to explain changes in the atmosphere that cause various weather phenomena

be able to describe and explain the supporting evidence, in simple terms, for the layered structure of the inner Earth

Level 10 understand the theory of plate tectonics and the contribution this process makes to the recycling of rocks

The relationship between attainment targets, programme of study, strands and levels is shown in the diagram below.

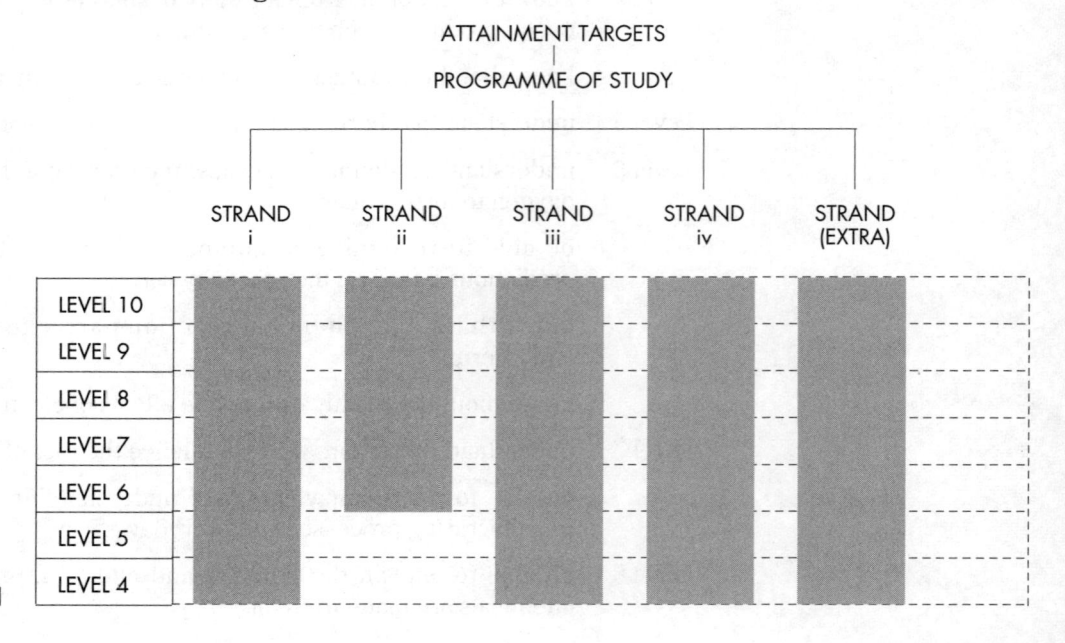

Fig. 1.1

3 > CERTIFICATES

GCSE (Key Stage 4) certificates report on levels 4 to 10.

Each *separate* science leads to a GCSE certificate e.g. Science: Biology; Science: Chemistry; Science: Physics. Success in all three subjects will give you a report of attainment in Science: Double Award as required by law.

Your GCSE certificate for chemistry will show the subject as **SCIENCE: CHEMISTRY**.

The relationship between Levels of Attainment for the National Curriculum and the GCSE grades is given below.

Levels of attainment	Grades
10	A⁺
9	A
8	B
7	C
	D
6	E
5	F
4	G
3	
2	U
1	

Fig. 1.2

4 > DIFFERENT SYLLABUSES

If you are studying at home, you will probably want a copy of the syllabus. If this is not available from your school or college, find out the **syllabus** that you are studying and write for a copy to the appropriate Examining Group (these are given on pages 17-18), remembering to enclose the cost of the syllabus and postage. If you are at a state maintained school you must also take the examination in Biology and Physics.

The syllabuses contain all the information that you will need to know about your examination including details on how many papers you will have to take and the time allowed for each paper.

The new syllabuses are similar in lay-out to previous syllabuses. They all have **aims, assessment objectives, subject content, scheme of assessment, weightings and grade decriptions.**

AIMS

Aims describe the *reasons* for studying chemistry and many of the aims are reflected in the Assessment Objectives and in the Scheme of Assessment. An example of an aim is *'to stimulate pupils' curiosity, interest and enjoyment in chemistry and encourage them to undertake further studies'*. Many aims, such as the example quoted, CANNOT be readily assessed.

ASSESSMENT OBJECTIVES

These are the objectives you *will be tested on* in the examination. They are divided into groups such as ***Scientific Investigations*** and ***Knowledge and Understanding of Chemistry***. Included in the latter is the ability to **communicate, handle data, evaluate and solve problems.** When an examination paper is written it must include questions testing the assessment objectives. Remember that the examination is trying to find out what you *know* about chemistry (not what you do not know). You may have heard the phrase **'positive achievement'**; this means demonstrating what you know, understand and can do in a subject such as chemistry.

SUBJECT CONTENT

The **subject content** will contain all the content from Attainment Target 3 (Materials and their properties) and the 'Environment' section from Attainment Target 4. The Coursework (see later) will contain about 25% of the investigations listed in Attainment Target 1 (scientific investigation).

SCHEME OF ASSESSMENT

There will usually be an examination taken at the end of year 12 (although some assessment schemes are modular) and this, together with your Coursework, is used to give you a grade. On your performance you will be awarded a grade of either A*, A, B, C, D, E, F or G; A* being the highest grade. A very few candidates do not get a grade; make sure you are NOT one of these candidates.

Remember that the examination is designed to find out what you **can do**. Papers are set at different **tiers**. Each tier will target specific levels, although it will be possible to obtain one level above or below the range of levels. You should discuss with your parents and teachers the tier for which you should be entered. The right tier will ensure that you will be able to demonstrate positive achievement. As a guide the table below might help you decide on your level of entry.

Expected Levels of attainment	Recommended tier of entry
4	
5	Basic or Foundation
6	
7	Central or Intermediate
8	
9	Further or Higher
10	

Fig. 1.3

WEIGHTINGS

The weightings of the papers is really for the benefit of the examiners. It is used to ensure that the examination papers cover all the skills required in chemistry and give a good coverage of the syllabus. There is also a weighting of the questions within each paper which will give you an idea of how to allocate your time. If a question has twice as many marks as another question it is worth your spending more time on that question.

SPELLING, PUNCTUATION AND GRAMMAR (SPAG)

In each written examination 5% of the total marks are given for the use of spelling, punctuation and grammar. The marks awarded will be based on your performance in the paper as a whole.

To gain maximum marks for SPAG you must be able to:

- spell, punctuate and use rules of grammar with sufficient accuracy to convey meaning;
- record and store information in an appropriate form;
- use and understand information gained from various sources;
- communicate ideas to others;
- summarise and organise information in order to communicate adequately;
- use appropriate language to explain the results of observations in a variety of contexts.

NATURE OF THE ASSESSMENT

The following tables outline the combinations of examination papers and coursework required by the different examination groups. (Do check with the latest version of your examination group's syllabus as these requirements sometimes change)

CHAPTER 1 **ESSENTIAL PRINCIPLES** 7

Group	Components	Length	Weighting	Description
MEG Chemistry	1 Paper 1 2 Paper 2 3 Paper 3 4 Coursework	90 minutes 120 minutes 135 minutes	75% 75% 75% 25%	Short answer and structured questions, some will require extended responses
All questions in all papers are compulsory Candidates for the basic tier take components Candidates for the central tier take components Candidates for the further tier take components			1 and 4 2 and 4 3 and 4	
Salters	Paper 1	90 minutes	60%	Multiple choice Short answer Structured
	Paper 2	135 minutes	60%	Structured Free response
	sba		40%	
Paper 1 together with sba is used to access levels 4 to 7 Paper 2 with sba is used to access levels 7 to 10				
Nuffield	Paper 1	90 minutes	75%	Short answer structured questions
	Paper 2	120 minutes	75%	Structured questions
	Paper 3	135 minutes	75%	Structured question and free response
	sba		25%	
Paper 1 together with sba is used to access levels 3 to 7 (basic tier) Paper 2 together with sba is used to access levels 5 to 9 (central tier) Paper 3 together with sba is used to access levels 7 to 10 (further tier)				
NEAB Syllabus A	Paper 1	120 minutes	80%	Multiple choice Short answer Structured
	Paper 2	90 minutes	50%	Structured Free response
	Practical	School based	20%	
For candidates who take paper 2, paper 1 will be weighted at 30% Levels 4 to 7 will be awarded on paper 1 and practical Levels 4 to 10 will be awarded on papers 1, 2 and the practical The scheme of assessment is the same for syllabus B except that the weightings are: For levels 4 to 7, paper 1 75%, sba 25% For levels 4 to 10, paper 1 25%, paper 2 50% and sba 25%				

Fig. 1.4 Assessment in the different syllabuses.

Group	Components	Length	Weighting	Description
NISEAC	1P 1Q 1R 2P 2Q 2R Coursework	60 minutes 120 minutes 120 minutes 90 minutes 120 minutes 120 minutes	38% 38% 38% 38% 38% 38% 24%	20 objective questions and a number of structured questions. All questions will be compulsory
	Candidates for the P tier take components 1 P, 2 P and Coursework Candidates for the Q tier take components 1 Q, 2 Q and Coursework Candidates for the R tier take components 1 R, 2 R and Coursework			
SEG	1 Coursework 2 Foundation 3 Intermediate 4 Higher 5 Foundation 6 Intermediate 7 Higher	75 minutes	20% 40% 40% 40% 35% 35% 35%	Structured questions and some extended responses
	Candidates for the Foundation tier take components Candidates for the Intermediate tier take components Candidates for the Higher tier take components		1,2 and 5 1,3 and 6 1,4 and 7	
ULEAC	Foundation Tier Paper 1 Paper 2F Paper 3F Paper 4F Intermediate Tier Paper 1 Paper 2I Paper 3I Paper 4I Higher Tier Paper 1 Paper 2H Paper 3H Paper 4H	 sba 90 minutes 90 minutes 90 minutes sba 90 minutes 90 minutes 90 minutes sba 90 minutes 90 minutes 90 minutes	 25% 25% 25% 25% 25% 25% 25% 25% 25% 25% 25% 25%	There will be a variety of questions on each written paper including structured questions involving both short answer and extended prose
	Foundation tier is aimed at levels 4 to 6 Intermediate tier is aimed at levels 6 to 8 Higher tier is aimed at levels 8 to 10			
WJEC	Option P Option Q Option R	90 minutes 120 minutes 150 minutes sba	75% 75% 75% 25%	Short answer Structured Structured and free response
	Levels 4 to 6 will be awarded on Option P Levels 6 to 8 will be awarded on Option Q Levels 8 to 10 will be awarded on Option R			

Fig. 1.4 contd.

SCHOOL BASED ASSESSMENT: INVESTIGATIONS

The Attainment Target 1 – Scientific investigations – is the same for all the separate sciences and has the same three strands:

Strand (i)   Ask questions, predict and hypothesise.
Strand (ii) Observe, measure and manipulate variables.
Strand (iii) Interpret their results and evaluate scientific evidence.

You must attempt at least one assessed investigation and show positive achievement in all three strands if you are to satisfy the requirements of the examination.

The strands are divided into levels.

Strand (i)   Ask questions, predict and hypothesise

You should carry out investigations in which you:

Level 4   ask questions, suggest ideas and make predictions, based on some relevant prior knowledge, in a form which can be investigated

Level 5   formulate hypotheses where the causal link is based on scientific knowledge, understanding or theory

Level 6   use scientific knowledge, understanding or theory to predict relationships between continuous variables

Level 7   use scientific knowledge, understanding or theory to predict the relative effect of a number of variables

Level 8   use scientific knowledge, understanding or theory to generate quantitative predictions and a strategy for the investigation

Level 9   use a scientific theory to make quantitative predictions and organise the collection of valid and reliable data

Level 10 use scientific knowledge of laws, theories and models to develop hypotheses which seek to explain the behaviour of objects and events you have studied.

Strand (ii)   Observe, measure and manipulate variables

You should carry out investigations in which you:

Level 4   carry out a fair test in which you select and use appropriate instruments and measure quantities such as volume and temperature

Level 5   choose the range of each of the variables involved to produce meaningful results

Level 6   consider the range of factors involved, identify the key variables and those to be controlled and/or taken account of, and make qualitative or quantitative observations involving fine discrimination

Level 7   manipulate or take account of the relative effect of two or more independent variables

Level 8   select and use measuring instruments which provide the degree of accuracy commensurate with the outcome you have predicted

Level 9   systematically use a range of investigatory techniques to judge the relative effect of the factors involved

Level 10 collect data which are sufficiently valid and reliable to enable you to make a critical evaluation of the law, theory or model

Strand (iii)   Interpret their results and evaluate scientific evidence

You should carry out investigations in which you:

Level 4   draw conclusions which link patterns in observations or results to the original question, prediction or idea

Level 5   evaluate the validity of conclusions by considering different interpretations of experimental evidence

Level 6   use results to draw conclusions, explain the relationship between variables and refer to a model to explain results

Level 7 use observations or results to draw conclusions which state the relative effects of the independent variables and explain the limitations of the evidence obtained

Level 8 justify each aspect of the investigation in terms of contribution to the overall conclusion

Level 9 analyse and interpret the data obtained, in terms of complex functions where appropriate, in a way which demonstrates an appreciation of the uncertainty of evidence and the tentative nature of conclusions

Level 10 use and analyse the data obtained to evaluate the law, theory or model in terms of the extent to which it can explain the observed behaviour

The level that will be counted towards the final assessment will be the highest level that has been achieved in that strand. You may hand-write, type or word process your work. Remember to store all your material very carefully.

6 TYPES OF QUESTION

Several types of questions are used in Key Stage 4 (GCSE) including objective questions, structured questions and free-response questions.

Questions are targeted at specific levels and strands within the National Curriculum. You should be able to identify the level simply by looking at the strands described in the previous chapter. Thus 8 (ii) would mean that the question is used to test strand (ii) at level 8.

OBJECTIVE QUESTIONS

The objective questions commonly used are either multiple choice questions or matching pairs.

Answers to multiple choice questions are usually made by marking a special answer sheet with a pencil. So make sure you take a soft pencil (at least HB) in to the examination and a rubber. A ruler is also useful to make sure you are making a mark against the question you are answering. Remember there is only one correct answer, therefore only make one mark. You have to answer all the questions. Don't try to work out the answers in your head too much; instead work out the answer either on rough paper or on the question paper.

Which of the following elements is a halogen? (Level 7, Strand (i))

A carbon B copper C iodine D sodium
A   B   C   D
( )   ( )   (–)   ( )

You have made a mark in C to indicate that your answer is C. (This is the correct answer!)

When you are allowed to start your objective paper, work through it quickly answering as many questions as you can and mark on the paper the questions you have missed out. Then go through the paper again, spending time over the questions you could not tackle first time. If you still find there are questions you cannot do, cross out any answers you know are incorrect and make a guess from those that are left.

The other type of objective question used is matching pairs.

The questions below consist of four possible answers followed by a list of numbered questions. For each question select the best answer. Each answer may be used once, more than once or not at all.

A argon B carbon dioxide C nitrogen D oxygen

Select from A to D the gas which

(1) is the third most abundant gas in air
(2) is produced together with water, when methane is burnt in air
(3) contains only one atom, per molecule
(4) is a by-product of the thermal decomposition of limestone.

In case you tried the questions the answers are:
1 A; 2 B; 3 A; 4 B

NOTE that the SAME answer can occur more than once, and that not all the responses were used. The correct answer is often called the *key*.

> **Objective or multiple-choice questions.**

STRUCTURED QUESTIONS

In these questions you will be asked very clearly for the answer the examiner is expecting. There is usually a *theme* in a structured question. The number of marks for each section is in brackets; you should write your answers to these questions in the spaces provided on the question paper using blue or black biro (ink tends to smudge). DO NOT USE OTHER COLOURED BIROS – examiners mark in red and they use other colours for checking papers.

The compound calcium carbonate occurs in nature as marble.
- (a) Name two other forms of calcium carbonate which occur in nature. (2)
- (b) Write down the chemical formula of calcium carbonate. (1)
- (c) Carbon dioxide can be detected using an aqueous solution of a calcium compound:
  - (i) Write down the common name of the aqueous solution of the calcium compound which is used to test for carbon dioxide. (1)
  - (ii) What is the chemical name for this compound? (1)

> Structured questions.

ESSAY QUESTIONS

The more difficult papers for chemistry tend to have essay questions. These questions usually draw on knowledge from various parts of the course. Make a plan of your essay and write neatly and legibly. There is no need to write pages; an essay that is short and to the point will gain as many marks as a long-winded answer. Essay questions are written either on the question paper or on paper supplied to you. Again, if your answers are to be written on the examination question paper use a biro.

> Essay or free-response questions.

Explain why the following cause pollution of our environment; (a) the discharge of acid waste into the rivers, (b) the incomplete combustion of petrol in car engines.

Note that the question is about pollution – but you do not have to write everything you know about pollution. Part (a) has nothing to do with acid rain, so don't waste time writing about it. Part (b) is about the incomplete combustion of petrol so there is no need to mention lead compounds in petrol. In other words, **you must read the question**.

Most questions begin with one of the following words. It is useful to know what these words mean!

Terms used in question papers

'**Calculate**' is used when a numerical answer is required. Working must be shown.
'**Define**' is intended literally, it means 'give the exact meaning of'.
'**Describe**' means to write down fully what you would do or observe.
'**Determine**' means that you must use the information given to work out the answer.
'**Explain**' means you must give some reasons.
'**Find**' is often used in place of 'calculate' or 'determine'.
'**Outline**' means keep your answer brief, only essential detail is required.
'**Predict**' means that you have to make a logical deduction either from your own knowledge or from information in the question, or from both.
'**State**' means that there is no unique answer but you are to give your own idea of the best answer.
'**Suggest**' means that there is no unique answer but you are to give your own idea of the best answer.
'**Write down**' is meant literally. You just write down the answer.

> Be familiar with these words.

Questions are targeted at specific levels and strands within the National Curriculum. You should be able to identify the level simply by looking at the strands decribed in this chapter. Thus 8 (ii) would mean that the question is used to test strand (ii) at level 8.

MATHEMATICAL REQUIREMENTS

Some of the questions in chemistry require some mathematics. The mathematical skills required will be those that you have learnt from your studies in your National Curriculum Mathematics course. The following list is not exhaustive but will act as a guide to the skills that you will require.

> Some useful mathematical skills.

- whole numbers; odd, even
- estimation/approximation to obtain reasonable answers
- the four rules applied to whole numbers and decimal fractions
- measures of weight, length, area, volume and capacity in current terms
- time: 24 hour and 12 hour clock
- reading of clocks and dials
- use of tables and charts
- interpretation and use of graphs in practical situations
- drawing graphs from given data
- simple solid figures
- collection, classification and tabulation of statistical data
- reading, interpretation and drawing simple inference from tables and statistical diagrams
- construction of bar charts and pictograms
- whole numbers: prime, square
- factors, multiples, idea of square root
- directed numbers in a practical situation
- vulgar and decimal fractions and percentages; equivalence between these forms
- cases; conversion from vulgar to decimal fraction with the help of a calculator
- scales, including map scales
- elementary ideas and applications of common measures of rate
- efficient use of a pocket calculator; application of appropriate checks of accuracy

Data books

A candidates' data book is available for use in the final examination. It contains data that you are not expected to remember. You should make sure that you are familiar with this booklet prior to the examination.

Units

You should be familiar with the following units and prefixes:

Quantity	Base Unit	Symbol
electric current	ampere	A
length	metre	m
mass	kilogram	kg
temperature	kelvin Celsius Centigrade	K °C
energy (heat)	joule	J
volume	litre or cubic decimetre	l or dm^3

Multiple	Prefix	Symbol
10^6	mega	M
10^3	kilo	k
10^{-2}	centi	c
10^{-3}	milli	m
10^{-6}	micro	μ
10^{-9}	nano	n
10^{-12}	pico	p

Fig. 1.5

Thus, kilometres would be represented by km, millilitres by ml and micro-seconds by µs.
You will be allowed to use a calculator.

Graphs

Most graphs that you draw in chemistry will be **straight lines**. The only *exceptions* are likely to be rate graphs (plotting mass or volume against time), radioactive decay (plotting count against time). Examples of **straight-line** graphs are:

(a) plotting mass of one element against another (to find formulae);
(b) electrolysis (plotting mass or volume against time);
(c) precipitation reactions (plotting mass precipitated against volume or mass added);
(d) plotting heat combustion of various hydrocarbons against number of carbon atoms.

With the more difficult papers you have to select your own scale for your graph. Make sure that your graph almost fills the graph paper. On other papers, the scales will be given to you. Make sure you understand the scale used.

Diagrams

It is difficult to draw diagrams clearly and accurately and you should practise. Diagrams (see Fig. 1.6) should be two-dimensional and you should **not** draw the bench, the stands used for holding the apparatus or people. The diagram must represent **real** apparatus. The apparatus should be labelled in pencil using **full names** of chemicals (i.e not formulae). Unless you are collecting a gas in a syringe, make sure the apparatus is not completely sealed (it would blow up!).

When water is added to calcium dicarbide, calcium hydroxide and the gas ethyne are formed. Ethyne contains impurities which can be removed by passing the gas through aqueous copper(II) sulphate solution. Ethyne is insoluble in water. Draw a labelled diagram of the apparatus you would use to prepare and collect pure ethyne.

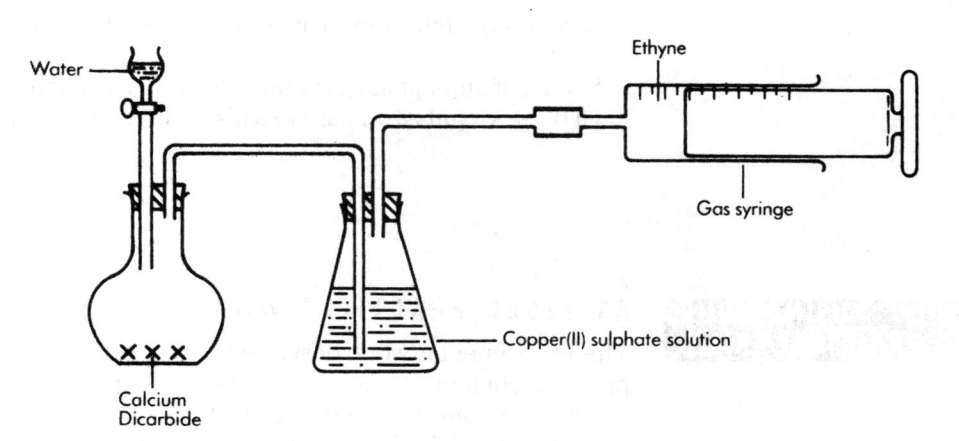

❝❝ A clear, well-labelled diagram is important. ❞❞

Fig. 1.6

Note that in this diagram a tap funnel has been used to prevent gas from escaping; the gas will bubble through copper(II) sulphate; there are corks in both flasks; the tubes are seen to pass through the corks; the gas is collected in a gas syringe (it could have been collected over water); lines are used for labelling (not arrows); the names of chemicals are written in full.

Study the other diagrams in this book; we have been very careful to make them accurate.

ADVICE

One of the best ways to improve your technique in answering questions is by practice. You should attempt as many questions as you can and check that you have got the answers right. In the objective questions make sure you know *why* the other answers given are wrong.

Learn all definitions. Learn formulae and how to write both word and symbol equations. Learn the charge on ions. Learn the test for gases. Practise looking for patterns. But there is no need to learn the periodic table! You will be given this in the examination.

Take into the examination: biros (either blue or black), calculator (make sure it is working properly beforehand, and that the battery is not about to run out), compass, pen (make sure that it is full of ink or that you have spare cartridges), a sharpened pencil, pencil sharpener, rubber, ruler and a watch. You will be supplied with writing paper, rough paper and blotting paper.

Try all the **exam-type questions** at the end of each topic-based chapter in this book *before* looking at the outline answers. Look carefully at the **examiner comments** on actual **student answers** to past exam questions throughout this book. Also try the **Review Sheets** which present questions at the end of each chapter to test your reading of that chapter. You can refer back to material in the chapter itself to find answers to these questions.

7 > COURSEWORK

Throughout the years of taking your Key Stage 4 (GCSE) examination in chemistry your coursework will be assessed by your teacher. You will get used to your teacher coming round the class with a clip-board in his or her hand. If you are having problems, do not hesitate to ask your teacher. It is better to do this than to score no marks in the assessment! In practical work always wear goggles and tie back long hair. Try to work tidily and logically. Do **not** start your experiment until you have understood what you are doing. Do not let your partner do all the work – **you** must become competent as well as him or her.

The Attainment Target 1 – Scientific investigations – is the same for all the separate sciences and has the same three strands:

Strand (i)   Ask questions, predict and hypothesise
Strand (ii) Observe, measure and manipulate variables
Strand (iii) Interpret their results and evaluate scientific evidence

You must attempt at least one assessed investigation and show positive achievement in all three strands if you are to satisfy the requirements of the examination.

8 > USING YOUR PRACTICAL SKILLS

ASSESSED PRACTICAL WORK

The experimental work described so far forms the basis of the internally assessed practical content of your GCSE course. Coursework will be worth 25% of your final mark. The courses are designed to allow you to show your ability in a range of experimental skills. You will be able to demonstrate that you can:

(i) Design investigations – suggest ideas or statements to investigate. Identify a problem based on your chemical knowledge and understanding and consider how it can be investigated.

(ii) Carry out investigations – use your investigative skills to observe, measure and manipulate variables in your investigation.

(iii) Interpret the results of your investigations – evaluate your findings in relation to your original design idea. Suggest improvements to the method based on your experience in carrying out the investigation.

PUTTING THESE CRITERIA INTO PRACTICE

You may be asked to suggest your own investigation. However, it is more likely that you will be given one to investigate. Consider the following:

You are asked to design and carry out an investigation to test the efficiency of three kettle-fur removing solutions, which are acids. You are told that kettle-fur is a form of calcium carbonate. You are also given the following equation as a guide to how these chemical solutions act.

$$\text{fur remover} + \text{fur} \rightarrow \text{solution} + \text{carbon dioxide}$$

(i) Designing the investigation

(a) First you must understand the problem and the information you have been given. It would help if you could try a preliminary experiment with one of the fur-removers and a little fur – mix them in a test tube. If this is not possible, you will see from the equation that a gas will be given off in the process of fur-removal.

So, measuring the gas given off might be an idea to pursue.

(b) Now you must interpret the meaning of 'efficiency'. Does most efficient mean fastest removal? Or does it mean removal of the most fur with the least fur-remover? You could decide to investigate one or both of these interpretations depending on the time available or your knowledge of chemistry.

Both can, in fact be investigated using the same apparatus so you must now choose that. Since the gas given off tells you that the fur-remover is working, the speed of the process is measured by the rate of evolution of gas. You now need to:

(i) choose a vessel to put the fur-remover and kettle-fur into;
(ii) choose a means of measuring the volume of gas given off;
(iii) choose how to measure the rate at which the gas is given off

(c) There are variables to identify and control in this investigation. They are:
- Temperature – the fur-remover may be used at any temperature between room temperature and the boiling point of water simply by switching on the kettle with the solution inside. Would fur-removal be more efficient at higher or lower temperatures? We can find out.
- Concentration of the fur-removing solution – it could be used 'from-the-bottle' but could also be diluted. So different dilutions could be investigated.
- State of the kettle-fur – are you given some genuine kettle-fur or are you given calcium carbonate (its chemical equivalent?) The fur-removers must each be tested against the same type of calcium carbonate for a fair comparison. If no genuine kettle-fur is available, calcium carbonate in a lump or in a powdered form can be chosen. If powdered, the sample must come from the same source each time. If lumps, the size must be the same for each experiment.

(d) The method of carrying out the investigation must be planned

> A fair comparison could be made by choosing room temperature, fur-remover straight from the bottle and three equal masses of the same sized lumps of calcium carbonate (usually in the form of marble chippings).

If we take the suggestion in the box above we will need a thermometer, a measuring cylinder, a chemical balance, a supply of marble chipping all of the same size, a vessel to carry out the reaction in and a stop-clock.

(ii) Carrying out the investigation

(a) Decide first what results you will be recording. You will need to measure the volume of the carbon dioxide gas collected in the gas syringe, say, every minute. You should record the temperature of the fur-remover to ensure that all are the same.

(b) Next decide how your results will be recorded. In this investigation the gas volumes are best recorded in a table with two columns. One column is for time in minutes, the other column is for gas volume in cm^3.

(c) Now carry out the investigation. Put a weighed sample of the marble chippings into the flask. Add, say, $10\ cm^3$ of one fur-remover and quickly stopper the flask. Start the stop-clock as the flask is stoppered. Record the volume of gas in the gas syringe every minute until the reaction stops and the reading becomes constant. Repeat the experiment to see if the results are consistent.

(d) Repeat the whole experiment using each of the other two fur-removers.

(iii) Interpreting the results

(a) The results as recorded – six tables – are difficult to interpret as they stand. They become easier to understand if they are plotted on a graph. Any set of results with two variables can be plotted on a graph.

(b) Graphs show trends and patterns more clearly than tables.

Usually, the *independent variable* (the one whose values are chosen by the investigator – in this case time) is plotted along the horizontal or *x*-axis. The *dependent variable* (so-called because the volume of gas depends on the times chosen to make the measurement) is plotted vertically on the *y*-axis.

The type of graph you will get is shown in Fig. 1.7.

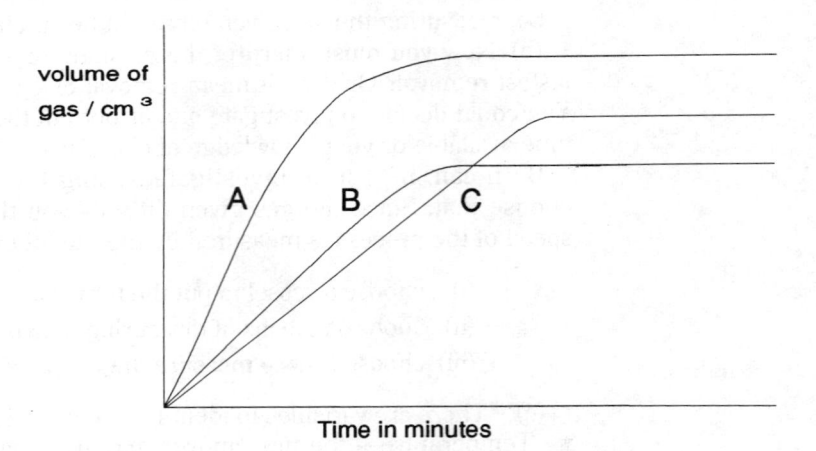

Fig. 1.7

(c) This set of graphs can be interpreted as follows.

The fur-removers are A, B and C.

The steeper the graph, the faster the gas is given off. The faster the gas is given off the faster the marble chippings (kettle-fur) is reacting and so dissolving.

Clearly the order of rate of dissolving marble chippings (removing kettle-fur) is

$$A > B > C$$
(fastest)   (slowest)

In terms of speed of removal as a measure of efficiency, A is the most efficient and C the least efficient.

Another feature of the graph needs interpretation however. Fur-remover A gave off more gas than the other two for the same volume used. What does this mean? The gas was not only produced faster but there was more of it. More gas means more marble dissolved. So the fur-remover which produces most gas will also remove most fur.

The graphs can now be interpreted in the second way to indicate that A removes more fur than C which removes more fur than B. So efficiency measured by the amount of fur removed gives the order

$$A > C > B$$
(dissolves most fur)   (dissolves least fur)

A final step is possible. The combined efficiency rating gives A more efficient than B or C, since it is both faster at removing fur and also removes more of it for a given volume of the solution used. No overall decision can be made about B and C since each is better than the other in either speed of action or mass of fur removed per unit volume of solution used.

(d) What suggestions can be made for improving the investigation?

It might be found that some of the carbon dioxide gas escapes before the bung can be placed in the flask. The way to overcome this is to place the fur-removing solution in a small test tube and hang it in the flask by a thread. Then the bung can be inserted taking care not to tip out the solution. Once the bung is on, the flask can be tilted to tip the solution out onto the marble chippings. This method has the added advantage of allowing a free hand to start the stop-clock.

(e) Extending the investigation.

(i) The investigations could be carried out at higher temperatures such as those that could be achieved in a kettle. A water bath would be used for obtaining temperatures up to about 80°C.

(ii) The fur-removers could be used at different concentrations. However, because these would be more dilute than the original, it is unlikely – though not entirely impossible – that the order of speed-efficiency would change.

SAFETY IN THE LABORATORY

In planned investigations like the one described above there are safety matters to consider.

(i) You should find out the hazards of all the chemicals you will be using and discover the safest way to use them. Always wear eye protection when carrying out experiments with chemicals.

(ii) Always support your apparatus where possible to free your hands for carrying out the experiments.

(iii) Be extra attentive if heating is involved. Be aware what a mishap might do and where your fellow students are working so that an accident will not harm them too.

(iv) Be as tidy as possible. Do not have books or personal belongings in the area where you are carrying out your experiment. Mop up liquid and solid spills as soon as they occur. Do not leave unclamped pieces of apparatus where it can be easily knocked off the bench onto the floor or into a sink.

(v) Do not rush; think about each operation and stop if you cease to understand what you are doing. Consult a teacher if you get into difficulties.

(vi) If an accident does occur seek your teacher's help immediately.

Experimental chemistry is usually interesting, sometimes exciting, rarely dull. The more you know of chemistry and its principles, the more delight you will find in practical work. Experimental work is the heart of chemistry. Whether qualified chemists are preparing substances, analysing them or researching new compounds, they are doing the sort of investigations that you will do at school or college. If you enjoy chemistry and succeed at it you may be joining them one day.

EXAMINATION GROUP ADDRESSES

ULEAC **University of London Examinations and Assessment Council**
Stewart House, 32 Russell Square, London, WC1B 5DN
Tel: 071 331 4000
Fax: 071 631 3369

MEG **Midland Examining Group**
1 Hills Road, Cambridge, CB1 2EU
Tel: 0223 61111
Fax: 0223 460278

NEAB **Northern Examinations and Assessment Board**
Devas Street, Manchester, M15 6EX
Tel: 061 953 1180
Fax: 061 273 7572

NISEAC **Northern Ireland Schools Examinations and Assessment Council**
Beechill House, 42 Beechill Road, Belfast, BT8 4RS
Tel: 0232 704666
Fax: 0232 799913

SEG **Southern Examining Group**
Stag Hill House, Guildford, GU2 5XJ
Tel: 0483 506505
Fax: 0483 300152

WJEC **Welsh Joint Education Committee**
245 Western Road, Cardiff, CF5 2YX
Tel: 0222 561231
Fax: 0222 571234

IGCSE **International General Certificate of Secondary Education**
University of Cambridge Local Examinations Syndicate
1 Hills Road, Cambridge, CB1 2EU
Tel: 0223 61111
Fax: 0223 460278

When contacting the examination Groups you will need to ask for the Publications Department and request an order form to be sent to you. On the order form indicate exactly which syllabus you are studying and be prepared to send a cheque or postal order with your order.

CHAPTER 21

THE CHEMICAL INDUSTRY AND ITS PLACE IN SOCIETY

THE ECONOMICS OF THE CHEMICAL INDUSTRY

THE WORK OF THE CHEMIST

TECHNOLOGICAL, SOCIAL AND ENVIRONMENTAL ASPECTS

POLLUTION

GETTING STARTED

As a reader of a GCSE guide, you will not be completely new to the study of chemistry. You will already have become aware of many of the achievements of professional chemists. One of the most important jobs of chemists in industry is to convert naturally occurring substances (raw materials) into more useful materials.

From these raw materials *industrial chemists* can separate elements, compounds or mixtures to make them into such everyday products as plastics, fertilisers, medicines, detergents, insecticides, dyes and paints.

Chemists not only *make* useful substances, they also use their knowledge and technical expertise to *analyse* substances to discover what is present in them. *Analytical chemists* play an important role in the fields of forensic science (crime detection), medical diagnosis, food inspection and quality control.

However, a very large section of the chemical industry relies upon *just five basic raw materials* for its huge range of products:

- crude oil/natural gas;
- ores and minerals (salt, limestone, metallic ores, sulphur);
- water;
- air;
- energy.

These sources of chemicals will be considered in detail in the following chapters. They are our chemical *resources*.

Unfortunately, the process of making useful chemicals almost always results in some undesired by-products. If these are not carefully handled they easily become pollutants. The chemical industry is not alone in this. Consider the unwanted by-products of everyday human activities – human and animal excrement, rotten and waste vegetable matter, waste paper, plastic packing, glass etc. All are potential pollutants if not properly disposed of or recycled. We realise the problem of waste more now than ever. There is a growing industry researching and developing methods of using waste or by-product materials.

1 THE ECONOMICS OF THE CHEMICAL INDUSTRY

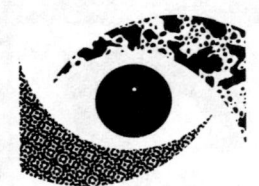

ESSENTIAL PRINCIPLES

(A) THE SITING OF A CHEMICAL PLANT

If you were to plot on a map the positions of the main chemical plants in the country, you would soon realise that the *sites* had been very carefully chosen. A chemical company must compete against other companies to sell its products. It must make its chemicals as cheaply as, or more cheaply than, its competitors, or it will not be profitable and will fail. An important factor in the profitability of a chemical plant is the site chosen. The main factors to consider are:

- easy access to *cheap* raw materials – ores, water, fuel and power;
- good transport – ships or rail for large tonnages, roads for smaller quantities;
- a good supply of skilled labour nearby.

A little thought given to these points will show how obvious they are. The siting of several important plants in the chemical industry will be considered in the following chapters. It should be realised, however, that the factors which influence the choice of site change continuously. In the days of poor transport, it was important for a chemical plant to be close to supplies of its raw materials. Houses, even small towns, would then often be built nearby for the labour force. Today, with more effective transport systems, it might be cheaper to site a factory close to the labour force and transport raw materials to the site. If the raw materials come from overseas, then the site may be close to a port where there is also a suitable labour force.

(B) RAW MATERIALS

For a chemical product to sell well it must be as cheap as its competitor's product – or cheaper. It is a big advantage to be able to buy the *raw materials* as cheaply as possible by building the plant *close to their source*. An iron works should be close to sources of coal, iron ore and limestone. A nitric acid plant must be built close to an ammonia plant. Compound fertilisers must be made where the components of the mixture are manufactured. Aluminium smelters would only be sited where electricity was cheap and bauxite could be cheaply shipped in from overseas, and so on.

(C) FUEL

The choice of *fuel* will depend upon its *cost* and also the ease of maintenance of heating equipment. Gas, oil and electricity are easy to 'transport' but coal requires a nearby mine or a good transport system. Here, again, correct siting can help. A plant producing heat as a by-product of its chemical processes may be in a position to provide heat energy to another plant nearby. This is just *one* reason why parts of the chemical industry tend to congregate in one area, such as Teesside.

(D) THE SEARCH FOR INCREASED EFFICIENCY

Finally, success can often depend upon a very small increase in *efficiency of operation* of the plant. *Catalysts* play an important role here. They can be expensive, but their role is to speed up chemical reactions and help to reduce costs. They are required in relatively small quantities and, with more research, even the small quantities now used will be reduced further. In theory, extremely minute amounts of catalysts could provide effective action if they could be spread *a mere one atom thick* on large surface areas of support material.

Since chemical reactions are mainly *exothermic*, there will frequently be a great deal of 'waste heat'. The sale or re-use of this 'waste heat' can sometimes be responsible for high profitability or low cost of the product (see Chapter 11). A plant requiring energy can be built close to one producing excess energy. Both plants can benefit from the sale of energy from one to the other.

2 > THE WORK OF THE CHEMIST

Chemists make use of a variety of reaction processes and separation techniques to convert natural resources into useful products.

The *processes* used include:

- dissolving
- precipitation
- crystallisation
- thermal decomposition
- oxidation – often combustion
- reduction
- electrolysis
- hydrolysis
- dehydration
- neutralisation

❝❝ Find examples of each of these processes in other chapters of this Guide and write them in your notebook for future reference. ❞❞

The *techniques* used include:

- filtration or centrifugation
- distillation and fractional distillation
- solvent extraction
- chromatography
- sublimation

❝❝ Try to draw diagrams of the apparatus used in each of these techniques *from memory*. After you have drawn them, look up the correct diagrams to check your work. ❞❞

The *techniques* of the chemist are the subject of Chapter 3. The chemical *processes* used by chemists will be discussed as they arise in the other chapters of this book.

3 > TECHNOLOGICAL, SOCIAL AND ENVIRONMENTAL ASPECTS

Britain's chemical industry earns money for the country by selling its products abroad. Its research effort is constantly improving the efficiency of the manufacturing processes and devising new ones. Chemists do not work in ivory towers, however. What they do can benefit, as well as damage, the real world in which they work and live. They fully realise this!

❝❝ Chemical waste ❞❞

Every chemical process which produces a **useful product** is likely also to produce a **waste product**. The simple process of burning fuel for the energy to heat our homes or cook our food gives waste products. The process of digestion of our food creates waste products which, incidentally, require huge expenditure to prevent them from polluting our environment.

We hope you will become aware, whilst studying the chapters of this guide, that most chemists work hard not only at making useful substances but also at protecting the environment in which we live. They help to feed and clothe us; help to house us and to cure our ills: and help to make life more pleasant and safer to live. Above all they produce, with a few exceptions, only what we **ask** them to make.

Major aspects of the work of chemists will be discussed **as they arise** in this study. The social and environmental impact of chemistry is now such an important part of its study, however, that some aspects of this are best discussed here.

(A) THE FUTURE OF OUR CHEMICAL RESOURCES

Most people are aware that our coal and oil resources will not last for very long if we continue to use them at the current rate. What is not so well known is that this concern extends to our mineral resources as well. Marvellous though the work of chemists often is, there is not much they can make from air and water only!

Ever since we have been able to use energy sources on a large scale – e.g. coal and oil – we have been extracting increasing quantities of chemical substances from the earth. We now realise that the earth cannot continue forever to provide the minerals we need.

You may share the concern for conservation. But why do we need to conserve our resources? *Total conservation* of chemical resources means that we do not use them at all. Will we benefit from ceasing to use them at all? Does it help to use them at a slower rate? The answer to these questions is that it also depends on what else we are doing.

(B) CONSERVING ENERGY AND MATERIAL RESOURCES

We could conserve energy by rationing it, by allowing a limited amount to be used daily. Our fuel resources would last longer but our standard of living would decrease and in the end we should still run short – it would simply take longer. It makes more sense.

> It is important to recognise the difference between renewable and non-renewable (fossil) sources of energy.

(i) to use **renewable sources** of energy, such as water, wind, solar power and vegetation;
(ii) to **recycle** the materials already in existence at a lower 'energy cost', thus conserving both the energy resource and the mineral resource and, at the same time, gaining the benefit of the re-use of the old material;
(iii) to devise more **energy-efficient** and **resource-efficient** ways of carrying out chemical processes;
(iv) to make better use of **'waste'** products.

The chemical industry is involved in all of these activities.

> Gasohol

(i) In Brazil, which has no oil resources and cannot afford to import all the oil it needs, sugar cane is grown as a source of ethanol for running motor vehicles. Sugar is extracted from the cane, **fermented** to **ethanol** solution and then **distilled** to produce nearly pure ethanol. The energy needed to carry out the distillation process comes from burning the cane waste, left after the sugar has been removed. Sugar cane will grow again and the process can be repeated. In sugar cane the Brazilians have a **renewable energy resource**.

> Recycled metals

(ii) In Western Europe, nearly a half of all aluminium used is eventually recycled. To make 'new' aluminium from scrap requires **only about 5%** of the energy spent in making the original aluminium from its ore. The saving of energy and mineral resources is obvious.

> Energy-efficient processes

(iii) The history of the production of aluminium illustrates point (ii) equally well. The metal is extracted by **electrolysis** of aluminium oxide. Energy consumption is large. However, the most recently built aluminium smelters use only 30% of the energy used by the very first smelters which were built a hundred years ago.

> Usable wastes

(iv) The use of 'waste products' can be beneficial in several ways. Firstly, it saves the expense of disposal and so makes the main product cheaper. Secondly, it makes more efficient use of natural resources. Thirdly, it can reduce environmental pollution.

> H_2SO_4 from waste SO_2

For example, many metal extraction processes produce large amounts of sulphur dioxide waste. If dispersed in the atmosphere, this oxide is a pollutant, producing 'acid rain' and an unhealthy atmosphere. The metal extraction industry uses the gas as a source of sulphur to make sulphuric acid. Pollution is reduced, a useful product is made, and the mineral ore has been more fully used.

4 > POLLUTION

(A) POLLUTION – ITS CAUSES

In the last section we touched on pollution from industrial activities. The problem has been with use ever since large-scale chemical manufacturing started. However, we must take care to be fair in our judgement of where the blame lies. It is a useful exercise to try to answer the question 'what would your daily life be like without the objects made with the products of the chemical industry?', mentioned in an earlier section. If we cannot honestly answer 'wonderful' then we ourselves must accept **some** of the responsibility for keeping the industry going. If we did not want its products, the chemical industry would not make a profit and would cease to exist.

All this **does not excuse** pollution by chemical processes, of course. There are strict rules for regulating the amounts of waste chemicals that can be dumped into our rivers and atmosphere or onto our land. However, because we demand more and more chemicals, even very small amounts of pollution for **individual** factories become large amounts **globally**.

What is being done to reduce or prevent pollution?

(B) POLLUTION – THE REMEDIES

> Less pollution now?

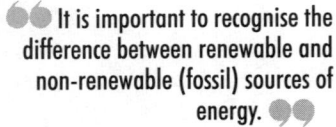

Although we do not have remedies for every situation, much has been done during the past century. Some processes which were serious pollutants of our environment a hundred years ago are no longer so. The chemical process used at that time for producing the alkali, used in soap and glassmaking, from salt, also produced hydrogen chloride as a waste product. The serious pollution caused by this acid gas led to the first law to control air pollution. This was the Alkali Act of 1863.

❝ No more smog! ❞

Even the 'smogs' of thirty-five years ago are no longer seen in Britain. The Clean Air Act of 1956 became law soon after the serious health risk from smog was recognised and smokeless zones were established in which the burning of coal was not allowed. This led to a big reduction in the concentration of smoke particles and sulphur dioxide in the air of our towns and cities.

❝ No more froth! ❞

Twenty years ago some of our rivers were polluted with detergent and almost permanently 'froth-covered'. Detergent manufacturers voluntarily took steps to change the chemical composition of their detergent so that it was 'biodegradable'. We no longer see frothy rivers, and bacteria have a new dish on their menu!

These improvements have been achieved by a combination of public concern and commercial responsibility. Those who run our industries also have to live with pollution if they cannot reduce it!

❝ More acid rain? ❞

One of the most important pollution issues at present is the atmospheric pollution from oxides of sulphur and nitrogen. These come mainly from coal-fired power stations and motor vehicles. Both sources can be made pollution-free – but at a cost.

Planned removal of oxides of sulphur from power station flue gases is making very slow progress. To date (1994) no commercial station operates a flue-gas desulphurisation plant. One is planned for the Drax station in Yorkshire by 1996. However, power producers plan to build more stations using natural gas which has almost no sulphur content and so will not require the costly flue-gas cleaning process.

(C) POWER STATION POLLUTION

The acidic oxides emitted by power stations can be **neutralised** and converted into salts by the use of **alkaline reagents**.

(i) Lime scrubbing

$$Ca(OH)_2(s) + SO_2(g) \rightarrow CaSO_3(s) + H_2O(l),$$

Lime + sulphur dioxide → calcium sulphite + water

$$CaSO_3(s) + \tfrac{1}{2}O_2(g) \rightarrow CaSO_4(s).$$

calcium sulphite + oxygen → calcium sulphate

The process can be expensive but it works well. The salt formed, usually calcium sulphate, $CaSO_4$, may have to be dumped, however. This could create another source of pollution, though a less unpleasant one. Calcium sulphate has a commercial use in the manufacture of wall plaster. If the product formed from the removal of sulphur dioxide could be made to the standard required for it to be made into plaster, the waste would be re-usable!

❝ Plaster from acid rain? ❞

It is interesting to note that many solid wastes can be dumped on land and eventually landscaped. When covered with a layer of topsoil, trees and shrubs and even crops can be grown. An ICI farm on Teesside grows crops on top of thirty feet of gypsum waste from the fertiliser industry!

(ii) Ammonia scrubbing

❝ More food from acid rain? ❞

An alternative process would be to convert oxides of sulphur and oxides of nitrogen into ammonium salts. The oxides react with water and air to form sulphuric and nitric acids. These acids are then neutralised by ammonia gas to form ammonium salts. Ammonium salts are used as fertilisers. This process uses waste to make a useful product.

$$2NH_3(g) + H_2SO_4(aq) \rightarrow (NH_4)_2SO_4(aq),$$

ammonia + sulphuric acid → ammonium sulphate

$$NH_3(g) + HNO_3(aq) \rightarrow NH_4NO_3(aq).$$

ammonia + nitric acid → ammonium nitrate

Nitrogen oxides can also be reduced by more efficient burning of the coal, for example by fluidised bed combustion. Sulphur oxides can be reduced by using coal with a lower sulphur content.

(D) MOTOR VEHICLE POLLUTION

Any high-temperature burning process using **air** will produce nitrogen oxides as pollutants – equation (1). If the fuel is a carbon compound, such as coal, oil or natural gas, then carbon monoxide may be produced also – by incomplete oxidation of the carbon in the fuel – equation (2).

$$N_2(g) + O_2(g) \rightarrow 2NO(g), \quad (1)$$

nitrogen + oxygen → nitrogen oxide

$$CH_4(g) + 1\tfrac{1}{2}O_2(g) \rightarrow CO(g) + 2H_2O(g). \quad (2)$$

methane + oxygen → carbon monoxide + water vapour

Atmospheric pollution from motor vehicles is often more noticeable than that from power stations because it is near ground level – power stations spread their pollution over a wide area by having very tall chimneys – as the inhabitants of Scandinavia will confirm!

A great deal of work has been done on the perfection of catalytic converters for motor vehicles, using petrol or diesel fuels to remove atmospheric pollutants from their exhaust gases. Countries such as the USA and Japan now insist on the fitting of exhaust emission control systems to all cars. The British company Johnson Matthey Chemicals Limited produce a converter called an **autocatalyst** which uses a platinum/rhodium catalyst to speak up the reaction of pollutant components of the exhaust gases with each other to produce harmless substances.

> Precious metals prevent petrol pollution.

The commonest pollutants from motor vehicles are carbon monoxide (CO) and nitrogen oxide (NO), both toxic gases, and unburned hydrocarbons (HC) from the fuel. These are removed in the autocatalyst by conversion to harmless carbon dioxide, water and nitrogen.

Typical reactions occurring in autocatalysts are:

$$2CO(g) + 2NO(g) \rightarrow 2CO_2(g) + N_2(g),$$

carbon monoxide + nitrogen(II) oxide → carbon dioxide + nitrogen

$$2CO(g) + O_2(g) \rightarrow 2CO_2(g),$$

carbon monoxide + oxygen → carbon dioxide

$$HC(g) + NO(g) \rightarrow CO_2(g) + H_2O(g) + N_2(g).$$

hydrocarbon + nitrogen(II) oxide → carbon dioxide + water vapour + nitrogen

> Reactions in autocatalysts.

(The last 'equation' is not a balanced equation; it is simplified to show the possible products. A typical hydrocarbon in petrol would be octane, C_8H_{18}. Try working out the balanced equation for the reaction to form the products shown.)

At present, autocatalysts require the use of **unleaded** petrol. This is because lead compounds in leaded petrol 'poison' the active surface of the catalyst, destroying its converting power. The polluting power of petrol engined cars registered after January 1993 has been much reduced by the compulsory fitting of catalytic converters. The progressive introduction of unleaded petrol will produce the **bonus** of less lead pollution of the atmosphere as well.

(E) POLLUTION OF WATER SOURCES

So far, discussion of pollution has centred around the atmosphere. Equally important, however, is pollution of the rivers and seas. River pollution is usually from two main sources – industry and sewage. Industrial pollutants are often complex chemical compounds and mixtures which are difficult to 'degrade' to harmless substances. Even so, there are ways of rendering most chemical wastes harmless.

A dozen or so water boards are responsible for the standard of drinking water in England and Wales. European standards have forced them to consider measures to reduce nitrate levels in areas where run-off from agricultural land causes these to be excessive, e.g. in East Anglia. Phosphate, largely from detergent mixtures, is also removed chemically in some areas, though on a small scale at the moment. The method is to precipitate phosphate as calcium phosphate. This can be recycled either as a constituent of washing powder or as a fertiliser.

(F) REMOVAL OF FACTORY WASTES

(i) Chemical methods

Industrial waste containing toxic matter can be incinerated at very high temperatures in specially designed furnaces. Such techniques, used by Rechem Limited of Southampton, can render many wastes harmless. The waste gases from these processes are carefully monitored during the combustion to ensure the formation of harmless gaseous products, which are then vented to the atmosphere. Thermal combustion processes can achieve a measure of saving by making use of the heat produced by the combustion processes – see also Chapter 14 (disposal of plastic waste).

Catalytic oxidation or **reduction** of solid and liquid chemical wastes offer ways of decomposing the **chlorinated hydrocarbons** which are so persistent in the soil and are responsible for the near extinction of many species of birds of prey.

(ii) Biochemical methods

Today, water containing toxic chemicals is often treated by sewage works and, because it is toxic, causes difficulties to the bacteria which 'work' there. Heavy metal compounds such as those of chromium and mercury, and toxic organic compounds such as phenol, are particularly difficult to treat. The wastes from many industrial processes such as paper making, sugar and mineral ore processing, textile treatment and agricultural processes cannot be accepted by many sewage works and are sometimes discharged into rivers either untreated or partly treated.

Even relatively simple compounds such as nitrates and phosphates are among the chemicals which are not completely removed by normal sewage treatment methods. In a later chapter we shall discuss the effects of allowing nitrates and phosphates into our rivers – causing **eutrophication** and damage to the ecology of the river.

Any method which allows treatment of such wastes at their place of origin, using inexpensive materials, has much to recommend it.

One such method in current use is the **root zone** method. This process uses the natural ability of certain water plants – reeds – in association with bacteria, to detoxify water percolated through their root systems. These plants can be grown on specially prepared beds close to the source of industrial pollution, and the effluent from that source becomes purified **before** entering a water course. This type of system, already in use for treatment of sewage and industrial waste, offers a more economical and socially acceptable waste treatment method than land fill and river disposal. The 'root zone' method will detoxify almost any waste, especially that from common polluting processes of the sugar, textile and mineral processing industries.

> Designer bugs

A novel treatment method which could become important in the future is the use of 'man-made' micro-organisms to degrade hazardous and toxic substances. Many micro-organisms are known which will digest substances that are toxic to humans. By the technique known as **genetic engineering**, it may be possible to **change** a micro-organism's digestive capabilities to enable it to digest almost any chemical substance we would like to be removed from waste. This exciting possibility is one for the future, perhaps the near future!

> Those wonderful chemists again.

We hope to have shown that the work of chemists is important to modern society. Their manufactures are useful and often vital to our daily lives. Their processes can pollute our environment, yet they work hard to reduce and even prevent that pollution. Their future efforts will extent the useful life of our material resources and generate products not yet imagined – who knows!

EXAMINATION QUESTIONS

QUESTION 1

This question is about pollution. Carefully study the map (Fig. 2.1) and answer the questions below

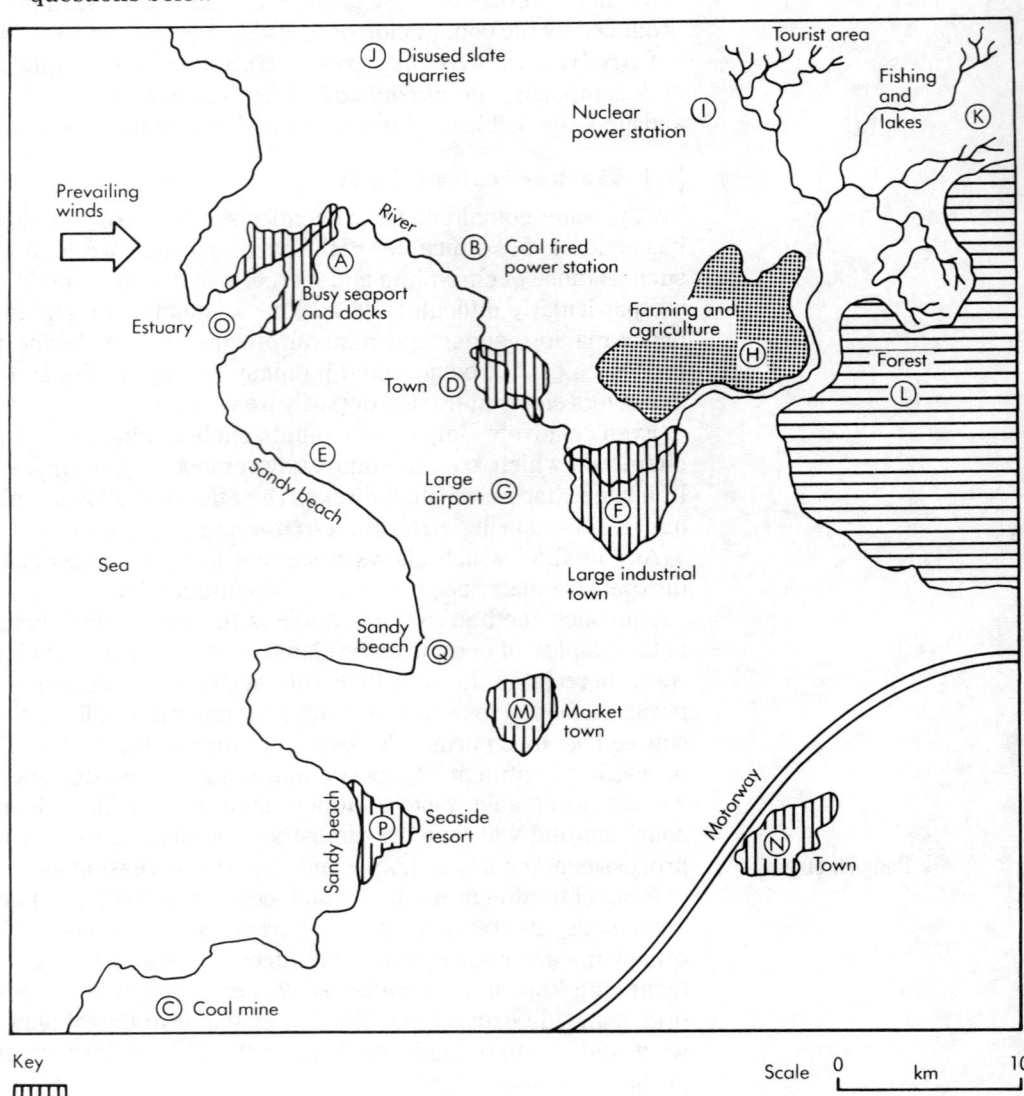

Fig. 2.1

Key
- Built-up areas
- Farming and agriculture
- Forest

Answer the first part of each question, using the letters A to Q, writing your answer in the space provided. Each letter may be used once, more than once or not at all. In each case give a reason for your choice of site.

Write the letter representing a place on the map **most likely** to be

(i) a **source** of radioactive waste;
Place ....
Reason ....(1 mark)

(ii) a **source** of pollution caused by nitrogenous chemicals;
Place ....
Reason ....(1 mark)

(iii) a **source** of factory effluent;
Place ....
Reason .... (*1 mark*)
(iv) a **source** of pollution which causes 'acid rain';
Place..
Reason .... (*1 mark*)
(v) **affected** by 'acid rain';
Place ....
Reason .... (*2 marks*)
(vi) **affected** by unsightly spoil heaps;
Place ....
Reason .... (*1 mark*)
....
(vii) **permanently affected** by oil spillages;
Place ....
Reason .... (*1 mark*)
....
(viii) **affected** by atmospheric lead pollution;
Place..
Reason .... (*1 mark*)
(ix) **affected** by noise pollution;
Place
Reason .... (*1 mark*)

QUESTION 2

Most petrol today contains small quantities of lead compounds. This means that more petrol can be made from the same amount of petroleum. When petrol burns in car engines lead compounds escape into the atmosphere.

The bar chart (Fig. 2.2) shows the average concentrations of lead in soil samples at different distances from the edge of a road.

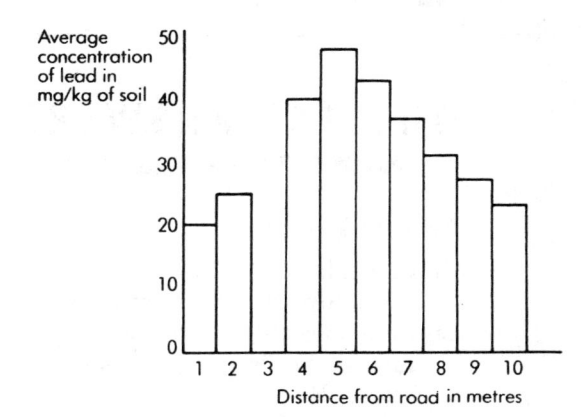

Fig. 2.2

(a) What is the average concentration of lead in the soil 7 metres from the edge of the road? (*2 marks*)
(b) At a distance of 3 metres from the road the average concentration of lead is 33 mg/kg of soil.
Complete the bar chart by putting in this result. (*1 mark*)
(c) At what distance from the road is the average concentration of lead in soil greatest? (1 line) (*1 mark*)
(d) Why is it wise to collect several samples at each distance to test for lead? (3 lines) (*2 marks*)
(e) Organolead plc, a company making lead compounds for adding to petrol, tried to get lead from soil by the side of a busy road.
Why is this not likely to be economically worthwhile? (2 lines) (*1 mark*)
(f) Why may it be unwise to eat vegetables grown in an allotment by the side of a busy road? (2 lines) (*2 marks*)
(g) Give one advantage and one disadvantage of using 'lead free' petrol in place of 'leaded' petrol.

Advantage (2 lines)
Disadvantage (2 lines)

(2 marks)
(Total 11 marks)

QUESTION 3

Margarine is produced (Fig. 2.3) when imported oils are 'hardened' by reaction with hydrogen.

The diagram shows a map of the area around salt deposits in Cheshire. Suggest two reasons why the place marked **X** would be suitable for building a factory to produce margarine.

1.
2.

(2 marks)

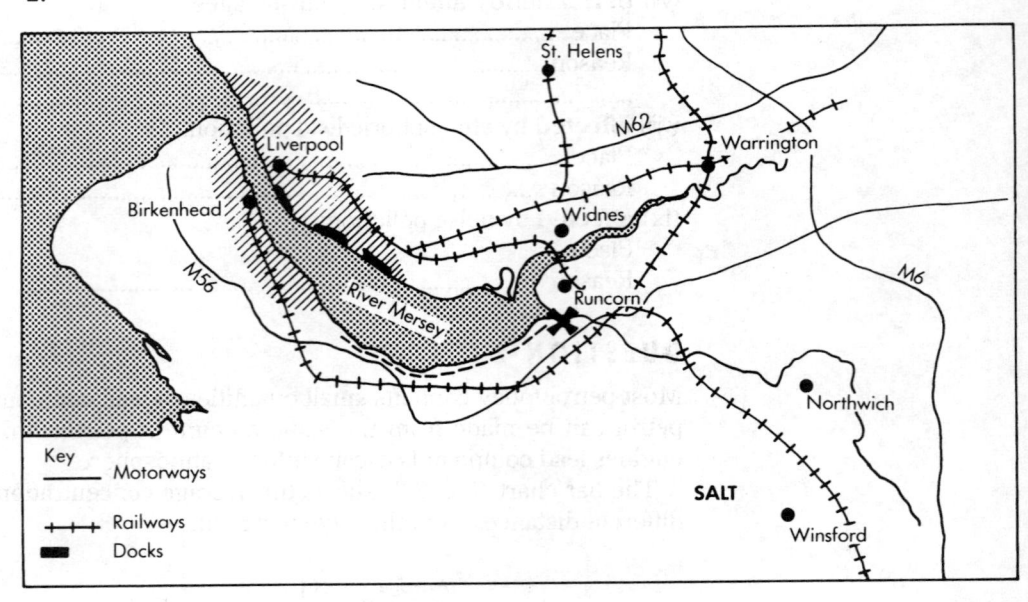

Fig. 2.3

OUTLINE ANSWERS

ANSWER 1

(i) **Place.** I.
   Reason. Nuclear power stations renew their fuel rods every few years. (The 'spent' nuclear fuel is radioactive and is sent for reprocessing to remove the waste products of the 'fission' process.)

(ii) **Place.** H.
   Reason. Farming and agriculture would use fertiliser, some of which is washed into nearby streams and rivers during rainy periods.

(iii) **Place.** F.
   Reason. Factories in a large industrial town will produce waste such as chemical wastes. These may be discharged into the river which flows through town F.

(iv) **Place.** B or F.
   Reason. Any coal-fired furnace such as is used in power stations and factories needing heat supply will produce sulphur dioxide and some nitrogen oxides. Both of these gases are atmospheric pollutants which are acidic in water (non-metal oxides).

(v) **Place.** K or L.
   Reason. The prevailing (commonest) wind direction is from the left. **Winds** will carry ***power station emissions*** towards the areas on the right of the map. Acid rain will affect forest, L, and lakes, K.

(vi) **Place.** J or C.
   Reason. Slate quarries, as do most quarries and coal mines, produce waste rock. Such waste is usually piled in heaps until of large enough size to landscape.

(vii) **Place.** O or A.

Reason. A busy port means many ships. Fuel oil leakage is impossible to avoid. Prevailing wind drives it into the estuary.

(viii) **Place**. N.

Reason. Lead compounds are present in motor car exhausts. The motorway, carrying a large volume of motor traffic, is only two or three kilometres downwind.

(ix) **Place**. N or F.

Reason. N is the town which is near a motorway. The edge is only 2 km from the noise of traffic. F is a town which will have aircraft flying overhead to **land into the prevailing wind** at airport G.

ANSWER 2

This is a comprehension question. Candidates are not expected to know all the details of the use of lead in petrol. *Some* chemical knowledge and an ability to **use information** which is given in the text of the question are required to succeed on this type of question.

The bar chart shows average lead concentrations in the soil as it changes with distance from the road where lead is emitted by motor vehicles.

(a) The average lead concentration in the soil at 7 metres from the road is 37 milligrams per kilogram of soil. A figure one mg/kg either way would be acceptable because the graph axis is marked every ten units and so an **estimate** has to be made of the required figure. **Units** are important as well as the **figure**. There is one mark for each.

(b) The top of the bar should come one-third of the distance between 30 and 40 on the vertical scale. It is a good practice to mark the side scale at 33 and **then** draw in the bar. In this way the examiner can see that you have attempted the estimate and not guessed it. You will also have made a more accurate estimate on the scale itself.

(c) Reading a **maximum** is usually easy if you know what the phrase **greatest average concentration** means. The answer is 5 metres. Can you see why?

(d) Collecting **several samples** is like doing an experiment **more than once** – we do it to make sure that we have not made an **error** in any **one** measurement. The first result **may be correct** but until the others **confirm it** we cannot be sure. Note also that even several measurements are likely to vary a little between themselves and so **an average** is taken because we cannot be sure **which one is most correct**.

(e) The concentration of lead in the soil in question is not very large – milligrams in every thousand grams of soil. 20 000 tonnes of soil would have to be treated to get one tonne of lead!

(f) The tests were done on roadside soil. The lead has probably come from motor vehicles. Fumes will deposit lead compounds *on* the leaves of vegetables and lead from the soil may get *into* the plants through their roots. The toxic effect of lead compounds makes it unwise to eat these vegetables regularly.

(g) Advantage.   No more lead compounds in exhaust fumes.

Disadvantage.   Lead-free petrol could be more expensive. Some cars cannot use it because their engines are not designed for it.

ANSWER 3

This **part-question** illustrates a type of question to be expected in GCSE papers. It tests understanding of the reasons for choosing a particular site for a chemical factory and the recognition that factories cannot simply be built where they are 'out of the way' of towns and people.

Factories are usually built close to supplies of raw materials, labour and transport routes.

Margarine manufacture, you are told, needs **hydrogen** and **imported natural oils**. Electrolysis of salt solution will produce hydrogen gas as a by-product of the production of chlorine, see Fig. 7.3.

❝❝ See Section 1 ❞❞

(1) Place X is close to a port for imports of the oils needed.

(2) It is close to salt supplies and so electrolysis of salt will probably be carried out in the area. Hydrogen will therefore be available.

Other reasons are: nearby supply of labour – several towns and a large city; plenty of good transport facilities for taking product to markets in other parts of Britain or even abroad.

STUDENT'S ANSWER – EXAMINER'S COMMENTS

(a) The first stage in the manufacture of sulphuric acid is the oxidation of sulphur dioxide to sulphur trioxide (SO_3) at 450°C with a vanadium(V) oxide catalyst
 (i) What do you understand by the term *catalyst*?

> A substance that speeds up a reaction without taking part in it.

(2 marks)

> 66 You have one essential property correct. But catalysts *do take part* in the reaction – they are *not used up* in the process. 99

 (ii) Of which group of elements in the Periodic Table is vanadium a member? (There is a copy of the Periodic Table in your Data Booklet.)

> It is a transition element

(1 mark)

> 66 Yes. Transition elements are a group of elements though not one of the groups numbered 1–8. 99

Suggest one other property you would expect for vanadium compounds.

> coloured compounds

(1 mark)

> 66 Good. 99

 (iii) Construct an equation for the catalytic oxidation reaction described above.

> $2SO_2 + O_2 \rightarrow SO_3$

(2 marks)

> 66 The formulae are correct but the *balance* is wrong – try $2SO_3$ 99

(b) The exhaust systems of American cars are fitted with special catalysts to convert carbon monoxide and nitrogen monoxide into safer products.

$$2CO + 2NO \rightarrow 2CO_2 + N_2$$

 (i) Name an additional pollutant present in the exhaust fumes of British cars. How does it get there?

> lead from the anti-knock

(2 marks)

> 66 Excellent answer. 99

 (ii) Explain briefly why carbon monoxide is dangerous.

> It is poisonous to people. It forms carboxyhaemoglobin in the blood.

(2 marks)

 (iii) Explain why carbon dioxide can also be considered an atmospheric pollutant.

> It is responsible for warming up the earth's atmosphere.

(1 mark)

> 66 Good – it's called the 'Greenhouse Effect'. 99

> 66 Excellent. 99

 (iv) How might nitrogen monoxide be formed in a car engine?

> from the nitrogen and oxygen in the air at the high temperature in the engine.

(2 marks)

 (v) From your knowledge of nitrogen monoxide, suggest one way in which its presence in the air might cause harmful effects.

> It forms nitrogen dioxide and this forms acid rain.

(2 marks)

> 66 Yes, it oxidises to nitrogen dioxide and this reacts with water to form nitric acid. 99

(c) In hard water areas concentrated nitric acid is sometimes added to irrigation water in greenhouses to clear scale from the piping
 (i) What is the origin of the scale?

> Limestone in the water supply.

(2 marks)

> 66 In fact 'limestone' in water is calcium hydrogencarbonate and heating or evaporation causes it to form the scale. 99

 (ii) Write an equation to show how the scale is removed.

> $CaCO_3 + HNO_3 \rightarrow CaNO_3 + H_2O + CO_2$

(2 marks)

> 66 Again, not quite correct. Try $Ca(NO_3)_2$ and $2HNO_3$. 99

 (iii) What is the other benefit of using nitric acid in the irrigation system?

> Nitrates are fertilisers.

(1 mark)

> 66 Good. 99

(SEG)

> 66 An excellent answer overall which would score very highly. 99

CHAPTER 3

ELEMENTS, COMPOUNDS AND MIXTURES

ELEMENTS

COMPOUNDS AND MIXTURES

SEPARATING PURE ELEMENTS AND PURE COMPOUNDS FROM MIXTURES

PURITY OF A SUBSTANCE

USE OF SEPARATION PROCESSES IN INDUSTRY

REACTION TECHNIQUES

GETTING STARTED

We can imagine that human beings have been using substances they found in the ground or obtained from the seas of our planet for as long as they have been on earth. Our ancestors will have used some of the *elements* that are to be found 'native', i.e. in a pure state naturally, such as gold for ornaments, sulphur for burning and perhaps medicinal purposes, and copper for tools. They will have found many uses for *mixtures* such as crude oil and sea water which are to be found widely throughout the globe. They will even have managed to produce some reasonably pure *compounds* for their use, such as common salt for preserving and flavouring food. However, the number of useful substances available to our ancestors was minute compared to those now used in our everyday lives.

- An **element** is a substance that cannot be separated into anything simpler. It is composed of atoms all of which have the same number of protons and electrons, but may have different numbers of neutrons.
- A **compound** is a substance formed by chemical reaction between two or more elements.
- A **mixture** consists of two or more components (elements, compounds or both) not chemically combined together. The properties of each component are not altered by the process of mixing.

Many of the compounds we find useful are soluble in water. They are prepared and purified from **aqueous solution**. An aqueous solution is a mixture of a *solute*, usually a solid, fully dissolved in the *solvent* – water. There is a fixed mass of any compound that is able to dissolve in a given mass of water. This mass is known as the *solubility* of the compound at the temperature of solution.

> The definition of **solubility** is therefore: The maximum mass of a solute that will dissolve in 100 g of water (or solvent) at a given temperature. The solution formed is called a *saturated* solution.

If more than that mass is added to 100 g of water, the excess will remain undissolved. If less is added, the solution will be unsaturated. An unsaturated solution can be made into a saturated solution by evaporating off water until crystals appear.

ESSENTIAL PRINCIPLES

1 ELEMENTS

> Draw a portion of the periodic table to contain the first twenty elements. Put the symbols of the elements onto your table and learn them.

Elements are the building blocks of all matter. There are 89 naturally occurring elements of which 21 are non-metals and 68 metals. Each element is a collection of atoms with identical numbers of protons in the nucleus. A knowledge of the symbols of the first twenty elements is required for GCSE courses.

The naturally occurring elements represent a global store of atoms which cannot be destroyed but which can become part of any of a larger number of different compounds. So the carbon atoms in the hydrocarbon molecules present in the petrol we buy at a garage were once possibly a part of the molecules in the body of a living creature and will, when used to power a motor car, become part of the gaseous carbon monoxide and carbon dioxide that comes out of the exhaust system. From there, these carbon atoms will eventually become part of yet other molecules – even possibly part of a human body. Atoms of elements are therefore re-usable 'building blocks' of matter.

Note: Synthetic elements are *not* made by chemical reactions. The synthesis of just a few atoms of a 'new' element requires a large expenditure of money, energy and ingenuity. Similarly, the destruction of atoms which occurs in atomic bombs and nuclear power plants and produces enormous amounts of energy is not a chemical reaction and so does not normally come within the study of chemistry.

2 COMPOUNDS AND MIXTURES

If elements are the 'building blocks' of matter then compounds are the 'buildings'. Compounds are formed when elements combine together to form new substances. They must be clearly distinguished from mixtures of elements. Two examples will make the difference clearer.

(A) COMPOUNDS

If we mixed the two elements hydrogen and oxygen, for instance in equal volumes, in a flask we could make them react or combine together by *heating*. There would be an explosion, heat would be produced, a liquid would appear on the sides of the flask as it cooled and we would find that there was some oxygen left which had not reacted! After heating, a product would be present which would not look like either oxygen or hydrogen. It would be a compound of the two elements oxygen and hydrogen called hydrogen oxide. Hydrogen oxide, commonly known as water, is a colourless, tasteless, non-toxic, non-flammable liquid quite different from the gases from which it was made.

What about the oxygen gas which had not reacted? Water is formed by the reaction of *exactly* twice as much hydrogen (by volume) as oxygen gas. Any extra hydrogen or extra oxygen is not used (we call it an *excess*) and is left over at the end of the reaction. **There is only one 'recipe' (formula) for the compound, water, whereas there are *many possible 'recipes' for mixtures of oxygen and hydrogen gases.***

Again, if we could *see* the particles of matter present in the reaction vessel after the explosion we should see *two* different types. *Water* molecules have three atoms, two of them hydrogen and one oxygen. In addition, there would be some *oxygen* molecules, unreacted because they were in excess, which have two identical atoms in the molecule. We would have a *mixture* of one *element* with one *compound*.

(B) SEPARATION OF THE ELEMENTS OF A COMPOUND

> Draw diagrams of oxygen molecules, hydrogen molecules and water molecules.

Unlike the separation of hydrogen and oxygen from a mixture of the two (see below), no *physical process* will separate the two elements from water. A chemical reaction is needed to obtain oxygen or hydrogen from water, e.g. reaction of sodium with water to get hydrogen or electrolysis to get both oxygen *and* hydrogen.

(C) MIXTURES

Hydrogen and oxygen are two elements. They are colourless gases and further they are both non-metals. If we put equal volumes of hydrogen and oxygen into the same flask and cork it, we will have a *mixture of two gaseous non-metallic elements*.

If we could see the particles in this mixture, we should see *two different types of molecules* consisting of pairs of atoms. Because the particles present are *not all identical*, we obviously have a **mixture**.

No noticeable change will occur in the flask no matter how long we leave the mixture there. The mixture formed here would, if used to inflate a toy balloon, cause the balloon to float in the air because the mixture of hydrogen and oxygen will be lighter than air. Also, we could mix oxygen and hydrogen in *other proportions* and still make a mixture of the two. Every mixture would look the same but those with the most hydrogen in would make the balloon rise faster than those with less hydrogen in. Animals could breathe in the mixtures which contained 20% or more of oxygen. Each element in the mixture behaves exactly as it does without the others being there! There can be *many* mixtures of these two gases, each one different from the others.

Separation of hydrogen and oxygen from a mixture

If we wished to separate the hydrogen from the oxygen in these mixtures it could be done by processes such as liquefying the oxygen, or allowing the hydrogen to diffuse through a palladium thimble which would not allow passage of the oxygen. Most mixtures can be separated by *physical processes* which are simpler than those mentioned for hydrogen and oxygen.

Solutions

Aqueous solutions are particular examples of mixtures. They are common because water is such a good solvent that many compounds dissolve in it. It is important to be able to determine the solubility of any compound in water.

The following method can be used to determine the **solubility** of a compound in water.

| To determine the solubility of a water-soluble compound |

1. Weigh out 100 g of water into a conical flask.
2. Warm the water to a few degrees above the temperature required.
3. Add the powdered compound a little at a time until no more will dissolve. Undissolved solid must be visible in the flask.
4. Filter the saturated solution rapidly under pressure and check the temperature.
5. Evaporate the water from this filtrate.
6. Weight the dry solid (M grams).

The solubility at the temperature of the saturated solution is the mass of dry solid per 100 grams of water, i.e. M grams per 100 g of water.

The determination can be repeated at any temperature up to 100°C.

An example of such a determination is given by the following results for the compound potassium dichromate.

Solubility in g per 100 g of water	7.7	12	18	25	33
Temperature in °C	10	20	30	40	50

Fig. 3.1

- **Designing and planning a solubility measurement**

It should be clear that it would have been quite valid and much more convenient to have used only 10 g of water in this determination. The results, when scaled up by a factor of ten would give the solubility value.

- **Evaluating the method**

There are obvious inaccuracies in the procedure:

(i) After filtration, some of the water used would remain in the crystals on the filter paper, and in the paper itself. So the water in which the compound is dissolved cannot weight 100 g.

(ii) The filtration process takes a little time and so the final portion of filtrate will be at a lower temperature than the first portion. The temperature of the measurement will therefore not be a specific value but a range of several degrees.

It is possible to overcome error (i) by weighing the filtrate and finding exactly the mass of water evaporated off to produce the dry solid. Error two can most easily be overcome by the simple process of rapidly tipping the saturated solution out of the flask through a plug of glass wool. The glass wool filters out the solid crystals with little cooling. The temperature of the filtrate should be measured immediately to obtain the correct temperature for the solubility value.

- **Trial plan**

Try working out the plan for this determination using 10 g of water. What vessel would you use? How would you heat the mixture? How would you ensure the glass wool was at the same temperature as the solution? In what vessel would you carry out the evaporation to dryness. Why could this latter procedure not be used to find the solubility of hydrated copper sulphate, $CuSO_4.5H_2O$?

- **Evaluating the results**

It is not easy to see what the figures in a table mean. However, the fact that we have measured two variables, the solubility and the temperature, enables us to draw a graph. The vertical axis will be the mass of compound dissolving in 100 g of water (the dependent variable). The independent variable, the one we have fixed, is the temperature; this is plotted horizontally.

Obtain a piece of graph paper and plot the above values. Then draw a smooth curve through the points. The curve can then be used to:

(i) Find the solubility of potassium dichromate at any temperature between 10 °C and 50 °C. Here we are interpolating the results – literally filling in the values in between the points we have measured.

(ii) Estimate a value for the solubility outside the range of temperature used. This is called *extrapolating* – extending the results curve outside the measured range.

(iii) Determine the mass of solid that would crystallise out from a saturated solution at a higher temperature on cooling it to a lower temperature (See the worked example below).

Dissolving an impure compound in hot water and cooling to room temperature or lower is a method used for purifying solids. Usually the small proportion of impurity present remains dissolved in the solvent, allowing purer crystals to deposit. If the process is repeated several times (if necessary) then a very pure product can be obtained. The difference between the 99% pure analytical grade chemicals sold by suppliers and the 95% general purpose reagents is often achieved simply by extra crystallisations given to the purer product.

WORKED EXAMPLE

(a) State what is meant by a saturated solution.
(b) The following tables shows the solubility of potassium carbonate in water at various temperatures.

Fig. 3.2

Temperature (°C)	20	30	40	50	60	70
Solubility (g per 100 g water)	110	114	117	121	127	133

Plot these results on the grid provided and draw the solubility curve for potassium carbonate.

(c) Use your graph to determine the solubility of potassium carbonate at 45 °C.
(d) How much potassium carbonate will be deposited if a saturated solution made with 50 g of water at 60 °C is cooled to 25 °C?

Solution

(a) *It is a solution which contains the maximum mass of dissolved solute at a given temperature.*

Fig. 3.3

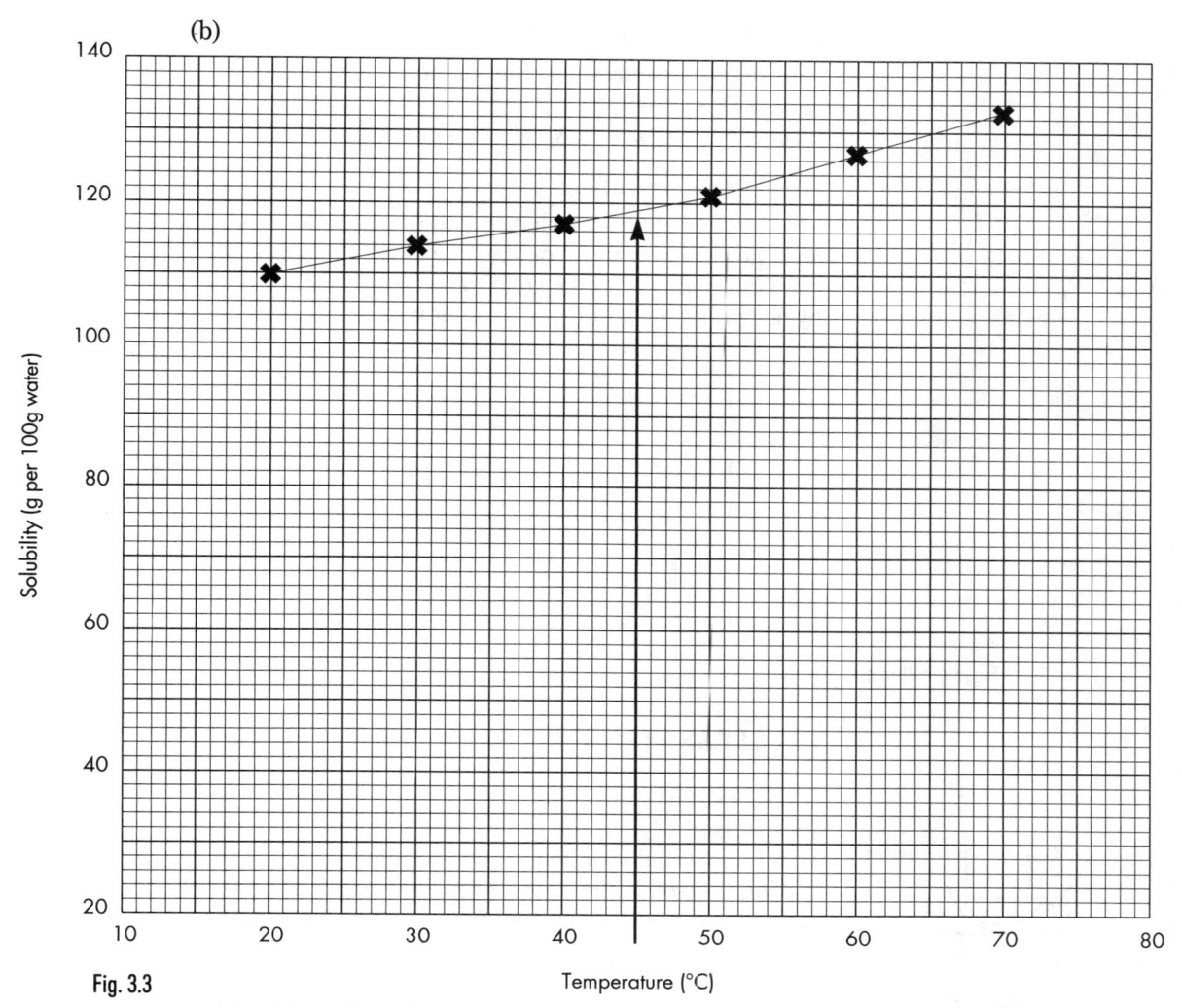

(b) [Graph: Solubility (g per 100g water) vs Temperature (°C)]

(c) The vertical line drawn at 45 °C shows the solubility to be 119 g/100 g water at 45 °C.

(d)
- at 60 °C the solubility is 127 g in 100 g water or 63.5 g in 50 g of water.
- at 25 °C the solubility is 112 g in 100 g water or 56 g in 50 g of water.

So (63.5 − 56) g of solid will deposit. The answer is 7.5 g of sodium carbonate.

The rest of this chapter will deal with methods of separating components of **mixtures**. All the methods are physical processes. Separating elements from their compounds involves chemical processes and will be discussed in the rest of the book. The following table gives some examples of elements, compounds and mixtures.

3 SEPARATING PURE ELEMENTS AND PURE COMPOUNDS FROM MIXTURES

Mixtures can be of several types:

(i) two or more elements, e.g. alloys or air;
(ii) two or more compounds, e.g. sea water or crude oil;
(iii) a mixture of elements and compounds, e.g. native gold or crude sulphur.

We usually want to obtain only **one** of the components of a mixture. The methods given below, however, will sometimes give more than one component in a pure state.

(A) SEPARATING A SOLID FROM A LIQUID IN WHICH IT DOES NOT DISSOLVE

(i) Filtration

This will separate a solid from a liquid (usually a solution) in which the solid is insoluble, e.g. sand from salt solution, a solid from its saturated solution or mud from water to be used for drinking. The solid remaining on the filter paper is called the **residue** (Fig. 3.4) and the solution running through the filter paper is the **filtrate**.

(ii) Decantation

This does the same as (i) but the liquid is carefully poured away from the solid which (Fig. 3.5) is usually heavy and at the bottom of the vessel, e.g. a saturated solution can be poured away from crystals, or wine from its sediment.

(iii) Centrifugation

This method also does what (i) and (ii) do. If the solid mixed with the liquid is very fine and slows down filtration by blocking the pores of the filter paper, then using a centrifuge will cause the solid to settle quickly. The solid and liquid are then separated by decanting the liquid into another vessel.

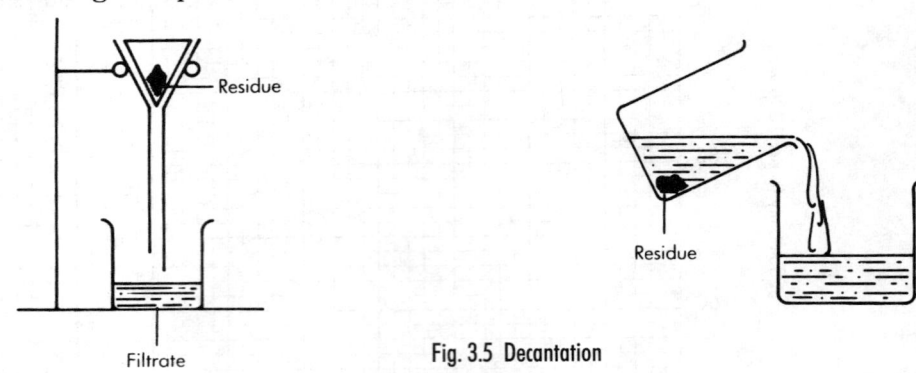

Fig. 3.4 Filtration

Fig. 3.5 Decantation

(B) SEPARATING A SOLID FROM ITS SOLUTION IN A SOLVENT

(i) Evaporation

This is used when a solid is to be **extracted** from its solution, e.g. salt from sea water or brine. Evaporation will allow the liquid part of the mixture to be lost into the air, leaving the solid (Fig. 3.6). If the liquid part of the mixture is needed then its vapour must be condensed and one of the methods in section (c) must be used.

(ii) Crystallisation

This is the process where **complete evaporation** of water from a solution would not produce the desired **crystalline** product. Many crystals **decompose** when heated to dry them. They may give off water to become powders.

Crystallisation is the process of evaporation which is **stopped** at the stage where a saturated solution has formed. The resulting solution is then cooled to room temperature and produces **crystals**. See also Chapter 10, Section 8(iii). The apparatus used is as for evaporation above.

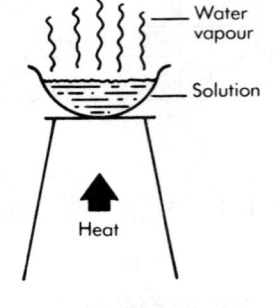

Fig. 3.6 Evaporation

(C) SEPARATING A LIQUID FROM A SOLUTION

Distillation

There are two types of distillation:

(i) **Simple distillation.** This is used to separate a single liquid from one or more solids in a solution, e.g. to obtain pure water from sea water or tap water (Fig 3.7).

(ii) **Fractional distillation.** This is used to separate several liquids from a mixture or a liquid from a solution of one liquid in another, e.g. getting 'fractions' from crude oil or ethanol from wine (Fig. 3.8).

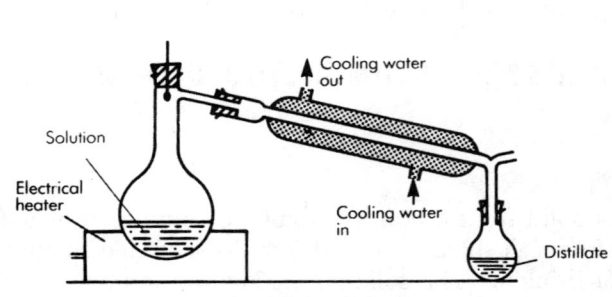

Fig. 3.7 Simple distillation

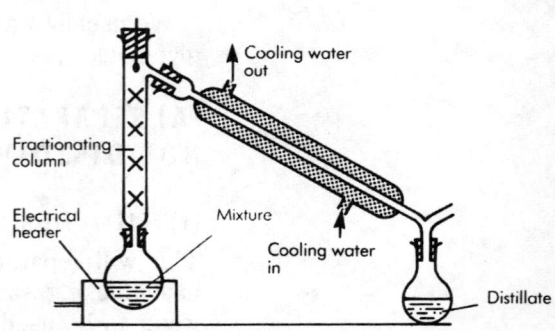

Fig. 3.8 Fractional distillation

Crude oil consists of more than 200 different hydrocarbons. The industrial separation of crude oil into its component fractions involves separating these into a dozen or so major 'fractions'. The fractions are not single compounds, but mixtures having a narrow boiling point range.

Fractional distillation of crude oil in the laboratory
For the purpose of the following description of fractional distillation, each fraction can be thought of as a component having a single boiling point. When the crude oil is boiled, the components vaporise. The vapours move up the fractionating column. The component with the *lowest* boiling point rises to the top of the column and passes into the condenser. On condensing, the liquid component collects as the distillate. The thermometer registers the boiling point of the component passing over. The temperature remains constant until all the component has distilled over. When this has happened, the next component will pass over, register its boiling point on the thermometer and condense into the receiver. The receiver must be changed everytime a new component distils. The last component to distil over is the one with the *highest* boiling point.

(D) SEPARATING LIQUIDS WHICH DO NOT MIX

Liquids which do not mix, of course, do not really form mixtures. However, the method of separating them is useful to know. Liquids which do not mix are said to be ***immiscible***, like mercury and water or oil and water. The 'mixture' is poured into a separating funnel or tap funnel (Fig. 3.9). The liquids are allowed to stand until they separate and a clear boundary can be seen. The lower (more dense or heavier) layer is then run out through the tap. If the top (less dense or lighter) layer is wanted, it can be poured out through the top of the separating funnel.

Fig. 3.9

(E) SEPARATING SEVERAL SOLIDS FROM A MIXTURE IN SOLUTION

Chromatography

It is sometimes necessary to separate several substances from a mixture in solution, e.g. mixed dyes in water (ink), or several sugars in water. Paper chromatography will do this quickly and efficiently (Figs 3.10 and 3.14).

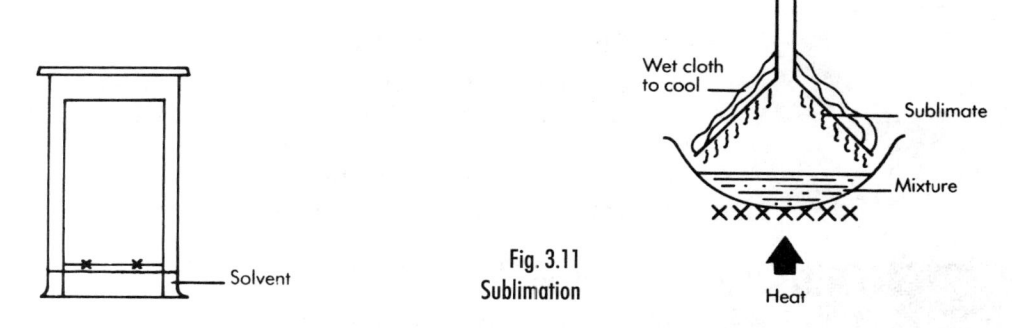

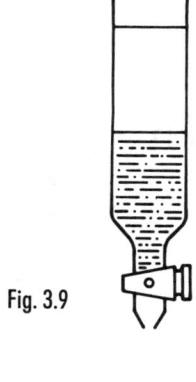

Fig. 3.10 Chromatography

Fig. 3.11 Sublimation

(F) SEPARATING ONE SOLID FROM A MIXTURE OF SOLIDS

Sublimation

This method has limited uses because very few solids will ***sublime***. Among those that will are iodine and ammonium chloride. Either of these can be separated from ***other*** solids by this process, which is similar to the process of distillation, but for purifying solids:

$$\textbf{\textit{sublimation}} \quad \text{solid} \xrightarrow{\text{heat}} \text{vapour} \xrightarrow{\text{cool}} \text{solid}$$

$$\text{compare} \quad \textbf{\textit{distillation}} \quad \text{liquid} \xrightarrow{\text{heat}} \text{vapour} \xrightarrow{\text{cool}} \text{liquid}$$

Sublimation is an unusual process. In it, the heated solid becomes a vapour without first melting, i.e. the solid boils before it melts! On cooling the vapour condenses to a solid rather than a liquid. The *two processes together* are called sublimation (Fig. 3.11).

4 PURITY OF A SUBSTANCE

A pure substance has a **sharp** melting point and a **fixed** boiling point. For example, pure water freezes at 0 °C and boils at 100 °C at normal atmospheric pressure. The presence of impurity lowers the freezing point (melting point) and increases the boiling point of a substance. The more impurity present, the greater its effect. For example, water containing about 4% common salt boils at 7 °C above its normal boiling point.

Adding about 20% of common salt to ice lowers the freezing temperature by some 20 °C. However, at all temperatures below 0 °C more and more ice will form as the temperature drops but the mixture will not freeze **completely** until the temperature reaches about −20 °C. So the freezing point is no longer sharp but occurs over a range of temperatures.

The melting point of lead (mp 327 °C) is lower by 2.3 °C for every 1% of tin added up to a maximum lowering at 62% of tin. As a quick test of your mathematical ability, what would be the melting temperature of the 62% tin: 38% lead mixture?

(A) MEASURING MELTING POINT AND BOILING POINT

Measuring boiling and melting points (Figs. 3.12 and 3.13) is a suitable way of finding out whether a substance contains small amounts of impurity. However, it will not tell us *how many* different substances are present in the mixture.

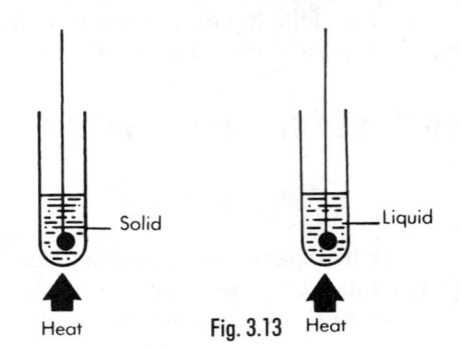

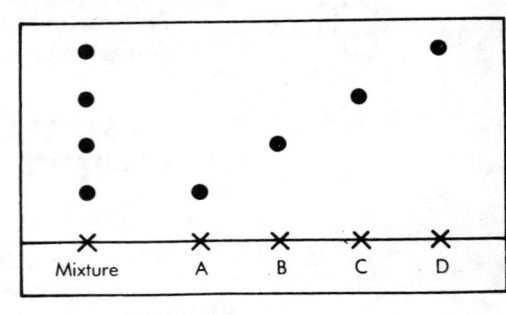

Fig. 3.12

Fig. 3.13

Fig. 3.14 Chromatography

(B) CHROMATOGRAPHY

An easy way of determining the number of substances present in a solution (liquid mixture) is by chromatography (Fig. 3.14). We can find out the number of different coloured dyes in an ink, for example. Chromatography can even be used where the substances are colourless. In this case colourless spots are present on the chromatogram and need a special chemical to show them up. See Chapter 14, Section 7(b).

5 USE OF SEPARATION PROCESSES IN INDUSTRY

Industrial chemistry deals with either:

(i) natural mixtures from which pure compounds are to be extracted; or
(ii) compounds from which elements are to be extracted; or
(iii) elements and compounds from which other substances are to be synthesised.

In almost every case, the raw materials have first to be purified by methods involving the processes described earlier in this chapter. A thorough understanding of these processes is therefore invaluable for further study.

Once pure chemicals are available, the chemist can use them to produce a wide variety of different substances. To do this a knowledge and experience of additional techniques will be required.

6 REACTION TECHNIQUES

Chemical reactions can be divided into several categories and different techniques are used to carry them out. Reactions may involve:

(a) heating
(b) gas collection/measurement
(c) crystallisation
(d) solid/vapour or gas combination
(e) combustion
(f) gas analysis

Fig. 3.15 shows pieces of apparatus suitable for carrying out reactions of the types listed in the following table. They may prove useful in designing and planning experiments. Study them and note the way each solves a different technical problem.

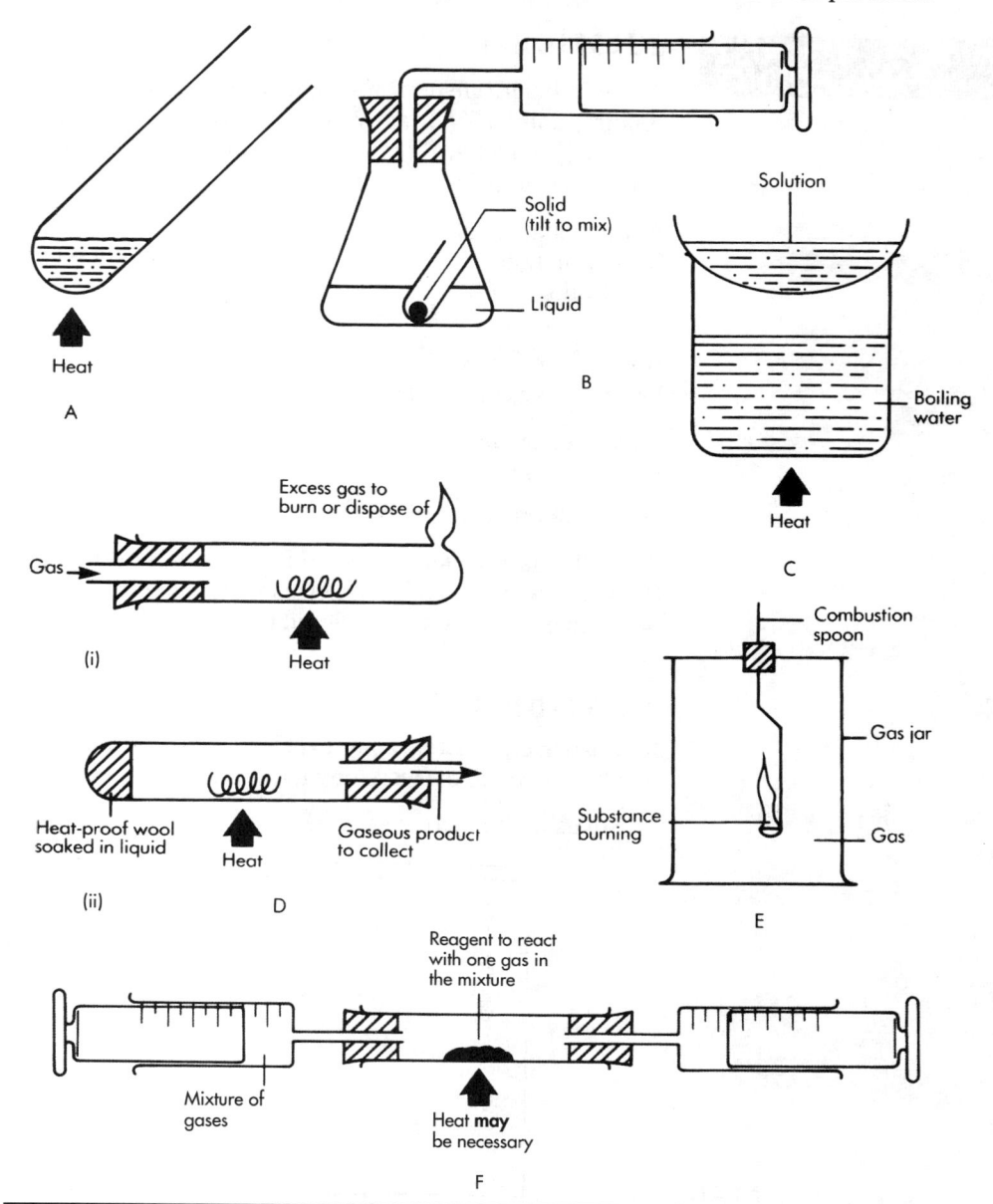

Fig. 3.15

Apparatus	What it is designed to do	Typical experiment in which it could be used
A	heating solids or liquids	decomposing a solid/testing for a gas produced
B	react solid with solution/collect gas	collecting O_2, H_2, CO_2, etc. measuring gas volumes if needed rates of reactions
C	crystallisation	getting pure salts from their saturated solutions
D	(i) passing a gas over a heated solid	reduction of metal oxides with H_2
	(ii) passing a vapour over a heated solid	reacting steam with a heated metal
E	burning solid or liquid in a gas	burning metals in oxygen or chlorine
F	removing one gas from a mixture, with measurement	finding percentage of O_2 in air or CO_2 in a mixture

EXAMINATION QUESTIONS

QUESTION 1

A public health inspector suspects that an ice cream contains traces of a green dye (boiling point 75°C), as well as an orange and a red dye (boiling points 69°C and 75°C respectively). Which of the following is the best method by which the green dye may be separated?

A fractional distillation
B chromatography
C filtration
D recrystallisation
E evaporation of the water present

QUESTIONS 2–4

From the list A to D below:

A condensation
B distillation
C evaporation
D filtration

Select the process which

2 can be used to separate sand from water most quickly and cheaply.
3 causes water to collect on classroom windows in cold weather.
4 involves the change of a liquid to a gas and of the gas back to a liquid.

(NEAB)

QUESTION 5

In a paper chromatography experiment to identify the dyes present in a mixture, the results shown below were obtained:

The dyes in the mixture were

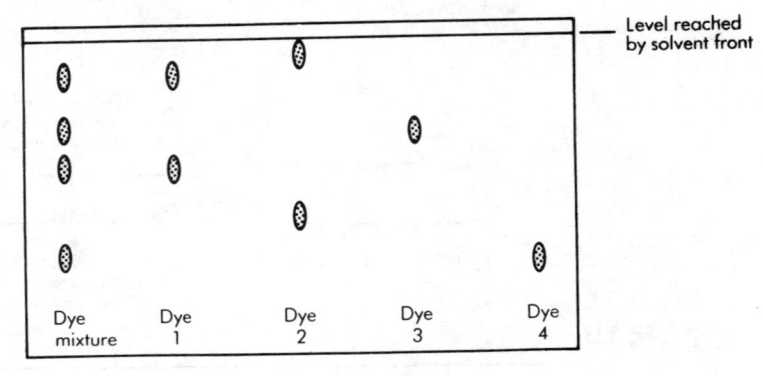

Fig. 3.16

A 1, 2 and 3
B 3 only
C 2, 3 and 4
D 3 and 4 only
E 1, 3 and 4

QUESTIONS 6–10

In questions 6–10 choose from the following list the letter representing the practical method which could be used to carry out each of the given processes. Each letter may be used once, more than once, or not at all:

A chromatography
B crystallisation
C filtration
D fractional distillation
E use of a separating funnel

6 Separate olive oil and water.
7 Separate undissolved material from river water.
8 Separate petrol from crude oil.
9 Obtain a sample of blue copper sulphate crystals from aqueous copper sulphate.
10 Obtain a sample of colouring from a soft drink.

(NISEAC)

QUESTIONS 11-13

The type of question represented by question 11-13 ask for the identification of a process.

Name the separation process shown in each of the following diagrams.
11 diagram (a) ....
12 diagram (b) ....
13 diagram (c) ....

(SEG)

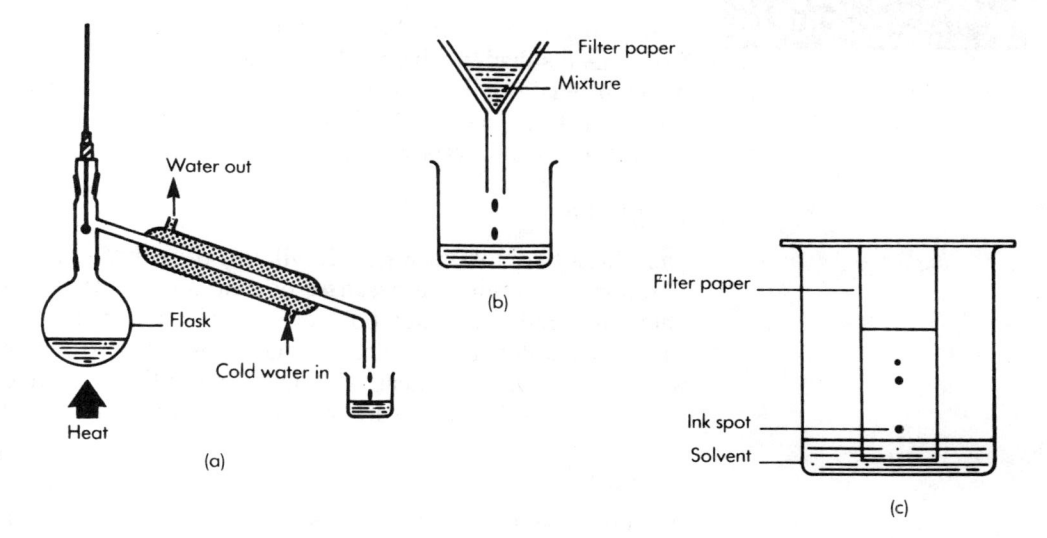

Fig. 3.17

STRUCTURED QUESTIONS

QUESTION 14

(a) (i) How is filtration of reservoir water carried out? (2 lines) *(1 mark)*
    (ii) What is the purpose of this filtration? (2 lines) *(1 mark)*
(b) (i) How may a sample of pure water be obtained from sea water? *(1 mark)*
    (ii) Explain the process of evaporation in terms of movement of molecules. (3 lines) *(3 marks)*
    (iii) Why does the salt in sea water not circulate through the atmosphere in the way the water does? (2 lines) *(2 marks)*

(SEG)

QUESTION 15

To show that a shampoo contains a mixture of colours, chromatography can be used. Two brands, X and Y, of yellow-coloured shampoo were compared and the chromatogram below was obtained.

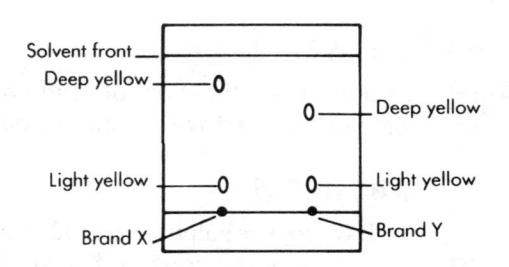

Fig. 3.18

(a) What is meant by the solvent front? (1 line) *(1 mark)*
(b) Name a suitable solvent to use in the experiment. (1 line) *(1 mark)*
(c) Explain whether you think brands X and Y contain the same coloured chemicals. (3 lines) *(3 marks)*

(WJEC)

OUTLINE ANSWERS

MULTIPLE CHOICE

ANSWER 1

The choice is between chromatography, which is usually used to separate dyes, and fractional distillation which will separate liquids of different boiling points. However, it is the green dye which must be separated and fractional distillation would not separate the green from the red dye because both have the *same* boiling point. The method must be chromatography. The key is B.

ANSWER 2

Sand is not soluble in water. It will not pass through a filter paper. The method of filtration will produce a *residue* of sand and a *filtrate* of water. The request for a cheap method eliminates both evaporation and distillation which will also separate sand from water. In these cases, energy is required for heating and these processes will therefore not be cheap. Condensation is the conversion of a vapour into a liquid and is not a method of separating a liquid from a solid. The key is D.

ANSWER 3

A. Condensation is the process by which water vapour from the air is cooled and becomes liquid water on the *cold* windows.

ANSWER 4

B. Distillation is the *two-part* process of vaporisation (liquid to gas) followed by condensation (gas to liquid).

ANSWER 5

E. The dye mixture was on the left-hand spot. The dyes present in the mixture have been separated by the process of chromatography. They are those dyes which have produced spots which are at the same level as spots of colour from the mixture. So dyes 1, 3 and 4 contain between them, the four dyes in the *mixture*.

ANSWER 6

E. Olive oil does not mix with water. The clue is in the word 'oil' if you did not already know this fact.

ANSWER 7

C. The undissolved material will not pass through a filter paper.

Section 3

ANSWER 8

D. Petrol is a 'fraction' of crude oil. It is a mixture of hydrocarbons of the correct flammability to drive a motor car engine.

Section 3

ANSWER 9

B. Blue copper sulphate crystals will form if the water is *carefully evaporated* from a solution of the crystals. Evaporation must be stopped *before* the solution dries up and the liquid left should be left to cool. The process is not the same as evaporation (to dryness). It is called crystallisation.

Section 3

ANSWER 10

A. Colouring in foods, soft drinks, etc., are dyes. They are separated by chromatography.

Section 3

ANSWER 11

This is a diagram of a *simple distillation* apparatus.

ANSWER 12

The process here is *filtration*.

ANSWER 13

This is *chromatography*.

2 > STRUCTURED QUESTIONS

ANSWER 14

(a) (i) Reservoir water is filtered through sand and gravel filter beds.
Filter paper would not be appropriate for the large-scale process – it would be expensive on paper and replacement of the filter would be time consuming.

(ii) The purpose is to remove any fine solid particles. (These will be trapped by the sand and gravel. Eventually the sand layer becomes clogged and must be washed clean to be reused. The washing process is carried out by 'back-flushing' – a process of pumping water *up* through the beds of sand and gravel and carrying the residue from the sand bed out of the filter vessel. When clean, the sand and gravel are allowed to settle again and are ready to be re-used.)

(b) (i) The process is distillation.
(Sea water contains salts. Water is easily vaporised but salts have high boiling points. Boiling the sea water will vaporise the water but not the salt. Passing the steam through a condenser will condense it to liquid water. The water will have been separated from the salt.)

(ii) Molecules of a liquid are always in motion. When heated, the molecules gain more energy. Those with the most energy are able to escape from the liquid and so form a vapour.
(All substances contain moving particles if they are not at absolute zero of temperature (–273 °C). Liquids, like water, contain particles which move about freely, at random, in all directions. Some of these molecules have enough energy to escape from the liquid into the space above the liquid. They are said to have vaporised. The higher the temperature, the more molecules are able to vaporise. In the vapour state molecules are much further apart than in the liquid state. They occupy at least one thousand times as much volume as the same number of molecules in the liquid.)

(iii) As explained above salts are not easily vaporised; they have high boiling points. Sea salts will not evaporate into the atmosphere.

ANSWER 15

(a) The solvent front is, as it suggests, the front edge of the solvent as it travels up the paper. On the finished chromatogram the solvent front shows the distance the solvent has travelled up the paper – for comparison with the distances travelled by the spots.

(b) The shampoos are soluble in water. Water could, therefore, be used as a solvent. *Any solvent* you might have used in chromatography would be accepted.

(c) The coloured spots from the two brands of shampoo show that both contain *the same* light yellow dye (spots at the same level) but each brand contains a *different* deep yellow dye (spots at different levels).

STUDENT'S ANSWER – EXAMINER'S COMMENTS

STUDENT TASK

You have been asked to discover by experiment which of TWO different indigestion tablets will give the fastest relief from acid indigestion. Give details of what you would do and how you would do it. Say how you would interpret the results of your experiments.
(An acid is provided which is similar to stomach acid.)

STUDENT ANSWER

> I would first take one of each of the two different tablets and put them in separate beakers. I would then add some of the acid, an equal volume, to each tablet. I would find the time taken to dissolve each tablet. The fastest tablet to dissolve would be the one which gives fastest relief from stomach ache.

❝ Your plan is a good one. It states clearly what you would do. It falls down on the detail of how you would do it. Remember that there are many ways of adding a liquid to a solid and you have not given precise details of your method. Would you add the acid slowly through a burette or quickly using a measuring cylinder? You do not state a volume of acid to be used. Would you use enough to dissolve the whole tablet? How would you find out how much this was? I presume you would use a stop watch to time the reaction though you do not say so. ❞

❝ A point about setting out your plans. Divide your answer up into paragraphs. One paragraph for the method to be used, another for the results you would expect to obtain and a third for the way in which you would interpret the results to find the answer to the problem. So many students, when they get a set of results, forget the aim of the experiment. Fortunately you did not.

Could you take the problem one step further? How could the slower of the two tablets be made to give faster relief from acid indigestion? ❞

REVIEW SHEET

- An element is _____

_____

Hydrogen and oxygen are two _____

- Compounds are formed when _____

_____

- A mixture consists of _____

_____

- Solubility is defined as _____

_____

- List 3 different types of mixtures, giving examples of each type _____
  1. _____
  2. _____
  3. _____

- Briefly explain each of the following methods of separation. In each case give an example for the type of separation involved

(a) Filtration _____

_____

_____

(b) Evaporation _____

_____

_____

(c) Crystallisation _____

_____

_____

(d) Fractional distillation _____

_____

_____

- Identify each process, then briefly explain it _____

(a)   **Process** _____

solid $\xrightarrow{heat}$ vapour $\xrightarrow{cool}$ solid   _____

Explanation _____

(b)   **Process** _____

liquid $\xrightarrow{heat}$ vapour $\xrightarrow{cool}$ liquid   _____

Explanation _____

- Draw and label the apparatus you might use in each of the following experiments

(a) decomposing a solid and testing for a gas produced

(b) collecting from an acid/carbonate reaction and a gas and measuring its volume

(c) getting pure salts from their saturated solutions

(d) finding the percentage of O_2 in air

CHAPTER 4

PARTICLES AND THEIR BEHAVIOUR

DIFFUSION
KINETIC THEORY
STATES OF MATTER
GAS LAWS

GETTING STARTED

The kinetic theory of matter
This is the hypothesis that best explains the behaviour of solids, liquids and gases. The theory states that:

  (i) matter is composed of tiny particles which may be atoms, molecules or ions;
 (ii) these particles are in unceasing motion at temperatures above absolute zero (0K or −273 °C);
(iii) at close quarters these particles attract each other, at larger distances the attractive force disappears;
(iv) the motion of the particles causes them always to be colliding with each other;
 (v) the higher the temperature of the matter, the greater the motion of its particles;
(vi) pressure in a gas is the result of bombardment of the sides of the containing vessel by the moving particles. The higher the rate of bombardment, the higher the pressure.

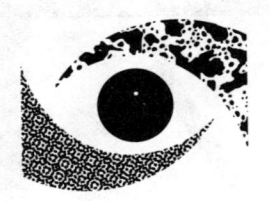

ESSENTIAL PRINCIPLES

The movement of particles within matter is called **DIFFUSION**. The *rate* of diffusion is affected by the following.

(i) **The distance apart of the particles – their concentration**. Particles are very far apart in gases but ten times closer in liquid and solids. Gases therefore diffuse many times faster than liquid because there is more space for movement and fewer collisions between particles. Solids hardly diffuse at all because the particles are so close there are no gaps through which they can pass to move from place to place.

(ii) **The energy of the particles**. The energy of particles depends upon temperature. The higher the temperature, the fast the diffusion.

(iii) **The mass of the particles**. The effect of mass is caused by the relationship between speed of particles and their temperature. This relationship is given by the equation

$$\text{temperature} \propto \tfrac{1}{2}mv^2$$

For a gas at a fixed temperature $\tfrac{1}{2}mv^2$ is fixed. So, the higher the mass, m, the lower the speed, v. Gases with heavy particles will diffuse at lower rates than gases with light particles – at the same temperature.

Hydrogen, whose molecules are the lightest known, will diffuse out of a toy balloon more quickly than any other gas. Weather balloons filled with hydrogen must have a special plastic coating to prevent the gas diffusing out and the balloon deflating. These principles are illustrated below.

1> DIFFUSION

(A) DIFFUSION IN GASES

Diffusion can be demonstrated using the apparatus shown in Fig. 4.1. The tube must be level to avoid the effect of gravity. The tube must be corked to prevent draughts moving the gases. The white compound formed where ammonia and hydrogen chloride meet is called ammonium chloride. Since this compound is formed nearer the hydrogen chloride end, it means that the ammonia molecules move further than the hydrogen chloride molecules in the same time, i.e. the ammonia molecules are moving faster than the hydrogen chloride molecules.

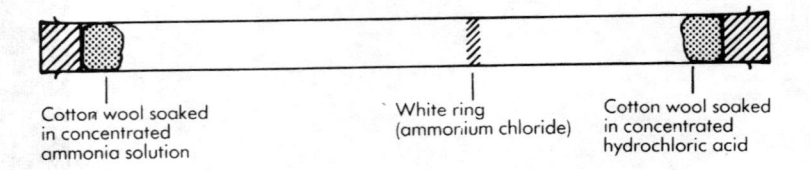

> Remember it is ammon*ium* chloride not ammonia chloride.

Fig. 4.1

(B) DIFFUSION IN LIQUIDS

Diffusion also takes place in liquids. This can be shown by placing a crystal of potassium manganate(VII) in a beaker of water. The solution slowly becomes uniformly purple in colour (Fig. 4.2).

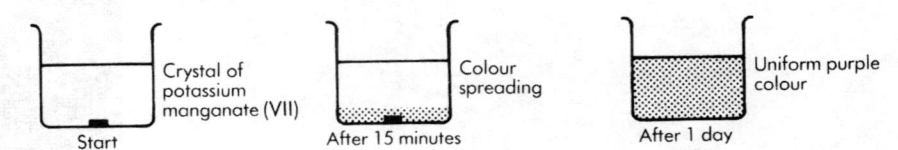

Fig. 4.2

Diffusion occurs more slowly in liquids than in gases because the particles are closer together and they therefore move more slowly because they collide with one another more frequently. Particles in a liquid are more closely packed than those in a gas.

(C) DIFFUSION IN SOLIDS

Diffusion can also take place in solids, but this process is very, very slow. The process can be speeded up by heating. This is the principle of spot welding. Welding is the joining together of two metals usually by heating the metals to a high temperature either with an oxy-acetylene flame or by using electricity.

(D) DIFFUSION AND POLLUTION

Diffusion has a major part to play in the removal of atmospheric pollutants.

> Fossil fuels contain sulphur and burn to produce sulphur dioxide.

Pollutants are usually formed in confined areas, e.g. from car exhaust pipes and factory chimneys. The pollutant from petrol engines is a mixture of carbon monoxide, unburnt petrol and oxides of nitrogen. This quickly spreads into the surrounding air and eventually into the world's atmosphere. The burning of fossil fuels in power stations causes a large amount of sulphur dioxide in the atmosphere and this reacts with water in the atmosphere to form *'acid rain'*. Power stations are built with tall chimneys to make sure that pollutants diffuse high into the atmosphere, thus keeping the concentration at ground level lower. This only removes the pollution problem from local areas to more distant parts. The tall chimneys release sulphur dioxide into the atmosphere and this is swept miles away, sometimes into other countries.

> Fuels such as hydrogen and ethanol are clean fuels.

2 KINETIC THEORY

> Energy cannot be created or destroyed. This is one of the basic laws of science.

Diffusion experiments provide evidence for the **kinetic theory**. Particles have kinetic energy – energy of movement. Gases have the greatest kinetic energy and solids the least. Energy cannot be created or destroyed, it can only be converted into another form of energy. Kinetic energy can be converted into heat energy, thus when a vapour condenses to a liquid, heat energy is given off. This explains why passing steam into cold water heats up the water. The kinetic energy of molecules of water in steam is converted into heat energy. This causes molecules in the water to move faster (their kinetic energy increases) and the water gets hotter.

3 STATES OF MATTER

(a) Solids, liquids and gases

All matter is either solid, liquid or gas (vapour).
- **Solids** have their particles arranged in an orderly manner within a crystal structure. The particles are touching and have strong forces of attraction. They are not able to move about within the structure (but they do vibrate) so solids retain their shape and volume.
- **Liquids** have particles that are slightly further apart than solids. The forces of attraction are therefore slightly less than in solids. This gives particles the ability and space to move about and around each other within the liquid giving it the property of a fixed volume but allowing it to take up the shape of its vessel.
- **Gases** have particles that are very much further apart than in liquids. The attactive forces are non-existent. The particles have completely free movement in all directions and are no longer held together so a gas will take up the volume and shape of its container.

(b) Changes of state of matter on heating

Particles in *solids* are not able to move about within the crystal but continuously vibrate about their mean position. If the energy of the crystal increases, by raising its temperature, the particles vibrate more strongly until at the melting point of the crystal, the particles become free to move about from place to place.

In *liquids*, the freely moving particles are still close together, as in solids. They have only a few per cent more space in which to move about. As a liquid is heated, however, its particles move about more rapidly since they now have more energy. At a specific temperature, the particles achieve enough energy to escape completely from the attraction of their neighbours – they escape into the gas or vapour state. The liquid state is unusual in one respect – particles are able to escape into the gaseous state at all temperatures and not just at the boiling point. The number escaping is small just above the melting point and increases up to the boiling point. This results in liquids which have quite high boiling points evaporating even at room temperature. For example petrol will slowly evaporate away completely at room temperature even though some of its constituents boil at 200 °C! Such liquids are said to be **volatile**.

Once vaporised, the particles have enough energy to move about at very high speeds and to become far apart. These changes are shown in graph form in Fig. 4.3. Because the particles are nearly ten times further apart in three dimensions, *gases* or vapours are one thousand times ($10 \times 10 \times 10$) less dense than liquids and solids.

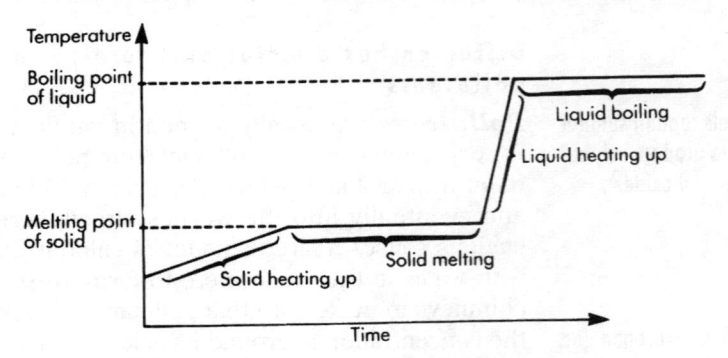

Fig. 4.3

On cooling, the reverse happens. The gas becomes first liquid and finally a solid (Fig. 4.4).

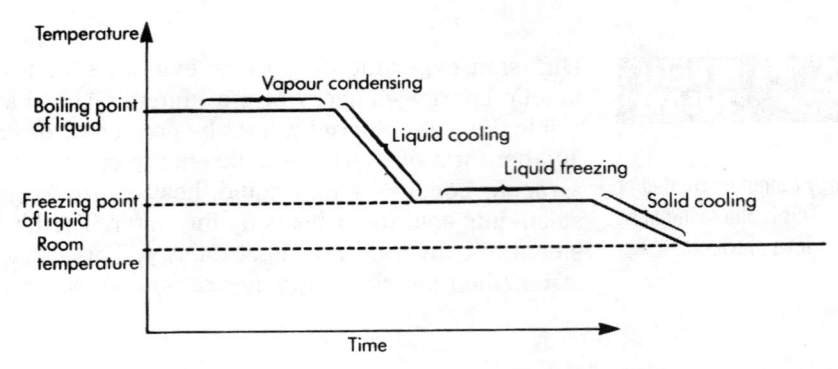

Fig. 4.4

Solid, liquid and gas are called the three **states of matter**. Fig. 4.5 shows the words used to describe the changes from one state to another.

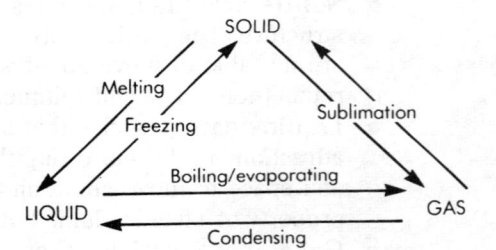

Fig. 4.5

(c) The effect of pressure changes of the change on melting and boiling

In addition to heating, a change of state can be brought about by a change of pressure. Reducing the pressure will vaporise a liquid; increasing the pressure will liquify a vapour. A vapour is a state that can be liquified by increased pressure alone. The term gas is used to describe a substance that cannot be liquified by pressure alone, but requires cooling also.

(d) Size of particles

If a crystal of a coloured substance such as potassium manganate(VII) is placed in a large beaker full of water, the whole solution becomes coloured. This solution can be diluted further and the colour can still be detected. We can explain this observation if we assume that potassium manganate(VII) crystals are made up of a very large number of very small particles.

(e) Brownian motion

Brownian motion is named after the botanist Robert Brown. He noticed that when he looked at pollen grains floating on water under a microscope, the pollen grains were moving in a random way. This movement is explained by assuming that water molecules are hitting pollen grains in a random way causing the pollen to move erratically. Brownian motion can be seen whenever small particles are suspended in a liquid or gas, e.g. smoke particles in air or toothpaste suspended in water.

(f) A fourth state of matter?

It used to be said that there existed a fourth state of matter – the **colloidal state**. This includes sols, gels, emulsions, aerosols and foams. We do not now regard these as different states of matter from solid, liquid or gas. They are mixtures with very special properties.

Each is a mixture of substances in two states. They are different from the mixtures we have discussed earlier because of the size of the particles present. In colloids the components of the mixture consists of particles which are bigger than atoms, molecules or ions of the other. Instead of the one component of the mixture **dissolving** in the other, we say that it is **dispersed**.

> Colloids are dispersions of one state of matter in another.

Some common colloids are shown in the table below. More are possible but outside your course of study. There are nine pair combinations possible, but the gas-in-gas mixture cannot be colloidal because gases cannot form the large particles necessary to form dispersions.

Colloidal mixture	Common name	Example
solid in gas	a smoke	cigarette smoke, insecticide smokes
liquid in solid	a gel	jelly, hair gel
liquid in gas	an aerosol	mist or fog, hair spray
liquid in liquid	an emulsion	emulsion paint, cosmetic creams, butter
gas in liquid	a foam	hair mousse, beer froth

Emulsions are dispersions of one liquid in another. We recognise two types in common use:
  (i) oil-in-water, such as salad cream – mainly oil;
  (ii) water-in-oil, such as moisurising cream mainly water.

To disperse one liquid in another liquid that it does not normally mix with requires an **emulsifying agent**. The emulsifying agent is a 'detergent-like' molecule. It has a water-loving head and an oil-loving tail. The head is attracted to the water, the tail is attracted to the oil. Fig. 4.6 shows the difference between the two diagramatically

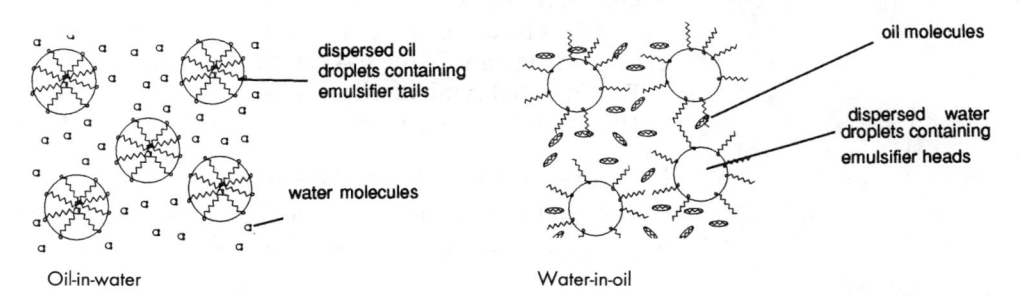

Fig. 4.6 Oil-in-water   Water-in-oil

4 GAS LAWS

These show the relationship between pressure (p), volume (v) and temperature (T) for a fixed mass (m) of gas.

If we accept the hypothesis that the pressure of a gas is proportional to the rate of bombardment of the sides of the gas container by its particles, we should be able to predict the effect of changing two of the variables.
  (i) Changing the volume of the gas whilst keeping the mass and temperature constant.

(ii) changing the temperature of the gas whilst keeping the mass and volume constant.

Remember we must only change one variable at a time if the results of an investigation are not to become meaningless!

Prediction (i) Suppose we reduce the volume of the gas. There will now be the same number of particles in a smaller space. An increased concentration of particles should result in higher rate of collision with the sides of the vessel. That means a higher pressure. We predict that reducing the volume of a given mass of gas at a constant temperature should increase its pressure. This is what happens in practice.

Prediction (ii) Suppose we increase the temperature of the gas. The particles will now be moving around faster. They will bombard the vessel sides at a higher rate. The pressure should therefore rise. We predict that raising the temperature of a given mass of gas at constant volume will raise its pressure. This is what happens in practice.

(i) Boyle's Law

When a gas is compressed by increasing the pressure upon it, the particles are forced into a smaller volume. Only the gas state is compressible because only in gases is there enough space between particles to allow for them to be squeezed closer together.

Robert Boyle discovered that the compression is proportional to the pressure. His Law is usually stated the other way round. The volume of a gas is inversely proportional to its pressure. This is written symbolically as

$$v \propto \frac{1}{p} \quad \text{also } p \times v \text{ is constant}$$

If 100 cm³ of air in a sealed gas syringe has the pressure on it doubled, its volume goes down to 50 cm³. Hence

initially $100 \propto \frac{1}{1}$ and finally $50 \propto \frac{1}{2}$ but $100 \times 1 = 50 \times 2$ that is pv is the same – constant.

> **Note that there is no degree (°) sign in front of the K**

The absolute temperature scale

The lowest temperature possible is –273 °C. This is called absolute zero of temperature and is given the value 0 K on the Kelvin scale of temperature.

To convert °C to K ADD 273   so 0 °C becomes 273 K
To convert K to °C SUBTRACT 273   so 0 K becomes –273 °C
Confirm for yourself that 500 °C is 773 K.

(ii) Charles's Law

When gases are heated, they expand. The particles gain energy and their more violent motion causes them to collide more often. This pushes them further apart.

Note: the particles themselves do not get bigger!

Jacques Charles discovered that the expansion was proportional to the increase in temperature. For every 1 °C rise in temperature Charles found the volume increased by 1/273 of its original volume. So by taking a gas at 273 °C and heating it by a further 273 °C, the volume of the gas can be doubled.

This is stated symbolically as $v \propto T$.

The volume of a gas is proportional to its absolute temperature.

(iii) The Combined Gas Laws

Boyle's and Charles' laws are usually combined, since both relate the volume of a gas to a change in another variable. Combined, the laws become

$$pv \propto T \qquad \textbf{equation (1)}$$

For a comparision of a fixed mass of gas under different conditions we can use equation 2.

$$\frac{p_1 v_1}{T_1} = \frac{p_2 v_2}{T_2} \qquad \textbf{equation (2)}$$

Doubling the absolute temperature of a fixed mass of gas at constant volume should double its pressue. This prediction arises from inserting the appropriate values into the general gas equation:

Initially $p_1 = 1$ atmosphere Finally $p_2 = ?$
$v_1 =$ constant, say 1 litre $v_2 =$ constant at 1 litre
$T_1 =$ say 300 K $T_2 = 600$ K

Applying the **equation (2)** above

step 1 $\dfrac{p_1 v_1}{T_1}$ is $\dfrac{1 \times 1}{300} = \dfrac{1}{300}$ must equal $\dfrac{p_2 v_2}{T_2}$ which is $\dfrac{p_2 \times 1}{600}$

step 2 that is $\dfrac{1}{300} = \dfrac{p_2}{600}$

step 3 rearranging we get $p_2 = \dfrac{600 \times 1}{300} = 2$ atmospheres pressure

So by doubling the absolute temperature of the gas we have doubled its pressure provided we keep the mass of gas at the same volume (that is, we change only one variable)

Try using the same equation to confirm that if the absolute temperature of a litre of gas is doubled from 273 K to 546 K, at constant pressure, the volume will double.

EXAMINATION QUESTIONS

MULTIPLE CHOICE

QUESTION 1
Which of the terms listed below describes the change from liquid to vapour?

A condensation
B distillation
C evaporation
D sublimation

(SEG)

QUESTION 2
Which one of the following processes involves a change of state?

A decanting
B evaporation
C filtration
D diffusion
E centrifuging

QUESTION 3
When water changes into steam, the molecules become

A much larger
B more widely separated
C less in mass
D separate atoms
E much smaller

QUESTION 4
When ice is changing from solid to liquid at its melting point

A heat is given out
B its particles become more ordered
C its particles gain energy
D its temperature increases

(SEG)

QUESTION 5
A gas jar containing nitrogen dioxide is placed on top of a gas jar containing air (Fig. 4.7).

Nitrogen dioxide is a dark brown gas and is denser than air.

Which one of the following correctly describes the colours inside the gas jars after a long period of time?

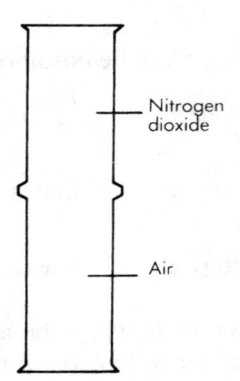

Fig. 4.7

	Upper gas jar	*Lower gas jar*
A	dark brown	colourless
B	brown	brown
C	dark brown	light brown
D	colourless	dark brown
E	light brown	dark brown

(SEG)

QUESTION 6

If fine pollen grains on the surface of water are examined under a microscope, it will be seen that the pollen grains are in random motion, frequently changing direction. The movement is most likely to be due to

A air draughts blowing on the water
B chemical reaction between the pollen and the water
C attraction and repulsion between charged particles
D collisions between water molecules and pollen grains
E electrolysis of pollen grains

(ULEAC)

STRUCTURED QUESTIONS

QUESTION 7

Diagram B shows the arrangement of the particles in a liquid (Fig. 4.8).

(a) Complete the diagrams A and C to show the arrangement of the particles in a solid and gas. *(2 marks)*
(b) How would you change liquid B into a gas? (2 lines) *(1 mark)*

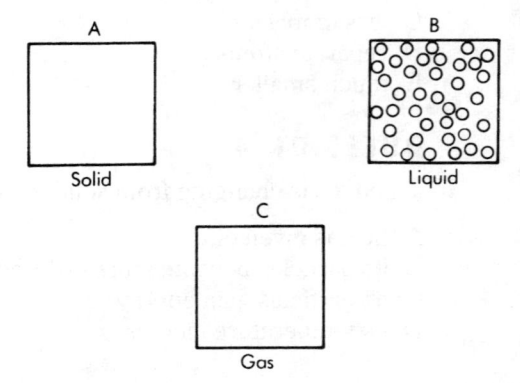

Fig. 4.8

QUESTION 8

A mixture of heptane (b.p. 100 °C) and 2,2-dimethylpentane (b.p. 80 °C) was separated by distillation. The graph below shows the temperature of the vapour entering the condenser over a period of time (Fig. 4.9).

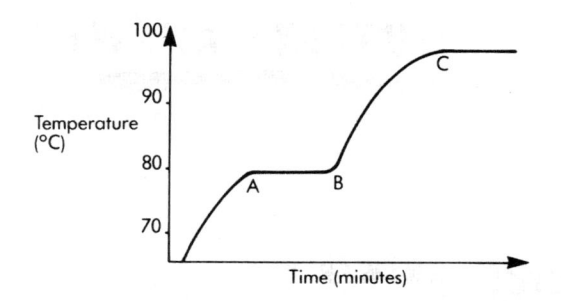

Fig. 4.9

(i) Why is the graph flat between A and B? (1 line) *(1 mark)*
(ii) Comment on the composition of the vapour entering the condenser between times B and C. (2 lines) *(1 mark)*

(NEAB)

QUESTION 9

(a) The diagrams below show two experiments to demonstrate diffusion. Describe what you would observe in each experiment (Figs 4.10 and 4.11).

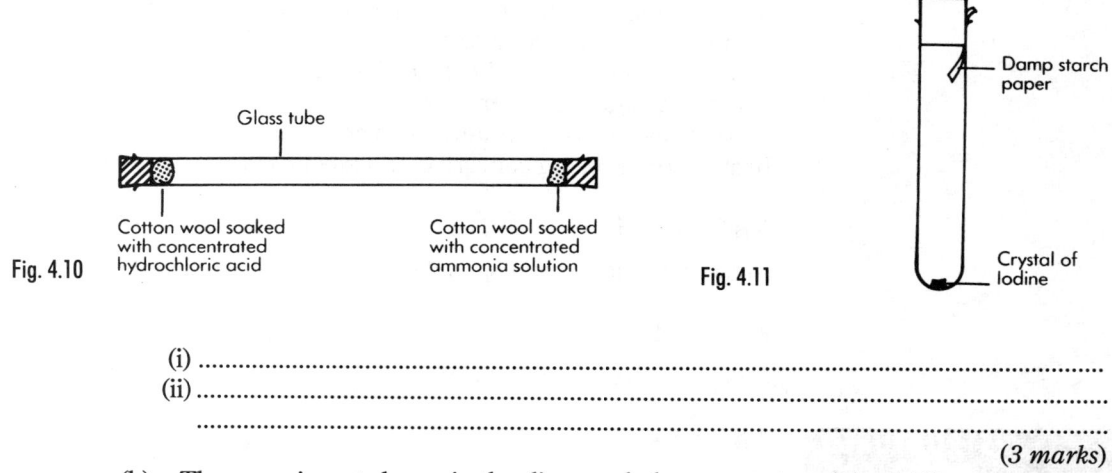

Fig. 4.10

Fig. 4.11

(i) ....
(ii) ....
....

(3 marks)

(b) The experiment shown in the diagram below was set up (Fig. 4.12).

How would you show that potassium hydroxide had diffused through the liquid? (2 lines) *(2 marks)*

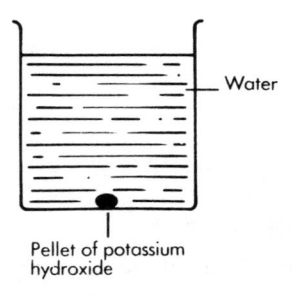

Fig. 4.12

(c) In the manufacture of ammonia by the Haber process, nitrogen and hydrogen are mixed and then passed along a pipe to the reacting vessel. If this pipe became porous would the gas mixture

(i) become richer in nitrogen
(ii) become richer in hydrogen
(iii) be unchanged

Answer..
Give an explanation (3 lines). *(3 marks)*

OUTLINE ANSWERS

MULTIPLE CHOICE

ANSWER 1
Liquid to vapour is evaporation – key C.

ANSWER 2
Answer: B (see above).
If you do not know the meanings of the other words look them up.

ANSWER 3
Answer B. Water molecules are identical to steam molecules; but in steam the molecules are further apart.

ANSWER 4
Ice is a solid and therefore its particles are arranged in an orderly way. When it is heated, energy is required to make the particles move, and therefore A is incorrect and since the particles become more disordered B is also incorrect. Heat energy is converted into kinetic energy, and hence the particles gain more energy – C is the correct answer. Temperature does not rise, because during the melting process all the heat energy is being converted into kinetic energy.

ANSWER 5
Answer: B, the gas will spread itself evenly through both gas jars.

ANSWER 6
Answer: D (see Section 3(e)).

STRUCTURED QUESTIONS

ANSWER 7
(a) (See Fig. 4.13).
Note in diagram A particles in a solid are orderly and vibrate in fixed positions. In diagram C, particles in a gas are far apart and move randomly.
(b) Liquid B would have to be heated to convert it into a gas.

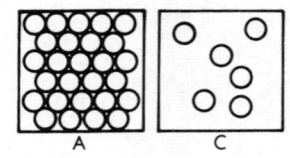

Fig. 4.13

ANSWER 8
(i) One of the vapours, 2,2-dimethylpentane, is condensing.
(ii) The vapour contains a little 2,2-dimethylpentane mixed with greater proportions of heptane until at 100°C the vapour is pure heptane.

ANSWER 9
(a) (i) A white solid is formed nearer the hydrochloric acid end.
(ii) A faint purple colour is seen in the tube (iodine vapour), and the starch paper turns blue. (Starch paper is used as a test for iodine.)
(b) Place a piece of red litmus paper in the top of the solution, eventually the paper will turn blue. (N.B. potassium hydroxide is a white solid and a solution of potassium hydroxide is colourless and alkaline.)

(c) The mixture becomes richer in nitrogen.
Hydrogen is less dense than nitrogen (hydrogen = 2, nitrogen = 28), therefore hydrogen will diffuse more quickly out of the porous pipe, leaving the mixture richer in nitrogen.

STUDENT'S ANSWER – EXAMINER'S COMMENTS

QUESTION

A plug of cotton wool was soaked in concentrated hydrochloric acid and placed in one end of a long dry glass tube and, at the same time, a similar plug soaked in concentrated ammonia solution was placed in the other end. After several minutes a white deposit of ammonium chloride formed in the tube in the position shown below.

(a) Explain why ammonium chloride was formed nearer the end of the tube soaked in concentrated hydrochloric acid.

> Because the molecules of ammonia move faster than the particles of hydrogen chloride therefore meeting at a point nearer the hydrogen chloride.
> (2 marks)

❝ Yes, but you should have said that HCl is denser than NH₃. ❞

(b) Explain why the tube must be
(i) level

> The tube must be level to make sure gravity has no effect on the movement of the molecules.

❝ Draughts would also affect the result. ❞

(ii) corked

> It has to be corked so that the molecules cannot go out into the air but are forced to join together and be concentrated

❝ No! Both the gases are soluble in water. ❞

❝ Good. ❞

(iii) dry.

> It has to be dry so that there is no water vapour affecting the movement of the molecules.
> (4 marks)

(c) What name is used to describe the movement of molecules?

> Diffusion
> (1 mark)

❝ More is needed here, as there are three marks for this section. It dissociates to give the gases NH₃ and HCl which combine again on cooling. ❞

(d) Molecules of ammonia and hydrogen chloride move at very high speeds. Explain why it took several minutes before ammonium chloride was formed.

> The molecules collide with molecules in the air which prevents them moving very quickly.
> (2 marks)

(e) Explain why, when ammonium chloride is heated in a test tube, the white solid disappears and then re-appears on the cold part of the test tube.

> It sublimes
> (3 marks)

❝ Yes, nearly all ammonium compounds are white. ❞

❝ Careless – should be ammonium. ❞

(f) If a similar experiment were repeated using concentrated hydrobromic acid (HBr) instead of hydrochloric acid, describe all you would see and name the product formed.

> A white deposit would be formed near the hydrobromic end. The product formed is ammonia bromide.
> (3 marks)

❝ Some good answers overall, but you have not used your Chemistry knowledge in (b) (iii). Also you have missed a few points. Still there is enough here for a mark of 9/15. ❞

REVIEW SHEET

- What does the Kinetic Theory of Matter state?
  (a) _____
  (b) _____
  (c) _____
  (d) _____
  (e) _____

- Diffusion is _____

- Complete the equation relating temperature to the mass (m) and speed (v) of particles!

  temperature ∝ [   ]

- Complete the box labels in this diagram for the change of steam to ice.

- What effect does **pressure** have on the different states of matter?
  _____
  _____
  _____
  _____

- What does the word **Colloids** mean?
  _____
  _____
  _____
  _____

- What is Brownian motion?
  _____
  _____
  _____
  _____

- What is the function of an emulsifying agent?

- State Boyle's Law.

- State Charles' Law.

- Use the Combined Gas Laws to show what will happen if you double the absolute temperature of a fixed mass of gas at constant volume.

CHAPTER 5

ATOMIC STRUCTURE AND BONDING

INSIDE THE ATOM
THE NUCLEUS OF AN ATOM
THE HYDROGEN ATOM
ISOTOPES OF ELEMENTS
RELATIVE ATOMIC MASS
THE ELECTRONS
PERIODS AND GROUPS
NOBLE GAS STRUCTURES
PROPERTIES OF MOLECULAR SUBSTANCES
PROPERTIES OF IONIC COMPOUNDS
IONIC AND MOLECULAR COMPOUNDS
MOLECULAR LIQUIDS AS SOLVENTS
MACROMOLECULES
METALLIC STRUCTURES

GETTING STARTED

As we discussed in Chapter 3, all elements are made up of atoms which are *characteristic* of those elements. Atoms rarely exist singly (noble gas atoms being an exception) but normally join with other atoms to form molecules or ionic structures.

An atom is the smallest particle of an element which can still have the *chemical properties of that element*. In this chapter we consider those particles which are *smaller* than atoms. We should understand that such particles do not have the properties of the elements of which they form part.

CHAPTER 5 ATOMIC STRUCTURE AND BONDING

ESSENTIAL PRINCIPLES

1 > INSIDE THE ATOM

Atoms are made up of particles which are even smaller than the atoms themselves. We call these particles *sub-atomic* particles. They are protons and neutrons (together called nucleons) and electrons. The relative masses and relative charges of these sub-atomic particles are shown in Fig. 5.1.

Sub-atomic particle	Relative mass	Relative charge
proton	1	1+
neutron	1	0
electron	negligible	1–

Fig. 5.1 Relative masses and charges of nucleons and electrons.

2 > THE NUCLEUS OF AN ATOM

> If an atom was magnified to the size of Wembley Stadium, its nucleus would be only the size of a flea!

The nucleus of an atom contains protons and neutrons (except the nucleus of a hydrogen atom). Compared with the size of the atom as a whole, the nucleus is minute, occupying only one thousand, million, million, millionth of the volume of the atom.

(A) ATOMIC NUMBER (PROTON NUMBER)

The number of protons in a nucleus is the *atomic number of the atom*.

3 > THE UNUSUAL HYDROGEN ATOM AND ION

(B) MASS NUMBER (NUCLEON NUMBER)

The sum of the numbers of protons and neutrons (nucleons) in an atom is its *mass number*.

The mass number and atomic number of an atom are usually shown as in Fig. 5.2. From these values the number of neutrons in this atom can be calculated to be 14.

Mass number 27   27 (neutrons + protons)
                                 Al
Atomic number 13   13 protons (13 electrons)

Fig. 5.2 The positioning of mass number and atomic number on the symbol of an element.

The hydrogen atom is the only atom which does not have neutrons (see the table below). It consists of a proton and an electron only.

Hydrogen ions are also unique among ions because they have **no electrons or neutrons**. Hydrogen ions are just **protons**.

Fig. 5.3 gives data for some important elements.

4 > ISOTOPES OF ELEMENTS

> Fixed number of protons

> Variable number of neutrons

A fixed characteristic of all the atoms of a given element is the *atomic number or number of protons in the nucleus of each atom of that element*.

However, a sample of almost any pure element will show the presence of several kinds of atoms *differing only in mass number. These are called isotopes*.

For example, there are three different kinds of hydrogen atom in any pure sample of hydrogen gas. The atomic number of each of the different hydrogen atoms is 1, which means they are all *identical* in *chemical properties*. They *differ* in the number of neutrons in each nucleus. *In chemical reactions there is no difference in the reactions of different isotopes of the same element*.

H-1 hydrogen	H 1 proton : 0 neutrons,	atomic number 1,	mass number 1,
H-2 deuterium	H 1 proton : 1 neutron,	atomic number 1,	mass number 2,
H-3 tritium	H 1 proton : 2 neutrons,	atomic number 1,	mass number 3.

Element	Atomic number	Number of protons	Number of neutrons	Mass number	Symbol
Hydrogen	1	1	NONE	1	$^{1}_{1}H$
Helium	2	2	2	4	$^{4}_{2}He$
Carbon	6	6	6	12	$^{12}_{6}C$
Nitrogen	7	7	7	14	$^{14}_{7}N$
Oxygen	8	8	8	16	$^{16}_{8}O$
Fluorine	9	9	10	19	$^{19}_{9}F$
Neon	10	10	10	20	$^{20}_{10}Ne$
Sodium	11	11	12	23	$^{23}_{11}Na$
Magnesium	12	12	12	24	$^{24}_{12}Mg$
Aluminium	13	13	14	27	$^{27}_{13}Al$
Sulphur	16	16	16	32	$^{32}_{16}S$
Chlorine	17	17	18	35	$^{35}_{17}Cl$
Argon	18	18	22	40	$^{40}_{18}Ar$
Potassium	19	19	20	39	$^{39}_{19}K$
Calcium	20	20	20	40	$^{40}_{20}Ca$
Iron	26	26	30	56	$^{56}_{26}Fe$
Copper	29	29	35	64	$^{64}_{29}Cu$
Zinc	30	30	35	65	$^{65}_{30}Zn$
Bromine	35	35	45	80	$^{80}_{35}Br$
Iodine	53	53	74	127	$^{127}_{53}I$

Fig. 5.3 Data for some important elements.

The element chlorine, atomic number 17, similarly has different kinds of atom.

Cl-35   chlorine-35   17 protons : 18 neutrons mass number 35,
Cl-37   chlorine-37   17 protons : 20 neutrons mass number 37.

5 > RELATIVE ATOMIC MASS

The *relative atomic mass* of an element is measured on a natural sample of the element. It is based on the *average mass of all the atoms in the sample*. You can see from the information above, about isotopes, that the presence of several kinds of atom of the same element with different masses will give the average mass of an atom a value which *will not be a whole number*. The relative atomic mass of chlorine is 35.5 because there are 25 atoms of mass 37 and 75 atoms of mass 35 in every 100 chlorine atoms. So, for 100 chlorine atoms chosen at random, the total *mass* is

$$(25 \times 37) + (75 \times 35) = 3550 \text{ units}$$

Therefore, the average relative atomic mass of a chlorine atom is

$$3550/100 = 35.5 \text{ units}.$$

6 > THE ELECTRONS

THE ELECTRON STRUCTURES OF ATOMS

The negatively charged *electrons* of an atom surround the positively charged nucleus as a 'cloud' of negative charge. This 'cloud' of electrons is normally considered to exist as spherical layers – like the skins of an onion – called *shells of electrons* (Fig. 5.4A). The number of electrons is the same as the number of protons in the nucleus of the atom. For each shell there is a limit to the number of electrons it can hold. This 'shell limit' is the same for all atoms.

The FIRST shell maximum is   2 electrons,
The SECOND shell maximum is   8 electrons,
The THIRD shell maximum is   18 electrons.

The symbol in brackets is the corresponding noble gas atom.

7 > PERIODS AND GROUPS

Examination of the contents of Fig. 5.4A will show that there are patterns in the arrangement of electrons in the atoms of the elements shown. Two patterns are seen: atoms may differ in

(i) the number of *shells* of electrons they contain;

and/or

(ii) the number of electrons they have in their *outer shell*.

Element	Electron Structure of the element	Electron Structure of the ion formed	Formula of ion
H		0	H⁺
He	2	NO IONS	NO IONS
Li	2 1	2 (He)	Li⁺
Be	2 2	NO IONS	NO IONS
B	2 3	NO IONS	NO IONS
C	2 4	NO IONS	NO IONS
N	2 5	2 8 (Ne)	N³⁻
O	2 6	2 8 (Ne)	O²⁻
F	2 7	2 8 (Ne)	F⁻
Ne	2 8	NO IONS	NO IONS
Na	2 8 1	2 8 (Ne)	Na⁺
Mg	2 8 2	2 8 (Ne)	Mg²⁺
Al	2 8 3	2 8 (Ne)	Al³⁺
Si	2 8 4	NO IONS	NO IONS
P	2 8 5	NO IONS	NO IONS
S	2 8 6	2 8 (Ar)	S²⁻
Cl	2 8 7	2 8 8 (Ar)	Cl⁻
Ar	2 8 8	NO IONS	NO IONS
K	2 8 8 1	2 8 8 (Ar)	K⁺
Ca	2 8 8 2	2 8 8 (Ar)	Ca²⁺

Fig. 5.4A The electron structures of the first twenty elements and their ions (where the ions exist).

Periods

The number of shells (not necessarily complete shells) an atom has tells us which **period** of the table the element is placed in, e.g. hydrogen is in period one; sodium is in period three (see Fig. 5.4A). **Periods** are **horizontal rows** of elements.

Groups

Period	Group 1	Group 2	Group 7	Group 0
2	Li 2 1	Be 2 2	F 2 7	Ne 2 8
3	Na 2 8 1	Mg 2 8 2	Cl 2 8 7	Ar 2 8 8
4	K 2 8 8 1	Ca 2 8 8 2	Br 2 8 18 7	Kr 2 8 18 8

Fig. 5.4B The electron structures of elements of groups 1, 2, 7 and 0.

The number of electrons in the outer shell of an atom (called **valency electrons**) tells us which **group** the element is in, e.g. lithium is in group 1; chlorine in group 7 (Fig. 5.4B).

Groups are **vertical** columns of elements having similar properties. It should be clear from Fig. 5.3 and Fig. 5.4A that the number of electrons in atoms increases by one as the atomic number increases by one. An increase of one electron in the atom of each successive element in a period will cause the outer electron shell to fill **as the eighth group is reached** (called Group 0). Since the eighth group contains noble gas elements, an outer shell of eight electrons evidently makes atoms very unreactive (stable).

The start of a new period occurs with the start of a new shell of electrons.

8 NOBLE (INERT) GAS ELECTRONIC STRUCTURES

The discovery of a group of elements which were **totally unreactive** to other elements was of great importance to chemists. What was the cause of this **inertness**? The electron structures of these gases gave the answer. The electrons of each element **filled the shells available to them**.

When chemists looked at what happened to the electrons in atoms of other elements when these elements reacted, they found that elements always reacted in such a way that their atoms gained the electron structure of the nearest noble (inert) gas atom.

There are many ways of drawing the electron structures of molecules. In this book we shall show you **two** ways. Both are perfectly acceptable and you may be familiar with one or with the other. Fig. 5.5 below shows one way, and Fig. 12.8 (Chapter 12.2, Section 1) another.

(A) NOBLE GAS STRUCTURES BY GAIN OR LOSS OF ELECTRONS

Anions

Cations

Ions with noble gain structures

If the process of achieving a noble gas structure occurs by **gain** of one or more electrons, then a negatively charged atom (called an **anion**) is formed. If the process occurs by **loss** of one or more electrons, then a positively charged atom (called a **cation**) is formed.

Where gain or loss of electrons happens, these electrons have to be given to, or taken from, the other reacting element. So if the atoms of one element **gain** electrons, the atoms of the other reacting element must **lose** electrons. At the end of the reactions the atoms of **both** elements will have full electron shells.

(B) SODIUM ATOMS AND CHLORINE ATOMS

In the reaction between sodium atoms and chlorine atoms

$$Na(g) + Cl(g) \rightarrow Na^+(s) + Cl^-(s).$$

The electron structures are

Atoms					Ions				
Na	2	8	1	→	Na$^+$(s)	2	8		1 electron lost,
Cl	2	8	7	→	Cl$^-$(s)	2	8	8	1 electron gained

To represent these electron structures **fully** we should use a diagram such as Fig. 5.5.

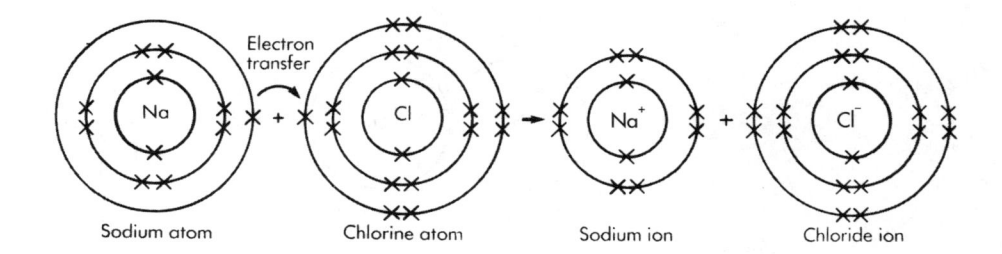

Fig. 5..5

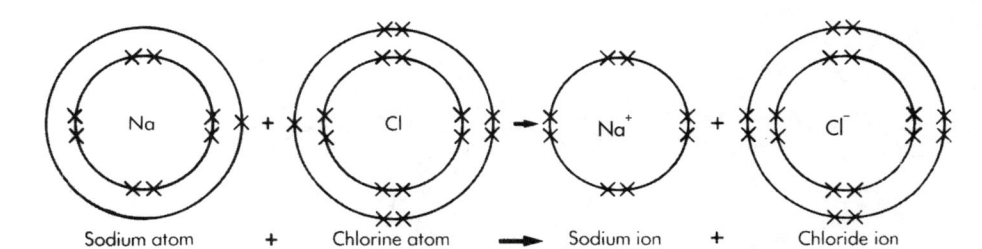

Sodium atom + Chlorine atom → Sodium ion + Chloride ion

Fig. 5.6

Sodium atom + Chlorine atom → Sodium ion + Chloride ion

However, since only the **outer electrons** are involved in the reaction, we can represent the combination as shown in Fig. 5.6.

Here only the outer two shells of each atom are shown. In this case the single electron in the outer shell of the sodium atom is lost to the chlorine atom and the next shell inside becomes the full outer shell. Similar changes occur in the formation of ions from other elements.

(C) ELECTRON SHARING

Fig. 5.4A above contains details of elements which **do not form ions**. The atoms of these elements achieve noble gas electron structures by electron **sharing**. For example,

(i) In elements

Single bond

Each **hydrogen atom** (Fig. 5.8), by contributing its single electron to the bond, gains the noble gas electron structure of **helium**. The sharing of two electrons in this way creates a **single bond**.

Each **chlorine** atom (Fig. 5.9) contributes **one** electron to the bond. The total number of electrons in the outer shell of each chlorine atom will then be **eight**.

Because **oxygen** atoms (Fig. 5.10) have **two** electrons fewer than eight, two oxygen

Metal atoms	Group	Electrons lost	Ion formed
lithium	1	1	Li⁺
sodium	1	1	Na⁺
potassium	1	1	K⁺
magnesium	2	2	Mg²⁺
calcium	2	2	Ca²⁺
aluminium	3	3	Al³⁺

Non-metal atoms	Group	Electrons gained	Ion formed
oxygen	6	2	O²⁻
sulphur	6	2	S²⁻
chlorine	7	1	Cl⁻
bromine	7	1	Br⁻
iodine	7	1	I⁻

Fig. 5.7 Some atoms and their ions.

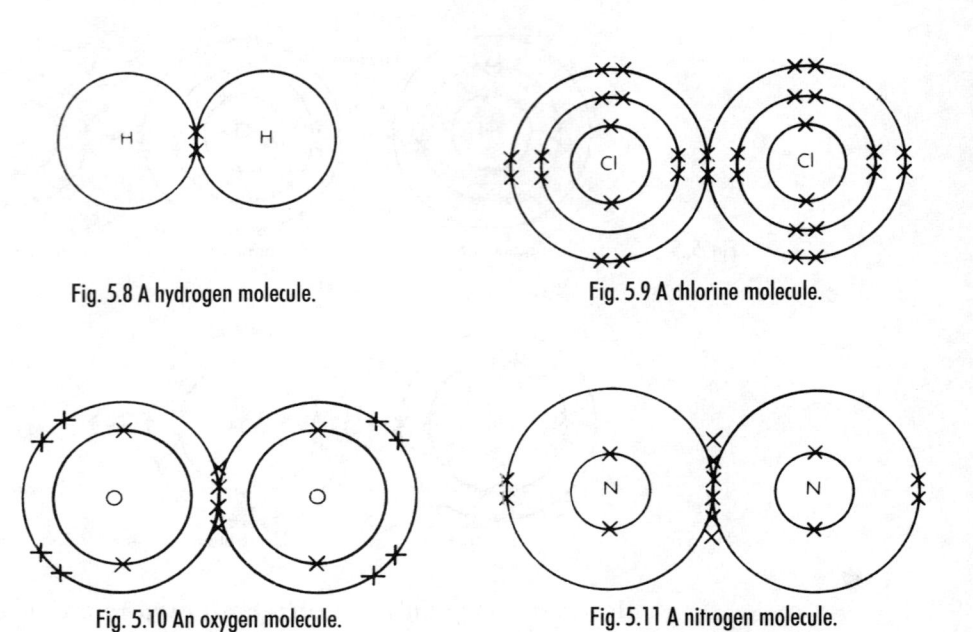

Fig. 5.8 A hydrogen molecule.

Fig. 5.9 A chlorine molecule.

Fig. 5.10 An oxygen molecule.

Fig. 5.11 A nitrogen molecule.

Double bond

atoms must *each* contribute two electrons to the bond. A four-electron bond is called a double bond. Each oxygen atom will then have the electron structure of the noble gas neon. The nitrogen molecule, N_2 is formed in a similar way with a triple bond by the sharing of six electrons (Fig. 5.11).

(ii) In compounds

The electron structure of *hydrogen* and *chlorine* atoms are:

    hydrogen   1
    chlorine   2   8   7

Hydrogen cannot achieve the electron structure of its nearest noble gas unless it gains one electron. However, that electron could only come from a chlorine atom. The chlorine atom can only achieve the electron structure of *its* nearest noble gas by **gaining an electron**. Since **both** atoms cannot gain one electron, they **share** two electrons – one from each atom. This gives *each* atom a noble gas electron structure. In Fig. 5.12, the outer shells only are shown. All inner shells are full.

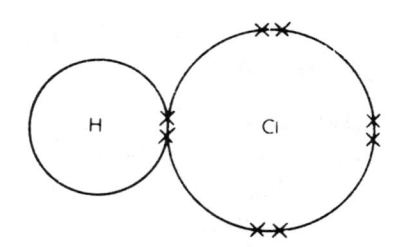

Fig. 5.12

The structures shown in this section are not all required for every syllabus. Consult the syllabus you are studying to see which structures you are expected to know.

(D) FORMULAE OF MOLECULAR COMPOUNDS

The relative numbers of atoms combining to form molecules determines the formula of the compound (Fig. 5.13).

A methane molecule

A tetrachloromethane molecule

A trichloromethane molecule

An ammonia molecule

A carbon dioxide molecule

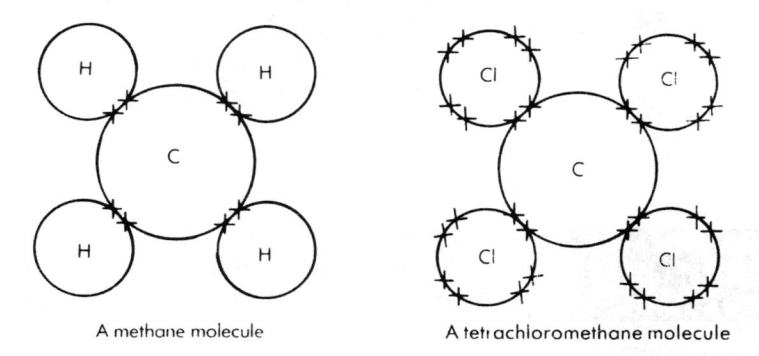

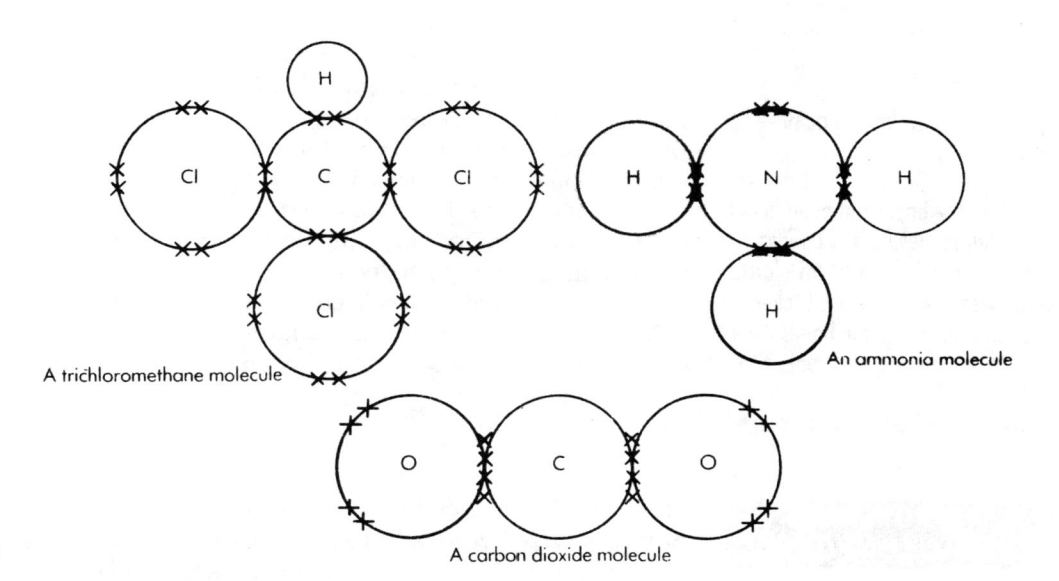

Fig. 5.13

(i) Methane

Carbon is in group four and so has four electrons in its outer shell. Hydrogen has a single outer electron. For both atoms to gain the electron structure of their nearest noble gas, four hydrogen atoms must share their outer electron with a single carbon atom. Each carbon—hydrogen bond is a single, two-electron bond.

(ii) Tetrachloromethane

Here the four electrons in the outer shell of the carbon atom need an additional four electrons from chlorine atoms for a complete octet of electrons. Chlorine atoms, however, need only a single extra electron each to achieve the octet. Both atoms gain the noble gas electron structure if four chlorine atoms share an electron each with the four outer electrons on a single carbon atom. Each of the four carbon—chlorine bonds is a single, two-electron bond, hence the formula is CCl_4.

(iii) Trichloromethane

This is similar to both methane and tetrachloromethane. The four single bonds form by sharing a pair of electrons contributed to equally by each of the atoms forming the bond. The carbon—chlorine bond forms as in (ii) above. The carbon—hydrogen bond forms as in (i) above.

(iv) Ammonia

Here, the nitrogen atom has five outer electrons. It needs three more for an octet. It gains these by sharing the outer electrons from three hydrogen atoms. At the same time the hydrogen atoms achieve the duet of electrons which is characteristic of helium. This gives a formula of NH_3.

(v) Carbon dioxide

As before, carbon requires a further four electrons from the atoms it combines with to make up the outer octet. Oxygen atoms require two electrons to give them an outer octet. Both atoms achieve the octet by contributing two electrons each to a carbon—oxygen bond. Two such bonds form, each with four electrons. There are two double carbon—oxygen bonds in the carbon dioxide molecule – hence the formula, CO_2.

9. PROPERTIES OF MOLECULAR SUBSTANCES

❝❝ Low melting point ❞❞

Molecules do not have a charge. Because of this, and unlike ions, molecules attract each other *only very weakly*. The forces of attraction holding molecules together in a solid molecular crystal can be easily overcome by adding quite small amounts of energy. Gently heating will thus cause the ***molecules*** of a molecular crystal to ***break free*** from each other, making the solid ***melt*** at a low temperature. Note that when the molecules break free from each other's attraction they ***do not break into atoms***. Melting is not the same as decomposing!

Even when molecules are in the liquid state and moving around freely amongst themselves, the forces of attraction between them are small. Therefore, it does not require very much added energy to cause the molecules to break ***completely free from each other*** and leave the liquid state altogether. This process is known as vaporisation – the substance boils or vaporises at a low temperature.

❝❝ Low boiling point ❞❞

❝❝ The important point here is that in *melting* and *boiling*, the bonds (or attractive forces) *between* molecules are broken. In *decomposing*, the bonds *within* molecules break. ❞❞

From what has been said earlier, the melting and boiling of ***molecular compounds*** require very little energy. The melting and boiling points are low and the amount of energy needed to melt or vaporise one mole of a molecular substance is much less than that for ***ionic*** compounds or ***giant molecular*** substances.

Because molecules are not charged, they cannot be conductors – they do not conduct electricity in solid or in molten form.

❝❝ Non-conductors ❞❞

10. PROPERTIES OF IONIC COMPOUNDS

The formation of ions by the reaction of the atoms of a ***metallic element and a non-metallic element*** produces particles which attract each other strongly. The ions, therefore, form an arrangement called a giant ionic lattice or structure. Such structures are always solids at room temperature (see Fig. 5.14).

Ions which collect together in a giant structure are held together by strong forces called ***ionic bonds***. These bonds are forces of attraction of oppositely charged particles. They are the cause of ***high melting and boiling points***.

❝❝ Melting and Boiling ❞❞

At room temperature, the ions in the structure are vibrating. As the temperature is raised, the ions vibrate more strongly. Eventually, a temperature is reached when the ions break free from the close-packed structure of the solid. As the ions begin to move around freely, the solid ***melts***. Further heating will give the mobile ions more energy until they ***vaporise*** at the boiling point of the compound.

❝❝ Electrolysis ❞❞

When molten, the ions of an ionic compound are mobile and can move towards the electrodes in an electrolysis cell. When ionic compounds dissolve in water, their ions also become mobile and can conduct electricity as they do in the molten state.

❝❝ Magnesium oxide ❞❞

The structure of magnesium oxide, MgO, is very similar to the structure of sodium chloride (Fig. 5.14). In the magnesium oxide structure, however, the ions have double charges, Mg^{2+} and O^{2-}, and are therefore much more strongly attracted to each other. This results in a very high melting point (2852 °C) and insolubility in water. Magnesium oxide is used as a lining for furnaces. You can deduce for yourself which property is crucial to this use (see also Chapter 11, Section 14 (d)).

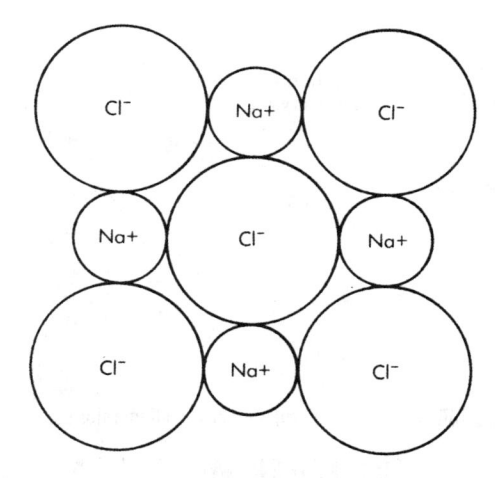

Fig. 5.14

11 IONIC AND MOLECULAR COMPOUNDS

Fig. 5.15 summarises the properties of compounds in which *ions* are present and those in which *covalently bonded molecules* are present.

Note that the temperatures given are intended to be a rule of thumb guide to deciding whether a substance is molecular or ionic by considering its melting or boiling point.

Property	Ionic compounds	Covalently bonded molecular elements and compounds
Melting point	high (>250 °C)	low (<250 °C)
Boiling point	high (>500 °C)	low (<500 °C)
Electrical conductivity	solid non-conductor molten – good conductor	non-conductor in any state
Solubility in water Solubility in organic solvents	usually soluble insoluble	usually insoluble soluble

Fig. 5.15 Properties of substances and their structure.

12 MOLECULAR LIQUIDS AS SOLVENTS

Any substance that will *dissolve* another substance is a *solvent* for the substance it dissolves. Water is a solvent for many ionic compounds. Organic compounds such as ethanol, propanone and xylene are solvents for many molecular compounds.

(A) WATER AS A SPECIAL SOLVENT

Water is a molecular compound with a difference! The structure of the water molecule is shown in Fig. 5.16A.

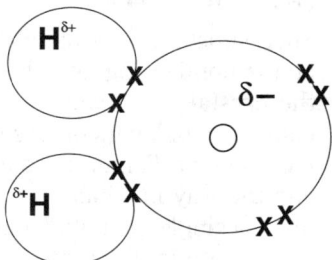

Fig. 5.16A The polar water molecule.

The bonds between the atoms of hydrogen and oxygen are covalent. However, the *electron pairs* forming these bonds are more strongly attracted to the oxygen atoms than to the hydrogen atoms. The result is a pair of POLAR bonds. The molecule has a slight positive charge ($\delta+$) on each hydrogen atom and a slight negative charge ($\delta-$) on the oxygen atom. See Fig. 5.16A above. The effect of these slight charges is to give the water molecule the power to attract particles which are charged, i.e. ions. Water molecules can, therefore, 'drag' ions out of ionic lattices: the ionic compound *dissolves* (Fig. 5.16B).

Water can also dissolve molecular compounds which are *similar to water* – polar compounds such as sugar, ethanol and propanone. Water will not dissolve molecular substances which are not polar, such as hydrocarbons (in petrol), or sulphur.

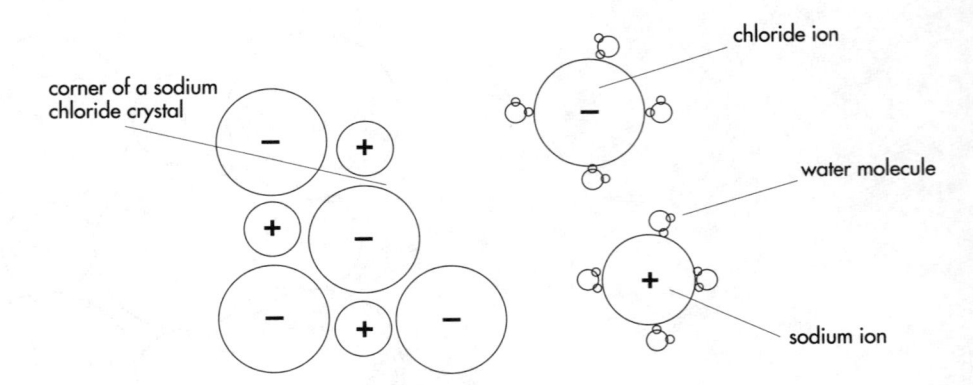

Fig. 5.16B How water molecules dissolve sodium chloride.

(B) OTHER MOLECULAR SOLVENTS (NON-AQUEOUS LIQUIDS)

Many of the liquids we use as solvents do not have polar molecules like water. They dissolve substances because of the attraction of their molecules for the molecules of the substance they are dissolving (SOLUTE). Thus, propanone will dissolve nail varnish, xylene will dissolve sulphur, ethanol will dissolve ball-pen ink dyes. They dissolve by the process of **attraction** of neutral molecules for each other. Molecules which can attract each other are able to mix freely and so form solutions.

One important use of non-aqueous liquids, as liquids *other than water* are called, is in 'dry' cleaning. The solvent here is called 'dry' because it is not water. The best dry-cleaning solvents are chlorinated hydrocarbons, such as perchloroethene, which dissolve grease and oil well but have low toxicity and are easily purified after use by distillation (low boiling points). These properties are characteristic of molecular compounds.

Another use of non-aqueous liquids is as general solvents for such everyday materials as paints, adhesives, inks and perfumes. Even Tippex, which is the standby of almost every student, contains a solvent for the white plastic coating. A glance at the small print on the bottle will show it to be 1,1,1 trichloroethane. This solvent is harmful, and the bottle should carry a hazard label to that effect.

13 MACRO-MOLECULES

Some substances have structures which do not fit the description given of ionic and molecular structures. These substances consist of extremely large molecules or even giant molecules. Such structures are sometimes called *macromolecules*. Figs 5.17 and 5.18 show the relationship between examples of giant and large molecules.

(A) GIANT MOLECULES – CARBON

Such substances as the allotropes of carbon - diamond and graphite – are made up of atoms bonded together by covalent bonds in a lattice which extends to the edges of the crystal. For diamond, any crystal is one giant molecule! For graphite, which is composed of layers of closely bonded atoms, each *layer* is itself a giant molecule. The hardness of diamond results from the strength of the bonds between carbon atoms and the way in which every carbon atom is bonded to its four nearest neighbours to make a single giant molecule the size of a diamond.

Graphite is different. A lump of graphite is composed of millions of layers - each layer being a giant molecule. What gives graphite its softness is the weak bonds *between* these layers which allow them to slide over each other and even completely separate from each other easily. The strength of the bonding *within* a graphite layer is in fact greater than that between atoms in diamond!

(B) GIANT MOLECULES – SILICON AND ITS OXIDE

The element silicon, well-known now for its use in microchips in computers, has a giant structure similar to that of diamond. The difference in hardness between the two structures arises because the bonds between carbon atoms are stronger than those between silicon atoms. By looking at the diamond structure in Fig. 5.17 above, and visualising silicon atoms in place of carbon atoms, the structure of the element silicon can be pictured.

Fig. 5.17   Diamond   Graphite

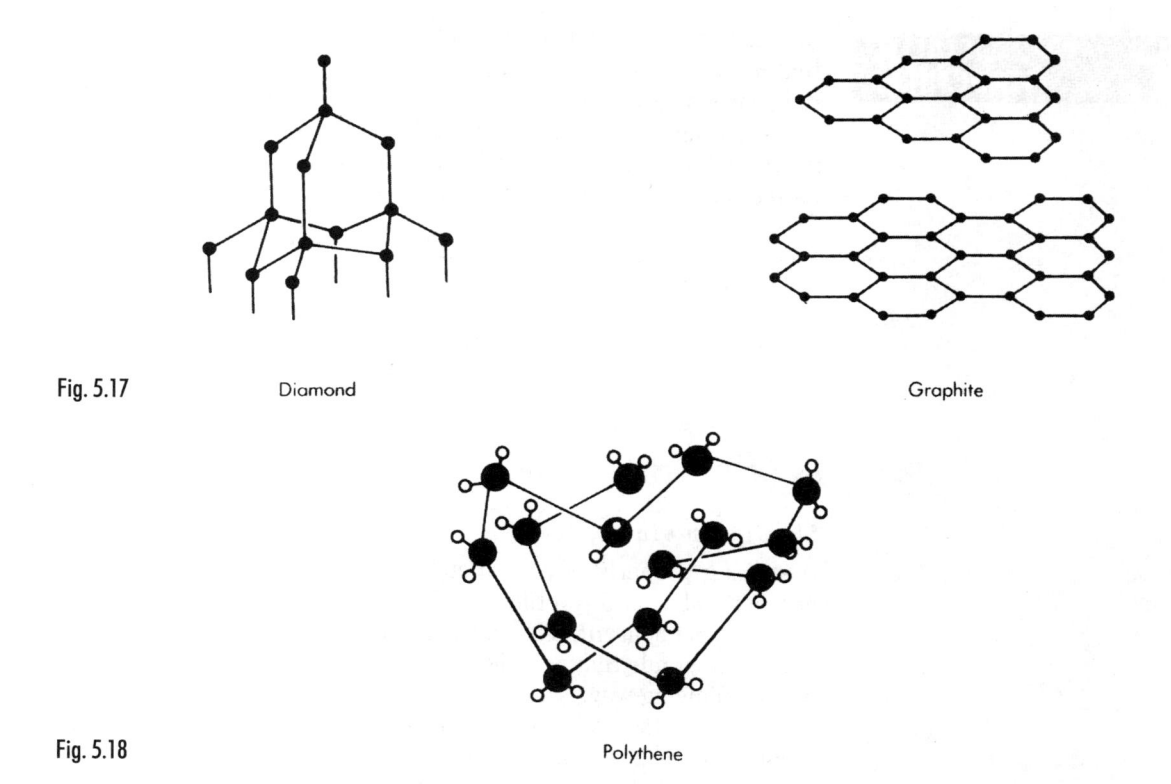

Fig. 5.18   Polythene

Silicon dioxide is a giant structure of silicon and oxygen atoms bonded by the covalent bond formed between silicon and oxygen atoms.

(C) PROPERTIES OF GIANT MOLECULES

The structures discussed above have no free electrons and so do not conduct electricity when solid. They also have no ions and so cannot conduct when molten either. The size of their molecules prevents them from dissolving in water and also, since the hardness of a substance is a measure of how strong the bonds are between atoms, these structures include the hardest known. The strong bonds also give the structures high melting and boiling points.

Graphite is something of an exception here. There are 'free' electrons between the layers of carbon atoms. These electrons allow the structure to conduct electricity like a metal (see also Fig. 5.19). The layers are also able to slide over one another when pressure is placed on them and this makes graphite smooth and slippery – quite unlike diamond and silicon. Because the layers are themselves giant structures, however, the element has a high melting point.

(D) LARGE MOLECULES – PLASTICS

This is another type of macromolecule. Large molecules are distinguished from giant molecules by the numbers of atoms in their molecules. Large molecules have thousands rather than billions of atoms per molecule. All polymers – starch, proteins and plastics – are large molecules.

(E) PROPERTIES OF LARGE MOLECULES

They have lower melting points than giant molecular structures but higher melting points than simple molecular compounds. The size of their molecules lies between the sizes of simple molecules (often called *small molecules*) and giant molecules. They do not conduct electricity for they have no ions or free electrons. They are not very soluble in water. An example of a large molecular structure is that of poly(ethene), Fig. 5.18.

The structures of diamond, graphite and poly(ethene) are shown in Fig. 5.18.
Chapter 14 deals with the structures and properties of plastics (Section 3) and fibres (Section 4).

14 METALLIC STRUCTURES

Metals form giant structures – but with a difference. There is ample evidence to suggest that *metallic structures* are composed of positively charged ions embedded in a 'sea of electrons'. The positively charged ions are held together by the electrons, giving the metal strength, hardness and high melting and boiling points. The electrons can be made to flow on application of a potential difference across the ends; in other words, the metal will conduct electricity in the solid state (see Fig. 5.19).

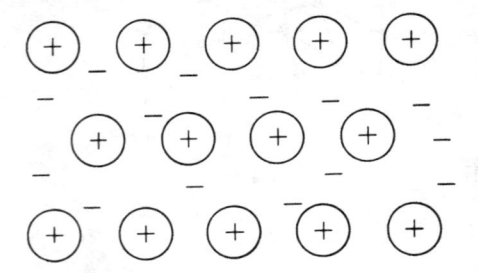

Fig. 5.19

Shaping metals

A striking property of pure metals is the ease with which they can be shaped – they are malleable and ductile. Gold can be hand-beaten into sheets so thin that they become transparent! This property is related to the structure. Metals do not have 'localised' bonds that exist in covalently bonded solids. The property can be explained in the following way.

Any atom (actually an ion) in the metal is surrounded by the 'sea of electrons' mentioned earlier. This sea acts as a 'glue' holding the ion in the metallic structure. Usually, solids break on being stressed because covalent or ionic bonds are broken and do not reform when the stress is removed. In metals, rolling or hammering causes layers of atoms to slide over one another. At each stage of this sliding process, the ions move from one place to another in which the bonding is constant – 'the sea of electrons'. Like a shoal of fishes moving through water, no matter where it stops it is in exactly the same environment as where it started. Only when a metal is stretched to the point where its atoms are pulled apart, does its structure fail.

The connection between the way in which the atoms, molecules or ions of a substance are arranged, and its properties, is an important part of the study of chemistry. A knowledge of the relationship between structure and properties helps to free us from the need to remember the individual properties of every substance we might use. An understanding of the principles discussed in this chapter will be crucial to success in any chemistry course.

EXAMINATION QUESTIONS

MULTIPLE CHOICE

QUESTIONS 1–3

Questions 1 to 3 refer to the following diagrams, which show the arrangements of atoms in four substances.

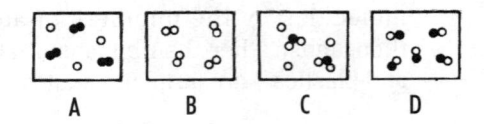

Fig. 5.20

Which diagram represents the arrangement of atoms in
1. a single element?
2. a single compound?
3. a mixture of two elements?

(SEG)

QUESTION 4

The isotope $^{35}_{17}X$ contains

A 17 neutrons
B 17 protons
C 35 neutrons
D 35 protons

(SEG)

CHAPTER 5 **ESSENTIAL PRINCIPLES** 73

STRUCTURED QUESTIONS

QUESTION 5
(a) Name two types of particle contained in an atom as well as the electron. (2)
    (i)............................. (ii)..
(b) In what part of the atom are they found? (1 line) (1)
(c) Show by means of a diagram how the electrons are arranged in an atom of aluminium (atomic number of aluminium is 13) (2)
(d) State how many of each of the three particles are contained in an atom of fluorine (atomic number of fluorine is 9, mass number is 19). (3)

Name of particle	Number
....	....
....	....
....	....

(e) State how a fluoride ion differs from a fluorine atom (1 line). (1)
(f) Draw a diagram to show how the electrons are arranged in the covalent compound NH_3. (2)
(g) Show by means of a diagram how the electrons are arranged in the ionic compound potassium chloride (KCl). (2)
(h) Describe two ways in which covalent compounds usually differ from ionic compounds in their physical or chemical properties. (2)

(*Total 15 marks*)

(NISEAC)

OPEN-ENDED OR 'ESSAY TYPE' QUESTIONS

QUESTION 6
(a) State three differences in the properties of sodium chloride and tetrachloromethane (carbon tetrachloride). (3)
(b) Explain in terms of the electronic structures of the compounds why they have these differences in properties. (6)
(c) Use your knowledge of chemistry to explain the following facts as fully as you can. (2)
    (i) Aluminium wire carries electricity in power lines.
    (ii) Graphite is used as a lubricant. (2)

(*Total 13*)

(NEAB)

OUTLINE ANSWERS

MULTIPLE CHOICE

ANSWERS 1–3

The diagrams represent the **molecules** in elements, compounds and mixtures. Black circles and white circles are atoms of **different** elements. A white circle *joined to* a black circle is a molecule of a compound.
1 B is the single element. Its molecules are **all identical**.
2 D is the single (i.e. pure) compound. Its molecules are **all identical**. They contain atoms of **two elements**.
3 A is a mixture of two elements. White atoms are molecules of one, pairs of black atoms are molecules of the other. Note here, that noble gas elements are the only elements which have only **one atom in the molecule**.

ANSWER 4

●● See Fig. 5.2 ●●

The isotope contains 17 protons, the answer is B.
The **superscript** (upper number) gives the mass number and the **subscript** (lower number) the atomic number. The isotope's identity can be 'read' from the symbol as **the atom of element 17 having 35 nucleons (protons plus neutrons)**. The atom, therefore has 17 protons and 18 neutrons – corresponding to the answer B.

ANSWER 5

This is a fairly wide-ranging question. It is largely based on recall but the answers can be worked out from a knowledge of the principles discussed in Chapter 5.

(a) and (b) require knowledge of the composition of the nucleus (see Section 2 above).
(c) Here the atomic number is given to enable you to deduce the number of electrons. The aluminium atom will have 3 shells. The arrangement is 2, 8, 3 (Fig. 5.4).
(d) requires a calculation of the numbers of the three types of sub-atomic particle in the atom of fluorine. 9 protons, 9 electrons and 10 neutrons.
(e) Fluorine is a non-metal. Will it gain or lose electrons to become an ion? In fact the ion has one more electron than the atom (Fig. 5.4).
(f) Ammonia contains an atom (nitrogen) which has five electrons in its outer shell. How will it share electrons with hydrogen to achieve an octet whilst hydrogen atoms achieve the duet of helium? See Fig. 5.13.
(g) Potassium chloride is similar to sodium chloride – sodium and potassium are in the same group. The structures of the two chlorides are similar, but not identical. Potassium has one more shell than sodium (see Fig. 5.4).
(h) Remember that ions attract each other strongly but molecules are weakly attracted to each other (Fig. 5.15). Physical properties are those in which the substance is not changed into a different substance – like melting and boiling points (Sections 9 and 10).

ANSWER 6

(a) (i) Sodium chloride would have much higher melting and boiling points than tetrachloromethane. This is usually judged to be ONE difference despite the mention of two physical properties.
(ii) Sodium chloride would conduct electricity when molten or in solution: tetrachloromethane would not.
(iii) Sodium chloride would give a positive test for chloride ions with silver nitrate solution; tetrachloromethane would give no reaction in this test.

(b) Sodium chloride is an ionic compound; tetrachloromethane is covalently bonded – a molecular compound. The explanation of the three differences stated in (a) are:
(i) The presence of charged particles, ions, in a structure creates strong bonds which require high temperatures to break, so the melting and boiling points will be high. Molecules do not attract each other strongly and so molecular compounds are easily melted and boiled.
(ii) The ions in sodium chloride allow it to conduct electricity when they become mobile – in a molten state or in solution. Tetrachloromethane molecules cannot carry an electric current.
(iii) Chloride ions will react with silver ions to form a white precipitate of silver chloride. Tetrachloromethane does not contain ions and this reaction cannot occur:

$$Cl^-(aq) + Ag^+(aq) \rightarrow AgCl(s).$$

(c) (i) Aluminium wires carry electricity because the structure of the aluminium is that of aluminium ions in a 'sea of electrons'. A diagram might attract credit here but in any case would help to reinforce the explanation. An electric current is a stream of electrons. Electrons entering the metal wire can push the electrons in the 'sea' along the wire to the other end, where they enter the electrical circuits of a building.
(ii) Graphite is a giant structure with a difference! It is made of giant structured *layers* which are weakly bonded *to* each other. *Putting a sideways force onto graphite causes* these layers to slide over each other very readily. The whole structure 'spreads' like a pack of playing cards pushed sideways whilst being held between the palms of two hands. The sliding layers of carbon atoms allow movement of metal surfaces over each other if graphite is present between them.

STUDENT'S ANSWERS – EXAMINER'S COMMENTS

❝ You have not read this carefully. Your answer refers to the same *group*. Perhaps you thought (ii) was the same question as (i), but for a different group! You have seven elements to chose from in the period Li → F. ❞

(a) Name an element in
 (i) the same group of the Periodic Table as chlorine; ..... bromine
 (1 mark)
 (ii) the same period of the Periodic Table as carbon. ..... silicon
 (1 mark)

(b) Write down or draw a diagram of the electronic structure of
 (i) an atom of carbon (atomic number = 6);
 (ii) an atom of chlorine (atomic number = 17).

carbon   C = 2.4

chlorine   Cl = 2.8.7

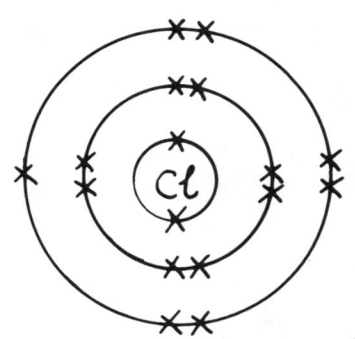

❝ Excellent diagrams. Full marks for accuracy and careful drawing. ❞

(2 marks)

(c) Draw a diagram to show the electron arrangement in a molecule of tetrachloromethane (CCl$_4$). Only the outer electron shells need to be shown in your diagram.

❝ Again – excellent. You noticed that the question allowed you to simplify the diagram by drawing outer electrons only. ❞

❝ This answer shows a good understanding of the nature of covalent bonding and electron structure. ❞

(NEAB)

(2 marks)

❝ Examiner's mark 5/6. ❞

REVIEW SHEET

- The nucleus of an atom contains _____

_____

- The **atomic number** is _____
- The **mass number** is _____
- Complete the following table

Element	Atomic number	Number of protons	Number of neutrons	Mass number	Symbol
Hydrogen	1	1	NONE	1	^1_1H
Carbon					
Nitrogen					
Oxygen					
Sodium					
Magnesium					
Aluminium					
Sulphur					
Chlorine					
Calcium					
Iron					
Copper					
Zinc					

- The number of shells an atom has tells us _____

_____

a) The FIRST shell maximum is _____
b) The SECOND shell maximum is _____
c) The THIRD shell maximum is _____

- Complete the table showing the electron structures of elements of groups 1, 2, 7 and 0

Period	Group 1	Group 2	Group 7	Group 0
2	Li 2.1.	Be	F	Ne
3	Na	Mg 2.8.2.	Cl	Ar
4	K	Ca	Br 2.8.18.7.	Kr

- **Periods** are _____ of elements
- **Groups** are _____ of elements
- The eighth group is called group _____

CHAPTER 5 ATOMIC STRUCTURE AND BONDING

- Draw a diagram to represent the following reaction between magnesium atoms and oxygen atoms.

$$Mg(g) + O(g) \rightarrow Mg^{2+}(s) + O^{2-}(s).$$

The electron structures are

Atoms					Ions			
Mg	2	8	2	$\rightarrow$	$Mg^{2+}(s)$	2	8	2 electrons lost,
O	2	8	6	$\rightarrow$	$O^{2-}(s)$	2	8	2 electrons gained.

- Ions are _____

- Ionic bonds are _____

- Ionic bonds cause _____

- Covalent bonds are _____

- Complete the following table to show the differences between ionic, molecular, giant molecular and metallic substances.

	Ionic	Molecular	Giant Molecular	Metallic
Melting point and Boiling point	High			
Solubility in water		Insoluble		
Solubility in propanone			Soluble	
Conduct electricity when solid		No		
Conduct electricity in aqueous solution				

CHAPTER 6

THE PERIODIC TABLE

METALS AND NON-METALS

THE PERIODIC TABLE

GROUPS AND THEIR PROPERTIES

GROUP 1 THE ALKALI METALS

GROUP 2 THE ALKALINE EARTH METALS

GROUP 7 THE HALOGENS

GROUP 0 THE NOBLE GASES

TRANSITION METALS

HYDROGEN

GETTING STARTED

The elements of the periodic table are arranged in order of their atomic numbers, from 1 to 107. This arrangement is, roughly, also the order of increasing relative atomic masses of the elements (see Chapter 5).

The simplest classification of elements is the metal/non-metal classification. This classification fits well into the broader classification of the periodic table.

The structure of the table was first devised by the Russian chemist Dmitrii Mendeleev in 1869. At that time there were only about sixty elements known and attempts to bring order to them had not been very successful.

Mendeleev's idea was to arrange elements in order of their relative atomic masses, at the same time placing elements with similar properties in vertical columns. To do this he had to leave gaps for elements which had not at the time been discovered. In this he differed from those chemists before him who had tried to classify only existing elements.

The table used today is much the same as Mendeleev's table. The gaps he left have now been filled and the table has been extended by the addition of a group of noble gases which Mendeleev knew nothing of, and more elements beyond bismuth, which had the highest relative atomic mass known to him.

The modern periodic table consists of horizontal rows of elements, called *periods*, and vertical columns, called ***groups***.

There are eight groups and seven periods. The reasons for arranging the elements in groups and periods lies in the electron structure of their atoms and has been discussed in Chapter 5.

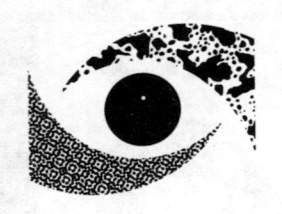

ESSENTIAL PRINCIPLES

The periodic table is useful to students of chemistry because it helps us to remember the properties of elements and also explains why elements have these properties.

1 METALS AND NON-METALS

A simple classification of elements is into **metals** and **non-metals**. These are fairly clearly separated within the periodic table as shown in Fig. 6.1.

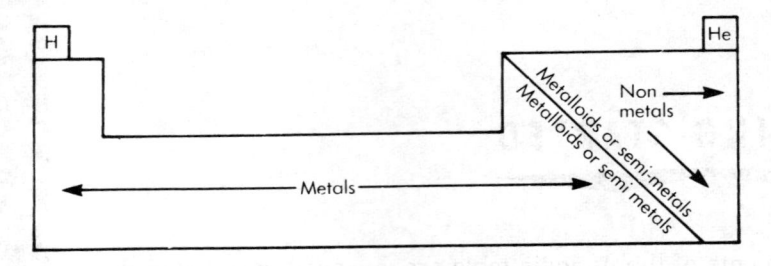

Fig. 6.1 The periodic table showing the division into metals and non-metals

SEMI-METALS OR METALLOIDS

The class of elements which lies on the borderline between metals and non-metals is often classified as **semi-metals** or **metalloids**. This class includes elements such as silicon. (See Fig. 6.1). The differences between metals and non-metals are shown in Fig. 6.2.

The differences between metals and non-metals are:	
Metals	Non-metals
Good conductors of heat and electrictiy	Poor conductors of heat and electricity
Shiny	Dull
Malleable	Brittle
Strong	Weak
React with oxygen to form basic oxides	React with oxygen to form acidic oxides
Usually high density	Usually low density
Usually high melting points except alkali metals	Usually low melting points except carbon
Many react with dilute acid to produce hydrogen	No reaction with dilute acid

Fig. 6.2 Table of elements showing the properties of metals and non-metals.

2 THE PERIODIC TABLE

We can start by looking at the change in properties of elements as their atomic number increases in single units. This sequence is a **period** and we refer to the changes in properties as **trends**.

(A) TRENDS IN PROPERTIES ACROSS A PERIOD

These trends are clearest across the second and third periods, that is elements Li—Ne and Na—Ar.
The information in Fig. 6.3 shows the following trends.

Going across Fig. 6.3 from left to right:

(i) The elements change from metals to non-metals.
This is easily shown by testing the elements for electrical conductivity using the apparatus of Fig. 6.4. **Metals** conduct and the bulb lights, **non-metals** do not conduct and the bulb does not light.

Metal/non-metal	Na m	Mg m	Al m	Si n/m	P n/m	S n/m	Cl n/m	Ar n/m
Outer shell electrons	1	2	3	4	5	6	7	8
Valency	1	2	3	4	3	2	1	0
Oxidation no.	+1	+2	+3	+4	−3	−2	−1	0
Melting point/°C	98	650	660	1410	44	113	−100	−189
Boiling point/°C	880	1100	2470	2355	280	444	35	−186
Oxide nature	basic	basic	amphoteric	acidic	acidic	acidic	acidic	− −
Formula of oxide	Na_2O	MgO	Al_2O_3	SiO_2	P_2O_3	SO_2	Cl_2O	− −
Formula of chloride	NaCl	$MgCl_2$	$AlCl_3$	$SiCl_4$	PCl_3	S_2Cl_2	Cl_2	− −

Fig. 6.3 The elements of the third period showing the periodicity of physical and chemical properties.

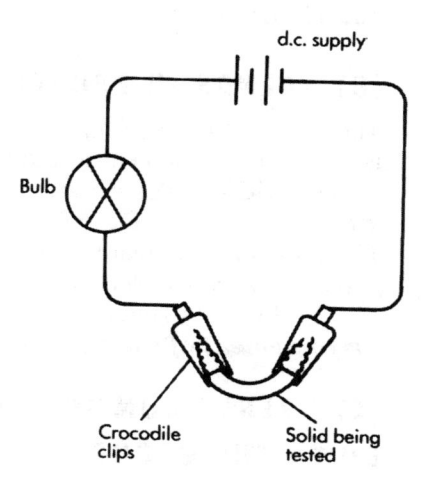

Fig. 6.4 Electrical conductivity testing apparatus.

(ii) **The number of electrons in the outer electron shell increases from 1 to 8.**

(iii) **The number of outer electrons equals the group number.**

Valency

(iv) **The valency of the elements increases from 1 to 4 in single units for the elements in the first group and then decreases by single units from 4 to 1 for the elements of groups 4–7.**

The reason for this is discussed in Chapter 5.

An alternative to valencies is the idea of *oxidation number*. Oxidation numbers have the same numerical values as valencies but additionally have a sign. Oxidation numbers (or states) of *metals* are valencies with a *positive* sign because positive ions are formed on reaction. For *non-metals*, which form negative ions or form molecules by accepting a share of electrons from another atom, the acceptance of electrons is indicated by a *negative* sign. In general, metals have positive oxidation numbers and also valencies in the range 1–3; non-metals have negative oxidation numbers and also valencies in the range 1–3.

Oxidation numbers

(v) **The melting points and boiling points of the elements increase to a maximum at group 4, decreasing again to group 0.**

The melting point of an element can be measured readily provided its value does not exceed the limits of measurement of the thermometer, and also provided the element does not catch fire at its melting point. The apparatus used is shown in Fig. 6.5.

(vi) **The oxides of the elements change from basic to acidic.**

This is connected with the change from metals to non-metals. *Metallic oxides* are basic; *non-metallic oxides* are acidic. The oxides of just a few elements have both acidic and basic properties – not at the same time, obviously. Such oxides are called

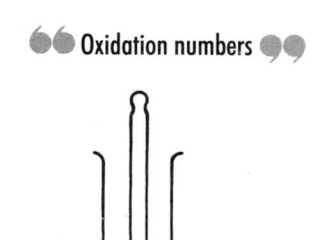

Fig. 6.5

amphoteric oxides. Elements which have amphoteric oxides are those positioned on the borderline of the change from metal to non-metal in the table.

There are two methods of determining the acid/base nature of an oxide.

> **Methods for determining nature of an oxide**

(a) Dissolve the oxide in water and find the pH of the solution using indicator paper. This can only apply to **soluble oxides**.
(b) For oxides which are **not soluble** in water, e.g. aluminium oxide and silicon dioxide, determine whether they are more soluble in acid or alkali than they are in water. If an oxide dissolves more in **acid** than in water then it is a **basic oxide**. If more soluble in an alkali than in water it is an **acidic oxide**.

Oxides which are more soluble in **both** acids and alkalis than they are in water alone are **amphoteric oxides**, e.g. aluminium oxide and zinc oxide.

(vii) The formulae of compounds of the elements shows the change in valency or oxidation number. The table (Fig. 6.3) shows this for oxides and chlorides.

(B) TRENDS IN PROPERTIES DOWN THE GROUPS

The phrase 'down a group' is a short way of saying that the change being considered is from the top element to the bottom element in the group. The groups studied in detail at GCSE level are groups 1, 2, 7 and 0. The electron arrangements of these groups are shown in Fig. 6.6.

The most obvious feature of the above electron structures is the presence of **the group number** of electrons in the outer shell.

The elements react in such a way as to achieve an **outer shell electron arrangement of the nearest noble gas (group 0 element)**.

(C) TRENDS COMMON TO ALL GROUPS
DOWN THE GROUP

(i) The atom gets larger: its diameter increases.

This is caused by the addition of an extra electron **shell** for each step down the group. The number of such shells corresponds to the number of the period in which the element is placed. For example, magnesium is in period 3 and so has three shells containing electrons – its electron structure is 2 8 2. Its atoms will be smaller than those of calcium, the element below it in the same group, because calcium atoms have four shells and an electron structure of 2 8 8 2.

(ii) The number of electrons in the outer shell is always equal to the group number.

See Fig. 6.6. All the elements in the same group have the same number of electrons in the outer shell.

Group 1						Group 2					
lithium	2	1				beryllium	2	2			
sodium	2	8	1			magnesium	2	8	2		
potassium	2	8	8	1		calcium	2	8	8	2	
rubidium	2	8	18	8	1	strontium	2	8	18	8	2
caesium	2	8	18	8	8	1	barium	2	8	18	18	8	2

Group 7						Group 0				
						helium	2			
fluorine	2	7				neon	2	8		
chlorine	2	8	7			argon	2	8	8	
bromine	2	8	18	7		krypton	2	8	18	8
iodine	2	8	18	18	7	xenon	2	8	18	18	8

Group 4		
carbon	2	4
silicon	2	8	4

Fig. 6.6 Electron structures of selected groups of elements.

(iii) The atoms lose their outer electron(s) more easily.

The effect of this is to make metals more reactive down the group and non-metals less reactive. This is because, to react, **metal** atoms must **lose** their outer electrons and form positive ions. The further from the **attracting** nucleus the outer electrons are the more easily they can be lost (transferred) to another atom.

The opposite is the situation for **non-metals**. They are the elements that **gain** electrons to achieve a full outer electron shell. In doing so they must attract electrons to the outer shell. This attraction is stronger the closer the outer shell is to the attracting nucleus of the atom, i.e. the smaller the atom. So the most reactive non-metal elements are at the top of their groups in contrast to the metals.

This difference in reactivity trend between metals and non-metals is the result of the basic difference between atoms of metals and atoms of non-metals. Metal atoms will always lose electrons in their chemical reactions; non-metal atoms will always gain electrons.

It is interesting to note that in group 4, the elements at the top are non-metals and the elements at the bottom are metals (tin and lead). This shows clearly how the increase in number of electron shells down a group increases the ease of removal of the outer electrons, in this case making the lower atoms metallic even though the elements higher in the group are non-metallic.

(iv) The density of the element increases

The densest elements in Fig. 6.7 are towards the bottom of each group.

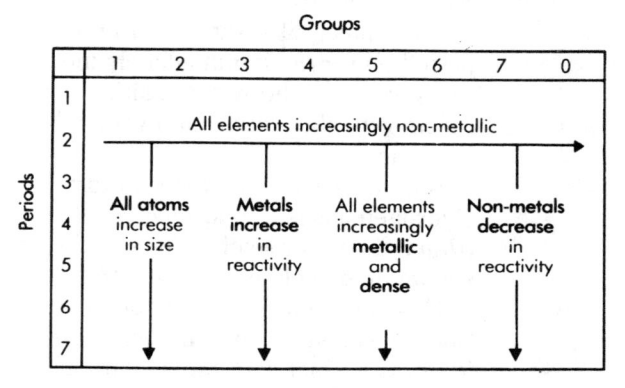

Fig. 6.7 A summary of group trends

3 GROUPS AND THEIR PROPERTIES

The elements of a *group* have similar properties. This fact is related to the similar electron structures of the atoms of the elements of the group. If every atom in a group has the same number of electron shells as well as the same number of electrons in the outer shell, then all elements in that group would have *identical properties. They would, of course, be one and the same element.*

What makes elements of the same group similar but not identical is the different number of electron shells but the same number of electrons in the outer one. Some groups show family properties better than others. These are the groups studied at GCSE level. They are groups 1, 2, 7 and 0.

4 GROUP 1 THE ALKALI METALS

Low m.p. Low density

The elements lithium, sodium, potassium, rubidium, caesium and francium are the *most reactive* metals in the periodic table. They are soft metals, easily cut with a knife to reveal a shiny cut surface which quickly tarnishes. Their softness is mainly due to their low melting points. In this property, and in their low densities, they differ from most other metals.

Because these metals are so reactive they must be kept out of contact with any of the substances they can react with. These include all non-metals except the noble gases, and most compound containing these non-metals. For this reason they are usually stored under a liquid hydrocarbon such as paraffin oil. This keeps the metal out of contact with oxygen, water vapour and carbon dioxide.

If alkali metals come into contact with **water or its vapour** the following reaction occurs:

$$2Na(s) + 2H_2O(l) \rightarrow 2NaOH(aq) + H_2(g)$$

sodium + water → sodium hydroxide + hydrogen.

With *oxygen or air*, the reaction is

$$4Na(s) + O_2(g) \rightarrow 2Na_2O(s).$$

sodium + oxygen → sodium oxide

Sodium hydroxide and sodium oxide are both white solids. These white solids are also alkalis and will react further with carbon dioxide in the air to form, finally, sodium carbonate as the end-product of the reaction of sodium with gases in the air. The rapid tarnishing of a cut surface of any of these metals is caused by reaction with oxygen, water vapour and carbon dioxide in the air.

As we have seen in Section 2 (c) (iii), the reactivity of these elements increases **down the group**. Lithium is the least reactive and francium is the most reactive. Francium is in fact a synthetic element and has only been made in minute quantities. Even so, its reactions have been found to be exactly as predicted from our knowledge of the group trend.

The reaction of the alkali metals with *water* is perhaps the most interesting of the reactions of alkali metals. Lithium, sodium and potassium all float on water – they are all less dense than water itself. If we take the reaction of *sodium* with water as a starting point we can compare the reaction of the others with it.

(A) REACTIONS OF SODIUM

(i) With water

A small piece of sodium can be cut easily with a knife from a larger lump. When placed on *water* it immediately melts, forming a small ball of metal and moves about the surface of the water making a hissing sound. It rapidly becomes smaller as it reacts with the water and eventually disappears, sometimes with a bang! What has happened?

Sodium reacts with water to form sodium hydroxide which dissolves in the water. Hydrogen gas is also formed but is not noticed because it is given off into the air from *above* the water level. To collect the gas and identify it as hydrogen would require the sodium to be held under water to fill a test tube full of water with the gas.

This can be a dangerous procedure if not done with care. It can be done using a 'sodium spoon' - a special metal gauze container at the end of a long handle (Fig. 6.8). Water can react with the sodium and hydrogen can escape through the holes in the gauze.

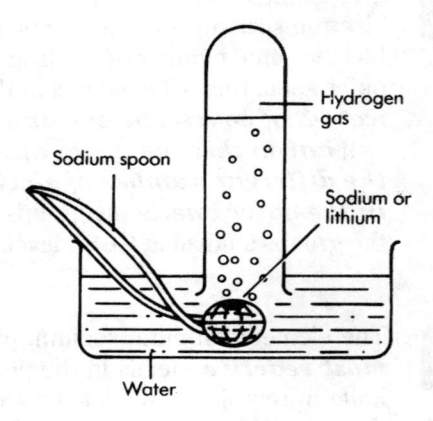

Fig. 6.8 The use of a sodium spoon in collecting hydrogen from the reaction of sodium with water.

The reaction is

$$2Na(s) + 2H_2O(l) \rightarrow 2NaOH(aq) + H_2(g).$$

sodium + water → sodium hydroxide + hydrogen

Substituting the symbol of *any other alkali metal for that of sodium* in the above equation gives the corresponding equation for the reaction of that element with water.

(ii) With air

Yellow flame

Sodium burns with a yellow flame if heated in air. Sodium oxide is formed. Testing the residue with damp indicator paper will confirm the alkaline nature of the oxide:

$$\text{sodium} + \text{oxygen} \rightarrow \text{sodium oxide}$$
$$4\text{Na(s)} + \text{O}_2\text{(g)} \rightarrow 2\text{Na}_2\text{O(s)}.$$

(iii) With chlorine

Sodium burns strongly in chlorine with a bright yellow flame:

$$\text{sodium} + \text{chlorine} \rightarrow \text{sodium chloride}$$
$$2\text{Na(s)} + \text{Cl}_2\text{(g)} \rightarrow 2\text{NaCl(s)}.$$

The product is common salt, sodium chloride.

(B) REACTIONS OF LITHIUM AND POTASSIUM

From the reactions and properties of sodium given above it is possible to **predict** – to foretell – the reactions of other alkali metals:

(i) *Lithium* will be *harder* than sodium; *potassium* will be *softer* - because the melting points decrease down the group and the lower the melting point the softer the metal.

(ii) For the same reason as in (i), *lithium* does *not melt* on reaction with water, whereas *potassium* will form a *globule* like sodium. **Both** will *float*.

(iii) *Potassium* will be *more reactive* than sodium; *lithium* will be *less reactive* than sodium. In fact, potassium catches fire or, rather, the hydrogen given off catches fire over potassium. A lilac flame is seen.

(iv) **Both** will produce **alkaline solutions** of the metal hydroxide and also hydrogen gas as shown by the equation above. Lithium hydroxide has the formula LiOH, and potassium hydroxide, KOH.

(v) **Both** will **burn in air** to form alkaline oxides of formula Li$_2$O and K$_2$O.

(vi) **Both** will **burn in chlorine**, producing white solid chlorides of formulae LiCl and KCl.

Alkali metals below potassium are more dense than water and much more reactive than potassium. We would predict them to be extremely violent in their reactions with any of the substances that lithium, sodium and potassium react with.

(C) COMPOUNDS OF THE ALKALI METALS AND THEIR PROPERTIES

66 Reactive metals 99

66 Ionic salts 99

66 Strong alkalis 99

These metals react strongly with the halogens and oxygen. The resulting compounds are alkali metal halides and oxides. In their reactions, alkali metal atoms lose their single outer electron. See Fig. 6.6 for the electron arrangements of group 1 elements.

Members of each set of compounds have similar formulae and properties.

The **chlorides**: LiCl, NaCl, KCl, etc., are all ionic salts which can be electrolysed when molten to give the alkali metal at the cathode and chlorine at the anode.

The **hydroxides**: LiOH, NaOH, KOH, etc., are all strong alkalis.

The **oxides**: Li$_2$O, Na$_2$O, K$_2$O, etc., are all strong alkalis which form the hydroxides when they react with water.

The **group** is called the **alkali metals** because of the alkalis formed by reaction with air or water. The pure metals themselves are not alkalis.

5 GROUP 2 THE ALKALINE EARTH METALS

The only members of this group studied at this level are **magnesium** and **calcium**. Examination questions will probably be set on the prediction of the properties and reactions of other metals in the group where these are *similar* to those of magnesium and calcium.

These metals are not as reactive as the alkali metals and also are harder so that they are difficult to cut with a knife. Their hardness compared with alkali metals can be seen to be connected with their higher melting points. Melting points **decrease** going **down the group** as with all groups of metals. **Density** also increases **down the group**.

REACTIONS OF GROUP 2 METALS

- In these the atoms lose two electrons from their outer electron shell, gaining a double positive charge in the process; see Fig. 6.6 for the electron arrangements in group 2 atoms.
- The metals tarnish in air but more slowly than group 1 metals.
- Their reaction with water is much slower and they are all denser than water. The products of reaction with water are hydrogen and a metal oxide or hydroxide.
- With the exception of magnesium, they are also kept under paraffin to stop reaction with water vapour, oxygen and carbon dioxide from the air.

The reactions of calcium

Calcium is a very reactive metal. It is kept under oil to reduce its reaction with air or water vapour. It reacts quickly with air to form a white oxide coating. It burns strongly in air or oxygen with a red flame:

> 66 Red flame 99

$$2Ca(s) + O_2(g) \rightarrow \rightarrow 2CaO(s)$$

calcium + oxygen → calcium oxide (quicklime).

Calcium oxide is a base. It reacts with water to form its hydroxide which is an alkali, $Ca(OH)_2$, common name slaked lime:

$$CaO(s) + H_2O(l) \rightarrow Ca(OH)_2(s)$$

calcium oxide + water → calcium hydroxide (slaked lime).

> 66 Compare this with the behaviour of sodium. Group 1 elements float on water, group 2 elements sink. 99

A small piece of calcium will sink as it reacts with water. A steady stream of gas bubbles is produced and a white residue appears in the water. The equation for the reaction is

$$Ca(s) + 2H_2O(l) \rightarrow Ca(OH)_2(s) + H_2(g)$$

calcium + water → calcium hydroxide + hydrogen.

The gas can be collected in an upturned test tube full of water as with sodium (see Section 4(a)). The gas will explode if put to a flame, showing it to be hydrogen. If the resulting solution is filtered and the filtrate shaken with some carbon dioxide gas, a milky precipitate forms:

$$Ca(OH)_2(aq) + CO_2(g) \rightarrow CaCO_3(s) + H_2O(l)$$

calcium hydroxide + carbon dioxide → calcium carbonate + water.

The filtrate is lime-water, calcium hydroxide solution. Calcium hydroxide is a strong alkali but is not very soluble in water.

Reactions of other alkaline earth metals

From its position in the group, *magnesium* would be expected to be less reactive than calcium. *Strontium*, which is just below calcium, would be expected to be more reactive than calcium. This proves to be so.

> 66 Lower reactivity of magnesium. 99

Magnesium is a light silvery metal. Its uses are given in Chapter 11. Magnesium does **not** react with **cold water** unless it is finely powdered (surface area effect on the rate of reaction). Even then, the reaction takes days rather than minutes.

Magnesium *will* react *with steam*:

$$Mg(s) + H_2O(g) \rightarrow MgO(s) + H_2(g).$$

magnesium + steam → magnesium oxide + hydrogen

This reaction can be carried out as in Fig. 6.9. In this case the *oxide* and not the *hydroxide* is formed.

Magnesium also *burns in air* or oxygen to form the oxide

$$2Mg(s) + O_2(g) \rightarrow 2MgO(s).$$

magnesium + oxygen → magnesium oxide

Magnesium *reacts rapidly* with *dilute* solutions of hydrochloric and sulphuric acids to form magnesium salts and hydrogen gas:

$$Mg(s) + H_2SO_4(aq) \rightarrow MgSO_4(aq) + H_2(g)$$

magnesium + sulphuric acid → magnesium sulphate + hydrogen.

A *similar reaction* occurs with **dilute hydrochloric acid**, HCl(aq); the salt magnesium chloride, $MgCl_2$, is formed. Try working out the equation.

Strontium should react more rapidly with water producing a fast stream of hydrogen and forming an alkaline solution which will be cloudy. It should burn in air or oxygen, but more vigorously than either magnesium or calcium. This is, in fact, what happens.

> **Predicting the reactions of other group 2 metals**

The reactions of ***barium*** can be predicted in the same way. Which is the most reactive metal in group 2?

Try constructing equations for the reactions of barium with water or dilute hydrochloric acid.

Compounds of alkaline earth metals and their properties

These metals react less strongly than the alkali metals do with the halogens and with oxygen. Members of each set of compounds have similar formulae and properties.

> **Electrolysis**

The ***chlorides***: $MgCl_2$, $CaCl_2$, etc., are all ionic salts which, when electrolysed in the molten state, give the metal at the cathode and chlorine at the anode. These metals are produced industrially by this process.

The ***oxides***: MgO, CaO, etc., are all bases. Calcium oxide and the oxides of the more reactive elements in the group react ***exothermically*** with water to form hydroxides:

> **This process is the slaking of quicklime (CaO) to form slaked lime (Ca(OH)$_2$).**

$$CaO(s) + H_2O(l) \rightarrow Ca(OH)_2(s)$$

calcium oxide + water → calcium hydroxide + heat.

Glass manufacture

Glass is a supercooled liquid. It is a mixture of silicates. Many different types of glass are in use. For example everyday glass is mainly calcium and sodium silicates. Other types of glass contain potassium silicates and boron compounds (pyrex glass) or lead silicates (crystal glass). Pure silica forms silica glass, a glass with a high melting point which resists cracking even when plunged, red-hot, into cold water!

Glass is made by mixing sand (silica), limestone and soda ash (sodium carbonate) together with broken glass added to speed up the melting. The mixture reacts to form a mixture of sodium and calcium silicates. This mixture is made into bottles and sheets of glass. Plate-glass used for high quality windows is made by floating molten glass onto a bath of liquid tin. The molten glass settles as a film of even thickness. The absolutely smooth surface of the molten tin gives the solidifying glass the same polished surface.

GROUP 7 THE HALOGENS

These are the ***reactive*** non-metals ***fluorine, chlorine, bromine*** and ***iodine***.
- The elements are all ***diatomic*** - they have two atoms per molecule, F_2, Cl_2, Br_2 and I_2.
- The elements are ***coloured***. Fluorine and chlorine are green, bromine is a brown liquid and iodine a grey solid which forms a purple vapour on heating.
- Unlike the groups of metal elements just discussed, non-metals have the ***most reactive*** elements at the top of the group. The most reactive is fluorine, the least reactive is iodine.

Fluorine is much too dangerous to use in a school laboratory, which gives a hint as to its extreme reactivity.

(A) EXPLANATION OF THE TREND IN REACTIVITY OF THE HALOGENS

Each halogen must ***accept*** an electron to achieve a noble gas electron structure of eight electrons in its outer shell; see Fig. 6.6 for the electron arrangements in atoms of group 7 elements. This it does by either:

(i) accepting an electron by ***transfer*** from a metal atom; or
(ii) accepting a ***share*** of an electron from another non-metal atom.

> Note that on *one* property, all group trends are alike. Namely the *density* of all elements increases 'down the group'.

In either case the electron which is being accepted is most strongly held if it enters an electron shell close to the nucleus, which strongly attracts electrons. So the element with its outer shell of electrons closest to the nucleus – fluorine – will most readily form compounds and will be the most reactive. The reactivity will decrease down the group as the outer shell of electrons gets further from the nucleus.

The trend in the melting points of these elements is also in the opposite direction to that with groups of metals. The melting point of fluorine is lowest and that of iodine the highest. Fluorine and chlorine are gases, bromine is a liquid and iodine a solid at room temperature.

(B) REACTIONS OF THE HALOGENS

These are best studied using *chlorine* as an example.

(i) Reaction with metals, iron

Iron is a metal of average reactivity (see the reactivity table). Knowing how it reacts with chlorine helps us to predict the reactions of other metals and other halogens.

If a stream of dry chlorine is passed over heated iron wool a strongly exothermic reaction occurs. The wool becomes red hot and a brown smoke of iron(III) chloride forms. This can be collected in a dry container where it crystallises on the cold sides as a black solid. The apparatus most often used for this reaction is shown in Fig. 6.10.

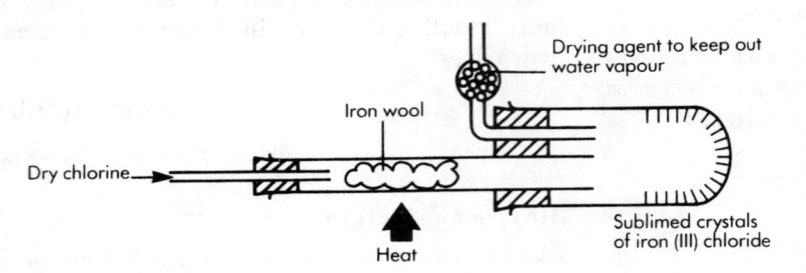

Fig. 6.10 Reacting a metal with chlorine.

The reaction between iron and chlorine is an *oxidation* of iron by chlorine:

$$2Fe(s) + 3Cl_2(g) \rightarrow 2FeCl_3(s)$$

iron + chlorine → iron(III) chloride.

(ii) Reaction with sodium

As a comparison, the reaction of sodium with chlorine is more vigorous still and forms sodium chloride – common salt.

$$2Na(s) + Cl_2(g) \rightarrow 2NaCl(s)$$

sodium + chlorine → sodium chloride.

It is useful to consider the differences between chlorine and sodium and the resulting salt, sodium chloride.

Whereas chlorine is a poisonous green gas, and sodium a very reactive soft metal, when reacted together the product is a tasty, non-poisonous, stable white solid. Why is this?

It is because each chlorine atom has accepted one electron from a sodium atom. The *atoms* of the two elements no longer exist as atoms and are now in fact *ions* - sodium and chloride ions. Obviously, the presence of *one more* or *one less* electron has had a tremendous effect on the properties of the atoms.

A similar change of properties occurs with the other halogens when they become halides, and other metals when they become metal salts.

Such is the nature of the *chemical reaction*!

(iii) Reaction of halogens with water

There is no strong reaction with water, with the exception of the reaction of fluorine with water.

Chlorine, bromine and iodine react to decreasing extents forming an acidic, bleaching solution. The bleaching power of these solutions decreases as the reactivity of the halogen decreases.

The usual **chemical test** for chlorine depends upon the formation of acid and bleach on reaction with water. A piece of **damp** universal indicator paper will first turn red and then colourless with chlorine. This also happens with bromine and iodine, but more slowly:

$$Cl_2(g) + H_2O(l) \rightarrow HCl(aq) + HOCl(aq)$$

chlorine + water → hydrochloric acid + chloric(I) acid (bleach).

(iv) Reaction of halogens with halides

Just as metals are able to displace each other from solutions of their ions (see Chapter 11, Section 3) so non-metals can do the same. A more reactive non-metal can displace a less reactive non-metal from a salt of the latter.

Remember - the more reactive halogen is **higher** in the group!

Chlorine can displace bromine from **ionic** bromides and iodine from **ionic** iodides:

$$Cl_2(g) + 2Br^-(aq) \rightarrow 2Cl^-(aq) + Br_2(aq)$$

chlorine + bromide ions → chloride ions + bromine.

If sodium bromide is the salt used the equation could also be written

$$Cl_2(g) + 2NaBr(aq) \rightarrow 2NaCl(aq) + Br_2(aq)$$

chlorine + sodium bromide → sodium chloride + bromine.

The reaction of chlorine with **iodides** is similar - iodine is displaced:

$$Cl_2(g) + 2KI(aq) \rightarrow 2KCl(aq) + I_2(aq)$$

chlorine + potassium iodide → potassium chloride + iodine.

The iodide used above could have been **any soluble metal iodide**.

- Try constructing an equation containing ions, for the iodine displacement. It should look something like the first equation given above with the symbol for iodine in place of the symbol for bromine.
- Try also writing an equation for the reaction between bromine and potassium iodide. Will a displacement occur?
(Note that all halide ions have a single negative charge.)

(C) FLUORINE

The study of **fluorine** is not on any GCSE syllabus. However, questions may be asked about its properties where these can be **predicted** from a knowledge of the properties of the other halogens and an understanding of the group reactivity trend.

Fluorine is at the **top** of the group.

- It would be expected to be a gas at room temperature because its boiling point should be lower than that of chlorine, which is also a gas.
- It would be expected to be the most reactive element in the group and will therefore react vigorously with iron and with sodium forming iron(III) fluoride and sodium fluoride.
- It should displace chlorine, bromine and iodine from their ionic compounds.

Can you predict some of the properties of the synthetic halogen astatine which is below iodine in the group?

The uses of the halogens are discussed in Chapter 12.

7 > GROUP 0 THE NOBLE GASES

The elements helium He, neon Ne, argon Ar, krypton Kr, and xenon Xe make up the group of almost totally unreactive gases called the **noble gases**.

They are all **monatomic** gases. That is, their molecules contain a single atom. This is because they have no need to combine with any other atom to achieve a full outer shell of electrons - they already have one!

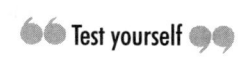

They are all gases because of the very small attractive forces between their molecules. Helium has the smallest molecule of the noble gases. Its molecules attract each other least and so the melting and boiling points of helium are the lowest in the group. Radon, with the largest molecules, has the highest melting and boiling points of the group. (Radon is the noble gas element below xenon; it is a radioactive element and is not studied at GCSE level. Its properties can, however, be predicted in the usual way from a knowledge of the properties of the other noble gases.)

(A) OCCURRENCE

These gases occur in the air, though only argon, at about 1% of the air, is common. Apart from helium, which is found in natural gas in some parts of the world, the gases are obtained by the fractional distillation of liquid air; see Chapter 12.3, Section 1.

(B) GROUP TRENDS - PHYSICAL PROPERTIES

The trend *down the group* is to higher melting points and boiling points and higher densities as with other non-metals (Fig. 6.11).

Noble gas	Density/g per litre	Melting point/°C	Boiling point/°C
helium	0.17	−270	−269
neon	0.84	−248	−246
argon	1.66	−189	−186
krypton	3.46	−157	−152
xenon	5.45	−112	−107
radon	8.90	− 71	− 62

Fig. 6.2 Some physical properties of the noble gases.

Note: The lowest possible temperature is −273 °C. The greater the negative value of the temperature in degrees Celsius, the lower is that temperature. Minus 62 °C is a higher temperature than minus 107 °C.

(C) CHEMICAL REACTIVITY

The lack of reactivity of the noble gases is caused by the inability of their atoms to transfer or share electrons. Each noble gas element has atoms with the outer electron shell full. For helium this is the first shell and contains just two electrons. The electron structures of the noble gases are shown in Fig. 6.6 above.

Noble gas atoms do not need to react with other atoms – not even with their own atoms – to achieve a full outer shell of electrons. They are therefore *inert* to other substances.

Until the early 1960s, no compounds of these elements had been prepared. At that time xenon was found to be capable of reacting with fluorine, the most reactive non-metal known. A knowledge of these reactions is not required for GCSE examinations.

The ability of xenon to form compounds illustrates very well the increased ability of electrons to be lost from the outer shell of the atom towards the bottom of a group. The most reactive noble gases are low down in the group – krypton and xenon.

(D) USES OF THE NOBLE GASES

The word 'noble' as used to describe these gases means *not very reactive*. This word 'noble' as used to describe these gases means *not very reactive*. This 'nobility' is very useful to chemists when they require the use of a non-reactive gas, for instance as an inert atmosphere to exclude reactive gases from a reaction vessel.

Helium is a non-flammable substitute for hydrogen in balloons and 'airships'. It is not used in 'hot air' balloons!

> It is a common error to believe that helium is used in 'hot air balloons'!!

Helium mixed with oxygen is supplied to deep sea divers. It prevents an unpleasant and sometimes fatal affliction called 'the bends'. Nitrogen in air dissolves in the blood as a diver descends and 'undissolves' forming gas bubbles in the capillaries as the diver ascends – resulting in great pain. Helium does not do this. It does, however, give the diver a squeaky voice whilst it is being breathed!

Neon is used in red illuminated signs and is also the 'starter' gas in sodium street lamps. Its tell-tale red glow is visible when these lamps are first turned on. The electric current conducted by the neon warms up the lamp which vaporises the solid sodium inside. When the sodium is fully vaporised it conducts the current, giving a yellow glow which mixes with the red of the neon to give the typical orange light of the sodium street lamp.

Argon is the main gas filling ordinary electric light bulbs. Its purpose is to prevent the tungsten filament from vaporising too rapidly and weakening itself.

Argon is the commonest of the noble gases and is available cheaply to industry. It is used wherever a non-reactive atmosphere is required cheaply and one such application is in welding, where the melted metal might react with oxygen in the air and cause failure of the weld. Here the argon is directed onto the metal being welded and keeps out air.

Krypton and **xenon** are also used as fillings for light bulbs. Krypton is used in miners' head-lamp bulbs which are much brighter, for the same size, than ordinary lamp bulbs; xenon is in the brightest bulbs in use – in lighthouses! These two gases prevent the filament of the bulb vaporising away and therefore allow the filament to be run at a much higher temperature, producing more intense light.

8 TRANSITION METALS

These metals are *not a group* of the periodic table – they do not all have the same number of electrons in the outer shell of their atoms. They are, in fact, a block of dense metals in the middle of the periodic table with many properties in common. They could be called a 'family' of elements.

Only some of the elements in the first row of this block will be considered.
The properties include

(i) **Metallic nature.** All are metals but they are harder than the alkali metal and have very little reaction with water – with the exception of iron!

(ii) **High densities.** Unlike the alkali metals, none of them floats on water. Densities vary from about 3 to 9 g/cm³ for elements 21–30.

> Students often believe that *all* metals have high melting points. This is untrue. Alkali metals, for instance, have very low melting points.

(iii) **High melting and boiling points.** Melting points range from 420°C to 1900°C and boiling points from 900°C to 3400°C.

(iv) Many of these elements are used as **catalysts** to speed up chemical reactions. Iron is the catalyst in the **Haber** process, nickel in the hydrogenation of vegetable oils to make margarine and vanadium(V) oxide the **Contact process**.

> Coloured in solution

(v) The compounds of most of the elements of this block are coloured in **aqueous solution**, e.g. copper(II) ions, $Cu^{2+}(aq)$, are blue and iron(II) ions, $Fe^{2+}(aq)$, are green.

(vi) The atoms of each of these elements can exist in **several different valencies** or **oxidisation states**, e.g. iron(II) and iron(III) compounds.

(vii) These elements are used in a number of important alloys (see Fig. 11.1).

The place of transition elements (heavy metals) in the periodic table is shown in Fig. 6.12.

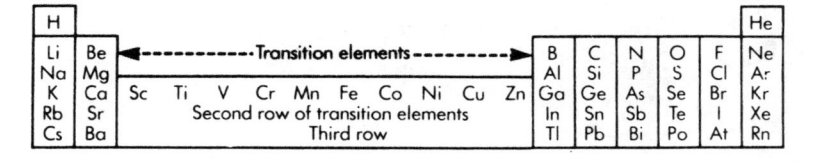

Fig. 6.12

H																	He
Li	Be											B	C	N	O	F	Ne
Na	Mg	←---------- Transition elements ----------→										Al	Si	P	S	Cl	Ar
K	Ca	Sc	Ti	V	Cr	Mn	Fe	Co	Ni	Cu	Zn	Ga	Ge	As	Se	Br	Kr
Rb	Sr	Second row of transition elements										In	Sn	Sb	Te	I	Xe
Cs	Ba	Third row										Tl	Pb	Bi	Po	At	Rn

9 HYDROGEN

Hydrogen is often placed in the middle at the top of the periodic table. However, it is also placed at the top of group 1. So, which group is it in? The answer is that hydrogen does not readily fit into any group.

The reason it is sometimes shown in group 1 is that:

- It has a valency/oxidation number of 1, e.g. it forms HCl, H_2O.
- It forms ions with a single positive charge, compare Na^+ with H^+.
- like the alkali metals its atom has one electron in its outer shell

The reason it is not always placed in group 1 is that:

- It is not a metal like group 1 metals
- It forms mostly covalent compounds whereas metals form ionic compounds
- It is a gas at normal temperatures, the alkali metals are all solids
- It does not have any of the metallic properties as elements of group 1 do.

It could be placed in group 7 with the halogens on the basis of its atomic structure. Its atom has one electron less than a full shell. However, ions (H^-) of the same charge as the halide ions are rare and do not exist in aqueous solution.

Hence hydrogen is best placed in the middle of the table at the top where it stands alone because of its unique properties.

THE PERIODIC TABLE AS A USEFUL TOOL FOR CHEMISTS

The periodic table is a useful tool that chemists use to summarise their knowledge and understanding of the chemistry of the elements. As you become more familiar with it you will be able to use it in the same way.

EXAMINATION QUESTIONS

MULTIPLE CHOICE QUESTIONS

QUESTIONS 1-4

Questions 1-4 concern the periodic table as shown in Fig. 6.13 where the letters A-E represent elements:

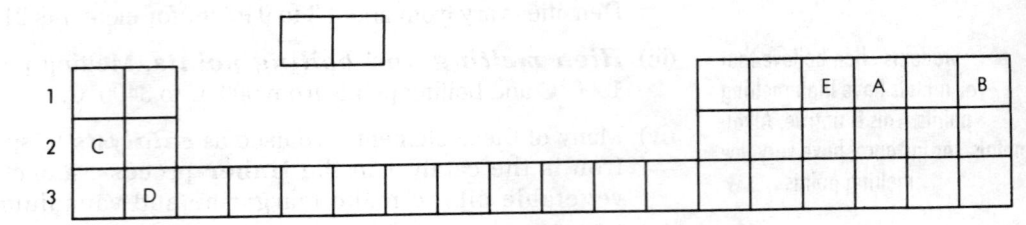

Fig. 6.13

Select the letter which represents:

1. A metal which produces hydrogen at a steady rate when added to water.
2. A metal which floats and reacts vigorously with water.
3. A gas that forms no compounds.
4. A gas that is an oxidising agent.

(WJEC)

QUESTIONS 5-8

Questions 5-8 concern the structures of an alkali metal atom. Match the numbers lettered A-E with the statements in questions 5-8. Each letter may be used once, more than once or not at all.

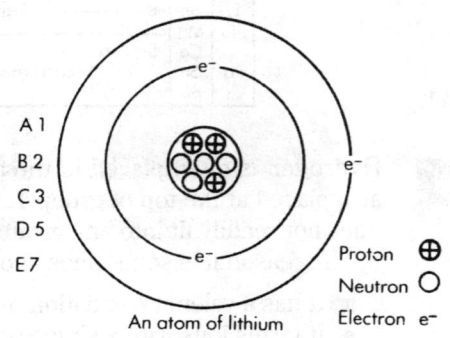

A 1
B 2
C 3
D 5
E 7

Fig. 6.14

5. The mass number of the atom.
6. The valency of the atom.
7. The atomic number of the atom.
8. The positive charge on the ion formed from the atom.

QUESTION 9

Chlorine is more reactive than bromine and bromine more reactive than iodine. To displace bromine from a solution of sodium bromide you could add

A chlorine water.
B iodine solution.
C potassium chloride solution.
D sodium chloride solution.

(SEG)

STRUCTURED QUESTIONS

QUESTION 10

An element X forms an ion X^{2-}.
(a) To which group of the Periodic Table does the element X belong? (1 line)
(1 mark)
(b) Write the formula of the compound formed between caesium and X. (Caesium has symbol Cs and is in group 1 of the Periodic Table.) (1 line)   *(1 mark)*
(c) The ion X^{2-} contains 54 electrons. How many protons are present in the nucleus of an atom of X? (1 line)
(1 mark)

(SEG)

QUESTION 11

This question is about the Periodic Table (Fig. 6.15).

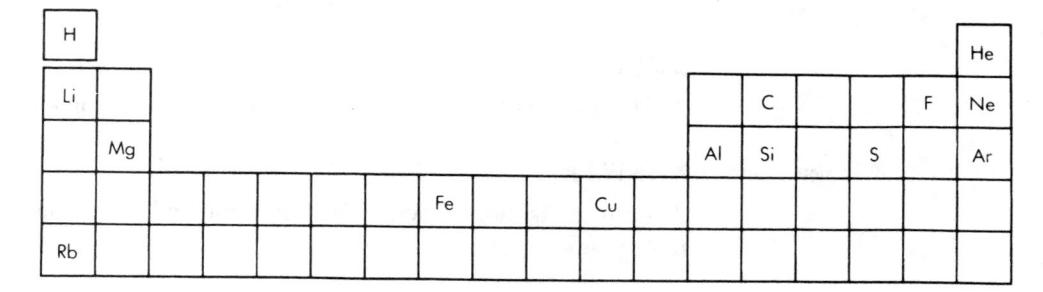

Fig. 6.15

(a) Using *only* the symbols in the table, give the symbol for:
   (i) an element which is in Group 3 of the Periodic Table,
   (ii) an element which is in the same period as carbon (C),
   (iii) a non-metal used in computer hardware,
   (iv) a metal that is used in light alloys,
   (v) an element that is used in illuminated signs,
   (vi) an element which forms an ion with a 2+ charge,
   (vii) the element that reacts most violently with fluorine (F).   *(7 marks)*
(b) Place the symbol for each of the following elements in its correct place in the Periodic Table of Fig. 6.15.

Element	Symbol	Atomic number
oxygen	O	8
calcium	Ca	20
bromine	Br	35

(3 marks)
(Total 10 marks)
(ULEAC)

OUTLINE ANSWERS

MULTIPLE CHOICE QUESTIONS

●● Section 2 ●●

ANSWER 1

D. Any group 2 metal other than magnesium will react with cold water to produce hydrogen at a 'steady rate'.

Section 2

ANSWER 2
C. Alkali metals float on water and react very vigorously with it.

ANSWER 3
B. The noble gases at the top of the group form no compounds. They are helium, neon and argon.

ANSWER 4
A. This is oxygen, at the top of group 6.

ANSWER 5
E. Mass number is the number of protons + neutrons in the nucleus of an atom.

ANSWER 6
A. The valency is the number of electrons in the outer shell of this atom.

ANSWER 7
C. The number of protons in the nucleus.

ANSWER 8
A. The atom will lose its single outer electron to become an ion.

Section 2

ANSWER 9
A. Chlorine is more reactive than bromine and will displace bromine from solutions of *bromides*.

STRUCTURED QUESTIONS

ANSWER 10
(a) The ion has two negative charges. It has been formed from an atom by gaining two electrons. The original atom must have had *two* electrons in its outer shell *less* than the number needed for stability – eight. This identifies its group number as group 6.

(b) Here candidates are asked to predict a formula of a compound containing an element they will never have seen or studied. One of the values of a knowledge of the periodic table is that such predictions are not difficult. Caesium is in group 1 – we are told. It will have *one* outer electron. Atoms of element X have two electrons less than an octet, (a) above. Therefore caesium atoms will transfer electrons to atoms of X until X has a full outer shell and each caesium atom also has a full outer shell. Each caesium atom can only donate *one* electron for its outer shell to be a full shell (loss of the outer single electron makes the *next shell* inwards *the new outer shell*). *Each X atom must accept* two electrons for a full outer shell. The formula is worked out by this kind of reasoning. Try it.

(c) Protons are positively charged particles in the nucleus of an atom. Because every atom is neutral in charge, overall, there must be as many negative charges as there are positive charges. Each electron has a single negative charge, so 54 of them will need to be balanced by 54 positive charges. However since the ion has a charge of 2 –, the number of protons must be 52.

ANSWER 11
A diagram of the periodic table is provided. Only those elements marked on the table can be used to answer the questions.

(a) (i) Group 3 is not marked as such. It is the third vertical column from the left – *omitting the transition element block*. The element is Al, aluminium. The symbol is required.

(ii) Lithium, fluorine and neon are elements in the same period as carbon: any one of the symbols for these will be acceptable.

(iii) Computer hardware means computers themselves. Si, silicon is used in their manufacture.
(iv) Mg, magnesium or Al, aluminium are used in light alloys.
(v) Ne, neon is used as the gas filling for illuminated sign tubes.
(vi) A 2+ charge would be found on an ion of a group 2 metal, Mg is an answer. However, Cu and Fe also have ions with 2+ charges and these answers would be equally acceptable even though they are transition metals.
(vii) Fluorine is the most reactive non-metal; rubidium is the most reactive metal shown on the table provided. Rb is the answer. Note, however, that caesium is even more reactive but it is not one of the symbols on the table and *would not be accepted as the answer to the question*.

(b) This part is testing your knowledge of the structure of the periodic table. Elements are arranged in *atomic number order*. Count the numbers out starting at hydrogen = 1. Oxygen will come just before F; calcium immediately under Mg (as a check Ca *is* a group 2 metal like Mg); Br is a halogen and in case, by now, you are finding difficulty counting to 35, it will be the third halogen down - two spaces below F.

STUDENTS' ANSWER – EXAMINER'S COMMENTS

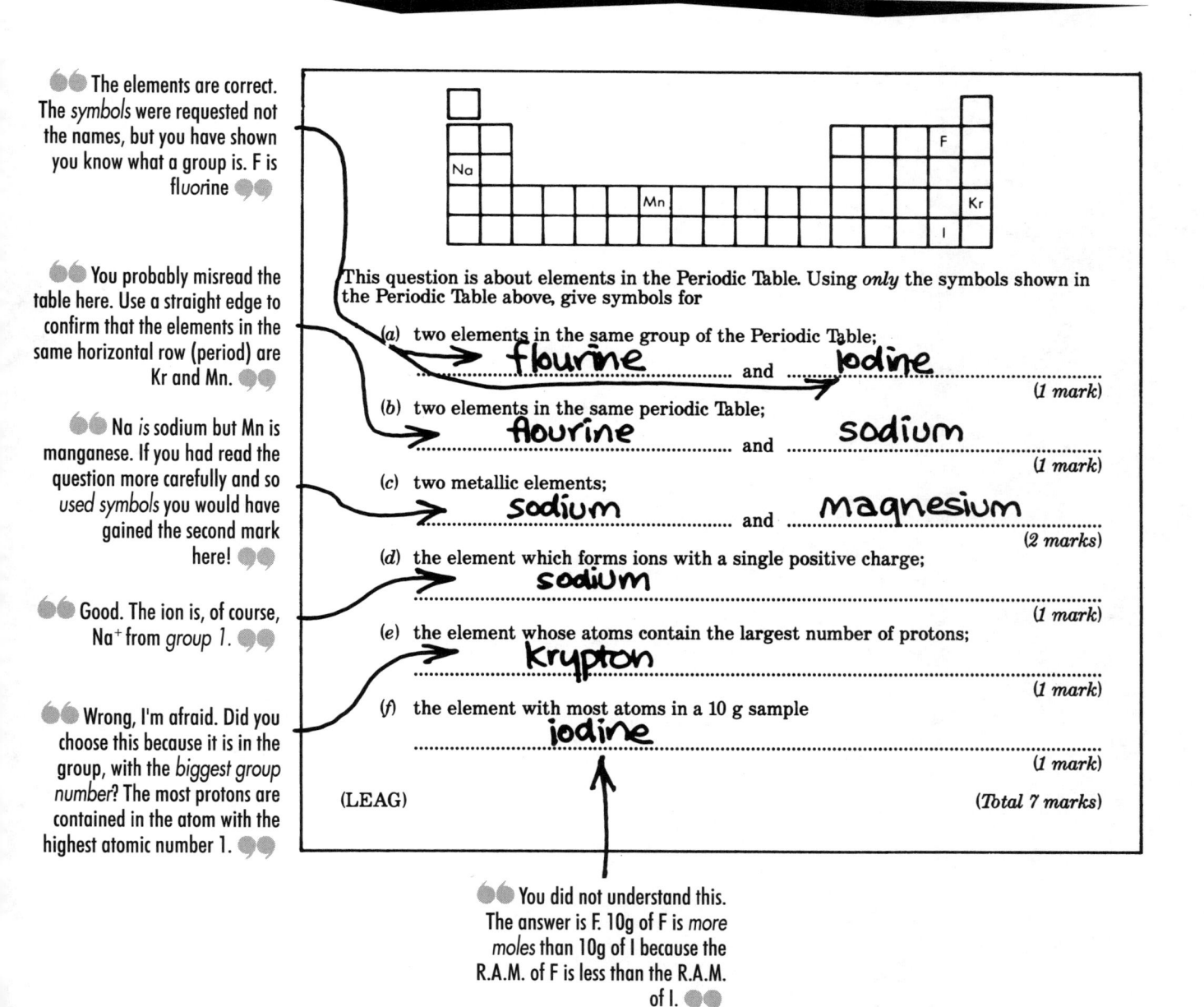

The elements are correct. The *symbols* were requested not the names, but you have shown you know what a group is. F is fluorine

You probably misread the table here. Use a straight edge to confirm that the elements in the same horizontal row (period) are Kr and Mn.

Na *is* sodium but Mn is manganese. If you had read the question more carefully and so used symbols you would have gained the second mark here!

Good. The ion is, of course, Na⁺ from *group 1*.

Wrong, I'm afraid. Did you choose this because it is in the group, with the *biggest group number*? The most protons are contained in the atom with the highest atomic number !.

This question is about elements in the Periodic Table. Using *only* the symbols shown in the Periodic Table above, give symbols for

(a) two elements in the same group of the Periodic Table;
   ....flourine........ and ....iodine........ (1 mark)

(b) two elements in the same periodic Table;
   ....flourine........ and ....sodium........ (1 mark)

(c) two metallic elements;
   ....sodium........ and ....magnesium........ (2 marks)

(d) the element which forms ions with a single positive charge;
   ....sodium........ (1 mark)

(e) the element whose atoms contain the largest number of protons;
   ....Krypton........ (1 mark)

(f) the element with most atoms in a 10 g sample
   ....iodine........ (1 mark)

(LEAG) (Total 7 marks)

You did not understand this. The answer is F. 10g of F is *more moles* than 10g of I because the R.A.M. of F is less than the R.A.M. of I.

CHAPTER 6 **ESSENTIAL PRINCIPLES** 97

REVIEW SHEET

■ Complete the table

The differences between metals and non-metals are:	
Metals	Non-metals
1.	
2.	
3.	
4.	
5.	
6.	
7.	
8.	

■ List some of the trends in properties **across a period.**

1. _____
2. _____
3. _____
4. _____
5. _____
6. _____

■ List some of the trends in properties down the groups.

1. _____
2. _____
3. _____
4. _____

■ If alkali metals come into contact with *water* the following reaction is:

■ If alkali metals come into contact with *oxygen or air*, the reaction is:

■ Describe an experiment to investigate the reaction of magnesium with steam. Draw the apparatus used.

_____
_____
_____
_____
_____
_____
_____

- List some characteristics of the reactions of group 2 metals.

- List some of the characteristic of the reactions of group 7, the Halogens.

- What properties do 'noble gases' have?

- List some of the properties of the 'transition metals'.

CHAPTER 7

GETTING STARTED

One of the many ways of classifying substances is on the basis of their ability to conduct electricity. We can divide all known substances into two groups: conductors and non-conductors. A substance which allows electricity to pass through it is called a *conductor*. Substances which do not conduct electricity are *non-conductors* or *insulators*.

ELECTROCHEMISTRY

TYPES OF CONDUCTOR

ELECTROLYSIS

MOLTEN ELECTROLYTES

AQUEOUS ELECTROLYTES

SOME IMPORTANT ELECTROLYSES

SUBSTANCES PRODUCED BY ELECTROLYSIS

OTHER USES OF ELECTROLYTIC PROCESSES

SIMPLE CELLS

CELL EMF'S AND THE REACTIVITY SERIES

RECHARGEABLE CELLS

FUEL CELLS

TAKING IT FURTHER

ELECTRICAL COSTS IN METAL PRODUCTION

ESSENTIAL PRINCIPLES

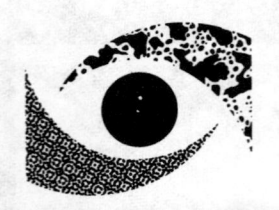

1 > TYPES OF CONDUCTOR

There are three sorts of conductors, shown in the following table:

Conductors		
A	B	C
Elements – all metals and all alloys, e.g. copper or aluminium or brass. Also graphite which is a non-metal	Compounds which contain ions which conduct when molten or in aqueous solution, e.g. salts or acids or alkalis.	Elements which have covalent molecules but conduct weakly, e.g. silicon or germanium.

> *Strictly speaking compounds should not be called conductors when electricity passes through them. Unlike metals which are not broken down as they conduct, compounds decompose as electricity passes through them. A better term for compounds would be 'electrolytic conductors' rather than just conductors.*

(A) GROUP A

Metals and alloys conduct by allowing a flow of electrons to pass through them. The valency electrons present in these structures form a 'sea of electrons' which allows electrons from the battery to flow through the structure (see Chapter 6, Section 14).

Graphite is unusual since it is a non-metal and would not be expected to be a conductor. It has a layer structure with 'free electrons' sandwiched between the layers of carbon atoms. These free electrons are able to move when graphite is placed between the terminals of a battery. Because graphite is not a very reactive element it serves a useful purpose in electrochemistry as an inert electrode.

(B) GROUP B

Compounds do not have the same structures as metals or graphite. Those compounds which contain ions are ***decomposed into elements*** by the electricity that passes through them. This process is called ***electrolysis*** and happens only when ions are free to move – as in a molten state (a melt) or in an aqueous solution. Ions in ***solid*** ionic compounds can only vibrate about fixed positions in the crystal lattice – they are not able to move from place to place.

A compound which is decomposed by an electric current is called an ***electrolyte***. Electrolytes are ionic compounds which are molten or dissolved in water.

(C) GROUP C

Group C substances contain no 'free electrons' and no ions. They allow very small currents indeed to pass through them by a mechanism that is outside the scope of this study. They are called ***semi-conductors***.

2 > ELECTROLYSIS

Electrolysis is the process of ***decomposing a compound*** by passage of an electric current. ***Elements*** cannot be electrolysed because an element cannot be broken down into anything simpler.

Electrolysis is carried out by inserting two ***electrodes*** into the electrolyte and passing a ***direct current*** through it. A convenient direct current source is a battery or a lab-pak. A d.c. source will have a positive and a negative terminal. The electrodes are made of graphite (a fairly inert non-metal) or an inert metal such as stainless steel, platinum or titanium. Sometimes the electrode is required to dissolve away during the electrolysis in which case it will not be made of an inert metal (see Section 10). The material chosen for the electrodes must be unreactive to both the electrolyte and to the electrode products – unless it is convenient or economical to allow reaction to occur (see the electrolysis of alumina).

The electrolyte must contain freely moving ions. As the current passes through the electrolyte, the ions move to the electrode which has ***a charge opposite to their own charge***.

Anode

The electrode connected to the positive terminal of the supply is called the **anode**. The anode attracts negatively charged ions called *anions*.

Cathode

The electrode connected to the negative terminal of the supply is called the *cathode*. The cathode attracts positively charged ions called *cations*.

Ions from the electrolyte are **discharged** at both electrodes forming products which are elements.

- The *cathode product* is always either a *metal or hydrogen*.
- The *anode product* is always a *non-metallic* element such as halogen or oxygen.
- The *electrode product* may be a *deposit* of a solid element or it may be a gas, in which case the gas bubbles to the surface of the electrolyte and can be collected if required (see Fig. 7.2 below).

Note: The use of an alternating supply (a.c. supply) would cause the electrodes to alternate between being anodes and cathodes fifty times per second and *no electrolysis* would occur.

3 > A TYPICAL ELECTROLYSIS CIRCUIT

The main features of the circuit are:

(i) A d.c. supply to provide an electrolysing current with positive and negative electrodes when connected.
(ii) A and C are the Anode (+) and Cathode (−).
(iii) The electrolyte is a molten ionic compound or an aqueous solution of a salt, an acid or an alkali. The important requirement of an electrolyte is that it contains mobile ions.

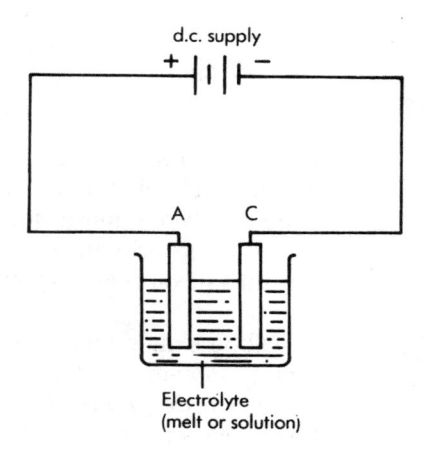

Fig. 7.1

(iv) The electrolysis is carried out in an electrolysis cell. This can be any vessel which will
   (a) contain the liquid electrolyte;
   (b) allow the insertion of the electrodes; and
   (c) allow the collection or removal of the products.

A beaker is best for electrolysis in which a metal is deposited on the cathode. The types of apparatus shown in Fig. 7.2 below are better if gases are to be collected.

4 > CIRCUITS FOR QUANTITATIVE ELECTROLYSIS

It is sometimes necessary to measure the **quantity of electricity** and the **mass or volume** of a deposited element. In such experiments an **ammeter** and a **variable resistor** must be included in the circuit shown in Fig. 7.1. The variable resistor is used to adjust the value of the current **to keep it constant** throughout the electrolysis. This allows the quantity of electricity passed to be calculated. The ammeter measures the current passing. To calculate the *quantity* of electricity passed a stop-clock is also needed.

5 > THE PRODUCTS OF ELECTROLYSIS

Ionic compounds usually contain one metal and one or more non-metallic elements. If there is one metal and one non-metal present, the compound will be electrolysed to the metal at the cathode and the non-metal at the anode, e.g. NaCl when molten will produce sodium at the cathode and chlorine at the anode.

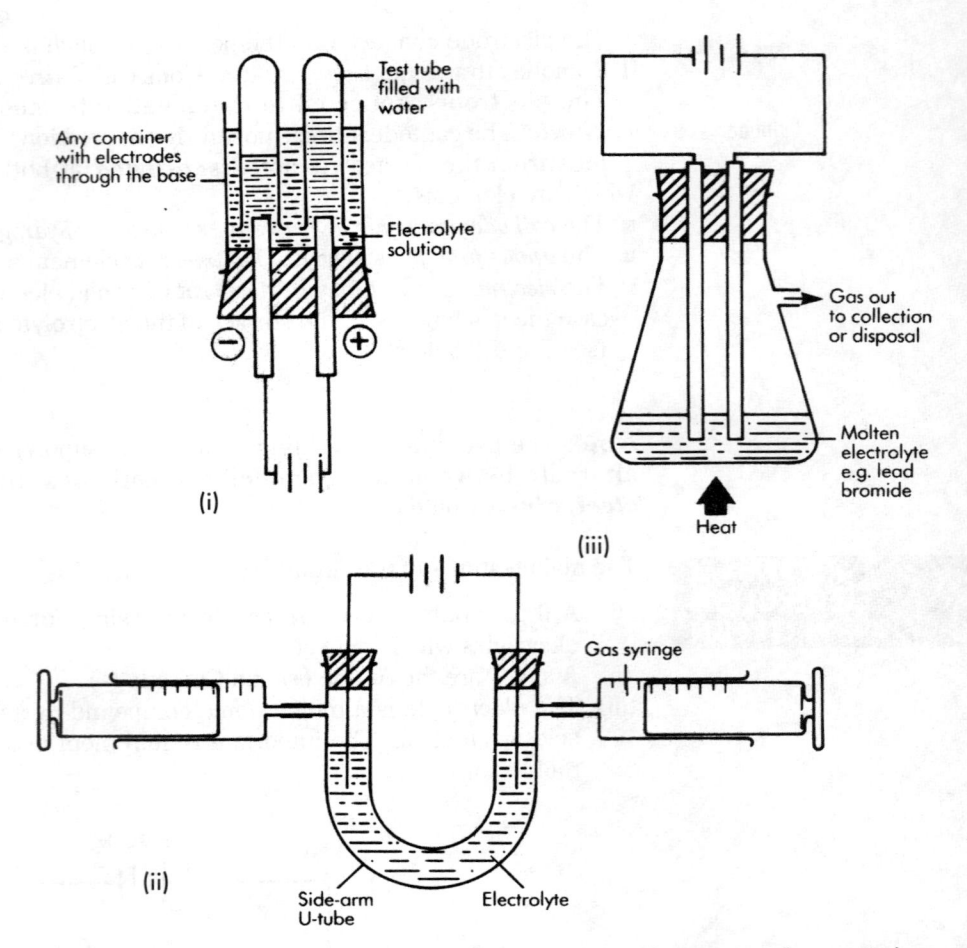

Fig. 7.2

Electrolysis of **molten** compounds containing **more than two elements** is more complicated and will not be used in GCSE papers. A knowledge of the electrolysis of compounds of two or more elements in **aqueous solution**, however, **is** required.

The following principles can be used to predict the products of electrolysis of molten and aqueous electrolytes.

6 MOLTEN ELECTROLYTES

These will be simple binary compounds, i.e. they will contain only two elements – a metal and a non-metal. The **metal** will be the **cathode product**; the **non-metal** will be the **anode product**.

An example is the electrolysis of molten lead bromide, $PbBr_2(l)$. A carbon anode and a steel cathode are suitably **inert** electrodes (see Fig. 7.2(iii)).

At the anode (+)

Anodes are positively charged because they are **lacking in electrons**. Anions, on the other hand are negatively charged ions – they are atoms or groups of atoms with an **excess** of electrons. In this example the anode accepts one electron from each anion. We say the anion is DIScharged at the anode:

$$2Br^-(l) - 2e^- \rightarrow Br_2(g).$$

bromide ions minus 2 electrons → bromine gas molecules

❝ Anodic oxidation ❞

Bromine gas is the product as the temperature of the molten lead bromide is above the boiling point of bromine.

Because the anion loses electrons to the anode the process is one of **oxidation** of the anion at the anode: anodic oxidation.

❝ The equations for the discharge of ions at the anode and cathode are often badly done in examination answers. Make the effort to understand them so that you do not lose marks on these easy equations. ❞

At the cathode (−)

Cathodes are negatively charged because they have an **excess of electrons**.

Cations are positively charged ions – they are atoms of groups of atoms with one or more electrons missing. They are electron **deficient**.

In this example the cathode gives two electrons to each lead cation. The lead cations are discharged at the cathode:

$$Pb^{2+}(l) + 2e^- \rightarrow Pb(l).$$

lead ions plus 2 electrons → lead metal atoms.

Molten lead is the product at the cathode since lead (m.p. 323°C) is a liquid at the temperature of the molten lead bromide, m.p. 373°C.

Cathodic reduction

Because the cation gains electrons from the cathode the process is one of **reduction** of the cation at the cathode: cathodic reduction.

Overall, the lead bromide is decomposed into the elements lead and bromine:

$$PbBr_2(l) \rightleftharpoons Pb(l) + Br_2(g).$$

7 > AQUEOUS ELECTROLYTES

These are really mixtures of two electrolytes – *the compound and water*. Water itself is a very weak electrolyte. It is slightly ionised:

$$H_2O(l) \rightleftharpoons H^+(aq) + OH^-(aq).$$

Because the hydrogen ions ($H^+(aq)$) and the hydroxyl ions ($OH^-(aq)$) are *in equilibrium* with water molecules in any aqueous solution, these ions will be replaced as quickly as they are removed. This means that these two ions from water behave *as if* they were present in large concentrations. They can be discharged as any other ions are discharged.

8 > PREDICTING THE ELECTROLYSIS PRODUCTS FOR AQUEOUS SOLUTIONS

It is possible to understand why aqueous solutions produce the observed products by looking at the *'reactivity series'* for cations and anions as shown in the table below. These are similar to reactivity series studied elsewhere in this book (see Chapter 11, Section. 3).

Reactivity series for cations	Reactivity series for anions	
potassium sodium calcium magnesium aluminium	sulphate nitrate carbonate	these ions are ***never*** discharged
hydrogen zinc tin lead copper silver	oxide/hydroxide chloride bromide iodide	

Stable ions don't discharge

The ion *lowest* in the tables above will be discharged at each electrode in preference to any other ion present. The *most* reactive metals *form the most stable ions*. Therefore, these ions will be difficult to convert back to metals. This will cause the least reactive metals to discharge instead. Similarly, the *least reactive non-metals* will be most *easily discharged*. By *listing* the ions present at each electrode and consulting the tables above, the main products can be found.

USING THE TABLE TO PREDICT THE PRODUCTS OF ELECTROLYSIS

For example, consider the electrolysis of aqueous zinc nitrate, $Zn(NO_3)_2(aq)$, using graphite (carbon) electrodes. When the current is switched on, one electrode becomes positively charged and the other becomes negatively charged. Negatively charged ions are attracted to the anode (+) and positively charged ions to the cathode (−).

At the anode (+)

The ions *attracted* will be (aq) from the water and Cl^-(aq) from the sodium chloride. Of the two ions, the chloride ion will be preferentially discharged since it is lower in the above table than the hydroxide ion.

$$4Cl^-(aq) - 4e^- \xrightarrow{\text{loss of 4 electrons (4e}^-\text{) to anode}} 2Cl_2(g)$$

At the cathode (−)

The ions *attracted* will be the H^+(aq) from water and the Na^+(aq) from the sodium chloride. Of the two, the lowest in the table will be preferentially discharged. This is the hydrogen ion.

$$4H^+(aq) + 4e^- \xrightarrow{\text{gain of 4 electrons from the cathode}} 2H_2(g)$$

It is a requirement of electrolysis that the same number of electrons should feature in both electrode equations. This is because the electrons that are picked up by the anode are passed round the circuit to the cathode where they are given to the discharging cations.

Overall reactions

$$2NaCl(aq) + 2H_2O(l) \rightarrow 2Na^+(aq) + 2OH^-(aq) + H_2(g) + Cl_2(g)$$

The ions that have not been discharged, remain in solution and are equivalent to a solution of sodium hydroxide. The products of electrolysis of sodium chloride are therefore:

aqueous sodium hydroxide + hydrogen + chlorine

When carried out industrially, this process is the basis of the **chlor-alkali** industry. The most important products are the sodium hydroxide (the alkali) and chlorine. Huge tonnages of these are used annually all over the world.

10 AN OUTLINE OF SOME IMPORTANT ELECTROLYSES

> **Aluminium is made only by this process. Electricity must be cheap for economical production.**

Electrolyte	Anode product	Cathode product	Other observations
1. The manufacture of aluminium			
Molten aluminium oxide	Oxygen at carbon anode. Anode slowly oxidised to carbon dioxide	Molten aluminium at carbon cathode	Electrolyte is a mixture of alumina (aluminium oxide) with cryolite to lower its melting point
Ions: Al^{3+}(l) and O^{2-}(l)			
Overall reaction: $2Al_2O_3(l) \rightarrow 4Al(l) + 3O_2(g)$			

Fig. 7.3. Some important electrolyses.

CHAPTER 7 **ESSENTIAL PRINCIPLES** 105

> One day this process may be used to produce hydrogen gas as a motor vehicle fuel. It will need a cheap source of electricity to become an acceptable fuel.

> The electrolysis of brine is the basis of the important Chlor-Alkali industry.

> Refined copper of 99.999% purity is obtained by this process. Zinc and lead are purified by similiar processes.

Fig. 7.3. (cont.) Some important electrolyses.

	Electrolyte	Anode product	Cathode product	Other observations
2.	**The electrolysis of concentrated hydrochloric acid**			
	Concentrated hydrochloric acid	Chlorine at inert anode	Hydrogen at inert cathode	Equal volumes of the gases are produced
	Ions: $H^+(aq)$ and $Cl^-(aq)$			
	$H^+(aq) + OH^-(aq)$ from water			
	Overall reaction: $2HCl(aq) \rightarrow H_2(g) + Cl_2(g)$			
3.	**The electrolysis of water**			
	Dilute aqueous sulphuric acid	Oxygen at inert anode	Hydrogen at inert cathode	In effect, water is decomposed. Sulphuric acid remains unaffected
	Ions: $H^+(aq)$ and $SO_4^{2-}(aq)$ and $H^+(aq) + OH^-(aq)$ from water			
	Overall reaction: $2H_2O(l) \rightarrow 2H_2(g) + O_2(g)$ water has been decomposed			
4.	**The manufacture of chlorine and sodium hydroxide*			
	Concentrated aqueous sodium chloride	Chlorine at inert anode $OH^-(aq)$ ions accumulate around anode	Hydrogen at inert anode $Na^+(aq)$ ions accumulate around cathode	The loss of hydrogen and chlorine leaves sodium hydroxide solution as product
	Ions: $Na^+(aq)$ and $Cl^-(aq)$			
	$H^+(aq) + OH^-(aq)$ from water			
	Overall reaction: $2NaCl(aq) + 2H_2O(l) \rightarrow 2NaOH(aq) + H_2(g) + Cl_2(g)$			
5.	**Electrolysis of aqueous copper salt**			
	Aqueous copper (II) sulphate at inert electrodes	Oxygen at inert anode	Copper at inert cathode	If **all** the copper sulphate is decomposed, sulphuric acid remains, and the solution becomes colourless
	Ions: $Cu^{2+}(aq)$, $SO_4^{2-}(aq)$ and $H^+(aq)$, $OH^-(aq)$ from water			
	Overall reaction: $CuSO_4(aq) + H_2O(l) \rightarrow Cu(s) + H_2SO_4(aq) + \frac{1}{2}O_2(g)$			
	Aqueous copper (II) chloride at inert electrodes	Chlorine at the anode	Copper at the cathode	Only the ions from copper (II) chloride discharge.
	Ions; $Cu^{2+}(aq)$, $Cl^-(aq)$ and $H^+(aq)$, $OH^-(aq)$ from water			
	Overall reaction: $CuCl_2(aq) \rightarrow Cu(s) + Cl_2(g)$			
6.	**The industrial refining of copper**			
	Aqueous copper (II) sulphate at copper electrodes	Copper anode dissolves	Copper deposits on cathode	Copper is transferred from anode to cathode. Electrolyte concentration remains constant
	Ions: $Cu^{2+}(aq)$, $SO_4^{2-}(aq)$			
	$H^+(aq) + OH^-(aq)$ from water			
	Overall reaction: $Cu(impure) \rightarrow Cu(pure)$ Copper has been purified			

11> USEFUL SUBSTANCES PRODUCED BY ELECTROLYSIS

Cathode product required or formed	Anode product required or formed	Electrodes required	Electrolyte required
Aluminium **Cathode reaction:** $4Al^{3+}(l) + 12e^- \rightarrow 4Al(l)$	oxygen **anode reaction:** $6O^{2-}(l) - 12e^- \rightarrow 3O_2(g)$	carbon carbon anode	MOLTEN aluminium oxide (Section 8.)
sodium **Cathode reaction:** $2Na^+(l) + 2e^- \rightarrow 2Na(l)$	chlorine **anode reaction:** $2Cl^-(l) - 2e^- \rightarrow Cl_2(g)$	steel cathode carbon anode	MOLTEN sodium chloride (Section 8.)
sodium hydroxide and hydrogen **Cathode reaction:** $2H^+(aq) + 2e^- \rightarrow H_2(g)$	chlorine **anode reaction:** $2Cl^-(aq) - 2e^- \rightarrow Cl_2(g)$	titanium anode nickel cathode	AQUEOUS sodium chloride (Section 8.)
Pure copper **Cathode reaction:** $Cu^{2+}(aq) + 2e^- \rightarrow Cu(s)$	none **anode reaction:** $Cu(s) - 2e^-(aq) \rightarrow Cu^{2+}(aq)$	Pure copper cathode impure copper anode	aqueous copper(II) sulphate

Fig. 7.4 Useful substances produced by electrolysis.

12> THE MERCURY ELECTRODE

Very pure sodium hydroxide solution is made by electrolysing brine using a mercury cathode. The process is unusual because, normally, no sodium would discharge from a solution containing water. The mercury cathode, however, allows metallic sodium to dissolve in it forming a mixture called an ***amalgam***. Sodium discharges in preference to hydrogen under these conditions.

When the amalgam is reacted with water a solution of sodium hydroxide of high purity is obtained:

$$2Na/Hg(l) + 2H_2O(l) \rightarrow 2NaOH(aq) + H_2(g) + 2Hg(l).$$

sodium amalgam + water → sodium hydroxide + hydrogen + mercury.

13> OTHER USES OF ELECTROLYTIC PROCESSES

(A) ELECTROPLATING

This is an electrolysis in which

(i) the cathode is an object to be ***metal coated***; and
(ii) the electrolyte must contain ***ions of the metal*** to be coated onto the cathode.

The anode is usually a piece of the plating metal, i.e. a piece of silver for silver plating. Examples include the silver plating of trophies, jewellery and cutlery; gold plating of microprocessor connections; zinc plating of steel (galvanising); chromium and nickel plating of parts for bicycles and cars.

A special example of an electroplating process is used to purify (refine) copper. This is called ***copper refining***, see Fig. 7.3 above. In this process, the anode is a plate of impure copper (about 90% pure). The cathode is a very thin plate of pure copper. Before the electrolysis, the cathode is very lightly greased. Electrolysis is carried out in an aqueous solution of copper(II) sulphate.

During the electrolysis the copper present in the impure copper anode dissolves into the electrolyte and is then plated onto the original, pure copper cathode. When all the copper from the anode has deposited on the cathode, the anode and cathode are replaced and the process is repeated (see Fig. 7.4 above).

Because of the light greasing of the original cathode, the deposited copper can be *peeled off* and the thin cathode reused. Pure copper of 'five-nines' (i.e. 99.999%) purity is used for electrical wires.

(B) ANODISING

Whereas electroplating is a process which occurs on the cathode, anodising occurs on the anode. ***Anodising*** is the electrolytic process of coating objects made of aluminium with a very thin ***oxide film*** to protect the metal from corrosion and dulling of the surface shine. To ensure a very thin film of oxide the oxidation is carried out by electrolysis using the aluminium object as the ***anode***. The electrolyte is usually dilute sulphuric acid which, it will be remembered, gives oxygen at the anode on electrolysis (Fig. 7.3 above). Under the correct conditions the oxygen reacts with the surface of the aluminium and coats it with a thin, invisible, but protective coating of aluminium oxide.

at the anode(+)

$$2Al\,(s) + 6OH^-\,(aq) \rightarrow Al_2O_3(s) + 3H_2O\,(l) + 6e^-$$
coating on aluminium

at the cathode(−)

$$6H^+\,(a) + 6e^- \rightarrow 3H_2(g)$$

Anodised aluminium can also be dyed, the oxide coating absorbing colour which cannot be washed out in normal use.

14> SIMPLE CELLS

The commonly used 'battery' is an example of a cell which uses a ***chemical reaction to produce electricity***. The process occurring inside such a cell is a ***reversal*** of the type of reaction occurring in electrolysis.

In electrolysis, an electric current is used to decompose a chemical compound. In simple cells (Fig. 7.5), electricity is produced by a reaction between chemicals, e.g. in the displacement reaction:

$$Mg(s) + Cu^{2+}(aq) \rightarrow Mg^{2+}(aq) + Cu(s)$$

magnesium + copper(II) ions → magnesium ions + copper.

This reaction can be carried out in a cell with the reacting chemicals separated from each other by a ***porous*** partition.

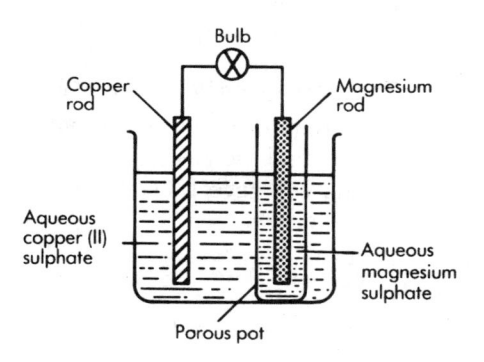

Fig. 7.5 A simple cell.

> A cell using magnesium and silver electrodes is included in the survival kit of military pilots who might ditch in the sea. It produces enough electricity to light a lamp using sea-water as the electrolyte.

The magnesium dissolves, releasing electrons and forming magnesium ions:

$$Mg(s) \rightarrow Mg^{2+}(aq) + 2e^-\ \text{electrons released.}$$

If the cell is connected to a circuit, the electrons travel through the circuit and eventually reach the copper:

$$Cu^{2+}(aq) + 2e^- \rightarrow Cu(s).$$

copper ion + 2 electrons → copper atom

Here they combine with copper(II) ions forming copper atoms.

> Electricity from a chemical reaction

You will see from this description that the reaction shown in the first equation above has occurred. The transfer of electrons from magnesium atoms to copper ions has taken place ***through*** the circuit ***and so an electric current has been produced*** that will light a bulb or drive a motor.

Any reaction between a ***reactive metal*** and the ***ions of a less reactive metal***

Reactivity series again

will produce electricity in the same way. Simply placing two metal plates, one of a more reactive metal than the other, into a solution containing ions will produce a current. ***The further apart the metals are in the reactivity table, the greater the voltage and current***.

15> CELL EMFS AND THE REACTIVITY SERIES

If simple cells are made up using one electrode of **copper** and the other of another, more, or less, reactive metal, the voltage readings (called electromotive forces, e.m.f.s) depend on the reactivity of the other metal. The table gives a set of results obtained by this method. The electrode position refers to the cell shown in Fig. 7.5.

left-hand electrode	right-hand electrode	E.M.F. in volts
copper	magnesium	1.6
copper	zinc	1.0
copper	silver	− 0.3

Interpreting the results

The e.m.f. is the greatest where the two metals in the cell are furthest apart in the reactivity series. The higher the e.m.f., the greater the difference in electron concentration between the electrodes.

Metals high in the reactivity series react more readily than copper. Reaction for metals means forming positive ions and electrons. Reaction, therefore produces electrons on the metal and ions in the surrounding solution.

The most reactive elements produce electrons more readily than less reactive elements. Hence magnesium produces electrons more readily than copper and this shows in the e.m.f. of 1.6 volts. Zinc reacts less readily than magnesium, so its e.m.f. in a cell with copper is less than that of magnesium with copper. Silver is *less* reactive than copper. Hence when coupled with copper in a cell the e.m.f. would show as a negative value. This is the same as saying that the silver has swapped places with the copper as the least reactive of the two metals in the cell.

Electromotive forces (e.m.f.s) are measures of the difference between two electrode **potentials**. The potential of a metal is a measure of the charge on that metal electrode when it is reacting with the electrolyte. The electrolyte used when comparing metals in these cells is usually dilute sulphuric acid. This provides a common electrolyte for a fair comparison of the e.m.f.s.

Predicting values for other pairs of metals

If we regard the electrode potential of copper as zero for the purpose of comparison, we can find the electrode potential of the other metal by difference. The magnesium – copper cell gave 1.6 volts. If copper is 0.0 volts, the magnesium must have a potential of 1.6 volts.

Reactivity Series	E.M.F.	
magnesium	1.6	The
aluminium		greater the
zinc		difference in
iron		reactivity,
lead		the
copper	0.0	greater the
silver	− 0.3	e.m.f. of
gold		the cell

Refering to the adjacent table, the e.m.f. of a cell with silver and magnesium would be obtained by adding together the e.m.f.s of the magnesium – copper and the copper – silver cells. It should be 1.6 + 0.3 = 1.9 volts.

The e.m.f. for a cell made with magnesium and aluminium should be between 1.0

and 1.6 volts. This is not the value usually observed because the aluminium has an oxide coating which stops it reacting. The e.m.f. will be much less. If the oxide film is removed, however, the expected value is observed.

16> RECHARGEABLE CELLS

Because electrolysis involves the *reverse* process of that producing electricity in a cell, it should be possible to recharge 'dead' cells by passing electricity into them. This can be done in a limited number of cells. A typical rechargeable cell is the lead–acid cell used in cars and for emergency lighting in hospitals and power stations (Fig. 7.6).

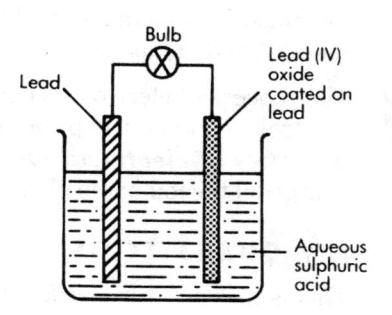

Fig. 7.6 The lead-acid cell.

The cell consists of two electrodes dipping in dilute sulphuric acid. One plate is of lead, the other of lead(IV) oxide. When connected to a circuit which uses the electricity produced, electrons will be produced at the lead plate and travel through the circuit to the lead(IV) oxide plate where they react with lead(IV) oxide to form lead(II) ions. When the lead(IV) oxide has all been consumed, the *reverse* reaction to regenerate the materials of the plates is carried out by passing electricity through the cell *in the reverse direction*.

Many other types of rechargeable cell are currently on the market.

17> FUEL CELLS

Fuel cells (Fig. 7.7) produce electricity from chemical reactions, just as in the cells described above. The difference is that the reaction occurring in a fuel cell is *essentially* a continuous flameless combustion. For example, the combustion of hydrogen in oxygen can be carried out in a fuel cell and electricity produced from the reaction.

The essentials are

(i) inert electrodes which also *catalyse* the reaction;
(ii) a fuel to be *continuously* fed in at one electrode;
(iii) oxygen to be *continuously* fed in at the other electrode;
(iv) an electrolyte into which the reaction product can be absorbed.

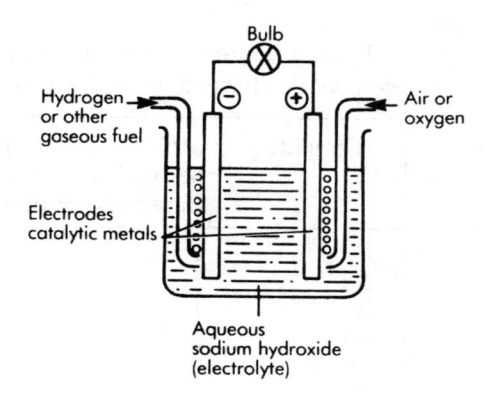

Fig. 7.7 A fuel cell.

The reactions occurring are the *reverse* of those in the electrolysis of water.

At the positive electrode

$$O_2(g) + 2H_2O(l) + 4e^- \rightarrow 4OH^-(aq).$$
oxygen + water + electrons → hydroxide ions

At the negative electrode

$$2H_2(g) + 4OH^-(aq) \rightarrow 4H_2O(l) + 4e^-.$$

hydrogen + hydroxide ions → water + electrons

Adding these two equations together gives the *overall* reaction

$$2H_2(g) + O_2(g) \rightarrow 2H_2O(l).$$

The fuel cell is much more efficient at converting fuels into electricity than the usual methods. Development has been slow, but there are now large-scale cells on trial in the USA and in Japan.

The process of electrolysis can be used to determine the *charge on an ion*. During electrolysis, ions accept or release electrons at the electrodes. By measuring the *quantity of electrical charge* involved in the discharge of *one mole* of ions, the charge on the ion of the element discharged will have been found.

(A) QUANTITY OF ELECTRICAL CHARGE

This is measured in *coulombs*. One coulomb is the charge which flows through an electrolyte when a current of 1 amp flows for 1 second. The quantity of charge passing through a circuit during an electrolysis is therefore found by the equation

quantity of charge (coulombs) = current (amps) × time (seconds).

(B) THE MOLE OF ELECTRICAL CHARGE

One *mole* of electrons has flowed through an electrolyte when 96 500 coulombs passed through. This quantity of charge is called a *faraday*. One faraday is equivalent to the total charge on 6×10^{23} electrons and one mole of atoms is 6×10^{23} atoms.

$$\text{quantity of electricity in faradays} = \frac{\text{coulombs passed}}{96\,500}.$$

If the amount of element discharged at the electrodes is then calculated in moles by the expression:

$$\text{moles of element discharged} = \frac{\text{mass (grams)}}{\text{relative atomic mass (grams)}},$$

a simple relationship will be seen between the moles of element discharged and the moles of electrons (faradays) passed through the circuit:

$$\text{charge on the ion} = \frac{\text{faradays passed}}{\text{moles of element}} = \frac{\text{moles of electrons}}{\text{moles of atoms of element}}.$$

Typical values for the number of moles of electrons per mole of atoms of the element discharged in electrolysis for some common elements are shown in Fig. 7.8.

Element	Moles of electrons per mole of atoms (faradays per mole)	Electrode where element is discharged	Charge on an ion of the element
H	1	cathode (−)	1+
Na	1	cathode (−)	1+
K	1	cathode (−)	1+
Ca	2	cathode (−)	2+
Mg	2	cathode (−)	2+
Al	3	cathode (−)	3+
Cl	1	anode (+)	1−
O	2	anode (+)	2−

Fig. 7.8 Faradays, moles of element and charge on the ion.

There is an obvious connection between the number of *moles of electrons* passing through the electrolyte for each mole of element discharged and the *charge on the ion of the element*. The following example should make the connection clear.

One mole of atoms of any element is represented in equations by the symbol for the element. Similarly, one mole of electrons is represented by the symbol for the electron, e^-.

(i) Cathode reactions

Metal ions, having positive charges, are discharged at the cathode. Using aluminium ions as an example, the discharge equation at the cathode is

$$Al^{3+} + 3e^- \rightarrow Al$$

1 mole of ions + 3 moles of electrons → 1 mole of atoms.

One mole of aluminium ions *accepts* three moles of electrons to become one mole of aluminium atoms. This shows the charge on a *single aluminium ion* to be three positive charges. *Each aluminium ion* with three positive charges accepts *three electrons*, each having a negative charge, to become a single aluminium atom with *no charge*.

(ii) Anode reactions

Non-metal ions, having negative charges, are discharged at the anode. Using chloride ions as an example, the discharge equation at the anode is

$$Cl^- - e^- \rightarrow Cl$$

1 mole of ions – 1 mole of electrons → 1 mole of atoms.

One mole of chloride ions *gives up* one mole of electrons to become a mole of chlorine atoms. This shows the charge on a *single chloride ion* to be a single negative charge. *Each chloride ion* with a single negative charge gives up *a single electron* having a negative charge to become a single chlorine atom with *no charge*.

We need to note here that chlorine atoms pair up to form diatomic molecules as soon as they form, so the *complete* equation for the formation of chlorine at the anode is

$$2Cl^- - 2e^- \rightarrow Cl_2.$$

Chlorine atoms pair

19 ELECTRICAL COSTS IN METAL PRODUCTION

Fig. 7.8 shows that the production of aluminium by electrolysis requires more electricity per mole than other metal elements shown. This is *one* of the reasons why aluminium is an expensive metal to produce.

As an exercise, compare the quantity of electricity to produce 1 g each of sodium, magnesium and aluminium, remembering that the quantities of electricity referred to in the table are *per mole* of element. You will need to look up the relative atomic masses of the three metals.

EXAMINATION QUESTIONS

MULTIPLE CHOICE

QUESTION 1

The reaction taking place at the negative electrode during the electroplating of copper can be represented by the equation

A $\quad Cu \rightarrow Cu^{2+} + 2e^-$

B $\quad Cu^{2+} + e^- \rightarrow Cu$

C $\quad Cu^{2+} + 2e^- \rightarrow Cu$

D $\quad Cu^{2+} + 2e^- \rightarrow 2Cu$

(NEAB)

QUESTION 2

A simple cell can be made by dipping two metal strips into dilute sulphuric acid. Which of the following would produce the greatest voltage? (In the reactivity series zinc is above iron and iron is above copper.)

(SEG)

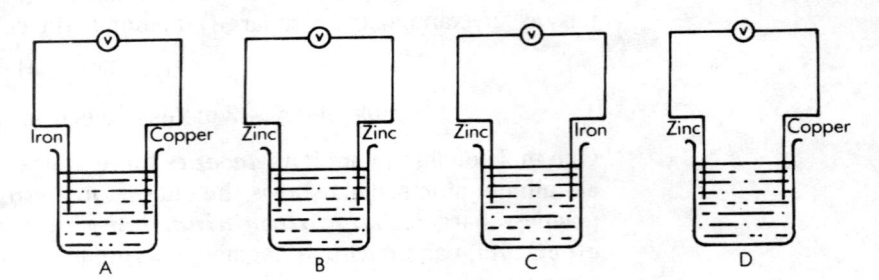

Fig. 7.9

QUESTION 3

A solution of copper(II) sulphate is electrolysed using carbon electrodes. The pinkish-brown coating found on the cathode is

A carbon sulphate
B copper
C copper(II) oxide
D copper(I) sulphate
E sulphur

QUESTION 4

Which one of the following elements forms at the cathode when a mixture of sodium chloride and potassium chloride in water is electrolysed?

A chlorine
B hydrogen
C potassium
D sodium

(SEG)

STRUCTURED QUESTIONS

QUESTION 5

(a) Potassium bromide, KBr, is a salt which can be electrolysed when it is molten. During this process, what product would you expect to be formed
  (i) at the positive electrode? ....
  (ii) at the negative electrode? ....
(2 marks)

(b) Why does solid potassium bromide *not* conduct electricity? ...

(2 marks)

(SEG)

QUESTION 6

The following diagram shows a method of nickel plating an object using a solution of nickel(II) sulphate (NiSO$_4$).

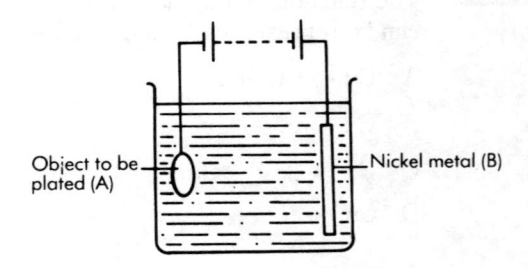

Fig. 7.10

(i) State the names of the electrodes represented as A and B in the diagram.
A... B...
(1)
(ii) Give equations to represent the reactions occurring at A and B.
At A ...... 2⁻ AB² → C₂O₂ ......
At B ...... B₂ + C₄ → BC₃ ......
(2)
(iii) If the object to be plated is made of plastic, it has to be painted in a suspension of graphite before the plating occurs. Explain the reason for this. ......
...... Because active as to ionize to Hydrochloric Acid ...... (1)

(WJEC)

QUESTION 7

The diagram below shows the electrolysis of sodium chloride solution.

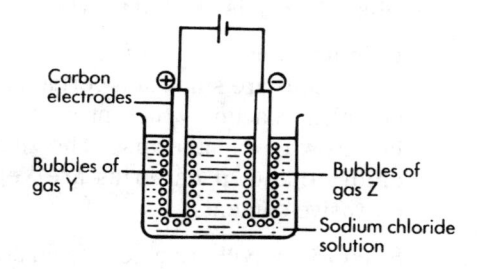

Fig. 7.11

(a) Name the gases Y and Z.
Y is ...... Carbon Dioxide ......
Z is ...... Sulphur Dioxide ......
(2 marks)
(b) If a few drops of universal indicator are added to the solution before electrolysis starts, the indicator is green. As electrolysis happens, the indicator gradually turns blue.
(i) What is the pH of the solution when the indicator is green? (1 line) (1 mark)
(ii) Explain why the electrolysis causes the indicator to go blue. (3 lines). (3 marks)
(iii) Name a compound produced on an industrial scale by electrolysis of sodium chloride solution. (1 line) (1 mark)
(c) In the electrolysis of copper(II) chloride solution the electron transfer at the negative electrode is shown by the following equation.

$$Cu^{2+}(aq) + 2e^- \rightarrow Cu(s)$$

(i) What does (aq) stand for? (1 line) (1 mark)
(ii) What would you expect to see at the negative electrode during this electrolysis? (2 lines) (2 marks)
(d) The table gives information about three substances A, B and C when they are solid and when they are molten.

Substance	Appearance of solid	Does the solid conduct electricity?	Does the melt conduct electricity?	Product at + electrode	Product at − electrode
A	white solid	no	yes	bromine	lead metal
B	yellow solid	no	no	(does not conduct)	
C	grey solid	yes	yes	none	none

(i) Suggest possible identities for substances A and B.
Substance A could be ....
Substance B could be ....
(2 marks)

(ii) What type of bonding does solid B have? (1 line) *(1 mark)*
(iii) What type of bonding does solid C have? (1 line) *(1 mark)*
(iv) When the melted substance A conducts electricity what particles are carrying the current? (1 line) *(1 mark)*

(e) (i) Predict the products of electrolysis of an aqueous solution of aluminium sulphate using inert electrodes. Explain how you arrive at your answer. (4 lines) *(1 mark)*

(ii) Why is cryolite added to aluminium oxide during the electrolytic manufacture of aluminium? (2 lines) *(1 mark)*

(SEG)

QUESTION 8

Three different types of cell for producing electricity are described below. In each case, energy released by a chemical reaction is made available as electrical energy when the cell is used to provide a current.

Primary cell (e.g. a dry cell)
These cells are small and portable. They use common materials and are cheap, but the chemical reaction which produces the electricity cannot be reversed so the cell must be thrown away after use. The zinc casing of a dry cell dissolves in use, forming zinc chloride and, if batteries are kept too long, the case may leak and spill out the corrosive contents.

Secondary cells (e.g. lead/acid accumulator)
These are larger and more expensive than primary cells and very heavy, but they can supply much larger currents. In use, both electrodes are converted to lead sulphate but this reaction can be reversed by passing an electric current through the cell (in the reverse direction to the current which is supplied by the cell when working). Thus some source of electricity is needed to recharge the cell.

Fuel cell (e.g. hydrogen/oxygen cell)
These also use an irreversible reaction but in this case the 'fuel' may be continuously added to the cell while it is running, so that it can operate for very long periods. In the cell shown, the chemical change is equivalent to burning hydrogen. Expensive catalysts are needed to make the cell work efficiently and containers are needed to store the hydrogen and oxygen.

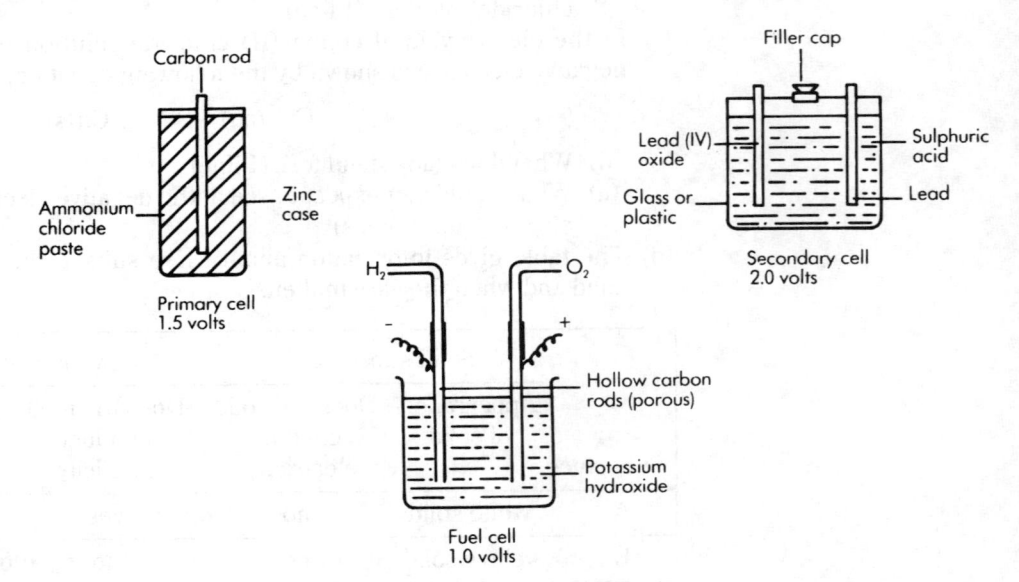

Fig. 7.13

(a) Give one advantage and one disadvantage of each type of cell. *(6)*

(b) Write a word equation for the chemical change which takes place while the fuel cell is being used to supply a current. *(1)*

(c) Explain what change you would expect to occur in the concentration of the acid in the lead/acid accumulator, while it is being used to supply electricity. *(2)*

(d) Explain, giving reasons, which type of cell from amongst those described would be the most suitable for each of the uses described below.
   (i) The power supply for a deaf person's hearing aid.
   (ii) The power supply for a milk float.
   (iii) The power supply for the light on a buoy marking a safe passage at sea.
   (6)

(e) Water from the sulphuric acid in a lead/acid battery gradually evaporates away and, from time to time, the battery must be 'topped-up' with distilled water. Explain why ordinary tap water is unsuitable for this purpose. (2)

OUTLINE ANSWERS

MULTIPLE CHOICE

ANSWER 1

C. The cathode is negative. Metals are formed there. The cathode supplies electrons, e^-, to positively charged metal ions, **dis**charging them. This appears to happen in B, C and D. Only C is a **balanced** equation (see Fig. 7.3).

ANSWER 2

D. Zinc and copper are the two metals **farthest apart** in the reactivity series and so produce the largest voltage, see Section 13.

ANSWER 3

B. Copper is a 'pink' metal produced at the cathode in electrolysis. It will coat the carbon electrode.

ANSWER 4

B. Neither sodium nor potassium will form when aqueous solutions are electrolysed. Metals more reactive than zinc do not deposit on the cathode even if their ions are present in solution. The cathode product is hydrogen formed from hydrogen ions which are present in all aqueous solutions.

STRUCTURED QUESTIONS

ANSWER 5

(a) See Section 6.
   (i) Bromine gas would be expected at the positive electrode. Bromide ions are Br^-. They are negatively charged and will be attracted to the positive electrode, where they will give up electrons to become bromine molecules, Br_2.
   (ii) Because there is no other positive ion present than the potassium ion, potassium metal is produced at the negative electrode.
(b) See Section 2.
   Solid potassium bromide is an ionic compound **but** its ions are **not free** to move to the electrodes to be discharged.

ANSWER 6

(i) The electrode names should be straightforward recall.
(ii) At A. During the process of electroplating, the cathode is the object to be plated. Therefore, the equation here is for the formation of nickel. The solution contains nickel(II) ions. This is a clue to the electrode equation. It is similar to that for the plating of copper.
At B. This is the nickel anode. It dissolves to supply the ions for plating the cathode. The reaction is the reverse of the cathode equation.
(iii) The coating of graphite is to make a non-conductor – the plastic – conduct, otherwise it could not be part of the circuit. Look up the reasons for this.

See Section 12

ANSWER 7

To answer the question well candidates require a good general understanding of qualitative aspects of electrolysis. The diagram is of an electrolysis of aqueous sodium chloride using carbon electrodes (Section 3). The circuit is of a simple electrolysis.

(a) The gas Y is chlorine. Chlorine is more easily discharged than oxygen from aqueous solutions of chlorides; the electrode is the anode (Section 8).

The gas Z is hydrogen. Hydrogen is more easily discharged than sodium from aqueous solutions of sodium salts; the electrode is the cathode (Section 8).

(b) (i) The starting solution is neutral (universal indicator green). Sodium chloride is a neutral salt. The pH is 7.

(ii) The change in pH indicated by the universal indicator turning blue (pH > 7) means that the solution has become alkaline. Hydroxyl ions have built up in the electrolyte. This is because, of the two ions present in the solution from the ionisation of water, OH^-(aq) and H^+(aq), the hydrogen ions have been discharged at the cathode to form hydrogen gas. The hydroxyl ions are ***not discharged*** and their concentration increases, making the remaining solution alkaline.

(iii) This electrolysis produces two elements (hydrogen and chlorine) but one compound – sodium hydroxide. The compound sodium chlorate(I) could also form if the chlorine from the anode was reacted with the sodium hydroxide solution formed. Sodium chlorate(I) is common bleach.

(c) This part is about a different electrolysis, that of aqueous copper(II) chloride.

(i) (aq) is short of aqueous. It means the solution is copper(II) chloride dissolved in water.

(ii) The negative electrode is the cathode. Positive ions are discharged there. The electrode equation shown indicates that copper is discharged at the cathode. A pink–brown deposit would be seen when the electrolyte was removed.

(d) (i) Substance A could be lead bromide because electrolysis produces lead and bromine (Section 6).

Parts of (d) are not strictly within the scope of this chapter. They are answered here for completeness.

Substance B could be sulphur since it is a yellow molecular (i.e. non-ionic) substance. It could be ANY yellow, molecular substance in fact but sulphur is the one most likely to be familiar to you.

(ii) B is not a metal – its solid form does not conduct electricity.
It is not ionic – its melt does not electrolyse (conduct). So B must be molecular and its bonding must be ***covalent***.

(iii) C conducts in the solid form. It must be a metal. Its bonding is ***metallic*** (Chapter 6, Section 14).

(iv) Molten A must contain **ions** because it does not conduct when solid.

(e) (i) aqueous aluminium sulphate contains two cations – aluminium ions and hydrogen ions. Hydrogen ions discharge more easily than aluminium ions because they are lower in the reactivity series than aluminium ions, i.e. less stable. Hydrogen gas will form. Of the two anions – sulphate ions and hydroxide ions – hydroxide ions discharge to form oxygen gas as in the electrolysis of sulphuric acid.

(ii) Electrolysis of aluminium oxide cannot occur unless it is molten or dissolved. Because the oxide is insoluble in water the only option is to melt it. It melts at 2070 °C! Adding cryolite lowers the melting point to a more reasonable temperature.

ANSWER 8

A 'comprehension' question. Most of the answers are in the text. Your task is to ***recognise and select*** appropriate information and explanations.

(a)

Type of cell	Advantage	Disadvantage
primary cell	small/portable	thrown away after use
secondary cell	supply large currents	bigger and more expensive
fuel cells	continuous fuel supply	expensive catalysts needed

There are *more* advantages and disadvantages given in the text – you have a good selection to choose from – make your own selection, perhaps adding some not mentioned in the text.

(b) This word equation is 'hinted at' in the text. It is said to be **equivalent to** the burning of hydrogen. So it will be

hydrogen + oxygen → water.

(c) The text tells you that both electrodes of a lead/acid accumulator are converted to lead sulphate. This removes sulphuric acid and so the electrolyte, the sulphuric acid, becomes more dilute – more nearly plain water!

(d) (i) A deaf person's hearing aid does not require much power but should not have too large a cell. A primary cell would be most suitable here.

(ii) Milk floats are likely to be heavy but not to move very fast. Throw away batteries (hundreds would be needed to propel a vehicle!) and fuel cells would be expensive and so a secondary (rechargeable) cell would be best.

(iii) A buoy at sea will be far from an electrical supply so a secondary (rechargeable) cell would be of little use. Primary cells would need frequent replacement. A fuel cell could run for a long period – the fuel supply could be stored easily on the floating buoy.

(e) Tap water is not suitable topping-up liquid because it contains dissolved substances (impurities) such as chlorides, which would react with the lead compounds in the cell forming insoluble lead chloride which would coat the electrodes.

STUDENT'S ANSWER – EXAMINER'S COMMENTS

The following results were obtained during the electrolysis of 500 cm³ of aqueous copper(II) sulphate using carbon electrodes

Total mass of copper deposited on the cathode/g	Time current was passed
0.70	30 minutes
1.40	1 hour
2.75	2 hours
3.00	2½ hours
3.00	3 hours
3.00	3½ hours

(a) Draw a labelled diagram of the apparatus you could use, including the electrical circuit, in order to carry out this electrolysis.

❝ A good diagram and labelling. The electrolyte is a *solution* – which you did not mention. ❞

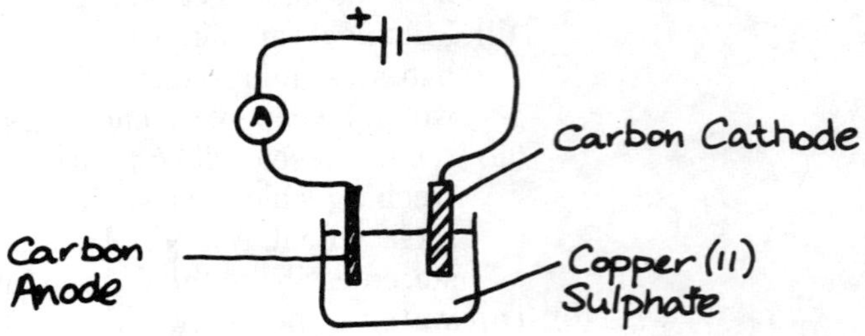

[Diagram: battery with ammeter, Carbon Anode and Carbon Cathode in Copper(II) Sulphate]

(2 marks)

(b) (i) Plot the results on the graph below.

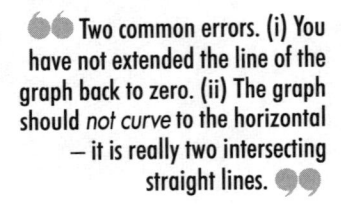

❝ Two common errors. (i) You have not extended the line of the graph back to zero. (ii) The graph should *not* curve to the horizontal – it is really two intersecting straight lines. ❞

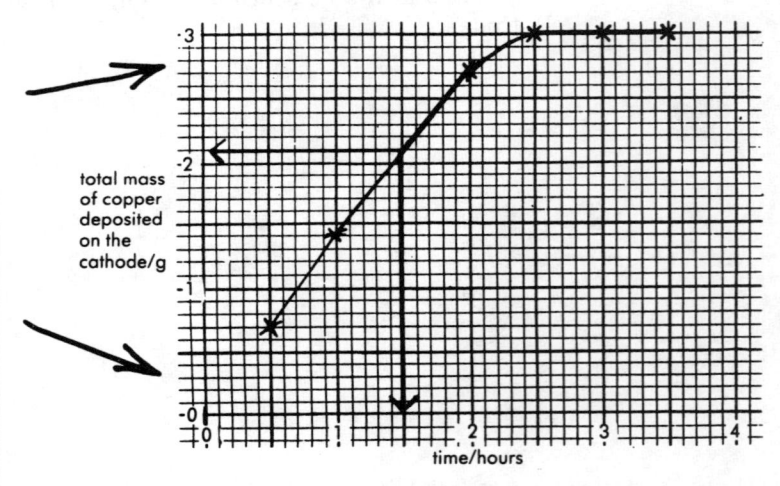

[Graph: total mass of copper deposited on the cathode/g vs time/hours]

❝ Good – clearly showing on the graph *how* you got your answer. ❞

(ii) What is the total mass of copper deposited on the cathode after the current has passed for 1½ hours? **2·1g**

(iii) Calculate the concentration, in mol/dm³, of the original aqueous copper(II) sulphate.

relative atomic mass of copper = 64

2·1g of copper = 2·1/64 moles = 0·033 m

∴ 0·033 moles copper from 0·033 moles copper sulphate in 500 cm³. The solution was 0·066 moles per dm³

(5 marks)

❝ Apart from the error of using 2.1g instead of 3.0g (the *whole* of the copper deposited) your calculation is excellent. You would lose half a mark or possibly one out of the 5 marks for (iii). Also note that M means molar and not moles. ❞

(iv) Suggest two reasons why some metal objects are copper plated.
1. plating stops rusting.
2. It makes objects look nicer.

(2 marks)

❝ Two good reasons. ❞

REVIEW SHEET

- Electrolysis is _____
  _____

- The electrode connected to the positive terminal of the supply is called the _____
  _____

- The anode attracts negatively charged ions called _____

- The electrode connected to the negative terminal of the supply is called the _____
  _____

- The cathode attracts positively charged ions called _____

- Ions from the electrolyte are _____
  at both electrodes forming products which are elements.

- The **cathode product** is always either a _____ or _____

- The **anode product** is always a _____
  such as a halogen or oxygen.

- The **electrode product** may be _____
  _____

- Draw the apparatus used for collecting gases in electrolysis.

- The *most* reactive metals form the stable ions _____
  Therefore these ions will be _____
  to convert back to metals. This will cause the reactive metals to discharge instead.

- List a reactivity (most to least) series for:

  cations   *anions*

120 CHAPTER 7 REVIEW SHEET

■ Complete as much as you can of the following table for some important electrolyses

Electrolyte	Anode product	Cathode product	Other observations
1. The manufacture of aluminium			
2. The electrolysis of concentrated hydrochloric acid			
3. The electrolysis of water			

CHAPTER 8

CALCULATIONS IN CHEMISTRY - THE MOLE

NAMING COMPOUNDS
WRITING FORMULAE
WRITING EQUATIONS
STATE SYMBOLS
IONIC EQUATIONS
RELATIVE ATOMIC MASS
RELATIVE MOLECULAR MASS
THE MOLE
AVOGADRO'S LAW
REACTIONS OF SOLUTIONS
INCOMPLETE REACTIONS
EXCESS REAGENTS
EMPIRICAL FORMULAE
MOLECULAR FORMULAE
CALCULATIONS IN ELECTROLYSIS

GETTING STARTED

Calculations in chemistry centre on an understanding of **the mole** as a unit of measurement. A mole is the mass of 600 000 000 000 000 000 000 000 (written as 6×10^{23}) of whatever particles a substance is made up of.

This huge number has a similar place in chemistry to that of the dozen or score or gross in everyday life. It is a counting unit. Its enormous size derives from the fact that the particles we count with it are so small that we need many billions of billions of them to make just a speck of matter!

- **The relative atomic mass** of any element is the mass in grams of *one mole of atoms* of the element. That is the mass of 6×10^{23} atoms.
- **The relative molecular mass** of a covalently bonded compound is the mass of *one mole of molecules* of that compound. That is the mass of 6×10^{23} molecules.
- **The relative formula mass** of a compound is the mass of *one mole of formula units* of that compound. That is the mass of 6×10^{23} formula units.

We can speak of one mole of atoms, ions, molecules, electrons or formula units (called formulae). In every case we simply mean 6×10^{23} of those particles.

Other measurements you will revise in this chapter are:
(i) **Percentage by mass** of an element in a compound:

Percentage by mass = $\dfrac{\text{mass of the element}}{\text{mass of the compound}} \times 100$

(ii) **The empirical formula** of a compound:
The simplest whole number mole-ratio of the atoms of the elements in a compound.
(iii) **The molecular formula** of a compound:
The actual whole number mole-ratio of the atoms of the elements in the molecule of a compound.
(iv) **The formula** of an ionic compound:
The simplest whole number mole-ratio of the ions in a compound.
(v) **The relative atomic mass** of an element is the average mass of the atoms in that element.
(vi) **The relative molecular mass** of an element or compound is the average mass of the molecules in the element or compound.
(vii) **The molarity of a solution** is the concentration in **moles per litre** of the element or compound present in the solution.

CHAPTER 8 CALCULATIONS IN CHEMISTRY – THE MOLE

ESSENTIAL PRINCIPLES

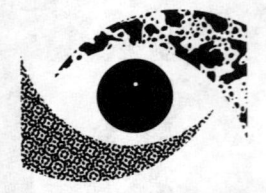

1. NAMING COMPOUNDS

Compounds of *two elements* have an *-ide* ending. The metal is always written down first. Thus a compound of magnesium and oxygen is called magnesium ox*ide* and a compound of sodium and chlorine is called sodium chlor*ide*. (Many metals end in the letters *-ium*.)

If the compound is made up of *two non-metals*, the non-metal that is either *lower down* the group (if they are in the same group), or *nearest to the left-hand side* of the periodic table, is placed *first*. Thus a compound of sulphur and oxygen is called *sulphur* dioxide and a compound of carbon and sulphur is called *carbon* disulphide.

If the compound is made up of *three elements*, one a *metal*, one a *non-metal* and the other *oxygen*, the compounds have *-ate* endings. A compound of copper, sulphur and oxygen is called copper sulph*ate* and a compound of calcium, carbon and oxygen is called calcium carbon*ate*.

If the compound contains a *metal*, *hydrogen* and *oxygen*, the compounds have a *hydroxide* ending. A compound of sodium, hydrogen and oxygen is called sodium *hydroxide* and a compound of calcium, hydrogen and oxygen is called calcium *hydroxide*.

2. WRITING FORMULAE

The *valency* of an element is a number which shows its combining power. In *ionic* compounds it is equal to the charge on the ions of the elements. In *covalent* compounds it gives the number of covalent bonds which the element can form.

SIMPLE COMPOUNDS

To write the formulae of simple compounds, e.g. aluminium oxide:

- Write the valency of the element to the top right-hand side of each element:

$$Al^3 O^2,$$

- Put the valency of the second element to the bottom right-hand side of the first element, and the valency of the first element to the bottom right-hand side of the second element:

$$Al_2 O_3.$$

- Do not write down 'ones' and simplify the numbers if possible.
- Thus the formula of the compound between carbon and oxygen is:

$$C^4 O^2 \qquad C_2 O_4.$$

This can be simplified to CO_2. Some ions contain more than one element. However, the same rules still apply, e.g. calcium hydrogencarbonate:

$$Ca^2 HCO_3^1 \qquad Ca_1(HCO_3)_2.$$

The formula is

$$Ca(HCO_3)_2.$$

Note: to show that there are two hydrogencarbonates, brackets are placed around the symbols. For lead(II) nitrate we have Pb^2 and $NO_3^{1,}$ hence the formula is $Pb(NO_3)_2$

> **Don't forget the *brackets*.** $PbNO_{32}$ means 1 atom of lead, 1 atom of nitrogen and 32 atoms of oxygen!

3. WRITING EQUATIONS

Chemical reactions can be summarised by writing *equations*, either in words or by using symbols. The most important thing to remember is that it must represent a reaction that is known to take place. We have seen that sodium burns in chlorine to form sodium chloride. This can be stated as:

sodium + chlorine → sodium chloride.

The *arrow* indicates that a reaction takes place from left to right. The reaction can also be represented by *symbols*:

$$Na + Cl_2 \rightarrow NaCl.$$

> **Never write $NaCl_2$.**

> This is important.

- Each substance must be represented by its correct formula.
- Remember that gases are diatomic.
- We have seen that atoms cannot be created or destroyed, but in the above example there are two chlorine atoms on the left-hand side and only one chlorine on the right-hand side. To **balance the equation for chlorine atoms** we need to put a '2' in front of the NaCl:

$$Na + Cl_2 \rightarrow 2NaCl.$$

We now have two sodium atoms on the right-hand side and only one on the left-hand side. To balance the sodium atoms we need to put a '2' in front of the Na:

$$2Na + Cl_2 \rightarrow 2NaCl.$$

The equation is now said to be balanced.
Here are two further examples:

(i) iron(III) oxide + carbon monoxide → iron + carbon dioxide.
Unbalanced: $Fe_2O_3 + CO \rightarrow Fe + CO_2$.

> When balancing equations, NEVER change the correct formula of a substance. Note that it is 2Fe NOT Fe_2.

Balanced: $Fe_2O_3 + 3CO \rightarrow 2Fe + 3CO_2$.

(ii) ammonia + copper(II) oxide → nitrogen + copper + water.
Unbalanced: $NH_3 + CuO \rightarrow N_2 + Cu + H_2O$.

Balanced: $2NH_3 + 3CuO \rightarrow N_2 + 3Cu + 3H_2O$.

4 STATE SYMBOLS

When we look at the equations we have written, they only tell us that the reaction has occurred. They do not tell us the speed of the reaction or the *state* of the substances. This last point is easily dealt with because we can use *state symbols*. We add (s) to represent a solid, (l) to represent a liquid, (g) to represent a gas and (aq) for a substance dissolved in water (an aqueous solution). Thus our two examples become:

$$Fe_2O_3(s) + 3CO(g) \rightarrow 2Fe(s) + 3CO_2(g),$$

$$2NH_3(g) + 3CuO(s) \rightarrow N_2(g) + 3Cu(s) + 3H_2O(g).$$

Note in this last reaction, water is formed as water vapour.

5 IONIC EQUATIONS

When iron is added to copper(II) sulphate solution, copper and iron(II) sulphate are formed:

$$\text{iron + copper(II) sulphate} \rightarrow \text{copper + iron(II) sulphate,}$$

$$Fe(s) + CuSO_4(aq) \rightarrow Cu(s) + FeSO_4(aq).$$

If we write this equation in terms of *ions* we get:

$$Fe(s) + Cu^{2+}(aq) + SO_4^{2-}(aq) \rightarrow Cu(s) + Fe^{2+}(aq) + SO_4^{2-}(aq).$$

We can see that the sulphate ions are unaffected by the reaction and therefore they can be left out. They are called *spectator ions*.

$$Fe(s) + Cu^{2+}(aq) \rightarrow Fe^{2+}(aq) + Cu(s).$$

> Check that both the number of *atoms* and the number of *charges* balance.

This is called an *ionic equation*. It balances in both the number of atoms and the number of charges on each side of the equation. Another example of an ionic equation is:

$$CO_3^{2-}(s) + 2H^+(aq) \rightarrow CO_2(g) + H_2O(l).$$

This is the reaction between a solid carbonate and an acid to form carbon dioxide, water and a salt, e.g. if calcium carbonate were added to hydrochloric acid the products would be carbon dioxide, water and, in this case, the salt calcium chloride. **The spectator ions are calcium ions and chloride ions.**

6 RELATIVE ATOMIC MASS

Relative atomic mass is a way of measuring how heavy an *atom* is. Carbon-12 (an isotope of carbon) is given a relative atomic mass of 12.00. The masses of all other atoms are compared with this value. The atoms of magnesium are twice as heavy as carbon atoms, they have a relative atomic mass of 24. The mass of the oxygen atom is one and one-third that of carbon, i.e. 16.

7 RELATIVE MOLECULAR MASS

❝ In Na_2CO_3 there are 2 atoms of sodium, 1 atom of carbon and 3 atoms of oxygen. ❞

Relative molecular mass is similar to relative atomic mass, but in this case *compounds* are used, i.e. it is the relative mass of a molecule on a scale in which the mass of one atom of carbon is 12 units. It applies to all compounds, even if they are ionic. Relative molecular mass is calculated by adding together the relative atomic masses of all the elements present. The relative molecular mass (M_r) of carbon dioxide (CO_2) is $12 + (2 \times 16) = 44$; the M_r of sodium carbonate (Na_2CO_3) is $(2 \times 23) + 12 + (3 \times 16) = 106$.

8 THE MOLE

❝ There are the same number of particles in one mole of *every* substance, but the type of particle present must be stated to avoid confusion ❞

The *mole* is the amount of a substance that contains the same number of particles as there are atoms in 12.00 grams of carbon-12. This number of atoms is 6×10^{23} and it is called the *Avogadro constant* or *number*.

Since relative atomic mass and relative molecular mass are based on carbon-12, then the relative atomic mass of an element and the relative molecular mass of an element or compound must contain Avogadro's number of particles. Thus the following all contain the same number of particles: 44 grams of carbon dioxide (molecules); 18 grams of water (molecules); 23 grams of sodium (atoms) and 100 grams of calcium carbonate. 100 grams of calcium carbonate contains 1 mole of calcium atoms (40 grams), 1 mole of carbon atoms (12 grams) and 3 moles of oxygen atoms (48 grams). You must make sure that you state the type of particles you are talking about; thus 1 mole of oxygen atoms has a mass of 16 grams and the mass of 1 mole of oxygen molecules is 32 grams.

9 AVOGADRO'S LAW

❝ Learn this law ❞

Avogadro's Law states that *equal volumes of all gases* under the same conditions of temperature and pressure *contain the same number of molecules*. It follows from this law that 1 mole of any gas under the same conditions of temperature and pressure must occupy the same volume. At room temperature and pressure this volume is 24 dm³ and it is called the *molar gas volume*.

EXAMPLE

❝ Make sure you understand this calculation ❞

What volume of carbon monoxide is required to reduce 160 g of iron(III) oxide at room temperature and pressure?
The equation for the reaction is:

$$Fe_2O_3 + 3CO \rightarrow 2Fe + 3CO_2.$$

Mass of 1 mole of iron(III) oxide is 160 g.
Moles of iron(III) oxide used = 1 mole.
From the equation, 1 mole of iron(III) oxide reacts with 3 moles of carbon monoxide.
Moles of carbon monoxide required = 3 moles.
Volume of carbon monoxide required = $3 \times 24 = 72$ dm³.

10 REACTIONS OF SOLUTIONS

Often calculations involve solutes dissolved in solvents. The concentrations of these solutions are given in mol/dm³ (mol/litre). Thus a solution of 2.0 mol/dm³ sulphuric acid contains 2 moles of sulphuric acid (196 g of sulphuric acid) in 1 dm³ (1 litre) of solution.

EXAMPLE

25 cm³ of 2.0 mol/dm³ of sodium hydroxide exactly reacts with 10 cm³ of sulphuric acid. What is the concentration of the sulphuric acid?
Equation:

$$2NaOH + H_2SO_4 \rightarrow Na_2SO_4 + 2H_2O.$$

❝ ...and that you understand this one!! ❞

Moles of sodium hydroxide used = $2 \times \dfrac{25}{1000} = 0.050$.

Since 2 moles of sodium hydroxide react with 1 mole of sulphuric acid, the number of moles of sulphuric acid in 10 cm³ must equal 0.05/2 = 0.025 moles.
Since there are 0.025 moles in 10 cm³ of the acid, the concentration of sulphuric acid = $0.025 \times \frac{1000}{10}$ = 2.5 mol/dm³.

11. INCOMPLETE REACTIONS

Sometimes reactions do not go to completion. It is possible to calculate either how much of the reactant has reacted or how much of the product has been formed.

EXAMPLE

The reaction between nitrogen and hydrogen to form ammonia is reversible:
$$N_2 + 3H_2 \rightleftharpoons 2NH_3.$$

... and this one!!

What is the percentage yield of ammonia, at room temperature and pressure, if 12 dm³ of hydrogen react to give 2 dm³ of ammonia?

Moles of hydrogen used = 12/24 = 0.5
3 moles of hydrogen produce 2 moles of ammonia if the reaction goes to completion.
Moles of ammonia that should be formed = $0.5 \times \frac{2}{3} = \frac{1.0}{3}$
Volume of ammonia that should be formed = $\frac{1.0}{3} \times 24$ = 8 dm³.
Percentage yield = $\frac{2}{8} \times 100$ = 25%

12. EXCESS REAGENTS

If one of the reagents is in excess not all of this reagent would be used up.

EXAMPLE

If 20 g of calcium carbonate is added to 50 cm³ of 2 mol/dm³ hydrochloric acid, how much calcium carbonate is left at the end of the reaction?

$$CaCO_3 + 2HCl \rightarrow CaCl_2 + CO_2 + H_2O.$$

This calculation must also be understood

Moles of hydrochloric acid used = $2 \times \frac{50}{1000}$ = 0.1.
From the equation, 1 mole of calcium carbonate reacts with 2 moles of hydrochloric acid.
Moles of calcium carbonate reacted = half of 0.1 moles = 0.05.
Mass of calcium carbonate reacted = 0.05×100 (M_r of $CaCO_3$ = 100) = 5 g.

Therefore mass unreacted = 20 – 5 = 15 g.

13. EMPIRICAL FORMULAE

The simplest formula which shows the ratio of each type of atom in a compound is called its ***empirical formula***. It can be calculated, from experimental results, for all compounds using the idea of moles.

EXAMPLE

4.14 g of lead is found to react with 3.20 g of bromine. What is the formula of lead(II) bromide?

To find the number of moles you must divide by the relative atomic mass

Moles of lead = $\frac{4.14}{207}$ = 0.02 moles of lead atoms.
Moles of bromine = $\frac{3.20}{80}$ = 0.04 moles of bromine atoms.
1 mole of lead atoms (Pb) reacts with 2 moles of bromine atoms (Br).
Formula of lead(II) bromide is $PbBr_2$.

14. MOLECULAR FORMULAE

The ***molecular formula*** shows how many of each type of atom are present in a molecule. If the relative molecular mass (M_r) is known, it is possible to work out the molecular formula.

EXAMPLE

A compound X contains 6 g of carbon and 1 g of hydrogen. The relative molecular mass of X is 56. What is the molecular formula of X?

> Note: the formula is NOT 4CH$_2$

Moles of carbon = $\frac{6}{12}$ = 0.5.

Moles of hydrogen = $\frac{1}{1}$ = 1

1 mole of carbon reacts with 2 moles of hydrogen.

Empirical formula is CH$_2$.

'M_r' of empirical formula = 12 + (2 × 1) = 14.

$\frac{56}{14}$ = 4. Therefore there must be four 'CH$_2$' in the molecular formula.

Molecular formula of X is C$_4$H$_8$.

15> CALCULATIONS IN ELECTROLYSIS

(a) **Electrolysis** is the decomposition of compounds into their elements by passage of a direct electrical current. There are two ways of recording the effect. For example, in the electrolysis of aqueous sodium chloride:

(i) **by an overall reaction equation**, e.g.
2NaCl(aq) + 2H$_2$O(l) → 2NaOH(aq) + H$_2$(l) + Cl$_2$(l)

(ii) **by two electrode reaction equations**, e.g.
At the anode (+)   2Cl$^-$(aq) − 2e$^-$ → Cl$_2$(g)
At the cathode (−) 2H$^+$(aq) + 2e$^-$ → H$_2$(g)

(b) We can calculate the mass of each element produced as follows.

(i) Writing the molar masses of the substances we are interested in beneath the equation we get
2NaCl(aq) + 2H$_2$O(l) → 2NaOH(aq) + H$_2$(l) + Cl$_2$(l)
2 × 58.5   2 × 18 g → 2 × 40 g   2 g   2 × 35.5 g

We can see that

117 g of NaCl reacts with 36 g of water to form 80 g of NaOH, 2 g of H$_2$ and 71 g of Cl$_2$

From this information we can calculate the mass of chlorine, hydrogen or sodium hydroxide obtainable from any specified mass of sodium chloride.

EXAMPLE

> What mass of *chlorine* can be manufactured from 58.5 tonnes of sodium chloride by electrolysis of its aqueous solution?
>
> From the equation above the molar masses below it, we see that
>
> 2 × 58.5 g of sodium chloride gives 2 × 35.5 g of chlorine gas. so
>   58.5 g of sodium chloride will give 35.5 g of chlorine gas. Therefore
>   58.5 tonnes of sodium chloride will give 35.5 tonnes of chlorine gas.
>   **35.5 tonnes of chlorine would be obtained**

Note that because we are dealing with *relative* formula masses, the units − grams or *tonnes* − do not alter the figures provided we do not mix units.

The same reaction can be used to illustrate the method of calculating the *volume* of gas evolved during a reaction. In the electrolysis of aqueous sodium chloride, brine, two gases are given off. Chlorine is produced at the anode and hydrogen at the cathode.

EXAMPLE

What volume of *chlorine* and *hydrogen* can be manufactured from 58.5 tonnes of sodium chloride by electrolysis of its aqueous solution?

From the equation above we see that

2 moles of sodium chloride gives 1 mole of chlorine gas + 1 mole of hydrogen gas
So 2×58.5 g of sodium chloride will give 1 mole of each gas.
Therefore: 58.5 g of sodium chloride will give 1/2 mole (12 litres) of each gas
Because we have mixed units (grams and tonnes) here we cannot get a volume in litres from tonnes of NaCl without a conversion.
To go from grams to tonnes we multiply by 1 million **[one tonne contains 1 million grams]** so we must multiply litres by one million also:
58.5 tonnes of sodium chloride will produce 12 million litres of chlorine and 12 million litres of hydrogen at 20°C and normal pressure.

12 million litres of each gas will be manufactured

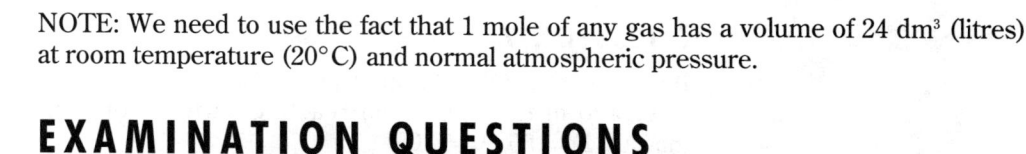

NOTE: We need to use the fact that 1 mole of any gas has a volume of 24 dm^3 (litres) at room temperature (20°C) and normal atmospheric pressure.

EXAMINATION QUESTIONS

MULTIPLE CHOICE

QUESTION 1

The equation below represents the reaction between sodium hydrogencarbonate and hydrochloric acid:

$$NaHCO_3 + HCl \rightarrow NaCl + H_2O + CO_2.$$

This equation shows that

A The hydrochloric acid is dilute.
B The sodium hydrogencarbonate is in aqueous solution.
C One mole of sodium hydrogencarbonate gives two moles of carbon dioxide.
D The hydrochloric acid is concentrated.
E One mole of hydrogen chloride gives one mole of carbon dioxide.

(NISEAC)

QUESTION 2

Which one of the following equations is balanced?

A $Zn + O_2 \rightarrow ZnO$
B $CO_2 + C \rightarrow CO$
C $Mg + Cl_2 \rightarrow MgCl_2$
D $H_2 + O_2 \rightarrow H_2O$
E $CH_4 + O_2 \rightarrow CO_2 + H_2O$

(NISEAC)

QUESTION 3

An important industrial pigment contains 4.8 g of titanium (Ti) combined with 3.2 g of oxygen. What is the formula of the pigment? (Relative atomic masses: Ti = 48, O = 16)

A TiO
B TiO$_2$
C Ti$_2$O
D Ti$_2$O$_3$
E Ti$_3$O$_4$

(ULEAC)

QUESTION 4

What is the mass of oxygen contained in 36 g of pure water?

A 16 g
B 32 g
C 48 g
D 64 g
E 70 g

QUESTION 5

A metal M forms a hydroxide $M(OH)_3$. The mass of one mole of the hydroxide is 78 g. What is the relative atomic mass of M? (Relative atomic masses: H = 1, O = 16).

A 27
B 30
C 59
D 61
E 78

(ULEAC)

QUESTION 6

What is the concentration in mol/dm^3 (mol/litre) of 250 cm^3 of a solution containing 1.0 g of sodium hydroxide ($M_r = 40$)?

A 0.025
B 0.1
C 0.25
D 1.0
E 2.0

QUESTION 7

It is found that 2.8 g of iron displaces 10.8 g of silver from a silver nitrate solution.
The ratio of the number of reacting particles of iron to silver is (Relative atomic masses: Fe = 56, Ag = 108).

A 1 : 2
B 2 : 1
C 1 : 1
D 3 : 1
E 2 : 3

(ULEAC)

STRUCTURED QUESTIONS

QUESTION 8–10

Complete the following word equations.

8 magnesium + oxygen → .... (1)
9 sodium hydroxide + hydrochloric acid → .... + ... (1)
10 aluminium + copper oxide → .... + ... (1)

(NEAB)

QUESTIONS 11–14

Complete the following symbol equations.
11 $Fe(s) + S(s) \rightarrow$ .... (1)
12 $MgO(s) + 2HCl(aq) \rightarrow$ .... + ... (1)
13 $CaCO_3 + 2HNO_3(aq) \rightarrow$ .... +........................ + ... (1)
14 $H^+(aq) +$ ....(aq) $\rightarrow H_2O(l)$ (1)

(NEAB)

QUESTION 15

The burning of ethane in air or oxygen forms water and carbon dioxide according to the equation:

$$2C_2H_6 + 7O_2 = 4CO_2 + 6H_2O$$
$[A_r(C) = 12; A_r(H) = 1; A_r(O) = 16.]$

(a) (i) Calculate the mass of one mole of carbon dioxide. (1 line) (1)
    (ii) Calculate the mass of carbon dioxide that is formed from 30 g ethane. (3 lines) (1)
(b) Describe or draw a diagram showing how you could collect some of the water formed during the burning. (5 lines) (2)
(c) How could you prove that the liquid collected was water. (1 line) (1)

(WJEC)

QUESTION 16

Magnesium sulphate crystals (MgSO$_4$.7H$_2$O) can be made by adding excess magnesium oxide (MgO), which is insoluble in water, to dilute sulphuric acid.

(a) Why is the magnesium oxide added in excess? (1 line) *(1 mark)*

(b) The following apparatus could be used to separate the excess magnesium oxide from the solution. Label the diagram by putting the correct words in each of the spaces below.

(4 marks)

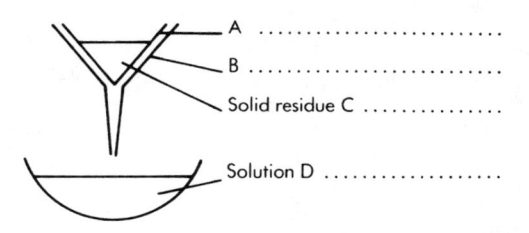

Fig. 8.1

A ....
B ....
Solid residue C ....
Solution D ....

(c) Given the relative atomic masses: H = 1, Mg = 24, O = 16, S = 32, calculate the relative formula mass of
   (i) Magnesium oxide, MgO..
   (ii) Magnesium sulphate crystals, MgSO$_4$.7H$_2$O (1 line) *(3 marks)*

(d) Use your answers in (c) to calculate the maximum mass of magnesium sulphate crystals that could be obtained from 2.0 g of magnesium oxide. (4 lines)

(2 marks)

(e) Describe how you would obtain pure, dry crystals of magnesium sulphate from magnesium sulphate solution (5 lines) *(4 marks)*

(ULEAC)

QUESTION 17

To find the formula of a compound formed between copper and bromine, copper was heated with an excess of liquid bromine in the apparatus shown below. The experiment was carried out in a fume cupboard.

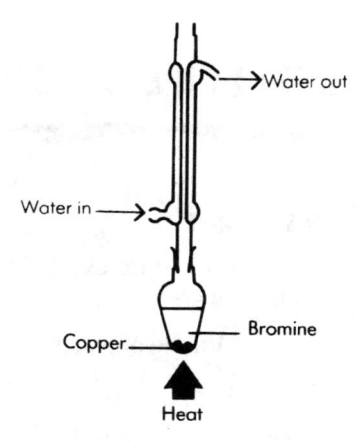

Fig. 8.2

After the reaction was over, any bromine which had not been used was removed, leaving the compound behind. From the readings made, the mass of bromine which had combined with the copper was calculated.

The experiment was repeated starting with different masses of copper.

(a) Why is a reflux condenser used in the apparatus? (1 line) *(1 mark)*

(b) Explain what should be done to remove the unreacted bromine. (3 lines)

(2 marks)

(c) Complete the list below, which gives the readings that need to be taken in order to calculate the masses of bromine and copper which have combined.
   (i) mass of empty flask
   (ii) ....
   (iii) ....

(2 marks)

The results from some of the experiments are shown plotted on the graph below.

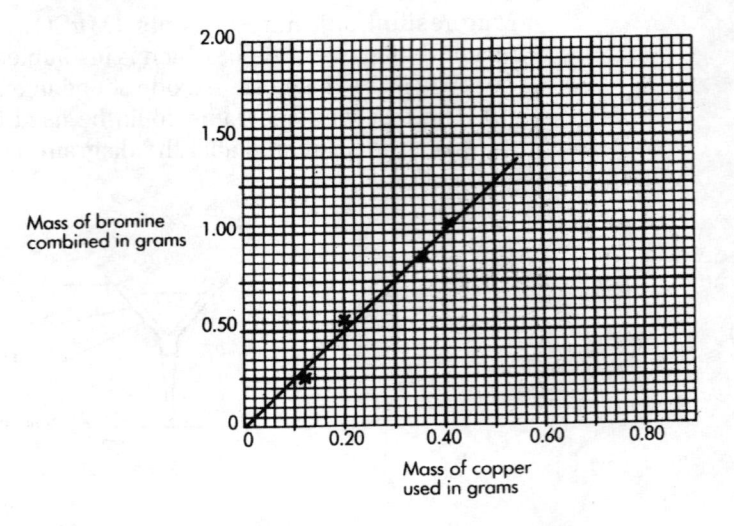

Fig. 8.3

(d) Use the graph to find out
  (i) what mass of bromine would combine with 0.30 g of copper; (1 line)
  (1 mark)
  (ii) what mass of compound would be formed from 0.50 g of copper. (1 mark)
(e) A further experiment found that 0.64 g of copper combined with 1.60 g of bromine.
  (i) Plot this result on the graph. (1 mark)
  (ii) How many grams of bromine would combine with 64 g of copper? (1 line)
  (1 mark)
  (iii) How many moles of bromine would combine with 1 mole of copper? (relative atomic masses: Cu 64; Br 80.) (1 line) (1 mark)
  (iv) Write the formula of the compound formed between copper and bromine in these experiments. (1 line) (1 mark)
  (v) Name the compound formed in these experiments. (1 line)
  (2 marks)

(SEG)

OUTLINE ANSWERS

MULTIPLE CHOICE

ANSWER 1

There are no state symbols in the equation, hence A, B and D are incorrect. The equations states:

1 mole of NaHCO$_3$ reacts with 1 mole of HCl to give 1 mole each of

NaCl, H$_2$O and CO$_2$

Hence the answer is E: 1 mole of hydrogen chloride does give 1 mole of carbon dioxide.

ANSWER 2

Count the number of atoms on each side; the only equation that balances is key C.

ANSWER 3

Moles of Ti = $\frac{4.8}{48}$ = 0.1.

Moles of O = $\frac{3.2}{16}$ = 0.2.

Ratio of moles of Ti to moles of O is 1:2.
Formula is TiO$_2$. This is key B.

ANSWER 4

Mass of 1 mole of water is 18 g ($(2 \times 1) + 16 = 18$).
Moles of water = $\frac{36}{18} = 2$.

Therefore 2 moles of water contain 2 moles of oxygen = $2 \times 16 = 32$ g of oxygen: key B.

ANSWER 5

Mass of hydroxide $OH^- = 17$. There are three hydroxides, therefore $3 \times 17 = 51$, $78 - 51 = 27$ which is the mass of 1 mole of M: key A.

ANSWER 6

1 g in 250 cm³ is 4 g in 1 dm³ (litre).
Mass of 1 mole of NaOH is 40.
$\frac{4}{40} = 0.1$: key B.

ANSWER 7

Answer: A.

STRUCTURED QUESTIONS

ANSWER 8

magnesium oxide.

ANSWER 9

sodium chloride + water.

ANSWER 10

copper + aluminium oxide.

ANSWER 11

FeS(s).

ANSWER 12

$MgCl_2(aq) + H_2O(l)$.

ANSWER 13

$Ca(NO_3)_2(aq) + H_2O(l) + CO_2(g)$.

ANSWER 14

$+ OH^-$.

If you had problems answering questions 11 to 14 look again at Sects. 3 and 5.

ANSWER 15

(a) (i) $12 + (2 \times 16) = 44$.
    (ii) Mass of 1 mole of ethane = 30 g.
        Moles of ethane used = $\frac{30}{30} = 1$.

From the equation 2 moles of ethane give 4 moles of carbon dioxide.
Moles of carbon dioxide formed = 2.
Mass of carbon dioxide formed = $2 \times 44 = 88$ g.
(b) Your diagram should look like Fig. 13.7.
(c) See Chapter 12.1, Section 2(c).

ANSWER 16

(a) To make sure that the reaction has gone to completion, i.e. all the sulphuric acid has reacted.

(b) A. filter paper; B. filter funnel; C. magnesium oxide; D. magnesium sulphate solution.
(c) (i) 40, (ii) 246
(d) 40 grams of magnesium oxide gives 246 grams of crystals, 2 grams gives $246 \times \dfrac{2}{40}$ = 12.3 g.

(e) See Chapter 10, Section 8(iii).

ANSWER 17

(a) To prevent bromine vapour from escaping (bromine is a volatile liquid).
(b) Remove the condenser and heat the mixture gently in a fume cupboard.
(c) (ii) mass of flask + copper.
(iii) mass of flask + copper bromide.
(d) (i) 0.75 g. (ii) 1.25 + 0.5 = 1.75 g.
(e) (i) See graph. Try plotting the point yourself – it should come close to the *extension* of the graph already drawn.

(ii) 160. (iii) 2 moles ($\dfrac{160}{80}$) of bromine atoms.

(iv) $CuBr_2$. (v) copper(II) bromide.

STUDENT'S ANSWER – EXAMINER'S COMMENTS

Pure zinc reacts slowly with dilute sulphuric acid to produce hydrogen. Addition of copper(II) sulphate solution increases the speed of the reaction because zinc displaces copper from copper(II) sulphate solution. The copper formed acts as a catalyst. The graph below plots the volume of hydrogen obtained when various volumes of 1.0 mol/dm³ copper(II) sulphate were added to excess dilute sulphuric acid and x g of zinc. The volume of hydrogen was measured at room temperature and pressure (r.t.p.) and the same mass of zinc (x g) was used each time.

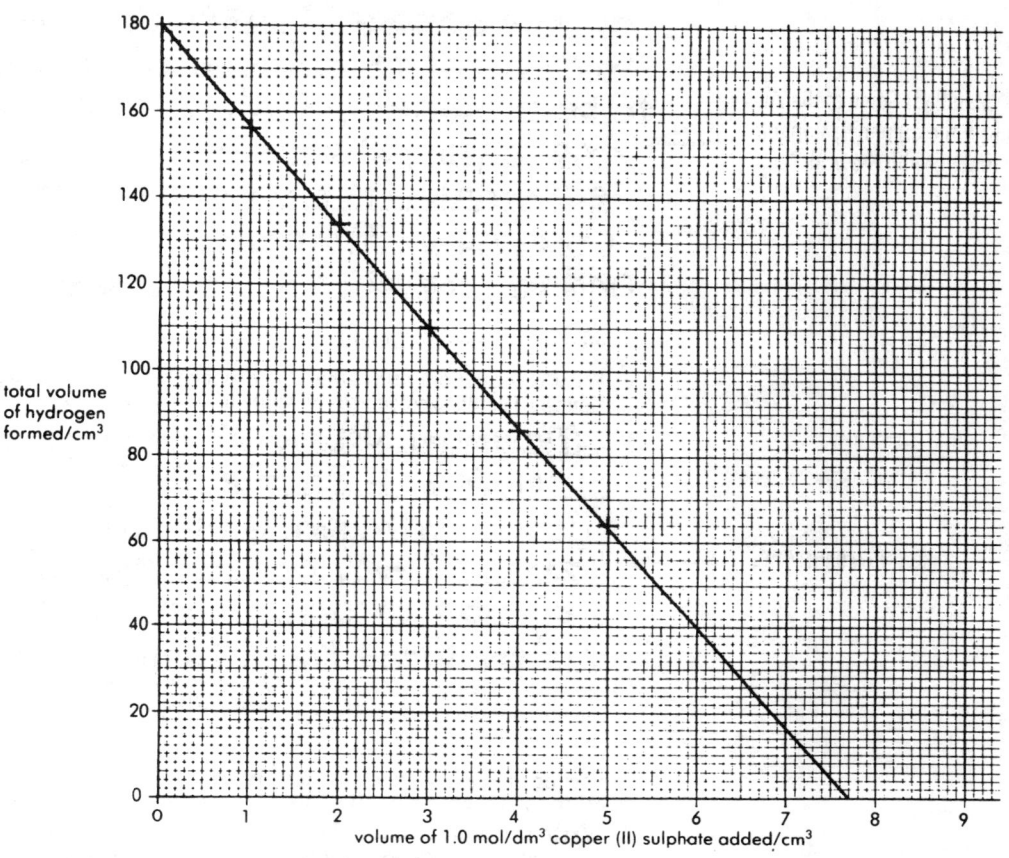

[Graph: total volume of hydrogen formed/cm³ (y-axis, 0 to 180) vs volume of 1.0 mol/dm³ copper(II) sulphate added/cm³ (x-axis, 0 to 9). A straight line decreases from approximately (0, 180) to approximately (7.5, 0).]

(a) Draw a diagram of the apparatus you would use to perform this experiment. Your diagram should clearly show how you kept the zinc and dilute acid separated before starting the reaction.

[Student's diagram: A conical flask containing "Solution of copper(II) sulphate and sulphuric acid", with a "Cotton wool stopper" on top, a "dish Containing zinc" inside, sitting on a "balance".]

"This would not work. All the gas would escape" ← examiner's comment pointing to the cotton wool stopper.

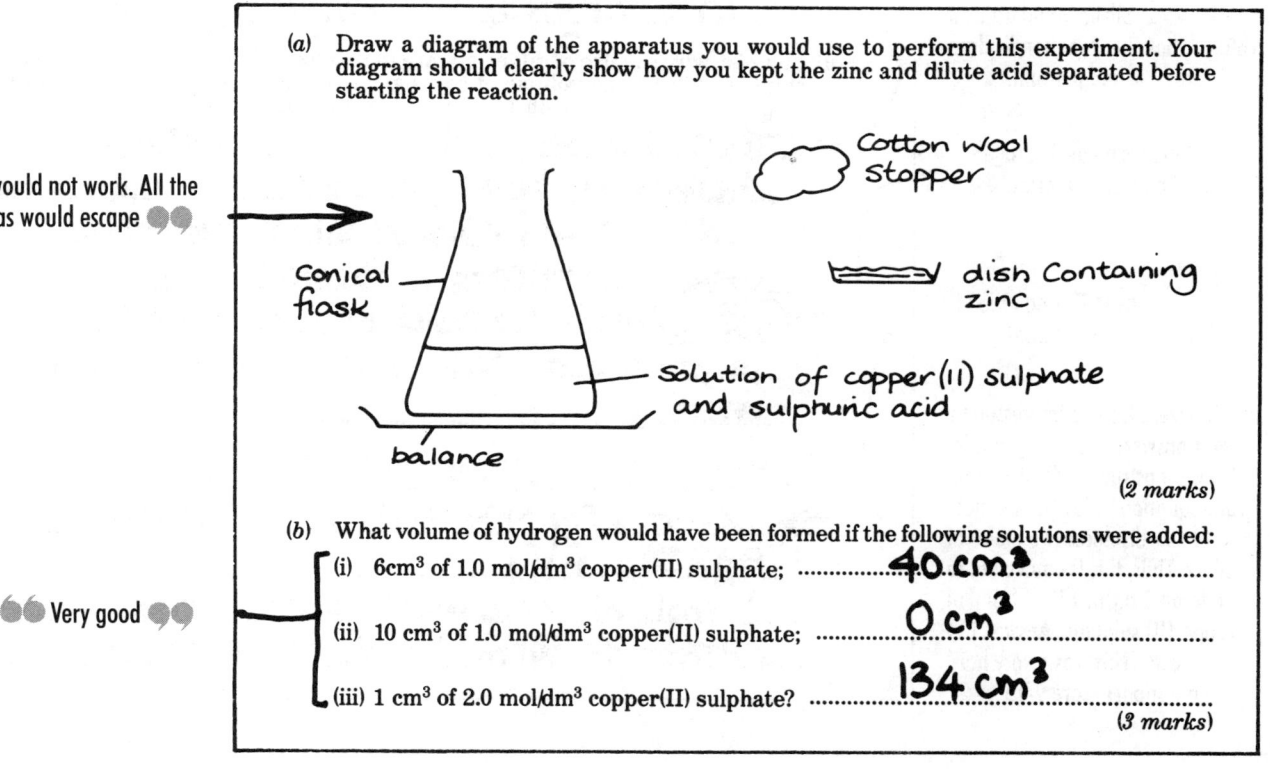

(2 marks)

(b) What volume of hydrogen would have been formed if the following solutions were added:

(i) 6cm³ of 1.0 mol/dm³ copper(II) sulphate; ......**40 cm³**

(ii) 10 cm³ of 1.0 mol/dm³ copper(II) sulphate; ......**0 cm³**

(iii) 1 cm³ of 2.0 mol/dm³ copper(II) sulphate? ......**134 cm³**

"Very good" ← examiner's comment on part (b).

(3 marks)

(c) (i) What is a catalyst?

A catalyst is a substance which will speed up a chemical reaction (without taking part) in the reaction. It can be collected at the end of the experiment and it should be the same mass as when it started.

> 66 Careful, catalysts are known to take part in reactions. 99

(ii) Explain why the volume of hydrogen formed decreases as the volume of copper(II) sulphate added increases.

As more copper (II) sulphate is added there are more particles in the solution. For hydrogen to be produced a fruitful collision between the copper (II) sulphate and the zinc is essential. As more particles are added, the chances of fruitful collisions decreases and so production of hydrogen is less.

> 66 Muddled! Some of the zinc reacts with the copper(II) sulphate, and *not* with the acid 99

(iii) What is the maximum volume of hydrogen that could be obtained in this experiment? Use this result to calculate the value of x (the mass of zinc) used in each experiment.

Maximum volume of hydrogen is 180 cm³.
$H_2SO_4 + Zn \rightarrow ZnSO_4 + H_2$
1 mol hydrogen is produced by 1 mol of zinc. 24000 cm³ of hydrogen is produced by 6.5 g of zinc, therefore 180 g of hydrogen is produced by $\frac{6.5 \times 180}{24000}$ g of zinc = 0.04875 g

> 66 Excellent 99

(5 marks)

(d) The order of reactivity of the metals used in this experiment is magnesium (most reactive), zinc, copper, silver (least reactive).

(i) Write the equation for the reaction between zinc and aqueous silver nitrate.

$Zn + 2AgNO_3 \rightarrow Zn(NO_3)_2 + 2Ag$

> 66 Silver would act as a catalyst, but zinc does not displace magnesium. 99

(ii) Suggest why the use of silver nitrate in this experiment in place of copper(II) sulphate affects the volume of hydrogen given off, but the use of magnesium sulphate has no effect on the volume of hydrogen given off.

This is because the valency of silver is one whereas the valency of copper and magnesium is two. Two moles of silver are produced when zinc nitrate is formed. The silver (reacts) with the acid and so more hydrogen is produced than with the other two metals.

> 66 Silver is below hydrogen in the reactivity series. 99

> 66 This equation is nonsense! 99

(iii) Calculate the volume of hydrogen formed if x g of zinc were added to 4 cm³ of 1.0 mol/dm³ aqueous silver nitrate and excess dilute sulphuric acid.

$Zn + 2AgNO_3 + H_2SO_4 \rightarrow Zn(NO_3)_2 + Ag_2SO_4 + H_2$
1 mol of zinc reacts with 2 mols silver nitrate to form 1 mol of hydrogen.

(5 marks)

> 66 Overall, I was impressed by your answers to part (b) and (c) You went astray in (d) (iii). From your equation in (d) (i) one mole of zinc displaces two moles of silver. Thus, this is equivalent to adding 2 cm³ of 1.0 mol/dm³ of copper(II) sulphate. Answer 134 cm³. (This was a very hard question!) Score 9/15 99

REVIEW SHEET

- The **relative atomic mass** is _____
  _____

- The **relative molecular mass** is _____
  _____

- The **relative formula mass** is _____
  _____

- Compounds of two elements have an _____
  ending to their name

- **Valency** of the element is _____
  _____

- In **ionic compounds**, the valency of an element is _____
  _____

- In **covalent compounds** the valency of an element is _____
  _____

- Describe the stages involved in developing the formula of **calcium hydrogencarbonate** $Ca(HCO_3)_2$
  _____
  _____
  _____
  _____
  _____

- Write down the symbol **equation** for the following reaction
  sodium + chlorine → sodium chloride
  _____

- What do you understand by a **balanced equation**?
  _____

- Balance the following equations
  (i) iron(III) oxide + carbon monoxide → iron + carbon dioxide.
      Unbalanced: $Fe_2O_3 + CO \rightarrow Fe + CO_2$.
      Balanced:
  (ii) ammonia + copper(II) oxide → nitrogen + copper + water.
      Unbalanced: $NH_3 + CuO \rightarrow N_2 + Cu + H_2O$.
      Balanced:

- What is a **mole**? _____
- State **Avogadro's Law** _____
  _____
  _____
  _____

- What volume of carbon monoxide is required to reduce 160 g of iron(III) oxide at room temperature and pressure?

  The equation for the reaction is:
  $$Fe_2O_3 + 3CO \rightarrow 2FE + 3CO_2.$$

  Mass of 1 mole of iron(III) oxide is 160 g.

  Moles of iron(III) oxide used = 1 mole.

  _____
  _____
  _____
  _____

- 25 cm³ of 2.0 mol/dm³ of sodium hydroxide exactly reacts with 10 cm³ of sulphuric acid. What is the concentration of the sulphuric acid?

  Equation:
  $$2NaOH + H_2SO_4 \rightarrow Na_2SO_4 + 2H_2O.$$

  _____
  _____
  _____
  _____

- A compound X contains 6 g of carbon and 1 g of hydrogen. The relative molecular mass of X is 56. What is the molecular formula of X?

  Moles of carbon $\frac{6}{12} = 0.5$.
  Moles of hydrogen $= \frac{1}{1} = 1$.
  1 mole of carbon reacts with 2 moles of hydrogen.
  Empirical formula is CH_2.

  _____
  _____
  _____
  _____

CHAPTER 9

CHEMICAL REACTIONS

ENERGETICS OF A REACTION
ACTIVATION ENERGY
FUELS
SPEED OF REACTION
COLLISION THEORY
REVERSIBLE REACTIONS
REDOX
TESTING FOR REDOX REACTIONS
FREE RADICALS
SUMMARY OF TYPES OF REACTION

GETTING STARTED

Chemical reactions occur whenever one or more substances react and change into different substances. They may

- give out energy or take in energy.
- need a push to get going.
- occur almost instantly or take millions of years
- go to completion and produce 100% products, or they may
- **reach equilibrium when some of the reactants remain unchanged.**

When you consider the fact that there are 89 elements to form compounds from and many thousands of naturally occurring substances to extract chemicals from, you will get some idea of the never-ending possibilities of chemistry. When we can create a huge dictionary full of words with just 26 letters, imagine the possibilities for creating chemical compounds from 89 elements!

In this chapter we shall look at how far and how fast chemical reactions occur and examine, too, the energy changes that occur, but first a few terms we will use:

- **Exothermic reactions** are those giving out heat – signified by a negative value for the energy change, preceded by the symbol ΔH eg

$$H_2(g) + Cl_2(g) \rightarrow 2HCl(g) \quad \Delta H = -191 \text{ kJ/mole}$$

- **Endothermic reactions** are those taking in heat – signified by a positive value for the energy change, preceded by the symbol ΔH eg

$$3O_2(g) \rightarrow 2O_3(g) \quad \Delta H = +285 \text{ kJ/mole}$$

- **Activation energy** is the energy required by the reactants to loosen the bonds to enable them to form new bonds in the products. It is the minimum energy needed, on collision, for molecules to react.

- **A reversible reaction** is any reaction that can be reversed by changing the conditions eg.

$$CuSO_4(s) + 5H_2O(l) \rightarrow CuSO_4.5H_2O(s) \quad \textbf{at room temperature}$$

but the reverse

$$CuSO_4.5H_2O(s) \rightarrow CuSO_4(s) + 5H_2O(l) \quad \textbf{on heating to 120°C}$$

ESSENTIAL PRINCIPLES

1. ENERGETICS OF A REACTION

(a) Bond breaking and bond making

When bonds between atoms are broken, energy is taken in. When new bonds form between atoms, energy is given out. The energy change of a reaction is due to the difference between these two quantities.

When hydrogen reacts with chlorine the reaction gives out heat – the mixture explodes! The energy given out when covalent bonds between hydrogen and chlorine atoms form is greater than the energy taken in to break the covalent bonds into hydrogen molecules and chlorine molecules. This is shown in Fig. 9.1 and is an example of an exothermic reaction.

When ozone is formed in the stratosphere (the ozone layer) ultraviolet light gives energy to oxygen molecules, O_2, to convert them into ozone molecules, O_3. This is shown in Fig. 9.2 and is an example of an endothermic reaction. The energy given out when bonds between oxygen atoms break is greater than the energy given out when bonds form to produce the ozone molecule.

Bonds	Covalent Bond energies in kJ/mole of bonds
H — H	436
Cl — Cl	242
H — Cl	431

The bond energy is the energy, in kJ, needed to break 1 mole of the covalent bond specified

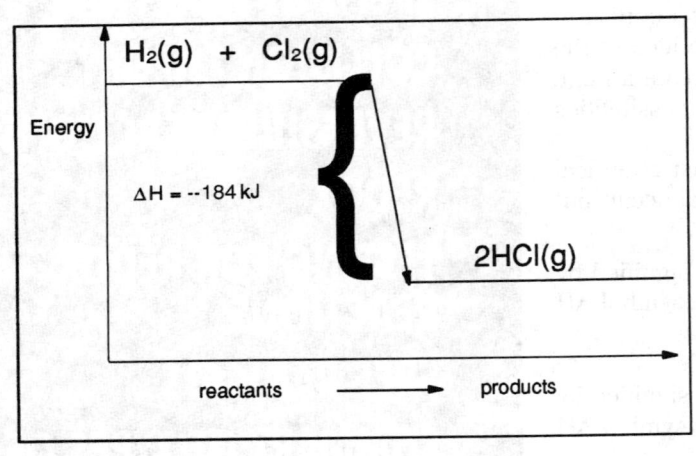

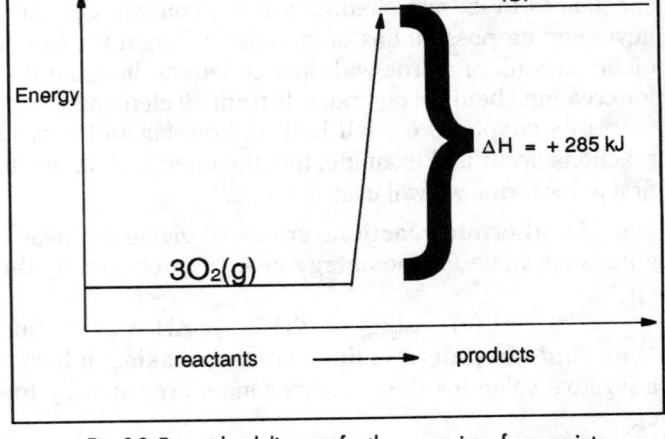

Fig. 9.1 Energy level diagram for the reaction of hydrogen and chlorine to form hydrogen chloride.

Fig. 9.2 Energy level diagram for the conversion of oxygen into ozone in the ozone layer.

(b) Bond energies

To study the energy diagram above in more detail we need to find the energies of the bonds involved. A data book will give the following information about bond energies.

Applied to the equation for the reaction of hydrogen with chlorine, we have

$$H_2(g) + Cl_2(g) \rightarrow 2HCl(g)$$

Energy needed to break 1 mole of H–H bonds = 436 kJ

Energy needed to break 1 mole of Cl–Cl bonds = 242 kJ

Energy given out on making 2 moles of H–Cl bonds = 2 × 431 kJ

Total energy to be added to break the bonds in 1 mole of hydrogen and 1 mole of chlorine = 436 + 242 = 678 kJ

Total energy given out in the formation of 2 moles of bonds in hydrogen chloride = 2 × 431 = 862 kJ

We see that more energy is given out in making the bond of the products than was taken in to break the bonds in the reactants. This leaves a surplus of energy, 184 kilojoules, given out. The reaction is exothermic. So the calculated value for the energy change of the above reaction is ΔH = –184 kJ.

(c) The significance of bond energies

Bond energies tell us the strength of covalent bonds in covalently bonded elements and compounds.

The table of bond energies given below shows that

(i) not all bonds are equal in strength
(ii) the strength of a bond can explain the reactivity, or lack of it in substances.

For example, the very strong bonds in nitrogen molecules would lead us to predict that nitrogen would not be very reactive – a prediction confirmed by observation. Alternatively, the bonds between chlorine atoms are rather weak by comparison and chlorine would be expected to be much more reactive than nitrogen – which it is.

bond	bond energy kJ/mole of bonds
O=O	497
N≡N	945
H–O	464
C=O	800
C–F	452
C–Cl	339

(d) Bond energies in calculations

We have earlier calculated the energy change for a simple chemical reaction involving only the making and breaking of covalent bonds.

Boiling a substance

Let us now consider a common misconception at this level of study – that boiling a substance splits the substance into its elements. A little thought will tell us that this is not what we observe. If it *were* so, the kitchen at home would soon fill with an explosive mixture of hydrogen and oxygen simply as a result of boiling an egg! We can show that this is not likely using bond energies. The reactions we are comparing are

$$H_2O(l) \rightarrow H_2O(g) \quad \text{vaporisation of water at } 100°C$$

and

$$H_2O(g) \rightarrow H_2(g) + \tfrac{1}{2}O_2(g) \quad \text{decomposing water into its elements.}$$

The energy to carry out the vaporisation is the heat of vaporisation of water, ΔH = + 44 KJ/mole. To calculate the energy needed to convert one mole of water vapour into hydrogen and oxygen gases, we can use bond energy data (Fig 9.3).

To **break** these bonds

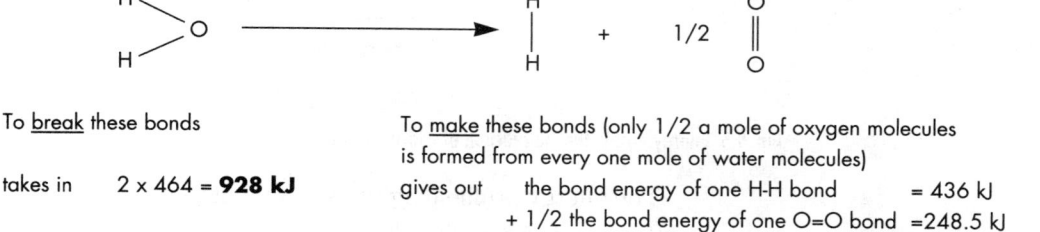

takes in   2 × 464 = **928 kJ**

To **make** these bonds (only 1/2 a mole of oxygen molecules is formed from every one mole of water molecules)
gives out   the bond energy of one H-H bond   = 436 kJ
          + 1/2 the bond energy of one O=O bond = 248.5 kJ
                                                  = **684.5 kJ**

Fig. 9.3

The energy change for the whole decomposition is the overall energy change for this reaction

928 kJ taken in less 684.5 given out = **+243.5 kJ**

We see now that vaporising one mole of water (18g) requires an input of 44 kJ whereas to decompose the same quantity requires, according to our calculation, more than five times as much energy. This comparison is shown in the energy level diagrams (Fig 9.4).

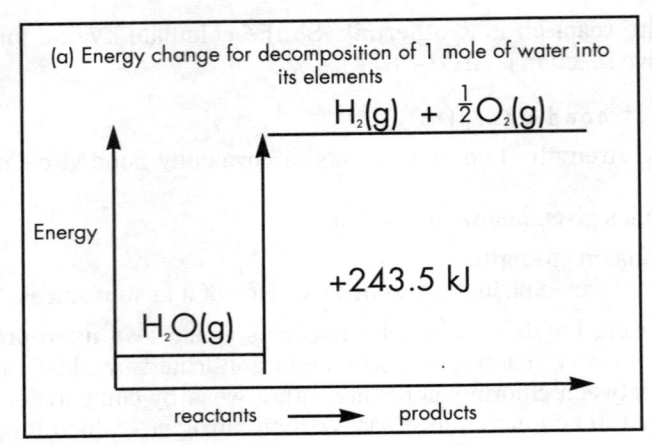

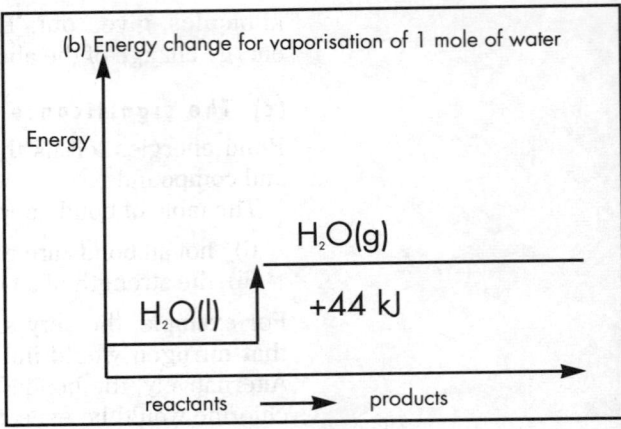

Fig. 9.4 Energy level diagrams.

(a) Energy change for decomposition of 1 mole of water into its elements: $H_2O(l) \rightarrow H_2(g) + \frac{1}{2}O_2(g)$, +243.5 kJ

(b) Energy change for vaporisation of 1 mole of water: $H_2O(l) \rightarrow H_2O(g)$, +44 kJ

Unreactive chlorofluorocarbons, CFCs

The reason why chorofluorcarbons – CFCs – are so unreactive in our atmosphere is related to the strength of the C—F and the C—Cl bonds they contain. The table above shows that the C—F bond is especially strong at 452 kJ/mole.

2. ACTIVATION ENERGY OF A REACTION

Most reactions will not start unless they are supplied with energy. A match must be heated by friction before it will ignite; light must be shone onto a mixture of hydrogen and chlorine before it will form hydrogen chloride as in the reaction discussed earlier in Section 1.

Energy must be added to reactants to loosen the bonds before reaction with the formation of new bonds takes place. This energy 'activates' the molecules and so is called the activation energy. The following energy diagram takes the energy level diagram from section 1(a) further by showing the activation energy. This type of diagram is called an **energy profile** (Fig. 9.5).

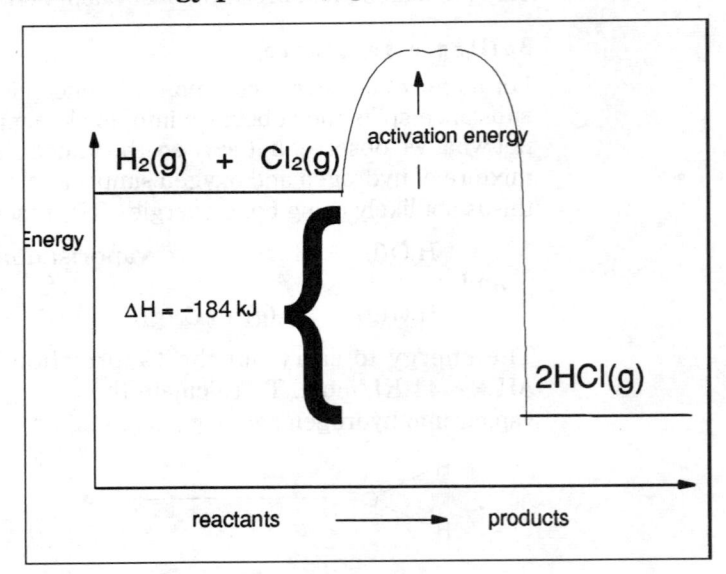

Energy profile: $H_2(g) + Cl_2(g) \rightarrow 2HCl(g)$, $\Delta H = -184$ kJ, with activation energy shown as a hill.

Fig. 9.5 Energy profile for the reaction of hydrogen with chlorine in UV light.

The energy profile diagram shows that to react, a mixture of hydrogen and chlorine requires energy to be added. This can be done by shining UV light on the mixture. The energy of the reactants is raised to the top of the 'hill' where the bonds are 'looser' and there they react to form the products. As calculated earlier, the bonds in the products are stronger than those in the reactants, resulting in hydrogen chloride formation and excess energy being given out in the form of heat. The overall energy change is still the difference in energy between the reactants and products despite the input of activation energy – as can be seen from the diagram.

The exothermic nature of most chemical reactions suggests that we can make use of a chemical reaction to heat our homes. This we do by burning fuels – an oxidation process usually called combustion.

3 > FUELS

Fuels give out energy when they burn in oxygen or in air. Fuels usually contain carbon and hydrogen and the products of combustion are carbon dioxide and water, together with lots of energy. Coal is mainly carbon and it burns in an excess of air to give carbon dioxide:

$$\text{carbon} + \text{oxygen} \rightarrow \text{carbon dioxide}$$

$$C + O_2 \rightarrow CO_2.$$

North Sea gas (natural gas) is mainly methane. It burns in an excess of air to give carbon dioxide and water:

$$\text{methane} + \text{oxygen} \rightarrow \text{carbon dioxide} + \text{water}$$

$$CH_4 + 2O_2 \rightarrow CO_2 + 2H_2O.$$

> *In a limited supply of air, all organic compounds burn incompletely and one of the products is carbon monoxide*

If a limited amount of air is used, the poisonous gas carbon monoxide is formed in both cases. This is why it is important that you keep a room well-ventilated when fuels are burning.

With so many different fuels to choose from, we would, if possible, choose the one that gives most heat energy per unit of cost to ourselves. This is not, however the only consideration. It may not always be possible to obtain the cheapest fuel, or to use it if it is available. The cheapest fuel may be dirty to use or just inconvenient. Consider all the available energy sources, electricity, coal, oil, natural gas, wood and bottled gas. Make a list of the advantages and disadvantages of each for use in your own home. The results of your analysis must be compared with the relative costs of these sources – roughly in order of cost for the same heat output (most expensive first) – electricity > oil > bottled gas > natural gas > coal > wood. However, the order will vary a little depending on the area in which you live; wood is cheaper in the countryside where there are trees than in areas where there are no trees.

4 > MEASURING THE HEAT ENERGY GIVEN OUT BY BURNING FUEL

To make the comparision referred to in Section 3, we need a method of finding the heat output per unit weight of a fuel. We do this in a calorimeter.

The principle of the method is that heat energy can best be measured if it is made to heat water. It is known that

> 4.2 kilojoules of energy will raise the temperature of 1 kilogram of water by 1°C
> therefore
> energy in kJ = mass of water in kg x 4.2 x temperature rise in °C

As a laboratory investigation, the following would be an acceptable way of comparing the heat output of different fuels.

(a) The investigation

The apparatus shown is set up. The metal can contains, say, 500g (half a kilogram) of water.
  (i)   the fuel, in its container, is weighed (w_1)
  (ii) the temperature of the water in the can is measured (T_1)
  (iii) the container of fuel is placed under the can of water and lit
  (iv) the water is stirred as the burning fuel heats it
  (v)   when the temperature of the water has risen by just under 10°C the flame is put out by excluding air.
  (vi) the highest temperature of the water is taken (T_2)*
  (vii) the fuel container is reweighed (w_2)

*The temperature may rise a little further because heat still in the bottom of the can continues to warm it after the flame has been extinguished

(b) Calculating the energy value of the fuel

Two quantities are needed to assess the fuel.
  (i) the energy given out which is measured by the amount that enters the water.
  (ii) the mass of fuel burnt which is $w_1 - w_2$.

(c) Calculation of the energy value

The energy value is now found by dividing energy by mass burnt to give an answer in kilojoules per gram of fuel burnt.

Energy in water/kJ	Mass of fuel burnt/g	Energy kJ/g
$0.5 \times 4.2 \times 10$ = 21 kilojoules	$w_1 - w_2$	$\dfrac{21}{w_1 - w_2}$

(d) Evaluating the results

It is evident that this cannot be an accurate method of determining the energy value. There are obvious areas of inaccuracy. You may see them if you answer the following questions

  (i)   Does all the heat from the burning fuel go into the water?
  (ii) If not, where does the rest go?
  (iii) Has the temperature rise been accurately measured?
  (iv) Has the mass of fuel burnt been accurately measured?

You are now in a position to suggest how the investigation could be improved.

5 > POLLUTANTS FROM FUELS

(A) ACID RAIN

Fossil fuels such as coal, oil and some natural gas contain sulphur. When these fuels burn one of the products is sulphur dioxide. It dissolves in rain water to form '*acid rain*' (sulphurous acid). Acid rain causes brickwork, statues and metal objects to corrode. It also decreases the pH of rain water, and, when this arrives in rivers and streams, it causes fishes and plants to die.

(B) BURNING PETROL

Incomplete combustion of petrol causes carbon monoxide, which is poisonous, to be formed. This is a very big problem in cities where there is a lot of traffic. Sometimes the petrol does not all burn and petrol fumes escape into the atmosphere. The sparking plugs that ignite the petrol and air mixture also cause nitrogen and oxygen in the atmosphere to combine and form oxides of nitrogen. These oxides are acidic and can damage the lungs. One way of removing pollutants from car exhausts is by the use of a catalyst. This would make carbon monoxide and oxides of nitrogen combine to form nitrogen and carbon dioxide which do not pollute the atmosphere. A compound of lead is often added to petrol to make it burn quietly. Lead, which would block the engine, is removed in the exhaust fumes by adding another compound. Lead compounds in the atmosphere cause brain damage. Many people would like their countries to follow the example of a few countries and use 'lead-free' petrol.

6 > SPEED OF REACTION

For molecules to react, they must collide with each other. Since we know that molecules are in unceasing, high-speed motion, this is likely to happen frequently. However, calculations show that not every collision results in a reaction. We can understand this with the aid of our energy profile for the reaction of hydrogen and chlorine, Fig. 9.5 above.

Reacting particles must have had their bonds 'loosened' by taking up energy – the activation energy. Only these molecules are able to react. However, as more of them do react, and energy is given out, this energy is absorbed by even more molecules. The number of molecules with enough energy to react increases and the reaction speeds up, finally becoming very rapid. In the reaction we are discussing this results in an explosion, started by a flash of light!

7 > COLLISION THEORY OF REACTIONS

The reason for an increase in the rate of a chemical reaction can be explained by the *collision theory*. In order for particles to react they must collide, and they must also have sufficient energy to react.

> Make sure that you understand this section

(a) If the size of the reacting particles is decreased, there is more surface area available for reacting and so the speed of the reaction increases

This is why powdered calcium carbonate reacts far more quickly than lumps of calcium carbonate (marble chips). This also explains why there is a danger of explosions in flour mills. The very fine flour can easily catch fire, and a very fast reaction occurs which causes an explosion. A similar problem occurs in coal mines where there can be a build up of coal dust and combustible gases. Bacterial spoilage of food is much quicker if the the surface area of food is increased as in minced meat, meat pies, and thin sliced meats. Most food poisoning by bacterial growth occurs in these products.

(b) When a solution becomes more concentrated, the number of particles present in the solution increases

The more particles there are the greater the number of collisions, and therefore the rate of the reaction increases. Gases can be concentrated by increasing the pressure. This squeezes more particles into a given volume. This is one reason why reactions between gases in industrial processes are usually carried out at higher than normal pressures.

(c) Increasing the temperature increases the speed of the particles

The faster the particles move, the greater the number of collisions, and therefore the rate of the reaction increases. A 10°C rise in temperature almost doubles the rate of most reactions. One way you may have at home of speeding up the cooking of vegetables is a pressure cooker. A pressure cooker enables water to boil at a higher temperature, and this increases the rate of cooking.

> If the temperature is increased by 70 °C the rate of the reaction is increased by a factor of about 128.

The faster the particles move the greater the number of collisions per second and therefore the greater the reaction rate. For **living organisms**, whose body chemistry must take place within a very narrow range of temperature of about 0°C to 40°C, the rate is roughly doubled for every 10°C rise in temperature*. Bacterial spoiling of food speeds up at higher temperatures (up to about 40°C) so refrigeration is necessary to slow down bacterial action. Many processes are carried out at higher temperatures to take advantage of this speeding up effect, for example, washing dishes and clothes, cooking, drying (though this is an evaporation process).

* For chemical reactions outside the organism, the temperature rise to double the rate can vary widely.

(d) One of the ways a catalyst is thought to work is by lowering the energy required before a reaction can take place

A catalyst speeds up a reaction by providing an alternative, lower energy route for the reactants to take in becoming products. This is shown on the energy profile (Fig. 9.6).

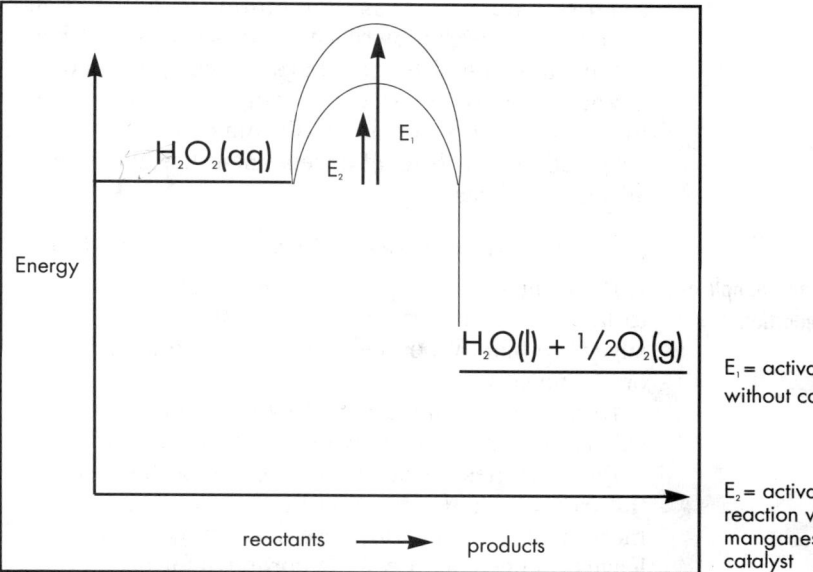

Fig. 9.6 Energy profile for the decomposition of aqueous hydrogen peroxide with a manganese(IV) oxide catalyst.

E_1 = activation energy without catalyst

E_2 = activation energy of reaction with the manganese(IV) oxide catalyst

In this reaction, the hydrogen peroxide molecules react with the manganese (IV) oxide catalyst, form water and oxygen which leave the catalyst which can now react with more oxide and so on. The catalyst reacts with the reactants but is reformed as the products are created. The equation for the example shown could more accurately be given as

$$MnO_2(s) + H_2O_2(aq) \rightarrow MnO_2(s) + H_2O(l) + \tfrac{1}{2}O_2(g)$$

because this shows that the catalyst is a **reactant** and that it is also a product, ie it is reformed after reacting and so is not used up. Chemical equations do not usually show formulae which occur on both sides of the equation, so the formula of a catalyst is usually left out and the equation becomes

$$H_2O_2(aq) \rightarrow H_2O(l) + \tfrac{1}{2}O_2(g)$$

> A catalyst speeds up a chemical reaction but is itself unchanged at the end of the reaction.

A catalyst can:
- make a reaction occur faster at a given temperature or
- make a reaction go quickly at a much reduced temperature

The above reaction is faster at room temperature with the catalyst than without it. It is also faster at room temperature with the catalyst than at 100°C without the catalyst.

Biological catalysts – enzymes

These have evolved to work at low temperatures, usually in the range 0°C–45°C. For example the enzymes in yeast will ferment sugars to ethanol at room temperature whereas with no catalyst, grape sugar solution would take centuries to become wine! The enzymes in our bodies will digest food and oxidise the digestion products thousands of times faster than could be done with 'chemical' catalysts used in the chemical industry. However, the structures of enzymes are broken down at temperatures above 45°C and enzyme activity ceases. For this reason, living organisms cannot survive at temperatures much above 45°C. We take advantage of this to kill bacteria in food by heat treatment.

❝ Enzymes are destroyed at temperatures a few degrees above room temperature ❞

Catalysts in industry

The use of catalysts in industry is widespread. A great deal of money can be saved if a reaction can be made to take place at a low temperature for two reasons
- less heat energy is used
- more of the product is made in a given time

The Contact process (vanadium (V) oxide) and the Haber process (iron) are examples of large industries using catalysts. (See Chapter 12.3, Sections 4 and 6).

Industrial chemists are always searching for better catalysts. In theory a catalyst for a reaction between gases need only form a layer one atom thick to work because any lower layers do not normally make contact with the gases. In some catalyst preparations this level of development has almost been reached. Can you suggest the advantage of this?

(e) Light affects the rate of a few reactions

❝ This is an example of reduction ❞

One example you may be familiar with is photography. When a silver salt is exposed to light, silver is formed. In black and white photography, the film is covered with silver bromide. When light shines on the film, silver is formed. This is the black part on the negative.

Light can also cause certain dyes to fade. This is very useful for certain farmers who can simply leave sheep's wool in the sunlight and it will become pure white.

Photosynthesis is one of the most important reactions involving light. Chlorophyll is the catalyst for the reaction between carbon dioxide and water to form starch. The more light there is, the more chlorophyll is formed. This is one of the reasons why leaves change colour when chlorophyll formation ceases.

Light can also cause certain chemicals to explode. If light is shone on a mixture of hydrogen and chlorine the mixture explodes.

8 > REVERSIBLE EQUILIBRIA

(A) REVERSIBLE REACTIONS

Many chemical reactions can be **reversed**. One example has been given in Getting Started at the beginning of this chapter. The industrial processes of extracting metals from their oxide ores is, in effect, the chemist's way of reversing the reactions which occur in nature. Iron that was present on the surface of the Earth when its crust formed, has been oxidised to iron(III) oxide by chemical attack from oxygen in the presence of water – rusting in fact. This oxide is found widely distributed in rocks and gives the brown colour to sand, clay and sandstone. We now reverse that process to make use of the metal. The same is true of other metals.

If a chemical reaction can be reversed, that is can 'go both ways', can it do so under the same conditions? The answer to that question is yes. For example, if white copper sulphate, $CuSO_4(s)$ reacts with water to form blue copper sulphate, $CuSO_4.5H_2O(s)$, and the reaction reverses at temperatures of 120°C, there is likely to be an intermediate temperature where the two processes are occurring together. This leads to an **equilibrium** situation.

(B) EQUILIBRIUM PROCESSES

(i) Physical equilibrium

The simplest example of an equilibrium process is the evaporation and condensation of water. We know that water evaporates to form water vapour at room temperature. We also know that it will evaporate faster at 100°C. We further know that water vapour will condense back to water and that this occurs faster at room temperature than at 100°C. What happens if we keep water in a closed vessel at a temperature between room temperature and 100°C? Both processes occur at the same time and a balance is achieved when the amounts of water in the liquid and vapour states no longer change. **Evaporation is occurring as fast as condensation**. We show this as:-

$$\text{water} \underset{\text{evaporation}}{\overset{\text{condensation}}{\rightleftharpoons}} \text{water vapour}$$

$$H_2O(l) \rightleftharpoons H_2O(g)$$

In this **equilibrium** the speed of evaporation of the water equals the speed of condensation of the vapour. Although the two processes continue for ever, they do so at the same speed so we detect no change in the proportions of vapour and liquid in the *closed vessel*. If the vessel were not closed, the vapour molecules could escape more easily than the liquid molecules; there would be less vapour to condense to liquid and so the speed of condensation would go down whilst the speed of evaporation would stay the same. This would eventually result in the water evaporating away completely. Equilibrium requires a closed vessel in this example.

(ii) Chemical equilibrium

As an example of a chemical equilibrium let us consider the synthesis of ammonia in the Haber process. The reaction is exothermic in the forward direction and so endothermic in reverse.

$$N_2(g) + 3H_2(g) \underset{\text{exothermic reaction}}{\overset{\text{endothermic reaction}}{\rightleftharpoons}} 2NH_3(g)$$

The ⇌ sign indicates that the chemical reaction is 'going both ways' at the same time. That is, nitrogen and hydrogen molecules are reacting together to form ammonia molecules at the same time as ammonia molecules are decomposing into nitrogen and hydrogen molecules. At equilibrium, these two opposing processes are happening at the same speed and the **equilibrium mixture** contains a constant proportion of each substance.

Effect of temperature change

An increase in temperature will cause equilibrium to be established more quickly. However, because this is an exothermic change, if the temperature of the equilibrium mixture is raised, the reaction which takes in heat is favoured. The reverse reaction takes in heat so the equilibrium mixture becomes less concentrated in ammonia molecules and more concentrated in hydrogen and nitrogen molecules. We see that increased temperature moves the position of equilibrium to the left. For high yield therefore, the reaction should be carried out at as *low a temperature as possible*. This is not done in practice because the reaction would become very slow.

Effect of pressure change

Changing the pressure of a gas changes it concentration. We increase concentrations of gases by increasing their pressure – squeezing more molecules into the same space. Increased pressure therefore means increased reaction speed and equilibrium is established faster. However, as with temperature change, the effect may not be the same on the forward and backward reactions. The effect depends on the change in the number of molecules in the reaction mixture as the reaction procedes. In the synthesis of ammonia, four molecules of reactants becomes two molecules of products. This decrease in molecules represents a decrease in volume. *Increased pressure favours the reaction by which there is a decrease in volume*. The opposite is true of a decrease in pressure. In ammonia synthesis, high pressures are used to give high yields of ammonia

Fig. 9.7 shows the effects of changing conditions on the position of equilibrium.
In summary,

Exothermic reaction + temperature rise = decreased yield of product
Endothermic reaction + temperature rise = increased yield of product
Molecules decrease on reaction + pressure rise = increased yield of product
Molecules increase on reaction + pressure rise = decreased yield of product

Variable	Reaction type	Effect on position of equilibrium	Example/Industrial process
Temperature increase / Temperature decrease	Exothermic	Moves to left - less product forms / Moves to right - more product forms	Contact process for sulphuric acid production $2SO_2 + O_2 \rightleftharpoons 2SO_3$ $\Delta H = -186$ kJ
Temperature increase / Temperature decrease	Endothermic	Moves to right - more product forms / Moves to left - less product forms	Production of steam from water $H_2O(l) \rightleftharpoons H_2O(g)$
Pressure increases / Pressure decreases	Decrease in molecules left to right	Moves to right - more product forms / Moves to left - less product forms	Haber process for ammonia production $N_2 + 3H_2 \rightleftharpoons 2NH_3$ 4 moles 2 moles
Pressure increase / Pressure decreases	Increase in molecules left to right	Moves to left - less product forms / Moves to right - more product forms	$2O_3 \rightleftharpoons 3O_2$

Fig. 9.7

9 REDOX

Redox reactions are those in which oxidation and reduction occur at the same time, e.g.:

(a) iron(III) oxide + carbon monoxide → iron + carbon dioxide.

Iron(III) oxide has been reduced to iron metal (removal of oxygen).
Carbon monoxide has been oxidised to carbon dioxide (addition of oxygen).
Iron(III) oxide contains Fe^{3+} ions; iron contains Fe atoms with no charge.
The change Fe^{3+} to Fe takes place by gain of three electrons

$$Fe^{3+} + 3e \rightarrow Fe$$

This gain of electrons confirms the change of iron(III) oxide to iron as a reduction.

(b) hydrogen iodide(aq) + chlorine → hydrogen chloride(aq) + iodine.

Hydrogen iodide has been oxidised to iodine (removal of hydrogen).
Chlorine has been reduced to hydrogen chloride (addition of hydrogen).
Hydrogen iodide solution contains iodide ions, I^-; iodine contains iodine molecules, I_2. The change from ion to molecule takes place by a loss of two electrons

$$2I^- - 2e^- \rightarrow I_2$$

This loss of electrons confirms that the change is an oxidation.

■ Test yourself by writing an equation to describe what happens to the chlorine molecules in equation (b) when they are changed to hydrogen chloride solution (Hint: hydrogen chloride solution contains chloride ions)

Respiration is an example of oxidation, photosynthesis is an example of reduction. Rusting and iron extraction are also examples of redox reactions.

10> TESTING FOR REDOX REACTIONS

❝❝ Learn these colour changes ❞❞

The easiest way to *test* for an oxidising agent is to add a substance that is easily oxidised, e.g. potassium iodide solution. Potassium iodide solution is colourless, but if it is added to an oxidising agent, such as chlorine, it will go brown because iodine is formed. This colour change, from colourless to brown, is a very sensitive test for an oxidising agent.

Similarly, a reducing agent can be tested for by adding a substance that is very easily reduced. Two main chemicals are used: acidified potassium manganate(VII) and acidified potassium dichromate(VI). Acidified potassium manganate(VII) changes from purple to colourless in the presence of a reducing agent and acidified potassium dichromate(VI) changes from orange to green.

11> FREE RADICALS

Free radicals are particles which have an unfilled shell of electrons. They are very reactive because of this and react with other particles to complete their outer octet. For example, oxygen molecules are split into oxygen atoms by the action of UV light in the ozone layer.

$$O_2 \longleftrightarrow 2O\bullet$$

molecules – each atom has an octet of electrons

atoms, free radicals – each atom has only six electrons

The oxygen free radical reacts with oxygen molecules to form ozone molecules in which all the oxygen atoms have eight outer electrons.

$$O\bullet + O_2 \longleftrightarrow O_3$$

free radical   oxygen molecule   molecule of ozone

These reactions are important in the stratosphere where they result in the formation of the ozone layer. The ozone layer absorbs damaging UV light rays from the Sun, preventing them damaging life on the surface of the planet.

12> SUMMARY OF TYPES OF REACTION

There are many types of chemical reactions

(A) ADDITION

When two or more compounds react together to form one compound:

ethene + bromine → dibromoethane.

(B) CRACKING

The breaking down of an organic molecule into smaller molecules:

butane → ethane + ethene.

(C) DEHYDRATION

The removal of the elements of water from a compound:

ethanol → ethene + water.

(D) DISPLACEMENT

(See Chapter 11, Section 3) when one element displaces another:

zinc + copper(II) sulphate → copper + zinc sulphate

potassium iodide + chlorine → potassium chloride + iodine.

(E) ELECTROLYSIS
When molten compounds or solutions are decomposed by an electric current. Anode reactions are oxidations, cathode reactions are reductions
Electrolysis of brine gives

$$\text{at the anode } 2Cl^-(aq) - 2e^- \rightarrow Cl_2(g)$$
$$\text{at the cathode } 2H^+(aq) + 2e^- \rightarrow H_2(g)$$

(F) EQUILIBRIUM
When a reversible reaction reaches a balance of reactants and products.

$$\text{sulphur dioxide + oxygen} \leftrightarrows \text{sulphur trioxide}$$

(G) EXOTHERMIC
When energy is given out in a chemical reaction: ΔH is negative

$$\text{methane + oxygen} \rightarrow \text{carbon dioxide + water + heat}$$

(H) ENDOTHERMIC
When energy is taken in during a chemical recation: ΔH is positive

$$\text{oxygen + energy from UV light} \rightarrow \text{ozone} - \text{heat}$$

(I) FERMENTATION
When sugar solutions are converted by enzymes to ethanol.

$$\text{glucose} \rightarrow \text{ethanol + carbon dioxide}$$

(J) HYDRATION
When water is added to a compound:

$$\text{anhydrous copper(II) sulphate + water} \rightarrow \text{hydrated copper(II) sulphate.}$$

(K) HYDROLYSIS
When water reacts with a compound:

$$\text{aluminium chloride + water} \rightarrow \text{aluminium hydroxide + hydrogen chloride}$$

(L) NEUTRALISATION
When an acid reacts with a base - see Ch. 10 Sect. 2:

$$\text{hydrochloric acid + sodium hydroxide} \rightarrow \text{sodium chloride + water.}$$

(M) OXIDATION
When an element or compound accepts oxygen, gives up hydrogen or loses electrons. They are the opposite of reductions. Oxidation and reduction usually occur together. The underlined substance is oxidised in the following equations

$$\underline{\text{hydrogen}} + \text{oxygen} \rightarrow \text{water}$$
$$\underline{\text{ammonia}} + \text{oxygen} \rightarrow \text{nitrogen + water}$$
$$\underline{\text{chloride ions}} \text{ minus electrons} \rightarrow \text{chlorine molecules}$$

(N) POLYMERISATION
When many small molecules link up to form a very large molecule

$$\text{ethene} \rightarrow \text{poly(ethene)}$$

(O) PRECIPITATION
When two soluble compounds react to form an insoluble compound:

$$\text{sodium sulphate(aq) + barium chloride(aq)} \rightarrow \text{barium sulphate(s) + sodium chloride(aq).}$$

❝ Remember the state symbols ❞

(P) REDOX IS A GENERAL NAME FOR OXIDATION OR REDUCTION

(Q) REDUCTION

When an element or compound accepts hydrogen, loses oxygen or gains electrons. They are the opposite of oxidations. Reduction and oxidation usually occur together. The underlined substance is reduced in the following equations

<u>copper oxide</u> + hydrogen → copper + water

<u>nitrogen</u> + hydrogen → ammonia

<u>hydrogen ions</u> + electrons → hydrogen molecules

(R) REVERSIBLE

A reaction that can go in either direction:

hydrated copper sulphate ⇌ anhydrous copper sulphate + water

(S) THERMAL DECOMPOSITION

A compound breaks down on heating into simpler substances which do not recombine on cooling:

sodium nitrate → sodium nitrite + oxygen.

> When a substance thermally decomposes it does NOT react with oxygen!

(T) THERMAL DISSOCIATION

A compound breaks down on heating into simpler substances which recombine on cooling:

ammonium chloride ⇌ ammonia + hydrogen chloride.

EXAMINATION QUESTIONS

MULTIPLE CHOICE

QUESTION 1

A chemical reaction occurs when

A   an electric current is passed through a copper wire.
B   salt solution is heated.
C   crude oil is distilled.
D   dilute hydrochloric acid is added to magnesium ribbon at room temperature.
E   ice melts to form water.

(ULEAC)

QUESTIONS 2–5

From the list, A to D, choose the type of reaction taking place in each of the examples given below.

A   direct combination of elements.
B   neutralisation.
C   precipitation.
D   thermal decomposition.

2   The preparation of ammonium chloride from ammonia and hydrochloric acid.
3   The formation of silver chloride from silver nitrate solution and dilute hydrochloric acid.
4   The formation of carbon dioxide from carbon.
5   The relief of acid indigestion by sodium hydrogencarbonate (bicarbonate).

(NEAB)

QUESTION 6

Which one of the following changes produces a new substance?

A burning powdered sulphur.
B condensing ethanol vapour.
C melting paraffin wax.
D vaporising iodine crystals.

(SEG)

QUESTION 7

Two pollutants produced by petrol engines are

A carbon and sulphur dioxide.
B carbon dioxide and steam.
C carbon monoxide and oxides of nitrogen.
D carbon monoxide and steam.
E oxides of nitrogen and steam.

QUESTION 8

A common rocket fuel consists of a mixture of liquid hydrogen and liquid oxygen. The exhaust gas produced by this fuel will contain

A carbon dioxide and steam.
B carbon monoxide and steam.
C steam only.
D carbon dioxide only.
E hydrogen peroxide.

QUESTION 9

The main reason for using catalysts in industry is that they

A increase the yield of the products.
B raise the temperature of reaction mixtures.
C remove impurities from reaction mixtures.
D speed up the rate of formation of the products.

(SEG)

STRUCTURED QUESTIONS

QUESTION 10

(a) Use **one** of the two words FAST or SLOW to describe the rate of the following reactions.
   (i) The action of potassium on water ....
   (ii) The rusting of the steel body of a motor car ....
   (iii) The decomposition of hydrogen peroxide using a catalyst ....
   (iv) The neutralisation of potassium hydroxide solution with an acid ....
                                                                                                   (4)

(b) (i) Name the solution formed in (a) (i) ....
   (ii) Name the gas formed and the catalyst used in (a) (iii).
      Gas .... Catalyst ....
   (iii) What type of energy change takes place in (a) (iv)?
      ....
                                                                                 (4)

QUESTION 11

Oxidation may be defined as

either   the addition of oxygen to an element or compound;
or   the removal of hydrogen from an element or compound.

Reduction is a reaction which is the opposite of oxidation.

For each reaction described below state whether the substance underlined has been oxidised, reduced or undergone neither of these changes.

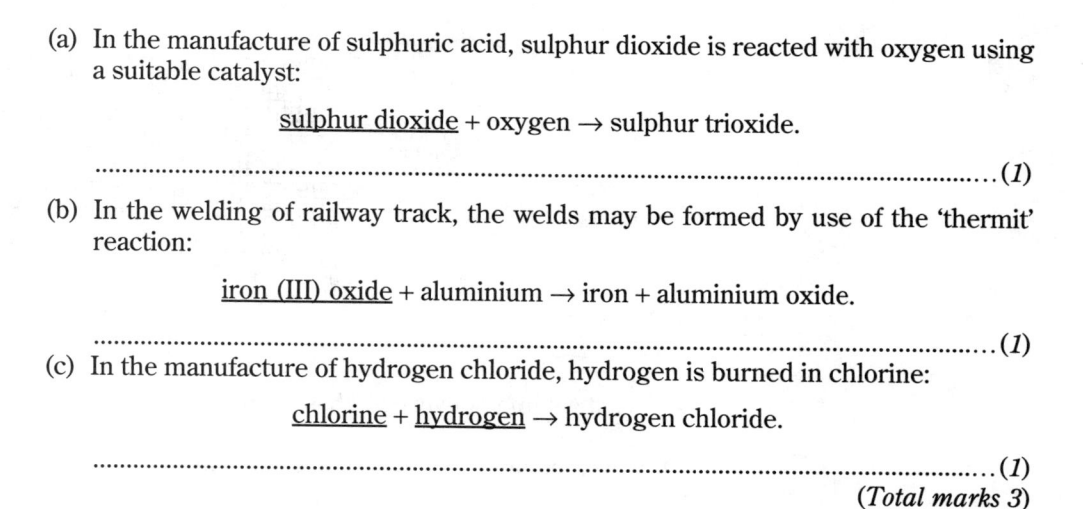

(a) In the manufacture of sulphuric acid, sulphur dioxide is reacted with oxygen using a suitable catalyst:

<u>sulphur dioxide</u> + oxygen → sulphur trioxide.

....(1)

(b) In the welding of railway track, the welds may be formed by use of the 'thermit' reaction:

<u>iron (III) oxide</u> + aluminium → iron + aluminium oxide.

....(1)

(c) In the manufacture of hydrogen chloride, hydrogen is burned in chlorine:

chlorine + <u>hydrogen</u> → hydrogen chloride.

....(1)

(Total marks 3)

QUESTION 12

The graphs below give information about fuels.

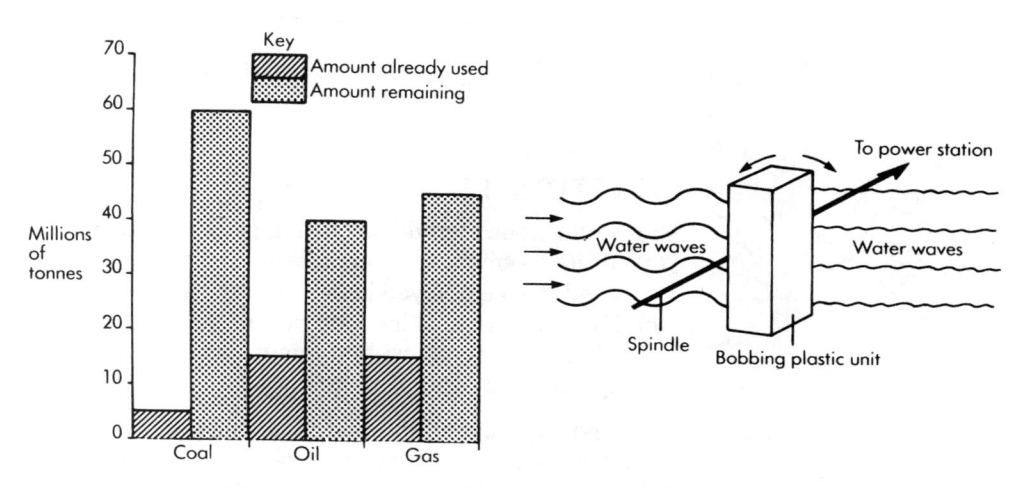

Figs. 9.8 and 9.9

(a) Use the graphs to help you answer the following questions.
  (i) Which fuel should last the longest? ....
  (ii) Which fuel is being used up fastest? ....
  (iii) How would the motor industry be affected if all the oil reserves were used up? (3)

(b) Coal is used to produce electricity in power stations, but is being replaced by nuclear fuels. For nuclear power stations compared to coal burning ones, give
  (i) **one** advantage, ...
  ....
  (ii) **one** disadvantage ....
  ....
  (2)

(c) One method proposed for the production of electrical energy in the future is by harnessing wave power. The diagram above shows waves making a plastic unit 'bob' back and forth turning a spindle. The spindle is attached to a generator in the power station.

  (i) Give **one** source from which the waves get their energy.
  (ii) Give **two** reasons why plastic is preferred to steel for the bobbing units.
  (iii) Give **one** advantage and **one** disadvantage of this system of producing electricity when compared with methods using coal, oil and gas. (5)

QUESTION 13

The graph below shows the total volume of hydrogen produced in the reaction of magnesium ribbon with excess dilute hydrochloric acid over a period of time.

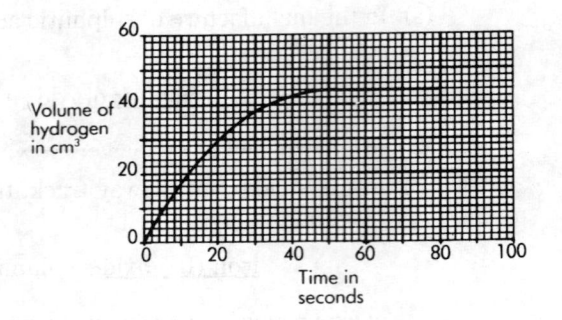

Fig. 9.10

(a) What volume of hydrogen has been produced after 15 seconds? .... cm³
(1 mark)

(b) How long does it take to produce 28 cm³ of hydrogen? .... seconds
(1 mark)

(c) Use the graph to work out the volume of hydrogen produced after 100 seconds .....
....cm³
(1 mark)

(d) Sketch *on the graph* the results you would expect to obtain if the same mass of magnesium was treated with more concentrated acid.
(2 marks)

(SEG)

QUESTION 14

(a) Outline one method for the industrial production of hydrogen. (3)
(b) Write a symbol equation for the conversion of hydrogen to ammonia and state the conditions employed in industry for this conversion. (4)
(c) Hydrogen is usually prepared in the laboratory by collecting the gas given off when zinc reacts with sulphuric acid. This reaction was investigated using the apparatus shown.

In a first experiment, the acid was added to the zinc and the volume of hydrogen was noted every 15 s. In a second experiment, five drops of copper sulphate solution were added to the zinc before the addition of the sulphuric acid, but otherwise the experiment was the same. The results obtained were plotted graphically and are shown below.

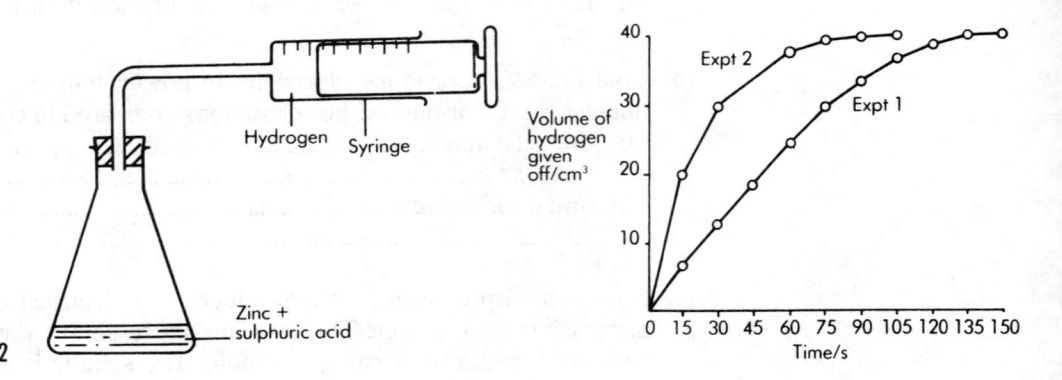

Figs 9.11 and 9.12

(i) What can you tell from the different curves resulting from the two experiments?
(1)
(ii) Suggest a possible explanation for the difference between the graphs. (2)
(iii) Describe an experiment which you would use to see whether or not your suggested explanation in (ii) is correct. (4)
(iv) Outline two other experiments to investigate more fully the reaction between zinc and sulphuric acid, and indicate the results that you would expect. (6)

(NISEAC)

OUTLINE ANSWERS

MULTIPLE CHOICE

ANSWER 1

Answer: D. A chemical reaction always involves the formation of a new substance. When hydrochloric acid is added to magnesium, the new substances formed are magnesium chloride and hydrogen. Changes in A, B, C and E are all physical changes, and can easily be reversed, e.g. the fractions from crude oil can be mixed together again.

ANSWERS 2, 3, 4 AND 5

If you could not do these questions read Section 10. 4: Answer 2: B. Answer 3: C. Answer 4: A. Answer 5: B.

ANSWER 6

Answer: A. Burning sulphur produces sulphur dioxide, all the others are physical changes.

ANSWER 7

Answer: C. Steam is NOT a pollutant. Oxides of nitrogen are formed at the high temperature of the spark. The pollutants from a petrol engine are carbon monoxide and oxides of nitrogen.

ANSWERS 8, 9

Answer 8: C. Answer 9: D.

STRUCTURED QUESTIONS

ANSWER 10

(a) (i) fast (ii) slow (iii) fast (iv) fast.
(b) (i) potassium hydroxide
  (ii) oxygen and manganese(IV) oxide
  (iii) exothermic (energy is given out).

ANSWER 11

(a) oxidised (b) reduced
(c) chlorine reduced and hydrogen oxidised.

ANSWER 12

(a) (i) coal (ii) oil
  (iii) There would be no petrol or diesel and hence they would have to either synthesise fuels or find alternative sources of energy.
(b) (i) One advantage of nuclear power stations is that they do not produce pollutants such as sulphur dioxide and smoke.
  (ii) One disadvantage is the disposal of radioactive waste.
(c) (i) Waves get their energy by gravitational pull of moon and sun (tides) and from winds.
  (ii) Plastic bobbins will not corrode and because they are less dense than steel bobbins less energy will be required to move them up and down.
  (iii) One advantage of this method is that there is no pollution, but one of the disadvantages is that it depends on there being a tide!

ANSWER 13

(a) 24 cm^3 (b) 18 seconds (c) 44 cm^3
(d) The curve would be steeper (because the reaction would be faster), but the same volume of hydrogen would be given off.

ANSWER 14

(a) See Chapter 12.1, Section 1(b).
(b) See Chapter 12.3, Section 4(a).
(c) (i) Experiment 2 was faster.
   (ii) Copper(II) sulphate (in fact copper) acts as a catalyst.
   (iii) Add powdered copper instead of copper(II) sulphate, if this speeded up the reaction then copper (from copper(II) sulphate) is acting as a catalyst.
   (iv) Same experiment as the one carried out but in one use the same mass of finely divided zinc and in the other the same volume of a more concentrated solution of sulphuric acid. In each case the reaction should be faster.

STUDENT'S ANSWER – EXAMINER'S COMMENTS

Excess of calcium carbonate was added to a known volume of dilute hydrochloric acid and a gas was produced. The volume of gas produced was recorded every ten seconds and the results are shown below.

Time/seconds	10	20	30	40	50	60	70	80	90	100
Total volume/cm³	130	225	300	360	410	480	490	500	500	500

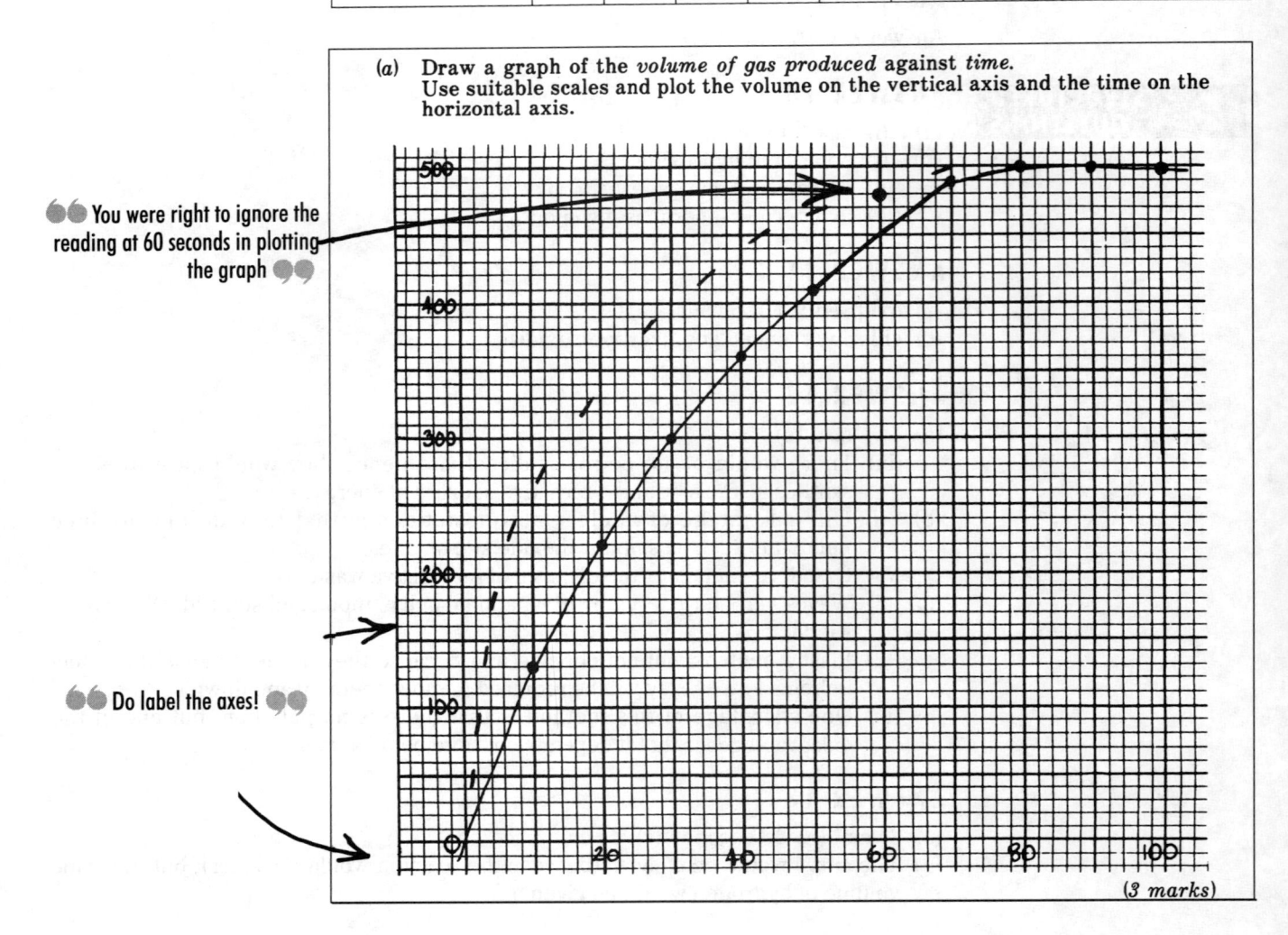

(a) Draw a graph of the *volume of gas produced* against *time*.
Use suitable scales and plot the volume on the vertical axis and the time on the horizontal axis.

❝ You were right to ignore the reading at 60 seconds in plotting the graph ❞

❝ Do label the axes! ❞

(3 marks)

CHAPTER 9 STUDENT'S ANSWER – EXAMINER'S COMMENTS 155

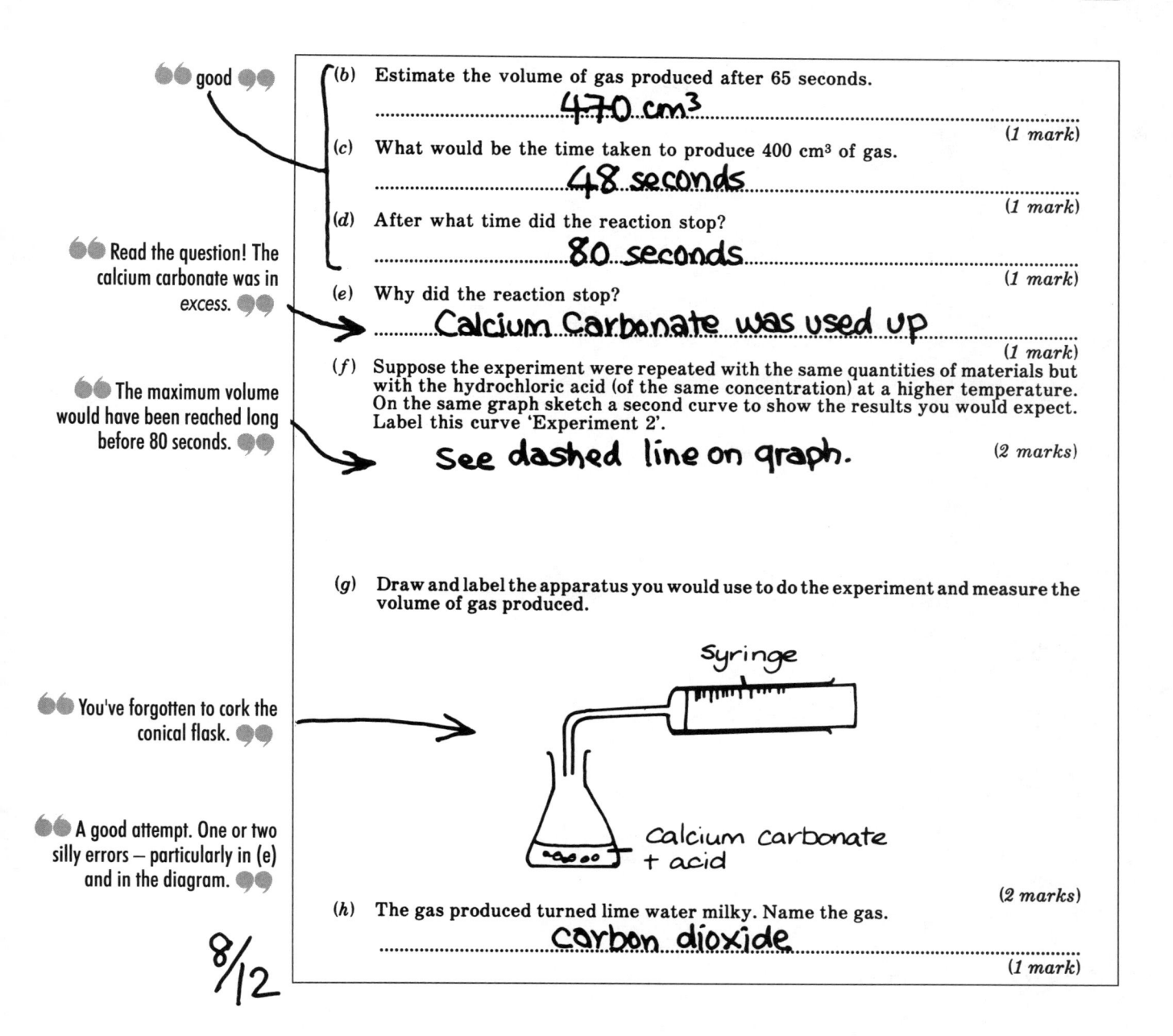

❝ good ❞

(b) Estimate the volume of gas produced after 65 seconds.
.... 470 cm³ ....
(1 mark)

(c) What would be the time taken to produce 400 cm³ of gas.
.... 48 seconds ....
(1 mark)

(d) After what time did the reaction stop?
.... 80 seconds ....
(1 mark)

❝ Read the question! The calcium carbonate was in excess. ❞

(e) Why did the reaction stop?
.... Calcium Carbonate was used up ....
(1 mark)

❝ The maximum volume would have been reached long before 80 seconds. ❞

(f) Suppose the experiment were repeated with the same quantities of materials but with the hydrochloric acid (of the same concentration) at a higher temperature. On the same graph sketch a second curve to show the results you would expect. Label this curve 'Experiment 2'.
See dashed line on graph.
(2 marks)

(g) Draw and label the apparatus you would use to do the experiment and measure the volume of gas produced.

❝ You've forgotten to cork the conical flask. ❞

[Diagram: conical flask containing calcium carbonate + acid, connected to a syringe]

❝ A good attempt. One or two silly errors – particularly in (e) and in the diagram. ❞

8/12

(2 marks)

(h) The gas produced turned lime water milky. Name the gas.
.... carbon dioxide ....
(1 mark)

REVIEW SHEET

■ **Exothermic reactions** are _____

_____

■ **Endothermic reactons** are _____

_____

■ **Activation energy** is _____

_____

■ **A reversible reaction** is _____

_____

■ The **energy change** of a reaction is due to the difference between _____

_____

_____

■ **Bond energies** tell us _____

_____

■ Calculate the value of the energy change in the following situation.

Applied to the equation for the reaction of hydrogen with clorine, we have

$H_2(g)$ + $Cl_2(g)$ → $2HCl(g)$

Energy needed to break 1 mole of H—H bonds = 436kJ

Energy needed to break 1 mole of Cl—Cl bonds = 242kJ

Energy given out on making 2 moles of H—Cl bonds = 2 × 431kJ

■ Describe a laboratory investigation to compare the heat output of different fuels ____

_____

_____

_____

_____

_____

_____

_____

- List some of the factors **increasing the speed** (or rate) of a reaction
    1. _____
    2. _____
    3. _____
    4. _____
    5. _____

- How does a **catalyst** speed up a reaction? _____

- How could you test for an oxidising agent? _____

- How could you test for a reducing agent? _____

- What do you understand by a free radical? _____

CHAPTER 10

ACIDS, BASES AND SALTS

TESTING FOR ACIDS
TESTING FOR BASES
ACIDS AND ACIDITY
SYMBOLS FOR PROTONS AND HYDRATED PROTONS
BASES
USES OF ACIDS
USES OF BASES
SALTS
USES AND ANALYSIS OF SALTS

GETTING STARTED

Nearly all compounds of the naturally occurring elements other than carbon fall into the categories of acids, bases or salts. There is a simple relationship between the three types of compound:

Salts are formed by the neutralisation of *acids* by *bases*.

The property that allows us to recognise acids is their *acidity*. It is this property of an acid which is immediately recognised when we taste a fruit. If the fruit is not ripe we immediately recognise its acidity by the sour taste! It is not, however, a good test to apply to unknown substances to discover whether or not they are acids. *Many chemicals are poisonous*.

For this reason, other properties of acids are much more useful in testing for acidic properties. Acids are also *corrosive*, which means they dissolve metals, stonework and many other substances. **Strong** acids will corrode these substances quite quickly but *weak* acids dissolve them much more slowly. The ability of acids to dissolve metals and carbonate rock is a type of reaction we use in testing for acids. You will see later that it is also a great nuisance to society.

The property which allows us to recognise a base is its ability to *neutralise* an acid. Bases are of two types. *Soluble* bases are also called *alkalis*; *insoluble* bases are simply *bases*.

A salt is the compound formed when an acid is neutralised by a base. Salts are *ionic* compounds.

ESSENTIAL PRINCIPLES

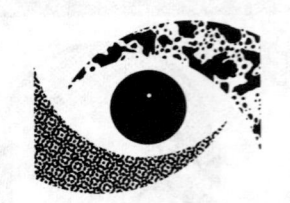

1 TESTING FOR ACID

(A) INDICATORS

It was clear to the very earliest chemists that 'tasting' for acids was a dangerous test. Soon, coloured substances from plants were found which changed their colour if added to acids. These coloured substances became known as *indicators* of acidity. Litmus was once a common indicator; its natural colour is blue and it becomes red in acids.

Other indicators are now used which not only change colour in acids but show different colours for different *strengths* of acids. They also show a range of colours for different strengths of alkalis. *Universal indicator* is of this type.

Universal indicator will *measure* the acidity or alkalinity of a substance on a scale called a *pH scale*. This scale runs from 1 to 14 with pH 7 being neither acid nor alkaline – that is, *neutral*. Universal indicator is a mixture of synthetic dyes, blended to produce a visibly distinct colour for each pH value. Paper chromatography can be used to separate the components of this mixture (see Section 4.4(b)).

The numbers on the pH scale represent decreasing acidities from 1 to 14. So, pH 1 is the strongest acid, pH 7 is neutral and pH 14 is the strongest alkali. An *acid* will have a pH of from 1 to 6.9; an *alkali* will have a pH of more than 7.

A *weak acid* has a pH of 3–6; a *weak alkali* has a pH of 8–12.

Most salts, and water, are neutral and have a pH of 7.

(B) OTHER TESTS FOR ACIDS

The following table (Fig. 10.1) gives a detailed summary of the important properties of *aqueous* solutions of acids.

> 66 Although litmus is a good indicator for distinguishing an acid from an alkali it has limitations. Unlike the universal indicator, litmus will not measure pH nor will it indicate that a substance is neutral. 99

> 66 Even *strong* alkalis can have pHs of 8–12 if they are in *dilute* solution. The distinction between *strong* and *weak* in alkalis, as with acids, is in the *proportion of molecules* which are ionised in solution 99

Reagent	Reaction	Comments
universal paper or solution	paper or solution turns red – yellow; pH 1 (red) to 6 (yellow–green)	colour or pH depends on *strength* of acid
magnesium or any metal *above copper* in the reactivity table	the acid gives off *hydrogen* gas and leaves a solution of the salt of the metal	any pure, grey powder which fizzes in acid will almost certainly be a metal
calcium carbonate or any other carbonate or hydrogencarbonate	*carbon dioxide* is given off from the carbonate or hydrogencarbonate	this reaction is also used as a test for carbonates or hydrogencarbonates
any *base* or *alkali* e.g. copper(II) oxide or sodium hydroxide	*neutralisation* occurs: heat is produced.	pH of acid will rise. A neutral solution is formed if *no excess* of alkali is added

Fig. 10.1 Properties of aqueous solutions of acids.

Any of the reactions given in the table can be used as a *test* for acidity. Equations for the reactions occurring in these tests **using hydrochloric acid as an example of an acid** are:

A base will react with an acid to form a neutral solution of a salt in water.

$$ACID + BASE \rightarrow SALT + WATER,$$

or

$$ACID + ALKALI \rightarrow SALT + WATER.$$

Indicator	Test 1	coloured dye	+ hydrochloric acid →	different colour dye	+ anion of acid
Metal	Test 2	magnesium	+ hydrochloric acid →	magnesium chloride	+ hydrogen gas
		Mg(s)	+ 2HCl(aq) →	MgCl$_2$	+ H$_2$(g)
Carbonate	Test 3	calcium carbonate	+ hydrochloric acid →	calcium chloride	+ carbon dioxide + water
		CaCO$_3$(s)	+ 2HCl(aq) →	CaCl$_2$(aq)	+ CO$_2$(g) + H$_2$O(l)
Base	Test 4	copper(II) oxide	+ hydrochloric acid →	copper(II) chloride	+ water
		CuO(s)	+ 2HCl(aq) →	CuCl$_2$(aq)	+ H$_2$O(l)
Alkali	Test 5	sodium hydroxide	+ hydrochloric acid →	sodium chloride	+ water
		NaOH(aq)	+ HCl(aq) →	NaCl(aq)	+ H$_2$O(l)

Fig. 10.2

2 TESTING FOR BASES

An alkali is a water-soluble base. So alkalis can be recognised by their effect on damp pH paper – they turn it any colour between blue – green (pH 8) and purple (pH 12–14). Using the indicator paper **damp** allows some of the alkali to dissolve in the water and the dyes in the paper respond more quickly. (Note that some pH indicators are 'short range indicators' and detect pH values of from 1–12 only.)

A base which does not dissolve in water will not affect universal indicator paper. It will, however, neutralise an acid.

Whether **a solid substance** is a base is shown in the following test. Put a small amount of acid solution in a beaker. Add a few drops of a pH indicator; the indicator will turn red. Now, add **the substance** a little at a time to the acid. If the pH, as measured by the indicator, **rises**, the indicator colour changes from red to green - then the substance being added is a base. The pH will eventually rise to 7 as the acid becomes completely neutralised. In fact, a solid compound which **dissolves** in an aqueous acid but **does not dissolve in water alone** must be a base.

In this reaction the base reacts with the acid forming a soluble salt and so a **solution** will be formed. Most salts are soluble in water, so most bases dissolve completely in acids.

3 ACIDS AND ACIDITY

It is important to realise that 'acids' become 'acidic' only on dissolving in – **in fact reacting with** – water. This is the reason for using damp indicator paper and for making the tests on **solutions of acids in water**.

Looking at the formulae of a few acids will show that they all contain hydrogen atoms. However, it is not true that **any** substance containing hydrogen will be an acid. **All acids contain hydrogen** but **not all substances which contain hydrogen are acids**.

The table below (Fig. 10.3) shows some compounds containing hydrogen. Some of these compounds are acids but some are not.

❝ Higher pH - lower acidity ❞

Acids	Formula	Not acids	Formula
hydrochloric	HCl	methane	CH$_4$
sulphuric	H$_2$SO$_4$	water	H$_2$O
nitric	HNO$_3$	ethanol	C$_2$H$_5$OH
phosphoric	H$_3$PO$_4$	ammonia	NH$_3$
ethanoic	CH$_3$CO$_2$H	sodium hydroxide	NaOH

Fig. 10.3 Compounds containing hydrogen.

If a compound containing hydrogen reacts with water to form hydrogen ions (see Section 4(b)), then that compound is an acid. The solution formed will contain hydrated protons.

4 SYMBOLS FOR PROTONS AND HYDRATED PROTONS

There are various acceptable ways of showing the presence of hydrated protons in **equations**. The following are all **equivalent** to each other:

$$H_3O^+(aq), H^+(aq), \text{ or just } H^+.$$

A hydrated proton is just what it says, H$^+$ plus a water molecule, H$_2$O(l) or (aq).

(A) TAKING IT FURTHER

❝ Hydrated protons are sometimes called *oxonium ions* or *hydronium ions* ❞

When a substance which we know to form acidic solutions 'dissolves' in water the reaction:

'acid' + water → hydrated proton + anion of the 'acid'

occurs. The hydrated protons formed in this reaction are the **ions responsible for acidity**. For example, when hydrogen chloride gas reacts with water:

$HCl(g) + H_2O(l) \rightarrow H_3O^+(aq) + Cl^-(aq)$

hydrogen chloride + water → hydrated proton + chloride ion.

A hydrogen ion (a proton) is *transferred from the hydrogen chloride* molecule to the water molecule. The $H_3O^+(aq)$ formed in this reaction is what makes hydrochloric acid *an acid*.

A similar reaction occurs when any pure acid is added to water – a hydrated hydrogen ion forms. Acids are therefore **proton donors**. Molecules of acids give protons to water molecules and in doing so create acidity in the resulting solution.

For acids to be able to donate protons to water molecules, or to any other molecules they must obviously contain **hydrogen atoms**. In Fig. 10.3 only those molecules capable of donating one or more protons to water molecules will be acids. Substances containing hydrogen which cannot be donated as protons to water are not acids.

Any substance which can *transfer protons* to another substance is an acid. All the tests given in Fig. 10.1 above are reactions in which protons are being transferred from the acid under test to the reagent being used to carry out the test. **THEY ARE ALL EXAMPLES OF PROTON TRANSFER REACTIONS**, as the following *ionic equations* will show.

Test 1	indicator dye	+	acid	→	(indicator + H)⁺	+	anion of acid	
Test 2	magnesium	+	acid	→	magnesium salt	+	hydrogen gas	
	Mg(s)	+	$2H^+(aq)$	→	$Mg^{2+}(aq)$	+	$H_2(g)$	
Test 3	metal carbonate	+	acid	→	metal salt	+	carbon dioxide + water	
	$CaCO_3(s)$	+	$2H^+(aq)$	→	$Ca^{2+}(aq)$	+	$CO_2(g)$	+ $H_2O(l)$
Test 4	metal oxide or hydroxide	+	acid	→	metal salt	+	water	
	CuO(s)	+	$2H^+(aq)$	→	$Cu^{2+}(aq)$	+	$H_2O(l)$	
	NaOH(aq)	+	$H^+(aq)$	→	$Na^+(aq)$	+	$H_2O(l)$	

Fig. 10.4

(B) STRONG AND WEAK ACIDS

If *equally concentrated* solutions of ethanoic acid and hydrochloric acid are tested with pH paper, the ethanoic acid will show a pH of about two units higher than the hydrochloric acid. The *ethanoic acid is a weaker acid than hydrochloric acid of the same concentration*. The explanation for this lies in the different reactions of the two acids with water.

Hydrogen chloride reacts with water and *completely ionises*:

$HCl(g) + H_2O(l) \rightarrow H_3O^+(aq) + Cl^-(aq)$

hydrogen chloride + water → hydrated proton + chloride ion.

All the molecules of hydrogen chloride are converted into hydrated protons (hydrogen ions). The acid is *fully ionised*. Ethanoic acid molecules, however, do not all react with water molecules. Only about 1% do so. The concentration of hydrated protons (hydrogen ions) is therefore much lower and the pH correspondingly higher.

Other strong acids are sulphuric acid and nitric acid. Other weak acids are carbonic acid and citric acid.

5 > BASES

A base *neutralises* an *acid* to form a *salt* and *water* only. *Oxides* and *hydroxides* of metal are bases. Most bases are not soluble in water, e.g. copper(II) oxide. Those bases that do dissolve in water are given the name *alkalis*. The oxides and hydroxides of group 1 metals are all alkalis, e.g. lithium, sodium and potassium oxides and hydroxides.

(A) TAKING IT FURTHER

Bases as proton acceptors

We have shown, above, that acids are **proton donors**. When acids react with bases the proton they donate is received by the base. Bases are **proton receivers or acceptors**.

There are bases which are not oxides or hydroxides. Carbonates and hydrogencarbonates, for example, are able to neutralise acids (see the section on uses of acids and bases). In fact, any substance which can **accept a proton** can neutralise an acid. Some examples are:

Metal oxides contain the oxide ion O^{2-}:

$$O^{2-}(s) + 2H^+(aq) \rightarrow H_2O(l)$$

oxide ion + protons → water (a neutral liquid).

Metal hydroxides contain the ion OH^-:

$$OH^-(aq) + H^+(aq) \rightarrow H_2O(l)$$

hydroxide ion + proton → water.

Metal carbonates contain the ion CO_3^{2-}:

$$CO_3^{2-}(s) + 2H^+(aq) \rightarrow H_2O(l) + CO_2(g).$$

carbonate ion + protons → water + carbon dioxide.

Metal hydrogencarbonates contain the ion HCO_3^-:

$$HCO_3^-(s) + H^+(aq) \rightarrow H_2O(l) + CO_2(g).$$

hydrogencarbonate ion + proton → water + carbon dioxide.

In each reaction the base **accepts** protons from the acid.

(B) STRONG AND WEAK ALKALIS

> Even *strong* alkalis can have pHs of 8–12 if they are in dilute solution. The distinction between *strong* and *weak* in alkalis, as with acids, is in the *proportion of molecules which are ionised in solution*

As with acids, there are strong and weak alkalis. Alkalis which produce a high concentration of **hydroxide ions** in solution are **strong** alkalis, pH 13–14. Those producing a low concentration are **weak** alkalis, pH 8–12.

Alkali metal hydroxides are strong alkalis; an aqueous solution of ammonia is a weak alkali. Alkali metal hydroxides are ionised to a greater extent than ammonia in solution.

6 > USE OF ACIDS

- The 'sourness' of acids has led to their use in soft drinks and sweets. Citric acid, for instance, is used to give a 'tang' to many sweets and fruit drinks; phosphoric acid is added to colas.
- A dilute (about 5%) solution of ethanoic acid (acetic acid) is **vinegar** (see Chapter 13, Section 7(a)) for its manufacture).
- Carbonates and hydrogencarbonates will react with most acids to give carbon dioxide gas. Release of carbon dioxide can be put to use in cake making where it helps the cake mixture to 'rise' to produce the foamed texture of a typical cake. Cooking 'sets' this structure and prevents its collapse on cooling.
- Cake mixtures contain sodium hydrogencarbonate and tartaric acid. On mixing with **water** the acid and hydrogencarbonate react to produce carbon dioxide which helps the mix to swell, like a balloon being blown up!

sodium hydrogencarbonate + tartaric acid ⟶ sodium tartrate + carbon dioxide + water

- A similar reaction – between **citric acid** and sodium hydrogencarbonate – produces the sharp fizziness of 'sherbet' and the refreshing effervescence of 'Health salts'. Flavouring and sugar are also added to sherbet for a more pleasant taste. 'Health salts' usually contain 'medicinal ingredients' as well.

- Kettle 'fur' and pipe 'scale' removers. Temporary hard water forms a scale when heated (see Chapter 12.5, Section 4). This is a nuisance and also a danger if it blocks pipes connected to water boilers. The scale is calcium carbonate. It also forms on the heating elements of electric kettles where it is called kettle 'fur'. We can make use of acids reaction to remove the 'fur' from kettles and the 'scale' from boiler pipes. As a precaution against the acid corroding (that is dissolving) the metal of the kettle heating element or the boiler pipe, weak acids are usually used for 'scale' or 'fur' removal. Examples of acids used are: citric acid, phosphoric acid, formic acid and sulphamic acid.
- Pickling. The sheet steel processing industry which makes cars and washing machines from steel uses dilute sulphuric acid or hydrochloric acid to remove rust from the steel before painting. The process is known as 'pickling'. Rust is iron oxide; iron oxide is a metallic oxide, metallic oxides are bases and so rust will dissolve in acids.

These facts also explain the use of phosphoric and hydrochloric acids in 'rust removers' which can be bought to remove rust from motor car bodies, etc.

7 > USES OF BASES

The human stomach contains hydrochloric acid of about 0.1 molar concentration. The acid takes part in the food digestion process. Sometimes an excess is produced which causes stomach pains. Clearly, a weak base – non-poisonous, of course – would be the ideal substance to 'cure' this acidity. Indigestion tablets, also called antacids, are mixtures of weak bases. They include calcium carbonate (chalk), magnesium carbonate, magnesium hydroxide, $Mg(OH)_2$, sodium hydrogencarbonate and aluminium hydroxide, $Al(OH)_3$. All these substances will neutralise the excess stomach acid and be harmless if present in slight excess.

Indigestion cure	Base(s) present
Boots' sodamints	$NaHCO_3$
'Rennies'	$CaCO_3 + MgCO_3$
'Settlers'	$CaCO_3 + MgCO_3$

Fig. 10.5

The reactions of these bases with acid in the stomach are follows:

$$NaHCO_3(s) + HCl(aq) \rightarrow NaCl(aq) + CO_2(g) + H_2O(l),$$
$$CaCO_3(s) + 2HCl(aq) \rightarrow CaCl_2(aq) + CO_2(g) + H_2O(l),$$
$$MgCO_3(s) + 2HCl(aq) \rightarrow MgCl_2(aq) + CO_2(g) + H_2O(l).$$

These indigestion tablets neutralise stomach acid and form carbon dioxide gas.

EXPERIMENT 1. A SIMPLE ANALYSIS OF INDIGESTION TABLETS

Using a solution of hydrochloric acid (a concentration of one mole per litre is convenient), find the volume of acid which can just react with one indigestion tablet.

Repeat for several different brands of tablet.

Compare the volumes (or number of drops), of acid and draw a conclusion about which is the most efficient antacid tablet i.e. the one which neutralises most acid.

The apparatus to be used can be as shown in Fig. 10.6. An alternative to a 20 cm³ plastic syringe would be a burette.

Add the acid half a cm³ at a time. There will be a fizzing as the tablet reacts with the acid. When fizzing has stopped, add a little more acid. Repeat until the size of the tablet is much reduced and then **add the acid a drop at a time** until you can detect no more fizzing.

The acid added has now **dissolved** the tablet. (There may remain a small amount of white powder, ignore this – it is starch added to the powdered antacid as it is pressed into tablet form. The starch binds the powder particles together helping the tablet to remain intact.)

An alternative to adding acid until there is no more fizzing is to put three drops of an indicator solution into the beaker with the tablet before the acid is added. An indicator that changes colour **distinctly** when the tablet has reacted is useful here. Such an

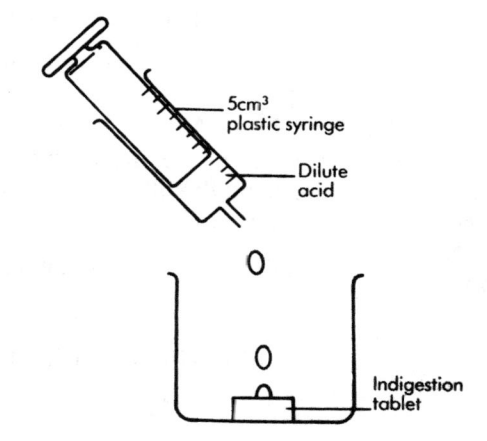

Fig. 10.6 Neutralising an indigestion tablet.

indicator is **screened methyl orange** which changes from green to red. Universal indicator would change very gradually from blue to pink and it would be difficult to find the exact point at which the tablet had *just* dissolved in the acid (green colour in the indicator).

Draw up your results in a form which displays the efficiencies of the tablets as acid-neutralising reagents – antacids – for comparison (i.e. bar chart, pie chart, etc.).

8 SALTS

Salts are formed as products of neutralisation of acids and bases. The methods of preparation of salts in laboratories or in industry, however, are not confined to neutralisation reactions.

METHODS OF PREPARING SALTS IN THE LABORATORY

The method of preparation of any salt depends on the solubility in water of the substances used to make it and on the solubility of the salt itself (Fig. 10.7).

Salts	Solubility	Method of preparation
carbonates	all insoluble *except* sodium, potassium and ammonium	precipitation if insoluble, e.g. $CaCO_3$ or $CuCO_3$
sulphates	all soluble *except* barium, calcium and lead sulphates	dilute sulphuric acid on metal, metal oxide or metal carbonate for soluble salts; precipitation for insoluble sulphates
nitrates	all soluble	dilute nitric acid on metal, metal oxide or metal carbonate
chlorides	all soluble *except* silver and lead chlorides	dilute hydrochloric acid on metal, metal oxide or metal carbonate; precipitation for insoluble chlorides

Fig. 10.7 Table of solubilities of salts and methods of preparation.

The method of preparation can be divided into four classes:

- direct reaction between the elements, e.g. iron(III) chloride;
- precipitation method for insoluble salts;
- metal, metal oxide or metal carbonate with acids for all soluble salts;
- titration method for sodium and potassium salts.

(i) Synthesis

Direct reaction has been illustrated elsewhere in the text, see Chapter 6, Section 6. The process is called **synthesis**. Compounds formed by this method include iron(III) chloride, sodium chloride and iron(II) sulphide:

sodium + chlorine → sodium chloride

iron + sulphur → iron(II) sulphide.

(ii) Precipitation

This involves the mixing of two solutions. One solution should contain the chosen **metal** ions and the other the chosen **non-metallic** ions. The salt forms immediately on mixing and can be filtered off, washed with water and dried in a warm oven:

lead(II) nitrate + sodium chloride → lead(II) chloride + sodium nitrate

$$Pb(NO_3)_2(aq) + 2NaCl(aq) \rightarrow PbCl_2(s) + 2NaNO_3(aq).$$

silver nitrate + hydrochloric acid → silver chloride + nitric acid

$$AgNO_3(aq) + HCl(aq) \rightarrow AgCl(s) + HNO_3(aq).$$

barium chloride + sodium sulphate → barium sulphate + sodium chloride

$$BaCl_2(aq) + Na_2SO_4(aq) \rightarrow BaSO_4(s) + 2NaCl(aq).$$

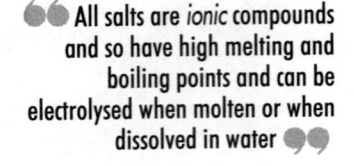

> All salts are *ionic* compounds and so have high melting and boiling points and can be electrolysed when molten or when dissolved in water

> Try writing the ionic equations for these reactions.

(iii) Reactions between an acid and a metal, metal oxide or metal carbonate

The above three types of reaction are very similar. They rely upon the fact that the three types of solid reactants are **not soluble in water**, but react with acid to form soluble salts and other products.

The method is almost identical for all three and so will be described as one method.

(1) The acid to be used is first chosen:

dilute sulphuric acid will form sulphates;
dilute nitric acid will form nitrates;
dilute hydrochloric acid will form chlorides.

(2) The metal-containing compound is then chosen:

metals will react with acid to product **hydrogen gas** and the salt solution required;
metal oxides neutralise the acid with **no gas production** to form the salt solution required;
metal carbonates react with acids to give **carbon dioxide** and the salt solution required.

(3) A quantity of the acid is measured into a beaker. The powdered solid chosen is then added, a little at a time until **no more will react**. In the cases of the metal and the metal carbonate, this will be shown by no further fizzing of the mixture (Fig. 10.8).

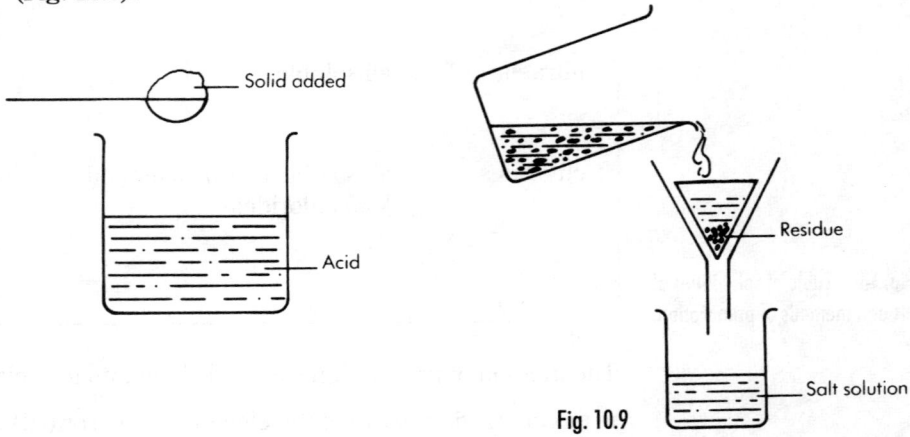

Fig. 10.8

Fig. 10.9

(4) The acid has now been neutralised and excess solid has only water to dissolve in. **Since none of these solids dissolve in water**, the excess will remain as a **residue**. The mixture is **filtered**. The **filtrate** is a solution of the required salt (Fig. 10.9).

(5) The pure crystalline salt can be obtained from the solution by concentrating it until it becomes **saturated** with the salt. This is done by careful evaporation to drive off **most of the water**, but not all. The solution is saturated when a sample

taken out and cooled gives crystals. When this occurs, the rest of the solution can be cooled and will deposit crystals (Fig. 10.10).

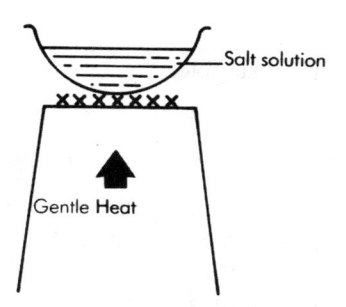

Fig. 10.10

Dry with tissue

(6) The salt can be filtered from the mixture and the crystals on the filter paper *washed* with a little distilled water and dried with *tissue*. Pure crystals should not be wet!

Salts prepared in this way include hydrated copper(II) sulphate, hydrated magnesium sulphate and hydrated iron(II) sulphate.

Copper(II) sulphate crystals cannot be made by reacting the *metal* with acid because copper metal is not reactive enough to dissolve in dilute sulphuric acid. Instead the oxide or carbonate is used:

$$CuO(s) + H_2SO_4(aq) \rightarrow CuSO_4(aq) + H_2O(l)$$

copper(II) oxide + sulphuric acid → copper(II) sulphate + water.

$$CuCO_3(s) + H_2SO_4(aq) \rightarrow CuSO_4(aq) + CO_2(g) + H_2O(l)$$

copper(II) carbonate + sulphuric acid → copper(II) sulphate + carbon dioxide + water.

Magnesium salts can be prepared from magnesium metal, the oxide or the carbonate. All react with acids to give the salt and water as the only products left after filtration, e.g.

$$Mg(s) + H_2SO_4(aq) \rightarrow MgSO_4(aq) + H_2(g)$$

magnesium + sulphuric acid → magnesium sulphate + hydrogen.

The equations for the reaction of the oxide and carbonate are similar to those for the copper compounds above.

Drying crystals of salts. The drying process must be done at a *low temperature* and not by heating using a burner. This is because many salts contain *water of crystallisation*, that is, they are *hydrated crystals*. If such crystals are heated to dryness they will *decompose* into the *anhydrous* salt, containing no water of crystallisation, and *water vapour*. Usually, the hydrated salt is the required product.

If, for example, copper(II) sulphate crystals are dried by heating the following *dehydration* reaction occurs:

$$CuSO_4 \cdot 5H_2O(s) \rightarrow CuSO_4(s) + 5H_2O(g).$$

hydrated copper(II) sulphate → copper(II) sulphate + steam

The result is a *white powder* instead of *blue crystals*. White *anhydrous copper sulphate* is formed.

Drying is quite easily done by soaking up excess liquid from the crystals and *leaving them in a warm place* to dry.

A crystalline salt which does not have water of crystallisation, such as sodium chloride, *can* be heated to dryness to obtain a product.

(iv) Titration method

All compounds of sodium and potassium are soluble in water. For this reason it is not possible to add one reagent in excess and to filter the excess off in order to obtain a solution of the required salt, as in method (iii).

To overcome this difficulty, exact quantities of the two reacting compounds are mixed by *titrating one into the other using an indicator to show when the correct reacting amount has been added*. These reactions are usually between an acid and an alkali:

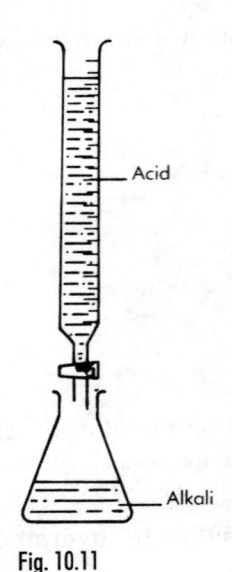

$$\text{acid} + \text{alkali} \rightarrow \text{salt} + \text{water}.$$

For example,

$$\text{hydrochloric acid} + \text{sodium hydroxide} \rightarrow \text{sodium chloride} + \text{water}$$

$$HCl(aq) + NaOH(aq) \rightarrow NaCl(aq) + H_2O(l).$$

The reaction can be followed by watching the colour of an indicator in the mixture. Acid is added, a little at a time from a burette to a flask containing a measured volume of alkali containing two drops of an acid–base indicator. When the colour of the indicator *just* changes, the titration is stopped. The correct volume of acid to neutralise the alkali has been found.

If the titration is now *repeated without the indicator* but using the volume of acid measured in the first titration, a salt solution will have been made *free from indicator*. Evaporation to crystallisation will give pure crystals of the salt. The crystals can be separated and dried by the method described above which, for sodium chloride, can be by heating.

Fig. 10.11

(v) Titration as a method of finding the concentration of an acid or an alkali

The method used in (iv) to prepare a salt can also be used to determine the unknown concentration of an acid or an alkali.

We shall take the results of a typical titration to show how this is done.

25.00 cm³ of a solution of sodium hydroxide of known concentration, 2 mol/dm³ is placed in a 250 cm³ conical flask. A burette is filled with hydrochloric acid of unknown concentration **M** moles/dm³. Two drops of phenolphthalein indicator is added to the flask of alkali (see Fig. 10.11).

Suppose that 23.50 cm³ of the acid is needed to change the colour of the indicator from pink to colourless. This volume of acid just neutralises the alkali in the flask. The concentration of the acid many now be calculated.

The equation for the reaction is:

$$\underset{\text{1 mole}}{NaOH(aq)} + \underset{\text{1 mole}}{HCl(aq)} \longrightarrow NaCl(aq) + H_2O(l)$$

The equation tells us that equal numbers of moles of acid and alkali have reacted. Hence

moles of acid = moles of alkali

$$\text{Moles of alkali} = \frac{25.00 \times 2}{1000}$$

$$\text{Moles of acid} = \frac{23.50 \times M}{1000}$$

These two must be equal

Therefore $\quad \dfrac{25.00 \times 2}{1000} = \dfrac{23.50 \times M}{1000}$

Leading to $\quad \dfrac{25.00 \times 2 \times 1000}{23.50 \times 1000} = M$

and $\quad M = \dfrac{25.00 \times 2}{23.50} = 2.12 \text{ mol/dm}^3$

The concentration of the hydrochloric acid is 2.12 mol/dm³.

9 USES AND ANALYSIS OF SALTS

(A) USES OF SALTS

Many of the most useful substances are salts. A few examples are given below, others will be discussed as their chemistry is studied elsewhere in the text.

salt	use
ammonium salts	fertilisers
barium sulphate	'barium meal' before a stomach X-ray
calcium sulphate	gypsum wall plaster: plaster of Paris for setting broken limbs
iron(II) sulphate	'iron tablets' for anaemia
magnesium sulphate	a laxative in some 'health salts'
silver chloride	photographic film emulsion
sodium carbonate	water softener

Fig. 10.12

(B) ANALYSIS OF SALTS

All salts contain **cations** and **anions**. The following tables summarise the reactions of cations and anions found in the most common salts. Using the reagents shown and noting the results of the tests should allow the identification of the cation and anion in any simple salt.

First dissolve the unknown solid in water to make a **solution**. To identify the **cation** in the salt, use the following scheme (Fig. 10.13):

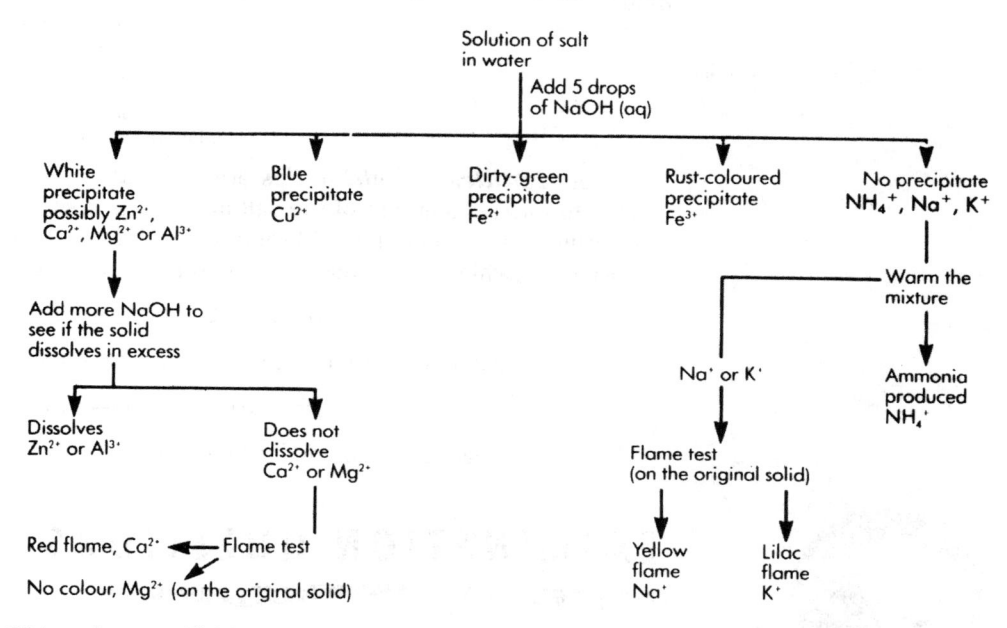

Solution of salt in water
Add 5 drops of NaOH (aq)

- White precipitate possibly Zn^{2+}, Ca^{2+}, Mg^{2+} or Al^{3+}
  - Add more NaOH to see if the solid dissolves in excess
    - Dissolves Zn^{2+} or Al^{3+}
    - Does not dissolve Ca^{2+} or Mg^{2+}
      - Flame test (on the original solid)
      - Red flame, Ca^{2+}
      - No colour, Mg^{2+}
- Blue precipitate Cu^{2+}
- Dirty-green precipitate Fe^{2+}
- Rust-coloured precipitate Fe^{3+}
- No precipitate NH_4^+, Na^+, K^+
  - Na^+ or K^+
    - Flame test (on the original solid)
    - Yellow flame Na^+
    - Lilac flame K^+
  - Warm the mixture
    - Ammonia produced NH_4^+

Fig. 10.13 Scheme to identify the *cation* in the salt.

This scheme will identify the cations included in all **non-Nuffield** syllabuses. Some Nuffield syllabuses do not require cation analyses. However, study your own syllabus carefully before using this scheme and the one below. No one syllabus requires all the above ions to be identified

Flame tests

Very few metal ions produce flame colours. Those that do, however, can easily be identified. The ***flame test*** is usually done on the solid salt. Dip a new piece of **nichrome wire** into some **concentrated** hydrochloric acid. ***Next dip the end of the wire into the solid to be tested***. This procedure produces a small amount of the ***chloride of the metal*** on the wire tip. This chloride will vaporise in the flame when the tip of the wire is put into it. If a coloured flame is seen the table below will help to identify the metal present. Flame tests are not used to identify non-metal ions.

Metal ion	Flame colour
sodium	persistent yellow
copper	blue/green
calcium	a 'flash' of red
potassium	faint purple/lilac

To identify the **anion** in the salt use the following scheme (Fig. 10.14):

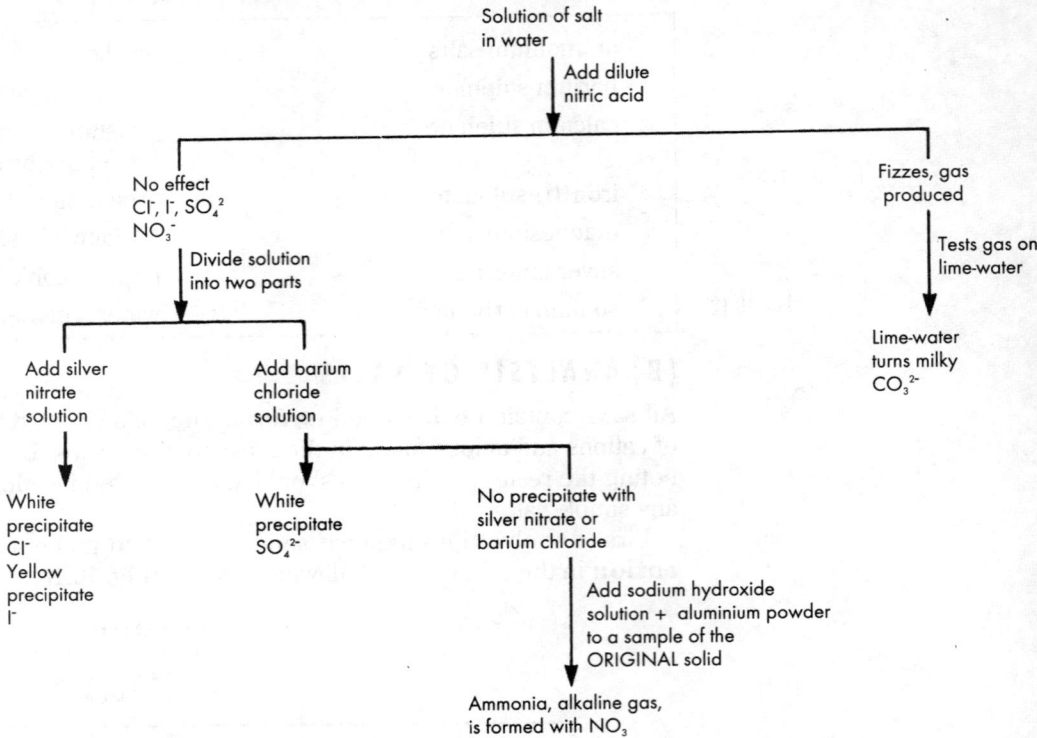

```
                    Solution of salt
                       in water
                          │
                       Add dilute
                       nitric acid
          ┌───────────────┴───────────────┐
       No effect                      Fizzes, gas
    Cl⁻, I⁻, SO₄²⁻                     produced
        NO₃⁻                              │
          │                          Tests gas on
    Divide solution                   lime-water
     into two parts                       │
          │                          Lime-water
    ┌─────┴─────┐                    turns milky
 Add silver  Add barium                 CO₃²⁻
 nitrate    chloride
 solution   solution
    │          │
    │      ┌───┴────────────┐
  White   White        No precipitate with
precipitate precipitate  silver nitrate or
   Cl⁻      SO₄²⁻       barium chloride
  Yellow                        │
precipitate              Add sodium hydroxide
   I⁻                   solution + aluminium powder
                          to a sample of the
                            ORIGINAL solid
                                │
                         Ammonia, alkaline gas,
                         is formed with NO₃⁻
```

Fig. 10.14 Scheme to identify the *anion* in the salt.

Where *iodides* and *chlorides* are to be identified on the same syllabus a better test is to make a solution of the salt and to add a solution of lead nitrate made acidic with dilute nitric acid. The chloride and iodide of lead are distinctly different. Lead chloride is a white precipitate and lead iodide a brilliant yellow precipitate:

$$Pb^{2+}(aq) + 2Cl^-(aq) \rightarrow PbCl_2(s)$$

lead ions + chloride ions → white precipitate of lead chloride.

$$Pb^{2+}(aq) + 2I^-(aq) \rightarrow PbI_2(s)$$

lead ions + iodide ions → yellow precipitate of lead iodide.

EXAMINATION QUESTIONS

MULTIPLE CHOICE

QUESTIONS 1–6

are about the pH of solutions.

A 1
B 4
C 7
D 10
E 14

Choose from A–E the pH of:

1. a strongly acidic solution.
2. pure water.
3. a weakly acidic solution.
4. a neutral solution.
5. bench dilute potassium hydroxide solution.
6. a mixture of ethanol and water.

(ULEAC)

STRUCTURED QUESTIONS

QUESTION 7

Complete the table below, which describes the preparation of some salts.

(6 marks)

(SEG)

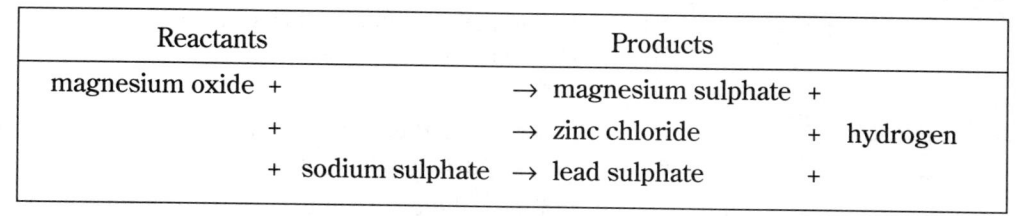

Reactants	Products
magnesium oxide +	→ magnesium sulphate +
+	→ zinc chloride + hydrogen
+ sodium sulphate	→ lead sulphate +

QUESTION 8

This question is about acids and their reactions.
(a) When a dilute acid reacts with a metal a gas is produced. What is the name of this gas? *(1)*
Name of gas ....
(b) Put names in the boxes below to form a word equation describing one reaction between a dilute acid and a metal. *(1)*

☐ + dilute ☐ → ☐ + ☐
(name of metal)   (name of acid)   (name of gas)   (name of other substance formed)

Sodium hydroxide solution reacts with dilute sulphuric acid.
(c) What type of substance is sodium hydroxide? (1 line) *(1)*
(d) What is this sort of reaction called? (1 line) *(1)*
(e) Write a word equation for this reaction. (1 line) *(2)*
(f) Write a symbol equation for this reaction. (1 line) *(2)*
(g) Describe how you would use this reaction in the laboratory to prepare a dry crystalline sample of the salt formed. Include all of the stages necessary to obtain the final product. (8 lines) *(5)*
(h) Vinegar is a mixture of ethanoic (acetic) acid and water. Vinegar is sometimes made from wine. What is it in the wine which is changed into ethanoic acid to make the vinegar? (1 line) *(1)*
(i) 'Heartburn' is a sensation caused by the presence of too much acid in the stomach. Name one substance often used to reduce the amount of acid and cure the heartburn. (1 line) *(1)*
(j) Aluminium nitrate is formed when aluminium hydroxide is dissolved in nitric acid. How much aluminium nitrate is produced when 7.8 g of aluminium hydroxide is completely dissolved in nitric acid

$$Al(OH)_3 + 3HNO_3 \rightarrow Al(NO_3)_3 + 3H_2O.$$ *(3)*

(Relative atomic masses: Al = 27, O = 16, N = 14, H = 1.
Answer ....g.

(18 marks)
(NISEAC)

QUESTION 9

Cadmium (Cd) is an element in the same group of the periodic table as zinc. Cadmium carbonate is insoluble in water and reacts in the same way as zinc carbonate with dilute acids. Cadmium sulphate is soluble in water and crystallises as a salt hydrate.
(i) Give the formulae of cadmium carbonate and cadmium sulphate. (1 line) *(1)*
(ii) Describe the preparation of a dry, crystalline sample of hydrated cadmium sulphate from cadmium carbonate. (8 lines) *(5)*

(WJEC)

CHAPTER 10 ACIDS, BASES AND SALTS

FREE RESPONSE QUESTIONS

QUESTION 10

Acid indigestion is caused by excess hydrochloric acid HCl in the stomach. There may be 1 dm³ of 0.10 M hydrochloric acid present.

Two brands of indigestion tablets contain the following 'active ingredients':

Brand A: Each tablet contains 0.75 g calcium carbonate $CaCO_3$ – cost £0.50 per 100.
Brand B: Each tablet contains 0.58 g magnesium hydroxide $Mg(OH)_2$ – cost £0.60 per 100

Calculate which of these tablets would neutralise more acid and hence be more effective in curing acid indigestion. Decide which is better value for money.

Devise and describe a simple experiment which would enable you to confirm which brand of tablet was most effective in neutralising acids.

(H = 1; O = 16; Mg = 24; Ca = 40.)

(10 marks)

QUESTION 11

The four substances listed in the table below are all chemicals used in the home. The table shows the results expected for each substance in each of three simple tests.

Substance	add water then indicator	Action of gentle heat on sample	Action of acid on substance
Sodium carbonate	Alkaline	No reaction	Odourless gas
Sodium hydrogencarbonate	Alkaline	Gas evolved	Odourless gas
Citric acid	Acidic	No reaction	No reaction
Calcium chlorate (I)	Alkaline	No reaction	Gas with a strong smell

Devise an identification key which will show how this information could be used to identify an unknown solid as one of these substances.

(5 marks)

OUTLINE ANSWERS

MULTIPLE CHOICE

ANSWERS 1–6

See Section 1 for the discussion of pH.
1. A. The **lowest pH** is the **most strongly acidic**.
2. C. pH 7 is neither acidic nor alkaline - it is neutral.
3. B. pH 4 is **less acidic** than pH 1.
4. C. pH 7 is neutral.
5. E. Potassium hydroxide (like sodium hydroxide) is a strong **alkali** so has the **highest** pH.
6. C. Ethanol and water are both neutral liquids. When mixed they do not react with each other, so the mixture will also be neutral.

STRUCTURED QUESTIONS

ANSWER 7

Salt preparations are discussed in Section 8 and summarised in Fig. 10.7.
This question can be answered from the information in these references.

ANSWER 8

66 See Chapter 12.1.1 99

(a) The gas is **hydrogen**. Hydrogen is produced by the reaction of **any metal** *which is higher in the reactivity series than hydrogen* with dilute sulphuric or hydrochloric acids.

See Chapter 12.1.1

(b) Any metal more reactive than copper will do. Do not choose dilute nitric acid, it does not produce hydrogen with metals.

See Chapter 12.1.1

(c) Sodium hydroxide is a **strong alkali**.
(d) Neutralisation occurs.
(e) Sodium hydroxide + sulphuric acid → sodium sulphate + water.
(f) $H_2SO_4(aq) + 2NaOH(aq) \rightarrow Na_2SO_4(aq) + 2H_2O(l)$.

Note that **two moles** of sodium hydroxide neutralises **one** mole **of sulphuric acid. This is because each molecule of** sulphuric acid has **two hydrogen atoms capable of becoming hydrogen ions**. Each of these hydrogen ions will react with **one** hydroxide ion from sodium hydroxide – hence two moles of sodium hydroxide are needed for every mole of sulphuric acid.

(g) The method is exactly as described in Section 8(iv), but the acid and alkali chosen are as required by the question. There are 5 steps for one mark each.

See Section 8(iv)

(h) Ethanoic acid is formed when ethanol is oxidised by bacterial action. It is oxygen from the air and enzymes from the bacteria that cause the oxidation or 'souring' of wine.

See Section 7

(i) 'Heartburn' or 'acid indigestion' may be cured by neutralising excess acid in the stomach with a **weak alkali**, e.g. sodium hydrogencarbonate.

(j) The equation must be 'read' here. It shows that **one mole of aluminium hydroxide** reacts with **three moles of nitric acid** to form **one mole of aluminium nitrate** and **three moles of water**.

In this reaction all the aluminium hydroxide will dissolve because **all nitrates are soluble in water**.

The mass of aluminium nitrate depends on the mass of aluminium hydroxide dissolved. Remember to 'read' the equation. **The calculation concerns only the aluminium hydroxide and the aluminium nitrate formed from it**. One mole of aluminium hydroxide forms one mole of aluminium nitrate.

Formula mass of $Al(OH)_3$ is $27 + (16 + 1) + (16 + 1) + (16 + 1) = 78$ g.

Formula mass of $Al(NO_3)_3$ is $27 + 3 \times (14 + 16 + 16 + 16) = 213$ g.

So 78 g of aluminium hydroxide gives 213 g of aluminium nitrate. Therefore 7.8 g (exactly one-tenth of a mole – for ease of calculation!) will produce 21.3 g of aluminium nitrate.

There are two marks for the two formula mass calculations and one mark for the final answer.

What happens if you make a mistake?

It is easy to make an arithmetical error in a calculation like the one above. An examiner does not give marks **only** for the correct answer. If you **carry through** your mistakes but use **the correct method of solving the problem** you will gain credit for **all correct steps other than the one you made your mistake in!** This could get you full marks minus one.

ANSWER 9

(a) (i) Cadmium is a metal which is **not directly studied** for the examination. For this reason, candidates are **given** information about it which should **enable them** to answer the questions that follow.

The **'message'** is that cadmium is **like zinc** in its chemistry. This should give the formulae of the two cadmium salts to a candidate who knows, or can work out the formulae, of the corresponding zinc salts. Zinc forms ions with **two positive charges**. The formulae of its compounds are similar to those of group two metals such as magnesium and calcium. The same will be true, therefore, of cadmium salts. $CdCO_3$ **and** $CdSO_4$ **are the salts in question**.

(ii) The salt preparation asked for here is of a **soluble salt from an insoluble compound**. The crystals must be dry and are in fact *hydrated*, so the drying method is important. The **five marks** will be for **five distinct steps**. The first step has been taken for you – the reactants have been chosen!

ANSWER 10

The cure of 'acid indigestion' is an important use of the chemical reaction called *neutralisation*. This question is one of the more difficult questions that candidates hoping for higher grades will have to attempt.

The amount of acid in the stomach of the indigestion sufferer is said to be about 1 dm^3 of 0.10 M hydrochloric acid. We must work in moles for the calculation.

(a) How many moles of hydrochloric acid? If 1000 cm^3 contains 0.10 moles (that is the meaning of 0.10 M) then there will be 0.10 moles of hydrochloric acid, HCl, in the stomach to be neutralised.

(b) How much 'active ingredient' is needed for the neutralisation? Here we need the equations for the two different neutralisation.

$$CaCO_3 + 2HCl \rightarrow CaCl_2 + CO_2 + H_2O$$

and

$$Mg(OH)_2 + 2HCl \rightarrow MgCl_2 + CO_2 + H_2O$$

You should notice that the equation tells us that *one mole of each 'active ingredient'* reacts with *two moles of acid*.

Both 'active ingredients' are the same *in this respect*, i.e. one mole of each neutralises two moles of acid.

(i) One mole of calcium carbonate, CaCO$_3$, is 40 + 12 + (16 × 3) = 100 g.
(ii) One mole of magnesium hydroxide, Mg(OH)$_2$, is 24 + (16 + 1) + (16 + 1) = 58 g
(iii) 58 g of magnesium hydroxide neutralises the same amount (2 moles) of acid as 100 g of calcium carbonate.
(iv) 0.58 g (1 Brand B tablet) of magnesium hydroxide will neutralise the same amount of acid as 1.0 g (1.33 Brand A tablets) of calcium carbonate.
(v) Conclusion: one Brand B tablet will be more effective than one Brand A tablet.
(vi) Value for money. This is quite a difficult idea to grasp.

Think of the cost of *equal 'amounts' of neutralisation*. One tablet of Brand A costs 0.50p so 1.33 tablets ((iv) above) will cost 1.33 × 0.50p = 0.67p.

One tablet of Brand B costs 0.60p and has the same effect as 1.33 Brand A tablets costing 0.67p. Brand B is therefore better value for money.

An experiment to confirm which brand was the most effective in neutralising acids is described in the earlier text. It should be modified to compare two tablets instead of three as in the text.

❝ See Section 7 ❞

Marking by impression

The question above is marked 'by impression'. This means that the examiner will look to see if the candidate has some sensible idea of how to do the calculation and how to devise, i.e., design an experiment. Neither a perfect calculation nor a perfect experimental design will be required for full marks.

ANSWER 11

There is more than one possible scheme to be suggested here. Remember that you are not being tested on your memory of having done this in the course! You should be able to work out a scheme for yourself using the information given.

One possible scheme is:

Three of the substances are alkaline, the fourth acidic. A test with indicator paper will immediately identify the 'odd-one-out' – the acid – which will turn the paper orange showing it to be a weak acid. This is citric acid.

Gentle heating will produce a gas with one of the remaining three substances, but no gas with the other two. The substance which gives a gas on heating is sodium hydrogencarbonate (bicarbonate of soda).

❝ Chlorine is the strong smelling gas. ❞

Adding an acid produces a strong-smelling gas with one of the remaining two substances, but an odourless gas with the other. The substance producing the strong-smelling gas is calcium chlorate; the other solid must be sodium carbonate as it is the only solid not so far identified.

The question asks for a key. One way of arranging a key is to ask questions about the results of the tests to which the answer is yes or no.

We could do the three suggested tests and ask the questions:

(1) Is the pH of the solution less than 7?   Yes – Citric acid
                                              No – Do the next test

(2) Is a gas produced on heating?   Yes – Sodium hydrogencarbonate
                                              No – Do the next test

(3) Is a strong-smelling gas formed on   Yes – Calcium chlorate(I)
    reaction with an acid?   No – Sodium carbonate

Another way is to display the results in the form of a pyramid:

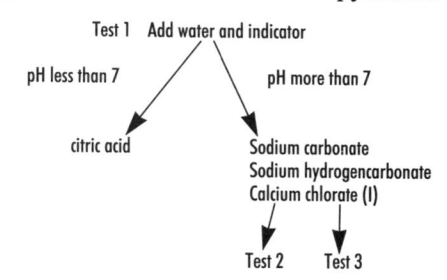

```
                  Test 1  Add water and indicator
              ↙                              ↘
     pH less than 7                     pH more than 7
         ↓                                    ↓
     citric acid                       Sodium carbonate
                                       Sodium hydrogencarbonate
                                       Calcium chlorate (I)
                                           ↓        ↓
                                         Test 2   Test 3
```

You should try to devise for yourself what test you would use as 2 and 3.

STUDENT'S ANSWER – EXAMINER'S COMMENTS

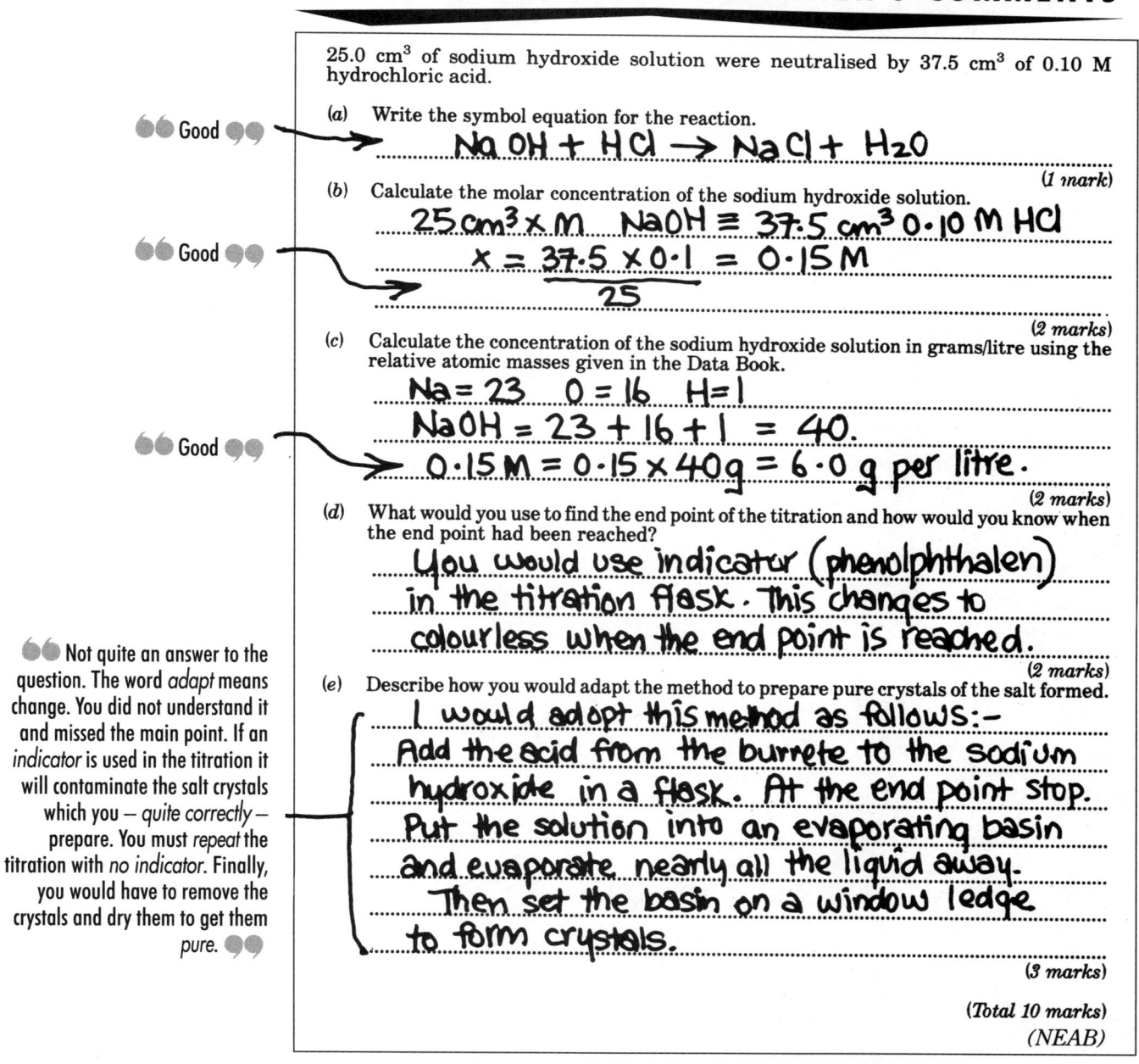

25.0 cm³ of sodium hydroxide solution were neutralised by 37.5 cm³ of 0.10 M hydrochloric acid.

(a) Write the symbol equation for the reaction.

❝ Good ❞ → NaOH + HCl → NaCl + H₂O

(1 mark)

(b) Calculate the molar concentration of the sodium hydroxide solution.

❝ Good ❞
$$25 \text{ cm}^3 \times M \text{ NaOH} = 37.5 \text{ cm}^3 \ 0.10 \text{ M HCl}$$
$$x = \frac{37.5 \times 0.1}{25} = 0.15 \text{ M}$$

(2 marks)

(c) Calculate the concentration of the sodium hydroxide solution in grams/litre using the relative atomic masses given in the Data Book.

❝ Good ❞
Na = 23   O = 16   H = 1
NaOH = 23 + 16 + 1 = 40.
0.15 M = 0.15 × 40 g = 6.0 g per litre.

(2 marks)

(d) What would you use to find the end point of the titration and how would you know when the end point had been reached?

You would use indicator (phenolphthalen) in the titration flask. This changes to colourless when the end point is reached.

(2 marks)

(e) Describe how you would adapt the method to prepare pure crystals of the salt formed.

❝ Not quite an answer to the question. The word *adapt* means change. You did not understand it and missed the main point. If an *indicator* is used in the titration it will contaminate the salt crystals which you – quite correctly – prepare. You must *repeat* the titration with *no indicator*. Finally, you would have to remove the crystals and dry them to get them pure. ❞

I would adopt this method as follows:—
Add the acid from the burrete to the sodium hydroxide in a flask. At the end point stop. Put the solution into an evaporating basin and evaporate nearly all the liquid away. Then set the basin on a window ledge to form crystals.

(3 marks)

(Total 10 marks)
(NEAB)

REVIEW SHEET

- **Salts** are formed by reacting _____
  _____

- **Universal indicator** will **measure** the acidity or alkalinity of a substance on a scale called a _____ **scale**. This scale runs from _____ to with pH being neither acid nor alkaline – that is, _____

- Why is **universal indicator** often preferred to **litmus paper** as a test for acids?
  _____
  _____

- A **base** is _____
  _____

- An **alkali** is _____
  _____

- Any substance which can **transfer protons** to another substance is called an
  _____

- Why is ethanoic acid a weaker acid than hydrochloric acid of the same concentration?
  _____
  _____

- Oxides and hydroxides of metals are _____
  _____

- Aklalis which produce a _____ concentration of **hydroxide ions** in solution are **strong** alkalis, pH 13–14. Those producing a _____ concentration are **weak** alkalis, pH 8–12.

- List some of the uses of acids _____

  1 _____

  2 _____

  3 _____

  4 _____

  5 _____

- List four types of method for preparing salts in a laboratory

    1 _____

    2 _____

    3 _____

    4 _____

    List five salts together with their uses

    1 _____

    2 _____

    3 _____

    4 _____

    5 _____

- Describe how you might identify a **cation** in a salt _____

    _____

    _____

    _____

    _____

    _____

- Describe how you might identify an **anion** in a salt _____

    _____

    _____

    _____

    _____

    _____

    _____

CHAPTER 11

METALS AND OTHER STRONG MATERIALS

- USES OF METALS
- ALLOYS
- THE REACTIVITY SERIES
- REACTIVITY AND DISPLACEMENTS
- THE EXTRACTION OF METALS
- THE ABUNDANCE OF METAL RESOURCES
- CHOICE OF THE METHOD OF EXTRACTION
- METALS IN HISTORY
- ALUMINIUM EXTRACTION
- THE CHEMICAL RESISTANCE OF ALUMINIUM
- THE EXTRACTION OF IRON IN A BLAST FURNACE
- IRON SMELTING
- ZINC AND LEAD EXTRACTION
- SILVER EXTRACTION

GETTING STARTED

Metals are elements which have *most* or *all* of the following *properties*.

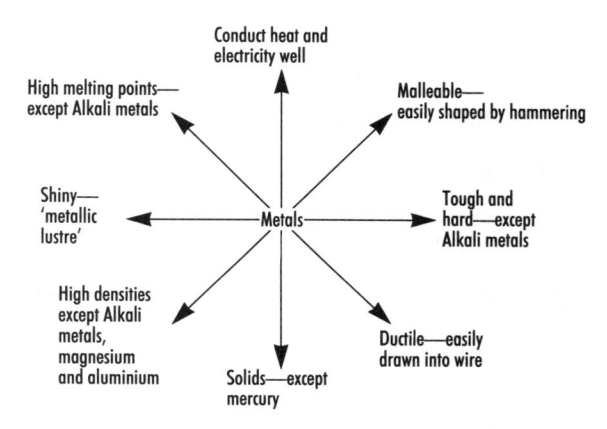

Diagram showing properties of metals radiating from the word "Metals":
- Conduct heat and electricity well
- High melting points—except Alkali metals
- Malleable—easily shaped by hammering
- Shiny—'metallic lustre'
- Tough and hard—except Alkali metals
- High densities except Alkali metals, magnesium and aluminium
- Ductile—easily drawn into wire
- Solids—except mercury

You will have noticed that there are exceptions to some of the general properties of metals. In fact, there are more exceptions than are mentioned above. The chart applies only to the properties of the metals studied at GCSE level.

The metal gallium, for instance would melt in the palm of your hand; tungsten is too hard to shape by hand-hammering. Gold is a soft metal - so soft it is rarely used pure for making any object that needs to retain its shape in use. Gold is usually alloyed with copper to harden it - for instance in much 'gold' jewellery.

There are also non-metals that have some of the properties of metals. Graphite, an allotrope of carbon, for example is a good conductor of electricity and is used as the positive terminal of dry cells in batteries. The semi-metal or metalloid, silicon, when 'doped' with small amounts of other elements, becomes a weak electrical conductor and is used in transistors and microchips.

Strong materials are used in the construction and fabrication of buildings and everyday items of equipment and consumer products. The commonest strong materials in use are **metals** and **ceramics**. **Composite** materials such as fibreglass reinforced resin and carbon-fibre composites are being used in a growing number of products.

ESSENTIAL PRINCIPLES

1 USES OF METALS

Fig. 11.1 shows those common *characteristics* of metals that are used in the manufacture of everyday items of equipment and machinery.

Property	Use	Metal
toughness	equipment and machinery that will be knocked about with use – steel	iron
metallic sheen	mirrors, reflectors	aluminium silver
reflecting heat and light	coating of firemen's protective clothing: space 'shuttle' heat shield of gold foil	aluminium gold
malleability	easy shaping of metal structures by presses, also 'hand beating' of metals into shape – brass	zinc copper
ductility	wide variety of wires – electrical and ornamental	copper aluminium gold
high melting point	wires for electric fires, metals for boilers, cookers, pans, electric light filaments	iron aluminium tungsten (m.p. about 3500°C)
good heat conductivity	radiators in central heating systems, copper for cooking pans	aluminium iron copper
good electrical conductivity	electrical wiring	copper aluminium
corrosion resistance	roofing, flashings, foil and food containers – soft drink and beer cans, zinc coating – 'galvanised' steel	lead aluminium iron zinc
low density	aircraft construction, lightweight vehicles and wheels	aluminium magnesium

Fig. 11.1 Common characteristics of metals.

Individual metals have characteristics of their own which make them more useful than other metals for a particular purpose. *Iron*, for instance, has the special property of being ***easily magnetised***; *gold*, the rare property of ***never corroding***. It would be pointless to try to make a magnet out of gold so that it would last forever, because gold will not magnetise! It would be equally pointless to make a wedding ring out of iron rather than gold just because iron is cheaper.

Though not strictly a characteristic of a metal, the ***cost*** of the metal must also be taken into account. Nails are more often made from steel than other metals because of the strength and cheapness of steel – there are metals that would be equally suitable but much more costly.

The choice of a metal or alloy for a particular use, then, depends on the special properties of that metal or alloy and its cost.

Testing Strong Materials

Most materials used in manufacturing and building are under **stress** of one type or another; stresses which are tending to pull, bend, twist or squash them. Every material has a measurable strength which relates to each of these stresses. Engineers must know whether their chosen materials will withstand the stresses they will encounter in service. Only then can they make a correct choice of material to use.

Any material that is to be made into a usable article must be **cast, pressed, machined or forged** into shape; they must be **fabricated**.

The terms used to describe the properties of metals and other strong materials are given below. In use, materials come under different types of stress. They may be subject to bending, twisting, squeezing or pulling forces. Their ability to withstand such stresses is measured by their **strengths** when tested with these forces.

- **Tensile strength** is a measure of the pull required to stretch and break the material. It measures strength under tension – a stretching or pulling force – as on the wires supporting a lift. This term is often shortened simply to strength.
- **Compressive strength** is a measure of the strength under a compressing force, as when a concrete foundation supports the weight of a building.
- **Hardness** is a measure of the material's resistance to being deformed. It is usually measured by scratching or denting the material.
- **Tough materials** resist cracking and breaking on being struck. It is important not to confuse hardness with toughness. A diamond is hard but hit it with a hammer and it will shatter. Diamond is brittle, not tough. On the other hand mild steel is tough – it bends but doesn't crack or break when treated in this way.
- **Brittle** materials crack and break easily, eg. glass. **Tough** materials do not snap or crack easily
- **Ductile** materials are easily drawn into wire.
- **Malleable** materials are easily shaped by rolling or beating.
- **Hard** materials do not dent or scratch easily.

2 ALLOYS

❝ For strength ❞

❝ For hardness ❞

❝ For ease of shaping ❞

Alloys are solid mixtures of metals (but steel is a mixture of iron and the non-metal, carbon). The most important method of increasing the strength of pure metals is by ***alloying them*** with other metals.

Mention above of the hardening of gold by alloying it with copper illustrates a major change that occurs to metals when they are mixed with other metals. Copper is hardened by alloying with zinc (to make brass) or nickel (to make 'nickel silver' for silver coins). Alloying can also make metals easier to shape, mould or cast.

Alloying combines the ***strength*** required of nearly all metals used in construction with the ***particular properties*** of the main metal in the alloy, the so-called 'parent' metal.

> Alloying can also be used to produce *coloured* metal as with *green* gold alloys and the gold coloured cupro-nickel alloy used to make one-pound coins.

Alloy	Composition	Property	Uses
brasses	copper, 66-70% zinc, 30-34%	harder and cheaper than copper, resists corrosion	ornaments, screws, rivets, cartridges, watertaps.
bronze	copper, 90% tin, 10%	hard, strong, can be cast into intricate shapes, corrosion-resistant	castings
coinage bronze	copper, 95% tin, 3.5% zinc, 1.5%	hard, strong and corrosion-resistant	coinage, penny and twopenny pieces
cupro-nickel	copper, 75% nickel, 25%	strong, corrosion-resistant, easy to shape cold without annealing	'silver' coins
duralumin	aluminium, 95% copper, 4% magnesium, 1%	higher strength/weight ratio than steel or aluminium, low density	aircraft framework
solder	lead, 67% tin, 33%	low melting point, stronger than tin or lead	joints in electrical work plumbing and tin-can making
steel	iron, 99% carbon, 0–1%	strong, cheap, easily shaped and welded	bridges, ships, vehicles, rails, gears
stainless steel	iron, 73% chromium, 18% nickel, 8% carbon, 1%	very resistant to rusting, strong and hard wearing	cutlery, kitchen utensils, chemical plant
type metal	lead, 74% antimony, 16% tin, 10%	easily cast but hardened by the antimony to keep its shape in use	printer's type

Fig. 11.2 Uses of alloys

Steels

STEELS are the commonest alloys in use. There are several types in common use:

Type	Composition	Properties	
low carbon	0.5%	Becomes less ductile. Hardness increases. More brittle & difficult to shape	Tensile Strength increases ↓
medium carbon	1.0%		Tensile Strength decreases ↑
high carbon	1.5%		
cast iron	>2.5%	very brittle, moderate strength and hardness	

Heat treatment of metals – especially steels

The rate of cooling of metals from the molten state controls the grain size and hence the properties of the solid metal. The smaller the grain size the harder the metal.

Different crystalline forms of metals have different properties. If a 'high-temperature' form has desirable properties the hot metal must be cooled very quickly to room temperature to retain the structure and properties. This is done by **quenching in cold water or oil**. **Quenching** and also **cold-working** of metals makes them stronger *and* harder. Cold-worked metals are said to be **work-hardened**. Hard metals can, however, be too brittle for use and must be softened. There are two softening processes:

> *Softening processes*

(i) **Annealing**. This involves heating the metal to a temperature below the melting point after work relieves stresses in the metal, making it less brittle (softer) but also reducing its strength. **Hot-working** allows stresses to be relieved at the same time so does not make the metal too hard as it gets stronger.

(ii) **Tempering**. This is carried out by heating the metal to a lower temperature than any previous heat treatment. Then the metal is allowed to cool naturally. It is intended to make steel tough and springy from being hard and brittle.

3 › STRONG METERIALS AND THEIR PROPERTIES

The variety of engineering and building materials is greater than it has ever been. Materials which were non-existent only a short time ago are now in common use. The average car now has up to 40% plastic in its construction where forty years ago there was virtually none. Fishing rods and tennis racquets were once only made of wood and now use the most advanced composites. We shall find a continuing substitution of specially designed materials with 'tailor-made' structures and properties in place of the more traditional metals and wood. Some of these are discussed in this section.

Ceramics

The term means 'of pottery'. Pottery and glass are common ceramics. Ceramics are materials other than metals formed by heating at high temperatures during their fabrication. They are heat and chemical resistant.

Composites

Normally of strong but brittle material in a crack-stopping matrix. The choice of fibre affects the strength and stiffness of the composite; the matrix largely governs its chemical resistance and temperature stability. The matrix prevents brittle fracture of the fibres so exploiting the best possible combination of properties of the composite structure. Ancient composites include 'wattle and daub' for house walls.

Examples of composites

- **bone** is a composite of collagen fibres in a matrix which is mainly calcium phosphate. Calcium phosphate on its own is brittle. The collagen prevents brittle fracture. Bone will withstand pressures up to 2 tonnes per square inch. Spaces in bone ensure lightness; long bones are hollow for part of their length.

- **carbon fibre** composites. Carbon fibres are even stronger than glass fibres. The composite contains carbon fibres in woven mat form in a resin matrix. For strength in all dimensions the fibres are inserted at right angles to each other in three dimensions. Carbon is less dense than glass and so carbon fibre composites have greater strength **and** lower densities than glass reinforced plastic (GRP).

- **concrete** consists of various sizes of rock particles (called aggregate) set in a matrix of sand and cement. It is very strong in compression but weak in tension. If steel reinforcing rods are laid in concrete in the same way that glass and carbon fibre mats are used as described above, tensile strength is much increased. This gives **reinforced concrete** and **prestressed concrete**. In the latter, the steel wires are tensioned before being set in concrete. The tensioned steel holds the concrete in compression – where it has the greatest strength.

- **glass fibre** composites are usually mats of woven glass laid parallel to each other in a resin matrix. Glass is strong but brittle. The matrix prevents surface cracks from reducing the fibre strength.

- **wood** is a naturally occurring composite cellulosic fibre (on average about 70%) bonded together by lignin. Wood is attractive to look at and generally light, tough and flexible. It has good chemical resistance. Unfortunately, wood must be seasoned or it shrinks and distorts in use. As a natural material, its characteristics can vary from sample to sample. Fig. 11.3 summarises the main properties of the materials discussed here.

Material	Structure	Properties	Examples and uses
Ceramics	Giant ionic structures	Strong, brittle, hard, temperature resistant chemically inert	Alumina (Al_2O_3) for bearings and abrasives. Aero engine parts, oven pottery, glass test tubes.
Metals and alloys	Metallic structure. Alloys are solid solutions	Malleable and ductile. Tough and strong. Some alloys very hard	Structural steels. Cutting and drilling metals. Sheet steel for car bodies. Wire and cable
Glass reinforced plastic	Glass fibre in an acrylic or epoxy resins matrix	Stronger than steel but not as stiff. Resistant to water and chemicals.	Canoes, boats, fishing rods, kitchen sinks, rooflights, shower cubicles
Carbon fibre	Carbon fibre in an epoxy resin matrix	Very strong and stiff. Chemical and water resistant. Expensive	Fishing rods, aeroplane and racing car bodies and seating
Concrete	Small stone pebbles in mortar matrix. Steel reinforcing wires	Strong in compression. Weak in tension unless reinforced. Cheap, high density	Foundations for buildings. If reinforced, bridge structures
Natural composites			
Bone	Collagen fibres in an inorganic matrix of calcium phosphate	Twice the strength of mild steel - weight for weight	Animals - bony limbs. Prehistoric people used bone as cutting and piercing tools
Wood	Celluose fibre in a lignin matrix	High strength to weight ratio. Flexible. Cheap	Building and carpentry. In the past boats and ships
Plastics	Long molecules tangled or cross-linked	Strength to weight ratio comparable with metals. Mouldable. Cheap	Common as cheap containers, plastic film, bags. Paints and glues

Property	Metals	Ceramics	Composites	Polymers
Density (water=1) g/cm³	1 - 22	2 - 16	2 - 3	1 - 2
Melting point/°C	100 - 3500	2000 - 4000	100 - 200	70 - 200
Tensile strength*	100 - 2500	10 - 400	50 - 1400	30 - 300
Stiffness*	40 - 400	150 - 450	10 - 200	0.5 - 3.5
Heat conductivity	High	Medium	Low	Low
Electrical conductivity	High	Low	Low	Low

* Units omitted for simplicity. Strength and stiffness are compared by comparing the values.

Fig. 11.3 Properties of materials.

Newer alloys

The metals and alloys described above have been in use for a long time - some of them for thousands of years. Since metallurgists began to understand why alloying changed the properties of metals, they have sought to 'tailor' alloys for particular purposes. The number of alloys in use increases yearly.

The use of the very strong, light and corrosion-resistant metal *titanium* in alloys for making gas turbine engines for aircraft and hip replacement parts is an example of the discovery of newer useful alloys.

4 THE REACTIVITY SERIES

Anyone experimenting with metals soon notices that **they are not all equally reactive**. Some metals react extremely vigorously with other substances, others are quite difficult to 'persuade' to react.

The ***reactivity series*** (***reactivity table***) of metallic elements is a list or table in which the most reactive metal is placed at the top of the series and the least reactive metal is placed at the bottom. It is an ***order of reactivity***.

The types of experimental results which need to be obtained in order to place metals in a reactivity order are discussed below.

(A) REACTION WITH DILUTE ACIDS TO PRODUCE SALTS AND HYDROGEN

Only metals ***above copper*** in the reactivity series react in this way:

$$Zn(s) + 2HCl(aq) \rightarrow ZnCl_2(aq) + H_2(g)$$

zinc + hydrochloric acid → zinc chloride + hydrogen.

$$Fe(s) + 2HCl(aq) \rightarrow FeCl_2(aq) + H_2(g)$$

iron + hydrochloric acid → iron(II) chloride + hydrogen.

Similar reactions occur with dilute sulphuric acid to produce metal sulphates and hydrogen.
- Dilute nitric acid does not react with metals in this way.
- Copper will not react with dilute acids in this way.

The usual method for producing hydrogen in the laboratory is by reacting zinc with dilute hydrochloric ***or*** dilute sulphuric acid.

(B) REACTION WITH OXYGEN TO FORM METAL OXIDES

The most reactive metals burn, less-reactive metals do not. Both types are oxidised, e.g.

$$2Mg(s) + O_2(g) \rightarrow 2MgO(s)$$

magnesium + oxygen → magnesium oxide

Only metals such as gold and platinum do not oxidise when heated in air.

(C) REACTION WITH WATER TO FORM HYDROGEN AND A METAL OXIDE OR HYDROXIDE

Where there is reaction, metals displace hydrogen and form hydroxides or oxides. (The results of a series of metals reacting with water are shown in Fig. 11.9).

(i) Cold water, e.g. sodium or calcium

$$2Na(s) + 2H_2O(l) \rightarrow 2NaOH(aq) + H_2(g)$$

sodium + water → sodium hydroxide + hydrogen.

$$Ca(s) + 2H_2O(l) \rightarrow Ca(OH)_2(aq) + H_2(g)$$

calcium + water → calcium hydroxide + hydrogen.

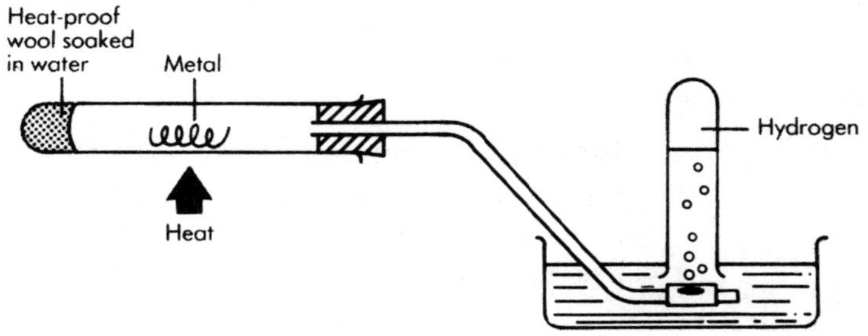

Fig. 11.4 The action of steam on metals.

(ii) Steam, e.g. magnesium, zinc and iron (see Fig. 11.4)

$$Mg(s) + H_2O(g) \rightarrow MgO(s) + H_2(g)$$

magnesium + steam → magnesium oxide + hydrogen.

Low down the reactivity series, at iron, the reaction with steam becomes reversible– an indication that metals less reactive than iron will not be reactive to steam:

$$3Fe(s) + 4H_2O(g) \rightleftharpoons Fe_3O_4(s) + 4H_2(g)$$

iron + steam ⇌ iron(II)diiron(III) oxide + hydrogen.

There are three common oxides of iron: FeO, Fe_2O_3 and Fe_3O_4. They are named iron(II) oxide, iron(III) oxide and iron(II) diiron(III) oxide. The last one is commonly called 'smithy scales' because it is the oxide formed when red hot iron is cooled in water, a practice common when metalsmiths make articles by shaping hot metals. This oxide, if very thin, can act as a protective coating preventing corrosion of iron. Fishhooks are treated in this way to coat them with this protective oxide.

(D) REACTION OF METALS WITH METAL OXIDES

This type of reaction is an obvious 'competition' between two metal atoms for oxygen atoms. The more-reactive metal atoms will remove the oxygen from the less-reactive metal oxide. This results in a transfer of oxygen from the less reactive metal oxide to the more reactive metal. The rule is that the more-reactive metal always takes the oxygen away from the less-reactive metal oxide:

magnesium + copper(II) oxide → copper + magnesium oxide

$$Mg(s) + CuO(s) \rightarrow Cu(s) + MgO(s)$$

more-reactive metal + less-reactive metal oxide → less-reactive metal + more-reactive metal oxide

(E) REACTION OF METALS WITH METAL SALTS (DISPLACEMENTS)

Metal salts react in the same way as oxides with other metals. **Heating** a reactive metal with the solid or molten salt of a less-reactive metal results in the formation of the less-reactive metal and a salt of the more-reactive metal, e.g.

$$Fe(s) + CuBr_2(l) \rightarrow Cu(s) + FeBr_2(s)$$

iron + copper(II) bromide → copper + iron(II) bromide

more-reactive metal + bromide of less-reactive metal → less-reactive metal + bromide of more-reactive metal

Easier in solution

However, because many metal salts are soluble in water, the reaction with a metal can be more easily carried out by mixing the metal with the salt **solution**. Usually no heat is needed. The products are also easily separated from each other by simple **filtration**. The technique may vary from dipping a piece of clean metal foil into a solution of a metal salt, to stirring a metal powder into the metal salt solution.

There is always an energy change in these 'displacement' reactions and stirring with a thermometer or feeling the bottom of the reaction vessel will show that the temperature has risen - the reactions are **exothermic**.

Testing the reactions of several metals with their salts

We would place a small piece of each metal into separate solutions of the salts of each of the metals. An easier way is to place some of each salt solution on a clock glass and insert thin slivers of each metal into the solution as shown in the diagram (Fig. 11.5).

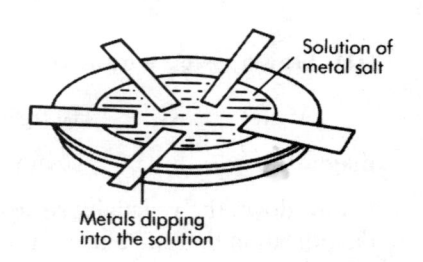

Fig. 11.5

If a reaction has occurred, a deposit will appear on the metal. This means that the metal of the sliver has displaced the metal element in the salt from its solution. For example, a sliver of zinc, placed in a solution of copper(II) sulphate, will become coated with a brown deposit. The deposit is copper. Copper has been displaced from copper(II) sulphate by the more reactive zinc:

$$Zn(s) + CuSO_4(aq) \rightarrow Cu(s) + ZnSO_4(aq).$$

zinc	+	copper(II) sulphate solution	→	copper	+	zinc sulphate solution
grey metal		blue solution		brown metal		colourless solution

> **The word *replacement* is also sometimes used instead of *displacement*. The reactive metal *displaces* the less reactive one and *replaces* it in the compound**

During the reaction the colour of the solution will change from blue to colourless if there is enough zinc to react with all the copper sulphate present.

It is found that the metals higher in the reactivity series displace the metals lower down from their salts (chlorides, nitrates, sulphates, etc.). The results of such a series of reactions would be:

Metals	Salts of: Mg	Zn	Pb	Cu	Conclusion
magnesium	×	✓	✓	✓	Mg most reactive – displaces 3 metals in this experiment
zinc	×	×	✓	✓	
lead	×	×	×	✓	
copper	×	×	×	×	Copper least reactive – displaces no metals
					× = no displacement, ✓ = displaced metal

(F) THE STABILITY OF METAL COMPOUNDS TO HEAT

Many metal compounds ***decompose*** on heating. The temperature at which the decomposition occurs depends on the reactivity of the metal in the compound.

The effect of heat on some metal compounds is summarised in Fig. 11.6.

Metal	Hydroxide	Nitrate	Carbonate
potassium sodium	none	nitrite + oxygen	none
calcium magnesium aluminium zinc lead copper	form oxide and water	form oxide and nitrogen dioxide and oxygen	form oxide and carbon dioxide
silver gold platinum	form metal, oxygen and water	form metal, oxygen and nitrogen dioxide	form metal, oxygen and carbon dioxide

Fig. 11.6 The effect of heat on metal compounds.

There is a clear connection between the reactivity and products of decomposition.

- ***Compounds*** of the most reactive elements decompose less easily than similar compounds of the least reactive elements. Example reactions are
- ***Copper(II) hydroxide*** and ***copper(II) carbonate*** decompose on heating:

$$Cu(OH)_2(s) \rightarrow CuO(s) + H_2O(g)$$

copper(II) hydroxide → copper(II) oxide + water.

$$CuCO_3(s) \rightarrow CuO(s) + CO_2(g)$$

copper(II) carbonate → copper(II) oxide + carbon dioxide

- The **hydroxides** and **carbonates** of sodium will **not** decompose on heating.

(G) REDUCTION OF METAL OXIDES

(i) By a more reactive metal

Removal of oxygen from metal oxides is the commonest method of obtaining the metal. The reduction of a metal oxide can be carried out by any metal *more reactive* than the metal contained in the oxide. For instance, sodium could be used to obtain iron from iron oxide ore. This process is not carried out in practice because:

(a) sodium is not available in sufficient quantities to produce all the iron required; and
(b) it would make the iron produced very expensive – more expensive than sodium.

The reduction of metal oxides by a more-reactive metal is, however, used in industry.

Chromium and **manganese oxides** are reduced by aluminium to obtain the metals

$$Cr_2O_3(s) + 2Al(s) \rightarrow 2Cr(s) + Al_2O_3(s)$$

chromium(III) oxide + aluminium → chromium + aluminium oxide.

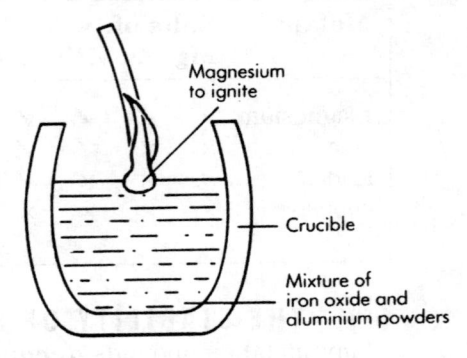

Fig. 11.7 The thermit reaction.

This is an example of the **thermit process** (Fig. 11.7) and you may have seen it demonstrated in a laboratory using iron(III) oxide and aluminium:

$$Fe_2O_3(s) + 2Al(s) \rightarrow 2Fe(s) + Al_2O_3(s)$$

iron(III) oxide + aluminium → iron + aluminium oxide.

By including carbon and hydrogen in the reactivity series of metals, it is possible to see that these two non-metallic elements can reduce many metal oxides to metals.

(ii) By hydrogen as a reducing agent

Hydrogen will reduce oxides of metals **lower than iron** in the reactivity series to the metal and water, e.g.

$$CuO(s) + H_2(g) \rightarrow Cu(s) + H_2O(l).$$

copper(II) oxide + hydrogen → copper + water

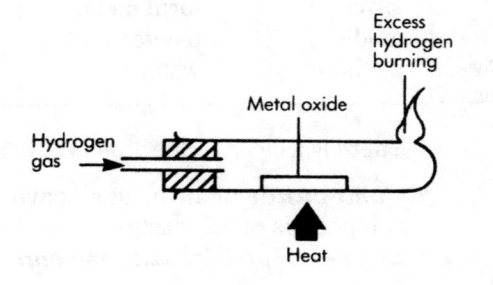

Fig. 11.8 Reduction of metal oxides.

Hydrogen in the reactivity series

The metal oxide must be heated in a stream of hydrogen (Fig. 11.8).
Aluminium and metals above it in the reactivity series cannot be formed by this type of

reduction. Hydrogen will not reduce oxides of metals higher than iron. This fact places hydrogen between zinc and iron in the reactivity series.

(iii) By carbon as a reducing agent

Carbon in the reactivity series

Carbon will reduce oxides of metals **lower down in the reactivity series than aluminium** to the metal and carbon dioxide. Zinc and iron oxides, however, ***just below aluminium***, need higher temperatures than can usually be obtained in a bunsen flame:

$$2CuO(s) + C(s) \rightarrow CO_2(g) + 2Cu(s)$$
copper(II) oxide + carbon → carbon dioxide + copper,

$$2PbO(s) + C(s) \rightarrow CO_2(g) + 2Pb(l)$$
lead(II) oxide + carbon → carbon dioxide + lead.

The oxides must be heated with powdered carbon. Lead forms as a liquid at the temperature of the reduction.

Metals	Reaction of the reactivity series metals with:		
	Water	Acids	Oxides and salts
potassium sodium calcium	rapid reaction with cold water giving hydrogen and a hydroxide	violent reaction to form H_2 and the metal salt	Each metal will DISPLACE any of
magnesium aluminium zinc	react with steam but not with cold water to give the oxide and hydrogen	react with decreasing vigour to form H_2 and the metal salt of the acid	the METALS below it in the TABLE from
iron	reversible reaction		their
lead copper silver	*no reaction* with water or steam	*no reaction* with dilute acids to form hydrogen	OXIDES or from
gold platinum	*no reaction* with any substance except 'aqua regia'		their SALT SOLUTIONS

Fig. 11.9. Reaction of the reactivity series metals.

Fig. 11.9 also serves as a **summary** of the reactions of the metals with common reagents.

5 › REACTIVITY AND DISPLACEMENTS

The reason why some metals are more reactive than others is because of their greater tendency to form ***ions***. The most reactive metals, the alkali metals, have a greater tendency to form ions than less reactive metals. Gold and platinum, the least reactive of all metals, have hardly any tendency to form ions at all.

When metals are combined, the particles present in their compounds are ions. When metals are uncombined, the particles present are atoms. For metals, the process of combining is one of ***formation of ions from atoms***:

Metal ***atoms*** form ***ions*** by loss of electrons. Metal ***ions*** form ***atoms*** by gain of electrons. Both of these types of process occur in a displacement reaction.

So, for the displacement of copper from any copper compound by magnesium we can write:

| Cu^{2+} | + | Mg | → | Mg^{2+} | + | Cu |
| copper ions | + | magnesium atoms | → | magnesium ions | + | copper atoms |

magnesium atoms $\xrightarrow{\text{oxidation}}$ magnesium ions

copper ions $\xrightarrow{\text{reduction}}$ copper atoms

There are copper ions in solid copper oxide and in aqueous copper sulphate. Magnesium **reduces** these copper ions to atoms and magnesium atoms are themselves **oxidised** to magnesium ions.

The higher in the reactivity series, the greater the tendency of the atoms of a metal to give up electrons to form ions and the lower the tendency of those ions to accept electrons to form atoms. The atoms of elements lower in the series have little tendency to give up electrons to form ions but their ions have a greater tendency to accept electrons to form atoms (Fig. 11.10).

Element	Atoms → ions	Ions → atoms
potassium	greatest tendency at the top of the series	smallest tendency at the top of the series
sodium		
lithium		
calcium		
magnesium		
aluminium		
CARBON		
zinc		
iron		
tin		
lead		
HYDROGEN		
copper		
silver		
gold	smallest tendency at the bottom of the series	greatest tendency at the bottom of series
plantinum		

Fig. 11.10

6 THE EXTRACTION OF METALS

Very few can be obtained from the ground as pure metals – called 'native' metal. Only the least reactive metals have been able to stand up to millions of years of exposure to oxygen, water, heat and pressure and remain uncombined.

Most metals over this period have combined to form oxides, carbonates, sulphides and chlorides. **The metals are present in these compounds as ions**.

When these compounds occur in the ground – usually mixed with more or less rocky substance – they are called 'ores'. Only a small number of metals can be extracted from their ores by heat alone – see Section 6(B).

From what we have seen in the previous section, to convert these compounds (the metal ions really) into metallic elements (metal atoms) requires a more reactive element to **reduce** them. It is **possible** to make any element from its ore by reduction with a more reactive element. In practice this will only be done if it is economical.

(A) THE CHOICE OF REDUCTION METHOD FOR EXTRACTING METALS FOR THEIR ORES

Carbon reduction

The reactivity series, as displayed in Fig. 11.10, shows that a non-metal, carbon, is a suitable reducing agent for obtaining many metals from their oxides. Carbon, in the form of coke, is cheap and abundant and very suitable for large-scale metal extraction such as for iron, lead, and zinc.

"Zinc and lead smelting"

Zinc and lead ores are mainly sulphides, ZnS and PbS, whereas iron ore is mainly found as the oxide, with the sulphide and carbonate also important in different parts of the world. Sulphide ores are roasted in air to form oxides before the carbon reduction begins.

All three oxides are reduced by **carbon monoxide** formed inside a blast furnace by reaction with air. The blast furnace for iron smelting is similar to those used for zinc and lead smelting. The reactions are

$$2C(s) + O_2(g) \rightarrow 2CO(g)$$

carbon(coke) + oxygen → carbon monoxide,

followed by

$$ZnO(s) + CO(g) \rightarrow Zn(g) + CO_2(g)$$

zinc oxide + carbon monoxide → zinc vapour + carbon dioxide,

or

$$PbO(s) + CO(g) \rightarrow Pb(l) + CO_2(g)$$

lead(II) oxide + carbon monoxide → molten lead + carbon dioxide,

or

$$Fe_2O_3(s) + 3CO(g) \rightarrow 2Fe(l) + 3CO_2(g)$$

iron(III) oxide + carbon monoxide → molten iron + carbon dioxide.

Electrolytic reduction

But what of those metals which are **more reactive** than carbon? Carbon will not reduce their oxides to metal.

For these metals **electrolysis** is the general method chosen. The process of **reduction occurs at the cathode** in electrolysis. In theory **any** metal can be made from its molten compounds by electrolysis. The cathode, as it were, is at the top of the reactivity series and will displace any metal from any metal compound that can be electrolysed!

"Reactive metals"

Metals obtained in this way are the alkali metals, magnesium and aluminium – metals of groups 1, 2 and 3.

The electrolysis reactions occurring are given in detail in Chapter 7, Fig. 7.4.

(B) METHODS WHICH DO NOT REQUIRE AN ADDED REDUCING AGENT

The **least reactive** metals can be extracted without the use of any of the methods discussed above.

"Copper"

Copper, for instance, is extracted by roasting its sulphide ore to convert it partly to its oxide and then heating the mixture strongly (reduction) to obtain the impure metal called 'blister copper'. No added reducing agent is used. The reactions are:

"In this process the ore is also being used as a fuel. Heat from its reaction with oxygen helps to make the process more energy efficient."

$$2Cu_2S(l) + 3O_2(g) \rightarrow 2Cu_2O(l) + 2SO_2(g) \text{ roast,}$$

followed by

$$Cu_2S(l) + 2Cu_2O(l) \rightarrow 6Cu(l) + SO_2(g) \text{ reduction.}$$

The 'smelting' of copper, as this method is called, produces a great deal of sulphur dioxide. If this is emitted to the atmosphere it is a major source of pollution. To prevent such pollution, copper smelting is usually coupled with sulphuric acid manufacture to make use of the sulphur dioxide and at the same time eliminate it as a pollutant (see Chapter 12.3, Section 6).

"Pollution control"

Mercury, found as the sulphide, is first roasted in air to convert it to its oxide. The oxide decomposes at 500 °C to the metal and oxygen:

"Mercury"

$$2HgO(s) \rightarrow 2Hg(g) + O_2(g).$$

mercury oxide → mercury + oxygen

7. TAKING IT FURTHER

Metallurgical chemists can go even further in their use of the principles of the reactivity series to extract metals. They make use of other metals and, in one case, hydrogen to reduce metal compounds:

(A) REDUCTION USING ANOTHER METAL

Titanium is produced by the reduction of its chloride using either sodium or magnesium (depending on the company of manufacture). This is called the Kroll process:

$$TiCl_4(l) + 4Na(l) \rightarrow Ti(s) + 4NaCl(s)$$

titanium chloride + sodium → titanium + sodium chloride,

or

$$TiCl_4(l) + 2Mg(l) \rightarrow Ti(s) + 2MgCl_2(l)$$

titanium chloride + magnesium → titanium + magnesium chloride.

Such a process must make the titanium more expensive than either sodium or magnesium. Look up the uses of titanium and it may be clear why such expense is justified.

(B) REDUCTION USING HYDROGEN

Hydrogen is used to reduce only one metal compound on a large scale – tungsten oxide:

$$WO_3(s) + 3H_2(g) \rightarrow W(s) + 3H_2O(g).$$

tungsten oxide + hydrogen → tungsten + water

8. THE ABUNDANCE OF METAL RESOURCES

The *cost* of production of a metal depends on many factors, see Chapter 2, Section 1. Some of these are:

- the abundance of its ore in the earth's crust;
- the richness of the ore;
- the amount of energy used in its extraction;
- the amount of metal that can be recycled;
- labour costs.

The most commonly used metals are those with useful physical and chemical properties. They are either

- abundant, such as iron or aluminium;
- less abundant but cheap to produce, such as copper, zinc and lead;
- less abundant and expensive to produce, but have very important uses like manganese which is used in many steels.

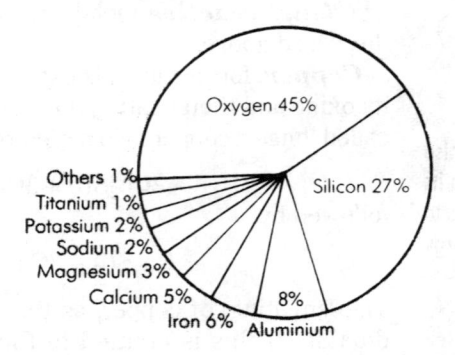

Fig. 11.11

Oxygen 45%
Silicon 27%
Aluminium 8%
Iron 6%
Calcium 5%
Magnesium 3%
Sodium 2%
Potassium 2%
Titanium 1%
Others 1%

The abundance of the most common metals in the earth's crust is shown in Fig. 11.11. The figures are rounded up to the nearest whole number.

(A) HOW LONG WILL OUR METAL RESOURCES LAST?

Since cheap sources of energy, in the form of coal, became available to industry during the Industrial Revolution, ever-increasing quantities of metals have been extracted from their ores. The increasing pace of the use of the world's resources has resulted in a concern for the future of the supply of these minerals.

Some metals are so abundant that it is difficult to believe that they could ever 'run out'. Aluminium and iron are examples. Yet even these two metals can only be extracted from concentrated ores and the supply of these is not large. Without recycling or the discovery of alternative materials, the extraction of these two metals could become difficult within 500 years.

The situation is more serious for other metals. Known sources suggest the following 'lifetimes':

> ❝ These figures are a rough guide to the lifetime of metal ores. New sources are being found continually and any set of figures becomes quickly out of date ❞

copper	50 years
lead	20 years
zinc	20 years
tin	20 years
gold	20 years

One way of extending the use of scarce metals is by recycling. For example, a large proportion of lead in use is recycled, extending the lifetime of the resource considerably.

(B) RECYCLING METALS

> ❝ Over sixty per cent of steel, tin and lead, and over forty per cent of copper and aluminium, is recycled in the UK annually ❞

Recycling makes metals cheaper as well as making our resources last longer. The energy needed to extract a metal from its ores has already been paid for in its first use. Re-melting and refining scrap needs only a small fraction of the energy needed to extract the metal from its ore. Scrap metal recycling is widely used for iron, aluminium, lead, zinc and precious metals. Lead-acid batteries are a source of lead scrap, drinks cans of aluminium, building scrap of lead and copper, old cars of scrap iron, etc.

There are, of course, other costs of recycling. The collection, transport, separation and cleaning of the scrap all add to the cost of the re-processed product.

(C) SITING A METAL EXTRACTION PLANT

The choice of site depends upon similar factors to those discussed in the siting of ammonia and sulphuric acid plant. (Chapters 12.4(K) and 12.7(B))
- For metals, the ores generally come from abroad. This leads to
- the siting of extraction plant close to deep-water ports to reduce transport costs.
- if electricity is required as in aluminium extraction, there must be a large power station nearby, supplying **cheap** electricity.
- if there are pollutant emissions, rarer now than in the past, the site must not be too close to a town or city and preferably downwind of it.
- a labour supply is required close by.
- the plant must not be built on valuable agricultural land. It is preferable to use reclaimed land.
- transport of the product to places within and outside the area of the plant must be convenient.

(D) ENERGY COSTS OF METAL PRODUCTION

Carbon offers the cheapest source of energy because of its abundance. ***Electrolysis*** is expensive and usually used only if no alternative method is available. The amount of electricity used depends upon the charge on the metal ion and also upon the temperature required for the electrolysis. For example, to produce sodium (ions, Na^+) should require only one-third of the electricity required to produce an equal amount (in moles) of aluminium (ions Al^{3+}).

9 ▶ CHOICE OF THE METHOD OF EXTRACTION

The reactivity series is a good guide to the choice of reduction methods for metals. The most reactive metals hold on strongest to the elements they are combined with. They will require the strongest reducing methods for their extraction. Metals of low reactivity, such as gold, require no reduction at all since they are found 'native', i.e. uncombined.

The use of carbon to reduce metal ores extends up the reactivity series only as far as zinc. Metals above zinc cannot be obtained by use of carbon. Although the use of a more reactive metal is possible, it is usually cheaper to use electrolysis for aluminium and more reactive metals (Fig. 11.12).

Metal	Source	Extraction method
potassium	potash, KCl	electrolysis (KOH(l))
sodium	rock-salt, NaCl	electrolysis (NaCl(l))
calcium	limestone, $CaCO_3$	electrolysis ($CaCl_2$(l))
magnesium	dolomite, $MgCO_3/CaCO_3$ sea water	electrolysis ($MgCl_2$(l))
aluminium	bauxite, Al_2O_3	electrolysis (Al_2O_3(l))
zinc	zinc blende, ZnS	carbon reduction (ZnO(s))
iron	haematite, Fe_2O_3	carbon reduction (Fe_2O_3(s))
lead	galena, PbS	carbon reduction (PbO(s))
copper	copper pyrites, $CuFeS_2$	roast-reduction of Cu_2S(s)
silver	native	the metals are usually dissolved from their ores and then redeposited by displacement with a reactive metal, e.g. zinc
gold	native	
platinum	native	

Fig. 11.12 Metals, Sources and Methods of Extraction

10 METALS IN HISTORY

Native metals

Early alloys

We get clues about the reactivity of metals by a study of their use in the past. The earliest metals to be used were those which could be found pure in the ground – gold, silver and, in some parts of the world, copper.

The discovery and use of fire would eventually have resulted in the heating of rock mixtures on wood (charcoal) fires. Metals which can be extracted by low-temperature reduction with carbon include copper and tin. Since many ores occur **mixed**, these would produce mixed metals – the early alloys such as bronze.

Higher temperatures from the use of coal would allow the production of iron and zinc, but metals, more reactive than these could not be produced by reduction with carbon and had to wait for the discovery of electricity.

Volta's discovery of the electric current in the early years of the nineteenth century led to the discovery of the more reactive metals. Group 1 and 2 metals could then be obtained by electrolysis of their **easily melted** compounds.

The extraction of aluminium proved difficult on a large scale until the discovery of a method of melting aluminium oxide by dissolving it in molten cryolite. The first large-scale production of aluminium was not until 1868! Since then, of course, metals which are even harder to extract from their ores have been obtained and are 'in service', e.g. titanium.

The reactivity series not only helps to explain why we find our metals combined in nature, but also helps us understand the difficulties in their extraction.

11 ALUMINIUM EXTRACTION

Pre-treatment

Aluminium is the third most abundant element and *the* most abundant metal in the earth's crust. Only one important ore is known – *bauxite* – which contains hydrated aluminium oxides, $Al_2O_3.H_2O$, with iron oxide as the main impurity.

Before use, bauxite is treated to remove iron oxide and water, both of which would interfere with the extraction process. Can you suggest how they would interfere? The purified product is dry alumina, Al_2O_3(s).

Like all the metals which are more reactive than zinc, aluminium is produced by electrolysis. However, the electrolyte in this case is the oxide of the metal dissolved in a molten salt.

The melting point of aluminium oxide is 2072 °C which is too high for practical use in electrolysis. The discovery that aluminium oxide could be electrolysed if **dissolved** in molten cryolite (sodium aluminium fluoride) at 970 °C made the electrolysis process possible.

The electrolysis cell consists of a steel container lined with carbon. The carbon acts as the cathode. The anodes are carbon rods which are suspended in the electrolyte. The anodes are consumed in the process.

The electrolyte is aluminium oxide (alumina) dissolved in molten cryolite. About 5% alumina in cryolite is used. The reactions occurring are:

Note the need to make the number of electrons involved in each electrode reaction equal.

At the anode(+) $\qquad 6O^{2-}(l) - 12e^- \rightarrow 3O_2(g).$

At the cathode(−) $\qquad 4Al^{3+}(l) + 12e^- \rightarrow 4Al(l).$

The overall reaction is:

$$2Al_2O_3(l) \rightarrow 4Al(l) + 3O_2(g).$$

Molten aluminium forms at the bottom of the cell and so automatically separates from the oxygen, which is taken from the top of the cell. Hence, no separator between the electrodes is needed. The carbon anodes are oxidised away slowly in the process:

$$2C(s) + O_2(g) \rightarrow 2CO(g)$$

carbon + oxygen → carbon monoxide

Aluminium of 99.9% purity is siphoned off daily. More alumina is added as it is decomposed (Fig. 11.13).

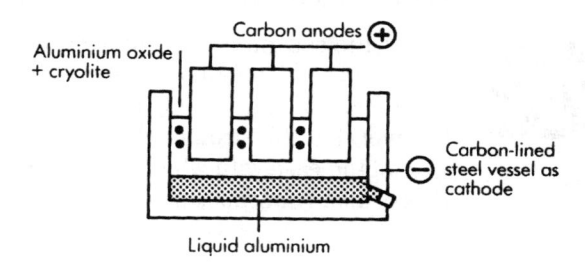

Fig. 11.13 Electronics of molten alumina; aluminium metal production

Aluminium is a useful metal because of its low density and its resistance to corrosion. But why is it resistant to corrosion when it is placed so high in the reactivity series? The position of aluminium in the reactivity series would suggest that it would react with steam and oxygen readily – as magnesium (above) and zinc (below) do. Yet aluminium is unaffected by either.

Cost of aluminium extraction

Aluminium is relatively expensive to extract from its ores because it requires the use of large amounts of electricity. Electricity is produced largely by combustion of coal (but at an efficiency of conversion level of only about 30%). So metals like iron which can use coke in their extraction have a fuel or energy 'advantage', this makes them potentially cheaper.

Use of recycled aluminium

Recycling aluminium is now common. Drink cans are collected and melted down; impurities are removed. The production consumes only 5% of the energy needed to extract the metals from its ore by electrolysis.

12 THE CHEMICAL RESISTANCE OF ALUMINIUM

It is the reactivity of aluminium to oxygen that protects it against attack by some chemicals. When a clean aluminium surface is exposed to air an invisibly thin oxide film forms immediately. The film covers the metal surface and protects it from attack by any chemical that cannot **dissolve** the film. This protective film prevents corrosion by water and air though common salt can attack it. Unprotected aluminium surfaces remain clean and shiny except in salty atmospheres, e.g. near or on the sea.

(A) BREAKDOWN OF THE PROTECTIVE FILM

Any chemical that can dissolve aluminium oxide will destroy the oxide film and the aluminium surface will be exposed and may react.

Aluminium oxide is an amphoteric oxide. It acts as **either** an acidic oxide **or** a basic oxide. It will, therefore, dissolve in acids **and** alkalis to form a salt and water. Dilute acids and alkalis will remove the protective film and expose the aluminium to reaction.

Since aluminium will react with both acids and alkalis to form soluble salts and hydrogen gas, then as soon as the oxide film is dissolved by an acid or an alkali, the exposed metal will also react and dissolve, with the formation of an aluminium salt and hydrogen gas:

aluminium oxide + acid/alkali → aluminium salt + water,

followed by

aluminium + acid/alkali → aluminium salt + hydrogen.

This breakdown of the oxide film in acids and alkalis shows us a limitation in the corrosion resistance of aluminium.

Aluminium is commonly used in the kitchen in foil, pans and cooker parts. None of these should be brought into prolonged contact with acids (vinegar, fruit juices, kettle-fur remover), or even brief contact with alkalis such as the caustic soda used to clean ovens, or aluminium will be dissolved. High concentrations of aluminium in food are dangerous.

(B) ANODISING

The thin oxide layer can be thickened by the process know as **anodising**, see Chapter 7, Section 13(B). This is done where extra corrosion resistance is required and also where aluminium is to be coloured by dyeing.

13> THE EXTRACTION OF IRON IN A BLAST FURNACE

Iron is the second most abundant metal and the fourth most abundant element in the earth's crust. It is found mainly as oxide, Fe_2O_3, sulphide, FeS_2, or carbonate, $FeCO_3$. Haematite contains mainly Fe_2O_3, magnetite is mainly Fe_3O_4 and pyrite is mainly FeS_2. The world is still strongly dependent on the use of iron as a constructional material in spite of the ease with which it corrodes.

This is mainly because it is:

- cheap;
- strong;
- easily worked into shape;
- easily and cheaply alloyed for increased strength or hardness.

Cheap iron arises from:

- the widespread occurrence of its ores;
- high concentration of iron in the ores;
- cheapness of the reducing agent (carbon) and the flux (limestone);
- large amounts of available scrap for recycling.

14> IRON SMELTING

Iron is smelted in a blast furnace (Fig. 11.14). Here, iron oxide is reduced to molten iron by carbon (actually carbon monoxide is the reducing agent). Iron ore contains much impurity – mainly silica – which would 'clog' the furnace if not removed. By adding limestone, silica can be converted to calcium silicate – a glassy substance which melts at the furnace temperature and flows from the furnace with the molten iron. In this way **all** the products are removed from the furnace as liquids. With constant addition of raw materials, the process can work continuously. **The extraction of iron from its oxide ores is equivalent to a reversal of the process of rusting.**

(A) THE CHEMICAL REACTIONS IN THE BLAST FURNACE

(i) Coke (carbon), iron oxide ore and limestone are added at the top.
(ii) A **blast** of hot air enters near the bottom.
(iii) Reduction occurs and iron is formed.
(iv) Molten iron falls to the bottom of the furnace and is tapped off when necessary.
(v) Slag (molten impurities) forms and runs to the bottom of the furnace. It floats on the iron, protecting the iron from oxidation by the air blast. Slag is tapped off when necessary.
(vi) Hot, waste gases containing carbon monoxide, carbon dioxide and nitrogen exit from the top of the furnace.

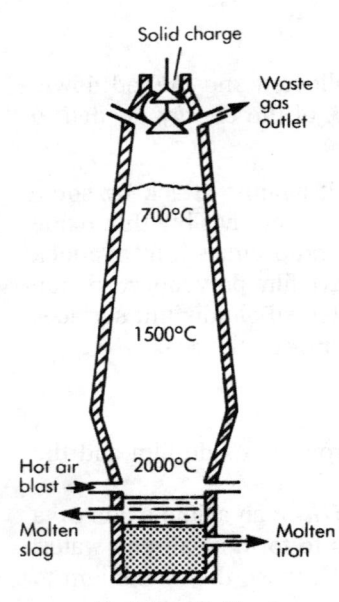

Fig. 11.14 The blast furnace.

(B) THE REACTIONS

(I) Coke is first oxidised by air to carbon monoxide:

$$2C(s) + O_2(g) \rightarrow 2CO(g)$$
carbon + oxygen → carbon monoxide

This occurs mainly round the air blast inlet at 2000 °C

(ii) Carbon monoxide **reduces** iron oxide to iron:

$$3CO(g) + Fe_2O_3(s) \rightarrow 2Fe(l) + 3CO_2(g)$$
carbon monoxide + iron oxide → iron + carbon dioxide

Molten iron flows to the bottom of the furnace

(iii) Limestone is decomposed by heat to calcium oxide at 1000 °C:

$$CaCO_3(s) \rightarrow CaO(s) + CO_2(g)$$
calcium carbonate → calcium oxide + carbon dioxide

(iv) calcium oxide (basic oxide) reacts with silica (acidic oxide) to form molten calcium silicate (slag):

$$CaO(s) + SiO_2(s) \rightarrow CaSiO_3(l).$$
calcium oxide + silicon dioxide → calcium silicate

The molten iron tapped from the furnace contains about 5% of carbon which dissolves in the iron on its way down the furnace.

The gases formed in these reactions are carbon monoxide and carbon dioxide. Nitrogen from the air blast passes through unchanged. The hot waste gases pass out through the top of the furnace. Their heat energy is used to **preheat** the incoming air blast. In this way economies in energy use are achieved. Over the years, the process has been made more economical. The weight of coke now needed to produce a tonne of iron is about one-third what it used to be.

❝ Economy ❞

(C) PIG-IRON/CAST IRON

The molten iron from a blast furnace is tapped off into large preheated containers. It is taken to the nearby steelworks where it is converted into a large number of different steels, many of them tailor-made to the customer's specification.

Some of the molten iron is cast into moulds called 'pigs'. This is **cast** or **pig-iron**, it has 5% carbon and is very brittle. It is used where cheapness and little strength combined with a greater corrosion resistance than ordinary steel is required - which is not often.

Wrought iron

If **all** the carbon is removed from pig iron, **pure iron** or **wrought iron** is formed. This is very easily bent to shape and is mainly used for ornamental ironwork such as gates and scrolls.

Steel

Steel is an alloy of iron and other elements. The commonest and cheapest steels contain carbon as the alloying element.

mild steel contains up to	0.25% carbon (easily pressed into complex shapes);
medium carbon steel contains	0.25–0.45% carbon;
high carbon steel contains	0.45–1.5% carbon (strong but brittle);
cast iron contains	2.5–5% carbon (weak and brittle).

Alloying elements other than carbon - alloy steels

- Manganese is added for increased strength and hardness;
- Chromium and nickel are added for increased corrosion resistance;
- Tungsten and vanadium are added for increased hardness, especially at high temperatures.

(D) MAKING STEELS

The basic oxygen process

The first requirement of steelmaking is to remove the carbon from the pig-iron which comes, molten, from the blast furnace. This is done by oxidising the carbon and other non-metal impurities to oxides by blowing in **pure oxygen** through a water-cooled lance under pressure.

❝ Oxidation ❞

Carbon oxides are gases and leave the reaction vessel – called a 'converter' – through the mouth of the vessel, usually burning as they do so.

Phosphorus oxides are not gases, but like all non-metal oxides they are acidic. They combine with the special 'basic' lining of the converter (magnesium oxide, see Chapter 5, Section 10) to form solid phosphates and are thereby removed.

> *Acid-base reaction*

Lime may also be added and this too reacts with non-metal oxides to form a slag which can be poured away. Up to 20% scrap steel can be used in this process. The resulting iron is mixed with the calculated amounts of alloying elements and steel results.

These processes, used in steelmaking, are all exothermic and this helps to keep the metal molten whilst the reactions are being carried out.

The electric arc process

Only used with scrap steel, this process uses an electric arc to provide the energy to melt the charge of scrap metal. Lime is added to convert impurities to slag. The slag can be poured off when the steel has reached the required composition.

Steel analysis

The analysis of steels can now be done very rapidly. A 'Polyvac' spectrometer can give a complete analysis in five minutes. This enables the correct amounts of the alloying elements to be determined and added without expensive delay in holding the steel at a high temperature.

(E) RUSTING AND ITS PREVENTION

Iron and steel rust readily in the presence of water and oxygen. The process is speeded up by the presence of acids in polluted air. Prevention takes several forms:

(i) **Covering up the surface to exclude air or water or both.** This is done by
- painting – cars, household machinery
- metal plating – chromium or nickel or zinc (galvanising) or silver (cutlery)
- plastic coating – dishwasher crockery racks, underground pipelines.

(ii) **Sacrificial anode protection.** This is done on underground pipelines in wet ground. The pipe is attached by conducting wires to large lumps of zinc or magnesium at intervals. Zinc and magnesium are more reactive than iron and dissolve slowly. The reaction is

$$Zn(s) \longrightarrow Zn^{2+}(aq) + 2e^-$$

or

$$Mg(s) \longrightarrow Mg^{2+}(aq) + 2e^-$$

The electrons released in the reaction travel through the wire into the iron pipe where they build up, preventing the rusting reaction from occurring. In effect they **reverse** the reaction below.

$$\underset{\text{iron pipe}}{Fe(s)} \underset{\text{protection}}{\overset{\text{rusting}}{\rightleftharpoons}} \underset{\text{rust on iron pipe}}{Fe^{3+}(aq)} + \underset{\text{from zinc or magnesium}}{3e^-}$$

In the process, the zinc or magnesium dissolves (hence the sacrifice) and must be replaced from time to time. This is cheaper than replacing the pipeline!

15. ZINC AND LEAD EXTRACTION

Zinc and lead occur as the sulphides, zinc blende, ZnS and galena, PbS.

The ore is first concentrated to about 55% zinc content and then roasted to form the oxides:

$$2ZnS(s) + 3O_2(g) \rightarrow 2ZnO(s) + 2SO_2(g)$$

and

$$2PbS(s) + 3O_2(g) \rightarrow 2PbO(s) + 2SO_2(g)$$

(i) ZINC EXTRACTION

Zinc oxide is then either

(a) reduced with carbon in a blast furnace; or
(b) extracted by electrolysis.

(a) Smelting in a blast furnace

At Avonmouth, near Bristol, the **smelting process** is used. The process is similar to the iron smelting process. Zinc oxide is mixed with coke and fed into a furnace through which hot air is blown.

The reactions are:

$$2C(s) + O_2(g) \rightarrow 2CO(g),$$
carbon + oxygen → carbon monoxide
$$ZnO(s) + CO(g) \rightarrow Zn(g) + CO_2(g)$$
zinc oxide + carbon monoxide → zinc + carbon dioxide

Zinc vapour is formed at the temperature of the furnace.

Zinc vapour leaving the furnace is condensed by a spray of *liquid lead*. The lead/zinc mixture is cooled further until the lead and zinc separate into *two layers*. The zinc layer is tapped off and the lead is returned to the condensers to condense more zinc vapour (Fig. 11.15).

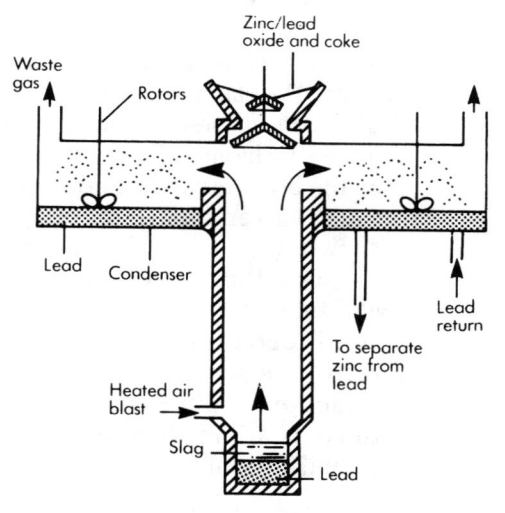

Fig. 11.15. Zinc smelting.

Use of data

Zinc made in this way contains about 1% lead and is purified by *fractional distillation* to 99.99% purity. The table of data below will be useful in understanding the principles of the purification process.

	Melting point (°C)	Boiling point (°C)
zinc	420	908
lead	328	1651

No pollution

About 12% of the world production of zinc is made by this process. The sulphur dioxide formed in the roasting process is not passed into the atmosphere but is made into sulphuric acid by the Contact Process, see Chapter 12.3, Section 6(G).

(b) Electrolysis

Most of the world's zinc is produced by *electrolysis* of zinc sulphate solution. This is formed by dissolving zinc oxide in sulphuric acid and purifying the solution before electrolysis. The electrolyte must be free from any metals lower down the reactivity series than zinc. Can you see why? This can be done by displacing these metals using zinc dust and filtering off the metal impurity:

zinc + salt of metal low in reactivity → displaced metal + zinc salt.

The solution is electrolysed in lead-lined cells using a lead anode and aluminium sheet cathodes.

From time to time the cathodes are removed and the zinc stripped off, melted and cast into ingots. The zinc is 99.96% pure. The electricity consumption of this process is only about one-quarter than for aluminium, weight for weight.

- at cathode $Zn^{2+}(aq) + 2e^- \longrightarrow Zn(s)$ deposited on the aluminium cathode
- at the anode oxygen gas is the product, the lead does not dissolve.

(c) Uses of zinc

Zinc is mainly used for galvanising steel to protect it against corrosion (35%). It is also used for diecasting alloys (25%) and brasses (20%). Smaller amounts are used to make the outer casings of dry cells (batteries) (Fig. 11.16).

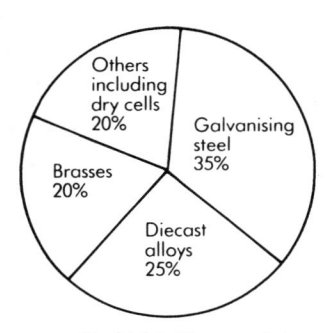

Fig. 11.16. The uses of zinc.

(ii) LEAD EXTRACTION

Lead oxide is extracted by reducton with carbon (coke) and limestone in a blast furnace. The furnace is not as large as iron smelting furnaces, however, the reactions are similar to those in iron smelting.

$$2C(s) + O_2(g) \longrightarrow 2CO(g) \quad \text{the blast}$$
$$PbO(s) + CO(g) \longrightarrow Pb(l) + CO_2(g) \quad \text{reduction}$$
$$PbO(s) + C(s) \longrightarrow Pb(l) + CO(g) \quad \text{reduction}$$

slag formation removes silica impurities:

$$\underset{\text{limestone}}{CaCO_3(s)} \longrightarrow CaO(s) + CO_2(g)$$

$$CaO(s) + \underset{\text{silica}}{SiO_2(s)} \longrightarrow \underset{\text{slag}}{CaSiO_3(l)}$$

As with iron in the blast furnace, the molten lead is tapped off at the bottom of the furnace. The slag is tapped off from **above** the molten lead.

The lead formed by this process is not pure. It contains small amounts of other elements including silver. These elements are removed and may be of value. The lead from the blast furnace is purified by one of two processes.

(a) **Desilverisation**. In this process silver is extracted from the molten lead by stirring it with molten zinc. The silver forms an alloy with zinc and lead and this rises to the surface and is skimmed off. A final treatment removes other impurities and pure lead results.

(b) **Electrolysis**. If electrical power is cheap this is the preferred process. Electrolysis produces lead at the cathode. The process resembles that for the production of pure zinc and pure copper. The anode is of impure lead, the cathode is a thin sheet of pure lead. The cathode grows thicker in the process; the anode dissolves.

$$\text{at the cathode} \quad Pb^{2+}(aq) + 2e^- \longrightarrow Pb(s) \quad \text{reduction}$$
$$\text{at the anode} \quad Pb(s) \longrightarrow Pb^{2+}(aq) + 2e^- \quad \text{oxidation}$$

16 > SILVER EXTRACTION

Silver is usually found associate with lead and zinc ores and with copper and nickel ores. It is usually extracted by dissolving the silver compounds from these ores with a cyanide solution. The silver is then extracted from the cyanide solution by electrolysis. The silver is formed on the cathode.

$$Ag^+(aq) + e^- \longrightarrow Ag(s)$$

EXAMINATION QUESTIONS

MULTIPLE CHOICE

QUESTION 1

In which one of the following sets are all the metals so reactive that they have to be extracted by electrolysis?

A calcium, copper, silver.
B calcium, magnesium, sodium.
C copper, iron, magnesium.
D iron, magnesium, silver.

(SEG)

Questions 2–5 concern the following metals:

A chromium
B copper
C tin
D zinc
E aluminium

QUESTIONS 2–5

Select from A to E the metal which is
2 used in galvanised iron.
3 alloyed with iron to produce stainless steel.
4 used as a coating on metals in food packaging.
5 a constituent of brass and bronze.

(ULEAC)

STRUCTURED QUESTIONS

QUESTION 6

Aluminium is manufactured by passing electricity through a molten mixture of aluminium oxide and cryolite (a mineral containing sodium, aluminium and fluorine). The cryolite is not used up in the process. The melting point of this mixture is much lower than that of pure aluminium oxide. The cell which holds the molten mixture is lined with carbon. Molten aluminium collects at the bottom of the cell. The current is supplied through carbon rods. Oxygen formed from the aluminium oxide burns these rods away as carbon monoxide.

(a) Answer the following questions about this process:
  (i)   Explain why it is necessary to melt the aluminium oxide.
  (ii) What are two advantages of the low melting point for the mixture in the cell?
  (iii) From the information given above, what factors are most likely to affect the cost of making aluminium?
  (6)

(b) The map shows the British Isles. The grey dotted areas are called **development** areas, where the Government will help to pay some of the costs of starting a new industry. The black circles show deep water ports. The arrow shows the direction of the prevailing winds. The ore of aluminium is imported by sea. Aluminium refineries may produce airborne fluoride fumes and should be placed where there are no large towns **downwind** of the factory.

Three possible sites for aluminium refineries are shown (A, B and C). For **each** of these sites list the **advantages** and **disadvantages** of siting a refinery at that place.
(6)

(c) Many drink cans are now made of aluminium and it has been suggested that used cans should be collected so that the metal can be recycled. Explain what factors must be considered when deciding whether the material from disposable items such as cans ought to be recycled.
(5)

QUESTION 7

The following diagram is a simple outline of a blast furnace.

(a) Complete the labelling of the diagram by writing the names of the raw materials A, B and C, and the names of the products D and E in the spaces provided. (5)
(b) Name the type of chemical reaction involved when iron ore is converted to iron
....(1)
(c) Complete the equation for the conversion of iron ore to iron.
   $Fe_2O_3 + 3CO \rightarrow$ .... + ...(2)
(d) Explain why aluminium is not extracted from its ore by a similar process to that used for iron. (4 lines)
(2)

(NEAB)

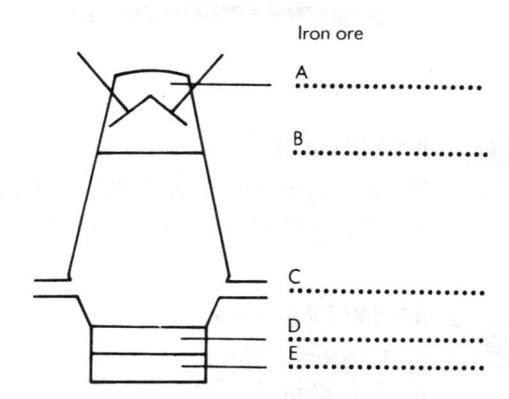

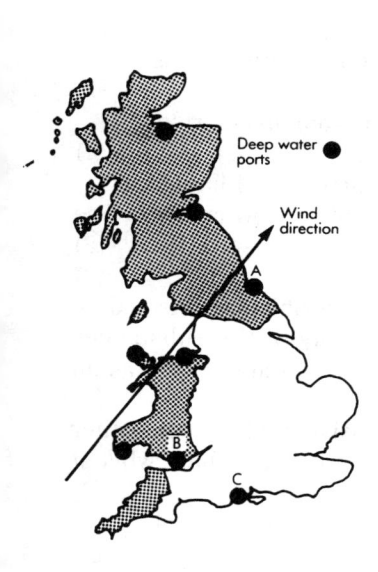

Fig. 12.17

QUESTION 8

Read the following passage through carefully. Using the information it contains and your knowledge of chemistry, answer questions (a)–(k) which follow it.

Sodium and its extraction

Of the many salt dissolved in sea water, common salt (sodium chloride) is the most abundant, comprising some 3% of mass of the world's oceans. In England, deposits of sodium chloride are found in Cheshire, Lancashire and Durham.

The production of sodium requires a high-energy process. It is produced by the electrolysis of molten sodium chloride in the Downs cell. Here the molten sodium chloride contains calcium chloride to lower its melting point. Once the process has been started, the very high current used keeps the electrolyte in the molten state. Sodium metal is produced at the cathode.

Very little waste material is produced from this process. The by-product of the reaction, chlorine, is of great commercial importance. It is, in fact, in greater demand than sodium itself!

Compared to some metals like aluminium, metallic sodium has relatively few uses. The annual world production of aluminium is about 14 million tonnes, while 0.2 million tonnes of sodium is produced each year. Sodium is used as a coolant in some nuclear reactors, in sodium vapour street lamps and in the manufacture of sodium salts.

(a) Name the chief natural source of the metal sodium (1 line) *(1)*
(b) By what method is sodium obtained from this source? (1 line) *(1)*
(c) State how the sodium chloride is kept in the molten state during the process (1 line) *(1)*
(d) Explain why it is desirable to lower the melting point of the sodium chloride. (2 lines) *(2)*
(e) Give the formula for the substance used to lower the melting point. (1 line) *(1)*
(f) State one advantage of this process from a pollution point of view and also one commercial advantage. (2 lines) *(2)*
(g) Give two uses of the by-product. (2 lines) *(2)*
(h) The electrodes used in the production of sodium must be capable of withstanding very high temperatures and must not react at all with any of the substances present (i.e. be inert). Name a substance which would be suitable to act as an electrode. (1 line) *(1)*
(i) Sodium is a very reactive metal which will react explosively with many other elements. Name two elements which must be kept away from the sodium while it is being formed and stored. (2 lines) *(2)*
(j) Suggest two reasons why sodium is suitable as a coolant in nuclear reactors. (2 lines) *(2)*
(k) Many street lamps give out yellow light. Explain why this tells you that there is sodium present in these lamps. (2 lines) *(2)*

(Total 17 marks)
(NISEAC)

OUTLINE ANSWERS

MULTIPLE CHOICE

ANSWER 1

B. The key phrase is **all the metals in the set**. There is at least **one** metal in every set that is extracted by the use of electrolysis but only set B in which **all** are – Fig. 11.12.

ANSWERS 2–5

2 D. Section 15(c).
3 A. Section 14(d).

See Section 12

4 C. So called 'tin cans' are really made from *tin coated* mild steel.
   Note: Tin is expensive but the coating is *very thin* and so does not make the can expensive to manufacture. The tin may also be recycled.

5 B. You may be tempted by zinc, which *is* present in brass but *not* in bronze.

STRUCTURED QUESTIONS

Questions 6 and 8 are comprehension questions. This type of question is not found on every chemistry paper. However, many questions have *new material* in them which may not be in the syllabus but which is presented with *enough information* for the candidate to produce an answer using known principles and techniques.

ANSWER 6

The question is about the process of aluminium extraction, how it is done, economic factors, pollution possibilities and recycling. It is therefore within the area of each syllabus which deals with the social, economic, environmental and industrial aspects of chemistry.

Look up the following section as you plan your answer:

(a) (i) Section 11.
     (ii) Common sense will help here.
     (iii) Re-read the passage looking for the expenses of the process.
(b) There are likely to be many questions of this sort in coming years. A little common sense comes in handy here. The factors to consider in each case are
     (i) wind-borne pollution.
     (ii) development area payments.
     (iii) deep water facilities.
One has all three, another only two and the third only one of these advantages. A total of six points for a mark each.
(c) There are many factors here. Look for some *cost reduction factors* and some *expenses* of the operation of scrap collection.

ANSWER 7

(a) A and B are coke (carbon) and limestone.
    C is air (sometimes enriched with oxygen).
    D is molten slag.
    E is molten iron.
(b) Iron ore contains an oxide. Removal of oxygen to convert this to a metal is called *reduction*. Reduction is a *type* of chemical reaction.
(c) The equation is given in Section 14.
(d) *Carbon reduction* of aluminium ore is not possible at temperatures below 2000 °C because carbon is not reactive enough to remove oxygen from aluminium oxide. Carbon is *lower* in the reactivity series than aluminium.

ANSWER 8

(a) Sodium chloride is the source of sodium but *natural sources* of sodium chloride are the sea and rock-salt deposits.
(b) Sodium is obtained from sodium chloride by electrolysis.
(c) The electrolyte is kept molten by the heat produced by the current passing through the cell. This can be as much as 30 000 amps!
(d) There are several answers here:
    (i) Lower temperature means less energy to keep molten.
    (ii) Less sodium vaporises at lower temperatures.
    (iii) Cheaper if energy use is less.
(e) The formula of calcium chloride is $CaCl_2$-calcium ions have *two positive charges* and chloride ions *one negative charge*, so two chloride ions must be present for every calcium ion - Ca^{++} $2Cl^-$.
(f) Little waste means little possible pollution. The chlorine by-product is valuable commercially.
(g) Chlorine is used in water sterilisation and as a bleach. It is also used to make poly(vinyl chloride). When asked for more than one use try to give uses which are not too similar if possible.

(h) An inert electrode material would be graphite (carbon) or steel for the cathode where sodium is formed. Carbon has few reactions other than burning in oxygen.
(i) Sodium must not be allowed contact with oxygen (air) or chlorine. Chlorine is a danger because it is formed in the same cell. Air must not be allowed to enter the part of the cell where the sodium collects.
(j) Coolants need to carry away heat – they must be liquids to circulate well (low melting point), conduct heat well and absorb a lot of it (high **heat capacity**).
(k) Sodium and its compounds impart a yellow colour to a flame. An electrical discharge through sodium vapour produces the same colour.

STUDENT'S ANSWER – EXAMINER'S COMMENTS

Titanium is the ninth most abundant element in the earth's crust. One form in which it occurs is rutile, TiO_2. In extracting titanium from its ore, rutile is first converted to titanium(IV) chloride, $TiCl_4$. This is then reduced to the metal by heating it with sodium or magnesium in an atmosphere of argon.

Magnesium and its alloys are used in aircraft construction. In spacecraft titanium is used rather than magnesium. In space the temperature is very low; on re-entering the atmosphere the surface temperature of the craft becomes very high.

	Melting Point °C	Boiling Point °C	Density in.g/m³	Relative Atomic Mass
Magnesium	650	1117	1.7	24
Titanium	1677	3277	4.5	48

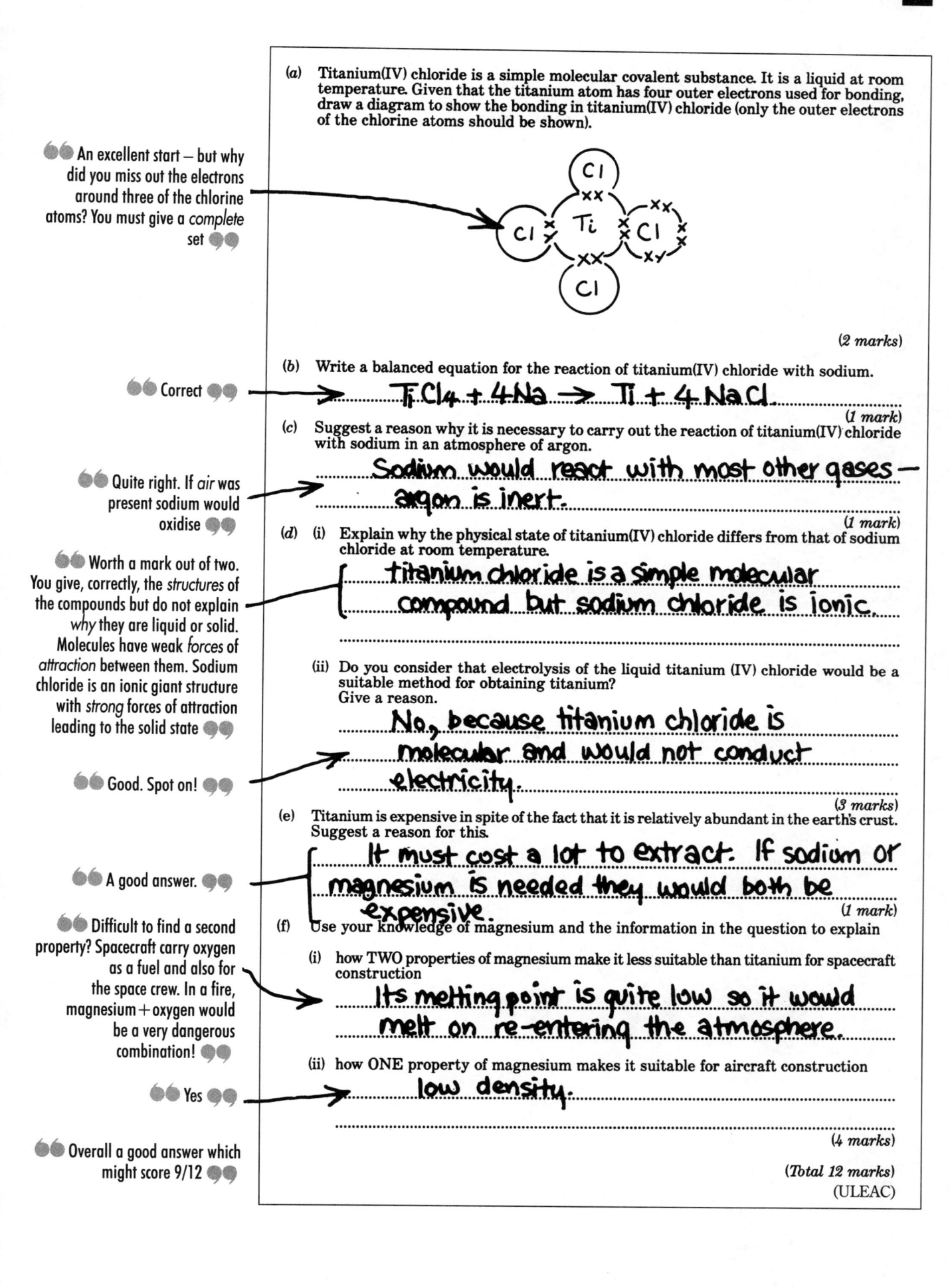

(a) Titanium(IV) chloride is a simple molecular covalent substance. It is a liquid at room temperature. Given that the titanium atom has four outer electrons used for bonding, draw a diagram to show the bonding in titanium(IV) chloride (only the outer electrons of the chlorine atoms should be shown).

> **An excellent start — but why did you miss out the electrons around three of the chlorine atoms? You must give a *complete* set**

[Diagram: Cl atoms arranged around central Ti, with one Cl showing xx electrons shared with Ti, and the other three Cl atoms without electrons shown]

(2 marks)

(b) Write a balanced equation for the reaction of titanium(IV) chloride with sodium.

> **Correct**

$$TiCl_4 + 4Na \rightarrow Ti + 4NaCl$$

(1 mark)

(c) Suggest a reason why it is necessary to carry out the reaction of titanium(IV) chloride with sodium in an atmosphere of argon.

Sodium would react with most other gases — argon is inert.

> **Quite right. If *air* was present sodium would oxidise**

(1 mark)

(d) (i) Explain why the physical state of titanium(IV) chloride differs from that of sodium chloride at room temperature.

titanium chloride is a simple molecular compound but sodium chloride is ionic.

> **Worth a mark out of two. You give, correctly, the *structures* of the compounds but do not explain *why* they are liquid or solid. Molecules have weak *forces of attraction* between them. Sodium chloride is an ionic giant structure with *strong* forces of attraction leading to the solid state**

(ii) Do you consider that electrolysis of the liquid titanium (IV) chloride would be a suitable method for obtaining titanium? Give a reason.

No, because titanium chloride is molecular and would not conduct electricity.

> **Good. Spot on!**

(3 marks)

(e) Titanium is expensive in spite of the fact that it is relatively abundant in the earth's crust. Suggest a reason for this.

It must cost a lot to extract. If sodium or magnesium is needed they would both be expensive.

> **A good answer.**

(1 mark)

(f) Use your knowledge of magnesium and the information in the question to explain

(i) how TWO properties of magnesium make it less suitable than titanium for spacecraft construction

Its melting point is quite low so it would melt on re-entering the atmosphere.

> **Difficult to find a second property? Spacecraft carry oxygen as a fuel and also for the space crew. In a fire, magnesium + oxygen would be a very dangerous combination!**

(ii) how ONE property of magnesium makes it suitable for aircraft construction

low density.

> **Yes**

(4 marks)

(Total 12 marks)
(ULEAC)

> **Overall a good answer which might score 9/12**

REVIEW SHEET

■ List some of the main properties of metals.

1. _____   5. _____
2. _____   6. _____
3. _____   7. _____
4. _____   8. _____

■ For each property you have identified give a **metal** which has that property and a **use** that can be made of that metal.

1. _____
2. _____
3. _____
4. _____
5. _____
6. _____
7. _____
8. _____

■ **Alloys** are _____
_____

■ Complete the following table

Alloy	Composition	Property	Uses
brasses	copper, 66–70% zinc, 30–34%		
bronze	copper, 90% tin, 10%		
cupro-nickel	copper, 75% nickel, 25%		
solder	lead, 67% tin, 33%		
steel	iron, 99% carbon, 0–1%		
Stainless steel	iron, 73% chromium, 18% nickel, 8% carbon, 1%		

■ Describe an experiment to measure the reactivity of metals with steam. Draw the apparatus used.

_____
_____
_____
_____
_____

CHAPTER 11 METALS AND OTHER STRONG MATERIALS

- Complete the following table:

Reaction of the reactivity series metals with:			
Metals	Water	Acids	Oxides and Salts
potassium sodium calcium			Each metal will _____ any of the METALS below it in the TABLE from their _____ or from their _____
magnesium aluminium zinc			
iron			
lead copper silver			
gold platinum			

- What does a **reducing agent** do? _____

- When would you use **carbon reduction**? _____

- When would you use **electrolytic reduction**? _____

- Outline the chemical reactions in a blast furnace where iron oxide is reduced to molten iron by carbon. _____

CHAPTER 12.1

HYDROGEN AND WATER

HYDROGEN

WATER

GETTING STARTED

Hydrogen is a very reactive element and therefore it is only found naturally in very small amounts. Gases from volcanoes and certain rocks contain a small amount of hydrogen. Free hydrogen occurs in the sun and other celestial bodies. Hydrogen occurs combined with a large number of elements, particularly oxygen and carbon. The most common compound containing hydrogen is water. Other compounds containing hydrogen are hydrogencarbonates, hydrocarbons and carbohydrates. Most animals and plants contain hydrogen.

1 HYDROGEN

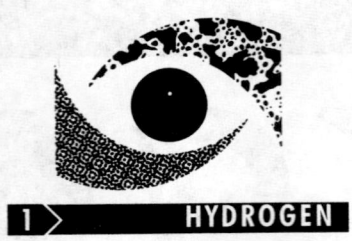

ESSENTIAL PRINCIPLES

Hydrogen is prepared by reacting a fairly reactive metal such as zinc with a dilute acid such as sulphuric acid (Fig. 12.1).

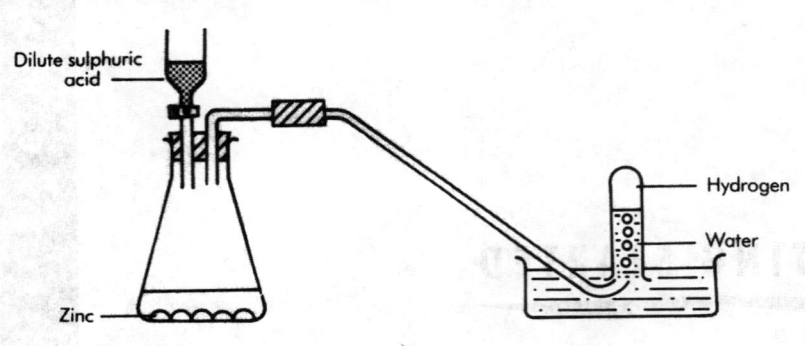

Fig. 12.1 Preparation of hydrogen

zinc	+	sulphuric acid	→	hydrogen	+	zinc sulphate
Zn	+	H_2SO_4	→	H_2	+	$ZnSO_4$.

This reaction is very slow. Copper acts as a catalyst for this reaction. A small amount of copper(II) sulphate is added to the zinc/sulphuric acid mixture. Zinc displaces copper, and this catalyses the reaction.

Sodium cannot be used to prepare hydrogen by this method because it is too reactive; and copper cannot be used because it is too unreactive.

You cannot make hydrogen using these acids and a metal.

Dilute nitric acid, concentrated nitric acid and concentrated sulphuric acid cannot be used because they are oxidising agents and they would oxidise hydrogen to water.

Hydrogen can also be made when a very reactive metal such as sodium reacts with water:

sodium	+	water	→	hydrogen	+	sodium hydroxide
2Na	+	$2H_2O$	→	H_2	+	2NaOH.

Hydrogen is formed when various aqueous solutions are electrolysed such as sulphuric acid, sodium hydroxide and magnesium nitrate. Hydrogen ions are discharged at the negative electrode:

hydrogen ions	+	electrons	→	hydrogen
$2H^+$	+	$2e^-$	→	H_2.

(A) PROPERTIES OF HYDROGEN

TEST FOR HYDROGEN

REACTION WITH CHLORINE

Hydrogen is a colourless gas. It has no smell. It is less dense than air. (It is the least dense of all gases.) It does not dissolve in water and therefore it has no effect on damp indicator paper. It is not poisonous.

Hydrogen burns with a squeaky pop in air or oxygen. This is used as a test for hydrogen:

Test for hydrogen

hydrogen	+	oxygen	→	water
$2H_2$	+	O_2	→	$2H_2O$.

It does not support the burning of a splint.

Reaction with chlorine

Hydrogen reacts with chlorine to form hydrogen chloride:

hydrogen	+	chlorine	→	hydrogen chloride
H_2	+	Cl_2	→	2HCl.

When hydrogen burns in chlorine the green colour of chlorine slowly disappears. The gas formed fumes in moist air and turns damp indicator paper red. When all the chlorine has reacted, the flame goes out because hydrogen chloride does not support burning (Fig. 12.2).

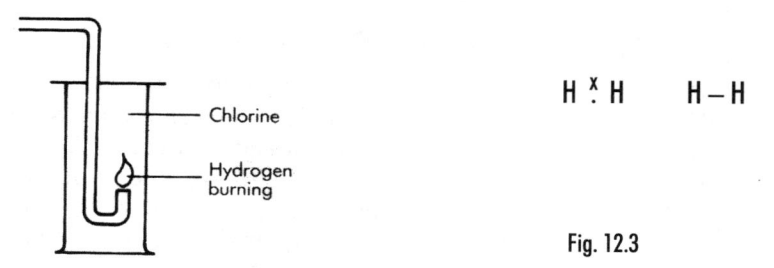

Fig. 12.2

Fig. 12.3

❝❝ Hydrogen is a reducing agent ❞❞

If light is shone on a mixture of hydrogen and chlorine it explodes.

Hydrogen is a powerful *reducing agent*. It reduces the oxides of metals low in the reactivity series to the metal:

copper(II) oxide + hydrogen → copper + water

CuO + H_2 → Cu + H_2O.

Hydrogen reduces chlorine to hydrogen chloride, nitrogen to ammonia and sulphur to hydrogen sulphide.

Hydrogen is a typical covalent molecule (Fig. 12.3). It is a gas which is insoluble in water. It does not conduct electricity.

❝❝ Structure ❞❞

Hydrogen has three *isotopes* of mass numbers 1, 2 and 3. These isotopes are given names. ^1H is called hydrogen, ^2H deuterium and ^3H tritium. Deuterium oxide, D_2O is known as *'heavy water'*.

❝❝ Ionic compounds ❞❞

Hydrogen forms ionic compounds with very reactive metals such as sodium. These compounds are unusual in that they contain a negatively charged hydrogen ion H^-. These metal hydrides react with water to form hydrogen.

(B) MANUFACTURE OF HYDROGEN

Industrially hydrogen is made by reacting natural gas (methane) with steam in the presence of a catalyst. The mixture of hydrogen and carbon monoxide formed is known as *synthesis gas* (Chapter 12.3, Section. 4):

methane + steam → hydrogen + carbon monoxide

CH_4 + H_2O → $3H_2$ + CO.

It can also be made by reacting red hot coke (carbon) with steam. The mixture of hydrogen and carbon monoxide formed is known as *water gas*.

carbon + steam → hydrogen + carbon monoxide.

Hydrogen is formed as the by-product of a number of industrial processes such as the manufacture of sodium hydroxide by electrolysis of brine (Chapter 7, Figs. 7.3 and 7.4).

(C) USES OF HYDROGEN

Hydrogen is used for making margarine, methanol and ammonia. It is used as a liquid fuel in rockets. It was used to inflate 'air-ships', but this was dangerous because a mixture of hydrogen and air is explosive. You may have seen a photograph or a film of the *Hindenburg* hydrogen balloon which was ignited by saboteurs in 1937.

❝❝ A mixture of hydrogen and carbon monoxide is used to make methanol. ❞❞

Hydrogen has possibilities as a fuel of the future. It is very abundant and it is a clean fuel because the only product on combustion is water.

2 ▶ WATER

About 80% of the world's surface is covered with water. It is therefore no surprise to find that water is the most common compound. It is present in almost all forms of living things. About 70% of you is water!

❝❝ Structure ❞❞

Water is a covalent molecule (Fig. 12.4). It is a liquid at room temperature because there are bonds holding water molecules to other water molecules called *hydrogen bonds*.

Fig. 12.4

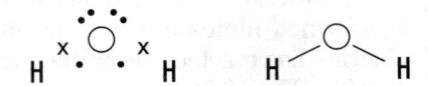

(A) POLLUTION OF WATER

> Note that fertiliser causes plants to grow. Also the plants get large and prevent light entering the water.

Because water is such a good solvent it dissolves a large number and variety of substances. Some of these substances **pollute** water. Water that has drained off roads contains grit, oil, petrol and lead compounds. Water that has fallen on land that has been recently fertilised dissolves the fertiliser. The fertiliser gets washed into rivers and streams and makes algae and other river plants grow. When these plants die there is then less oxygen for the fish and they also die. This collapse of a natural cycle is known as *eutrophication*.

A similar problem occurs when sewage is allowed to flow into rivers and seas. There are now very strict rules about the type and amount of waste that can be dumped into rivers and seas.

(B) PURIFICATION

> Chlorine sterilizes water.

> Energy is expensive.

Water must be *purified* in order to make it fit for drinking. The water is first filtered through sand filter beds. The layers of sand become finer towards the bottom of the beds. The filtering process removes organic and inorganic debris. The water leaving the filter beds is relatively clear but it still contains fine particles. These are removed by adding potassium aluminium sulphate (potash alum) which causes the fine particles to settle. This process is called **sedimentation**. The clear water contains harmful bacteria. Carefully controlled amounts of chlorine are added to kill the bacteria. Ozone is sometimes used instead of chlorine. It leaves no smell or flavour in the water. Bacteria can also be killed by boiling water but this is uneconomical on a large scale.

Purified water is not strictly *pure*. It contains many dissolved substances whereas pure water should really contain only water.

(C) DETECTION OF WATER

> If anhydrous copper(II) sulphate turns blue in a liquid, the liquid contains water, but it may not be pure water.

The *presence of water* can be shown by adding either anhydrous copper(II) sulphate which changes from white to blue or by adding anhydrous cobalt(II) chloride which changes from blue to pink.

To show that *pure water* is present you should measure either its freezing point (0 °C) or its boiling point at normal pressure (100 °C).

(D) PROPERTIES OF WATER

Cold water reacts vigorously with reactive metals such as sodium and potassium:

sodium + water → sodium hydroxide + hydrogen

2Na + 2H$_2$O → 2NaOH + H$_2$.

Fairly reactive metals such as magnesium and iron react when heated in *steam*:

magnesium + steam → magnesium oxide + hydrogen

Mg + H$_2$O → MgO + H$_2$.

Note: that with cold water the metal hydroxide is formed, but with steam the metal oxide is formed.

> Iron reacts to give the oxide Fe$_3$O$_4$ and H$_2$

Water does not react with copper under any conditions and this is why copper is used for cooking pans. (Aluminium does not react with water because it has a protective oxide layer, which is why we have aluminium pans and utensils.)

(E) USES OF WATER

Water is used in the home for cooking, drinking, washing and waste disposal. A large amount of water is used in farming and for cooling waste products, particularly in power stations. Water, in the form of steam, is used to turn turbines which then generate electricity. Water is used in the manufacture of sodium carbonate, ammonia, nitric acid and sulphuric acid. It is used to extract sulphur, sodium chloride and oil from the earth. Water is used as a solvent for many substances, both in the laboratory, in the home and in industry.

(F) WATER AS A SOLVENT

Water is often said to be the universal solvent. This is not true, of course, but many substances do dissolve in it.

(i) Oxygen dissolves in water. Without dissolved oxygen aquatic plants and animals could not survive. Gases dissolve less well in hot water than in cold water. For this reason aquatic animals have difficulty obtaining their oxygen supplies if the water is warm. Power stations emit warm water to rivers. Aquatic life disappears from the river section where the temperature is high enough to reduce the available oxygen. Fish will sometimes die in a garden pond that has become overheated in summer for the same reason.

(ii) Carbon dioxide dissolved in aqueous solutions of sugar and flavouring makes a refreshing drink – lemonade or cola, these drinks become flat if warmed.

(iii) Ionic solids, such as salts, dissolve well in water. The sea is a solution of many ionic compounds. The main compounds present are sodium chloride, magnesium and potassium sulphates with small amounts of compounds of calcium, bromine and carbon (as carbonate). The oceans contain about 3.5% dissolved solids. Some inland seas, like the Dead Sea, contain more.

(iv) Limestone or chalk dissolved in rain water produces the hard water characteristic of areas where such rocks underlie the surface (see Chapter 12, Section 4).

EXAMINATION QUESTIONS

MULTIPLE CHOICE

QUESTION 1

The table below gives the results of tests on four gases A, B, C and D. All four gases are colourless. Which gas is hydrogen?

Gas	Colour seen when tested with damp indicator paper	Effect of lighted splint
A	Blue	Splint extinguished
B	No change	Gas ignites
C	No change	Splint burns more brightly
D	Red	Splint extinguished

(SEG)

QUESTION 2–5

These questions are about the five gases labelled A–E.

A argon
B carbon dioxide
C hydrogen
D nitrogen
E oxygen

From this list of gases, choose the one which:

2. is not usually present in air.
3. reacts with hydrogen to make ammonia.
4. is used to make margarine from vegetable oils.
5. could be used to fill a weather balloon.

QUESTION 6

Which ONE of the following reactions would result in an element being formed?
A neutralising an acid with a base.
B burning charcoal in air.
C heating copper sulphate.
D the rusting of iron.
E reducing a metallic oxide.

(NISEAC)

COMPLETION AND STRUCTURED QUESTIONS

QUESTION 7

What is the purest form of water which occurs naturally? (NEAB)

QUESTION 8

Drinking water which is good for the growth of healthy teeth and bones contains ions of which elements?

QUESTION 9

(a) (i) How is filtration of reservoir water carried out? (2 lines) *(1 mark)*
    (ii) What is the purpose of this filtration? (2 lines) *(1 mark)*
(b) (i) How may a sample of pure water be obtained from sea water? (1 line)
    (1 mark)
    (ii) Explain the process of evaporation in terms of movement of molecules. (3 lines) *(3 marks)*
    (iii) Why does the salt in sea water not circulate through the atmosphere in the way the water does? (2 lines) *(1 mark)*
(c) (i) Name one pollutant of river water other than an agricultural fertiliser. (1 line) *(1 mark)*
    (ii) State the source of this pollutant and describe its effect. (2 lines) *(2 marks)*
(d) (i) Why is chlorine added to water supplies? (1 line) *(1 mark)*
    (ii) Tap water usually contains chloride ions rather than chlorine itself. Describe chemical tests that would show:

      (I) that tap water does not contain chlorine,
      (II) that tap water does contain chloride ions.
      (In each case you should name the substances you would use and describe what you would observe.) (4 lines) *(6 marks)*
    (iii) Explain in terms of electron transfer what happens when chlorine is converted into chloride ions. (2 lines) *(2 marks)*

(SEG)

QUESTION 10

(a) From the reactivity series in Chapter 11, Section 4 choose
    (i) an element that can occur uncombined in the earth's crust. (1 line) *(1 mark)*
    (ii) an element that reacts vigorously with cold water. (1 line) *(1 mark)*

(b) A gas may be made by passing steam over heated zinc using the apparatus shown below (Fig. 12.6).
    (i) Name the gas collected. (1 line) *(1 mark)*
    (ii) Name the other product of the reaction. (1 line) *(1 mark)*
    (iii) Write an equation for the reaction. (1 line) *(1 mark)*
    (iv) Name one metal that should not be reacted with steam in this way. Explain your choice. (2 lines) *(2 marks)*

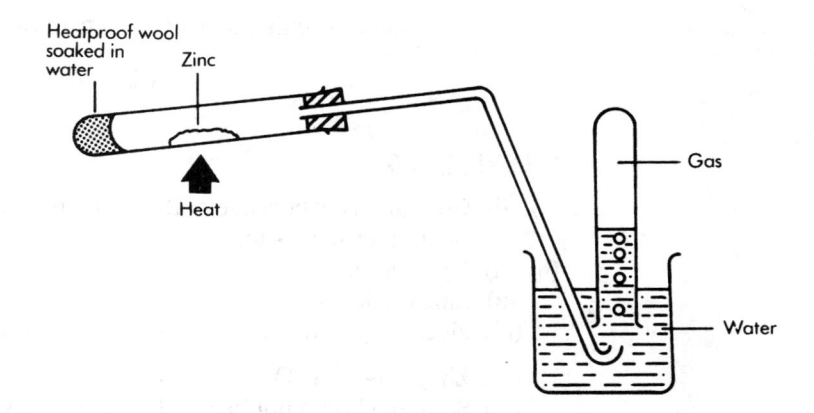

Fig. 12.6

OUTLINE ANSWERS

MULTIPLE CHOICE

ANSWER 1

Hydrogen is a colourless gas that is neutral to indicator and burns (ignites) with a pop. This is key B. Gas A is ammonia, it is an alkaline gas. Gas C is oxygen; it is neutral and supports burning. Gas D is an acidic gas such as sulphur dioxide or hydrogen chloride.

ANSWER 2

Answer: C, hydrogen diffuses so quickly it escapes from the atmosphere.

ANSWERS 3, 4, 5

Look at Section 1(c) above: 3 D; 4 C; and 5 C.

ANSWER 6

Answer: E - hydrogen is a reducing agent and reduces metal oxides to metals (see Section 1(a) above).

COMPLETION AND STRUCTURED QUESTIONS

ANSWER 7

Rain water.

ANSWER 8

Fluorine or calcium.

ANSWER 9

If you had problems answering this question read Sect. 2(b) above
(a) (i) Filter through filter beds made of sand.
 (ii) To remove inorganic and organic debris.
(b) (i) Distillation.
 (ii) Molecules in a liquid are in a continuous state of movement. Some of these molecules have sufficient energy to escape from the surface of the liquid and go into the air. This process is known as evaporation.
 (iii) Salt (sodium chloride) is a high melting point solid and hence it is not volatile.
(c) (i) Phosphates from (ii) washing powders. They cause algae to grow in water, which eventually leads to a shortage of oxygen and then fishes die.
(d) (i) To sterilise or kill bacteria.
 (ii) (I) Add pH paper; if paper is not bleached, then no chlorine is present.
  (II) Add nitric acid and silver nitrate. A white precipitate (of silver chloride) shows that chloride ions are present.

(iii) Chlorine molecule gains two electrons and becomes two chloride ions:

$$Cl_2 + 2e^- \rightarrow 2Cl^-$$

ANSWER 10

(a) (i) Gold or silver because of their lack of reactivity.
    (ii) Sodium or potassium.
(b) (i) Hydrogen.
    (ii) Zinc oxide.
    (iii) zinc + steam → zinc oxide + hydrogen
        Zn + H$_2$O → ZnO + H$_2$.
    (iv) Sodium should not be reacted in this way. It is a very reactive metal and the reaction with steam would be explosive.

STUDENT'S ANSWER – EXAMINER'S COMMENTS

Hard water is water which has passed over rocks such as limestone. It contains certain dissolved substances.

(a) What is the chemical name for limestone?

calcium carbonate

(1 mark)

(b) Describe a simple experiment to show that a sample of hard water contains dissolved substances.

→ **boil the water**

(1 mark)

❝ You should have answered 'carefully to dryness'. ❞

(c) Table 1 compares the properties of sodium carbonate and sodium hydrogencarbonate.

	Solubility in water	pH of aqueous solution
Sodium carbonate	Readily soluble	11
Sodium hydrogencarbonate	Not very soluble	8

Give one disadvantage of using bath salts containing

(i) sodium carbonate,

→ **It is fairly alkaline (pH11)**

(1 mark)

❝ good ❞

(ii) sodium hydrogencarbonate

→ **It takes away the natural oils.**

(1 mark)

❝ It tells you in the question that it is *not* very soluble. ❞

Table 2 gives the volume of solution required to give a lasting lather with different samples of water.

Experiment	Volume of soap solution
25 cm³ distilled water	1.0 cm³
25 cm³ of water sample A	7.0 cm³
25 cm³ of water sample A which is boiled before adding soap solution.	4.0 cm³
25 cm³ of water sample A after addition of bath salts.	1.0 cm³

(d) Name a piece of apparatus suitable for

(i) measuring out 25 cm³ of distilled water, **measuring cylinder**

(1 mark)

❝ For accurate work you would use a pipette. ❞

(ii) adding soap solution **burette**

(1 mark)

❝ correct ❞

(iii) Give the name and formula of the dissolved substance that causes hardness in water.

→ **calcium hydrogen carbonate**

(1 mark)

❝ The question also asks for the *formula* $Ca(HCO_3)_2$ ❞

(iv) Write the equation for the reaction which takes place when hard water is boiled.

→ **water + calcium hydrogen carbonate → calcium carbonate + water + carbon dioxide**

(2 marks)

❝ No need for water on the left-hand side ❞

(v) What might be suitable as the main ingredient of bath salts?

→ **sodium carbonate**

(1 mark)

❝ Correct ❞

(WJEC)

❝ Overall, quite good but you should write symbolic equations. Score 6/10 ❞

CHAPTER 22

OXYGEN

PREPARATION OF OXYGEN

OXYGEN FROM THE AIR

PROPERTIES OF OXYGEN

RESPIRATION

BURNING

COMMON FUELS

OXIDES

RUSTING

USES OF OXYGEN

COMPOSITION OF THE AIR

GETTING STARTED

Oxygen is the most abundant element in the earth's crust forming nearly 50% by mass. It is found in compounds mainly as oxides, carbonates and silicates. 89% by mass of water is oxygen. Oxygen occurs as the free element in air; about 21% of air by volume is oxygen (this is about 23% by mass).

Oxygen has not always been a component of the Earth's atmosphere. The first signs of the free element appear about half way through the 4.5 billion years of the Earth's existence. As photosynthesising plants evolved, however, the proportion of carbon dioxide would have diminished and that of oxygen increased. The formation of oxygen has led to the production of a protective layer of ozone in the stratosphere which filters out the more harmful wavelengths of UV light from the Sun.

ESSENTIAL PRINCIPLES

1. PREPARATION OF OXYGEN

Oxygen is prepared by adding a catalyst, such as manganese(IV) oxide, to hydrogen peroxide. The catalyst makes the hydrogen peroxide break down at room temperature (Fig. 12.7).

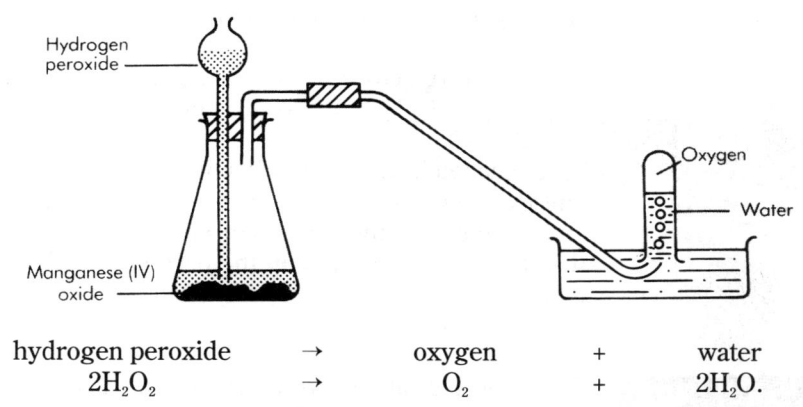

Fig. 12.7 Preparation of oxygen.

$$\text{hydrogen peroxide} \rightarrow \text{oxygen} + \text{water}$$
$$2H_2O_2 \rightarrow O_2 + 2H_2O.$$

N.B. The products are oxygen and water NOT oxygen and hydrogen. The catalyst, manganese(IV) oxide is not written in the equation.

Oxygen is obtained industrially from the atmosphere. Air is filtered to remove dust and other particles and dried to remove water vapour. Air is then cooled under pressure and it turns into a liquid. Liquid air is fractionally distilled. Nitrogen boils off first because it has the lowest boiling point and then oxygen. Argon and other noble gases are also obtained by this process.

Oxygen is formed by the electrolysis of certain aqueous solutions, e.g. sulphuric acid, sodium hydroxide and magnesium sulphate. Hydroxyl ions are discharged at the positive electrode.

Learn this equation

$$\text{hydroxyl ions} - \text{electrons} \rightarrow \text{oxygen} + \text{water}$$
$$4OH^- - 4e^- \rightarrow O_2 + 2H_2O.$$

Fig. 12.8

Oxygen is a typical covalent, diatomic molecule (Fig. 12.8). It is a gas and only slightly soluble in water. It does not conduct electricity.

2. OXYGEN FROM THE AIR

Oxygen is extracted from liquid air by distillation. Air is liquified by a repeated cycle of compression, cooling and expansion. The liquid formed at -200°C (73K) is warmed. Nitrogen boils at 77K and distils off as a gas. Oxygen remains a liquid since its boiling point is 90K. Both nitrogen and oxygen are sold as gases or liquids.

The boiling point of nitrogen is -196°C and the boiling point of oxygen is -183°C, -183°C is a higher temperature than -196°C

3. PROPERTIES OF OXYGEN

Oxygen is a colourless gas. It has no smell. It is slightly denser than air. It dissolves slightly in water. (In fact, oxygen is more soluble in water than nitrogen.) Fish breathe oxygen that is dissolved in water. Oxygen has no effect on damp pH paper. It is not poisonous. Oxygen does not burn.

Oxygen relights a glowing splint. This is used as a test for oxygen.

Test for oxygen

CHEMICAL PROPERTIES OF OXYGEN

- Most elements react with oxygen to form oxides.
- Metals react to form ***basic*** oxides. These oxides are ionic and have high melting points.
- Non-metals react to form ***acidic*** oxides. These usually have very low melting points. Many non-metallic oxides are gases that are soluble in water to form acids.
- Some oxides react with both acids and bases. These are called ***amphoteric*** oxides. These oxides have both basic and acidic properties. Some examples of amphoteric oxides are aluminium oxide, lead(II) oxide and zinc oxide.

- There are also **neutral** non-metallic oxides, e.g. water (H_2O), carbon monoxide (CO) and nitrogen(II) oxide (NO).
- All reactions involving oxygen are **exothermic**.

4 > RESPIRATION

Carbohydrates in our bodies are oxidised by oxygen that we breathe in to form carbon dioxide and water. Some of the energy produced helps to keep us warm. A well-known carbohydrate that we eat is sugar:

$$\text{sugar (glucose)} + \text{oxygen} \rightarrow \text{carbon dioxide} + \text{water}$$
$$C_6H_{12}O_6 + 6O_2 \rightarrow 6CO_2 + 6H_2O.$$

This reaction is very slow when it occurs in our bodies; however, the same amount of energy is given out when sugar burns. The energy given out can easily be measured and is known as the **calorific value** of sugar. Most brands of packaged food have the calorific value stated on the packet – this is very useful information for people on diets.

5 > BURNING

Putting out fires

When we talk about **burning**, we are usually referring to the burning of fuels to produce heat and light. Before burning can start, three things are needed: fuel, heat and oxygen (Fig. 12.9). If any one of these is missing burning stops. If you have to put out a fire there are three things that you should do.

(1) Turn off the supply of fuel. This would mean that you would turn off the gas, oil or petrol tap. Turn off the electricity switch.
(2) Lower the temperature by covering the flame with foam or water. **Water must not be used on petrol and oil fires because these substances float on water causing the fire to spread out**. To put out these types of fire you should cover them with soil, sand, foam or carbon dioxide. If a chip pan catches fire in your kitchen, the quickest action would probably be to cover the pan with a damp towel.
(3) Cut off the supply of oxygen by covering the fire with sand, a blanket or foam.

- Water is often used to put out fires because it lowers the temperature of the fire. The heat turns water to steam and the presence of steam removes the air supply.
- Carbon dioxide is also used to put out fires. It does not support burning and it is denser than air. It therefore helps to keep away the air supply.
- If you see someone with their clothes on fire, you should wrap them in a blanket or carpet.
- If you are in a fire in a building and it is too difficult for you to put it out, you should shout 'fire', get everyone out of the building, close all doors and windows and 'phone for the emergency services.

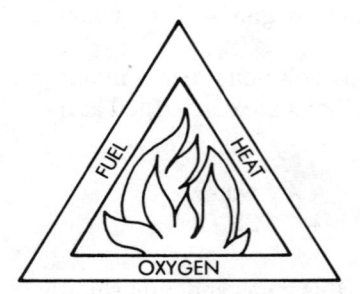

Fig. 12.9 The triangle of fire.

6 > COMMON FUELS

When you write an equation for burning, one of the reactants must be oxygen

The most common fuel we burn is **North Sea gas**, which is mainly methane:

$$\text{methane} + \text{oxygen} \rightarrow \text{carbon dioxide} + \text{water}$$
$$CH_4 + 2O_2 \rightarrow CO_2 + 2H_2O.$$

Another common fuel we burn is **petrol** to power our motor cars. Petrol is mainly octane:

$$\text{octane} + \text{oxygen} \rightarrow \text{carbon dioxide} + \text{water}$$
$$C_8H_{18} + 12\tfrac{1}{2}O_2 \rightarrow 8CO_2 + 9H_2O.$$

Another term that is used to describe burning of elements and compounds in oxygen (air) is **combustion**.

7 > OXIDES

Oxides are of three types, metallic, non-metallic and metalloid. These have different, distinguishing properties as is shown in the table below.

Property	metal oxides	non-metal oxides	metalloid oxides
acid/base nature	bases or alkalis	acidic or neutral	amphoteric – both acidic and basic
structure	ionic	molecular/covalent	ionic
examples	Na_2O, CuO, MgO	CO_2, SO_2, NO_2, H_2O	Al_2O_3, PbO

8 RUSTING

Rusting is an oxidation process

As we have seen, metals react with oxygen. When this process involves iron it is known as ***rusting***, and the flaky brown solid formed on the surface of iron or steel is called rust. In order for rusting to take place, both oxygen and water must be present. Other chemicals, such as the presence of salt in the water, can speed up the rusting process.

Iron can be protected from rusting by preventing air from reaching the surface. This can be done by painting, oiling, galvanising, covering with plastic or electroplating the iron surface. These coatings tend to peel off after some time. This would be very inconvenient and, in some cases, it would be impractical to replace the protective covering, e.g. ships' hulls or underground pipes. In these cases blocks of magnesium or zinc are attached to the iron. The magnesium and zinc are oxidised in preference to the iron. This is described as ***sacrificial protection***. Rusting is a reversal of the process of extraction of iron from its oxide ores.

9 USES OF OXYGEN

Oxygen is used in steelmaking. It is used in oxygen tents in hospitals to help recovery of normal breathing of people having breathing difficulties. Ethyne (acetylene) when burnt in oxygen produces a very hot flame. The temperature produced is hot enough to melt metals. The oxy-acetylene flame is used for welding and cutting metals. Oxygen is also used in rocket engines to enable fuels to burn.

10 COMPOSITION OF THE AIR

The third commonest gas in the air is argon, not carbon dioxide.

Air is a mixture, and its composition varies from time to time and from place to place and at different altitudes. The normal composition of unpolluted dry air is (by volume): 78% nitrogen; 21% oxygen; and 1% other gases. The main part of the 'other gases' is argon, but other noble gases are present and there is a little carbon dioxide. In most areas of the Earth, water vapour is also present in the air.

One of the reasons that the composition of air varies is because of the presence of ***pollutants***. Pollutants are largely caused by the burning of fuels. These introduce into the atmosphere carbon monoxide (due to incomplete burning) and sulphur dioxide (due to sulphur or sulphur compounds in the fuels burning). Carbon monoxide is very poisonous. Sulphur dioxide dissolves in water to form 'acid rain'. This has the effect of dissolving bricks and stonework and also of lowering the pH of water. Sulphur dioxide attacks the lungs and can cause bronchitis.

There are other pollutants from burning of petrol in motor cars. These include oxides of nitrogen, lead compounds and unburnt hydrocarbons.

One way the level of air pollution can be estimated is by looking at the lichens that grow on trees. They only exist where the level of pollution is low.

Uses of air

Air is used in the blast furnace for the manufacture of iron. It is also used in the manufacture of sulphuric acid and nitric acid. In these cases it is used as a cheap source of oxygen.

EXAMINATION QUESTIONS

1 MULTIPLE CHOICE

QUESTION 1

Which ONE of the following will rekindle a glowing splint?
A carbon dioxide   D ammonia
B hydrogen   E oxygen
C chlorine

(NISEAC)

QUESTION 2

When air reacts with hot copper, which gas is removed from the air?
A carbon dioxide
B nitrogen
C oxygen
D water vapour

(SEG)

QUESTION 3

Which one of the following will never rust?
A aluminium
B galvanised iron
C steel
D well oiled iron

(SEG)

QUESTIONS 4–6

Concern the following gases:
A argon
B carbon dioxide
C nitrogen
D oxygen
E sulphur dioxide

Select, from A to E, the gas which

4 does not occur naturally in the air.
5 is the third most abundant gas in air.
6 is not composed of molecules containing more than one atom.

(ULEAC)

STRUCTURED QUESTIONS

QUESTION 7

The gases of the atmosphere together with their approximate percentage are: oxygen (approx. 20%), nitrogen (approx. 80%), carbon dioxide (approx 0.04%), noble gases (approx. 1%).
(a) Shade and label the following pie diagram to show how much of the *two* most abundant gases is present in the atmosphere (Fig 12.10). (2)

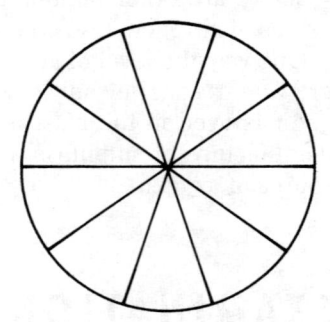

Fig. 12.10

(b) To separate oxygen from nitrogen, the air must be liquified and then allowed to evaporate. The boiling points of liquid oxygen and nitrogen are respectively $-180°C$ and $-196°C$. Explain which liquid evaporates first and give a reason. (2 lines) (2)
(c) Give *two* large scale uses of oxygen. (2 lines) (2)
(d) Explain why carbon dioxide is used in a lemonade bottle. (2 lines) (2)
(e) The following apparatus was used to determine the percentage of oxygen in air (Fig 12.11).

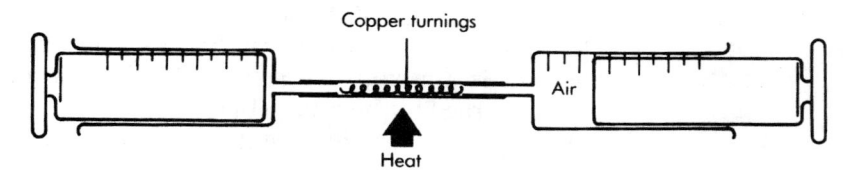

Fig. 12.11

The air was passed, to and fro, over the heated copper turnings until there was no further change in volume. The volume of gas at the start was 80 cm³.
(i) What is the volume of gas at the end? (1)
(ii) The copper turnings changed colour during the experiment, and became black. Explain what happens. (2 lines) (1)
(iii) Write an equation for the reaction taking place. (1 line) (1)
(WJEC)

QUESTION 8

The diagram shows apparatus which can be used to find the composition of the air. 100 cm³ of air were placed in syringe A with syringe B empty. The copper was heated strongly and the air was passed to and from syringes A and B over the hot copper and finally returned to syringe A (Fig. 12.12).

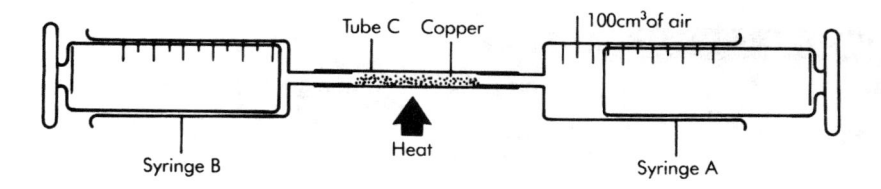

Fig. 12.12

(a) (i) Which gas does copper remove from the air? (1 line)
(ii) Name the compound that is formed. (1 line)
(ii) Describe the colour change you would observe during the reaction. (2 lines)
(iv) Which would be the most abundant gas in the mixture remaining in syringe A at the end of the experiment? (1 line) (4 marks)
(b) The gas involved in the reaction is also used up during breathing.
(i) Describe in chemical terms another process which would result in this gas being removed from the air. (2 lines)
(ii) What volume of gas would be present in a 100 cm³ sample of air? (1 line)
(iii) Describe how you would test for the presence of this gas and state the result you would expect. (2 lines) (5 marks)
(Total: 9 marks)
(ULEAC)

QUESTION 9

A chemist wanted to investigate whether gloss paint absorbs air when it dries. The apparatus shown below was used (Fig. 12.13).

Fig. 12.13

At the start of the experiment the total volume of air inside the apparatus was measured and found to be 200 cm³. The apparatus was left for a week. Every day the air was passed back and forth over the painted splints. At the end of the week, the volume of gas in the syringes had gone down by 38 cm³. Finally, the painted splints were taken out of the centre tube and examined. The paint was still sticky.

(a) What volume of air was in the apparatus after one week? (1 line) (1)
(b) What percentage of the air had been absorbed by the paint? (1 line) (1)
(c) Air is a mixture of gases. Which gas in the air is most likely to have been absorbed by the paint? (1 line) (1)
(d) How could you test the gas left in the apparatus to see whether your answer to (c) was right?
Test: (1 line)
Expected result: (2 lines) (2)
(e) The paint could have been placed in a dish inside the tube. Why was it better to coat it onto the splints? (2 lines) (1)
(f) Gloss paint is normally dry to touch after a day. Why, in this case, was it still sticky after a week? (3 lines) (3)

OUTLINE ANSWERS

MULTIPLE CHOICE

ANSWER 1
Answer: E (see Section 3 above).

ANSWER 2
Copper only reacts with oxygen in this list – hence the answer is C. This is a good way of removing oxygen from air.

ANSWER 3
Look at Section 8 above. The only element that **rusts** is iron, hence the answer must be aluminium – key A. Aluminium forms an oxide layer but this is **NOT rusting**.

ANSWER 4
Answer: E – sulphur dioxide is a pollutant.

ANSWER 5
Answer: A – about 1% of the atmosphere is argon, much more than one expects!

ANSWER 6
Argon is monatomic (one atom per molecule), hence key is A.

STRUCTURED QUESTIONS

ANSWER 7
(a)

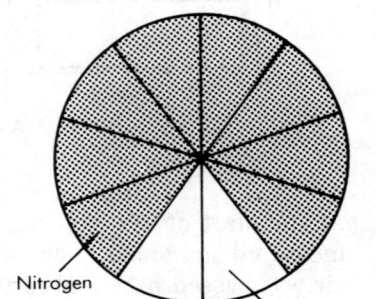

Fig. 12.14

(b) Nitrogen would evaporate first because it has the lowest boiling point (see Section 2 above).
(c) Two uses of oxygen are in the manufacture of steel and as a rocket fuel (see Section 9 above).
(d) It makes lemonade fizzy and gives it a sharp taste.
(e) (i) Nitrogen and noble gases would be left at the end of the experiment, which is about four-fifths of air.
$$\text{Volume left} = 80 \times 4/5 = 64 \text{ cm}^3.$$
(ii) Copper has reacted with oxygen in air to form copper(II) oxide which is black.
(iii) 	Copper + oxygen → Copper(II) oxide
 	2Cu + O_2 → 2CuO.

ANSWER 8

(a) (i) Oxygen (see answer 2); (ii) copper(II) oxide; (iii) pink to black (copper is pink; copper(II) oxide is black); (iv) nitrogen.
(b) (i) Burning or rusting (see either Section 5 or Section 8).
(ii) 21 cm³ (see Section 10).
(iii) Oxygen relights a glowing splint (see Section 3).

ANSWER 9

(a) 162 cm³ (200 minus 38).
(b) % absorbed = $38 \times \frac{100}{200} = 19\%$.
(c) Only oxygen (the other gases in air are *more or less unreactive*).
(d) Oxygen supports burning. If a lighted splint was put in the gas, *it would go out*.
(e) By putting paint on splints a greater surface area was exposed to air. (This would increase the rate of reaction.)
(f) Because the container was sealed, the *solvent vapour* was not able to escape. Also there might not have been *enough oxygen* to react with all the paint.

STUDENT'S ANSWER – EXAMINER'S COMMENTS

The two most abundant gases in the air are nitrogen (approximately 80%) and oxygen (approximately 20%).

(a) Shade in and label the pie-chart to show this approximate compostion of air.

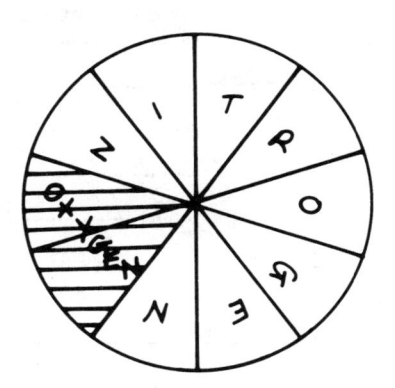

(2 marks)

well done

(b) To separate nitrogen from oxygen, the air is first liquefied. Use the Data Book to find which of these elements is easier to liquefy. Explain your answer.

Oxygen because it liquefies at a higher temperature than nitrogen.

(2 marks)

(c) How is nitrogen separated from liquid air?

Fractional distillation.

(1 mark)

Oh dear! For making ammonia and filling electric light bulbs.

(d) Give two large scale uses of nitrogen.

As a fuel (nuclear power?)
For breathing underwater etc.

(2 marks)

(e) A pupil designed an experiment to measure the amount of oxygen in a sample of air. The diagrams below show the apparatus at the beginning and end of the investigation.

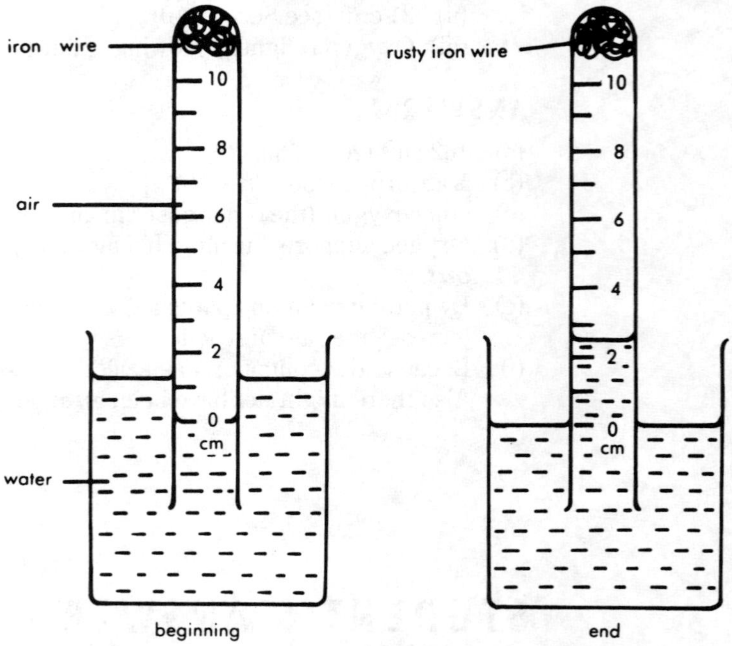

Oxygen is used up in the rusting process and the water rises to replace the 'lost' oxygen.

(i) Explain as fully as you can why the water rose up the test tube.

Because the gases in the air which are heavy come out of the test tube letting water in.

(2 marks)

No allowance has been made for the air above the 10 cm³ mark. Also no attempt was made to measure the volumes at the same pressure. The water levels should be equal in the test tube and the beaker.

The water level rose by 2.5 cm and so the pupil calculated that 25 per cent of the air in this sample was oxygen.

(ii) Explain why the apparatus did not give the known value for the percentage of oxygen of 20 per cent.

I have no idea!

Overall, after a good start, the answers got worse! Score 5/11.

(2 marks)

(Total 11 marks)
(NEAB)

CHAPTER 12.3

NITROGEN AND SULPHUR

N.P.K.
NITROGEN FIXATION
FOOD SUPPLY
AMMONIA
NITRIC ACID FROM AMMONIA
SULPHUR
CONVERSION OF SULPHUR TRIOXIDE TO SULPHURIC ACID
SULPHUR DIOXIDE

GETTING STARTED

The composition of the atmosphere of the Earth in its early life is very uncertain. Nitrogen was very possibly not present. However, it is probable that ammonia, NH_3, was. With the gradual release of oxygen into the atmosphere, the ammonia would be oxidised to nitrogen and water. Denitrifying bacteria which take oxygen from nitrates and release nitrogen may also have contributed to the present high percentage of nitrogen in the air.

The element *nitrogen* is a colourless, unreactive gas. It is the most common gas in the atmosphere (80% by volume). Its molecule contains two atoms joined by a triple bond, shown as N_2 or $N\equiv N$ (see Fig. 6.11). The triple bond is very strong and a large amount of energy is needed to break it. Hence, nitrogen is not very reactive, see bond energies Chapter 9.

The air is the only source from which nitrogen is extracted. Air can be liquefied by a process involving compression, cooling and expansion. The cycle of these operations is repeated until liquid air at about $-200°C$ is produced. The liquid air is then fractionated to produce liquid oxygen, liquid nitrogen and liquid argon. *Nitrogen gas* is formed from the liquid element by allowing it to warm and vaporise.

Liquid nitrogen boils at $-196°C$. It is a very cold liquid. For this reason it can be used to freeze those fruits which do not freeze well by normal methods, e.g. strawberries. It is also used to 'freeze-dry' coffee to make instant coffee granules.

Nitrogen gas is very *unreactive* and is used as an 'inert atmosphere' in *food storage*, e.g. in a bag of crisps it stops the oil used in cooking them from going rancid; in *chemical plant reaction vessels* where air would interfere with the reaction process; and in *flushing out* flammable vapours from oil pipes and fuel tanks.

Plant and animal life need food for growth. Since animals are wholly dependent upon plants for their food, the careful culture of plant crops is vital to the health of humans. Nitrogen is one of the essential elements for plant growth.

ESSENTIAL PRINCIPLES

1> N.P.K.

Nitrogen is the most important of the three main plant nutrients. The others, phosphorus and potassium, are required in smaller quantities since they are not removed from cultivated soil in such large amounts when crops are harvested.

It is important to recognise that the need of plants for these three elements does not mean that these elements can be applied to the soil *as elements*. Nitrogen gas cannot normally be absorbed by any part of a plant and the same is true of the elements phosphorus and potassium. If you remember what happens to yellow phosphorus when it comes into contact with air or what happens to potassium in contact with water you will understand the point being made. The phrase 'a plant needs nitrogen, phosphorus and potassium' is a convenient way of saying that the plant needs these elements *in the form of compounds*.

These compounds are nitrates (supply N), phosphates (supply P) and potassium compounds (supply K) in which the named elements are present as ions.

Typical compounds containing these ions are

Compound	Nutrient ion	Nutrient element
NH_4NO_3	NO_3^-	nitrogen
	NH_4^+	nitrogen
$(NH_4)_2SO_4$	NH_4^+	nitrogen
$(NH_4)_3PO_4$	NH_4^+	nitrogen
	PO_4^{3-}	phosphorus
$Ca_3(PO_4)_2$	PO_4^{3-}	phosphorus
K_2SO_4	K^+	potassium
KCl	K^+	potassium

Fig. 12.15

All these ions, if present in the soil or the compost the plant is growing in, will be acceptable as nutrients. Small amounts of sulphur are required by plants but are normally already present in the soil in large quantities. A good biology book should be consulted for the principles of plant nutrition.

Although plants need adequate supplies of the three main nutritional elements for balanced growth, only *one* of them is normally in short supply in the soil – nitrogen. For this reason the greatest need in agriculture for fertiliser is for the **nitrogenous type** – nitrates and ammonium compounds. The nitrogen in these compounds is converted within the plant to proteins.

❝❝ Human need for protein ❞❞

Because of our need for proteins, we grow and harvest plants which contain plenty of this nutrient and so in eating the plant as food we remove nitrogen previously in the soil. The more such plants we grow, such as wheat, barley, rye and maize, the more nitrogenous fertiliser we need to add to the soil to replace what we have removed. Failure to do this results in reduced yields of these vital foods.

THE NITROGEN CYCLE

This shows how the element nitrogen is used and re-used, much as water and carbon are in their 'cycles' (Fig. 12.16).

Much nitrogen in food for animals (including human animals) is passed through the body unused and becomes a waste product. Such wastes can be recycled as manure. In effect the nitrogen which animals have been unable to use goes back into the soil to be fertiliser for the next crop. The same could be said of the dead remains of plants and small animals.

2> NITROGEN FIXATION

The conversion of the *element* nitrogen into *compounds of nitrogen* is called **fixation**. It is both a natural and a synthetic process.

Natural fixation occurs through lightning and bacterial action called **nitrification**.

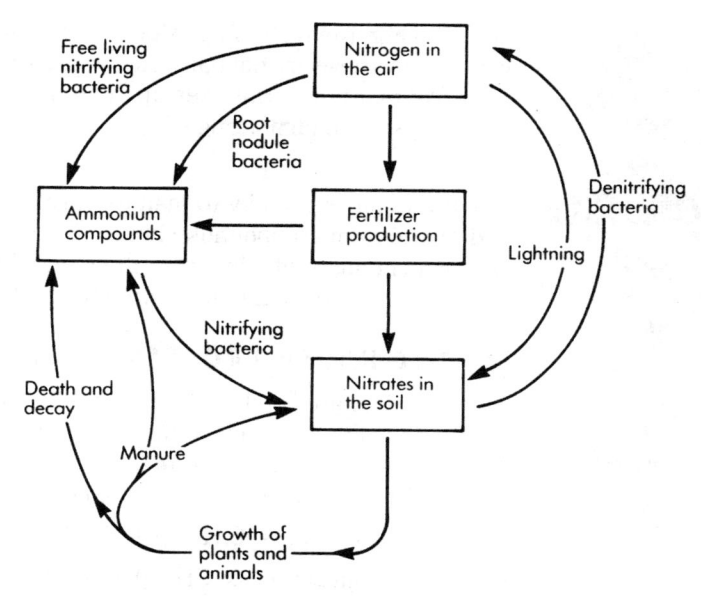

Fig. 12.16. The nitrogen cycle.

The reverse process also occurs through bacteria (denitrification) and through decay of animal and plant remains.

About 40% of the total amount of nitrogen *fixed* per year comes from artificial processes. The Haber process accounts for 30% and nitrogen oxide pollution from motor vehicle about 10%.

Natural nitrogen fixation produces 60% of all the fixed nitrogen, worldwide, each year. Nature is still our biggest supplier of fertiliser.

3 > FOOD SUPPLY

It is obvious that as the population of the world increases, so the volume of food production must increase if many people are not to die of hunger. The changes in population and fertiliser production this century is shown in Fig. 12.17.

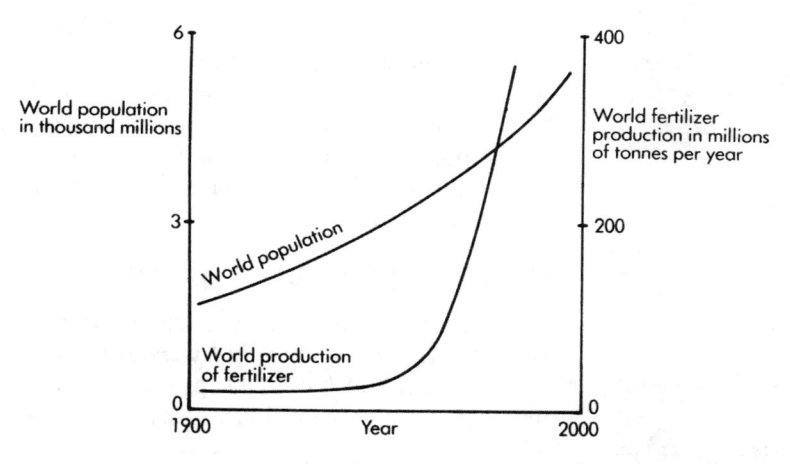

Fig. 12.17. World population and fertiliser production.

The need for more and more food has forced us to increase the amount of food we grow. This has been done in many ways, such as:

(i) Growing varieties of plants which give bigger yields of wheat, barley, maize etc. This has been described as 'making two ears of corn grow where one grew before'. **More fertiliser is needed** but the saving is on the area of land required.
(ii) Reducing the amount of food wasted by pest damage and rot. For (ii) pesticides and fungicides are in widespread use. The use of such chemicals has to be carefully controlled to avoid their toxic effects on animals and humans.
(iii) The contribution of the chemist to feeding the world's starving millions is also seen in the vast amounts of chemical fertiliser being used in today's agriculture.

DISADVANTAGES OF SYNTHETIC FERTILISER USE

Used without an understanding of their properties, fertilisers have been responsible for the pollution of some of our rivers and lakes. If fertiliser gets into water in which plants are growing, the fertilising effect causes increased growth of water plant life. Unlike land plants, these are not harvested and, like all plants, eventually die. Bacterial decay of the dead plant material uses up oxygen from the water and results in foul-smelling waterways in which nothing will grow. This process is called *eutrophication*.

4 > AMMONIA

The credit for our ability to manufacture large quantities of ammonia to make nitrates and ammonium compounds cheaply belongs to Fritz Haber and Herman Bosch, two German chemists who invented the method and engineered the machinery to produce ammonia from its elements – nitrogen and hydrogen gases.

(A) THE HABER PROCESS – SYNTHETIC NITROGEN FIXATION

The elements are produced from the cheapest sources available. For nitrogen this is always the air, free and abundant! Hydrogen was *once* produced from *water* by electrolysis and later from *coal*, but is now made from either *naphtha* or *natural gas*, whichever happens to be more economical at the time and place of manufacture:

> ❝ Economy ❞

- Naphtha process: $C_6H_{14}(g) + 12H_2O(g) \rightarrow 6CO_2(g) + 19H_2(g)$;
- Natural gas process: $CH_4(g) + 2H_2O(g) \rightarrow CO_2(g) + 4H_2(g)$.

> ❝ The easier process to carry out is the natural gas process. This is used where possible. ❞

In both cases the **hydrocarbon** chosen is heated with steam and carbon dioxide and hydrogen are produced.

Carbon dioxide is removed by

(i) dissolving in water or in an alkali; or
(ii) liquefaction by pressure and cooling.

The hydrogen gas flows on to the next stage of the process.

A mixture of three parts of hydrogen to one part of nitrogen (synthesis gas) is compressed to a pressure 200 times that of the normal atmosphere, heated to about 400°C and passed over an iron catalyst:

$$3H_2(g) + N_2(g) \rightleftharpoons 2NH_3(g).$$

The reaction is exothermic and reversible. The high pressure and relatively low temperatures are the conditions used to push the position of the equilibrium as far to the right as is practicable, see equilibria in Chapter 9.

The gas leaving the reaction vessel contains about 15% ammonia. Ammonia can be liquefied by cooling at this pressure. The unreacted gases are *recycled* after mixing with more synthesis gas.

(B) THE ECONOMICS OF THE PROCESS

It is valuable to look briefly at the *savings* gained by the change from using coal to make the hydrogen to using *hydrocarbons for that purpose* (Fig. 12.18).

The change of feedstock produced considerable savings in most areas and an increase in ammonia yield by nearly four times.

Process	Annual ammonia production (thousand tonnes)	Land use (hectares)	Labour (hundreds)	Capital (£ millions)	Energy use (gigajoules)
Coal based	225	20	23	75	75
Hydrocarbon based	800	7	24	80	40

Fig. 12.18. Difference between coal-based and hydrocarbon-based ammonia plants.

(C) LABORATORY PREPARATION OF AMMONIA

In the laboratory it is more convenient to make ammonia from its solid salts – ammonium compounds. The principle here is that ammonium compounds are products of the neutralisation of ammonia with an acid. For example: ammonium chloride NH_4Cl is a salt of ammonia and hydrochloric acid – $(NH_3 \cdot HCl)$. An added alkali or base will react with the hydrogen chloride *part* of the ammonium compound, HCl, leaving the ammonia, NH_3, to be released as a gas.

So any ammonium salt wil react with any base to form ammonia:

ammonium chloride + calcium hydroxide → ammonia + water + calcium chloride
(a salt)   (a base)

$2NH_4Cl(s) + Ca(OH)_2(s) \rightarrow 2NH_3(g) + 2H_2O(l) + CaCl_2(s)$

A similar reaction would occur with ammonium sulphate or ammonium nitrate in place of ammonium chloride, and also with sodium or potassium hydroxide in place of calcium hydroxide.

This same reaction can be used to identify any **ammonium salt** which will contain ammonium ions. Addition of sodium hydroxide solution to a salt suspected of containing ammonium ions will result in the characteristic smell of ammonia on gentle warming:

$NH_4^+ + OH^-(aq) \rightarrow NH_3(g) + H_2O(l)$

ammonium salt + alkali → ammonia + water
(ammonium ions) hydroxide ions gas

The simplest *chemical* test for ammonia is its effect on damp universal indicator paper. Ammonia is the only common alkaline gas and the paper turns from orange to blue/green.

Collecting ammonia

Because ammonia is very soluble in water and less dense than air, it must be collected by delivering it **upwards** into an **open collecting vessel**. If a **closed vessel** such as a **gas syringe** is used the air in the apparatus will not be able to escape and the ammonia collected will be mixed with air.

(D) THE CHEMICAL AND PHYSICAL PROPERTIES OF AMMONIA

Ammonia is a colourless, pungent smelling, alkaline gas. It is about half as dense as air. It is extremely soluble in water, producing a weakly alkaline solution of pH about 12.

$NH_3(g) + H_2O(l) \rightleftharpoons NH_4^+(aq) + OH^-(aq)$

ammonia gas + water ⇌ ammonium ions + hydroxyl ions

A concentrated solution of ammonia gas in water has the surprisingly low density of 0.880 g/cm³ and is often referred to as '880 ammonia'. Warming this solution will produce large volumes of damp ammonia gas. Passing the gas through calcium oxide (an alkaline drying agent) will produce a convenient supply of dry ammonia gas.

(E) OTHER SOURCES OF AMMONIA

> Ammonia gas opens up the nasal passages and smelling salts are therefore also sold to relieve catarrh

Ammonia is given off continuously by certain unstable ammonium compounds such as ammonium carbonate and ammonium hydrogencarbonate. Such compounds are used as 'smelling salts' to revive people who have fainted. Ammonia stimulates heart action which pumps more oxygen-containing blood to the brain, reviving the patient:

ammonium carbonate → ammonia + carbon dioxide + water
$(NH_4)_2CO_3(s) \rightarrow 2NH_3(g) + CO_2(g) + H_2O(g)$

Ammonia is produced naturally by bacterial decay of animal and plant wastes. A manure heap, a heap of old grass cuttings and a baby's wet nappy all smell of the gas for this reason.

> pH 12

Ammonia is the only common alkaline gas, so a simple test for it is to use damp pH paper which will turn blue. Because the gas is usually formed by the reaction of an alkali with an ammonium salt, it is important to place the pH paper in the **gas only**.

> Household ammonia

Ammonia solution will 'dissolve' grease because of its alkalinity. The solution is used as a household alkali for this purpose where the grease is not thickly coated. As a weak alkali it is not harmful to the skin.

Ammonia will also react with **acid gases**, neutralising them and forming salts. All salts are solid at room temperature so the reaction of ammonia and acid gases produce a smoke (a dispersion in air of fine solid particles). The most convenient acid gas to use for this test is hydrogen chloride which comes from concentrated hydrochloric acid as steamy fumes.

Test for ammonia

Mixing the fumes from concentrated hydrochloric acid and ammonia will make a white smoke, confirming the presence of ammonia. This last reaction can be used to compare the relative speeds of diffusion of ammonia and hydrogen chloride molecules in air, see Chapter 4, Section 1(a).

(F) ANALYSIS OF AMMONIA

Chemists carry out *two* types of analysis. They first have to discover **what elements or ions** a compound or mixture contains. This is called **qualitative analysis**. It answers the question 'What is present?' The second type of analysis answers the question 'How much is present?' This is **quantitative analysis**.

Qualitative analysis of ammonia gas can be carried out using the apparatus in Fig. 12.19.

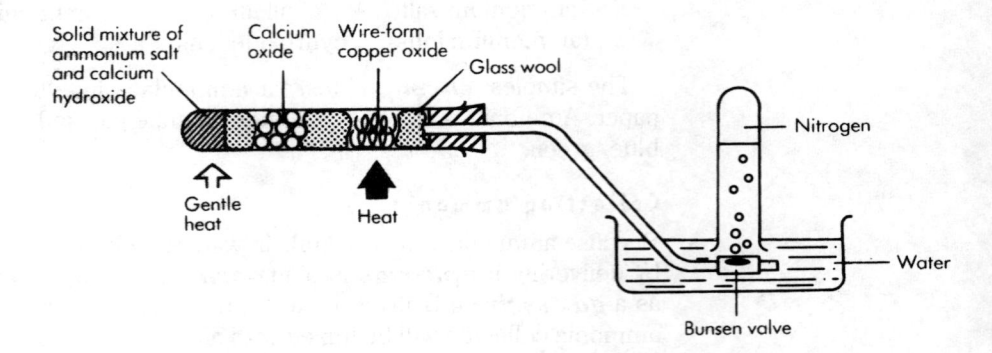

Fig. 12.19. Qualitative analysis of ammonia.

The ammonia is produced as in Section 4(c) above. The gas is dried by passing it over calcium oxide lumps. It is then passed over heated **copper(II) oxide** which oxidises the hydrogen in the ammonia to water. Nitrogen is unaffected by the copper(II) oxide and collects in the tube over water.

The gas is not usually **positively** identified as nitrogen because nitrogen is such an unreactive gas that there are few reactions it will take part in which will serve to identify it. However, the gas which collects has none of the properties of hydrogen or oxygen and does not turn lime-water cloudy. It has no smell. We accept such **negative** chemical properties as indicating the gas to be **nitrogen**:

$$3CuO(s) + 2NH_3(g) \rightarrow 3Cu(s) + 3H_2O(l) + N_2(g)$$
copper(II) oxide + ammonia → copper + water + nitrogen.

(G) AMMONIUM COMPOUNDS

When an acid is neutralised by ammonia, an ammonium salt is formed:

$$NH_3(g) + HNO_3(aq) \rightarrow NH_4NO_3(aq)$$
ammonia + nitric acid → ammonium nitrate.

The compound formed is a 'nitrogenous fertiliser'. The reaction of ammonia with **phosphoric acid** produces the salt ammonium phosphate, which is a valuable fertiliser because it contains both nitrogen and phosphorus.

Try writing similar equations for the reaction with $HCl(aq)$ and $H_2SO_4(aq)$, to give ammonium chloride and ammonium sulphate respectively.

(H) THE USES OF AMMONIA

The main use is as a fertiliser by direct addition to the soil (rare in Britain) or to make ammonium nitrate (common now) and ammonium sulphate (less common now than in the past) as fertilisers.

Direct addition of liquid ammonia to the soil is common in some countries because it is economical. Pure ammonia has a high **proportion** of nitrogen and is not combined with unnecessary material such as water or sulphuric acid, both of which are not in short supply for plants and add to the **transportable weight** and **cost**. Pure ammonia, however, is damaging to growing plants and can make the soil too **alkaline** for plants to grow. But **carefully** used, it is efficient and economical on transport costs.

In Europe, ammonium nitrate is now more commonly used than ammonium sulphate as a ntirogenous fertiliser. The reason will be apparent from the table of percentages of nitrogen in various nitrogenous fertilisers in common use in the world (Fig. 12.20).

Fertiliser	Formula	Percentage nitrogen by mass
Ammonia (g)	NH_3	$14/17 \times 100 = 82$
Urea (s)	CON_2H_4	$2 \times 14/60 \times 100 = 47$
Ammonium nitrate (s)	NH_4NO_3	$2 \times 14/80 \times 100 = 35$
Ammonium sulphate (s)	$(NH_4)_2SO_4$	$2 \times 14/132 \times 100 = 21$

Fig. 12.20 Percentages of nitrogen in common fertilisers.

Ammonium nitrate has a lower percentage of nitrogen than ammonia or urea but is higher in nitrogen than ammonium sulphate. When transport charges are so high, the more concentrated the source of nitrogen the more economical it will be to transport it.

Can you suggest the conditions that might make this **soluble alkaline gas** be less economical to use than a solid fertiliser such as an ammonium salt?

❝ Transport costs ❞

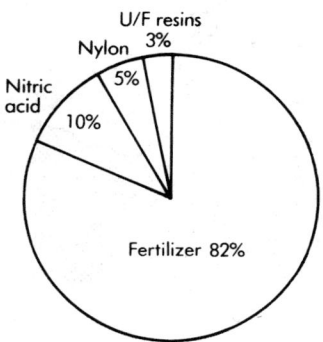

Fig. 12.21. Amonia uses.

❝ Urea in granular form is coated with sulphur to slow down further its release into the soil. This slow release form of urea will not be washed out of the soil as quickly as other fertilisers ❞

(I) OTHER USES OF AMMONIA

Apart from its use in the manufacture of fertilisers, ammonia is used to make nitric acid, HNO_3, nylon and urea–formaldehyde resins.

Urea itself is **conveniently** made on the same site as ammonia because its manufacture also utilises one of the **by-products** of the ammonia manufacturing process, carbon dioxide. In this way transport costs are eliminated.

$$CO_2(g) + 2NH_3(g) \rightarrow CO(NH_2)_2(s) + H_2O(l)$$
carbon dioxide + ammonia → urea + water

Urea breaks down slowly in the soil into carbon dioxide and ammonia. It is a 'slow nitrogen release' fertiliser.

(J) THE SITING OF AN AMMONIA PLANT

The place chosen to make an important industrial chemical is vital to the economic success of the process, see Chapter 2, Section 1(a). The following flowchart shows the processes involved in ammonia manufacture and sale:

RAW MATERIALS	→	FACTORY	→	PRODUCT	→	MARKET
natural gas or oil, air and water		labour and other costs		transport provision – roads, rail, port for exports; costs of transport		advertising costs

Ammonia 'plants' as factories are called, must be sited near to the supplies of raw materials and must be able to transport the product to the customer. The site will be close to oil or to natural gas supplies (this is transported by a national pipeline). Air of course is everywhere and free! Water will have to come from a river since the quantities needed cannot be supplied through the piped water system.

Two major sites are at Billingham on Tees and Severnside near Bristol (Fig. 12.22). Both are close to a deep water port, a river, gas pipeline or oilfields and good road and rail transport systems.

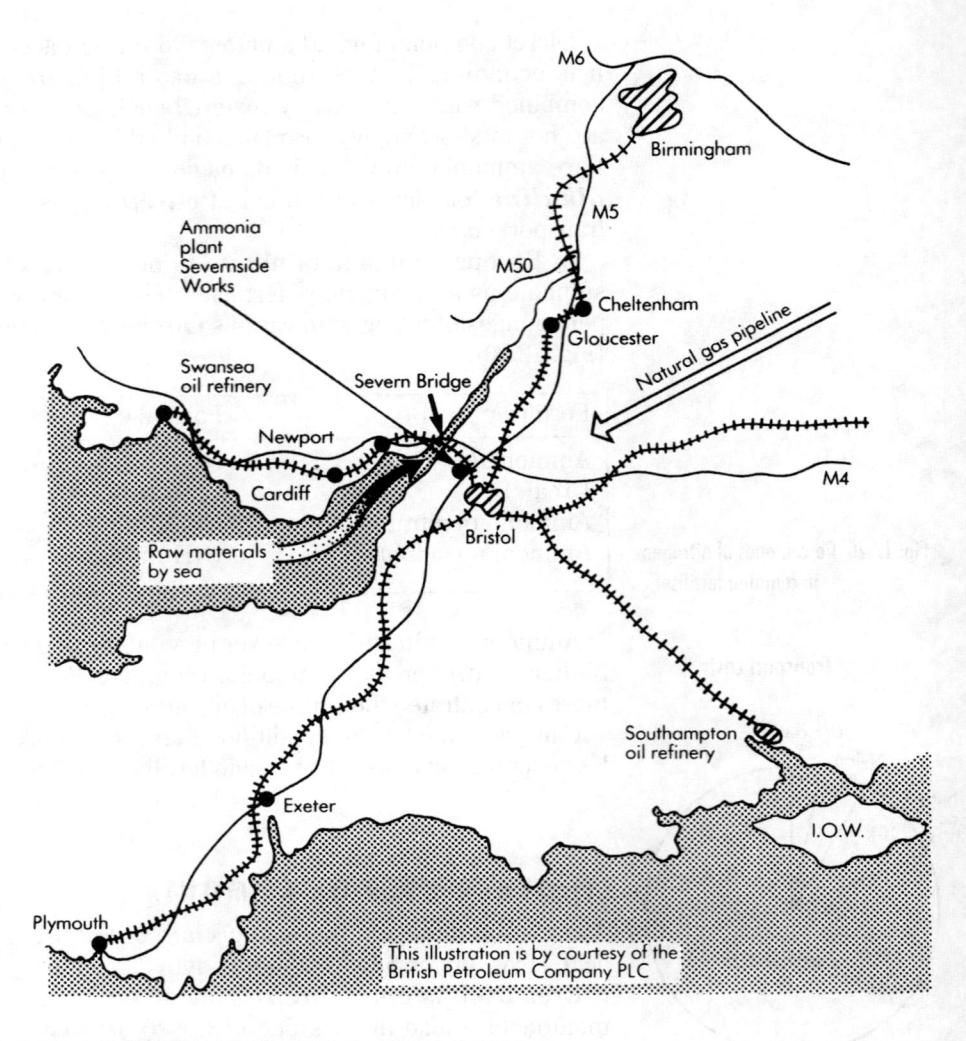

Fig. 12.22. Map of the Severnside Industrial Complex.

(K) LABORATORY USES OF AMMONIA

A solution of ammonia contains hydroxide ions which are responsible for its weakly alkaline properties, see Section 4(d) above. Ammonia solution will react with many metal salts to form insoluble hydroxides, some of which are soluble in *excess* ammonia (Fig. 12.23).

Metal ions	Precipitate formed	Colour	Does it dissolve in excess?
aluminium	Al(OH)$_3$	white	no
copper(II)	Cu(OH)$_2$	blue	yes – deep blue solution
iron(II)	Fe(OH)$_2$	green	no
iron(III)	Fe(OH)$_3$	brown	no
zinc	Zn(OH)$_2$	white	yes – colourless solution

Fig. 12.23. The ions of metal salts which react with ammonia solution.

Reaction occurs between the hydroxide ions from the ammonia solution and the metal ions from the salt solution.

$$Al^{3+}(aq) + 3OH^-(aq) \rightarrow Al(OH)_3(s),$$

and

$$Fe^{2+}(aq) - 2OH^-(aq) \rightarrow Fe(OH)_2(s).$$

The reactions of ammonia as a *weak* alkali with metal *ions* are slightly different from those of sodium hydroxide, a strong alkali.

5 > NITRIC ACID FROM AMMONIA

The conversion of ammonia into nitric acid is a three-stage process:

(i) Ammonia can be oxidised to oxides of nitrogen and water:

$$4NH_3(g) + 5O_2(g) \rightarrow 4NO(g) + 6H_2O(l)$$
ammonia + oxygen → nitrogen monoxide + water

> **Heat exchange**

A mixture of air and ammonia (10% ammonia) is burnt over a platinum catalyst at 850°C. The heat produced by this exothermic reaction is ***recovered*** by a heat exchanger.

(ii) Nitrogen monoxide is readily oxidised further to nitrogen dioxide:

$$4NO(g) + 2O_2(g) \rightarrow 4NO_2(g)$$
nitrogen monoxide + oxygen → nitrogen dioxide.

(iii) The nitrogen dioxide is reacted with water and more oxygen:

$$4NO_2(g) + 2H_2O(l) + O_2(g) \rightarrow 4HNO_3(aq)$$
nitrogen dioxide + water + oxygen → nitric acid.

(A) USES OF NITRIC ACID

The main use is in the production of ammonium nitrate (see Fig. 12.24).

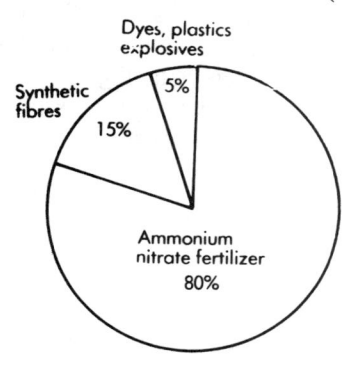

Fig. 12.24. Uses of nitric acid.

The main use of explosives such as dynamite is in the construction of roads, mining and quarrying operations.

(B) FACTORY SITING

As would be expected, nitric acid is made close to the plant producing the ammonia from which it is made. This means that wherever nitric acid is made there will be an ammonia plant nearby and usually on an adjacent site.

6> SULPHUR

> **A basic raw material**

Sulphur is element 16 in the periodic table. It is a yellow solid non-metallic element. It has no smell or taste. It is insoluble in water but soluble in many organic liquids such as toluene and xylene. Because of the amount of sulphur used and the wide variety of processes that use it, it is one the five basic raw materials of the chemical industry. The others are salt, limestone, coal and oil.

Its properties are typical of those of non-metals generally. It is a non-conductor of both heat and electricity, it is brittle and has a low density and a low melting point.

(A) ALLOTROPES OF SULPHUR

Sulphur occurs in two different crystalline forms – rhombic or alpha sulphur and monoclinic or beta sulphur. These different crystalline forms of the same element are called ***allotropes***. They are made up of ***the same S_8 molecules arranged differently in the two crystal structures***. The molecules of rhombic sulphur are more tightly packed than those of the monoclinic allotrope, giving densities of 2.07 g cm³ and 1.96 g cm³ respectively. The different packing of the molecules gives the two allotropes different melting points also. Rhombic sulphur melts at 113°C and monoclinic sulphur at 119°C. However, the rhombic form normally converts to the monoclinic form on heating to 96°C or above, making the melting point of rhombic sulphur difficult to measure in the normal way (see Fig. 3.9).

(B) SOURCES OF SULPHUR

As an ***element***, i.e. 'native', it is found chiefly in sedimentary and volcanic deposits. In its elemental form sulphur is found in the USA, Mexico, Poland, Iraq and Sicily. It is usually found mixed with gypsum, $CaSO_4$, and limestone, $CaCO_3$. Sulphur mining is normally carried out by the Frasch process which does not involve digging or excavation.

(C) THE FRASCH PROCESS

The extraction of native sulphur is part of only one GCSE syllabus. The method is, however, of great interest as a technological innovation of the late nineteenth century. Also, questions may appear on matters outside the syllabus if sufficient details are provided in the paper for candidates to show their knowledge and understanding of chemical facts and principles.

Up to the end of the nineteenth century sulphur was obtained as native sulphur, most of it from Sicily. It was extracted by shaft-mining methods and heated in furnaces. The sulphur melted and flowed away from the unmeltable rock and other substances.

In the early days of the oil rush in the USA, oil drillers in Louisiana discovered a sulphur deposit 100 feet thick beneath 400 feet of clay, gravel and quicksand. The sulphur could not be extracted by normal mining methods because of the quicksand and also the poisonous hydrogen sulphide from the deposits. The solution to these problems came from a petroleum chemist, Herman Frasch, in 1890.

Frasch recognised that the low melting point of sulphur would allow the sulphur to be removed as a liquid in much the same way as oil was obtained. His plan was to use superheated water to melt the sulphur and compressed air to pump it to the surface.

A Frasch well (Fig. 12.25) is installed by sinking a protective casing down as far as the upper part of the sulphur deposits. Three **concentric** pipes are put down this casing. They consist of:

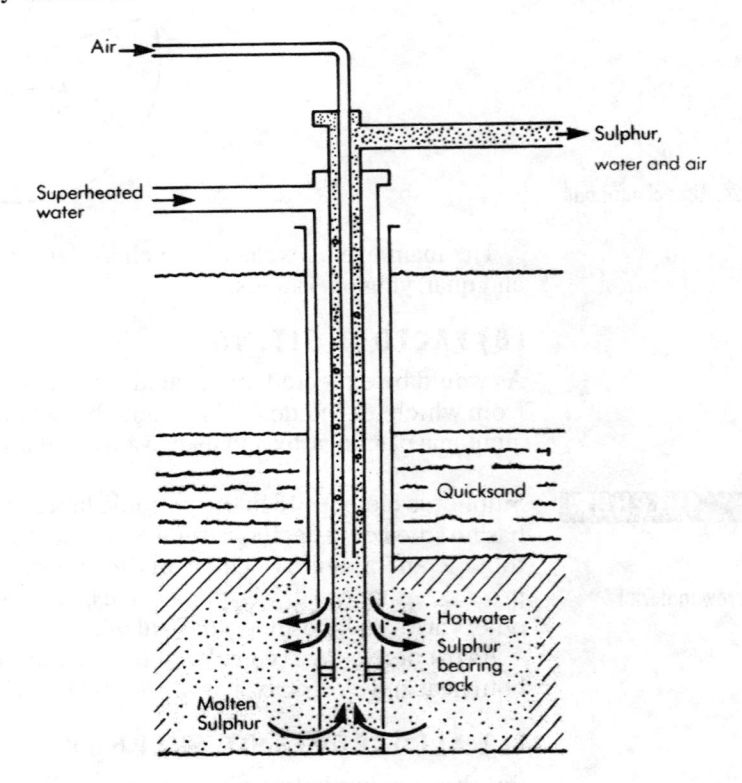

Fig. 12.25. The Frasch well.

(i) A 20 cm diameter pipe which reaches the bottom of the well. The lower end of this pipe has small holes in it. The lowest holes are to let the sulphur *in*; the holes higher up are to let the superheated water *out* into the rock. Inside this pipe is:
(ii) A 10 cm diameter pipe which reaches to within a short distance of the bottom of the well at a point below the upper set of holes but above the lowest set of holes. Lastly:
(iii) A 2.5 cm diameter pipe that reaches about halfway to the bottom of the well.

Water, heated to well above its normal boiling point (under pressure), is pumped down the space between (i) and (ii). The water flows through the holes into the sulphur deposit. The sulphur melts. Because molten sulphur is denser than water, it forms a pool at the bottom of the well. Compressed air pumped down the 2.5 cm pipe foams the sulphur so that it rises to the surface.

Once at the surface the sulphur can be solidified in huge vats or kept molten for

> **Liquid sulphur transport**

transfer to heated tankers or ships to be transported to industry in molten form. Most sulphur imports to Britain are now in the liquid state. Why do you think this is?

The method invented by Frasch shows how he overcame the difficulties of extracting sulphur caused by its occurrence in ground unsuitable for 'shaft-mining' methods. It is a good example of 'lateral thinking' – instead of puzzling about how to mine sulphur by overcoming the problems of sinking shafts, Frasch looked in another direction and devised a method based on extracting oil.

The method is very economical to work; it offers no danger to those working it; and there is no waste to be dumped (all the useless material is left at the bottom of the well).

It requires a nearby cheap source of fuel to heat the water and provide compression for the water and air. It was not until oil and natural gas were discovered near the sulphur deposits that they were able to be brought into production.

(D) OTHER SOURCES AND EXTRACTION METHODS

Because of its reactivity with most other elements sulphur is found also as sulphides and sulphates. For example, the sulphides of copper and lead, Cu_2S and PbS, from which the metals are extracted, and sulphates of calcium, $CaSO_4$, and magnesium, $MgSO_4$, which are useful chemicals in everyday life.

- Sulphur compounds are present in some crude oil and natural gas supplies. Such supplies are said to be 'sour'.
- When fossil fuels containing sulphur compounds are burned, sulphur dioxide is formed and enters the atmosphere (see Section (F) below on pollution).

> **Sour gas**

- Sour natural gas is now an important source of sulphur. Sour gas is found in southern France, western Canada and the Middle East. When partially burned, hydrogen sulphide extracted from sour gas forms sulphur:

$$2H_2S(g) + O_2(g) \rightarrow 2H_2O(l) + 2S(s)$$
$$\text{hydrogen sulphide} + \text{oxygen} \rightarrow \text{water} + \text{sulphur}$$

- Sulphur from sour gas and oil now forms a large part of all sulphur used in industry.

The easy availability of these new sources has sharply cut the cost of sulphur.

(E) USES OF SULPHUR

Most of the world's production of sulphur is converted into sulphuric acid. Other uses are as a fungicide, for vulcanising rubber to make it harder and less plastic for use in car tyres, and for making sulphites for bleaching wood pulp before it is made into paper.

Sulphuric acid manufacture

The raw materials for sulphuric acid manufacture are sulphur dioxide gas and air.
There are two main sources of sulphur dioxide gas:

(i) Sulphide ores. The first stage of the extraction of lead or zinc from their sulphide ores produces large quantities of sulphur dioxide as a by-product:

$$2PbS(s) + 3O_2(g) \rightarrow 2PbO(s) + 2SO_2(g)$$
$$\text{lead sulphide} + \text{oxygen} \rightarrow \text{lead(II) oxide} + \text{sulphur dioxide}$$

To prevent atmospheric pollution this sulphur dioxide has to be absorbed. The most favoured process is to turn it into sulphuric acid.

This method of production accounts for about 10% of UK production and about 40% of world production of sulphuric acid.

(ii) Sulphur. As stated above, sulphur is available from the Frasch process, from purification of 'sour' natural gas and from the removal of sulphur from crude oil.
Burning sulphur produces sulphur dioxide:

$$S(s) + O_2(g) \rightarrow SO_2(g)$$
$$\text{sulphur} + \text{oxygen} \rightarrow \text{sulphur dioxide}$$

(F) POLLUTION CONTROL

A third source of sulphur dioxide gas may be important one day. More sulphur dioxide is emitted from burning coal in the UK than is needed to make sulphuric acid. If, or perhaps when, pollution controls on sulphur dioxide emissions become law in the UK, it may be more economical to make sulphuric acid from the absorbed sulphur oxides than to dispose of it in other ways.

> *A trial process at Fiddler's Ferry power station near Warrington makes sulphuric acid from the sulphur dioxide extracted from the gases given off by coal-burning boilers*

(G) THE CONTACT PROCESS

In this process, sulphur dioxide is mixed with oxygen (air) and passed through a converter containing several beds of catalyst.

The catalyst is vanadium(V) oxide, supported on porous silica and promoted with potassium sulphate. The catalyst is only active at temperatures above 402°C. The reaction is:

> *Promotion makes catalyst better*

$$\text{sulphur dioxide} + \text{oxygen} \rightleftharpoons \text{sulphur trioxide}$$
$$2SO_2(g) + O_2(g) \rightleftharpoons 2SO_3(g)$$

The reaction is reversible and exothermic. This means that the product is a mixture of sulphur dioxide, oxygen and sulphur trioxide. The essential conditions are therefore 450°C, normal pressure, with a vanadium (V) oxide catalyst.

The effect of temperature on the equilibrium

If a reversible reaction is exothermic (gives out heat) then, in theory, *the higher the temperature the less product is obtained*. Applying this principle to the above reaction shows that *more* product, which is what is desired, is obtained at lower temperatures. Because the catalyst requires at temperature of at least 400°C the temperature chosen must be at least that value.

The effect of temperature on the speed of reaction

Reactions go faster at higher temperatures. *If possible* then, the highest possible temperature would be chosen.

There are now *three* requirements for the process to work *economically*:

(i) a temperature of at least 400°C for the catalyst to work;
(ii) as low a temperature as possible to push the equilibrium as far to the side of products as possible;
(iii) as high a temperature as possible for a fast reaction.

Requirements (ii) and (iii) conflict. A temperature is chosen which is as far above 400°C as possible, whilst producing a good yield of the desired sulphur trioxide. The process is run at 450°C with a yield of 99.5%.

Pollution control in the contact process

Sulphur oxides are atmospheric pollutants. If the conversion of sulphur dioxide to sulphur trioxide is not nearly 100% then waste gases containing these oxides will be passed into the atmosphere. Because there are now strict pollution controls applied to this process, these 'emissions', as waste gases passed to the atmosphere are called, are not allowed.

This requires sulphuric acid manufacturers to make their processes extremely efficient to reduce pollution. The level of efficiency required is achieved by having a sulphur trioxide absorption section *after* the mixture has passed through three catalyst beds. Removal of the product of a reversible reaction assists formation of products. The final stage will then remove most of the remaining unreacted sulphur dioxide. Emissions from such a process can be as low as 300 ppm of sulphur dioxide. (ppm is parts per million, a common unit of measurement for pollution. One cubic centimetre of pollutant gas in one thousand litres is 1 ppm.)

> *Emission control*

7 > CONVERSION OF SULPHER TRIOXIDE TO SULPHURIC ACID

Sulphur trioxide reacts strongly with water to form sulphuric acid:

$$SO_3(g) + H_2O(l) \rightarrow H_2SO_4(aq) \quad \textbf{highly exothermic}$$

If this is carried out as shown a dangerous acid mist is produced which cannot be

easily condensed to the acid. This apparently simple process is, therefore, carried out in two stages:
  (i) Sulphur trioxide, $SO_3(g)$ is dissolved in 98% sulphuric acid $H_2SO_4(l)$ without mist formation. This produces 98.5% sulphuric acid $H_2S_2O_7$ (known as oleum).
  (ii) The acid concentration is then reduced to 98% by adding water.

(A) ECONOMICS OF THE PROCESS

Costs

The economics of a chemical process demand that the product be made as quickly as possible. 'Time is money' when labour is paid for by the hour and bank interest has to be paid on money borrowed to build the factory and its chemical plant. It is for these reasons that catalysts and high temperatures are used where possible.

The oxidation of sulphur to sulphur trioxide, followed by reaction with water, produces a lot of heat. This heat is removed by 'heat exchangers' and is sold as steam to nearby users.

The running costs of a sulphuric acid plant include the cost of sulphur, maintenance materials and wages of workers at the plant. However, the income from the sale of steam normally covers all running costs except the cost of the sulphur.

(B) SITING OF A SULPHURIC ACID PLANT

Several existing sulphuric acid plants were originally sited close to a source of sulphur — calcium sulphate. It is now more economical, however, to import sulphur from overseas, than to use the naturally occurring sulphur compounds nearby

The acid is expensive to transport. It requires stainless steel lined tankers. There are dangers from tanker accidents. The plant is normally built close to places of use. If imported liquid sulphur is used to make the sulphur dioxide, then the plant must be close to a port or have good rail access.

(C) USES OF SULPHURIC ACID (FIG. 12.26)

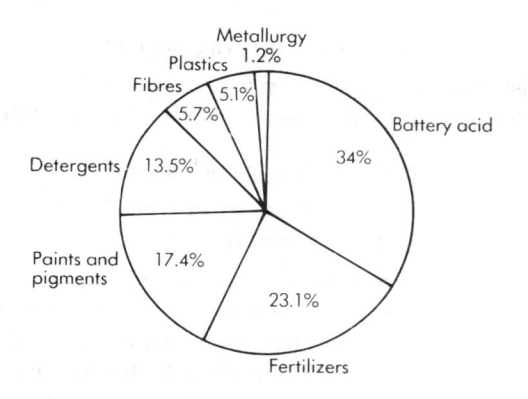

Fig. 12.26. Uses of sulphuric acid.

- Metallurgy 1.2%
- Plastics 5.1%
- Fibres 5.7%
- Detergents 13.5%
- Paints and pigments 17.4%
- Fertilizers 23.1%
- Battery acid 34%

(D) SUPERPHOSPHATE MANUFACTURE

Rock phosphate, an ore containing calcium phosphate, is being mined in many parts of the world as a phosphatic fertiliser. The phosphate in it is not, however, very soluble in water and so is not rapidly available to plants. Plants use phosphates for root development and a good supply is vital for strong growth. Rock phosphate can be made more soluble by treatment with concentrated sulphuric acid. In the process calcium 'superphosphate' is formed which is quite soluble in water.

Rock phosphate can also be converted into phosphoric acid by reaction with sulphuric acid. The phosphoric acid is then neutralised with ammonia to form ammonium phosphate which is both a nitrogenous and a phosphatic fertiliser.

Prosperity and acid production

The production of sulphuric acid used to be an indicator of industrial prosperity. The more sulphuric acid used, the more a country's industry was producing. This is no longer so. Industrial production has remained fairly level in Britain since 1980 but manufacture of sulphuric acid has dropped by 33%.

(E) THE PROPERTIES OF SULPHURIC ACID

(i) Reaction with water

The reaction is strongly exothermic. Because sulphuric acid is much denser than water the mixing must be done **correctly** to be done **safely**. Water added to the acid will float on the acid. Reaction between the acid and water will occur in the top layer which will boil vigorously. Sulphuric acid and water will spit out. Acid in the eyes or on the skin is harmful and corrosive.

> The safe way

The correct method of mixing is to add the denser acid to water. In sinking through the water the acid mixes thoroughly and heat is spread throughout the mixture, which gets hot but does not boil.

$$H_2O(l) + H_2SO_4(l) \rightarrow H_3O^+(aq) + HSO_4^-(aq)$$

The product of the reaction is dilute or aqueous sulphuric acid, $H_2SO_4(aq)$.

(ii) As a dehydrating agent

Because of its reaction with water, sulphuric acid will extract water from

(a) hydrated salts, e.g. $CuSO_4 \cdot 5H_2O(s)$; and
(b) compounds in which the elements of water are present, e.g. carbohydrates such as sugar and starch.

An example of (a) is the **dehydration** of the copper(II) sulphate crystals, which are blue. When concentrated sulphuric acid is added, the product is white, anhydrous copper(II) sulphate and dilute sulphuric acid:

$$CuSO_4 \cdot 5H_2O(s) + H_2SO_4(l) \rightarrow CuSO_4(s) + H_2SO_4(aq)$$

An example of (b) is the dehydration of sugar (sucrose) which produces carbon and dilute sulphuric acid.

$$C_{12}H_{22}O_{11}(s) + H_2SO_4(l) \rightarrow 12C(s) + H_2SO_4(aq) + 11H_2O(l)$$

In each example sulphuric acid reacts with water and itself becomes dilute sulphuric acid. The reactions are exothermic.

(iii) As a drying agent

> Ammonia cannot be dried by this method

Sulphuric acid can be used to dry moist gases, e.g. chlorine, oxygen, nitrogen, provided the gas does not react with the acid.

(iv) As a typical acid

All the properties of typical acids as described in Chapter 10, Section 1 apply to dilute sulphuric acid. It will:

- neutralise bases and alkalis;
- give hydrogen with reactive metals;
- give carbon dioxide with carbonates (with the exception of those which, like calcium carbonate, form an insoluble coating with the acid); and
- turn universal indicator red.

> Hydrogen

Hydrogen gas is usually prepared in the laboratory by the action of dilute sulphuric acid on zinc (Chapter 12.1, Section 1).

$$Zn(s) + H_2SO_4(aq) \rightarrow ZnSO_4(aq) + H_2(g)$$

Pure sulphuric acid, however, is not acidic. It does not have any of the properties of a typical acid. The reason for this unusual situation is the absence of **hydrated protons** in the pure acid. Addition of water, however, produces hydrated protons (hydrated hydrogen ions) which have all the properties of acids (see Chapter 11, Section 4). Thus:

$$H_2SO_4(l) + H_2O(l) \rightarrow H_3O^+(aq) + HSO_4^-(aq)$$
$$H_2SO_4(l) + \text{water} \rightarrow H^+(aq) + HSO_4^-(aq)$$

The same reaction occurs when concentrated sulphuric acid removes water from hydrated salts, sugars and gases. The reaction shown above explains why concentrated sulphuric acid is less corrosive to some metals than the dilute acid. Metals that will react with hydrated hydrogen ions (hydrated protons) will not always react with the concentrated acid, which contains none, e.g. lead and steel can withstand concentrated sulphuric acid.

Concentrated sulphuric acid is, however, also an oxidising agent. Metals which can be oxidised by it will be corroded. Metals such as copper and zinc are rapidly dissolved by oxidation.

(F) TESTING FOR SULPHATES

When identifying sulphuric acid it is obviously not enough to add an indicator and prove that an acid is present. All acids will respond to this test. An additional test for sulphate ions will show the acid to be **sulphuric acid**.

All sulphates contain sulphate ions in solution. Sulphate ions react with barium ions to form a ***precipitate*** of insoluble barium sulphate. Unless it is known that other ions that might also react with barium ions are absent, dilute hydrochloric acid must also be added (dilute nitric acid could be used instead) to react with these other ions (carbonate ions for example) so that they do not form a precipitate. The reaction is

$$BaCl_2(aq) + H_2SO_4(aq) \rightarrow BaSO_4(s) + 2HCl(aq),$$
barium chloride + sulphuric acid → barium sulphate + hydrochloric acid

or

$$Ba^{2+}(aq) + SO_4^{2-}(aq) \rightarrow BaSO_4(s)$$

It can be seen that ***any*** sulphate will give a positive test if it forms sulphate ions in solution. This is a general test for ***sulphates***. The test is performed as follows:
(i) Dissolve a little of the 'unknown' substance in 5 cm³ of dilute hydrochloric or nitric acid. (If there is a fizzing at this point and the 'unknown' is not a grey metallic looking powder, then a carbonate is probably present.)
(ii) Add a few drops of barium chloride solution to the mixture from (i).
(iii) A white precipitate indicates the presence of a sulphate (sulphate ions) in the 'unknown'.

8 SULPHUR DIOXIDE

Sulphur dioxide is formed by:
(i) burning sulphur in air or oxygen:

$$S(s) + O_2(g) \rightarrow SO_2(g)$$
sulphur + oxygen → sulphur dioxide

(ii) burning sulphur-containing fossil fuels, e.g. FeS_2 in coal:

$$2FeS_2(s) + 5\tfrac{1}{2}O_2(g) \rightarrow Fe_2O_3(s) + 4SO_2(g)$$
iron pyrites + oxygen → iron(III) oxide + sulphur dioxide

Try to construct for yourself an equation for the burning of hydrogen sulphide (found in 'sour' natural gas). Sulphur dioxide is formed in this combustion also.

(iii) burning sulphur as in the contact process (Section 6(G)). Sulphur burns readily with a pale blue flame which becomes very bright blue if oxygen is used instead of air:

$$S(s) + O_2(g) \rightarrow SO_2(g).$$

(A) PROPERTIES AND USES OF SULPHUR DIOXIDE

❝❝ SO₂ ❞❞

- Sulphur dioxide is a pungent, choking gas. It is very soluble in water. The gas is toxic.
- Sulphur dioxide is used as a sterilising agent in some food and equipment, e.g. fruit juices, wines and wine-making equipment. The gas is toxic to bacteria.

❝❝ Bleach ❞❞

- Sulphur dioxide is a powerful reducing agent and as such is used to bleach wood pulp for paper making. Because this bleaching occurs by ***reduction*** (removal of oxygen), the paper made from bleached wood pulp will eventually go yellow again as oxygen from the air reverses the bleaching process.

❝❝ Pollution ❞❞

- Sulphur dioxide is a well-known atmospheric pollutant because of its formation from the burning of fossil fuels in power stations and other industrial combustion processes dependent on fossil fuels.
- When it reacts with water, sulphur dioxide forms sulphurous acid:

$$H_2O(l) + SO_2(g) \rightarrow H_2SO_3(aq)$$
water + sulphur dioxide → sulphurous acid

A practical use of the sterilising power of sulphur dioxide in the home is its use to sterilise home-made wine-making equipment. If a 'Campden tablet', which contains sodium sulphite and citric acid as a solid mixture, is added to water, sulphur dioxide gas is produced. Wine-making equipment can be washed with this to prevent unwanted bacterial spoilage of the wine.

(B) ACID RAIN

Sulphurous acid is easily oxidised by air to sulphuric acid. In this way sulphur dioxide pollution of the atmosphere eventually produces 'acid rain' i.e. rain containing sulphuric acid.

The toxic nature of sulphur dioxide on humans at low concentrations causes breathing difficulties. The London 'smogs' (smoke plus fog) of the 1950s were believed to have killed many thousands of old and young people who suffered from asthma. At the time the sulphur dioxide concentration was as much as twenty times the yearly average. Since then the Clean Air Act of 1956 has forced a reduction in pollution from this gas.

Power station emissions

Pollution from power stations affects mainly those areas that are in the path of the gas as it is carried by the wind. It has been shown that this process can carry the gas many hundreds of miles and it is now accepted that much pollution is carried to Scandinavian countries by the prevailing south-westerly winds common in Britain. The gas attacks plants, stonework and metal causing damage to vegetation and corrosion to stone and metal structures (see Chapter 3, Section 4(c)).

EXAMINATION QUESTIONS

QUESTION 1

Sulphuric acid is essential to any country with a chemical industry.

(a) The charts below show the uses of sulphuric acid in an industrialised country and a developing country in 1990 (Fig. 12.27). By 1994, the chart for the industrialised country had hardly changed, but the chart for the developing country had changed significantly.

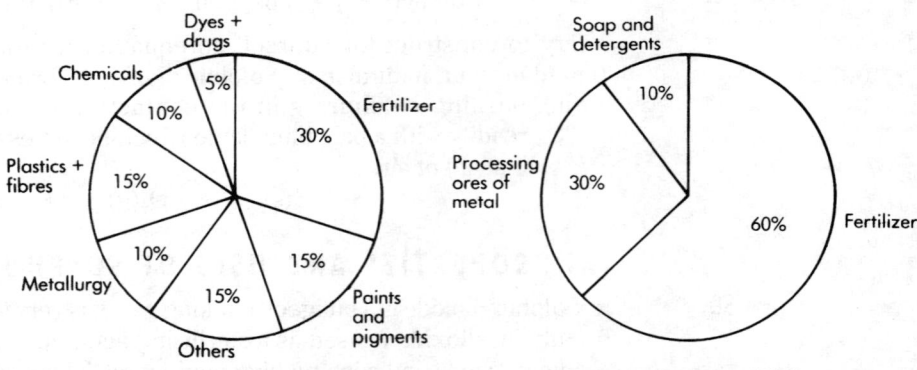

Fig. 12.27 — Industrialised country (1990): Fertilizer 30%, Dyes + drugs 5%, Chemicals 10%, Plastics + fibres 15%, Metallurgy 10%, Others 15%, Paints and pigments 15%.

Developing country (1990): Fertilizer 60%, Processing ores of metal 30%, Soap and detergents 10%.

(i) What were the two major industries in the developing country in 1990?
(1 line) (*2*)

(ii) Draw a chart for the developing country in 1994, showing the likely changes as the country becomes more industrialised (Fig. 12.28).

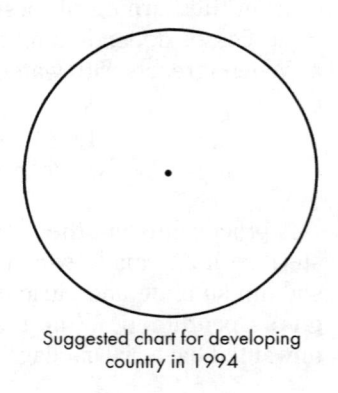

Fig. 12.28 — Suggested chart for developing country in 1994

(b) Sulphuric acid is manufacturered by the Contact Process. The reactions involved are as follows.

$$\text{sulphur} + \text{oxygen} \longrightarrow \text{gas A}$$

$$\text{gas A} + \text{oxygen} \xrightarrow{\text{catalyst B}} \text{sulphur trioxide}$$

$$\text{sulphur trioxide} + \text{liquid C} \longrightarrow \text{oleum}$$

$$\text{oleum} + \text{liquid D} \longrightarrow \text{sulphuric acid}$$

Give the name of:
gas A.. (*1*)
catalyst B .... (*1*)
liquid C... (*1*)
liquid D .... (*1*)

(*Total = 8*)
(IGCSE)

QUESTION 2

Sulphuric acid is an important industrial acid, about 130 million tonnes were made in 1982. The following flow diagram shows the main steps in its manufacture, by the Contact Process (Fig. 12.29).

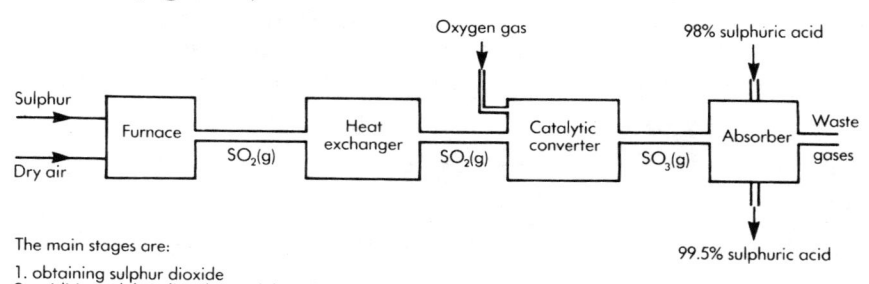

Fig. 12.29

The main stages are:
1. obtaining sulphur dioxide
2. oxidising sulphur dioxide to sulphur trioxide
3. converting the sulphur trioxide to sulphuric acid

(a) Write an equation for the burning of sulphur. (1 line) (*1*)
(b) Name another substance that would react with dry air on heating to form sulphur dioxide. (1 line) (*1*)
(c) What is the use of the heat exchanger? (1 line) (*1*)
(d) Write the equation for the reaction taking place in the catalytic converter and name the catalyst used. (1 line) (*2*)
(e) The sulphur trioxide is absorbed in 98% sulphuric acid and not in water, give a reason for this and write the equation for the absorption. (2 lines) (*2*)
(f) Explain why manufacturers build sulphuric acid plants near other chemical works. (2 lines) (*2*)
(g) Sulphur dioxide is one pollutant that forms 'acid rain'. Give one important source of this sulphur dioxide. (1 line) (*1*)
(h) Give one reason why 'acid rain' is a problem. (*1*)

(WJEC)

QUESTION 3

(a) Ammonia is a starting marterial in the manufacture of fertilisers.
   (i) Give the chemical name for a fertiliser made from ammonia. (1 line) (*1*)
   (ii) Name the element present in the compound named in (a)(i) which makes it useful as a fertiliser. (1 line) (*1*)
   (iii) Why do some farmers add fertiliser to their soil? (2 lines) (*1*)
(b) Study the reaction scheme shown and answer the questions below (Fig. 12.30).

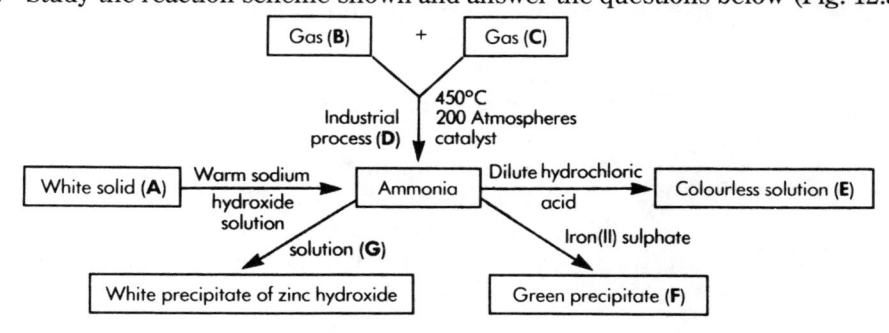

Fig. 12.30

(i) Give the name or formula of ....
solid (A), ...
gas (B), ...
gas (C), ...
solution (E), ...
precipitate (F), ...
solution (G), ... *(6)*
(ii) Name the industrial process (D), ... *(1)*
(Total 10)
(NEAB)

QUESTION 4

(a) Outline briefly how sulphur is produced commercially *(4)*
(b) Write equations for the reactions of oxygen with
   (i) sulphur to produce sulphur dioxide, *(1)*
   (ii) sulphur dioxide to produce sulphur trioxide. *(2)*
(c) Describe with a reason how sulphur trioxide is converted into sulphuric acid commercially (equations are not required). *(3)*
(d) (i) Describe **two** reactions which you have done in the laboratory, which show how dilute sulphuric acid behaves as an acid. *(6)*
   (ii) Concentrated sulphuric acid can act as a dehydrating agent. Describe **two** reactions which illustrate this property. *(4)*
(NISEAC)

QUESTION 5

Carefully read the following passage and then answer the questions which follow it. The map (Fig. 12.31) shows the location of a fertiliser factory and two power stations in the Belfast area.

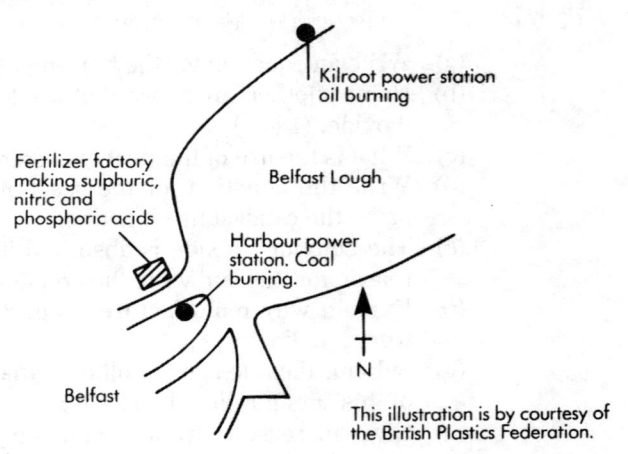

Fig. 12.31

All the raw materials needed at the power stations and fertiliser factory must be imported although it is hoped to generate power from locally mined lignite at some time in the future.

The location of the power stations means that the giant cooling towers seen at power stations in England are not needed.

Both sulphuric and nitric acids are manufactured in the fertiliser factory. The sulphuric acid produced at the fertiliser factory is used to make phosphoric acid from phosphate rock. The fertiliser factory markets fertilisers which are mixtures of the ammonium salts of the acids made at the factory. A plume of brown smoke is often seen rising from the nitric acid plant, and this, and other gases from the factory and power stations, contributes to the atmospheric pollution in the area.

(a) List **four** raw materials which must be imported for use either in the power stations, or the fertiliser factory. *(4)*
(b) (i) Name the main chemical found in phosphate rock. *(1)*
   (ii) Write a word equation for the reaction between sulphuric acid and phosphate rock. *(1)*

(iii) Write a word equation for the reaction between ammonia and phosphoric acid. *(1)*
(c) Write a symbol equation for the reaction between ammonia and sulphuric acid. *(2)*
(d) Name another chemical made at the factory which is an ingredient of the mixed fertilisers. *(1)*
(e) (i) Name the brown gas in the smoke given off at the fertiliser factory. *(1)*
   (ii) Name **two** other gases which pollute the atmosphere over these industries and state which process gives off the gas. *(4)*
(f) Winds in the Belfast area blow mostly from the south-west. Does this have any effect on atmospheric pollution over Belfast caused by these industries?
(g) (i) Why are large cooling towers not needed at the power stations? *(1)*
   (ii) How does this affect the environment? *(1)*
(h) Would burning lignite make much change to atmospheric pollution? Give a reason for your answer. *(2)*

(NISEAC)

OUTLINE ANSWERS

ANSWER 1

(a) (i) The two major industries in the developing country were farming (fertiliser manufacture uses much of the sulphuric acid) and metal mining (metal ore processing used the next largest quantity of acid).
   (ii) The chart should show at least one **new industry** such as plastics and fibres, though it would not be expected to take such a big portion of the total acid production as in a developed country at an early stage. Which particular new industry is chosen is not important.
(b) Gas A is sulphur dioxide.
Catalyst B is vanadium(V) oxide.
Liquid C is concentrated sulphuric acid.
Liquid D is water.

ANSWER 2

This question is mainly about the Contact Process and its processes discussed in Section 6(G).

(a) Sulphur burns in the **oxygen** of the air.

$$S(l) + O_2(g) \rightarrow SO_2(g)$$
$$\text{sulphur} + \text{oxygen} \rightarrow \text{sulphur dioxide}$$

No sulphur trioxide is formed when sulphur burns in air.
(b) Most sulphur compounds will **burn** in air to give sulphur dioxide. H_2S, hydrogen sulphide, will burn to give sulphur dioxide.
(c) The heat exchanger shown in the flow diagram absorbs heat from the waste gases before they are disposed of. It is an **economising measure**.
(d) In the converter, sulphur dioxide is oxidised to sulphur trioxide. The catalyst is vanadium (V) oxide:

$$2SO_2(g) + O_2(g) \rightarrow 2SO_3(g)$$

See Section 6(G)

(e) Sulphur trioxide reacts violently with water producing a mist, which is difficult to condense, and a considerable quantity of heat. Absorption in concentrated sulphuric acid reduces both these effects.

$$H_2SO_4(l) + SO_3(g) \rightarrow H_2S_2O_7(l)$$

(f) This will cut costs of transport, reduce risks of accidents with the acid and also will enable the sale of recovered heat energy to other plant operators if they are very close.

(g) Sulphur dioxide is emitted by any coal-burning process. Coal-fired power stations emit large amounts because they burn enormous quantities of coal per year. Crude oil often contains sulphur compounds and if burnt would also pollute the air. Most oil products for burning have had much of their sulphur removed before use.

(h) Acid rain is said to damage forests. It acidifies lakes and so kills fish and aquatic plants.

ANSWER 3

Part (a) is about nitrogenous fertilisers and their effect on crops.
  (i) Fertilisers made from ammonia are nitrogenous fertilisers. Ammonium nitrate is one.
  (ii) It is the nitrogen which makes the fertiliser useful to plants.
  (iii) Farmers use fertiliser to **increase the yield** of their crops.
(b) Solid (A) is any **ammonium salts**, e.g. NH_4Cl.
Gas (B) and Gas (C) are **nitrogen** and **hydrogen** used to make ammonia in the Haber process.
Solution (E) is **ammonium chloride solution** made by neutralising ammonia (alkali) with hydrochloric acid

$$NH_3(g) + HCl(aq) \rightarrow NH_4Cl(aq)$$

Precipitate (F) is **iron(II) hydroxide**. Ammonia solution is an alkali and contains $OH^-(aq)$ ions. These react with $Fe^{2+}(aq)$ ions to form the insoluble hydroxide of iron, which is green.
Solution (G) is **any zinc salt solution** since the precipitate is named as zinc hydroxide, which forms in the same way as was described for iron(II) hydroxide but requiring **zinc ions** instead of iron ions.
Industrial process (D) is the **Haber process** for the synthesis of ammonia.

ANSWER 4

(a) Commercial production of sulphur is by the Frasch process. This is described in detail in Section 6(C) above.
(b) These equations are given in the answer to question 2.
(c) This is given in the answer to question 2.

66 See Sect. 6(c) 99

(d) (i) Sulphuric acid behaving as an acid with:
      (a) universal indicator. It turns it red.
      (b) a reactive metal. A fizzing is observed, hydrogen is formed which explodes when put to a flame.

66 See Sect. 7(e) 99

      (c) any carbonate. A fizzing is observed. The gas produced turns limewater milky, proving it to be carbon dioxide.
    (ii) Sulphuric acid behaving as a dehydrating agent:
      (a) When added to sugar a vigorous reaction occurs and a voluminous black mass of carbon is formed.
      (b) When added to blue copper(II) sulphate crystals, the colour slowly changes to white as the crystals lose their **water of crystallisation** and become **anhydrous**.

ANSWER 5

This is a comprehension excercise. Apart from some chemical knowledge, you will need to keep looking to the text for information you may not have.
(a) The materials required are those needed to make the two acids, nitric and sulphuric, together with the imported raw material for phosphate production. There are **more than** four so **any four** will do. Note that **all materials** must be imported – brought in from aboard.
(b) (i) and (ii) are connected. If (i) is not known (ii) can only be guessed at (see

Section 7(D)). (iii) is straightforward, leading to the ammonium salt which is a dual-nutrient fertiliser.
(c) Remember that sulphuric acid has *two* hydrogen atoms to be replaced by ammonium ions.
(d) Another ammonium salt is required.
(e) (i) The brown gas is nitrogen dioxide, one of the chemicals formed in the manufacture of nitric acid. (Modern plants would not emit such pollution.)
   (ii) You must give two pollutants *and* two processes which produce them. Look again at the map – do you see other sources of pollution?
(f) The effect of wind direction is important in factory siting. In this case, the prevailing wind is favourable – you must *say why*.
(g) (i) and (ii) are probably general knowledge. Remember that absence of cooling towers does not mean the local engineers have discovered a way of producing power without cooling!
(h) This question asks for your considered judgement about a situation you may not be familiar with. Marks are awarded in such questions for reasonable comments relevant to the problem rather than the 'correct answer'.

STUDENT'S ANSWER – EXAMINER'S COMMENTS

Information about some common fertilisers is given in the following table.

Name	Formula	Solubility in water
Ammonium phosphate	$(NH_4)_3PO_4$	Readily soluble
	NH_4NO_3	Readily soluble
Potassium nitrate	KNO_3	Readily soluble
Urea	$CO(NH_2)_2$	Dissolves slowly

> 🙶 Ammonium nitrate would be the usual name. Did you notice the clue in the first name in the table? 🙷

(a) Name the compound whose formula is NH_4NO_3.

→ ammonia nitrate

(1 mark)

> 🙶 Good – and well set out too. 🙷

(b) Calculate the mass of 1 mole of urea.
(Relative atomic masses: H 1; C 12; N 14; O 16.)

→ $CO(NH_2)_2 = 12 + 16 + (14+2) \times 2 = 28 + 32 = 60g$

(1 mark)

(c) Why is urea a slow-acting fertilizer?

> 🙶 Answer couldn't be better. 🙷

It dissolves slowly. That means it will take a long time to act on the plant.

(1 mark)

(d) How can good plant growth be maintained if chemical fertilizers like those in the table are not used?

> 🙶 Nice to see you applying your experience! Yes natural manures often do smell! 🙷

I think the farmer would have to use manure from cows or pigs or waste from breweries – as they do near my home – phew!!

(2 marks)

(e) Another substance which may be added to soil is hydrated lime $Ca(OH)_2$.

(i) What is the chemical name for hydrated lime?

> 🙶 Good – you have 'read' the formula (Ca for calcium, OH for hydroxide). 🙷

→ calcium hydroxide

(1 mark)

(ii) What is the main reason for adding hydrated lime to soil?

> 🙶 If you added a great deal it might do that, but the main reason is to *neutralise* acidity in the soil. This is usually caused by use of ammonium compounds as fertiliser. 🙷

→ To make it alkaline.

(1 mark)

(iii) Why should hydrated lime and ammonium phosphate **not** be applied to the soil at the same time?

> 🙶 Yes it would. But TWO marks are given – and three lines for the answer. You could have guessed that TWO points should be made. '*They react* to form *ammonia* gas which would escape and be lost to the crops'. 🙷

→ ammonium phosphate would react with the lime.

(2 marks)

ISEG-Nuffield Alternative I

CHAPTER 124

HYDROGEN CHLORIDE, CHLORIDES AND CHLORINE

HYDROGEN CHLORIDE
HYDROCHLORIC ACID
CHLORINE
CHLORIDES

GETTING STARTED

Chlorine is a very reactive element and therefore it does not occur naturally in the free state. It occurs in a large number of compounds, the most common being ***sodium chloride***. Sea water contains sodium chloride, potassium chloride and magnesium chloride. About 2.5% by mass of the sea is sodium chloride. When inland seas dry up, sea beds are formed. Sodium chloride is mined from these sea beds as rock salt. Gases from volcanoes often contain a small amount of ***hydrogen chloride***. Sodium chloride is essential to animal life.

Sodium chloride is used to make hydrogen chloride, chlorine and sodium hydroxide (see Chapter 7, Section 11).

ESSENTIAL PRINCIPLES

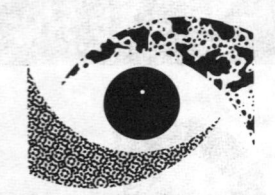

1 HYDROGEN CHLORIDE

Hydrogen chloride is **prepared** by reacting concentrated sulphuric acid with sodium chloride (Fig. 12.32):

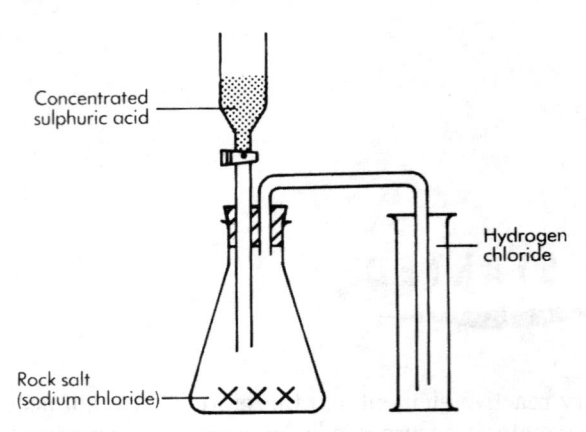

Fig. 12.32

>> Sodium hydrogensulphate is formed, *NOT* sodium sulphate <<

sodium chloride + sulphuric acid → hydrogen chloride + sodium hydrogensulphate
$NaCl(s)$ + $H_2SO_4(l)$ → $HCl(g)$ + $NaHSO_4(s)$

Hydrogen chloride is **manufactured** by **direct synthesis**. Hydrogen is burnt in chlorine:

>> Remember, hydrogen and chlorine are diatomic <<

hydrogen + chlorine ⟶ hydrogen chloride
$H_2(g)$ + $Cl_2(g)$ ⟶ $2HCl(g)$

(A) PROPERTIES OF HYDROGEN CHLORIDE

Hydrogen chloride is a colourless gas that fumes in moist air. It has a sharp, irritating smell.. It is denser than air. It is very soluble in water; the solution formed is known as **hydrochloric acid**. It turns damp pH paper red. It is poisonous. Hydrogen choride does not burn in air or oxygen. It does not support the burning of a splint.

(B) TEST FOR HYDROGEN CHLORIDE

>> Learn this test <<

Hydrogen chloride reacts with ammonia to form ammonium chloride. Ammonium chloride appears as a white smoke. This reaction is often used as a test for hydrogen chloride:

>> Ammon*ium* chloride not ammonia chloride <<

hydrogen chloride + ammonia → ammonium chloride
$HCl(g)$ + $NH_3(g)$ → $NH_4Cl(s)$

A solution of silver nitrate in water can be used as a test for a chloride. It forms a white precipitate of silver chloride. Thus if a drop of silver nitrate solution is held in hydrogen chloride gas it turns white:

>> Most metal chlorides are soluble in water <<

silver nitrate (aq) + hydrogen chloride (aq) → silver chloride(s) + nitric acid (aq)
$AgNO_3(aq)$ + $HCl(aq)$ → $AgCl(s)$ + $HNO_3(aq)$

(C) STRUCTURE OF HYDROGEN CHLORIDE

Hydrogen chloride is a fairly typical covalent, diatomic molecule (Fig. 12.33). It is a gas and a non-conductor of electricity. However, it is very soluble in water because it reacts with water to form hydrochloric acid:

hydrogen chloride + water → hydrochloric acid
$HCl(g)$ + $H_2O(l)$ → $H_3O^+(aq) + Cl^-(aq)$

H ˣ⋅ Cl :

Fig. 12.33

2 HYDROCHLORIC ACID

Hydrochloric acid is a colourless solution. It behaves as a typical strong acid both when it is concentrated and when dilute. The reactions of concentrated hydrochloric acid are much faster than reactions of dilute hydrochloric acid.

(A) REACTIONS OF DILUTE HYDROCHLORIC ACID

(i) Hydrochloric acid turns indicator paper red.
(ii) It reacts with metals above hydrogen in the reactivity series to form the metal chloride and hydrogen, e.g.

magnesium + hydrochloric acid → magnesium chloride + hydrogen gas
$Mg + 2HCl → MgCl_2 + H_2$

If the metal can form more than one chloride, it will form the chloride containing least chlorine. Iron reacts with hydrochloric acid to form iron(II) chloride and not iron(III) chloride.

(iii) It reacts with all carbonates to form the metal chloride, water and carbon dioxide, e.g.

calcium carbonate + hydrochloric acid → calcium chloride + water + carbon dioxide
$CaCO_3 + 2HCl → CaCl_2 + H_2O + CO_2$

❝ acid + base → salt + water ❞

(iv) It reacts with bases to give the metal chloride and water. A base is a metal oxide or hydroxide, e.g.

copper(II) oxide + hydrochloric acid → copper(II) chloride + water
$CuO + 2HCl → CuCl_2 + H_2O$

(B) REACTIONS OF CONCENTRATED HYDROCHLORIC ACID

Concentrated hydrochloric acid is oxidised to chlorine by oxidising agents such as manganese(IV) oxide and potassium manganate(VII):

❝ Another use of manganese (IV) oxide is as a catalyst in the preparation of oxygen ❞

hydrochloric acid + manganese(IV) oxide → manganese(II) chloride + water + chlorine
$4HCl + MnO_2 → MnCl_2 + 2H_2O + Cl_2$

(C) USES OF HYDROCHLORIC ACID

Hydrochloric acid is used to clean metals (by removing the oxide layer) before they are coated with other metals. This process is known as **pickling**. To prevent iron from rusting it is pickled and then covered with zinc. Covering iron with zinc is known as **galvanising**. Hydrochloric acid is also used for making printed circuits in the electrical industry and in the manufacture of dyes.

3 CHLORINE

Chlorine is prepared by oxidising concentrated hydrochloric acid with either manganese(IV) oxide or potassium manganate(VII). If potassium manganate(VII) is used, no heating is required (see Fig. 12.34).

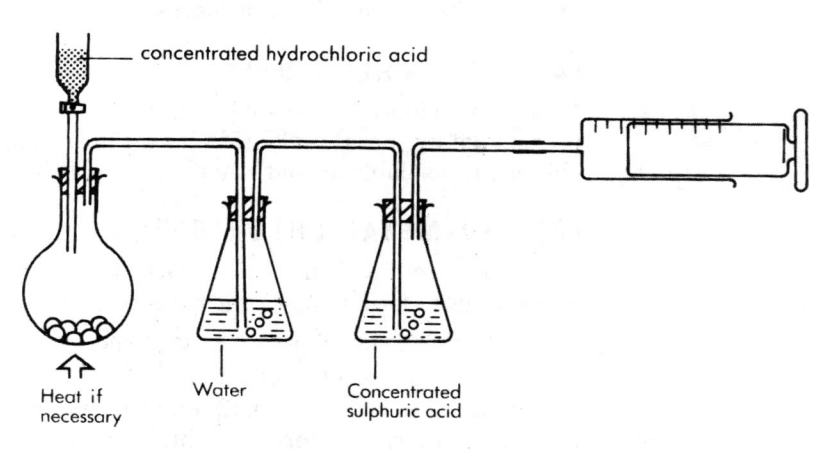

Fig. 12.34

hydrochloric + manganese(IV) → manganese(II) + water + chlorine
acid   oxide   chloride

$$4HCl + MnO_2 \xrightarrow{heat} MnCl_2 + 2H_2O + Cl_2$$

hydrochloric + potassium → manganese(II) + potassium + water + chlorine
acid   manganate(VII)   chloride   chloride

$$16HCl + 2KMnO_4 → 2MnCl_2 + 2KCl + 8H_2O + 5Cl_2$$

Chlorine is formed when molten metal chlorides are electrolysed (see Chapter 8, Section 11).

(A) MANUFACTURE OF CHLORINE

Chlorine is manufactured by the electrolysis of either molten sodium chloride or of aqueous sodium chloride (see Chapter 8, Section 11). The gas is released at the positive electrode which is usually made of carbon or titanium. Chlorine does not react with carbon or titanium. The electrode reaction is

$$2Cl^- - 2e^- → Cl_2$$

This process is an example of oxidation by electron loss.

(B) PROPERTIES OF CHLORINE

❝ Test for chlorine ❞

Chlorine is a pale green gas. Chlorine has a choking smell. It is denser than air. It is fairly soluble in water.

❝ Learn this test ❞

Chlorine turns damp pH paper red and then bleaches the paper. This is used as a test for chlorine. Chlorine is very poisonous. Although chlorine is very reactive, it does not burn in air or oxygen. A splint does not burn in chlorine.

(C) STRUCTURE OF CHLORINE

Chlorine is in group 7 of the periodic table and has seven electrons in its outer shell. It is a fairly typical covalent, diatomic molecule (Fig. 12.35). It is a gas and a non-conductor of electricity. However, it is soluble in water because it reacts with water to form a mixture of hydrochloric acid and chloric(I) acid:

chlorine + water → hydrochloric acid + chloric(I) acid
$$Cl_2 + H_2O → HCl + HClO$$

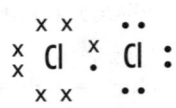

Fig. 12.35

(D) ISOTOPES

Chlorine has two *isotopes* of mass numbers 35 and 37. Its relative atomic mass is 35.5 because the ^{35}Cl isotope is more common than the ^{37}Cl isotope.

4 CHLORIDES

Chlorine forms ionic chlorides with metals and covalent chlorides with non-metals. Chlorine is a powerful oxidising agent. If an element can form more than one chloride, it will form the chloride containing most chlorine. Iron reacts with chlorine to form iron(III) chloride and not iron(II) chloride:

❝ Metal chlorides are ionic, non-metal chlorides are covalent ❞

iron + chlorine → iron(III) chloride
$$2Fe + 3Cl_2 → 2FeCl_3.$$

In this reaction, chlorine molecules are reduced to chloride ions by gain of electrons from the two iron atoms.

(A) METAL CHLORIDES

Most metal chlorides are soluble in water. This is why the sea contains such a high percentage by mass of chloride ions. Silver chloride is insoluble in water. Lead(II) chloride is insoluble in cold water, but soluble in hot water.

(B) NON-METAL CHLORIDES

Chlorine reacts with many non-metals to form covalent chlorides. It reacts with phosphorus to form phosphorus pentachloride:

phosphorus + chlorine → phosphorus pentachloride
$$2P + 5Cl_2 → 2PCl_5$$

Non-metal chlorides are easily hydrolysed and tend to fume in moist air because hydrogen chloride is formed. Chlorine does not react with carbon. However, the compound tetrachloromethane CCl_4 does exist.

(C) OXIDISING PROPERTIES

Chlorine is a powerful **oxidising agent** because it is easily reduced to chloride ions. It oxidises sulphites to sulphates, iron(II) compounds to iron(III) compounds, bromides to bromine and iodides to iodine (see Chapter 6, Section 6):

sodium sulphite + chlorine + water → sodium sulphate + hydrochloric acid
Na_2SO_3 + Cl_2 + H_2O → Na_2SO_4 + $2HCl$

iron(II) chloride + chlorine → iron(III) chloride
$2FeCl_2$ + Cl_2 → $2FeCl_3$

Here iron in its +2 oxidation state is oxidised by electron loss to iron in the +3 oxidation state. The oxidising agent is chlorine gas.

sodium bromide + chlorine → sodium chloride + bromine
$2NaBr$ + Cl_2 → $2NaCl$ + Br_2
sodium iodide + chlorine → sodium chloride + iodine
$2NaI$ + Cl_2 → $2NaCl$ + I_2

> Chlorine, bromine and iodine are diatomic

> The compounds of these elements are called chlorides, bromides and iodides

(D) CHLORIC(I) ACID

Chlorine is moderately soluble in water; the solution formed is known as chlorine water. Chlorine water is a mixture of hydrochloric acid and chloric(I) acid:

chlorine + water → hydrochloric acid + chloric(I) acid
Cl_2 + H_2O → HCl + $HClO$

Chloric(I) acid readily decomposes into hydrochloric acid and oxygen. This reaction takes place more quickly in sunlight.

Chloric(I) acid is a bleaching agent: it oxidises many coloured dyes to colourless substances. It bleaches indicator paper and this reaction is used as a test for chlorine.

(E) SODIUM CHLORATE(I)

Salts of chloric acid are called chlorate(I) salts. Sodium chlorate(I) is made by reacting chlorine with sodium hydroxide solution.

sodium hydroxide + chlorine → sodium chlorate(I) + sodium chloride + water
$NaOH$ + Cl_2 → $NaClO$ + $NaCl$ + H_2O

Chlorine also reacts with solid calcium hydroxide to form bleaching powder.

(F) USES OF CHLORINE

> Do not just say in swimming pools; you must say *why it is added*. Do not just say manufacture of plastic; you must name a plastic made from chlorine.

Chlorine is used for making liquid bleaches, e.g. sodium chlorate(I). (This compound is also known as sodium hypochlorite solution.) This is found in bleaches such as Domestos and Milton.

Chlorine when dissolved in water is a good disinfectant. It is used to kill bacteria in drinking water and in swimming pool water.

Chlorine is used to manufacture plastics such as PVC (polyvinyl chloride).

When chlorine is substituted for hydrogen atoms in various hydrocarbons, the products formed are often good solvents for organic compounds, e.g. perchlorethene is used to dry clean clothes; 1,1,1-trichlorethane is a solvent for liquid paper. Chemicals that are used as pesticides or weed killers are often compounds of chlorine, e.g. DDT (**d**ichloro**d**iphenyl**t**richloroethane) has been used as a pesticide. DDT is very stable and it is very poisonous to wildlife, it has been banned in most countries. Because it is very stable it tends to become concentrated towards the end of a food chain.

(G) SODIUM CHLORATE(V) NaClO₃

Sodium chlorate(V) is used as a weed killer. It is a very powerful oxidising agent and must be handled with care. It will ruin clothes if it is spilled on them.

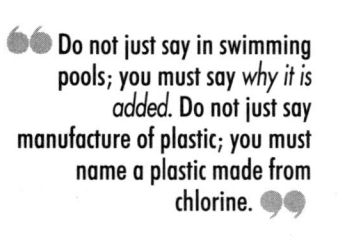

CHAPTER 12.4 HYDROGEN CHLORIDE, CHLORIDES AND CHLORINE

EXAMINATION QUESTIONS

MULTIPLE CHOICE

QUESTIONS 1-3

Choose from the following list the letter representing the gas described by the statement in the question. Each letter may be used once, more than once, or not at all.

- A ammonia
- B chlorine
- C hydrogen
- D nitrogen
- E sulphur dioxide

1 A gas which is coloured.
2 A gas which forms white fumes in contact with hydrogen chloride.
3 A gas which bleaches damp blue litmus paper.

(NISEAC)

QUESTION 4

Which one of the substances listed below could produce a solution of pH 7 if it was added, in the correct proportions, to a strongly alkaline solution?

- A distilled water
- B hydrochloric acid
- C lime-water
- D sodium hydroxide solution

(SEG)

QUESTION 5

Salt is necessary in your diet because

- A it helps in cooking
- B it is lost in sweat
- C it makes food taste better
- D it preserves food

(SEG)

QUESTION 6

Which one of the following is used to make a bleach?

- A hydrogen
- B carbon monoxide
- C carbon dioxide
- D chlorine
- E oxygen

COMPLETION AND STRUCTURED QUESTIONS

QUESTION 7

Identify the substances described below.

(a) Greenish-yellow gas; book on safety says 'very harmful gas which can cause skin damage on contact and severe lung damage if breathed in'.
Substance is ....
(1 mark)

(b) Colourless liquid which conducts electricity; turns pH paper red; reacts with silver nitrate solution forming a dense white precipitate.
Substance is ....
(2 marks)
(SEG)

QUESTION 8

The information shown below is taken from a 'data card' for common salt (sodium chloride). You will need to refer to this information in order to answer the question.

DATA CARD:	Salt.
MAIN MINERAL:	Rock salt.
TECHNICAL NAME:	Halite.
COMPOSITION AND FORMULA	Sodium chloride, NaCl.
HOW FOUND:	As undergound layers (strata). As evaporated material around inland seas.
WORLD SUPPLY:	Very plentiful
WHERE FOUND:	Very widespread. Countries with the largest production are those with large populations, e.g. USA, China, USSR.
MINING METHODS:	1. Undergound mining. 2. 'Solution mining'.
WORLD PRODUCTION:	Around 165 million tonnes per year.
UK PRODUCTION:	1.6 million tonnes of rock salt by underground mining and 1.2 million tonnes of solution-mined salt per year.
HOW USED:	To make chlorine and sodium hydroxide 37%
	To make sodium carbonate (mainly for glass) 21%
	Food preservation and flavouring 17%
	Road de-icing 10%
	Other (e.g. animal feed, water treatment) 15%
PRICE (1990):	£22 per tonne.
PROBLEMS ASSOCIATED WITH MINING THIS MINERAL:	Very few problems of health, safety or damage to the environment. Modern methods have largely overcome the problems of subsidence (ground collapsing at the surface, causing dips in roads and buildings to fall down), which have occurred previously.

(a) Explain which of the given information shows that Britain is not a major world producer of salt. (2 lines) .... (2)
(b) Rock salt contains a small amount of insoluble impurities. Describe how it could be purified for use in food. (6 lines) .... (4)
(c) Draw a bar chart to show the major uses of salt ....(4)

QUESTION 9

A company called CHLORMAN makes chemicals from rock salt (sodium chloride) which is found in rocks underneath Cheshire. This is a sketch of the factory.
The sodium chloride arrives at the factory by pipeline as brine.

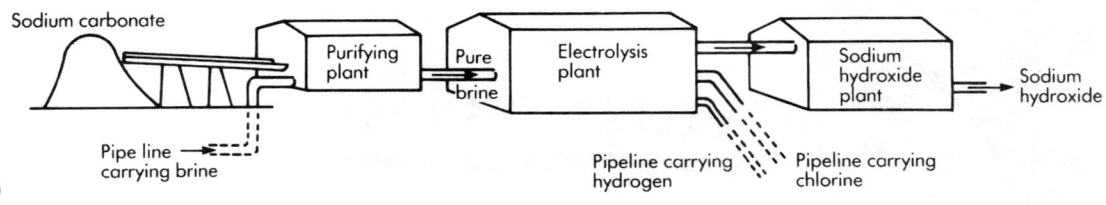

Fig. 12.36

(a) What is brine? (1)
(b) What would be the SIMPLEST way of obtaining brine from the underground rock salt deposits? (1)
(c) Where in Britain would you expect CHLORMAN to have built their factory? (1 line)
Explain why it would be sensible to build the factory there. (2 lines) (2)
(d) The brine contains calcium salts as impurities. These are removed by adding solid sodium carbonate to the brine.

(i) Complete this word equation to explain how the solid sodium carbonate reacts with the impurities.

sodium carbonate + calcium chloride → sodium chloride + ...

(ii) After this reaction the solid unwanted product must be removed from the brine. What method would you suggest to do this? (1 line) (2)

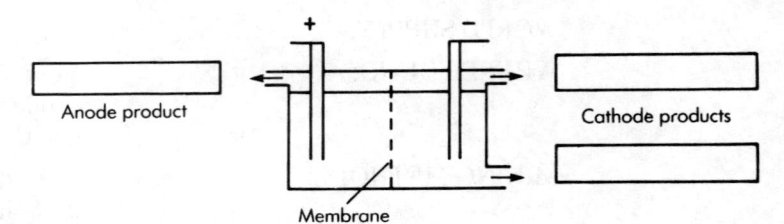

Fig. 12.37

(e) In the electrolysis plant there are many electrolysis cells like this (Fig. 12.37) in which sodium chloride is electrolysed.
Fill in the names of the three products in their correct boxes on the diagram. (3)

(f) Two of the products of this factory can be used to make hydrochloric acid. Which are they? (1 line) (1)

(g) CHLORMAN have to buy their supplies of brine and sodium carbonate. What else do the company need to pay for that will be a major part of the cost of operating this factory? (1 line) (1)

(h) CHLORMAN sells most of its products to these buyers:
Sodium hydroxide — to a soap manufacturer
Chlorine — to a PVC manufacturer
Hydrogen — to a margarine manufacturer

(i) How does the soap manufacturer use the sodium hydroxide in making soap? (1 line) (1)

(ii) If the PVC manufacturer goes out of business, CHLORMAN must find a new market for its chlorine AT ONCE. Why must CHLORMAN do so? (2 lines)
Suggest another use for which CHLORMAN might sell its chlorine. (1 line) (3)

(iii) The margarine manufacturer uses hydrogen to react with vegetable oils. These oils have unsaturated hydrocarbon chains as part of their molecules. The hydrogen turns these into saturated hydrocarbon chains which are present in the margarine.
   How would you show that the vegetable oil has unsaturated hydrocarbon chains in its molecule?
Test: add ....
Observation: If unsaturated hydrocarbon chains were present, I would expect to see (1 line)
What would you observe if you did the same test on a substance with only saturated hydrocarbon chains? (2 lines) (3)

(Total marks 18)
(MEG)

OUTLINE ANSWERS

ANSWER 1

Chlorine is the only coloured gas in the list, hence key is B (see Section 3(B) above).

ANSWER 2

One of the tests for hydrogen chloride is that it fumes with ammonia. Key is A (see Section 1(B) above).

ANSWER 3

Answer: B (see Section 3(B) above).

ANSWER 4

Answer: B (see Chapter 10).

ANSWER 5

The word to look at in this question is *necessary*. Salt does make food taste better and it preserves food, but is *necessary* because it replaces sodium chloride lost by sweating – key B.

ANSWER 6

Answer: D (see Section 4(F) above).

ANSWER 7

(a) Chlorine.
(b) Hydrochloric acid – the white precipitate is silver chloride.

ANSWER 8

(a) The UK production of salt is 1.6 + 1.2 = 2.8 million tonnes per year. This is very small compared with the world production of 165 million tonnes per year.
(b) Rock salt is crushed into small pieces and dissolved in water, heating if necessary. The mixture is filtered to remove insoluble impurities. The filtrate is then carefully evaporated to dryness leaving a white solid which is sodium chloride.
(c) You should be able to construct a bar chart (make 1 cm equivalent to 10%).

ANSWER 9

(a) Brine is a concentrated solution of sodium chloride in water.
(b) The simplest way of obtaining brine from rock salt would be to pump down water.
(c) CHLORMAN would be built in Cheshire where the salt deposits are found. It is cheaper to build the factory nearer the deposit of rock salt to reduce transport costs.
(d) (i) Calcium carbonate.
 (ii) Unwanted solid products can be removed by filtration.
(e) Anode product is chlorine.
 Cathode products are hydrogen and sodium hydroxide.
(f) Hydrogen and chlorine.
 (When hydrogen is burnt in chlorine it makes hydrogen chloride.)
(g) CHLORMAN would have to pay for electricity in order to carry out electrolysis.
(h) (i) Soap is made by reacting sodium hydroxide with vegetable oils such as castor oil.
 (ii) CHLORMAN would have difficulty in disposing of excess chlorine; it is poisonous and difficult to store for long periods. CHLORMAN could sell chlorine to hydrogen chloride or bleach manufacturers.
 (iii) To test for an unsaturated hydrocarbon, bromine water is added. If the hydrocarbon is unsaturated bromine water will be decolourised. If this test was carried out on a saturated hydrocarbon bromine water would stay orange see Chapter 13, Section 5(D).

STUDENT'S ANSWER – EXAMINER'S COMMENTS

The electrolysis of a concentrated solution of sodium chloride is an important industrial process for the production of chlorine, hydrogen and sodium hydroxide. Three types of cell may be used: diaphragm cells, mercury cathode cells, and membrane cells which are a recent modification of diaphragm cells. A diagram of a membrane cell is shown below. The electrode materials and the chemical reactions involved in the membrane cell are the same as in the diaphragm cell.

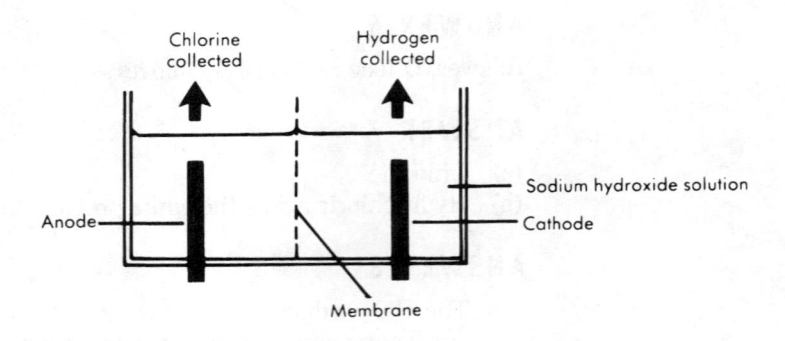

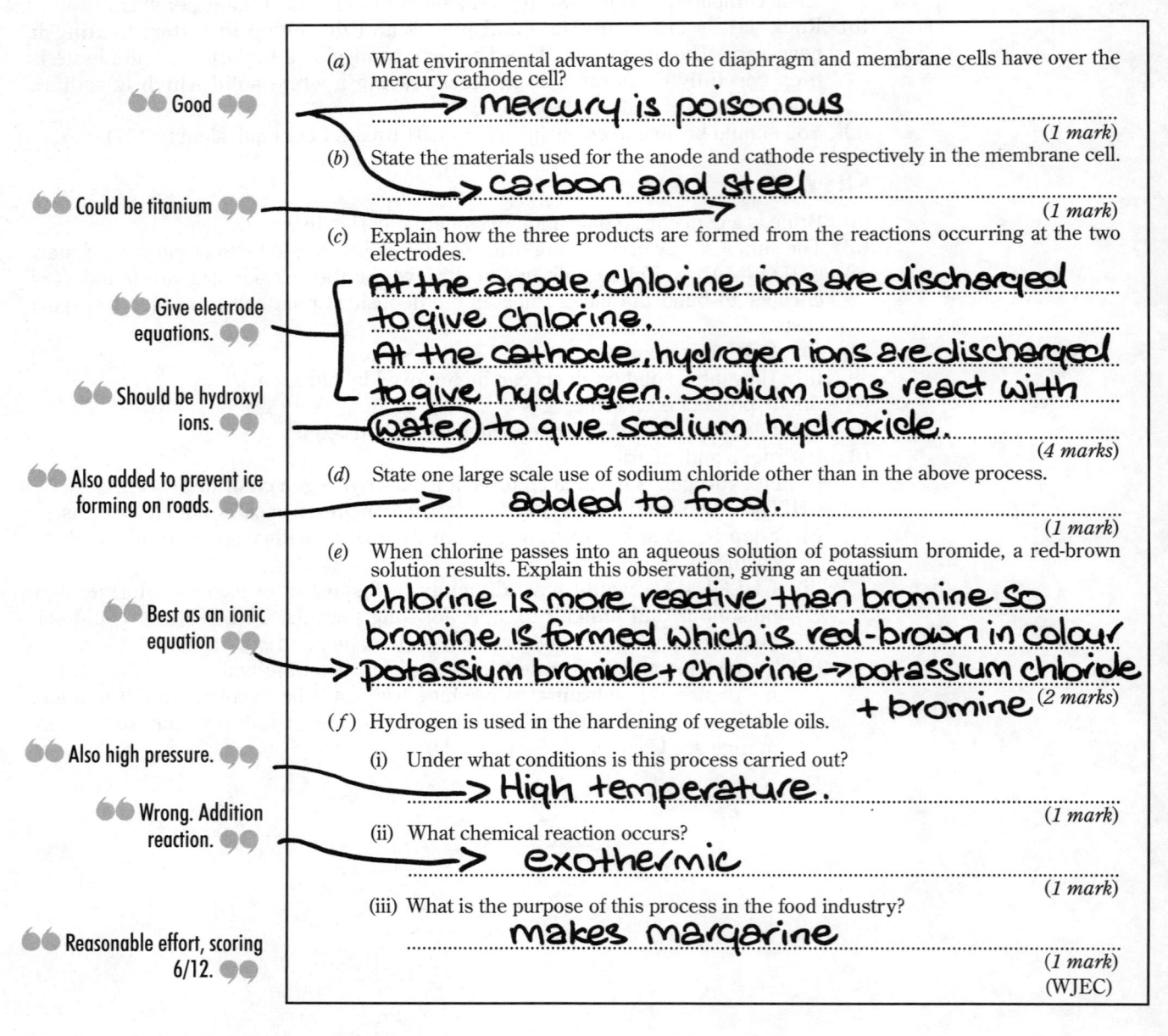

(a) What environmental advantages do the diaphragm and membrane cells have over the mercury cathode cell?

mercury is poisonous — *Good*
(1 mark)

(b) State the materials used for the anode and cathode respectively in the membrane cell.

carbon and steel — *Could be titanium*
(1 mark)

(c) Explain how the three products are formed from the reactions occurring at the two electrodes.

At the anode, chlorine ions are discharged to give chlorine. — *Give electrode equations.*
At the cathode, hydrogen ions are discharged to give hydrogen. Sodium ions react with (water) to give sodium hydroxide. — *Should be hydroxyl ions.*
(4 marks)

(d) State one large scale use of sodium chloride other than in the above process.

added to food. — *Also added to prevent ice forming on roads.*
(1 mark)

(e) When chlorine passes into an aqueous solution of potassium bromide, a red-brown solution results. Explain this observation, giving an equation.

Chlorine is more reactive than bromine so bromine is formed which is red-brown in colour
potassium bromide + chlorine → potassium chloride + bromine — *Best as an ionic equation*
(2 marks)

(f) Hydrogen is used in the hardening of vegetable oils.

(i) Under what conditions is this process carried out?

High temperature. — *Also high pressure.*
(1 mark)

(ii) What chemical reaction occurs?

exothermic — *Wrong. Addition reaction.*
(1 mark)

(iii) What is the purpose of this process in the food industry?

makes margarine
(1 mark)
(WJEC)

Reasonable effort, scoring 6/12.

CHAPTER 12.5

CARBON AND CARBON COMPOUNDS

- ALLOTROPY
- PROPERTIES OF CARBON
- OXIDES OF CARBON
- CARBON IN MINERALS
- HARDNESS OF WATER
- COMPARISON OF TEMPORARY AND PERMANENT HARDNESS IN WATER
- CALCIUM OXIDE
- CARBON CYCLE

GETTING STARTED

The element *carbon* occurs naturally as graphite and diamond. These are pure forms of the element. It occurs widely in mixtures such as oil, coal, natural gas and in compounds such as carbon dioxide and limestone (calcium carbonate).

ESSENTIAL PRINCIPLES

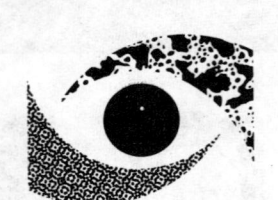

1> ALLOTROPY

Allotropes

Do not confuse allotropes with isotopes.

Allotropy is the existence of more than one form of an element in the same physical state. The different forms are known as **allotropes**. The allotropes of carbon are *diamond* and *graphite*.

(A) COMPARING DIAMOND WITH GRAPHITE

Properties of diamond	Properties of graphite
hardest known natural substance (Mohs' scale = 10)	relatively soft substance (Mohs' scale = 3)
does not conduct electricity	conducts electricity
good conductor of heat (explains why diamonds feel cold)	poor conductor of heat
density 3.5g/cm³	density 2.2g/cm³
colourless, transparent solid	dark grey solid

Diamond and graphite can be shown to be pure forms of carbon by completely burning equal masses of each in oxygen. They both give the **same amount** of carbon dioxide as the **only** product:

$$\text{carbon} + \text{oxygen} \rightarrow \text{carbon dioxide}$$
$$C + O_2 \rightarrow CO_2$$

As we saw in the table above, diamond and graphite are very different and the different arrangement of the carbon atoms in the two allotropes explains these differences.

The 'large' distances between the layers in graphite explains why its density is less than that of diamond.

Both allotropes have macromolecular structures and hence they have high melting points and boiling points. (Graphite in fact **sublimes** at 4200 °C.)

In diamond (Fig. 12.38) each carbon atom is joined to four other carbon atoms by strong single, covalent bonds, producing a giant lattice in three dimensions. This giant atomic structure is the reason for the hardness of diamond. All the outer electrons of the carbon atoms are being used for bonding and therefore there are no free electrons to move through the structure, so diamond does not conduct electricity.

In graphite (Fig. 12.39), each carbon atom is joined to only three other carbon atoms by strong single, covalent bonds. This produces a giant lattice in two dimensions. The remaining electrons from the atoms are **delocalised** between the layers. Since the forces between these layers in the graphite structure are relatively weak, the layers can slide over one another. This explains why graphite can be used as a dry lubricant. The free electrons between the layers allows graphite to conduct electricity (see Chapter 5, Section 13).

Practice drawing the structures of diamond and graphite

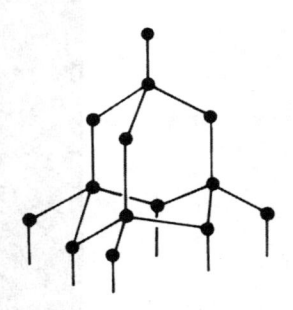

Fig. 12.38. Diamond.

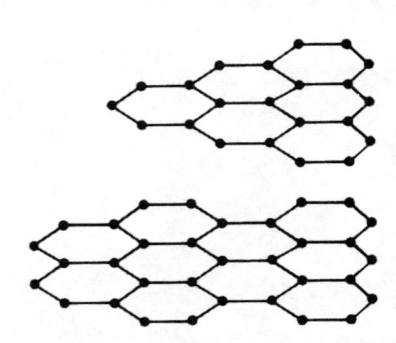

Fig. 12.39. Graphite.

(B) USES OF DIAMONDS

Diamonds, because they are rare, are valued as gemstones and because they are hard they are used as tips for drills and in saws and other cutting tools. Synthetic diamonds are made from graphite using high temperatures and high pressures. These artificial diamonds are only used in industry. They have no value as gemstones.

(C) USES OF GRAPHITE

Graphite, because it is a conductor of electricity and relatively unreactive, is used to make electrodes, for use e.g. in dry cells and the manufacture of aluminium.

> One of the disadvantages of graphite as an electrode is that it reacts with oxygen (to form carbon dioxide)

- Because graphite is slippery it is used as a dry lubricant, particularly when oil cannot be used.
- Graphite is used in pencils because the layers slide off.
- Graphite is also used to make graphite fibres which are used to reinforce metals.
- There is a great demand for both diamonds and graphite. Synthetic graphite can be made by purifying coal.

2 > PROPERTIES OF CARBON

Apart from burning, carbon is unreactive under normal conditions. It does not dissolve in any of the common solvents. It does not react with dilute acids or with dilute alkalis.

Carbon burns in a plentiful supply of air or oxygen to form carbon dioxide:

$$\text{carbon} + \text{oxygen} \rightarrow \text{carbon dioxide}$$
$$C + O_2 \rightarrow CO_2$$

This reaction is highly *exothermic*. This is the source of heat from carbon fuels.

If a limited supply of air or oxygen is used, the poisonous gas, carbon monoxide, is formed:

$$\text{carbon} + \text{oxygen} \rightarrow \text{carbon monoxide}$$
$$2C + O_2 \rightarrow 2CO$$

This reaction is also exothermic.

(A) CARBON AS A REDUCING AGENT

Carbon acts as a *reducing agent*. It will reduce copper(II) oxide to copper and lead(II) oxide to lead:

$$\text{copper(II) oxide} + \text{carbon} \rightarrow \text{copper} + \text{carbon monoxide}$$
$$CuO + C \rightarrow Cu + CO$$

It is often used as a reducing agent in industry because it can reduce a number of metal oxides (see Chapter 11, Section 5), and it is a common element which is relatively cheap. It is used for the manufacture of iron in the blast furnace.

(B) CHARCOAL

Charcoal, which is a porous form of graphite, can absorb substances. Charcoal is used to remove dyes, such as vegetable dyes from solutions; to remove the brown coloration in preparing white sugar; in gas masks to remove poisonous gases; in carbon filters for extractor fans in kitchens to remove cooking smells and it is placed in shoes (in a container) to remove foot odour.

3 > OXIDES OF CARBON

(A) CARBON MONOXIDE

Carbon monoxide is a colourless, poisonous odourless gas. It is almost insoluble in water. It burns with a bright blue flame to give carbon dioxide:

> This is the way to recognise carbon monoxide

$$\text{carbon monoxide} + \text{oxygen} \rightarrow \text{carbon dioxide}$$
$$2CO + O_2 \rightarrow 2CO_2$$

(B) POISONOUS NATURE OF CARBON MONOXIDE

Carbon monoxide is a very poisonous gas. It combines with haemoglobin in the blood to form *carboxyhaemoglobin*. This compound is about two hundred times more stable than the compound formed with oxygen, ***oxyhaemoglobin***. Carboxyhaemoglobin cannot carry oxygen around the body, and the victim dies from lack of oxygen.

Carbon monoxide is an ***atmospheric pollutant***. It is formed in the manufacture of iron and steel, in the paper industry and in petroleum refineries. It is formed during the incomplete combustion of carbon-containing compounds such as petrol, diesel, coal and cigarettes. Large quantities of carbon monoxide are formed when there are forest fires. Fortunately, there are many soil micro-organisms using their enzyme catalysts to convert carbon monoxide into carbon dioxide, therefore keeping the percentage of carbon monoxide in the atmosphere low.

(C) CARBON MONOXIDE AS A REDUCING AGENT

Because carbon monoxide has a strong tendency to form carbon dioxide, it is a good ***reducing agent***. It reduces some metal oxides to the metal. In the blast furnace carbon monoxide reduces iron(III) oxide to iron:

iron(III) oxide + carbon monoxide → iron + carbon dioxide
Fe_2O_3 + $3CO$ → $2Fe$ + $3CO_2$

(D) CARBON DIOXIDE

About 0.038% by volume of the air is carbon dioxide. This value is kept constant by the equilibrium between its removal from the air by photosynthesis and dissolving in water, and its replacement by respiration and combustion of carbon-containing compounds. Carbon dioxide is also formed in the manufacture of alcohol and in the manufacture of lime.

There is a fear that, with the large-scale cutting down of forests and with the sea becoming saturated with carbon dioxide, there will be a build up of carbon dioxide in the atmosphere. This may lead to an increase in temperature, commonly known as the ***greenhouse*** effect.

(E) PREPARATION OF CARBON DIOXIDE

Carbon dioxide is usually prepared by the reaction between a dilute acid and a metal carbonate or hydrogencarbonate. The usual reactants are calcium carbonate (in the form of marble chips) and dilute hydrochloric acid:

calcium carbonate + hydrochloric acid → carbon dioxide + water + calcium chloride
$CaCO_3$ + $2HCl$ → CO_2 + H_2O + $CaCl_2$

Note that dilute sulphuric acid cannot be used in place of hydrochloric acid in this reaction. It reacts with calcium carbonate to form an insoluble layer of calcium sulphate. This prevents any further reaction.

(F) PROPERTIES OF CARBON DIOXIDE

Carbon dioxide is a colourless, odourless gas. It turns directly into a solid (i.e. it sublimes) at -78°C. Solid carbon dioxide is known as ***'dry ice'***. Carbon dioxide is denser than air and fairly soluble in water to form a weak acid called ***carbonic acid***. Carbon dioxide does not burn and it does not support burning.

(G) CARBON DIOXIDE AS AN OXIDISING AGENT

Magnesium is a metal high in the reactivity series. Magnesium burns strongly enough in carbon dioxide to break carbon–oxygen bonds and hence continues to burn in the oxygen released.

carbon dioxide + magnesium → carbon + magnesium oxide
CO_2 + $2Mg$ → C + $2MgO$

❝ Sodium and potassium would also burn in carbon dioxide ❞

In this reaction carbon dioxide acts as an oxidising reagent. It also acts as an oxidising reagent in the blast furnace where it oxidises carbon to carbon monoxide:

carbon + carbon dioxide → carbon monoxide
C + CO_2 → $2CO$

Carbon dioxide reacts with water to form carbonic acid. This is a weak acid. It has a pH of about 5 or 6. Carbonic acid readily decomposes into water and carbon dioxide.

The reaction is reversible:

$$\text{carbon dioxide} + \text{water} \rightleftharpoons \text{carbonic acid}$$
$$CO_2 + H_2O \rightleftharpoons H_2CO_3$$

Carbon dioxide reacts with alkalis to form either the carbonate or with excess carbon dioxide to form the hydrogencarbonate.

When carbon dioxide is passed into a solution of calcium hydroxide in water (lime-water), a white precipitate of calcium carbonate is formed. This is used as a test for carbon dioxide:

$$\text{carbon dioxide} + \text{calcium hydroxide} \rightarrow \text{calcium carbonate} + \text{water}$$
$$CO_2(g) + Ca(OH)_2(aq) \rightarrow CaCO_3(s) + H_2O(l)$$

If carbon dioxide is passed, in excess, into this mixture, the white precipitate first formed disappears because soluble calcium hydrogencarbonate is formed:

$$\text{carbon dioxide} + \text{calcium carbonate} + \text{water} \rightarrow \text{calcium hydrogencarbonate}$$
$$CO_2(g) + CaCO_3(s) + H_2O(l) \rightarrow Ca(HCO_3)_2(aq)$$

(See Section 4 below, Hardness of water.)

> 66 Test for carbon dioxide 99
>
> 66 Learn this test 99
>
> 66 formula of calcium hydroxide is $Ca(OH)_2$ not $CaOH_2$ 99

(H) CARBON-CONTAINING COMPOUNDS

If a substance contains carbon, e.g. starch, it will react when heated with excess copper(II) oxide (or any other oxidising agent) to form carbon dioxide. Carbon dioxide can be tested for with lime-water:

$$\text{starch} + \text{copper(II) oxide} \rightarrow \text{carbon dioxide} + \text{water} + \text{copper}$$

We can use this reaction to test for the presence of carbon and hydrogen in compounds. If a dry compound forms carbon dioxide and water when it is heated with dry copper(II) oxide, then the substance must contain carbon and hydrogen.

> 66 Water would be given off from the copper(II) oxide and the compound if they were not dry. 99

(I) STRUCTURE OF CARBON DIOXIDE

Carbon dioxide is a fairly typical covalent, triatomic molecule (Fig. 12.40). It is a gas and a non-conductor of electricity. However, it is soluble in water.

Fig. 12.40

(J) USES OF CARBON DIOXIDE

- Carbon dioxide is used in fizzy drinks. The dissolved carbon dioxide gives water a sharp taste. The gas is dissolved under pressure. When the pressure is released by opening the can or bottle, carbonic acid decomposes and releases bubbles of carbon dioxide.
- Carbon dioxide is used in fire extinguishers because it does not support burning and it is denser than air and therefore smothers the fire. Fires cannot burn when there is no air (see Chapter 12.2, Section 5).
- Carbon dioxide is also used in the manufacture of carbamide (urea) which is used as a nitrogenous fertiliser. (See Chapter 12.3, Section 4(i)).

> 66 The sharp taste is really carbonic acid. 99

4 CARBON IN MINERALS

(i) Carbon is present in minerals and combines with oxygen and metal ions as carbonates. Calcium and magnesium carbonates are common sedimentary rocks known as limestones.
(ii) Peat and coal are largely carbon.

The world's deposits of peat, coal and limestones have been formed millennia ago by extraction of carbon dioxide from the atmosphere. Burning coal or decomposing limestone puts that carbon dioxide back into the air.

Limestone has many uses but its presence in rocks causes problems with domestic water supplies. Limestone readily dissolves in rain-water.

5 HARDNESS OF WATER

Rain water is a very weak solution of carbonic acid. It has a pH of 5 or 6:

$$\text{water} + \text{carbon dioxide} \rightleftharpoons \text{carbonic acid}$$
$$H_2O + CO_2 \rightleftharpoons H_2CO_3$$

When rain water falls on areas of the earth that contain calcium carbonate or magnesium carbonate a reaction occurs and the rock dissolves. This reaction produces calcium hydrogencarbonate or magnesium hydrogencarbonate. Both these compounds are very slightly soluble in water:

carbonic acid + calcium carbonate ⇌ calcium hydrogencarbonate
H_2CO_3 + $CaCO_3$ ⇌ $Ca(HCO_3)_2$

carbonic acid + magnesium carbonate ⇌ magnesium hydrogencarbonate
H_2CO_3 + $MgCO_3$ ⇌ $Mg(HCO_3)_2$

Other compounds present in the earth also dissolve in water. These compounds prevent water from forming a lather easily with soap. The water is said to be **hard**. There are two types of hardness: ***permanent hardness*** and ***temporary hardness***.

Hardness in water is caused by the presence of calcium ions and magnesium ions. Compounds present in hard water containing these ions are calcium hydrogencarbonate, magnesium hydrogencarbonate, magnesium sulphate, magnesium chloride, calcium sulphate and calcium chloride.

> **Temporary hardness**

When calcium hydrogencarbonate and magnesium hydrogencarbonate are heated they decompose and form insoluble carbonates. The calcium ions and magnesium ions are removed from the water. Since the ions are removed by heating water, they are said to cause temporary hardness:

calcium hydrogencarbonate → calcium carbonate + water + carbon dioxide
$Ca(HCO_3)_2$ → $CaCO_3$ + H_2O + CO_2

> **Make sure you know the difference between temporary and permanent hardness.**

magnesium hydrogencarbonate → magnesium carbonate + water + carbon dioxide
$Mg(HCO_3)_2$ → $MgCO_3$ + H_2O + CO_2

The precipitation of calcium carbonate and magnesium carbonate causes ***furring*** in kettles and ***scaling*** in boilers. This fur can be removed using a weak acid such as ethanoic acid, citric acid, sulphamic acid or phosphoric acid. A strong acid would react with the metal kettle or boiler (See Chapter 3, Section 7).

The other compounds that cause hardness in water, such as calcium sulphate, are not deposited by heating the water. They are said to cause permanent hardness.

> **Permanent hardness**

The calcium ions and magnesium ions can be removed by:

> **Softening of water**

(i) ***Distillation***, the compounds are left behind in the distillation flask. Water formed by this process is very pure and is known as ***distilled water***;

(ii) ***Ion exchange water softening resins***. These are used in industry and are also found in dishwashers. The process is described by the equation which applies equally to magnesium ions.

Ca^{2+}(aq) + sodium-form of ion-exchange resin ⇌ $2Na^+$(aq) + calcium-form of ion-exchange resin

When the ion exchange resin no longer has any sodium ions to exchange for calcium ions it must be recharged. This is a reversal of the above process. Sodium chloride solution is run through the spent resin. The reaction shown above reverses. The calcium ions are flushed away in solution.

Water formed in these processes is called ***soft water***. Soft water easily forms a lather with soap.

(iii) ***Sodium carbonate***. Water can also be softened by adding sodium carbonate (washing soda). This precipitates calcium ions and magnesium ions as insoluble carbonates:

> **If excess sodium carbonate is added, the water becomes alkaline**

calcium chloride + sodium carbonate → calcium carbonate + sodium choride
$CaCl_2$ + Na_2CO_3 → $CaCO_3$ + $2NaCl$

magnesium suphate + sodium carbonate → magnesium carbonate + sodium sulphate
$MgSO_4$ + Na_2CO_3 → $MgCO_3$ + Na_2SO_4

(A) THE ADVANTAGES OF HARD WATER

It is healthier to drink (it is thought to prevent heart attacks) and gives water a pleasant taste.

(B) THE DISADVANTAGES OF HARD WATER

(i) When it is heated it deposits calcium carbonate in pipes, boilers and kettles. This makes them less efficient and they might become blocked.
(ii) When it is added to soap it forms a scum which floats on the surface of the water. Scum is a calcium or magnesium compound of the soap; e.g. calcium stearate or calcium oleate.

6. COMPARISON OF TEMPORARY AND PERMANENT HARDNESS IN WATER

Some water supplies have temporary hardness, some permanent hardness and others a mixture of the two. To determine which type is present the following test investigation is carried out.

Titration with soap solution

Titration with soap solution is to discover how much soap reacts with the calcium or magnesium ions in the water sample. The more soap used, the higher the concentration of the calcium and magnesium ions. An indication that all these ions have reacted is seen when the water plus soap sample, shaken for ten *seconds*, supports a froth which lasts for *one minute*.

Procedure

(i) 10 cm^3 of each water sample is titrated wth soap solution. The sample is shaken after each 0.5 cm^3 addition of soap. The volume of soap solution needed to create the required lather is recorded. The results are noted.
(ii) 100 cm^3 of each water sample is boiled for 20 minutes to remove temporary hardness.
(iii) 10 cm^3 of each 'boiled water sample' is titrated with soap solution and the results again noted.

Results

Consider the following set of results

Sample number	volume of soap solution in cm^3/ unboiled sample	volume of soap solution in cm^3/ boiled sample	temporary hardness as a fraction of total hardness
1	0.1	0.1	0
2	2.4	1.6	1/3rd
3	4.0	4.1	0

Interpretation of the results

Permanent hardness is unaffected by boiling the water. Calcium sulphate is a cause of this.
Temporary hardness is removed by boiling. Calcium hydrogencarbonate is a cause of this.

With these guidelines we can interpret the results to mean:
(i) sample 1 has little *or no* hardness
The 0.1 cm^3 is the smallest volume of soap solution that can be added. It may not have been needed. ***This is probably distilled water.***
(ii) sample 2 loses one third of its hardness on boiling. This sample is hard water with 1/3 temporary hardness and 2/3 permanent hardness.
(iii) sample 3 loses no hardness on boiling and is the hardest sample tested. Its hardness is all permanent hardness. The difference of 0.1 cm^3 is experimental error.

7. CALCIUM OXIDE

Quicklime (calcium oxide) is made by heating limestone (calcium carbonate) to 1000 °C for several hours in a kiln (Fig. 12.42).

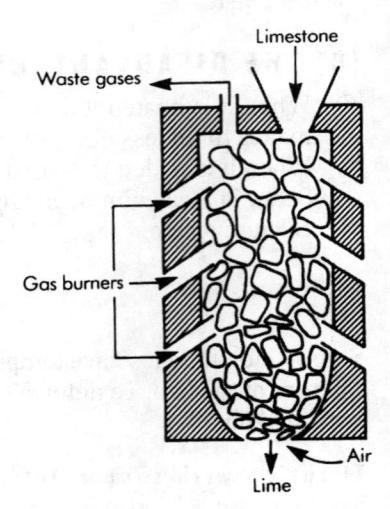

Fig.12.42. Preparation of calcium oxide.

$$\text{calcium carbonate} \rightarrow \text{calcium oxide} + \text{carbon dioxide}$$
$$CaCO_3 \rightarrow CaO + CO_2$$

The manufacturing process can cause a great deal of pollution. The kilns are heated by coal or gas which can produce carbon monoxide if incomplete combustion takes place. A large amount of dust is also formed in the process and unless this is removed by electrostatic precipitators it will cause a pollution problem.

(A) USES OF LIME

- Lime is used to neutralise acids, in particular **acid waste** from industry. If this acid waste was thrown into lakes, rivers and seas it would lower the pH of the water and kill fish and plants.
- Farmers use lime to neutralise acidic soil. Many plants will not grow if the pH of the soil is low. The ideal pH for plants is in the range 6–8.
- Lime is also used in the manufacture of steel (see Chapter 11, Section 14(E)).
- Slaked lime (calcium hydroxide) is made by adding water to lime. Slaked lime is often used instead of lime to neutralise water and acid soil.

(B) USES OF CALCIUM CARBONATE

Calcium carbonate is used in the manufacture of cement by heating it with clay. Calcium carbonate is also used in the manufacture of iron, sodium carbonate, glass and concrete.

(C) SOLUBILITY OF CARBONATES

Most carbonates are insoluble in water. Only carbonates of group 1 metals are soluble in water. If a solution of sodium carbonate is added to a solution of barium chloride, a white precipitate of barium carbonate is formed. This is an example of a precipitation reaction.

8. CARBON CYCLE

The amount of carbon dioxide in the air remains approximately constant at about 0.038% (by volume). The process by which this happens can be summarised by the carbon cycle (Fig. 12.43).

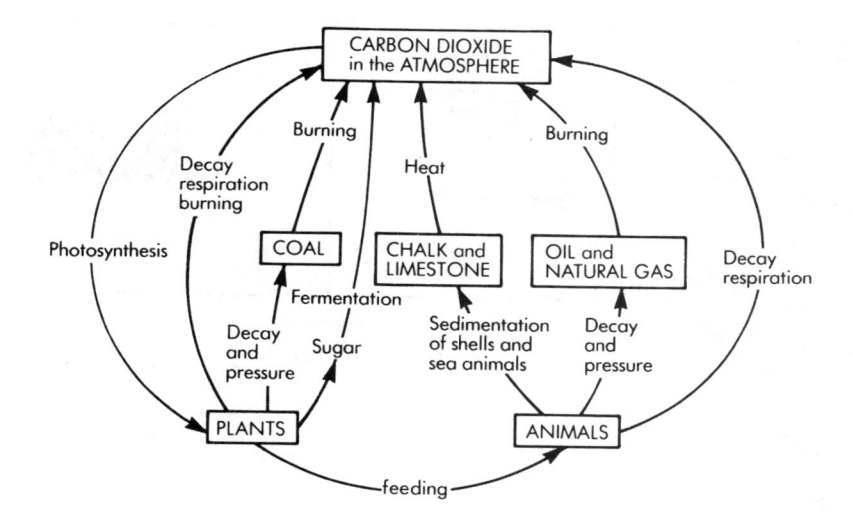

Fig. 12.43. Carbon cycle.

Some of the important reactions that take place are

(1) Photosynthesis: plants take in carbon dioxide and water which react to form starch and oxygen:

carbon dioxide + water → starch + oxygen
$6nCO_2$ + $5nH_2O$ → $(C_6H_{10}O_5)_n$ + $6nO_2$

where n is a large number

Chlorophyll acts as a catalyst in this reaction. Sunlight provides energy for photosynthesis to take place.
(2) Dissolving: carbon dioxide is soluble in water; a large amount of carbon dioxide dissolves in the sea.
(3) Respiration: animals, including you, produce carbon dioxide during respiration. It is eventually breathed out.
(4) Decay: when animals and plants decay, one of the products is carbon dioxide.
(5) Industrial processes: the manufacture of iron, beer and lime produce large amounts of carbon dioxide.

EXAMINATION QUESTIONS

MULTIPLE CHOICE

QUESTION 1

Which ONE of these substances is NOT a form of carbon?

A   diamond
B   calcium
C   coke
D   charcoal
E   graphite

(NISEAC)

QUESTION 2

A substance has a high melting point, is insoluble in water and will not conduct electricity in any state (Fig. 12.44). Its structure could be A, B, C, D or E?

(ULEAC)

QUESTION 3

The amount of carbon dioxide in the air is decreased by

A   respiration
B   burning of fuels
C   extraction of iron
D   photosynthesis
E   manufacture of lime from limestone

(WJEC)

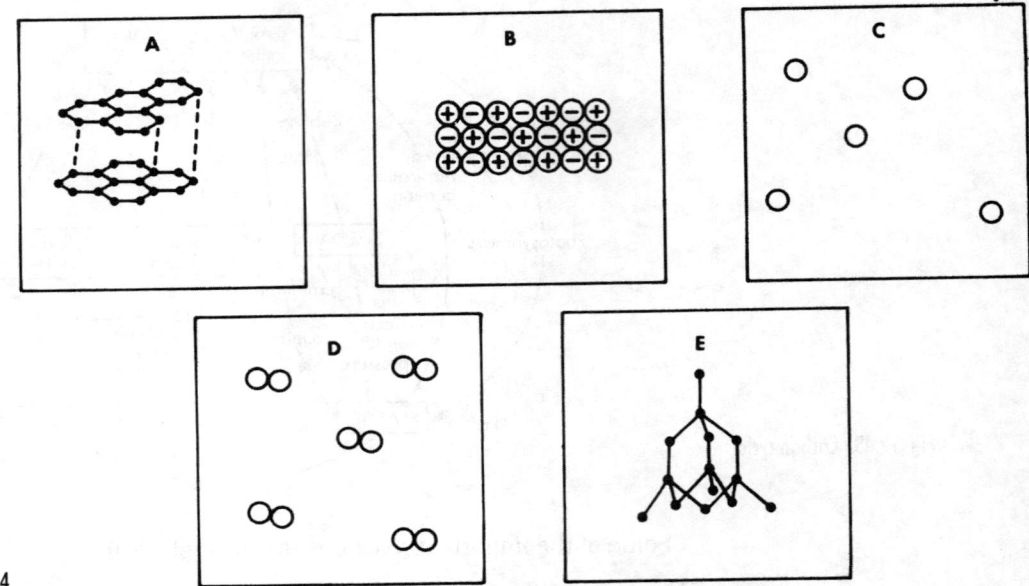

Fig. 12.44

QUESTION 4

Carbon monoxide is a dangerous gas because it

A dissolves in rain water, forming an acid solution.
B can corrode metal structures such as bridges.
C reduces the oxygen content of the atmosphere.
D reduces the blood's ability to absorb oxygen.
E easily forms carbon dioxide.

QUESTION 5

When air is bubbled through water in a fish tank the pH gradually changes from 7 to 6. The gas in air which could be responsible for this change is

A argon   D nitrogen
B carbon dioxide   E oxygen
C hydrogen

(ULEAC)

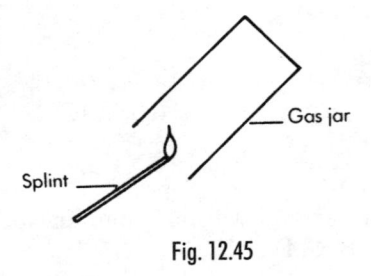

COMPLETION AND STRUCTURED QUESTIONS

QUESTION 6

Carbon dioxide can be prepared by adding hydrochloric acid to calcium carbonate.
(a) (i) Name the salt produced by the reaction. (1 line)
    (ii) What else is produced by the reaction, besides the salt and carbon dioxide? (1 line)

(2 marks)

(b) When a gas jar containing carbon dioxide is upturned over a burning splint, the flame goes out (Fig. 12.45).
What TWO properties of carbon dioxide does this illustrate?
(i) ....
(ii) ....
(iii) What piece of equipment used widely in every day life makes use of these properties? (1 line)

(3 marks)

Fig. 12.45

(c) If a piece of magnesium is burned in a gas jar of carbon dioxide, a white powder and particles of a black solid are formed.
(i) What is the black solid?...
(ii) What is the white powder?..
(iii) Write a word equation for the reaction in (c). (1 line)

(3 marks)
(Total 8 marks)
(SEG)

QUESTION 7

A drink such as cola might be sold in either glass or plastic bottles.

Name *three* raw materials which are used for making glass.

1. ....(1)
2. ....(1)
3. ....(1)

QUESTION 8

Limestone is calcium carbonate, $CaCO_3$.

Limestone is an important mineral. It is used to make many things, including cement, concrete, steel and lime.

One important use of limestone is making quicklime (calcium oxide, CaO). The limestone is heated strongly in a lime kiln. As well as quicklime, a gas is formed which turns lime-water milky.

(a) Name the gas... (1)
(b) When 100 tonnes of limestone are heated, 56 tonnes of quicklime are formed. What mass of the gas would also be formed? (1 line) (1)
(c) A student heated 100 g of limestone in a container in the school laboratory. She expected to get 56 g of quicklime but she found the residue after heating weighed 71 g. Suggest why it weighed more than she expected. (1 line) (2)
(d) Quicklime can be turned to slaked lime (calcium hydroxide, $Ca(OH)_2$), by adding water. Slaked lime is a cheap alkali. Farmers use large quantities of slaked lime. What do they use it for? (1 line) (1)
(e) A quarrying company wants to start a big quarry in the Chilterns in Buckinghamshire, near a well-known beauty spot. Many people protest against the quarry.
   (i) Give ONE group of people who might object. (1 line) (1)
   (ii) What might the objection of this group be? (1 line) (1)
   (iii) Give ONE argument the quarrying company might use to justify opening the quarry. (2 lines) (1)

Total marks (8)

QUESTION 9

Fizzy drinks can be made by dissolving carbon dioxide gas, under pressure, into water. The drink is kept in a tightly stoppered bottle until needed. When the stopper is removed bubbles of carbon dioxide form making the drink fizzy.

The carbon dioxide first dissolves in the water and some of the dissolved gas may react with water to form carbonic acid.

$$CO_2(g) + aq \rightleftharpoons CO_2(aq) \quad \textbf{Equation 1}$$
$$CO_2(aq) + H_2O(l) \rightarrow H_2CO_3(aq) \quad \textbf{Equation 2}$$

(a) Use Equation 1 to explain the appearance of bubbles of carbon dioxide when the stopper of a fizzy drink bottle is loosened. (2 lines)

(2 marks)

(b) Unless the bottles are tightly stoppered, these drinks tend to lose their fizziness quickly on warm days. Use Equation 1 to explain why this happens. (2 lines)

(1 mark)

(c) What advantage may be gained by keeping bottles of water in the fridge before making fizzy drinks? (2 lines)

(1 mark)

(d) Write an equation to show how H_2CO_3 can behave as an acid in water. (1 line)

(2 marks)

When carbon dioxide is bubbled into lime-water a white precipitate of calcium carbonate forms. An equation for the reaction may be written as follows.

$$H_2CO_3(aq) + Ca(OH)_2(aq) \rightarrow CaCO_3(s) + 2H_2O(l) \quad \textbf{Equation 3}$$

If more carbon dioxide is bubbled into the mixture, the cloudiness disappears and a solution of calcium hydrogencarbonate is formed as shown below:

$$H_2CO_3(aq) + CaCO_3(s) \rightleftharpoons Ca(HCO_3)_2(aq) \quad \textbf{Equation 4}$$

(e) Write two separate ionic equations to summarise the reactions indicated by Equation 3. (2 lines) *(2 marks)*

(f) Use Equation 4 to explain how domestic water supplies in many places contain calcium ions (Ca^{2+}). (6 lines) *(3 marks)*

(g) How do the equations given explain the formation of white deposits (such as kettle fur) in vessels used to boil tap water in hard water districts? (4 lines) *(2 marks)*

(h) Sodium stearate ($C_{17}H_{35}CO_2Na$) is a typical simple soap. Why is its use as a soapy detergent limited by the calcium ions which are often present in water? (4 lines) *(2 marks)*
(SEG)

OUTLINE ANSWERS

MULTIPLE CHOICE

ANSWER 1
Answer: B calcium is a metal, the rest are forms of carbon (see Section 1(A)).

ANSWER 2
A is the structure of graphite. It has a high melting point and is insoluble in water but it **does** conduct electricity.
B is the structure of a solid electrolyte such as sodium chloride. They have high melting points, and they are usually soluble in water but they will conduct electricity when molten.
C is the structure of a noble gas such as neon. Noble gases are insoluble in water and they do not conduct electricity but they have very low melting points.
D is the structure of a diatomic gas such as oxygen which is slightly soluble in water; it has a low melting point and it does not conduct electricity.
E, you might have recognised this structure as diamond. You will have read in Chapter 6, Section 13 that diamond has a high melting point because it has a macromolecular structure, it is insoluble in water and it has no free electrons to conduct electricity. Hence the answer is E (see Section 1 (A)).

ANSWER 3
During photosynthesis, carbon dioxide reacts with water in the presence of sunlight and chlorophyll to form starch and oxygen. This removes carbon dioxide from the atmosphere. This gives the key as D. During respiration we breathe out carbon dioxide and water vapour. Burning hydrocarbons produces carbon dioxide and water. In the extraction of iron, iron(III) oxide is reduced to iron by carbon monoxide. Carbon monoxide is oxidised to carbon dioxide. Limestone is calcium carbonate. When it is heated it forms calcium oxide (lime) and gives off carbon dioxide.

ANSWER 4
Answer: D (see Section 3(B)).

ANSWER 5
Answer: B (see Section 3(G)).

COMPLETION AND STRUCTURED QUESTIONS

ANSWER 6
(a) (i) Calcium chloride (look up the definition of a salt).
    (ii) Water.

Remember
ACID + CARBONATE → CARBON DIOXIDE + SALT + WATER
(b) (i) Carbon dioxide is denser than air,
(ii) and does not support burning.
(iii) Fire extinguishers (see Section 3(J)).
(c) (See Section 3(G)) (i) Carbon. (ii) Magnesium oxide.
(iii) magnesium + carbon dioxide → carbon + magnesium oxide.

ANSWER 7

Silica, calcium carbonate, sodium carbonate.

ANSWER 8

If you had problems with this question read Section 4 and Chapter 8, Section 8.
(a) Carbon dioxide.
(b) 44 tonnes.
(c) Not all the limestone had decomposed or not heated long enough.
(d) To neutralise the soil.
(e) (i) Either naturalists or local people.
(ii) Either destroy the beauty of the area, or it would pollute the local area (dust, carbon monoxide, noise).
(iii) Bring employment to the area or reduce pollution.

ANSWER 9

(a) When the stopper is loosened, carbon dioxide is given off as the reaction in equation 1 goes to the left. The *reverse* of dissolving in water.
(b) Gases are less soluble in hot water than cold water. Therefore on hot days, equation 1 moves to the left and carbon dioxide is given off.
(c) Gases are more soluble in cold water, therefore keeping water in a fridge allows more carbon dioxide to dissolve.
(d) $H_2CO_3 + H_2O \rightarrow H_3O^+ + HCO_3^-$
(e) $Ca^{2+}(aq) + CO_3^{2-}(aq) \rightarrow CaCO_3(s)$
$H^+(aq) + OH^-(aq) \rightarrow H_2O(l)$
(f) Rain water is a weak solution of carbonic acid (H_2CO_3). Rain water reacts with limestone (calcium carbonate) to form the ionic compound calcium hydrogencarbonate which is soluble in water. This solution contains calcium ions and hydrogencarbonate ions.
(g) When hard water is heated calcium hydrogencarbonate decomposes to form calcium carbonate, water and carbon dioxide, i.e. equation 4 moves to the left. The deposit of calcium carbonate is known as 'fur'.
(h) Sodium stearate reacts with calcium ions to form calcium stearate which is insoluble. Calcium stearate is known as 'scum'.

STUDENT'S ANSWER – EXAMINER'S COMMENTS

Carbon dioxide can be prepared by adding hydrochloric acid to calcium carbonate.

(a) (i) Name the salt produced by the reaction.

calcium chloride

❝ Good ❞

(ii) What else is produced by the reaction, besides the salt and carbon dioxide?

water

(2 marks)

(b) When a gas jar containing carbon dioxide is upturned over a burning splint, the flame goes out.

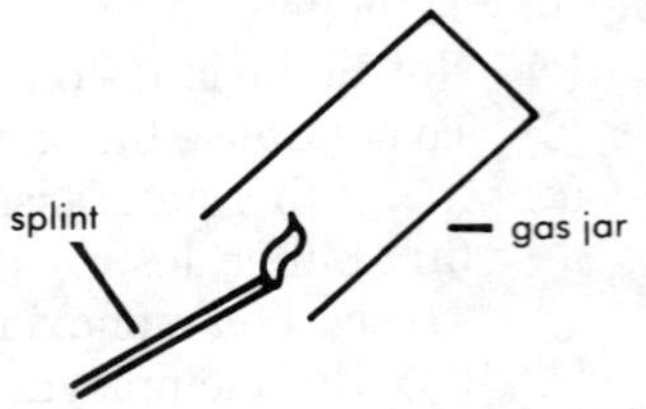

[diagram: splint and gas jar]

What TWO properties of carbon dioxide does this illustrate?

❝ Good ❞

(i) **does not aid burning**

❝ Better to say air than oxygen. ❞

(ii) **more dense than oxygen**

(iii) What piece of equipment used widely in every day life makes use of these properties?

❝ Strange answer! Should have been fire extinguishers. ❞

cars

(3 marks)

(c) If a piece of magnesium is burned in a gas jar of carbon dioxide, a white powder and particles of a black solid are formed.

❝ You've got them the wrong way round. ❞

(i) What is the black solid? **magnesium oxide**

(ii) What is the white powder? **carbon**

(iii) Write a word equation for the reaction in (c).

magnesium + carbon dioxide → magnesium oxide + carbon

❝ Quite a good answer overall. A pity you muddled the two products in (c). Remember, carbon is a black solid. Score 6/8 ❞

(3 marks)
(Total 8 marks)

REVIEW SHEETS, CHAPTER 12.1 to 12.5

REVIEW SHEET

These Review Sheets cover Chapters 12.1 to 12.5 inclusive.

- Complete the following table.

Gas	Hydrogen	Oxygen	Carbon dioxide	Carbon monoxide	Chlorine	Hydrogen chloride	Nitrogen	Amonia	Sulphur dioxide
Colour									
Smell									
Density									
Solubility in water									
Does it burn?									
Does it support burning?									
Effect on damp pH paper									
Is it poisonous?									
Uses									

- Compounds containing hydrogen include _____

- Describe a method for preparing hydrogen. Draw (and label) the apparatus you would use.

- Oxygen is found in compounds mainly as _____

- Describe a method for preparing oxygen. Draw (and label) the apparatus you would use.

- What is **respiration**? _____

- When writing an equation for burning, one of the _____ must be oxygen.

- The nitrogen molecule contains _____

- Name two other plant nutrients besides nitrogen
  1. _____
  2. _____

- Draw (and label) a diagram showing the **nitrogen cycle**

- **Fixation** of nitrogen is the _____

- Describe the laboratory preparation of **ammonia**

- Draw (and label) the apparatus used in the **qualitative analysis** of ammonia

- List some of the properties of **sulphuric acid** _____

REVIEW SHEET, CHAPTER 12.1 to 12.5

_____
_____
_____
_____
_____

- Describe how you would prepare **hydrogen chloride**. Draw (and label) your apparatus

- Allotropy is _____
_____

- The allotropes of carbon are _____
  and _____

- Complete the following table.

Properties of diamond	Properties of graphite

- Draw (and label) a diagram showing the carbon cycle

276 REVIEW SHEETS, CHAPTER 12.1 to 12.5

- Organic chemistry is _____
  _____

- Fossil fuels are formed from _____
  _____
  _____

- Petroleum is a mixture of _____

Complete the following table

Boiling range (°C)	Fraction	Use
<30		
20–200		
175–250		
200–350		
300–400		
350–450		
350–500		
<500 (solid)		

- Groups of compounds with similar chemical properties are known as _____
  _____

- List the properties of organic compounds that are in the same homologous series.

  1. _____
  2. _____
  3. _____
  4. _____

- Complete the following tables

Number of carbon atoms	Start of name
1	
2	
3	
4	
5	

Functional group	Name ending	Homologous series
C–C		
C=C		
C–O–H		
CO$_2$H		

- **Alkanes** are _____
  and have the general formula _____

- **Ethene** is _____

- Complete the following table

Test reagent	Alkanes	Alkenes
React with bromine solution		
React with acidified solution of potassium manganate(VII)		
Combustion		

- List some of the uses of **ethanol** _____

CHAPTER 13

MAKING A START IN ORGANIC CHEMISTRY

FOSSIL FUELS
HOMOLOGOUS SERIES
ALKANES
ISOMERS
ALKENES
ALCOHOLS
ORGANIC ACIDS
FUELS

GETTING STARTED

Organic chemistry was originally defined as the chemistry of substances found in living things. However, in the 1880s urea, an organic compound found in our bodies, was made from inorganic substances. Since then, organic chemistry has been defined as the study of compounds containing carbon.

How organic compounds are formed

Organic compounds are composed of just a few elements combined to form covalently bonded molecules. These elements are chiefly carbon, hydrogen, oxygen, nitrogen, phosphorus, sulphur and the halogens.

It is possible to *synthesise* (make a compound by chemical reaction outside a living organism) without the help of plants or animals, but the biggest source of organic chemicals is still the plant and animal kingdom – past or present. The huge deposits of coal and oil are fossil *chemical reserves* from the past. Plants and animals existing today also supply large quantities of chemicals such as fats, oils, perfumes, drugs and medicines and fuels.

It is important, for the future of the human race, that energy sources are developed that do not use up these fossil chemical reserves.

ESSENTIAL PRINCIPLES

1> FOSSIL FUELS

Coal, petroleum and natural gas are all formed from deposits of plant and animal remains hundreds of millions of years ago.

(a) Coal

Two hundred million years ago, the remains of trees and plants became covered with water in the swamps where they had grown in abundance. This slowed down the normal rapid bacterial decay and so preserved the plant material. Coal results from the long-term effect of pressure and heat on this slowly decomposing mass of vegetation.

(b) Crude Oil (petroleum –'rock-oil')

Petroleum is believed to have formed from the remains of animals and plants which lived in the sea in a similar way to the formation of coal from plant remains. These remains accumulated in fine-grained sediments on the sea bed. Heat, pressure and time have combined to force out the oily products. This oil moved upwards through permeable rock until it met rock that stopped its flow. Here it accumulated – to be found by oil prospectors for the first time about a century ago.

Crude oil extraction

(a) Location of oil. A petroleum reservoir consists of a dome shaped porous rock stratum enclosed within a cap of impervious rock. The whole structure resembles an upturned basin and is typically from 5–30 miles across. The oil and/or natural gas collects at the top of the dome. It is stored in the pores in the limestone or sandstone strata that make up the reservoir. The cap rock which has stopped the upward movement of the oil is usually of clay or shale through which the oil cannot penetrate. Beneath the oil there is usually salt water which traps the oil under pressure.

(b) How oil is found. Geologists are often able to recognise surface features which tell them of the likelihood of oil being found beneath the ground. Often, however, prospecting for oil involves seismic surveys. These explore and map the layers of rock under the surface. The dome-shaped formations can be recognised from these surveys.

(c) Siting of oil wells is not a matter of choice. Prospectors must go where the oil is found. However, the site will determine how easily the oil can be extracted. Oil found on land is much easier to tap than that under the sea. Environmental concerns may make the process very expensive, e.g. the Alaskan oilfields.

(d) Extraction is usually carried out by drilling a well. Diamond-tipped drills penetrate rock layers until the oil well is penetrated. The oil gushes out under pressure, being pushed upwards by the salt-water beneath the oil. The well is capped with a well-head to control the flow.

(e) Transport is by pipeline, ocean tanker or road tanker. The former is expensive to set up but cheap to run. The road tankers are cheap to buy but expensive to use.

(f) Hazards of handling oil are illustrated by the numerous ocean oil spills that hit the news at regular intervals. Oil is harmful to wild life, flammable and its fumes are toxic. Strict control of naked flames and sparks is required in the vicinity of oil or oil products.

SEPARATION OF CRUDE OIL INTO FRACTIONS

Petroleum is a complex ***mixture*** of liquid hydrocarbons - compounds of carbon and hydrogen only. It is ***fractionally distilled*** into various ***fractions***. These fractions are not pure substances but a mixture of hydrocarbons with similar boiling points. In this process the oil is heated, giving off a mixture of vapours. These are allowed to condense at different temperatures in a fractionating column. Each condensate is a different fraction. Some fractions and their uses and boiling temperature ranges are listed in the table below.

Boiling range (°C)	Fraction	Use
<30	liquefied gases	Calor gas, butane
20–200	petrol	petrol for cars, solvents
175–250	paraffin (kerosene)	oil stoves, aircraft fuel
200–350	diesel oil	diesel engine fuel in trains, lorries, tractors, etc.
300–400	lubricating oil	lubricant
350–450	fuel oil	fuel for power stations and ships
350–500	wax, grease	candles, wax paper, lubricant
>500 (solid)	bitumen	road making, roofing material

The higher the boiling temperature, the less volatile the fraction, ie. the less easily vaporised it becomes. Since it is the vapour that burns, the higher the boiling temperature of a fraction the more difficult it is to ignite. Hence, higher boiling fractions are not useful as fuels (see **cracking**).

Why are there so many organic compounds?

Over 2 million carbon compounds are known. This is more than all the compounds of the **other 88** elements added together. How is carbon able to form so many compounds? Carbon atoms are the only atoms able to bond together extensively in chains and rings. Hydrocarbons are known containing from one to several hundred carbon atoms joined in chains. As the chain length increases, the possibility of **isomerism** multiplies the number of different compounds possible. Substitution of other atoms in place of the hydrogens, in alkanes, multiplies the possibilities further. The existence of rings of carbon atoms and their variants adds more permutations until the huge number of compounds known begins to look small by comparison with those that can be imagined!

2 > HOMOLOGOUS SERIES

Organic compounds are divided into groups of compounds with similar chemical properties. Each group is known as an **homologous series**. Organic compounds that are in the same homologous series have the following properties in common:

(1) they can be represented by a **general formula**;
(2) they have **similar chemical properties** (because they contain the same functional group);
(3) they can be **made by similar reactions**;
(4) there is a **regular change in their physical properties**, i.e. the melting points increase as the relative molecular masses increase.

(A) NAMING COMPOUNDS

The ***first part*** of the name indicates the number of carbon atoms in the compound:

Number of carbon atoms	Start of name
1	meth-
2	eth-
3	prop-
4	but-
5	pent-

(B) FUNCTIONAL GROUPS

The **name ending** shows the homologous series of the compound. Compounds in the same homologous series contain the same **functional group**:

Functional group	Name ending	Homologous series
C—C	-ane	alkane
C=C	-ene	alkene
C—O—H	-ol	alcohol
CO_2H	acid	acids

> Make sure your writing is clear. 'Ethane' would be marked wrong

Thus methane is an alkane with one carbon atom.
Ethene is an alkene with two carbon atoms.
Propanol is an alcohol with three carbon atoms.
Butanoic acid is an acid with four carbon atoms.

(C) PHYSICAL PROPERTIES

These include boiling point, melting point, density, viscosity.
These vary with the relative molecular mass of the members of the series, increasing as the molecular mass rises. The change of boiling point with molecular mass for alkanes is shown below.

m.p. 135K
b.p. 273K
densiy 0.58g/cm³

```
  H H H H
  | | | |
H-C-C-C-C-H
  | | | |
  H H H H
```

m.p. 114K
b.p. 261K
density 0.56g/cm³

```
  H H H
  | | |
H-C-C-C-H
  | | |
  H | H
  H-C-H
    |
    H
```

Fig. 13.1 Butane

Fig. 13.2 2-methylpropane

3 > ALKANES

Alkanes are hydrocarbons. Alkanes have the general formula C_nH_{2n+2}.

(A) STRUCTURE OF METHANE (ELECTRONIC)

The first member of the homologous series of alkanes is methane.
The formula of methane is CH_4.
There is a pair of electrons between each hydrogen atom and the carbon atom (Fig. 13.3.).

```
    H
    |
  H-C-H
    |
    H
```

```
     ·×
  H ×·C·× H
     ×·
      H
```

Fig. 13.3

```
  H H
  | |
H-C-C-H
  | |
  H H
```

Fig. 13.4

(B) STRUCTURE OF ETHANE

The next member of the series is ethane, C_2H_6. This contains a pair of electrons between the carbon atoms. The molecule contains a carbon—carbon single bond (Fig. 13.4).

Alkanes are said to be **saturated** hydrocarbons.
They contain no double bonds. Other members of the alkane series are propane, C_3H_8 and butane, C_4H_{10}.

(C) PROPERTIES OF METHANE

Methane is a colourless, odourless gas. It is less dense than air. It is insoluble in water and neutral. It burns in an excess of air to give carbon dioxide and water.

methane + oxygen → carbon dioxide + water
CH_4 + $2O_2$ → CO_2 + $2H_2O$.

In a limited supply of oxygen, carbon monoxide and water are formed. You will remember that carbon monoxide is very poisonous, therefore if you are burning natural gas in your home, your rooms must be well ventilated.
A burning splint does not continue to burn in methane.
Alkanes react with chlorine and with bromine in the presence of sunlight:

> Substitution reactions

methane + chlorine → chloromethane + hydrogen chloride
CH_4 + Cl_2 → CH_3Cl + HCl.

CHAPTER 13 ESSENTIAL PRINCIPLES

Learn this definition

This is called a substitution reaction. ***A substitution reaction is a reaction in which a hydrogen atom is replaced by another atom or groups of atoms.***

(D) USES OF ALKANES

Alkanes are mainly used as ***fuels***. Methane is the main part of natural gas. Butane is used in camping gas and in lighter fuel and octane is used in petrol. Alkanes are used to make alkenes by a process known as cracking (see below).

4 > ISOMERS

Do not confuse with isotopes

Isomers are compounds with the same molecular formula but different structural formulae eg. there are two isomers of molecular formula C_4H_{10}. Their structural formulae are displayed below. The melting points and boiling points of alkanes are affected by their structures. The two isomers of formula C_4H_{10} above, can be seen to have different molecular shapes. The forces of attaction between molecules in each compound differ. The branched molecules of 2-methylpropane do not attract each other as strongly as the linear molecules of butane. Hence, lower temperatures are required to separate them from each other as required in melting and boiling.

5 > ALKENES

Alkenes have the general formula C_nH_{2n}.
The first member of the homologous series of alkenes is ethene.

(A) STRUCTURE OF ETHENE (ELECTRONIC)

The formula of ethene is C_2H_4.

There are two pairs of shared electrons between the carbon atoms. The molecule contains a carbon - carbon double bond (see Figs. 13.5 and 13.6).

Figs 13.5 and 13.6

(B) OTHER ALKENES

Alkenes are said to be **unsaturated** hydrocarbons. Other members of the alkene series are propene, C_3H_6, and butene, C_4H_8.

Note that methene CH_2 cannot exist, because it leaves carbon with two unshared electrons and only six electrons in the outermost energy level. You will remember that carbon needs eight electrons in the outermost energy level (outer shell) to be stable.

Note that ethene is made by dehydrating ethanol. Ethanol can be made by hydrating ethene

(C) PREPARATION OF ETHENE

Alkenes can be made by dehydrating the corresponding alcohol. Ethene is made by heating ethanol with an excess of concentrated sulphuric acid:

$$\text{ethanol} \rightarrow \text{ethene} + \text{water}$$
$$C_2H_5OH \rightarrow C_2H_4 + H_2O.$$

Ethene can also be dehydrated by passing ethanol vapour over a catalyst of hot aluminium oxide.

Propene can be made by dehydrating propanol, and butene by dehydrating butanol. Alkenes can also be made by cracking saturated hydrocarbons from crude oil distillation. (See Section F).

(D) PROPERTIES OF ETHENE

Ethene is a colourless gas. It has a slight sweet smell. It is slightly less dense than air. It is insoluble in water and therefore it is neutral. It burns in an excess of air to give carbon dioxide and water. A burning splint does not continue to burn in ethene.

Alkenes are very reactive because they are unsaturated. They undergo **addition reactions**. *An addition reaction is a reaction in which two or more molecules react together to form one molecule only*:

Addition reactions

compound *AB* + compound *CD* → compound *CABD*

AB + *CD* → *CABD*.

Test for unsaturation

Bromine dissolves in 1,1,1-trichloroethane. If this mixture is shaken with an alkene, a colourless product is formed very quickly. This reaction is used as a test for an alkene:

ethene + bromine → 1,2-dibromoethane

C_2H_4 + Br_2 → $C_2H_4Br_2$.

(brown) (colourless)

Learn this test

This reaction can also be used to distinguish between an alkane and an alkene. Alkanes decolorise bromine very, very slowly.

(E) COMPARING ALKANES WITH ALKENES

Test reagent	Alkanes	Alkenes
React with bromine solution	no reaction	bromine solution is decolourised rapidly
React with acidified potassium manganate (VII) solution	no reaction	the reagent is decolourised
Combustion	burns with clean yellow flame	burns with a sooty yellow flame

Ethene reacts with steam in the presence of a catalyst of phosphoric(V) acid to form ethanol:

ethene + water → ethanol

C_2H_4 + H_2O → C_2H_5OH.

Examples of addition reactions

Ethene reacts with hydrogen in the presence of a hot catalyst of nickel to form ethane:

ethene + hydrogen → ethane

C_2H_4 + H_2 → C_2H_6.

The addition of hydrogen to a carbon—carbon double bond is an important reaction in the conversion of vegetable oils into margarine.

Addition polymerisation

Because ethene is unsaturated it will also undergo **addition polymerisation**.

Ethene polymerises to form the polymer ***poly(ethene)***, commonly known as polythene. The conditions required are a high pressure and a catalyst. ***Propene*** polymerises to form ***poly(propene)***.

Polymer

A polymer is a long-chain molecule formed by the joining together of many small molecules called monomers.

Learn this definition

In a plentiful supply of air, ethene, like all hydrocarbons, burns to form carbon dioxide and water:

ethene + oxygen → carbon dioxide + water

C_2H_4 + $3O_2$ → $2CO_2$ + $2H_2O$.

In a limited supply of air, carbon monoxide and water are the products.

(F) CRACKING

Cracking always produces a mixture of alkanes and alkenes. Usually hydrogen is formed also. The high temperature causes the bonds in the compounds to 'loosen' and break, producing smaller molecules with lower boiling points, lower viscosities and greater flammability. These smaller molecules are therefore more useful for motor vehicle fuels and feedstock for polymer production.

Ethene can be manufactured by cracking. Long-chained hydrocarbons are not as

> Learn this definition

useful as those with shorter chains. ***The process of breaking long-chained molecules into small molecules is called cracking***. The reaction needs a high temperature and a catalyst:

$$\text{decane} \rightarrow \text{ethene} + \text{octane}$$
$$C_{10}H_{22} \rightarrow C_2H_4 + C_8H_{18}.$$

(G) USES OF ETHENE

Ethene is used for the manufacture of ethane-1,2-diol, (also known as ethylene glycol) which is used as an antifreeze and ethanol which is used as a solvent. Ethene is also used to make the well-known polymers poly(ethene), poly(styrene) and poly(vinyl chloride) (PVC).

6 ALCOHOLS

Alcohols have the general formula $C_nH_{2n+1}OH$. The first member of the homologous series of alcohols is methanol. The formula of methanol is CH_3OH. The structures of the first five straight-chain members of the alcohols homologous series are:

methanol

ethanol

propan-1-ol

butan-1-ol

pentan-1-ol

Other members of the alcohol series are ethanol, C_2H_5OH, propanol, C_3H_7OH and butanol, C_4H_9OH.

(A) PROPERTIES OF ETHANOL

> Note the difference between this reaction and burning.

Ethanol is a colourless liquid. It has no smell. It is completely miscible (mixable) with water and it is a neutral liquid. It burns in an excess of air to give carbon dioxide and water. Ethanol is slowly oxidised by the air and bacteria to ethanoic acid:

$$\text{ethanol} + \text{oxygen (from the air)} \rightarrow \text{ethanoic acid} + \text{water}$$
$$C_2H_5OH + 2[O] \rightarrow CH_3CO_2H + H_2O.$$

This is why wine and beer turn sour after a period of time if they are not kept in sealed containers.

The oxidation process can be speeded up by using an oxidising agent such as acidified potassium manganate(VII). The solution changes from purple to colourless.

In a plentiful supply of air, ethanol burns to form carbon dioxide and water:

$$\text{ethanol} + \text{oxygen} \rightarrow \text{carbon dioxide} + \text{water}$$
$$C_2H_5OH + 3O_2 \rightarrow 2CO_2 + 3H_2O.$$

In a limited supply of air, carbon monoxide and water are the products.

(B) MANUFACTURE OF ETHANOL

Ethanol can be manufactured by reacting ethene with steam in the presence of a catalyst of phosphoric(V) acid. The reaction needs a temperature of about 3000°C and 65 atmospheres pressure. This is a **continous process**. Reactants are fed in at one end and products are removed from the other. This is much more convenient and faster than having to fill reaction vessels at the beginning and empty them at the end as happens in a batch process.

$$\text{ethene} + \text{steam} \rightarrow \text{ethanol}$$
$$C_2H_4 + H_2O \rightarrow C_2H_5OH.$$

Ethanol can also be manufactured by ***fermentation***. Yeast is added to a sugar (e.g. glucose) solution and the mixture is kept at room temperature until all the carbon

Remember that enzymes are destroyed at about 45°C

dioxide has been given off. It is important to prevent air from entering the reaction vessel, otherwise ethanoic acid will be formed. Yeast contains biological catalysts known as *enzymes*. This is a batch process and so production is slow.

$$\text{glucose} \rightarrow \text{ethanol} + \text{carbon dioxide}$$
$$C_6H_{12}O_6 \rightarrow 2C_2H_5OH + 2CO_2.$$

Ethanol can be obtained from this mixture by *fractional distillation*.

Bread

A similar reaction takes place when bread is made. Yeast is added to the mixture of flour, water and sodium chloride. Carbon dioxide is given off and this causes the bread to rise. Ethanol escapes as a vapour during baking.

(C) USES OF ETHANOL

Ethanol is used as a solvent. *'Tincture of iodine'*, which is used as an antiseptic, is iodine dissolved in ethanol. *Shellac* dissolved in ethanol is used as a liquid polish. Perfumes are solutions of fragrances in ethanol or in an ethanol–water mixture.

Ethanol is used as a fuel and is the main constituent of methylated spirits which is used in burners for cooking. Methylated spirits has chemicals added to it to make it unsuitable for drinking. This process is called *denaturing*.

Carboxylic acids have the general formula $C_nH_{2n+1}CO_2H$. The first member of the homologous series of acids is methanoic acid. The formula of methanoic acid is HCO_2H and its structure is:

$$H-C\overset{\displaystyle O}{\underset{\displaystyle O-H}{}}$$

The old name for methanoic acid was formic acid, because it is found in ants. (The Latin word 'formica' means 'ant'.)

Other members of the acid series are ethanoic acid (acetic acid), CH_3CO_2H, propanoic acid, $C_2H_5CO_2H$, and butanoic acid, $C_3H_7CO_2H$. Organic acids are sometimes known as "fatty acids" because they are found in natural fats.

Alcoholic drinks

Ethanol is present in spirits, beers and wines. Unfortunately some people become addicted to alcohol and this can lead to mental and physical problems which, in the most serious cases, cause death.

Renewable versus non-renewable sources of ethanol

Fermentation is a renewable source of ethanol, ethene from crude oil is not. However, it would be difficult in many countries to produce enough fermentable plant material to create the quantity of ethanol required by industry or as a fuel for cars. For this reason only a small fraction of the ethanol used in Europe is made by fermentation.

7 > ORGANIC ACIDS

(A) FORMATION OF CARBOXYLIC ACIDS

Carboxylic acids are formed when alcohols are oxidised by the action of atmospheric oxygen in the presence of certain bacteria:

$$\text{ethanol} + \text{atmospheric oxygen} \rightarrow \text{ethanoic acid} + \text{water}$$
$$C_2H_5OH + 2(O) \rightarrow CH_3CO_2H + H_2O.$$

This is the reason why beers and wines turn sour if they are left open to the atmosphere. The sour taste is because ethanoic acid has been formed.

Ethanol can also be oxidised to ethanoic acid by using oxidising agents such as acidified potassium dichromate(VI) and acidified potassium manganate(VII).

methanoic acid   ethanoic acid

(B) USES OF ETHANOIC ACID

Pure ethanoic acid is used as a solvent.

Dilute ethanoic acid is used as an acid for purposes for which mineral acids would be too corrosive, e.g. removing fur from inside kettles (see Chapter 11, Section 6). Ethanoic acid is a component of vinegar. (Vinegar is used as a food preservative, e.g. in pickles.) Ethanoic acid is also the starting material for important plastics such as cellulose acetate.

8 FUELS

(a) Domestic fuels

A fuel is any combustible matter that burns in air to give out heat.
Domestic fuels must have additional properties. Some of these are considered below.

Fuel	storage needed	renewable or fossil source?	polluting rate	cost
Coal	storage	Fossil	high SO_2	low
Oil	storage	Fossil	medium	high
Natural gas	none	Fossil	low	medium
Wood	storage	Renewable	high	low
Bottled gas and paraffin	storage	Fossil	low	high

(b) Industrial fuels

Industry uses all of the available fuels. However, fuels which could not be used in homes are sometimes chosen for economic advantage. For example, sulphur may be burned as a cheap source of energy. The highly polluting sulphur dioxide that is formed in nearly 100% yields is converted to sulphuric acid – a valuable by-product with a ready market! The initial cost of the acid plant must be met but the use can be economically advantageous if much energy is used. Ethanol is not exploited as a fuel in many countries. It could be used instead of fuel oil but it cannot be supplied in such large quantities to compete.

Motor vehicle fuels of the future?

Here we have little choice as yet. Although there are about a million vehicles worldwide (1994) running on methane, and many more using mixtures of petrol and ethanol, the chief fuel is petrol or diesel. These are liquids with high energy-densities.

The energy per gram for petrol is higher than any fuel except liquid methane. To replace petrol would require the development of high energy-density fuels with the same ease of use as petrol. Among the suggested alternatives are liquid methane (bp. –160°C) and hydrogen (bp. –253°C). Both are gases at normal temperatures but would have to be much compressed or liquified for storage in fuel tanks on vehicles. Methane is stored as a refrigerated liquid and some success has been achieved in its use. Hydrogen can only be stored in a combined form as a hydride of, for example, magnesium or nickel. Unfortunately the storage tanks must be strong and therefore heavy to avoid explosion. The situation may improve by development of electric vehicles but electricity is not itself a fuel and is mostly produced by burning fossil fuels.

All fuels are explosive when mixed with air. If fuel tanks leak, methane and hydrogen will rapidly diffuse upwards into the air whereas petrol vapour is denser than air and hangs around the vehicle. Thus, the gases may be safer although more explosive!

Nuclear fuels

By harnessing the power of a slowed-down nuclear explosion we obtain heat for producing steam to generate electricity. This is essentially what happens in a nuclear power station. Electricity generated in this way conserves fossil fuel reserves for use as chemical feed-stock. There is much controversy about the merits of nuclear power. The process produces no gaseous pollution of the sort emitted by combustion processes, since the nuclear fuel does not actually 'burn'. However, there are radioactive waste products to be disposed. If mishandled these will be dangerous and pose a worse hazard than atmospheric pollutants from fossil fuel burning.

Pollution from fuel burning

This problem was discused in detail in Chapter 2, Section 4.

All fossil fuels produce carbon dioxide, a 'greenhouse gas'. They will also produce some carbon monoxide if inefficiently burned. Within a very short time, carbon monoxide is converted to carbon dioxide in the atmosphere and in the soil. Coal, in addition, contains sulphur compounds and these give sulphur dioxide which causes acid-rain. Petrol, diesel, natural gas and bottled gas are all relatively free from sulphur compounds. All high temperature combustion using air for combustion produce nitrogen oxides. This is because nitrogen and oxygen will combine together at high temperature in the combustion chambers of cars or the furnaces of industry.

Reducing pollution from fuel burning

The catalytic converter effectively reduces emissions of oxides of nitrogen and carbon monoxide. Sulphur dioxide from power stations can be reduced by fitting desulphurising plant which removes the pollutant in an alkaline scrubbing process. Benzene pollution from unleaded petrol is likely to be reduced by finding a substitute additive.

EXAMINATION QUESTIONS

MULTIPLE CHOICE QUESTIONS

QUESTION 1

Which one of the following is the formula of an organic compound?

A CH_4 ✓
B NaCl
C NH_3
D SO_2

(SEG)

QUESTION 2

Which one of the gases listed below burns in oxygen to form carbon dioxide and water vapour and also decolorises bromine water?

A carbon monoxide (CO)
B ethane (C_2H_6)
C ethene (C_2H_4) ✓
D methane (CH_4)

(SEG)

QUESTION 3

Crude oil can be separated into different fractions because each fraction has a different

A boiling point ✓
B density
C melting point
D solubility

(SEG)

QUESTION 4

Which ONE of the following is the structural formula of an alkane?

QUESTION 5

Gas from a cylinder burns in air to produce a mixture which turns lime-water milky and turns anhydrous copper(II) sulphate from white to blue.
The gas could be

A   hydrogen   D   ammonia
B   carbon monoxide   E   nitrogen
C   propane ✓

(ULEAC)

QUESTION 6

Cracking of a hydrocarbon mixture results in the

A   formation of small molecules from larger ones. ✓
B   combustion of the hydrocarbons.
C   formation of ethanol. ✗
D   formation of polythene.
E   separation of the hydrocarbons into groups of substances with similar boiling point.

QUESTIONS 7–9

concern the following substances:

A CH_3CH_2OH D CH_4
B $CH_3CH_2CH_3$ E $C_6H_{12}O_6$
C $CH_3CH=CH_2$

Choose, from A to E, the structure which represents
7   a substance which can be polymerised.
8   the substance with the highest melting point.
9   the substance that needs three molecules of oxygen for complete combustion of one molecule.

(ULEAC)

QUESTION 10

In an effort to conserve its fuel reserves and reduce pollution, Amazonia decided in 1978 that all new motor cars should use ethanol (CH_3CH_2OH) instead of petrol.
    The gas that would NOT be found coming out of the exhausts of new cars in 1979 is

A   carbon dioxide   D   sulphur dioxide
B   carbon monoxide ✓   E   water vapour
C   nitrogen

(ULEAC)

QUESTION 11

Which one of the following is an isomer of butane?

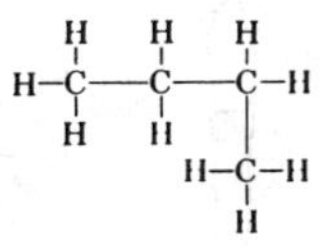

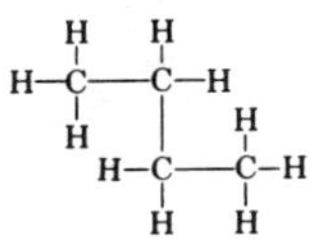

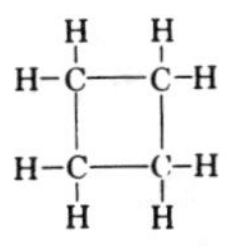

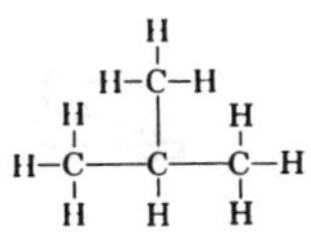

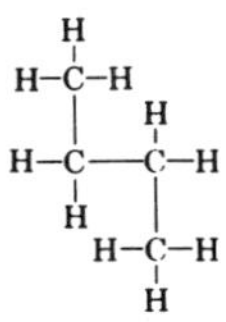

QUESTION 12

What substance catalyses the fermentation of sugar?

A   an enzyme ✓   D   oxygen
B   carbon dioxide E   water
C   ethanol

STRUCTURED QUESTIONS

QUESTION 13

Compound	Formula	Boiling point
A	CH$_4$	−162°C
B	C$_2$H$_6$	− 89°C
C	C$_3$H$_6$	− 48°C
D	C$_3$H$_8$	− 42°C
E	C$_4$H$_{10}$	
F	C$_5$H$_{12}$	+ 25°C

(a) Five of the six hydrocarbons listed above belong to the homologous series called alkanes. (1 line)

    (i) Which hydrocarbon listed does **not** belong to the alkanes? *(1)*
    (ii) Is compound F a solid, a liquid or a gas at 35°C? (1 line) *(1)*
    (iii) By studying the table predict the boiling point of compound E. (1 line) *(1)*
    (iv) Which **one** of the hydrocarbons is the main compound in natural gas? (1 line) *(1)*

(b) Hydrocarbon B is said to be saturated and has the structural formula

$$\begin{array}{c} \text{H} \quad \text{H} \\ | \quad | \\ \text{H}-\text{C}-\text{C}-\text{H} \\ | \quad | \\ \text{H} \quad \text{H} \end{array}$$

State what would happen if this compound was bubbled into bromine. *(1)*

QUESTION 14

The gas which is used for gas fires and bunsen burners consists mainly of methane (CH$_4$). When it is burned in a bunsen burner which gives a good supply of air, carbon dioxide and steam are formed. Complete the equation for this reaction:

(a) CH$_4$(g) + 2O$_2$(g) → *(2)*
(b) What does the symbol (g) tell us about the substances which are used up in this reaction? (2 lines) *(1)*
(c) What is meant by the number 2 in front of the formula of oxygen? (1 line) *(1)*
(d) Give the name and formula of another compound which might be formed if methane is burnt in a limited supply of air.
Name: ....
Formula: .... *(2)*

The apparatus shown below was used to identify the substances formed when methane burns.

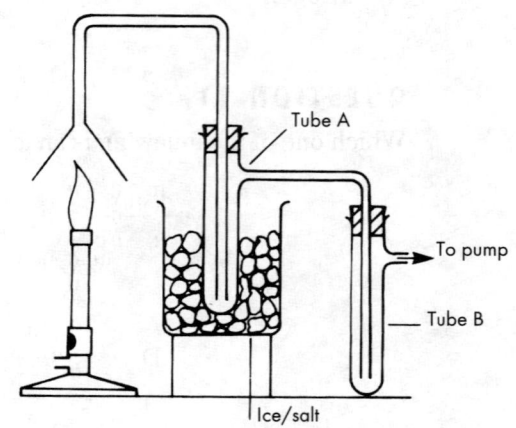

Fig. 13.7

(e) A colourless liquid collected in tube A. How could you test it to show it contains water?
Test: ....
Result: .... *(2)*
(f) What liquid could be placed in tube B to detect carbon dioxide?
Liquid: ....
Result if CO$_2$ present: .... *(2)*

QUESTION 15

The general formula for the alkene series of hydrocarbons is C_nH_{2n}. Ethene, C_2H_4, is the first member.

(a) (i) Work out the molecular formula of the fifth member, hexene. (1 line)
    (1 mark)
   (ii) Ethene may be prepared by passing ethanol vapour over a heated aluminium oxide catalyst. Sketch an apparatus which you might use to carry out this reaction, showing how you would collect the ethene. *(4 marks)*
   (iii) What would you do when using the apparatus shown in your answer to part (ii) to make sure that the ethene was reasonably free of air? (2 lines) *(1 mark)*
   (iv) Write an equation for the reaction in (ii). (1 line) *(1 mark)*

(b) An organic compound X undergoes the following reactions.
   (i) It burns completely in oxygen forming carbon dioxide and water only.
   (ii) It rapidly decolorises bromine water.
   (iii) It dissolves in sodium carbonate solution with fizzing.

State as fully as possible what you can deduce about the structure of compound X from each reaction. (5 lines) *(6 marks)*

(SEG)

QUESTION 16

(a) In oil refineries, petroleum, which is a mixture of an homologous series of alkanes, is distilled in a fractionating column to give various fractions. Some of these are used directly as fuels, some are subjected to catalytic cracking to give chemical feedstocks, and others are used to make plastics and other polymers.
   (i) Why are oil refineries usually found close to ports? (1 line) *(1)*
   (ii) State what is meant by an homologous series of alkanes. (2 lines) *(2)*
   (iii) State what is meant by a fuel, giving an example of a fuel produced directly in an oil refinery. (2 lines) *(2)*
   (iv) State two properties necessary for a good fuel. (2 lines) *(2)*
   (v) Explain what is meant by catalytic cracking and give an example. (2 lines) *(2)*

OUTLINE ANSWERS

MULTIPLE CHOICE

ANSWER 1

Organic chemistry is the study of compounds containing carbon. The only compound containing carbon is CH_4, key is A.

ANSWER 2

Since the compound burns to form carbon dioxide and water only it must contain carbon and hydrogen, therefore it cannot be carbon monoxide. Because it decolorises bromine water it must be an alkene (see Section 5(D) above). The only alkene in the list is ethene, key C.

ANSWER 3

A, see Section 1.

ANSWER 4

B (propane), see Section 3. A is an alcohol (ethanol), C is an alkene (ethene), D is an ester (methyl ethanoate) and E is an acid (ethanoic acid).

QUESTION 5

The gas that turns lime-water milky is carbon dioxide, hence the gas must contain carbon. The compound that turns anhydrous copper(II) sulphate from white to blue is water, hence the gas must contain hydrogen. The only gas in the responses that contains both carbon and hydrogen is the hydrocarbon propane. This is key C.

Hydrogen burns to form only water, carbon monoxide burns to form only carbon dioxide. Ammonia and nitrogen do not burn in air.

ANSWER 6
A – see Section 5(F).

ANSWER 7
C (propene, the compound must be unsaturated before it will polymerise – see Section 5(E)).

ANSWER 8
E - the larger the molecule, the higher the melting point.

ANSWER 9
Each carbon atom will need 1 molecule of oxygen and each pair of hydrogen atoms will need half a molecule of oxygen -but look out for compounds that already contain oxygen. A: this will need 3 molecules of oxygen; B: 5 molecules; C: 4 molecules; D: 2 molecules and E: 6 molecules (6 for carbon atoms, 3 for hydrogen atoms minus 1 for the oxygen already present). The answer is A.

ANSWER 10
D.

ANSWER 11
D (note that B and E are identical - they are both butane).

ANSWER 12
A (see Section 6(B)).

ANSWER 13
Some tips to help:
(a) (i) Look at general formulae (see Section 5).
     (ii) If the boiling point is below 35°C it is a gas.
     (iii) Look for a pattern – you are NOT expected to get the exact answer!
     (iv) See Section 3(D).
(b) See Section 5(E).

ANSWER 14
(a) $CO_2 + 2H_2O$.
(b) (g) means they are gases.
(c) Two moles of oxygen are used.
(d) Carbon monoxide, CO.
(e) Add anhydrous copper(II) sulphate, turns from white to blue.
(f) Lime-water - turns cloudy.

ANSWER 15
(a) (i) C_6H_{12}
     (ii) See Fig. 12.4B (ethanol is used instead of water and aluminium oxide instead of zinc).
     (iii) Either wait to collect first test tube full of gas or throw away first test tube full of gas.
     (iv) $C_2H_5OH \rightarrow C_2H_4 + H_2O$.
(b) (i) Contains carbon and hydrogen.
     (ii) Unsaturated organic compound.
     (iii) Organic acid.

ANSWER 16

(a) (i) Petroleum is transported by ships, the oil can be pumped straight from the ship to the refineries.
 (ii) An homologous series is a series of compounds with similar chemical properties and can be represented by a general formula, e.g. alkanes have the general formula C_nH_{2n+2}.
 (iii) A fuel is a chemical which, when burnt, gives out a large amount of energy, e.g. two fuels obtained from an oil refinery are petrol and paraffin.
 (iv) The properties of a good fuel include: does not burn to give poisonous products, easily transported, easily stored, easily mined, leaves little residue on burning.
 (v) Catalytic cracking is the breaking down of large molecules into smaller molecules, e.g.

$$C_{10}H_{22} \rightarrow C_2H_4 + C_8H_{18}.$$
$$\text{decane} \rightarrow \text{ethene} + \text{octane}$$

CHAPTER 13 **MAKING A START IN ORGANIC CHEMISTRY**

STUDENT'S ANSWER – EXAMINER'S COMMENTS

This question is about the formation of alcohol (ethanol) form sugars and its possible use as an alternative to petrol as a fuel for car engines.

One source of sugars is sugar cane which is crushed and the juices mixed with yeast. The mixture is allowed to stand for two to three days at around 30°C.

The liquid product is then fractionally distilled, most of the ethanol being in the middle of the three fractions.

(a) Name **one** other crop which is a useful source of sugars.

> Sugar beat

(1 mark)

❝ Spelling! Should be beet. Yours sounds like a pop group! ❞

(b) The equation for the reaction which changes the sugar glucose into ethanol in the presence of yeast is given below.

$$C_6H_{12}O_6(aq) \rightarrow 2\ C_2H_5OH(aq) + 2\ CO_2(g)$$

(i) What does the symbol (aq) indicate about the glucose?

> aqueous solution

(1 mark)

❝ You've really repeated the question. It means it's dissolved in water. ❞

(ii) What is the purpose of the yeast in the reaction?

> creates carbon dioxide

(1 mark)

❝ No – it is a catalyst. ❞

(iii) Why is the reaction **not** speeded up if the mixture is boiled?

kills yeast

(1 mark)

(iv) Give the name of the process which converts glucose into ethanol in this way.

> distillation

(1 mark)

❝ Should be fermentation ❞

(v) Why is the same reaction important in bread-making?

> makes bread rise

(1 mark)

❝ To be exact, the gas given off makes bread rise. ❞

(c) One of the advantages of ethanol over petrol is that, unlike petrol, ethanol is a *renewable energy source*.

Explain the meaning of the term *renewable energy source*.

> can be used again

(1 mark)

❝ Made from plants which can be grown again ❞

(d) What other possible advantages might ethanol have over petrol as a fuel for car engines?

> no lead needed
> no carbon monoxide produced

(2 marks)

❝ Good ❞

❝ All organic compounds can give carbon monoxide. However, ethanol does not burn to give sulphur dioxide. ❞

(e) Methylated spirits is a mixture of ethanol (about 90%) and methanol (about 10%) together with a small quantity of purple dye.

Explain why the ethanol is treated in this way before being sold as "meths".

To stop people drinking it.

(3 marks)

(SEG)

❝ Overall score 5/12. Some careless errors here reduced the mark. Make sure you read, and understand, the questions asked... ❞

CHAPTER 14

THE ORGANIC CHEMISTRY OF LARGE MOLECULES

GETTING STARTED

Large molecules or *macromolecules* are important to us for several reasons. Firstly, they have useful properties which we can turn to our advantage. Secondly, they are often found in living things and so can be obtained from a renewable resource. An example is wool which is a protein-like macromolecule. Unfortunately, our requirement for some of these macromolecules exceeds their supply from natural resources and chemists have been forced to *synthesise* them, or substances like them, from more abundant materials. This chapter is concerned with these natural and synthetic (man-made) macromolecules.

Macromolecules, or large molecules, are common in living things. Starch and protein, found in plants and animals, are examples of *natural* macromolecules.

Synthetic, or *man-made*, macromolecules are now produced on a large scale. They have the useful properties of natural macromolecules tailored to the needs of modern-day living.

The structure of macromolecules in general has been discussed in Chapter 5, Section 13. You should re-read this section before proceeding. One type of macromolecule is the *polymer* molecule.

- THE STRUCTURE OF POLYMERS
- SYNTHETIC POLYMERS
- THE EFFECT OF HEAT ON POLYMERS
- THE STRUCTURE OF PLASTICS
- THE USE OF PLASTICS
- WHAT POLYMERS ARE MADE OF
- NATURAL POLYMERS

CHAPTER 14 THE ORGANIC CHEMISTRY OF LARGE MOLECULES

ESSENTIAL PRINCIPLES

1. THE STRUCTURE OF POLYMERS

Because polymers are very large molecules, their structures can be complicated. They are made up of many (sometimes thousands of) small molecules joined together in a 'chain'. The small molecules making up the chain are called **monomers**. The chain is called the **polymer**. The chemical reaction in which monomers combine to form a polymer is called **polymerisation**.

Strictly, we should use the term monomer to mean the chemical **substance** and not the monomer **molecule**. Similarly, we should use polymer to mean the chemical and not the polymer molecule. To have to write 'polymer molecule' or 'monomer molecule' each time we are referring to the molecule results in tedious repetition. In what follows, the term 'monomer' will mean the molecule of monomer *or* the chemical substance. 'Polymer' will mean the polymer molecule *or* the chemical polymer. It should be clear from the context whether 'molecule' or 'chemical' is meant and no confusion should arise.

Monomer	Polymer	Properties	Uses
ethene (H₂C=CH₂)	poly(ethene)	'Polythene'. Cheap, strong, resists food acids, and solvents. Waterproof. No need for plasticiser	Film and bags. Containers, water pipes, kitchenware. Food wrapping.
chloroethene (H₂C=CHCl)	poly(chloroethene)	'PVC' Tough, strong rubbery and very flexible when plasticised. Flame resistant. Electrical insulator. Resists solvents.	Raincoats, wellingtons, artificial leather, electrical wire insulation.
phenylethene (H₂C=CHC₆H₅)	poly(phenylethene)	'Polystyrene'. Strong, flexible, but brittle. Retains strength when cold. Easily worked with hand tools.	Food containers, toys and 'fridge parts. Foam is used for heat insulation and packing.
propene (H₂C=CHCH₃)	poly(propene)	Harder, more rigid than polythene. Higher softening temperature (>100°C).	Moulded furniture, carpet fibre, ropes.
methyl methacrylate (H₂C=C(CH₃)CO₂CH₃)	poly(methyl methacrylate)	'Perspex'. Glass-like but tough. Easily moulded and machined. Shatterproof.	Sterilizable bottles. Aircraft windows, baths, camera lenses. Motorcycle windshields.
tetrafluoroethene (F₂C=CF₂)	poly(tetrafluoroethene)	'PTFE'. Unaffected by everyday chemicals. Non-stick, low friction. Heat- and solvent-resistant.	Non-stick pans. Acid-resistant containers in chemical plant.

Fig. 14.1 Monomers, polymers and their uses.

2 SYNTHETIC POLYMERS

How does polymerisation occur? Molecules that polymerise have to be capable of reacting with each other by one of two types of reaction – *addition* or *condensation*.

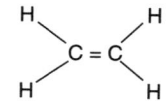

(A) ADDITIONAL POLYMERISATION

Some monomers are simple molecules, e.g. ethene, C_2H_4, which is obtained by cracking petroleum:

The carbon-carbon double bond in ethene is very reactive and allows ethene molecules to link together to form the polymer **poly(ethene)**, polythene.

This reaction needs a catalyst (strictly an initiator), a temperature of 200°C and high pressure. Under these conditions up to 10 000 ethene molecules will link to form a long-chain molecule -poly(ethene).

Usually, the number of monomers is variable, so the exact molecular formula of a polymer is rarely known. For this reason we show the number of monomer units in a polymer as the number n, which represents the number of times the unit is repeated – usually a *large unknown number*, e.g. poly(ethene) is represented as

$$-[CH_2-CH_2]-_n.$$

Polythene polymer molecules have very large relative molecular masses – 100 000 upwards!

The equation for the formation of poly(ethene) is therefore

$$n CH_2=CH_2 \xrightarrow[\text{high temperature and pressure}]{\text{initiator}} -[CH_2-CH_2]-_n$$

the polymer formed has none of the properties of ethene, the double bond is absent from the product. The monomer is an **unsaturated** hydrocarbon but the polymer is a **saturated** hydrocarbon.

Other addition polymers

Any molecule having the carbon—carbon double bond will polymerise in the same way as ethene. This will include all alkenes and their derivatives.

The structure of ethene and monomers derived from ethene are simple enough to show *in full* in their reactions.

It should be clear from the table above that the structure of the polymer derived from the monomer consists simply of a chain of monomer units linked together. In the process of linking, *the monomer units lose the double bonds between carbon atoms*.

To deduce the structure of the monomer from which a polymer is made:

(i) identify the repeating unit; then
(ii) insert a double bond between the carbon atoms that had been part of the chain; finally
(iii) eliminate the unused bonds at the ends of the unit, e.g.

in the polymer poly(chloroethane)

repeating unit

repeat unit with double bond inserted and without 'end bonds'.

Reversing the polymerisation process

Many of the polymers formed by **addition** reactions can be converted back to their monomers by heating. This is called **depolymerisation**. Because most of the alkene-type monomers are gases at room temperature, this process is usually illustrated in the laboratory by the depolymerisation of polymer Perspex which gives a liquid monomer.

On heating, Perspex is decomposed into its liquid monomer which boils at a temperature close to 100 °C. The monomer will therefore vaporise as soon as it forms. The usual apparatus for this depolymerisation, therefore, allows the two processes to take place together. The polymer is decomposed to the monomer. The monomer distils off from the residue (Fig. 14.2).

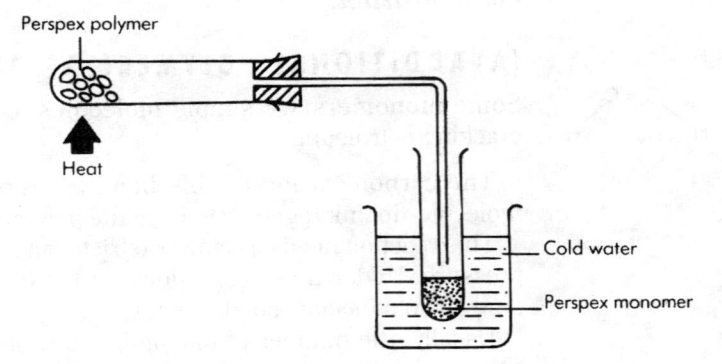

Fig. 14.2 Depolymerisation of Perspex

Testing with bromine solution will show the monomer to be an unsaturated compound. What would you expect to happen in the test? (see Chapter 13, Section 5(d))

Polymerisation of the resulting monomer can be carried out by addition of a tiny portion of an initiator to the warm monomer. The liquid will set to a hard, glassy plastic in a few hours if left.

$$\text{Perspex} \xrightarrow{\text{heat}} \text{monomer}.$$

$$\text{monomer} \xrightarrow{\text{initiator}} \text{polymer}$$

(B) CONDENSATION POLYMERISATION

Monomers with **reactive groups at each end of the molecule** polymerise in a different way from those having carbon—carbon double bonds.

Unlike addition polymers, condensation polymers are formed from their monomers by **loss of a small molecule** during the linking reaction. This small molecule is usually either a **water molecule** or a molecule of **hydrogen chloride**.

Because condensation polymerisation involves more complex monomers we shall use the **simplified monomer** structures **shown below**.

Monomer	Represented as	Reactive group at the end of the monomer
Terephthalic acid*	HO₂C — ▧▧▧▧ — CO₂H	— CO₂H group
Ethylene glycol*	HO — ▧▧▧▧ — OH	— OH group
Diaminohexane*	H₂N — ▧▧▧▧ — NH₂	— NH₂ group
Adipyl chloride*	ClOC — ▧▧▧▧ — COCl	— COCl group

Fig. 14.3

Monomers are represented in diagrams as in Fig. 14.3.

* These are traditional names of these compounds. The names recommended by the International Union of Pure and Applied Chemistry (IUPAC) are:

❝ IUPAC names ❞

benzene-1,4-dicarboxylic acid for terephthalic acid;
ethane-1,2-diol for ethylene glycol;
hexane-1,6-diamine for diaminohexane;
hexanedioyl dichloride for adipyl chloride.

The linking of monomers in condensation polymerisation

For monomers to polymerise they must be capable of reacting together. Each of the monomers shown in Fig. 14.3 has a **reactive group at each end**. Reaction between these groups causes them to link together to form polymers. During this process, a water molecule or a hydrogen chloride molecule is produced for every two monomers that react. Because the monomers have a reactive group at **each end**, the polymer can continue to grow in both directions.

(C) EXAMPLES OF CONDENSATION POLYMERS

Nylon – a polyamide

Nylon can be made by polymerising hexamethylenediamine with adipyl chloride. The reaction is easily done in the laboratory by carefully pouring aqueous hexamethylenediamine onto a solution of adipyl chloride in 1,1,1-trichloroethane (or any suitable organic solvent). A film of nylon forms where the liquids make contact. This film can be pulled out with tweezers and a continuous 'strand' of nylon can be wound out of the liquids around a rotating glass rod. The experiment is sometimes called the 'nylon-rope trick' (Fig. 14.4).

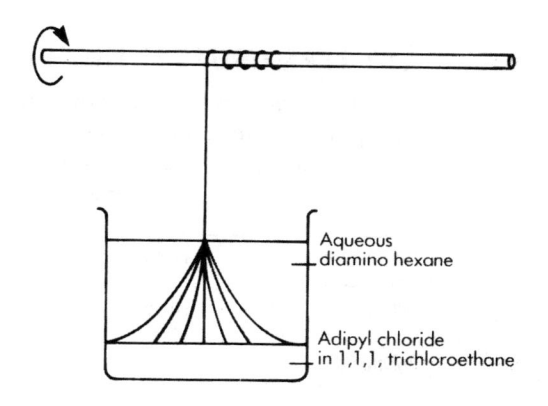

Fig. 14.4 The 'nylon rope trick'

During the process an —NH_2 group and a —COCl group react together to form a linkage called an **amide** linkage, producing a molecule of **hydrogen chloride** in the process (Fig. 14.5).

nH_2N —▨— NH_2 + nClOC —▩— COCl → ─[HN —▨— N—C—▩—CO]$_n$—

+nHCl(aq)

Fig. 14.5

Because the polymer contains **many amide** linkages, nylon is called a **polyamide**.

Properties and uses of nylon

Nylon has a similar structure to natural protein, such as that from which spider's webs are made. Nylon is very strong even in thin threads. It is not easily decomposed by bacterial or fungal attack - it is 'rot-proof'. It is also water-repellent.

Nylon is a thermosoftening plastic (Section 3 below), easily made into continuous fibres by forcing molten nylon through a 'showerhead' type of structure and cooling the thin streams of molten nylon as they emerge.

The strength, wear resistance and water-repellent properties of nylon determine many of its uses: fabric, carpet, tights, anoraks and climbing ropes, lightweight gears and other machine parts.

Terylene - a polyester

Terylene is made by polymerisation of benzene-1,4-dicarboxylic acid (**ter**ephthalic acid) with ethane-1,2-diol (eth**ylene** glycol). The reaction occurs between the —CO_2H group of the acid and the —OH group of the diol. These two groups react to form an **ester** linkage and eliminate a water molecule:

nHO$_2$C —▨— CO$_2$H + nHO —▩— OH → ─[—O$_2$C —▨— CO$_2$ —▩—]$_n$ + nH$_2$O

Because the polymer contains **many ester** linkages, Terylene is called a **polyester**.

Properties and uses of Terylene

Terylene is a thermosoftening polymer, like nylon, and is made into fibres by a similar process.

Its best-known use is as a fibre in cloth. It has properties similar to cotton but is more resistant to wear and chemical attack and takes permanent creases. The polymer is also made into audio and video tapes and the familiar plastic lemonade and cola bottles.

3 THE EFFECT OF HEAT ON POLYMERS

Some natural polymers decompose on heating, others soften and become pliable. Polymers which soften on heating are said to be *thermosoftening* or *thermoplastic*. Tortoise shell is one such natural polymeric material that was once much used to make shaped objects, such as ladies' hair-brushes, because of this property.

(A) THERMOSOFTENING PLASTICS - THERMOPLASTICS

Thermoplasticity is a property of most synthetic plastics. Those in common use are nylon, polythene, PVC, polystyrene, Terylene and Perspex. These plastics can be heated to soften them and then shaped, by a number of different processes, into everyday articles. For example:

Thermoplastic	Process	Finished article
PVC	blow moulding	bottles and other containers
Polythene	extrusion	sheet, film and tubing/piping
Perspex	vacuum forming	baths and record player covers

A glance at the above table will show how the uses of many plastics are related to their ability to be easily shaped by heat.

(B) THERMOSETTING PLASTICS – THERMOSETS

Thermosets cannot be melted once they have been formed. This makes them resistant to softening when heated. Examples include Bakelite, melamine and Araldite resin.

They find uses in making heat-proof containers and surfaces (melamine), electrical fittings and pan handles (Bakelite). Araldite resin is a strong, heat-resistant adhesive.

4 THE STRUCTURE OF PLASTICS

The different properties of the two types of plastic discussed above are related to their structures.

Thermoplastics, such as polythene, are composed of long polymer molecules in a state of constant motion. These molecules vibrate, rotate and generally become entangled with each other. The entangled molecules are attracted to each other by weak forces which increase as the molecules come closer together, Fig. 14.6.

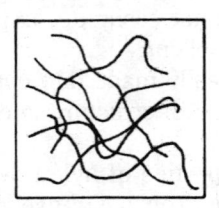

Warming increases the motion of the polymers, increasing the distance between them and reducing the forces of attraction. The mass then changes shape more easily when force is applied. Cooling reverses this series of changes.

Polythene behaves in this way. There are, however, two types of polythene, high- and low-density. They differ, as would be expected from their names, on the closeness of packing of their molecules.

In high-density polythene (HDP) the molecules are much closer together, lying parallel to each other for much of their length, and so attractive forces between them are greater. HDP is more rigid, stronger and has a higher softening temperature than low-density polythene (LDP), Fig. 14.7.

HD polythene is used instead of LD polythene where increased wear and tear is expected, e.g. polythene buckets, or where extra rigidity is required as in large containers, or where a higher softening temperature is vital as in sterilisable vessels.

Thermosets are quite different. In effect a single molecule is built up from polymer molecules by a 'cross-linking' process which chemically links them together. The polymer is rigid and, since warming cannot cause increased motion of the interconnected chains, will not soften at higher temperatures, Fig. 14.8.

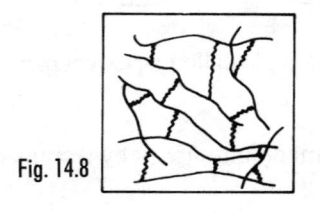

Thermosets such as Bakelite have been used for decades to make electrical fittings which might become hot in use (Fig. 14.9).

Fig. 14.6

Fig. 14.7

Fig. 14.8

Fig. 14.9

Plastics consumption	
Packaging	36%
Building	20%
Electrical	10%
Transport	5%
Furniture	5%
Toys/leisure	5%
Others	19%

Biopol – a biodegradable polymer

Biopol is a new polymer manufactured by ICI from carbohydrates. The process of its manufacture and biodegradation is

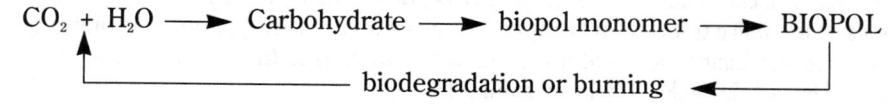

$$CO_2 + H_2O \longrightarrow \text{Carbohydrate} \longrightarrow \text{biopol monomer} \longrightarrow \text{BIOPOL}$$

$$\longleftarrow \text{biodegradation or burning} \longleftarrow$$

Fibres

Polymers are made into fibres by the process of extrusion. Molten polymer – nylon, poly(propene), terylene etc. – is forced by pressure through a spinneret. A spinneret is a 'shower head' like nozzle which allows continuous thin jets of molten polymer to be extruded into conditions where they set solid. Many hundreds of strands are produced by a single spinneret head. On cooling, threads are formed which are wound onto separate bobbins. As this is happening, the threads are stretched to six times their extruded length.

Remarkably, this gives the fibre increased strength. Stretching draws out the tangled molecules into parallel groups as in figure 14.10.

Parallel close-packed molecules are strongly attracted to each other and give the fibre high tensile strength – high resistance to stretching and breaking whilst being pulled.

Fig. 14.10

5 > THE USE OF PLASTICS

(A) ADVANTAGES

The greatest advantage of plastics is their wide range of desirable properties. They can be literally 'tailor-made' to suit the product. Many of these properties are shown in Fig. 14.1. Such properties allow a wide range of applications.

A summary of the most important properties of plastics:

- cheap and easy to make into intricate shapes;
- lightweight;
- uncorrodable;
- easily self-coloured;
- resistant to decay and chemical attack;
- tough and waterproof.

Write down a few everyday uses of plastics for each of the properties listed. Can you think of other properties not listed?

(B) DISADVANTAGES

(i) Fire risk

Plastics are polymers of substances obtained from crude oil. It is not surprising, then, that many plastics are flammable. The ease with which a plastic will burn is a constant hazard to be guarded against wherever plastics are in use.

Plastics used in the manufacture of furniture are responsible for many of the deaths in housefires each year. Toxic gases are produced when plastics burn in inadequate supplies of air, such as you would expect in closed rooms, and death from poisoning often occurs before the fire reaches the inhabitants.

Plastics used in furniture also emit smoke. A sensible precaution against poisoning by combustion gases would be the installation of smoke alarms in every household. These would give a warning before flames had taken a hold.

(ii) Pollution problems

The most useful properties of polymers are their strength, resistance to corrosion, water resistance and resistance to bacterial decay. These properties, however, are not enough to ensure that plastic objects will remain *usable for ever*. Synthetic fabrics wear, nylon gears break, polythene basins become scratched and may split. When the time comes to dispose of our polymer waste these *same properties become disadvantages*.

One 'problem' of disposing of plastic waste is that it will not rot away if dumped on refuse tips or buried. This problem is not limited to plastics, since concrete, brick and many metals are also resistant to decay, but we do not grumble as much about these materials. So why is there a problem with plastics?

Chiefly, it is that plastic waste is often light and easily blown about, spreading around the environment - like paper, but much more permanent. Carelessly disposed plastic waste quickly becomes a *permanent eyesore* in the environment.

The *proposed* solution to this problem is to develop plastics which can be decomposed by bacteria in the same way that paper and vegetable matter are. This solution, namely *biodegradable* plastics – as they are called – is becoming more widely available.

The development of biodegradable plastics would be a big step in reducing the effect of careless disposal of unsightly plastic waste in rural areas. *Collected waste* would be *more usefully* recycled or used as an energy source. The following methods of disposal are currently in use:

> Yet another possible solution has been tried out recently. Polystyrene treated with a special chemical was found to be degraded by sunlight. Such a plastic, lying outside for a few months, would disappear completely.

Disposal and recycling of plastics

- burning (incineration) in a good supply of air to form carbon dioxide and water - two products obtained from most combustion processes. The energy from this burning *can* be used to supply households with heating and factories with power. Britain lags behind some countries in the use of heat from this source. West Germany, for example recovers heat energy from 90% of its incinerators compared with only 6% in Britain. In Britain only about 4% of crude oil is made into polymers. Burning the waste from this could therefore save (only?) 4% of the crude oil for other purposes.

The presence of PVC as a common constituent of plastic waste can cause pollution problems. When PVC is burned one of the products is hydrogen chloride, HCl(g), which is an acidic gas. PVC burning will therefore contribute to 'acid rain'. However, HCl gas is produced from non-plastic waste as well. About 50% comes from this source. In fact the danger to the environment of such pollution 'countrywide' is very small since HCl emissions are controlled by law.

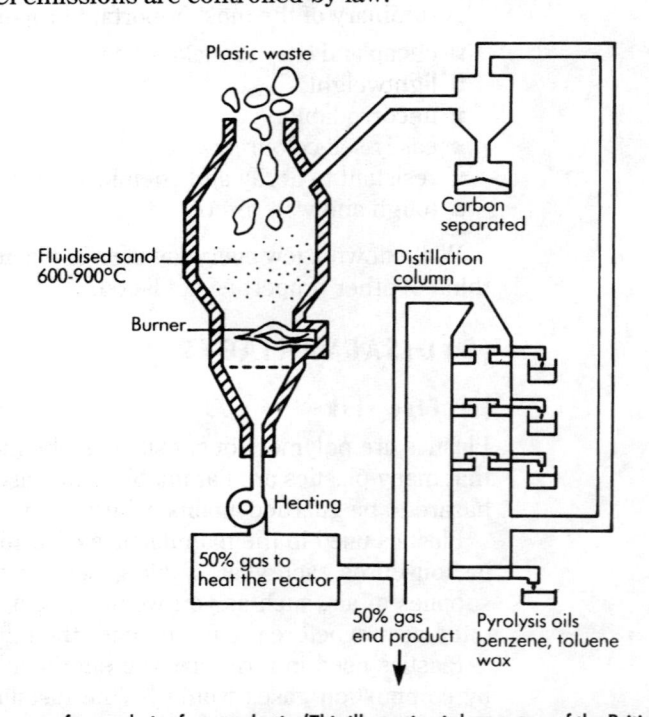

Fig. 14.11 Fluidised bed reactor for pyrolysis of waste plastic. (This illustration is by courtesy of the British Plastics Federation).

- recycling so that the energy and raw material used in their manufacture is not wasted. Bottle-crates and bin-liners are made from recycled plastic but it is rarely possible to re-use plastic waste to make more of the ***original*** plastic. This is simply because it is almost impossible to separate the waste into pure polymers. What will be obtained is a mixture, and on re-melting this will give a plastic 'alloy' which will be unsuitable for many uses.

Pyrolysis

- conversion of mixed plastic wastes back to simple petrochemical raw materials. By heating waste in the absence of air - a process known as ***pyrolysis***, which literally means 'splitting by fire' - a mixture of re-usable hydrocarbons can be obtained. These can be used as fuels or to synthesise more monomers (Fig. 14.11).

6 WHAT POLYMERS ARE MADE OF

The presence of carbon, hydrogen and nitrogen in natural polymers can be shown by the following tests:

(i) Oxidising the substance by heating with copper(II) oxide. This oxidation will result in the formation of carbon dioxide from any ***carbon*** present and water from any ***hydrogen*** present. The presence of oxygen cannot be found by this method because the oxidising agent used contains oxygen and this 'masks' the presence of oxygen in the substance.

(ii) Heating the substance with soda-lime (a mixture of sodium hydroxide and calcium hydroxide) will release ammonia gas if the polymer contains ***nitrogen*** (e.g. a protein). The nitrogen in the ammonia can only have come from the protein.

A summary of these results is shown below (Fig. 14.12).

Reagent	Starch/carbohydrates	Fats/oils Proteins
$CuO(s)$	$CO_2(g) + H_2O(l)$	$CO_2(g) + H_2O(l)$
$NaOH/Ca(OH)_2$	no reaction	$NH_3(g)$
Elements shown to be present	carbon hydrogen	carbon hydrogen nitrogen

Fig. 14.12

7 NATURAL POLYMERS

Like synthetic polymers, natural polymers are made mainly of the four elements carbon, hydrogen, oxygen and nitrogen. The element chlorine, a constituent of one of the most common synthetic polymers, PVC, is never found in natural polymers.

(A) STARCH

Starch is a polymer in which the repeating monomer unit is glucose. Its structure can be represented as:

$$\{O-\boxed{}-O-\boxed{}-O-\boxed{}-O\}_n$$

The formation of starch occurs in all green plants by the process of ***photosynthesis***. Photosynthesis results in the conversion of carbon dioxide and water into glucose and oxygen, aided by the catalytic action of chlorophyll and plant enzymes:

$$6CO_2(g) + 6H_2O(l) \rightarrow C_6H_{12}O_6(aq) + 6O_2(g)$$

carbon dioxide + water → glucose + oxygen.

Plants convert glucose to starch for storage within their seeds, many of which we use as food, e.g. wheat, maize, peas, beans, barley, etc.

The linking of glucose molecules involves the —OH group at each end of the monomer. A condensation polymerisation eliminates water and the starch polymer containing many thousands of glucose units is produced:

$$n\text{HO}-\boxed{}-\text{OH} \longrightarrow \{O\boxed{}-O\}_n + n\text{H}_2\text{O}$$

n monomers → a polymer of n monomers + water,

or

glucose ⟶ starch + water

$$nC_6H_{12}O_6 \longrightarrow (C_6H_{10}O_5)_n + nH_2O.$$

> Compare this definition with the definition of a hydrocarbon. The two are frequently mixed up.

Starch is a carbohydrate – it is a compound of the elements carbon, hydrogen and oxygen, in which the hydrogen and oxygen atoms are present in the same ratio as in water. The -hydrate part of the name indicates this fact.

Breakdown of starch – hydrolysis

(i) Hydrolysis of starch with an acid catalyst produces **glucose** as the only product. This reaction is the *reverse* of the process of starch formation:

$$(C_6H_{10}O_5)_n + nH_2O(l) \xrightarrow{acid} nC_6H_{12}O_6(aq)$$
$$\text{starch} + \text{water} \longrightarrow \text{glucose.}$$

(ii) Hydrolysis of starch by the enzymes amylase and ptyalin in saliva produces **maltose**, $C_{12}H_{22}O_{11}$:

$$2(C_6H_{10}O_5)_n + nH_2O(l) \xrightarrow{enzyme} nC_{12}H_{22}O_{11}(aq)$$
$$\text{starch} + \text{water} \longrightarrow \text{maltose.}$$

The maltose molecule is about twice the size of the glucose molecule. Evidently, acid catalysts work differently from the saliva enzyme in aiding the reaction of starch with water.

Starch hydrolysis in the laboratory

It is a simple matter to hydrolyse starch with the aid of acids or saliva. Two 10 cm³ samples of 1% starch solution are placed in separate boiling tubes. To one tube is added 1 cm³ of dilute hydrochloric acid. The contents are then boiled. To prevent the contents of this tube from boiling dry, a water-cooled condenser or a cold-finger is used to condense the steam formed back to water. To the other tube is added 1 cm³ of a saliva solution. This tube may be kept at room temperature, or at body temperature whilst the enzyme is working. It is easy to follow the progress of these reactions by detecting the change in the amount of starch remaining as time goes by.

> Blue colour

Starch solution gives a blue colour when mixed with iodine solution. So, the presence of starch in the mixtures can be tested at any time by removing a drop of solution from each test tube and mixing it with iodine solution. It will be found that the 'saliva' mixture gives no blue colour after a few minutes – all the starch has been hydrolysed. The enzyme in saliva is a very efficient catalyst for the hydrolysis of star Chapter By contrast, the starch will still be detectable in the 'acid' mixture for as long as half an hour.

It is also possible to follow the progress of the hydrolysis of starch by detecting the **products** of the reaction as they are formed. For this we need to test for the presence of simple sugars.

> Fehling's or Benedict's

Glucose and maltose can be detected by heating with Fehling's reagent or Benedict's reagent. These reagents are similar and give a change from a deep blue coloration to a yellowy-orange **precipitate**. The more sugar that is present, the greater the amount of precipitate and the quicker it is formed.

The products of these **hydrolysis** reactions are **hydrolysates**. The 'acid hydrolysate' is glucose. The 'saliva hydrolysate' is maltose. They can be separated and distinguished by chromatography.

(B) SEPARATION AND IDENTIFICATION OF SIMPLE SUGARS

The technique of chromatography can be used to **separate** different sugars, such as glucose and maltose, from one another. The method can also be used to **identify** a sugar.

A piece of chromatography paper is marked as in Fig. 14.13, using a pencil.

A drop of the enzyme hydrolysate (E) and a drop of the acid hydrolysate (A) are placed on separate marked spots. Drops of sugars thought to be present in the hydrolysates are also placed onto other marked spots. For starch hydrolysis these sugars are maltose (M) and glucose (G).

The chromatogram is 'run' by placing it into a closed container with a carefully measured volume of solvent in the bottom. The solvent must not cover the spots of sugars or these will dissolve off the paper rather than running up it. The solvent will be seen to move up the paper. When it reaches the top the chromatogram is removed and dried. At this stage the separated sugars are not visible on the paper.

The paper is next sprayed with a locating agent. On heating in an oven the position of the sugars on the paper become visible as coloured spots. The final chromatogram looks like this (Fig. 14.14):

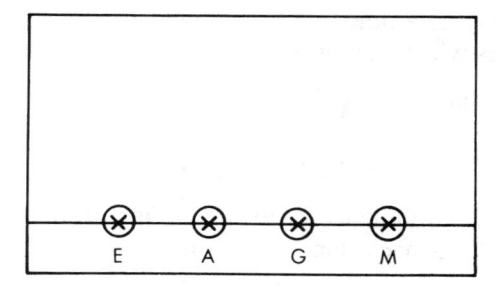

Fig. 14.13. Setting up a chromatogram.

Fig. 14.14 Chromatogram of sugars from starch hydrolysis.

Spots which are on the same *horizontal* level are from identical sugars. By this means we can see that the enzyme hydrolysate (E) contains **maltose but not glucose**, whereas the acid hydrolysate (A) contains **glucose but not maltose**.

(C) PROTEINS

Proteins are nitrogen-containing polymers found in plants and animals. Proteins are polymers of **amino acids**. There are about twenty naturally occurring amino acids.

Different amino acids can be represented as

$$H_2N - \boxed{} - CO_2H$$

Protein polymers contain several different amino acids and no part of the polymer repeats itself in a way that allows us to use the notation of n monomers making a polymer. A protein can be simply represented:

$$-[HN - \boxed{} - CO_2NH - \boxed{} - NHCO_2 - \boxed{} - CO_2NH - \boxed{} - NHCO]-$$

A 'simple' protein, such as the hormone insulin, contains 51 molecules, of 14 different amino acids, which illustrates the complexity of natural polymers.

A careful look at the structure of the protein molecule above will show that the **linkage** between amino acids is the same as that in nylon (a synthetic polyamide). The linkage is the amide or peptide linkage.

Breakdown of proteins – hydrolysis

Like starch, protein is broken down by hydrolysis into its constituent monomers – amino acids.

$$\text{protein} + \text{water} \xrightarrow{\text{acid}} \text{amino acids.}$$

The process of hydrolysing proteins is extremely slow with water alone. It is quicker using an acid as a catalyst. Boiling protein with dilute hydrochloric acid for several hours will hydrolyse much of it to its constituent amino acid monomers. These amino acids can be separated and identified by chromatography (see Section 7(B)).

The technique is the same as for sugars but a different solvent and locating agent are used.

Enzymes

Enzymes are biological catalysts and also proteins. In living organisms, there is often a different enzyme for each of the hundreds of chemical reactions that are taking place at any moment. An enzyme is a long, coiled molecule with an 'active site' where its chemical reactions take place. The active site accepts molecules that fit into it – as a key fits a lock. The molecule that fits is accepted onto the site, reacts, and is released.

The site becomes available to be used again. There are two ways in which the active site can be inactivated.

(i) If the site is damaged – as it is by heat – the catalysed reaction cannot occur e.g., as in fermentations using yeast enzymes at temperatures over 40°C.

(ii) If a 'foreign' molecule fits onto the site it competes with the normal process. Such molecules are called inhibitors. If the effect is to stop a vital process, poisoning is the result e.g. heavy metal toxicity. (Aspirin and Penicillin, however, have different effects.)

Aspirin When cells are damaged by injury, prostaglandins are produced. Aspirin acts by blocking the action of an enzyme which makes substances called **prostaglandins** which aggravate these symptoms. Thus

$$\text{cell damage} \xrightarrow{\text{enzyme}} \text{prostaglandins} \longrightarrow \text{inflammation}$$

ASPIRIN acts here

Penicillin acts to inhibit an enzyme in the final step which makes the bacterial cell wall. This prevents the bacterium multiplying.

(D) FATS

Fats are compounds formed by the reaction of fatty acids and glycerol. They usually contain one glycerol monomer linked to three fatty acid monomers, making a triglyceride. Fats are composed of **large molecules**. The linkages between the fatty acids and the glycerol are **ester** linkages, the same linkages as are present in Terylene.

A fat or oil can be simply represented as

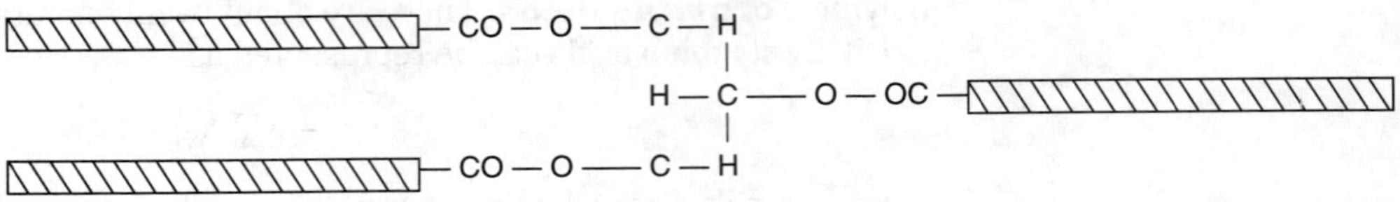

When reacted with a solution of sodium hydroxide, fats and oils **saponify**. That is, they are hydrolysed to soap and glycerine, e.g. beef tallow is glyceryl tristearate:

glyceryl tristearate + alkali → sodium stearate + glycerine.

The products of saponification of one molecule of glycerol tristearate:

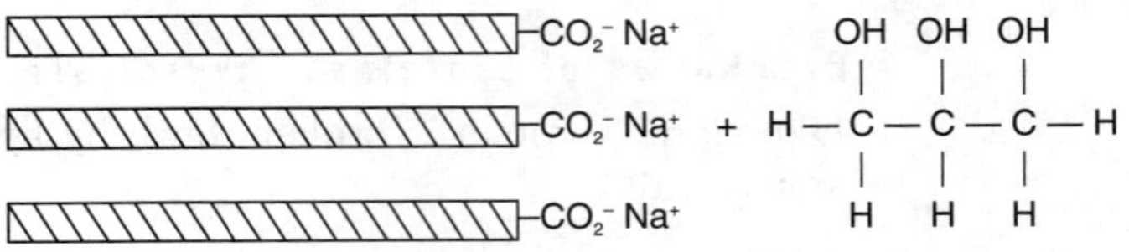

The fatty acids monomers in fats are saturated. That is, there are no carbon – carbon double bonds in them. Vegetable oils, on the other hand, have similar structures to fats but the fatty acid components are unsaturated. If these fatty acid monomers contain more than one carbon-carbon double bond they are polyunsaturates. They can each contain up to three such double bonds. The presence of unsaturated fatty acid parts in the oil lowers the melting point and ensures that oils are liquids at room temperature. Complete saturation of these oils using hydrogen gas – to saturate the carbon – carbon double bonds – results in a fat which is solid at room temperature. Partial hydrogenation gives soft fat/oil mixtures which are known as margarines of soft fat spreads.

Unsaturated oils are more chemically reactive then saturated fats. Oxidation produces fatty acids which alter the flavour, causing rancidity. This will also happen with saturated compounds, but more slowly.

(E) FOOD

Starch, protein and fat are necessary components of our everyday diet. Our diet must also include vitamins and minerals.

Fat
Carbohydrate } Energy-giving
Protein

Minerals } Body-building
Vitamins } needed to 'activate' enzymes

- **Carbohydrates** are oxidised in the body – respiration – to provide our main source of energy.
- **Protein** is used mainly for muscle body-building but excess is 'burnt' to provide energy. If the diet contains inadequate supplies of carbohydrate, muscular tissue will be used to supply the deficiency of energy.
- **Mineral** elements are necessary to combine with vitamins in order to make enzymes effective catalysts in the chemical reactions that occur in the body. Enzymes regulate these reactions so that normal metabolism occurs. This leads to a healthy body. Lack of vitamins and minerals causes some of these reactions to fail, leading to deficiency diseases, see below.

Vitamin	Source	Deficiency disease	Type	Stability
A	liver, eggs dairy-foods	reduced resistance to disease.	fat-soluble	stable to heat destroyed by air
D	'sunlight'	rickets.		stable to heat
C	fruit and vegetables	scurvy.	water-soluble	unstable to heat and air
B	cereals, milk offal, eggs	beri-beri, B_1, pelagra, anaemia, B_{12}		stable to heat

Vitamins, their sources, types and protective function

- **Vitamins** number more than a dozen. They are divided into water-soluble and fat-soluble types. Four of the major vitamins and their sources are shown above. A knowledge of the stability of vitamins to heat, oxygen in the air and to dissolving in water is important if vitamins are not to be lost in cooking and storage of food. For example, some vitamin C is lost from vegetables on cooking as it dissolves in the cooking water and also is destroyed by heat. Citrus fruit juices are preserved by treatment with sulphur dioxide. Sulphur dioxide removes oxygen from the juice, stopping destruction of the vitamin C by oxygen. Vitamin C itself can be used to preserve foods that are affected by air because it reacts so readily with oxygen. Fats, for example, go rancid in contact with air for long periods.

Detection and measurement of Vitamin C in foods

Vitamin C is easily deteced in food. It is water soluble and so may be detected in juices of fruit or vegetables. If an analysis of the total vitamin C content of the fruit or vegetable is required, a known mass of it must be macerated with water so that the vitamin has a chance to leave the cells and dissolve in water. Vitamin C decolourises the blue dye dichlorophenolindophenol (DCPIP).

The Vitamin C content of a fruit

(i) a solution of vitamin C of known concentration is made by dissolving a vitamin C tablet in a known volume of water and filtering. A **0.1% aqueous vitamin C** solution would be suitable. It will contain 1 mg/cm³ of vitamin C.

(ii) a **0.1% aqueous solution of DCPIP** is also made.

Calculating the Vitamin C content

(iii) 100g of fruit is liquidised and filtered to extract the vitamin C. Measure the volume of the extract. All the following steps must be done in the shortest possible time to avoid loss of vitamin C by enzyme reactions in the extract.

(iv) The volume of vitamin C solution required to just decolourise 2 cm³ of the DCPIP solution is determined. This is volume **A**.

(v) The volume of fruit extract to decolourise 2 cm³ of DCPIP is also determined. This is volume **B**.

Volume A contains A mg of vitamin C.
Volume B contains the same mass of vitamin C as volume A.

Therefore, the vitamin C content of 100g of the fruit is:

$$\frac{\text{volume of extracted juice} \times A}{B} \text{ mg of vitamin C}$$

(F) DETERGENTS

(a) Soaps

Soaps are sodium or potassium salts of long-chain fatty acids such as stearic acid ($C_{17}H_{35}CO_2H$), octadecanoic acid.

Preparation of a simple soap

Saponification is easily carried out as follows. Mix 2 cm³ of castor oil with about 10 cm³ of 5 M sodium hydroxide solution in an evaporating basin. Warm the mixture, with constant stirring, for fifteen minutes. During this time the oil will have been hydrolysed to its component fatty acids and glycerine. At this stage the soap is still mainly dissolved in the solution and must be precipitated. The addition of 10 cm³ of saturated sodium chloride solution, with stirring, will cause the solid soap to separate out as a crust on the mixture. The product is filtered off and washed free from alkali with distilled water.

The active particle in soaps is the ***ion***:

$$\boxed{\text{\\\\\\\\\\\\\\\\\\}}-CO_2^- \text{ the stearate ion is } C_{17}H_{35}CO_2^-$$

Sodium ions are 'spectator ions' in the activity of soaps. The complicated stearate ion (octadecanoate ion) is often more simply represented as

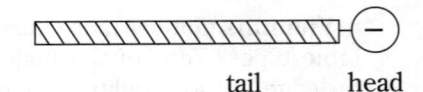

$$\boxed{\text{\\\\\\\\\\\\\\\\\\}}-\ominus$$
tail   head

It has a water-loving 'head', a carboxylate group CO_2^-. The 'tail' is a hydrocarbon chain $C_{17}H_{35}^+$ which is grease/oil-loving.

Detergent action

Soaps and detergents have the ability to reduce the surface tension of water and so to 'wet' surfaces and fabrics. that normally shed water. They are also able to emulsify oils and greases.

Emulsification is the process of aiding the dispersal of an oil in water or a water in oil.

Two types of emulsion are possible

- water droplets dispersed in a larger volume of oil – water-in-oil eg. cold creams.
- oil droplets dispersed in a larger volume of water – oil-in-water emulsion, e.g. salad cream, milk, many liquid medicines.

> An emulsion is a dipersal of an oil in water or water in an oil. The dispersed droplets are very small, containing only about a thousand molecules and so will pass through a filter paper.
> Emulsions are opaque and very often white like milk.

The process of emulsification converts oil or grease into minute droplets, each having many soap or detergent ions embedded in it. This happens when the oil-loving tail of the soap or detergent ion buries itself in the oil. The water-loving heads remain on the outside of the oil, giving the oil a negative charge. Agitation during the washing process dislodges the oil, as negatively charge droplets. These repel each other (like charges repel). In this way soaps and detergent **emulsify** oil and grease. The droplets are prevented from joining together again – they have been dispersed into the water as millions of minute droplets which are then easily rinsed away. It is often said that washing powders and liquids 'dissolve' grease. The process of dispersing the grease into minute droplets has much the same effect as dissolving but is strictly not the same process at all.

Oil Spill dispersal

We have all read of the devastating effects on wild-life of oil spills. Detergents are often used to disperse oil spills. The process is identical to that described above. But here, note, the correct terminology has entered common speech for we never talk of oil spills dissolving! The detergent again acts as an emulsifying agent.

(b) Synthetic detergents – syndets

Synthetic (soapless) detergents are sodium salts of long-chain sulphonic acids made by the reaction of sulphuric acid with hydrocarbons derived from crude oil.

A typical syndet has the formula $C_{18}H_{29}SO_3^-Na^+$. The syndet ion, $C_{18}H_{29}SO_3^-$, is the active detergent. It can be represented as (Fig. 14.15):

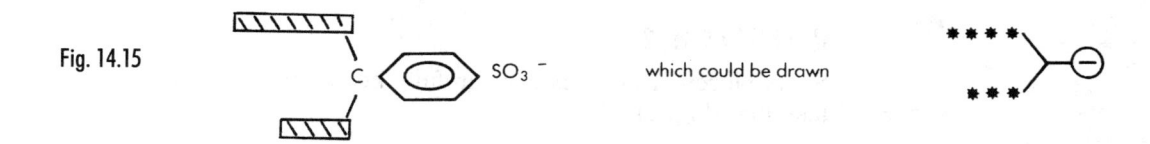

Fig. 14.15

The sulphonate group, SO_3^-, is water-loving and the hydrocarbon chain oil-loving. Syndet ions function in a similar way to soap ions in their washing action. Try to draw a diagram of a syndet emulsifying oil.

E-Numbers

Packaged food contains a number of chemical additives – some natural, some synthetic. The ones permitted by European Law are identified by E-numbers. Some examples are:

Acetic acid (Ethanoic acid)	– E 260	Permitted colours	E 100 – E 180
Ascorbic acid (vitamin C)	– E 300	Preservatives	E 200 – E 290
Carbon dioxide	– E 290	Antioxidants	E 300 – E 321
Calcium oxide (quicklime)	– E 529	Emulsifiers	
Bicarbonate of soda	– E 500	and others	E 322 – E 494
(sodium hydrogencarbonate)		Sweetners	E 420 – E 421
Sulphur dioxide	– E 220		

Medicine and drug development and testing

Many medicines are natural products or synthetic products that have been in use for a long time. Pharmaceutical chemists have found ways of improving on these products. Synthetic products are easier to obtain pure and are not subject to shortages for lack of raw materials. They are also usually more effective than natural medicines; because the cost of development would not be worthwhile if they were not. Drugs and medicines developed by large pharmaceutical companies are usually related to natural products that are known to have a curative effect. By skillful research, often aided by computer design programmes, promising compounds are recognised. They are then synthesised, purified and tested.

310 CHAPTER 14 THE ORGANIC CHEMISTRY OF LARGE MOLECULES

(i) First tests are on cells in flasks and test tubes – called *in vitro* screening from Latin vitrum – glass.
(ii) If the cell responses are favourable, the compounds are often tested on laboratory animals – called *in vivo* – Latin vivus – alive. Eventually, larger animals such as dogs and monkeys are used. The effect of the medicine on the animals metabolism is measured.
(iii) If the compound has no toxic effects it can be tested on healthy human volunteers – called *clinical trials* – from Greek clinikos – a bed.
(iv) Next it is tested on volunteer patients.
(v) Finally, if safe and effective in clinical trials the manufacturers obtain a licence to make and sell the product.
(vi) A follow-up period follows when the medicine is in use and its effects are recorded by doctors. If unwanted or hazardous side-effects are noted the medicine may have to be withdrawn – as happened to Thalidomide.

EXAMINATION QUESTIONS

MULTIPLE CHOICE

QUESTION 1

Which of the following is the main reason that plastics are a pollution problem?

A Plastics are organic compounds.
B Plastics are resistant to bacterial decay.
C Plastics do not react with acid.
D Plastics burn easily.

QUESTION 2

Some pieces of Perspex are carefully heated in a boiling tube connected to a cooled test tube (Fig. 14.16).

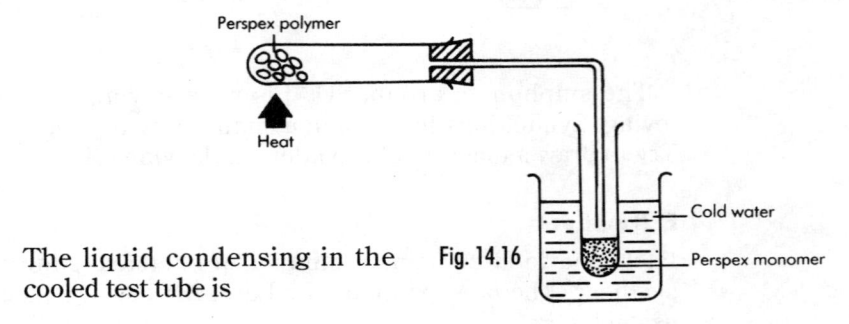

The liquid condensing in the cooled test tube is   Fig. 14.16

A liquid Perspex
B Perspex monomer
C Perspex polymer
D water

(SEG)

QUESTION 3

Which of the following types of chemical reaction occurs when poly(ethene) is formed from ethene?

A reduction
B oxidation
C neutralisation
D depolymerisation
E polymerisation

(ULEAC)

STRUCTURED QUESTIONS

QUESTION 4

The table below includes the structural formulae of some monomers and the polymers that can be made from them (Fig. 14.17).

(a) Which one of the monomers is a hydrocarbon? (1 line)   *(1 mark)*
(b) The molecular formula of propene is C_3H_6. Write the molecular formula of chloroethene. (1 line)   *(1 mark)*

Fig. 14.17

Monomer	Polymer
F\C=C/F, F/ \F tetrafluoroethene	[-C(F)(F)-C(F)(F)-]ₙ polytetrafluoroethene
H\C=C/Cl, H/ \H chloroethene	polychloroethene
CH₃\C=C/H, H/ \H propene	[-C(CH₃)(H)-C(H)(H)-]ₙ polypropene

(c) What similarity in structure exists in the three monomers? (1 line) (1 mark)

(d) What colour change would you see if propene gas was bubbled through a solution of bromine?
The solution changes from .... to .... (2 marks)

(e) Write the structural formula of polychloroethene in the table above. (2 marks)

(f) When polychloroethene is burned in an incinerator a gas is produced which is strongly acidic. If the gas is mixed with ammonia (NH₃), dense white fumes of ammonium chloride (NH₄Cl) are formed.
  (i) What is the gas present in the waste gases which is strongly acidic?
  (ii) Give **one** disadvantage of letting this acidic gas escape into the atmosphere.
  (iii) Name **two** other gases produced when polychloroethene is burned
  ....and ....(4 marks)

(g) Ethene (C₂H₄) can be polymerised under different conditions to form either low- or high-density polyethene. Both forms of polyethene can be easily moulded using heat and vacuum methods.
Low-density polyethene is cheaper to produce but it has a lower melting point and is less strong than high-density polyethene.
  (i) What is the usual industrial source of ethene? (1 line)
  (ii) In which form of polyethene are the chains of atoms more closely packed? Give a reason for your answer. (2 lines) (2 marks)

(h) Washing-up bowls used to be made of steel coated with paint. They are now often made of polyethene.
  (i) Suggest **two** reasons why polyethene is more suitable than painted steel for this purpose.
  (1) ....
  (2) ....
  (ii) Suggest a reason why high-density polyethene is more suitable than low-density polyethene for this purpose. (3 marks)

(i) The table below contains information about four materials in household refuse.

Material	Added to water
Polymers	float on water
iron	sinks in water
aluminium	sinks in water
paper	sinks when soaked

Assuming household refuse is a mixture only of polymers, paper, iron and aluminium, how could
  (i) iron be removed from the refuse (1 line)
  (ii) polymers be removed from the refuse? (1 line) (3 marks)

(j) It is impossible at present to separate polyethene from the mixture of polymers found in household refuse. Usually the mixture of polymers is melted and made into cheap block for lining walls.
  (i) What properties of polymers are important in making and using these blocks?
  Making the blocks ....

Using the blocks ....
(ii) What would be the economic advantage of being able to separate pure polyethene from household refuse? *(3 marks)*

(Nuffield)

QUESTION 5

The following is a list of the typical contents of a dustbin for a family of four in one week:

aluminium	0.55 kg
polythene/plastic	0.25 kg
waste food	4.50 kg
iron	1.30 kg
glass	1.75 kg
paper	4.15 kg

Much of the waste in this dustbin can be changed back into useful metal, glass or paper products if it is processed correctly. First, some of the parts of the rubbish must be separated from the rest.

(a) (i) Give **one** method which could be used to separate objects made of iron from domestic rubbish. (1 line) *(1 mark)*
(ii) Most scrap iron is converted into steel. What must be added to pure iron to change it into steel? (1 line) *(1 mark)*
(iii) Give one important use of steel and state a property of steel which makes it particularly suitable for this purpose.

Use: ....
(1 mark)

Property: ....
(1 mark)

(b) (i) Waste glass can be re-melted and used again. Give one problem which might be found when using empty bottles in this way. (3 lines) *(1 mark)*
(ii) Outline one other way in which the waste of glass containers can be avoided. (2 lines) *(1 mark)*
(c) (i) What percentage of the family's total waste is plastic? *(1 mark)*
(ii) Give one reason why plastic causes a serious pollution problem. *(1 mark)*
(iii) Plastic waste can be disposed of by burning it. Give one advantage and one drawback of this method.
Advantage: (2 lines) *(1 mark)*
Drawback: (2 lines) *(1 mark)*
(d) Explain why so many manufacturers use plastic packaging in spite of the pollution problems. *(3 marks)*

(SEG)

OUTLINE ANSWERS

MULTIPLE CHOICE

ANSWER 1

Plastics are certainly organic (carbon-containing) compounds, but that does not make them a pollution problem since, normally, organic compounds are easily decomposed by bacterial action. Bacteria cannot decompose plastics because they are not adapted to digest synthetic polymers, so dumped plastic waste can be unsightly and so an environmental pollution problem. B is therefore the correct answer (the key). It is true that plastics do not react with acids but acids are not used in rubbish dumps or present in the soil. Most plastics burn easily; burning them is one *solution* to the pollution problem, not a cause of it.

ANSWER 2

Heating Perspex will melt it, but attempts to boil it result in **decomposition** into the monomer. The liquid in the cooled tube will therefore be the liquid formed by condensing the **monomer vapour** – Perspex monomer. The key is B. No polymer vapour is possible and so no polymer liquid can condense. Molten polymer cannot escape from the heated tube either. Perspex polymer is a solid whereas the cooled tube contains a liquid. Water is not present in Perspex.

ANSWER 3

E. See Section 2 above.

2 STRUCTURED QUESTIONS

ANSWER 4

(a) Propene is a hydrocarbon. It contains only carbon and hydrogen.
(b) From the structure of the propene molecule we can see that it has three carbon atoms and six hydrogen atoms; its formula is therefore C_3H_6. Therefore the formula of chloroethene is C_2H_3Cl.
(c) They all have a **carbon—carbon double bond** in the molecule – the three monomers are all derived from alkenes.
(d) Propene gas is an **unsaturated hydrocarbon** similar to ethene. Its **C=C** reacts with bromine solution, which is red-brown, **decolorising** the solution.
(e) Polymers have structural formulae derived from the formula of the monomer by, first, **substituting** a C—C (single bond) in place of a C=C (double bond), then **placing a square bracket on either side of the formula, and finally** adding a single bond **to each end carbon atom as in the other polymer** formulae. The main point is that the double bond has been lost in the polymerisation process. (See Fig. 14.1)
(f) (i) Poly(chloroethene) is PVC. On burning, hydrogen chloride is produced which forms hydrochloric acid with water. Hydrochloric acid is a strong acid.
    (ii) As this gas escapes into the atmosphere it will eventually produce some acid rain. Acid rain corrodes metal and stonework and harms plant and animal life.
    (iii) Poly(chloroethene) molecules contain atoms of three elements. The carbon forms carbon dioxide on burning; the hydrogen forms water. The chlorine forms HCl as we have seen in (f)(i). Carbon monoxide is also formed.
(g) This is about the two forms of poly(ethene), see Section 4, LD and HD polythene.
    (i) Ethene is made by cracking petroleum products, e.g. naphtha.
    (ii) The high density of the HD form is caused by the closer packing of the molecules - more mass packed into the same volume.
(h) (i) Plastics generally are lighter than metals. They are also more easily moulded to shape and do not corrode as a painted steel one would if the paint became chipped.
    (ii) HD polythene is more rigid and stronger than LD polythene. It will resist the impact of cutlery better and will not soften as much with hot water.
(i) Concerns the materials in household refuse.
    (i) Iron is removed by magnets and
    (ii) polymers will float if the refuse is mixed with water (note that the paper will eventually sink as it soaks up water).
(j) (i) The blocks can be made easily because plastics can be melted to shape them. Also plastics are poor conductors of heat and so insulate the building from heat loss.
    (ii) Separation of pure polythene would allow recycling to make more **polythene** rather than less valuable 'plastic alloy' – made from mixtures of plastics – which has fewer uses. See Section 5(b) above.

ANSWER 5

The question is mainly about waste - how it originates, how it can be avoided and how it can be recycled.
(a) is about iron (normally steel) in waste. Iron must be separated before it can be recycled as scrap. These are questions about steel which can be answered by reading Chapter 12, Section 14(d).
(b) is about waste glass. This should be general knowledge. Empty bottles must be

separated into colourless and coloured glass before re-melting or colourless (clear) glass cannot be made from the scrap. Waste can be **avoided** by re-use of the intact bottles - as with milk bottles.

(c) is about plastic waste. The percentage of plastic is calculated by dividing the mass of polythene/plastic by the total mass of waste and then multiplying by 100. The answer is 2% – try it! Serious pollution from carelessly discarded plastic and the advantages and disadvantages of burning plastic are dealt with in Section 5.

(d) The use of plastics in packaging is given three marks -an indication of the need to mention three reasons. Think of why a piece of meat on sale might be covered with plastic rather than paper for instance.

STUDENT'S ANSWER – EXAMINER'S COMMENTS

A mixture of sucrose ($C_{12}H_{22}O_{11}$), water and yeast is placed in a conical flask and kept in a warm place for several days. Carbon dioxide is given off and a dilute solution of ethanol (C_2H_5OH) is formed in the flask.

The first stage of the process is the conversion of sucrose to a simpler sugar, glucose ($C_6H_{12}O_6$). This reaction can be represented by the equation

$$C_{12}H_{22}O_{11} + H_2O \rightarrow 2C_6H_{12}O_6$$

The second is the conversion of glucose to ethanol.

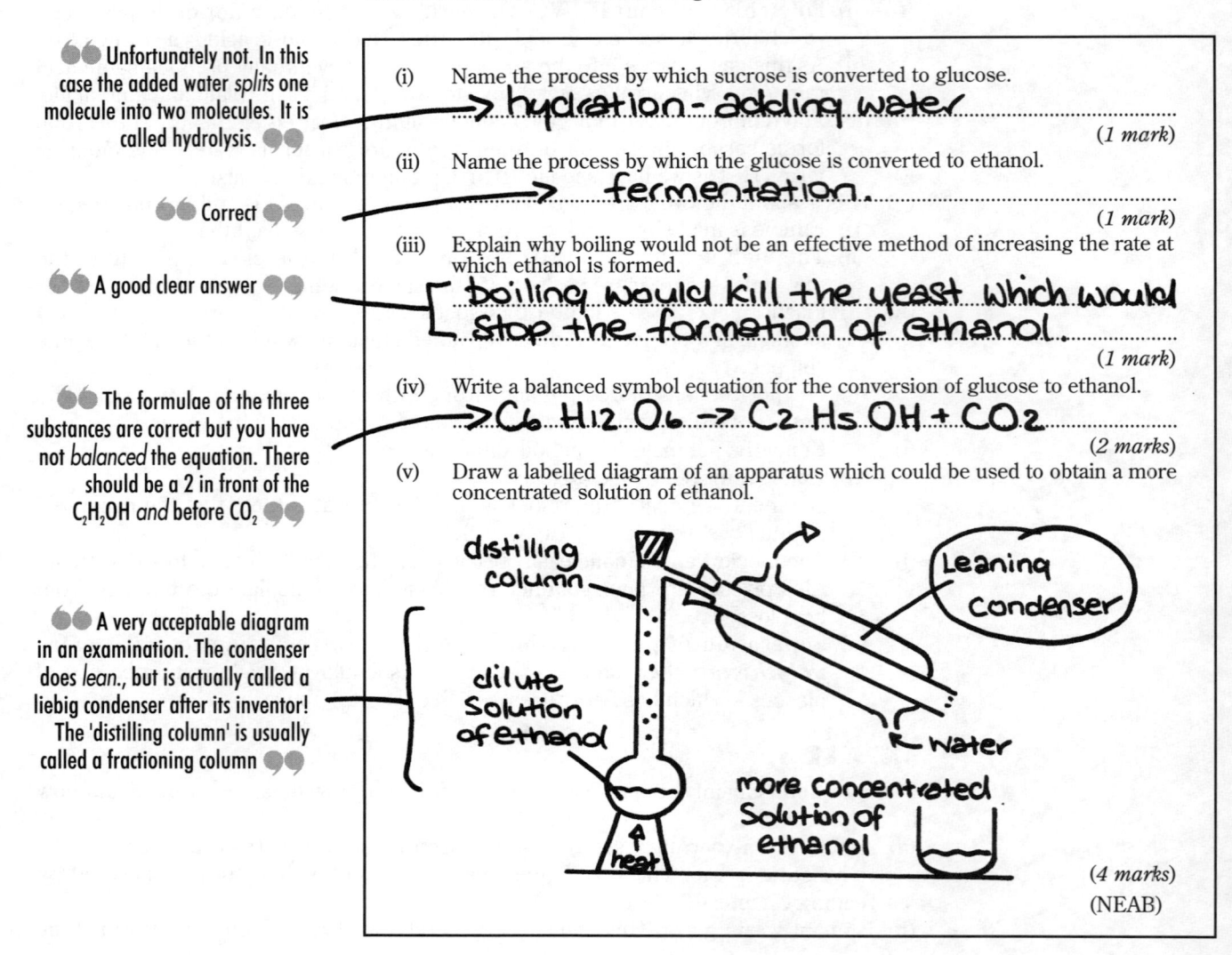

(i) Name the process by which sucrose is converted to glucose.

→ hydration - adding water

(1 mark)

❝ Unfortunately not. In this case the added water *splits* one molecule into two molecules. It is called hydrolysis. ❞

(ii) Name the process by which the glucose is converted to ethanol.

→ fermentation.

(1 mark)

❝ Correct ❞

(iii) Explain why boiling would not be an effective method of increasing the rate at which ethanol is formed.

boiling would kill the yeast which would stop the formation of ethanol.

(1 mark)

❝ A good clear answer ❞

(iv) Write a balanced symbol equation for the conversion of glucose to ethanol.

→ C6 H12 O6 → C2 H5 OH + CO2

(2 marks)

❝ The formulae of the three substances are correct but you have not *balanced* the equation. There should be a 2 in front of the C_2H_5OH and before CO_2 ❞

(v) Draw a labelled diagram of an apparatus which could be used to obtain a more concentrated solution of ethanol.

[Diagram labelled: distilling column; Leaning condenser; dilute solution of ethanol; water; more concentrated solution of ethanol; heat]

❝ A very acceptable diagram in an examination. The condenser does *lean*., but is actually called a liebig condenser after its inventor! The 'distilling column' is usually called a fractioning column ❞

(4 marks)
(NEAB)

REVIEW SHEET

- **Polymers** are _____
  _____

- **Monomers** are _____
  _____

- **Polymerisation** is _____
  _____

- Molecules that polymerise have to be capable of reacting with each other by one of two types of reaction _____ and _____

- Ethene and other molecules having the carbon-carbon double bond will polymerise by _____

- Monomers with **reactive groups at each end of the molecule** polymerise in a different way from those having carbon-carbon double bonds, namely by _____
  _____

- Complete the following table.

Monomer	Represented as	Reactive group of the end of the monomer
Glucose		
Terephthalic acid		
Ethylene glycol		
Diaminohexane		
Adipyl chloride		

- Briefly describe how nylon can be made _____
  _____
  _____
  _____
  _____
  _____

- List some of the properties and uses of nylon _____
  _____
  _____
  _____
  _____
  _____

- Polymers which soften on heating are called _____ plastics.
- _____ plastics cannot be melted once they are formed.
- List some of the important properties of plastic _____
  _____
  _____
  _____
  _____

- List some of the problems/disadvantages of using plastic _____
  _____
  _____
  _____
  _____

- Natural polymers are made mainly of which 3 elements? _____
  _____

- Describe briefly starch hydrolysis in a laboratory _____
  _____
  _____
  _____
  _____
  _____
  _____

- **Chromatography** can be used to _____
  _____

- Proteins are _____
- Proteins can be broken down by _____
  into their constituent monomers.
- When reacted with a solution of sodium hydroxide, fats and oils react to form _____
  _____

- Soaps are _____
- An emulsion is _____
- List 4 types of vitamin, the source of each vitamin and the disease which result from that vitamin deficiency

Vitamin	Source	Deficiency disease
1.		
2.		
3.		
4.		

CHAPTER 15

RADIOACTIVITY – NUCLEAR CHEMISTRY

TYPES OF RADIOACTIVITY
NUCLEAR EQUATIONS
NUCLEAR ENERGY
USES OF RADIOACTIVITY

GETTING STARTED

A chance discovery in 1896 by Henri Becquerel led to the idea of *radioactivity*. He found that a piece of photographic plate enclosed in some black paper and covered with crystals of a uranium salt became fogged just as if it had been exposed to light. This discovery could only be explained by assuming that the uranium salt was emitting particles that passed through the black paper.

Most people will have heard about radioactivity through either an accident with the reactor in Three Mile Island in America or the Chernobyl disaster in Russia

CHAPTER 15 RADIOACTIVITY–NUCLEAR CHEMISTRY

ESSENTIAL PRINCIPLES

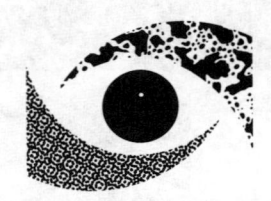

1 > TYPES OF RADIOACTIVITY

- **Alpha (α) particles** which are **helium nuclei**. These particles are easily stopped e.g. by paper.
- **Beta (β) particles** which are electrons. These are stopped by thin metal sheets. The particles that caused the fogging of the photographic plates in Becquerel's experiment must have been beta particles.
- We have seen that elements can be represented as $^{23}_{11}$Na. The bottom number, in this case 11, is the atomic number of sodium. It means that sodium has 11 protons in its nucleus. Since it is a sodium atom it must also contain 11 electrons. The top number of 23 is called the mass number and represents the number of protons and neutrons in the nucleus. The sodium atom therefore has 11 protons and 12 neutrons (23 - 11).

  Alpha particles can be represented as $^4_2$He^{2+} and beta particles as $^0_{-1}$e$^-$.

- **Gamma (γ) rays** are also sometimes emitted during radioactive decay. There is no change in mass number or atomic number when (γ) rays are emitted.
- **Radioisotopes** emit (α) or (β) particles or gamma rays from their **nuclei** to make them more stable. Some of these isotopes occur naturally, such as uranium-235 and carbon-14, and others are synthetic, such as plutonium-239 and iodine-128.

❝ Make sure you know the difference between mass number and atomic number ❞

2 > NUCLEAR EQUATIONS

When writing a nuclear equation the atomic numbers and mass numbers must balance.

Examples of natural radioactivity are:

(i) uranium-238 losing an alpha particle:

$$^{238}_{92}U \rightarrow {}^{234}_{90}Th + {}^4_2He,$$

(ii) carbon-14 losing a beta particle:

$$^{14}_{6}C \rightarrow {}^{14}_{7}N + {}^0_{-1}e^-$$

and examples of production of radioactive elements are:

(iii) nitrogen-14 being bombarded with alpha particles to produce oxygen-17 and a **proton**:

$$^4_2He + {}^{14}_{7}N \rightarrow {}^{17}_{8}O + {}^1_1H,$$

(iv) magnesium-24 bombarded by alpha particles to produce silicon-27 and a neutron:

$$^{24}_{12}Mg + {}^4_2He \rightarrow {}^{27}_{14}Si + {}^1_0n.$$

3 > NUCLEAR ENERGY

When radioactive atoms break down there is a release of energy in the form of heat and radiation. The energy given out is used in medical diagnosis and treatment.

(A) HALF LIFE

❝ Learn this definition ❞

❝ Do not confuse nuclear reactions with chemical reactions ❞

Each radioactive isotope has its own **half life. Half life is the time taken for the radioactivity of a substance to fall by half**. The half life is constant whatever the conditions. The rate at which particles are emitted from a nucleus is unaffected by temperature, concentration, light, catalysts or the compound of the radioactive isotope used. Half lives can be extremely small or extremely large or anything between.

(B) POLLUTION

Spent nuclear fuel is very radioactive and there is a large problem in disposing of this material. One method used is to surround the isotope with a large mass of concrete and dump it in the sea. One of the problems is the long half life of some of these isotopes and therefore it takes many years before the isotope is safe. Another problem is that gamma rays have a tremendous penetrating power and hence a large amount of concrete is needed to contain the radiation.

(C) NUCLEAR FISSION

Nuclear fission is when atoms split with the release of a large amount of energy.

It is not the same as radioactive decay. This is the principle of nuclear power stations when uranium-235 splits and releases a large amount of energy.

One of the fissions that occurs can be represented by:

$$^{235}_{92}U \rightarrow {}^{90}_{38}Sr + {}^{142}_{54}Xe + 3{}^{1}_{0}n.$$

> Calcium and strontium are both in Group II of the Periodic Table

Most of the isotopes produced by this fission emit beta particles. Strontium-90 is very dangerous because it can replace calcium in our bone structure.

Power generation

The energy from nuclear fission can be used to produce electrical power. The energy is used, however, in just the same way that heat energy from any other source is used in power generation – to heat water to create steam. The sequence of processes is as follows:

Source of heat energy
Nuclear
Coal
Natural gas $\rightarrow$ steam $\rightarrow$ turbine motion $\rightarrow$ electricity $\rightarrow$ national grid $\rightarrow$ point of use
Oil
Old tyres
Household waste

Disposal of fission products

The products of nuclear fission are radioactive elements of lower atomic number. Some of these products have short half-lives, others long half-lives. They are not allowed to enter the environment. They are kept under cooling water until the fierce initial radioactivity is gone before being separated into low-level and high level wastes.

(D) NUCLEAR FUSION

Nuclear fusion is the joining together of atoms with the release of a large amount of energy. This type of reaction is thought to occur on the sun to give us energy. Four hydrogen atoms combine to form helium and release a positron and energy:

$$4{}^{1}_{1}H \rightarrow {}^{4}_{2}He + 2{}^{0}_{1}e^+ + \text{energy}.$$

4. USES OF RADIOACTIVITY

Radioactivity is used either to trace pathways taken by chemicals or in radiotherapy. It is used to trace the uptake of fertilizers in plants or finding where there is a leak in a pipe or if there is a blockage in an artery or vein preventing the passage of blood. In radiotherapy, cobalt-60 is used to treat certain types of cancer.

You may have heard of carbon dating. This method uses the radioisotope carbon-14 which has a half life of 5736 years. Using this technique scientists have calculated the age of various carbon-containing substances such as materials found in the pyramids.

Rocks can also be dated by measurement of their remaining radioactivity. Since rocks tend to be very old, the long-lived radioactive isotopes, uranium – 235, (half-life 4.5 thousand million years) and potassium-40 (half life 1310 million years) are used for the very old or relatively young rocks respectively. (See Chapter 16).

EXAMINATION QUESTIONS

MULTIPLE CHOICE

QUESTION 1

The first nuclear reactors to be built depended on the fission of atoms of the less common form of uranium which can be represented by $^{235}_{92}U$. The more common form of uranium can be represented by $^{238}_{92}U$. These symbols show that the different forms of uranium have the:

A same number of neutrons but a different number of protons.
B same number of electrons but a different number of protons.
C same number of neutrons but a different number of electrons.
D same number of protons but a different number of electrons.
E same number of protons but a different number of neutrons.

QUESTION 2

Which one of the following is produced when radium ($^{226}_{88}$Ra) loses an alpha particle ($^{4}_{2}$He)?

A actinium ($^{226}_{89}$Ac)
B francium ($^{222}_{87}$Fr)
C lead ($^{210}_{82}$Pb)
D radon ($^{222}_{86}$Rn)

(SEG)

QUESTION 3

The most important reason for handling radioactive chemicals with care is that they

A decay to form compounds of lead.
B emit particles which are electrically charged.
C emit particles which make other substances radioactive.
D give off rays which can damage body tissues.

(SEG)

COMPLETION AND STRUCTURED QUESTIONS

QUESTION 4

(i) $^{40}_{19}$K is radioactive and gives $^{40}_{20}$Ca as a product.
Deduce the type of radioactivity emitted by potassium. (1 line)
(ii) The half life of $^{40}_{19}$K is 1×10^9 years. If 1 g of the isotope decays, what mass would be left after 2×10^9 years? (1 line)

(WJEC)

QUESTION 5

(a) Nuclear power stations have been producing electricity from radioactive elements for about 30 years.
   (i) Name one radioactive metal which is used in nuclear power stations after extracting it from ores found in the earth's crust. (1 line) *(1)*
   (ii) Name another metal from which nuclear power can be obtained and which is made in nuclear reactors. (1 line) *(1)*
   (iii) State one of the dangers which must be avoided in nuclear power stations and describe the precaution which is taken to avoid that danger. (4 lines) *(2)*
(b) The half life period of carbon-14 (^{14}C) is 5736 years. What does the term "half life" period mean? (2 lines)
(c) State two other sources of energy which do not depend on the burning of fuels or the use of radioisotopes and which can be used to make electricity.
   (i) First source ....
   (ii) Second source ....*(2)*

(Total 7)
(NEAB)

OUTLINE ANSWERS

MULTIPLE CHOICE

ANSWER 1

In Section 1 we saw that the bottom number is the atomic number, which is the number of protons in the nucleus, and the top number is the mass number, the number of protons and neutrons. Thus $^{235}_{92}$U contains 92 protons and 143 neutrons and $^{238}_{92}$U contains 92 protons and 146 neutrons. Hence they have the same number of protons but a different number of neutrons – answer E. These different forms of uranium are known as *isotopes*.

ANSWER 2

We looked at nuclear equations in Section 2. If an alpha particle is lost the mass number goes down by 4 units and the atomic number down by 2 units. The new element will have a mass number of 222 (226 minus 4) and an atomic number of 86 (88 minus 2) – answer D.

ANSWER 3

The answer is D, radioactive rays/particles can damage body tissues. This can cause cancer.

COMPLETION AND MULTIPLE CHOICE

ANSWER 4

(i) You should be able to work this answer out from the hints in question 2. The answer is a beta particle.

(ii) In Section 3(a) we saw a definition of half life in terms of count rate. It can also be defined as ***the time taken for the mass of radioactive atoms present to be reduced to half their initial mass.***

In 1×10^9 years the mass would be reduced to 0.5 g and in another 1×10^9 years the mass would reduce to 0.25 g which is the answer to this question.

You can see that the mass reduces by half its value every half life, and therefore after 3×10^9 years the mass of radioactive atoms left would be 0.125 g.

ANSWER 5

(a) See Section 3(c)
(b) See Section 3(a) or Answer 4(ii).
(c) (i) and (ii) See Chapter 2, Section 3(a).

STUDENT'S ANSWER – EXAMINER'S COMMENTS

(a) What is meant by the following statement?
There are three isotopes of oxygen: their mass numbers are 16, 17 and 18.

> Oxygen always has 8 protons in its nucleus. Mass number is the number of protons, plus the number of neutrons. Therefore isotope 16 has 8 neutrons, isotope 17 has 9 and isotope 18 has 10.

❝ Well answered. ❞

(3 marks)

(b) The half life of Bismuth 214 is 5 days.
(i) What is meant by the term 'half life'?

> Half life is the time taken for half the mass of the atom to decay.

❝ A 'loose' definition. It is the time taken for the radioactivity of a substance to fall by half. ❞

(2 marks)

(ii) What fraction of the original number of radioactive atoms will be left after 20 days?

> In 5 days there would be ½ left, after another 5 days ¼, then 5 more days ⅛ and after another 5 days there would be 1/16.

❝ Correct answer. ❞

(2 marks)

(c) What is an 'alpha particle'?

> helium nucleus.

(1 mark)

Bismuth has an atomic number of 83 and is in Group V of the Periodic Table. If Bismuth 214 decays by the loss of an alpha particle to form element x,

(i) What is the atomic mass of x?

> 214 − 4 = 210

(1 mark)

(ii) What is the atomic number of x?

> 83 − 2 = 81

(1 mark)

(iii) In which Group of the Periodic Table is x?
Explain your answer.

> Group III

❝ Give the reason. Elements are arranged in order of their atomic number, thus if two less, it must be two places to the left in the periodic table. ❞

(2 marks)

❝ Overall, quite well answered scoring 9/12. Do learn the definition of 'half life'. ❞

REVIEW SHEET

- Alpha (α) particles are _____ These particles are easily stopped e.g. by _____
- Beta (β) particles are electrons. These are stopped by _____
- There is no change in mass number or atomic number when _____
- rays are emitted. _____
- Some _____ occur naturally, such as uranium –235.
- In the expression $^{23}_{11}$Na, the bottom number is the _____ of sodium and the top number is the _____ of sodium.
- Complete the following nuclear equations.

> When writing a nuclear equation the atomic numbers and mass numbers must balance.
> Examples of natural radioactiity are:
> (i) uranium-238 losing an alpha particle:
> $^{238}_{92}$U → ☐ Th + ☐ He,
>
> (ii) carbon -14 losing a beta particle:
> $^{14}_{6}$C → ☐ N + ☐ e⁻
>
> and examples of production of radioactive elements are:
> (iii) nitrogen-14 being bombarded with alpha particles to produce oxygen-17 and a ***proton***
> $^{4}_{2}$He + ☐ N → ☐ O + ☐ H,
>
> (iv) magnesium-24 bombarded by alpha particles to produce silicon-27 and a neutron:
> $^{24}_{12}$Mg + ☐ He → ☐ Si + ☐ n.

- Half life is _____

- Nuclear fission is _____

- Nuclear fusion is _____

- List 3 uses of radioactivity

CHAPTER 16

EARTH AND ITS ATMOSPHERE

PROPERTIES OF THE EARTH

THE ATMOSPHERE

STRUCTURE OF THE EARTH

FORMATION OF ROCKS

ROCK TYPES AND THE ROCK CYCLE

THE AGE OF ROCKS

MINERALS AND ROCKS

SOIL FORMATION AND SOIL TYPE

PLATE TECTONICS

GETTING STARTED

The Earth as we know it today has evolved over a period of **four and a half thousand million years**. What has happened to the Earth in that time is still largely unknown, but a study of rocks (**geology**) has given many clues about the processes that have occurred and are still occurring in the evolution of the planet on which we live. This chapter is about the Earth and its atmosphere. We shall look at the Earth's origins and the changes that have occurred in it and that are still happening today.

Modern **plate tectonic** theory offers a satisfying explanation of the major changes that have occurred in the Earth's crust – both in the past and in the present. The theory explains the origin of **igneous**, **metamorphic** and **sedimentary rock** deposits; **volcano** and **earthquake activity, continental drift** and **ocean spreading, ocean ridge** and **ocean trench** formation as well as the more spectacular event of the **mountain building** which gave rise to the Himalayas and the Andes

CHAPTER 16 EARTH AND ITS ATMOSPHERE

ESSENTIAL PRINCIPLES

1 PROPERTIES OF THE EARTH

The Earth is a globe with a structure rather like an apple. Like an apple, the Earth is found to be made up of recognisable layers. A thin skin we call the crust, a central part we call the core and the layer in between we call the mantle. The rocks that we can see – that we use for building and as a source of chemicals, that have formed the soil on which we grow crops – are a very small part of the whole Earth.

The Earth is a sphere which is very slightly flattened at the poles. Fig. 16.1 shows a cross section through the centre of the Earth illustrating its layered structure.

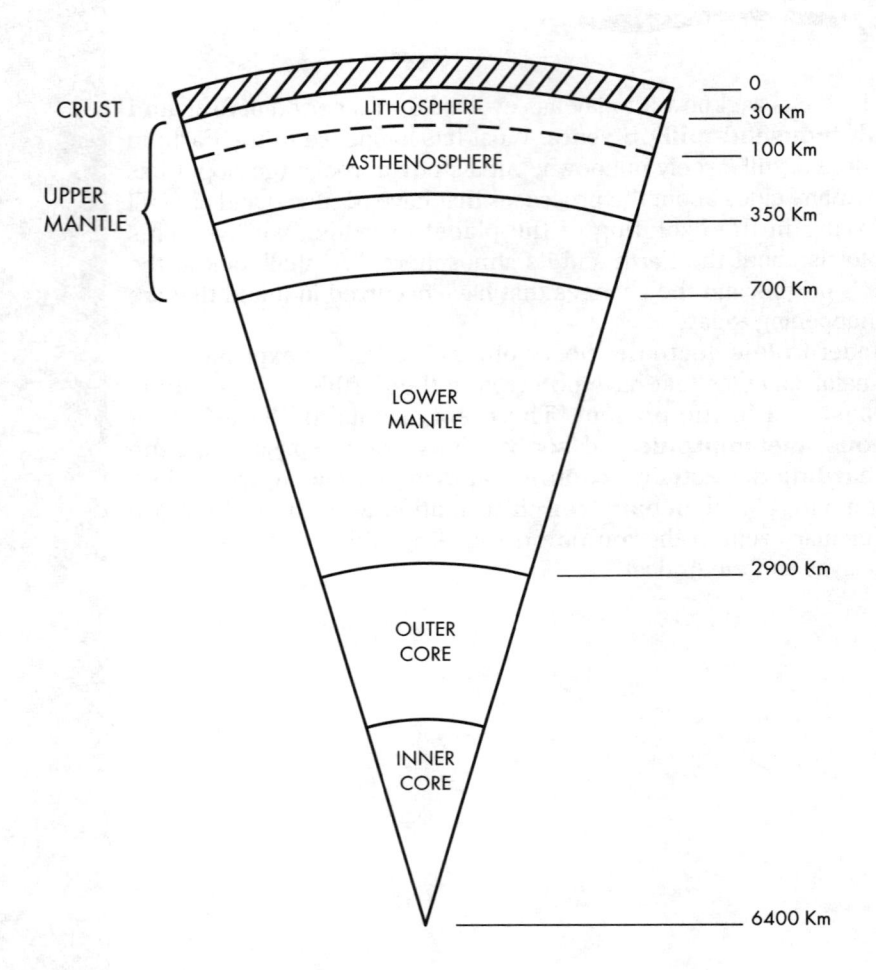

Fig. 16.1 A Section of the Earth showing its layers (in kilometres)

CRUST — LITHOSPHERE — 0, 30 Km
UPPER MANTLE — ASTHENOSPHERE — 100 Km, 350 Km, 700 Km
LOWER MANTLE — 2900 Km
OUTER CORE
INNER CORE — 6400 Km

Above the crust, sit the oceans and the atmosphere. The highest point of the crust is the top of mount Everest at about 9000 metres above sea level. The deepest part of the oceans is 11 000 metres below sea level. The thickness of the atmosphere cannot be so easily measured because there is no obvious upper boundary. However, most of the atmosphere is held in the lower 30 000 metres from the surface. The atmosphere (and the changes that go on in it) is of such importance in our daily lives that we shall look at this region first. Table 16.1 present some interesting facts about the earth.

Mass	6 000 million, million, million, million, grams	(M)
Volume	1 100 million, million, million, million, cm³	(V)
Density	5.5 grams per cubic centimetre	(D)

[the density (D) is $\frac{(M)}{(V)}$ the million, million, million, million, cancels leaving $\frac{6000}{1100} = 5.5$]

Its radius is about 6 400 kilometres
Its circumference around the Equator is about 40 000 kilometres
Its diameter pole-to-pole is about 20 kilometres shorter than its diameter across the equator
Total surface area 500 million square kilometres
Land area is 30% of the total surface area
Ocean area is 70% of the total surface area
Largest continent – Eurasia – 36% of the total land area
Largest Ocean – Pacific – 50% of the total ocean area
Highest point on land – top of Mt. Everest at 8848 metres above sea-level
Lowest point under the sea – bottom of the Marianas Trench, 11 033 metres below sea-level
Age of the Earth – about 4 600 million years
First solid crust – about 4 000 million years ago
First surface water – about 3 800 million years ago
First life on Earth – bacteria and blue/green algae about 3 000 million years ago
Oxygen appeared on Earth – about 2 000 million years ago
The first green algae appeared on Earth – about 1 000 million years ago
Animals appeared on Earth – about 1 000 million years ago
First land plants appeared – about 400 million year ago
Coal forests appreared 300 million years ago
Age of the Dinosaurs – about 200 million years ago
Flowers evolved – about 150 million years ago
Humans appeared on Earth – about 2 million years ago
The Earth is a great magnet. Its magnetic poles are close to the geographical N- and S- poles at present, but they have wandered about the globe in times past.

Table 16.1 Some interesting facts about the Earth

2 > THE ATMOSPHERE

The **atmosphere** is what we usually call the air. It makes up only a tiny fraction of the mass of the whole Earth – about one ten thousandth of one percent! Its composition is accurately known (Table 16.2) but changes slightly from place to place on the globe – largely because of variation in the water vapour composition.

Gaseous components in the present atmosphere	Percentage by volume
Nitrogen	79
Oxygen	20
Argon	0.9
Carbon dioxide	0.04
Water vapour	variable
Others ('pollutants')	variable

Table 16.2 Composition of the atmosphere

The composition of the atmosphere

The atmosphere of the Earth early in its development would have been very different from the present composition. Apart form CO_2, N_2 and water vapour, there would have been HCl, H_2S and probably CH_4 and NH_3 as well. Many of these would not have survived for long without reacting. **However, one gas that would certainly not have been present in the early atmosphere is oxygen gas.** Even so, there is evidence for the presence of oxygen gas as long ago as 2 000 million years in rocks of ironstones in which iron is in its most oxidised form, iron(III) oxide. This oxygen is believed to have been of biological origin.

3> STRUCTURE OF THE EARTH

COMPOSITION

The Earth's composition is not uniform. There are three main components.

1 The Earth's Crust (thickness 8–35 km)

The oldest rocks date back some 4 500 million years. As time went by, volcanic activity would have continually changed the appearance of the surface crust. Many cycles of mountain building and erosion may have occurred over this time. More recently – the past one thousand million years – change has been slower and the crust has taken on an appearance that we would recognise. There is clear evidence, however, that continents and oceans have been changing in size and shape even during this period.

The present continents and oceans are now believed to have formed from a single very large land mass called **Pangaea** which had formed about 275 million years ago and began to break up about 100 million years ago. Surrounding Pangaea was a single very large ocean. The break-up of Pangaea created the present-day continents and oceans although the process took some 50 million years.

The present crust is of two different types called **oceanic** and **continental**. Oceanic crust is formed below oceans and is relatively thin – only about 8 km deep. Continental crust is much deeper and is between 20 and 70 km thick. The differences are summarised in Table 16.3.

Layer	Average thickness in km	Density compared with water	Composition	Temperature	Age in millions of years
crust	Oceanic–8 Continental–35	Oceanic –3.0 Continental –2.7	solid basalt solid granite	10–600°C	200 3-500
mantle	2 900	3.5–5.5	semi-plastic rocky material	600–1200 °C	
outer core	} 3 400	10–12	liquid iron/nickel	} 3 000 °C	} 4 500
inner core		12–18	solid– mainly iron with some nickel		

Table 16.3 The Earths' layered structure

Rocks of the continental crust are granite and sedimentary rocks such as sandstones or shales. These are composed of oxides of silicon with aluminium and some iron in the form of silicates. They are low density rocks.

Rocks of the oceanic crust are the denser basalts made of oxides of silicon with iron and magnesium and smaller amounts of aluminium, sodium and potassium – all in the form of silicates. Oceanic crust rock is denser than continental crust rock. No oceanic crust older than 220 million years is known.

The whole crust of the Earth is itself very thin by comparison with the Earth as a whole. The crust is only one ninetieth the thickness of the inner part of the Earth at its thickest part – it is thickest over the land masses where mountains have arisen and thinnest where it has formed beneath oceans.

It is now widely accepted that the crust is made up of separate plates which are continuously growing by addition of new material from the mantle in a process called seafloor-spreading (see **plate tectonics**).

2 The Mantle (thickness 2 900 km)

Beneath the crust is the region called the **mantle**. The mantle material is subdivided by its strength into an upper layer (about 100 km thick) called the *lithosphere*, (rock-sphere). Beneath this is a 'weaker sphere' called the *asthenosphere* (about 250 km thick). This layer is easily deformed, having the consistency of warm tar. The Earth's crust floats and moves about on the upper mantle (asthenosphere). During volcanic eruptions the material of the mantle bursts through the crust to the surface. The release of pressure causes the mantle material to liquify and this fluid is called magma.

3 The Core (thickness 3 400 km)

The central part of the Earth is its **core**. This is the densest part – 12 to 18 times denser than the crust. It is believed to be composed mainly of iron and some nickel. The core contains an inner and an outer sphere.

- The outer part is liquid because of the high temperature and the lower pressure there.
- The inner part is solid because of the higher temperature and higher pressure – temperatures of 3 000°C plus may exist in this region.

(Unlike water, the melting points of most other substances increase with increase in pressure.)

Temperature and pressure inside the Earth

The temperature and pressure increase from surface to core. The source of heat is believed to be the radioactive decay of uranium, potassium and thorium isotopes contained in the material of the mantle. The pressure increase arises from the weight of material pressing on the inner layers.

Magnetic field of the Earth

The liquid outer core is possibly the source of the Earth's magnetic field. The exact cause is not known but it has been suggested that the motion of the fluid caused by the Earth's rotation might account for the observed magnetism.

The Earth's magnetic field has been recorded in solid rock whenever molten material reaches the surface and crystallises. By analysing rock from many places on earth and of many different ages, geologists have found that the magnetic field of the Earth has changed in intensity and in direction many times during its history. Magnetic field measurements (and other evidence) in Britain show that this country was situated in an equatorial region 200 million years ago!

EXPLORATION OF THE EARTH'S STRUCTURE BY EARTHQUAKE WAVES

The thickness of the three main layers of the Earth, see Fig 16.1, have been calculated from the measured speed of earthquake waves.

(i) Discovery of the core

Earthquake waves radiate from the centre (called the epicentre) of an earthquake and are detected at numerous places on the surface of the Earth. The way these waves bend as they spread out and are detected at points on the surface far away from the origin shows that they have been bent by reflection from the core of the planet. This was first noticed in 1906 by R. Olham. These wave measurements have also been used to measure the density of the core of the planet. The denser the material through which the waves pass, the higher their speed (See Table 16.3 above).

(ii) Discovery of the mantle

In 1909, an earthquake in Croatia produced records of unusual wave signals. Dr. A Mohorovicic, suggested that these indicated the presence of a boundary about 60 km beneath the crust. This boundary is now called the Mohorovicic discontinuity after its discoverer. The density of the mantle has been calculated from the measurement of the speed of waves in this layer in the same way as with the core. (Table 16.3)

THE ORIGIN OF THE EARTH

Radioactive dating of the oldest rocks of the Earth gives a date more than 3750 million years ago. Dates obtained for the rock of the moon and for rocky meteors which are not likely to have been molten, give ages of 4 500 million years. It is believed that all the planets and other bodies in our Solar System came into being at the same time. This gives the age of the Earth as 4 500 million years.

The structure of the Earth as worked out from earthquake wave measurements can be used to suggest possible origins of our planet. However, the evidence does not lead to a single conclusion.

CHAPTER 16 EARTH AND ITS ATMOSPHERE

>> Volcanoes. <<

>> Atmosphere. <<

>> Oxygen. <<

It is currently thought that the material from which the Solar System formed could have been dust and gas which became formed into planetary spheres. Larger bodies like our Earth underwent an internal heating process which first made them almost completely molten. Radioactive decay is believed to be responsible for the internal heat supply of the present Earth. This radiation would have been greater in the past but gravitational forces and frictional heating would have created much of the heat of the newly forming Earth. Gravitational forces would have carried the denser material to the centre of the Earth, leaving the lighter material towards the outside. A sphere of largely molten material would cool on the outside, forming first a surface crust. The matter inside the crust would continue to heat by radioactive decay and would expand, cracking the crust and thrusting molten material from the interior up through the cracks in the crust. These upthrusts would have been the first volcanoes. With the quantity of radioactive material inside the sphere decaying, heating would slow down but contraction of the outer cooling parts would still put pressure on the inner contents: volcanic action would continue. Further cooling would eventually cause the crust and mantle to become solid – as they are today. Volcanic activity today is caused by frictional heating at tectonic plate boundaries which melts the rock moving down into the mantle and causes local pressure increase which is relieved when the molten material breaks through to the surface. The vast quantities of gas – nitrogen, methane, carbon dioxide, sulphur compounds and water vapour – that would have been driven out of the once molten interior of the Earth were the beginnings of the atmosphere and oceans we have today (see the atmosphere). Eventually, cooling would allow rain to start the process of erosion. Surface water formation would follow and seas would begin to form. The proportion of oxygen has, of course, been increased, probably by ultraviolet decomposition of water vapour followed by photosynthesis in green plants. The proportion of carbon dioxide will have been decreased by the fast growth of plants and shelled sea creatures whose dead bodies have locked up great quantities of carbon dioxide in the form of limestone rock, coal and petroleum.

4 FORMATION OF ROCKS

The Earth's crust is 75% igneous, 20% metamorphic and 5% sedimentary rock. At the surface it is 75% igneous and 25% sedimentary rock. Fig. 16.2 presents an outline of rock formation.

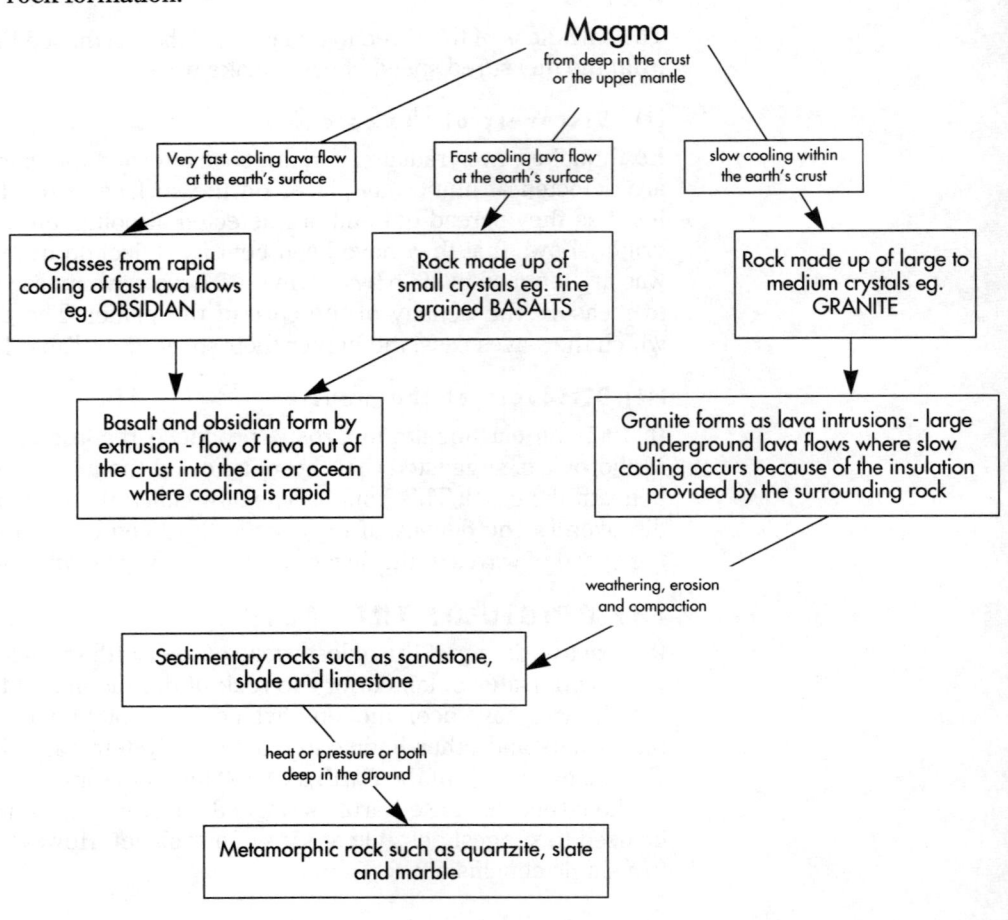

```
                        Magma
                  from deep in the crust
                   or the upper mantle
         ┌──────────────┼──────────────┐
  Very fast cooling   Fast cooling lava flow   slow cooling within
  lava flow at the    at the earth's surface   the earth's crust
  earth's surface
         ↓                    ↓                      ↓
  ┌─────────────┐      ┌─────────────┐        ┌─────────────┐
  │ Glasses from│      │ Rock made up│        │Rock made up │
  │rapid cooling│      │of small     │        │of large to  │
  │of fast lava │      │crystals eg. │        │medium       │
  │flows eg.    │      │fine grained │        │crystals eg. │
  │OBSIDIAN     │      │BASALTS      │        │GRANITE      │
  └─────────────┘      └─────────────┘        └─────────────┘
         ↓                    ↓                      ↓
  ┌────────────────────────────────┐     ┌───────────────────────┐
  │ Basalt and obsidian form by    │     │Granite forms as lava  │
  │ extrusion - flow of lava out of│     │intrusions - large     │
  │ the crust into the air or ocean│     │underground lava flows │
  │ where cooling is rapid         │     │where slow cooling     │
  │                                │     │occurs because of the  │
  │                                │     │insulation provided by │
  │                                │     │the surrounding rock   │
  └────────────────────────────────┘     └───────────────────────┘
                                             weathering, erosion
                                              and compaction
                           ┌──────────────────────────┐
                           │Sedimentary rocks such as │
                           │sandstone, shale and      │
                           │limestone                 │
                           └──────────────────────────┘
                                       ↓
                           heat or pressure or both
                              deep in the ground
                                       ↓
                           ┌──────────────────────────┐
                           │Metamorphic rock such as  │
                           │quartzite, slate and marble│
                           └──────────────────────────┘
```

Fig. 16.2 Mineral types in the Earth's rock formation

Molten material from the mantle is called **magma**. In the past, as now, this would have solidified, at the Earth's surface, into a hard rock called *basalt* – a dense form of igneous rock. The oceanic crust contains much basalt. Later the magma may have solidified into a different igneous rock called *granite* – which is not as dense as basalt. The continental crust is largely made of granite. Two other types of rock are common – *metamorphic* and *sedimentary*. These rock formations were not formed early in the Earth's history. Metamorphic rock is created when sedimentary rock is changed by the action of heat or heat and pressure. Thus, until the formation of sediments by weathering and erosion, metamorphic rock formation was not possible.

> *Metamorphic and sedimentary rock*

The igneous rocks would weather and erode and the fine particles they produced would enter the ocean and form sediments. Further sediments would originate from the remains of dead shelled sea-creatures whose shells are formed from calcium carbonate – a process that would have reduced the proportion of carbon dioxide in the atmosphere. These sediments would later become subjected to high pressure that would compact them into sedimentary rock. Sedimentary rock, if subjected to high temperature and/or high pressure, becomes transformed into metamorphic rock. The oldest rock known is metamorphic rock dated at 3750 million years ago.

The lower density granite would have floated on the denser underlayers. Rafts of granite would grow and move about on the plastic mantle layer (the asthenosphere). When these layers collided, large land masses would form lifted high by the growth of less dense rock on top of denser basalt and by the folding of sediments at the collision boundaries. The lower-lying land would fill with water, forming the oceans. Early land masses would break up by the continuing activity in the molten interior. This process of formation and breakup of continents and ocean beds has continued down to present times. The process of continuous change described here is now thought to have occurred by continuous movement and collision of floating crusts, called plates. This is discussed further in the section **plate tectonics**.

5 ROCK TYPES AND THE ROCK CYCLE

1 IGNEOUS ROCK (LATIN *IGNIS* = FIRE)

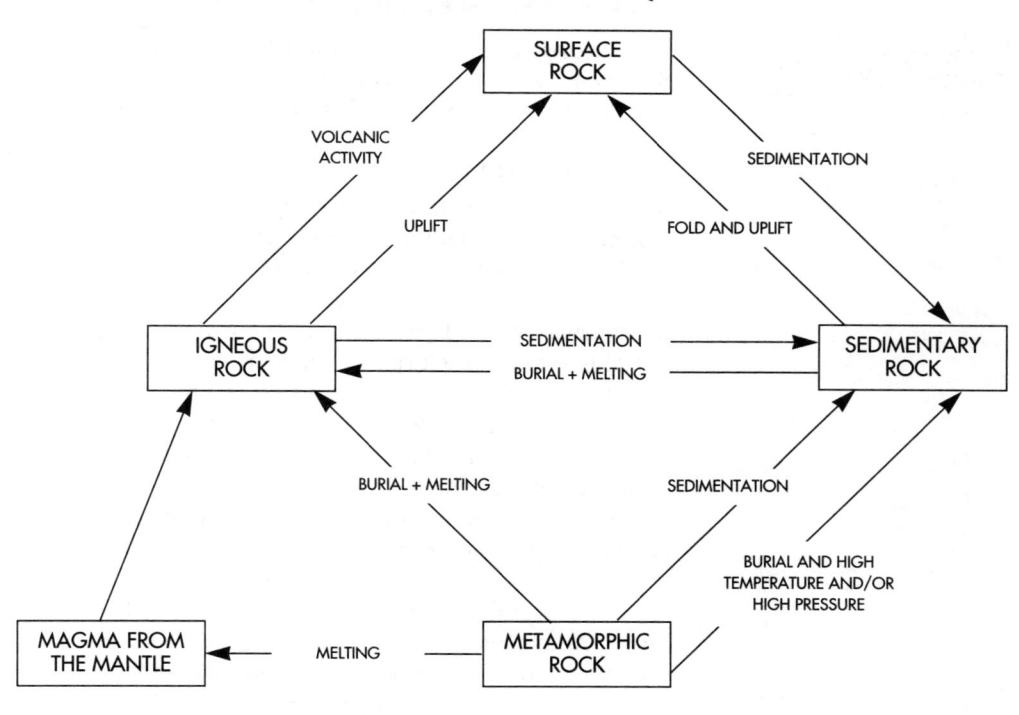

Fig. 16.3 The rock cycle

SEDIMENTATION = WEATHERING, EROSION, TRANSPORT AND DEPOSITION

They are of two main types of **igneous rock** associated with volcanic activity.

- **Extrusive** – formed by extrusion (pushing out) of magma through vents in the Earth's crust into the air or into the ocean. If cooling is rapid, crystals are small and the resulting rock is *basalt* (under the ocean) or *obsidian* (a glass) on land. *Pumice*, also land-formed, is solid volcanic froth with bubbles inside making it light enough to float on water.

- **Intrusive** – formed when magma from below the crust forces it way upwards into vertical fractures (forming *dikes*) or sideways between existing horizontal rock strata (forming *sills*). Where a hugh mass of magma makes a space for itself, a dome shaped mass forms on cooling: this is a *batholith*. Intrusions cool slowly, have large crystals and are granites.

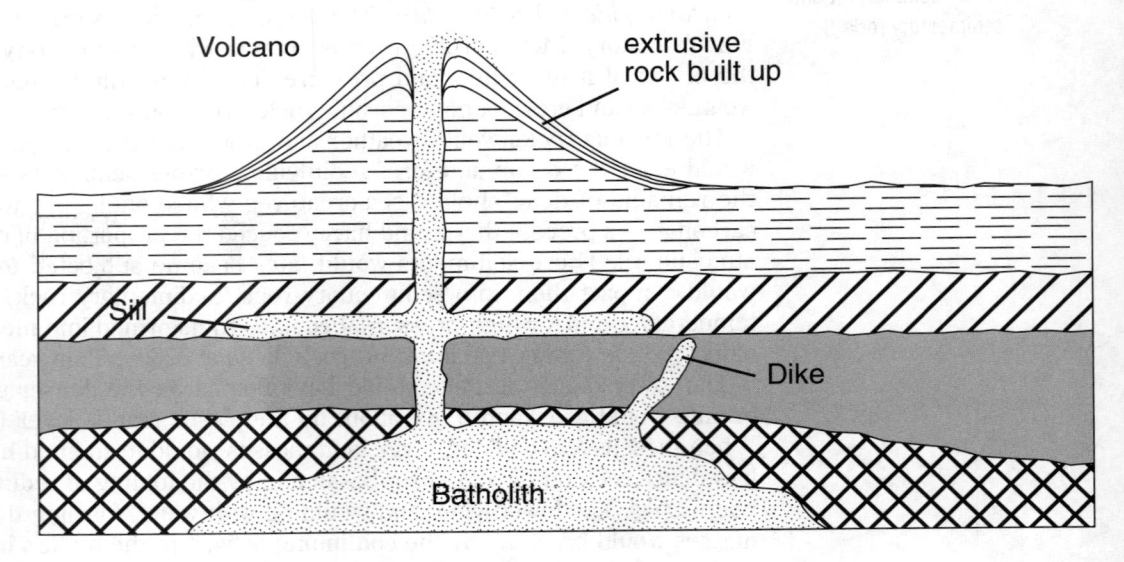

Fig. 16.4 A cross section through a volcanic region showing igneous rock formation

2 SEDIMENTS AND SEDIMENTARY ROCK (LATIN *SEDIMENTUM* – TO SIT)

Sedimentary rock is formed by compaction and cementation of sediments. Sediments are collections of small particles resulting from the erosion of weathered igneous rock or from depositis of dead shelled sea creatures.

(a) Weathering of rock

(i) *Chemical weathering – decomposition*

Igneous rock was the first type of rock formed in the Earth's crust. Because of the conditions under which it is formed, this type of rock is unstable under the conditions at the Earth's surface where temperature and pressure are much lower. Chemical weathering occurs largely due to the action of carbon dioxide dissolved in water. The unstable igneous rock reacts relatively easily with the acidic rain-water. Part of the rock dissolves and the remainder is weakened by the process and erodes more readily.

(ii) *Mechanical weathering – disintegration*

This is the result of a number of processes.

At low temperatures, cracks in the rock can fill with water which then freezes. On freezing, water expands and forces the rock apart. This eventually fragments the rock and exposes it to more rapid weathering by other processes.

It is possible that daily heating also fragments rock in a similar way.

Where weathered rock forms on slopes, the mineral grains are washed away rapidly, exposing more rock to the weathering process.

(iii) *Biological weathering – disintegration and decomposition*

The growth of roots of shrubs and trees in rock crevices is capable of forcing the rock apart, causing fracture and fragmentation. Further weathering occurs due to organic matter which produces acidic products which attack rock as described above.

(b) Erosion

Sediments form by erosion – wearing down – of weathered rock by moving water or ice, wind or waves. Unweathered rock – fresh igneous rock for example – is not easily eroded. The process of weathering softens igneous rock allowing fragments to be more readily swept clear by the eroding forces. The weathered particles eventually find their way into rivers, lakes and the sea.

(c) Transport of sediment

This is by water (river), wind or ice (glaciers). Whichever process has occurred, the fragments become sorted, en route, according to size. The largest particles settle out first and the finest particles last. If a river has deposited sediments in a large lake, for example, the coarsest bits of rock will be near the shore and the fine mud will be much further out, with sand in between.

When these sediments finally form rock, the rocks will be:

- conglomerate – coarse particles
- sandstone – sand particles
- shale or mudstone – very fine mud or clay particles

A similar 'assortment' is evident where all the sediment is forced to pile into a small area of deep water. Here the coarsest layer is on top and the finest at the bottom.

Quarrying for material to make concrete is usually done in such sedimentary rock sites. The coarse material produces gravel; finer material is used for concrete and sand is used to make mortar.

(d) Compaction and cementation

Sedimentary rock is formed when sediments are subject to high pressure compaction.

When thick piles of sediments are produced by erosion of weathered rock compaction under pressure occurs lower down in the pile due to the weight of material above. In time the sediment becomes cemented together forming a solid aggregate called sedimentary rock. The commonest cause of the cementation is via minerals deposited from solutions present in the layers. A feature of sedimentary rock is its layered structure. It is most often found on top of igneous and metamorphic rocks and may contain fossils.

(e) Sedimentary rocks not formed by weathering and erosion

Limestone, chalk, rock-salt and coal are sedimentary rocks. The formation of these sedimentary rocks is different from the process described above.

- **Limestone** is compacted sediment formed from the dead bodies of countless millions of shelled sea creatures. The internal structure of the body has long since decayed but the shell material remains and has become rock. Limestone is mainly calcium carbonate – the chemical of the shells.
- **Chalk** is a finer-grained rock than limestone but has the same calcium carbonate composition. The calcium carbonate that formed chalk arose from the remains of a tiny sea plant whose dead bodies form a white mud of almost pure calcium carbonate (calcite).
- **Rock-salt** has formed from a mixture of sediments with the salts deposited from evaporated sea-water. The process of compaction described above hardens the sediment into a rock.
- **Coal** began forming two hundred million years ago from plant and tree remains in swamp conditions. Such conditions slow down the natural decay of the organic material which eventually becomes covered in mud and sand. Compaction by pressure converts the soft deposits to harder coal; the mud and sand also become compacted, to mudstone and sandstone, and these sedimentary rocks are always found with coal deposits.

3 METAMORPHIC ROCK
(GREEK – *META* = AFTER, *MORPHE* = FORM)

Metamorphic rock forms from sedimentary rock under any of the following conditions:

- the rock is close to a high temperature granite intrusion. The heat from the instrusion changes the form of the sedimentary rock e.g. limestone into marble, sandstone into quartzite.
- the rock is subject to high pressure. This occurs when shale becomes converted into slate.
- the rock is subject to high pressure and high temperature. Shale becomes *schist* in such a process and *gneiss* (pronounced 'nice') is formed in a similar manner.

The formation of all types of rock other than those formed by extrusion of lava from volcanoes has taken many tens of millions of years (see **plate tectonics** below).

6 > THE AGE OF ROCKS

(a) Radioactive decay

The age of rock can be estimated with reasonable accuracy from a knowledge of the rate of decay of its radioactive components. The technical details are beyond the scope of this chapter, but in principle, any radioactive element found in rock will have been decaying since the rock formed. If the decay products and the remaining radioactive element are both collected, it is possible to calculate how long the element has been in the rock, ie. the age of the rock.

Every radioactive element has a known half-life. The half-life is the period of time in which the mass of that element drops to one half of its original mass. For example suppose analysis of a rock shows it to contain, say, 1 gram of a radioactive element. Also suppose that analysis of the products formed by decay of this element shows that there must originally have been 2 grams present. Then half of the original mass of the element has decayed over the age of the rock. If the half-life of the element is known to be, for example, 4 000 million years, (e.g. uranium –238) then that rock would be 4 000 million years old. All rocks contain radioactive material and so can be aged.

(b) The fossil record

Fossils are the petrified (made into rock) remains of animals and plants preserved in sediments at the time of their death. Rock containing the same fossils can reasonably be regarded as being of the same age or in the same age-range. Also, if particular fossils are found in widely separated parts of the world, then either the living organism must have been widely distributed or else the separated parts of the globe were at one time joined together. Fossil evidence of this sort supports the theory of continental drift.

(c) Magnetic field

Reversals of the magnetic field of the Earth can be used to date rocks. Since the dates of magnetic reversals are known, the sequence of these found in the oceanic rocks formed outwards from a spreading centre at a mid-ocean ridge has been used to date the oceanic crust. The oldest such crust is 165 million years.

7 > MINERALS AND ROCKS

- A **mineral** is a naturally formed substance of definite composition.
- A **rock** is a naturally formed, non-living, aggregate of minerals.

INDENTIFYING MINERALS AND ROCKS

Minerals and rocks often differ in colour, hardness and size of the crystals in the rock. The commonest tools for identifying minerals and rocks are therefore a hand lens – to examine the crystals – a pen-knife to scratch the sample and, of course, the naked eye to assess the results.

These variables can be incorporated into **keys** to identify different minerals or rocks.

Identifying minerals

An example of a key for identifying **minerals** is given in Fig. 16.5.

The identification of minerals is based on three different properties of rocks.

(i) That rocks differ in hardness. Attempting to scratch a rock with a knife will distinguish some rocks from others. (Some very soft rocks can be scratched by a fingernail – giving a further test of identity)

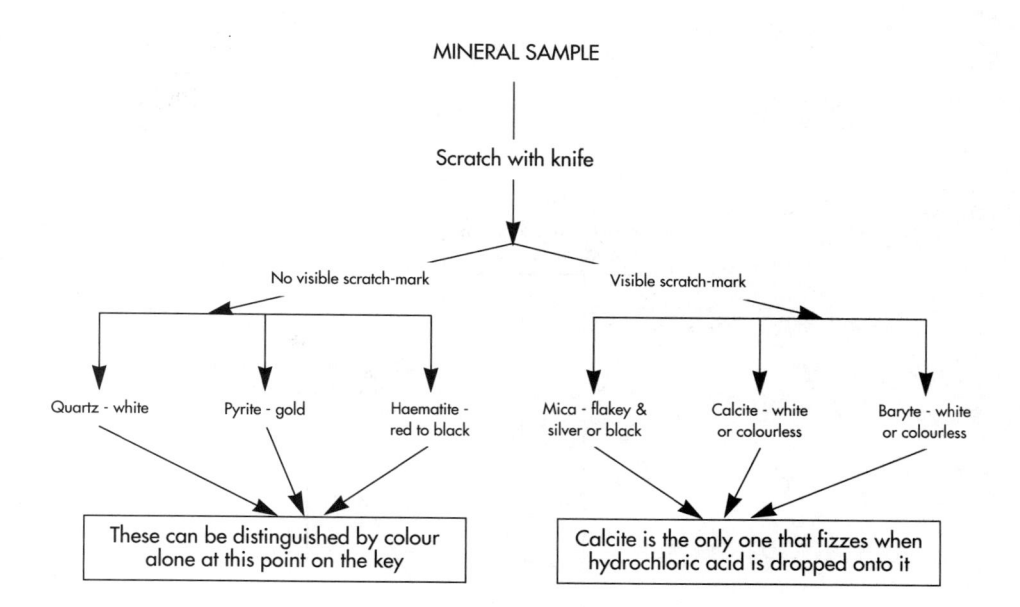

```
                        MINERAL SAMPLE
                              |
                       Scratch with knife
                              |
           ┌──────────────────┴──────────────────┐
     No visible scratch-mark              Visible scratch-mark
     ┌────────┼────────┐              ┌────────┼────────┐
     ↓        ↓        ↓              ↓        ↓        ↓
  Quartz   Pyrite   Haematite      Mica -    Calcite -  Baryte -
  - white  - gold   - red to       flakey &  white or   white or
                    black          silver    colourless colourless
                                   or black

  ┌─────────────────────────────┐   ┌─────────────────────────────┐
  │ These can be distinguished  │   │ Calcite is the only one that│
  │ by colour alone at this     │   │ fizzes when hydrochloric    │
  │ point on the key            │   │ acid is dropped onto it     │
  └─────────────────────────────┘   └─────────────────────────────┘
```

Fig. 16.5 Identity for minerals

(ii) Rocks have many different colours.

(iii) Carbonate rocks react with dilute hydrochloric acid. They fizz, giving off **carbon dioxide**.

Identification of Rocks

Rock types are identified by the key, in Fig. 16.6. This is based on the appeareance and scratch-hardness of the rock. Some of the identifying features are:

(i) That fossils must have formed in sediments and so can only exist in sedimentary or metamorphic rock. Sediments can have sand grains which will be a visible feature, e.g. sandstone.

(ii) Sedimentary rock that has been metamorphised is likely to show the original layers and be of one type of mineral.

(iii) Igneous rock has been formed from molten mixtures of materials and so is likely to form a mixture of several different types of mineral crystals on solidifying. Some lavas are glass-like solids.

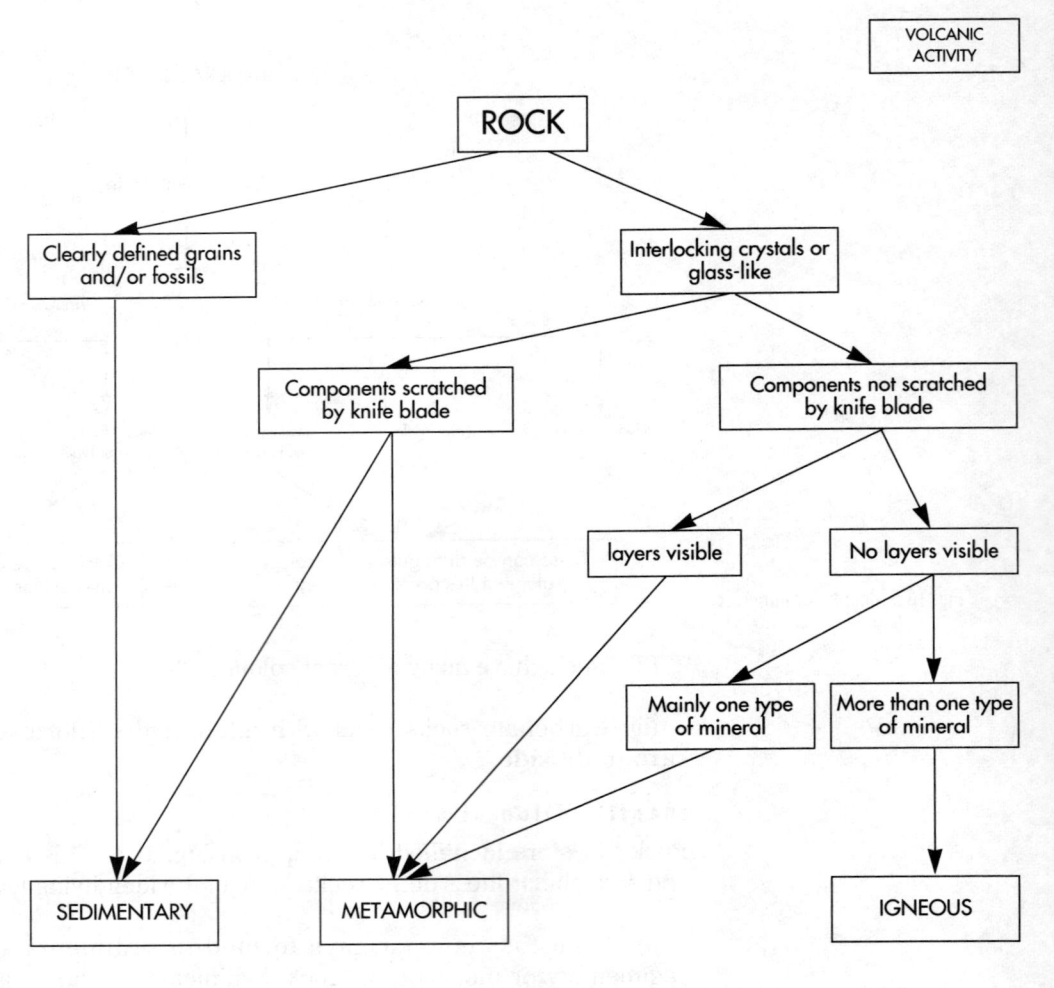

Fig. 16.6 Key for identifying rock types

```
                              VOLCANIC
                              ACTIVITY

                    ROCK
                   /    \
       Clearly defined   Interlocking crystals or
       grains and/or     glass-like
       fossils
          |              /        \
          |    Components     Components not
          |    scratched by   scratched by
          |    knife blade    knife blade
          |        |          /        \
          |        |    layers    No layers
          |        |    visible   visible
          |        |       |         \
          |        |   Mainly one    More than one
          |        |   type of       type of
          |        |   mineral       mineral
          ↓        ↓       ↓            ↓
     SEDIMENTARY  METAMORPHIC         IGNEOUS
```

Some details of the appearance of rocks and their type can be found in Table 16.4.

Rock Type Examples	Rock Type	Mineral Content	Visible Characteristics
granite	igneous	quartz, feldspar and mica	Random interlocking crystals – crystal size depends on cooling rate, see Rock Cycle.
sandstone limestone	sedimentary	quartz, haematite. calcite	Layered structure. Many contain fossils.
marble	metamorphic	calcite	Bands of interlocking crystals

Table 16.4 Common rocks and their type

8 > SOIL FORMATION AND SOIL TYPE

The weathering process which produces the material for the formation of sediments also produces soils. Fine clay, sand(silica) and organic matter in varous proportions is called **soil**.

The organic matter in soil derives from the bacterial decay of plant material. It is often refered to as humus. Plants grow in soils by utilizing the nutrients from the decaying organic material and from the minerals which they take up, in solution, through their roots. The nature of the underlying rock will mostly dictate the soil type. (See Table 16.5).

Soil type	underlying rock	appearance	feel	characteristics
sandy soil	sandstone and/or granite	grey to brown	Gritty. Will not hold together in a ball, even when wet.	Fail to retain moisture, poor in nutrients.
loam (clay +sandy)	shale, sandstone	grey to brown	Holds together in a ball when wet but is not sticky.	Ideal texture and nutrient-rich.
clay soil	shale	grey to brown	Sticky and holds together in a ball when wet.	Nutrient rich but waterlogs easily.

Table 16.5 Soil types and mineral content

Minerals in solution result from the weathering of rocks by physical and chemical processes. The carbon dioxide in soil – largely produced by the respiration of soil animals and bacteria – when dissolved in soil moisture, forms an acidic solution. This is capable of chemically decomposing some of the minerals in rocks, releasing a mineral solution which is used in plant growth.

The organic matter supplies much of the essential nitrogenous matter. The minerals supply most of the phosphorus, potassium and trace elements required for healthy plant growth. So plants extract most of the elements they need from minerals in the soil and, at death and decay, return those elements to the soil in the form of humus which recycles plant nutrients. The longer plants have been growing and decaying in soil, the richer in nutrients the soil is likely to be. Plants make their own fertiliser!

Soil profile

Soil begins as weathered rock or sediment of a more or less fine texture. This is an *immature soil*. The soil type is determined by this sediment (See Table 16.5 above).

Rain water is acidic enough to dissolve small amounts of minerals from the sediments and plant life invades the immature soil. As plants die, their remains become organic matter or humus. As the mass of humus builds up, the soil water extracts acids from the humus which dissolve more mineral nutrients from the rock fragments. Plants attract small animals and the presence of plants and animals further enriches the soil with organic matter; living organisms also 'work' the soil, mixing its components and incorporating more of the sub soil. Over a period of thousands of years the soil develops into a *mature soil* (see Fig. 16.7).

Soil X-section	Horizon	Layer name	Content
	'A'	TOPSOIL	Fine mineral and organic matter - dark colour. Animal and plant life abundant.
	'B'	SUBSOIL	Rock fragments and fine clay. Compacted with little air. Often waterlogged.
	'C'	BEDROCK	Solid rock in the process of weathering and becoming subsoil.

Fig. 16.7 Profile of a mature soil

Soil erosion

Erosion occurs when soil is removed from the place of its origin by wind or water. It happens when the soil is deprived of the plant cover which holds the soil in place by root penetration. Soils are most vulnerable to wind erosion when the existing vegetation has been removed by ploughing, leaving bare soil. In very dry conditions, wind can strip huge areas of agricultural land of all the top soil in a very short time. This has happened in this century on a large scale in the Western USA and in Australia. In African countries bordering on the Sahara desert, overgrazing by cattle can leave the land vulnerable to erosion by wind and flash floods. Water can often remove soil down to the bedrock.

Prevention of soil erosion depends upon good farming practice. In dry countries, soil should not be left without vegetation cover. Grassland can be ploughed in strips which alternate with grass cover reducing the chance of total soil loss. Shelter belts can reduce wind erosion. Terracing of steep slopes stops water washing soil down gradients.

9 > PLATE TECTONICS

CONTINENTAL DRIFT

It is believed that 200 million years ago, there was a single large supercontinent surrounded by sea (Fig. 16.8a). This land-mass is called **Pangaea** ('all lands'). When this land-mass broke up the parts separated into what we see as the present continents (Fig. 16.8b). The break-up and separation of the fragmented supercontinent is thought to have occurred by a process known as **continental drift**.

Fig. 16.8(a) The major continents 200 million years ago – Pangaea. Key: White area is the position of ancient ice cover. Shaded areas show the overlap of present-day land shapes used in this construction

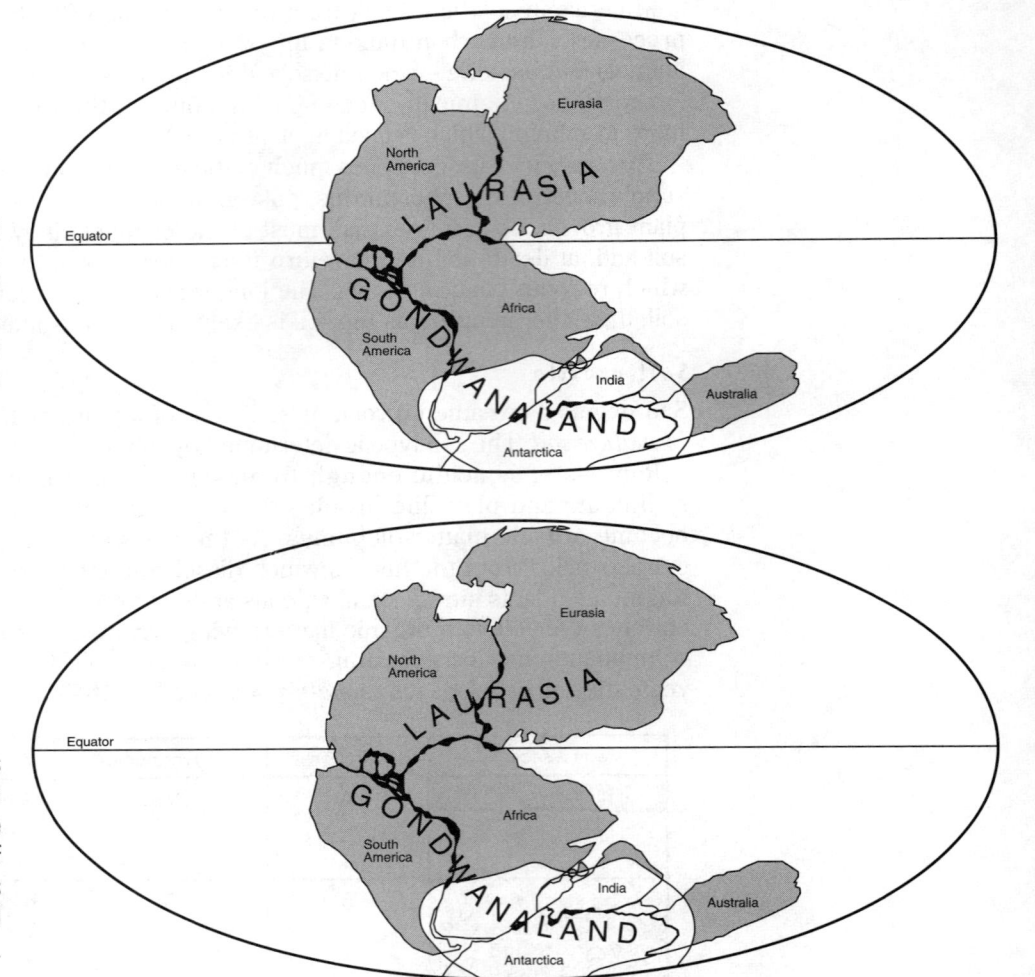

Fig. 16.8 (b) Present-day continents – the result of continental drift from the original Pangaea. Key: White areas show the ice covered areas of ancient Pangaea. Continent outlines show position of the continental shelf.

The evidence for continental drift is in several parts:

(i) The shape of the present-day continents, especially South America and Africa, is distinctive enough to have prompted the idea that the two were once joined together.

(ii) Fossils found in Africa are also found in parts of the world very far away – in S. America, India and Australia in fact. The fossil remains of Glossopteris is found in all the southern continents now separated by ocean. Fossils of the small freshwater reptile Mesosaurus are found in South Brazil and South Africa. It seems unlikely that a freshwater reptile could have made its way across an ocean!

(iii) The magnetic record stored in rock as it solidified shows that all the southern continents were located close together about 150–200 million years ago

(iv) Sedimentary deposits of glacial origin are found in many southern continents. They were formed at about the time the present continents are thought, from the evidence in (i)–(iii) above, to have been joined. This leads to the suggestion that these parts were covered by the same ice sheet and so were part of the same land mass. This evidence brings Antarctica and Australia into the proposed ancient supercontinent.

That continental drift was possible is explained by the modern theory of **plate tectonics**. If we were able to run the geological record backwards over 200 million years, we believe we would find the present continents moving in reverse to their positions when they were joined in one supercontinent – Pangaea. The fit is only approximate at the coastal boundaries but is better at the continental shelf boundaries, (see Fig. 16.8a above).

PLATE TECTONIC THEORY (GREEK – *TECTON* – A BUILDER)

The theory assumes that the present Earth's crust consists of six large and several smaller **plates**. The **crustal plates** are of lower density than the mantle and so float on it. It helps to visualise this situation to think of the whole crust as if it were a sheet of ice covering the surface but broken into six large and several small, irregular, sheets.

The map, Fig. 16.9, shows these plates and their direction of movement. The position of these plates is deduced from the volcanic and earthquake activity where plates meet the plate margins.

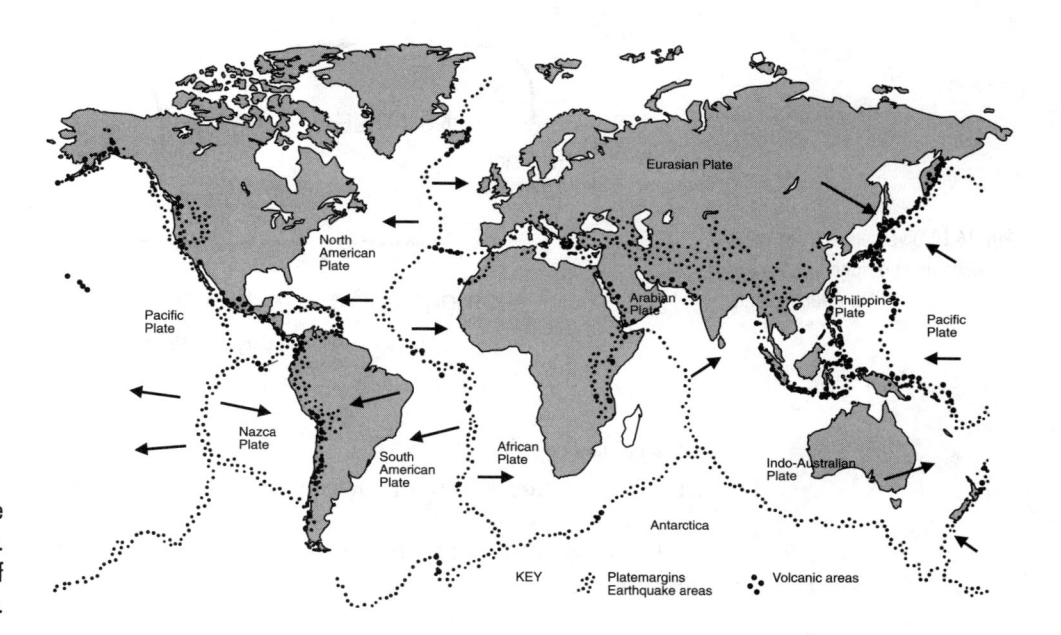

Fig. 16.9 The major plates of the Earth showing active plate margins. Key: arrows indicate direction of movement of the plates.

Plate movement is only a few centimetres a year but can now be measured from satellites by laser beams. The present continents and the surface features such as mountains and volcanoes are believed to be the result of movement of these plates over many millions of years.

The theory of plate tectonics therefore explains continental drift. It also explains more observable phenomena such as volcanic and earthquake activity, sea-floor spreading and crustal structures – in a single unifying theory.

The Plate Tectonics theory states that:

(a) the surface of the Earth is covered by a series of thin, rigid plates. Total surface area of these plates is believed to be constant, which means that if some crust is destroyed in one place an equal area must be formed elsewhere. The rigidity of plates means that deformation – as occurs in mountain building – must occur at the plate margins. Plate motion is believed to be driven by convection currents in the magma, see Fig. 16.10.

(b) the plates are always in motion.

(c) at the plate margins, the movement causes **volcanic** and **earthquake** activity and sometimes **mountain building** and **oceanic trench formation**.

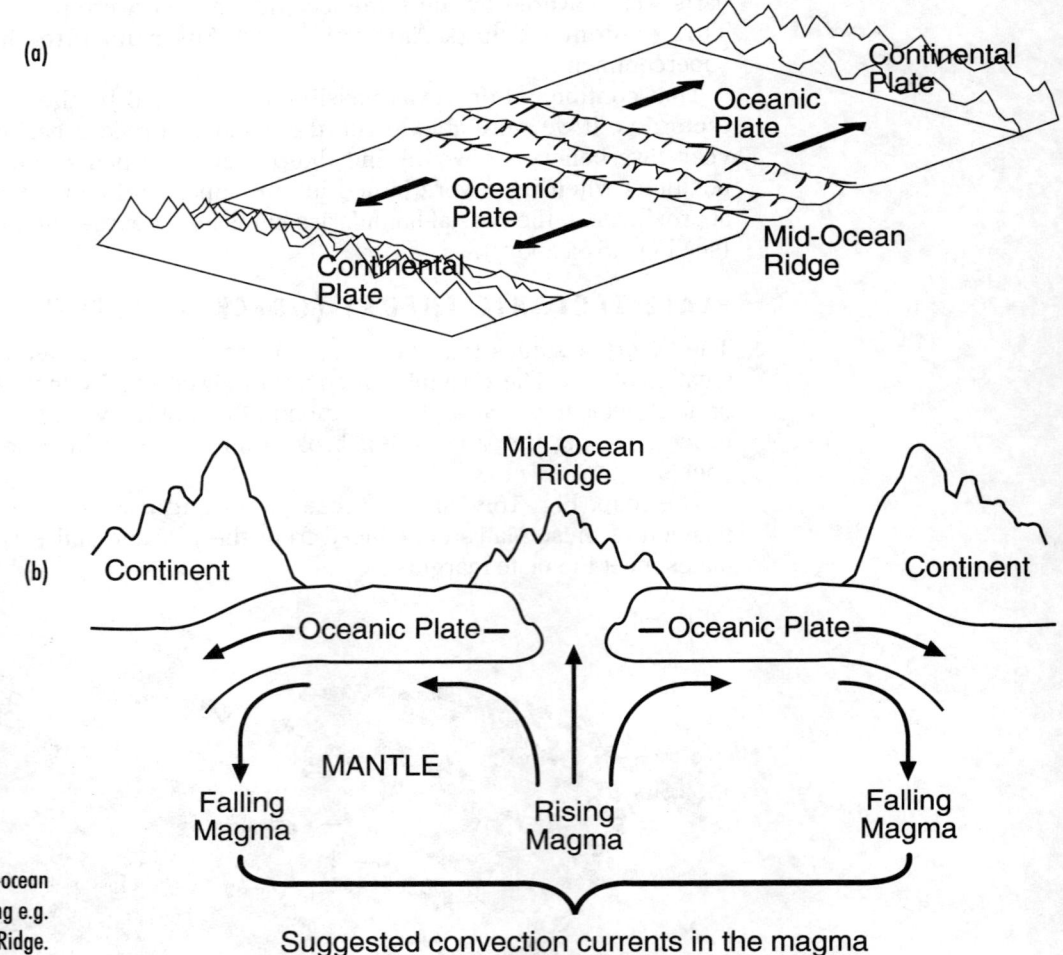

Fig. 16.10 Divergent margin-ocean widening and ridge forming e.g. Mid-Atlantic Ridge.

(a) = schematic diagram (b) = sectional diagram

Plate margins

The **plate margins** are the places where change in the crust occurs.

The margins are of three types:

(i) **divergent margins**: these are found where crust boundaries separate. This occurs at

- ocean crust-ocean crust margins where ocean widening is the result and earthquake activity and pillow lavas form, e.g. the Atlantic Ocean is slowly widening and the Mid-Atlantic Ridge has formed.
- continental crust – continental crust margins where there is earthquake activity, volcanic activity and a rift valley results, e.g. the African Rift Valley

(ii) **convergent margins**: these happen where crusts collide. This occurs at

- ocean crust – ocean crust margins where a seafloor trench forms and volcanoes result, e.g. the Peru-Chile Trench
- continental crust – continental crust margins where the crust folds, producing young mountain ranges but no volcanic acitivity, e.g. the Himalayas, the Alps.
- ocean crust – continental crust margins where a seafloor trench forms and volcanic activity produces a mountain range parallel to a trench, e.g. the Andes of Peru and Chile in South America

(iii) **conservative margins**: here the plates simply slip past each other. No surface crust is lost or gained (so the crustal area is conserved). This occurs at

- ocean crust – ocean crust margins where ridges and valleys form but volcanoes are rare, e.g. Kane Fracture Zone in the Atlantic
- continental crust – continental crust margins which slide past each other causing earthquakes but no volcanoes, e.g. the San Andreas Fault.

Fig. 16.9 above shows the plates and their boundaries today. Since the whole surface of the globe is covered by these plates, any movement of the plates must cause separation at one boundary and collision at another. Some of the consequences of these processes are described below.

Mountain formation (convergent margin activity)

When two continental plates converge, folding occurs and fold mountains result, like the Himalayas.

When an oceanic crust converges on a continental crust, the denser oceanic crust slips under the continental crust at an angle of 45°. Oceanic crust at the plate boundary is destroyed in this process. The process is called **subduction**. An oceanic or seafloor trench results. The process also causes heating, melting and eventually volcanic eruption as the crustal material moves down into the mantle. Mountain building also results from this type of change with the build-up of sediments which are scraped off the oceanic crust as it slides beneath the continental mass. These sedimentary masses build up to great heights, as is happening on the west coast of S. America where the Andes mountain range is the result. (Fig. 16.11).

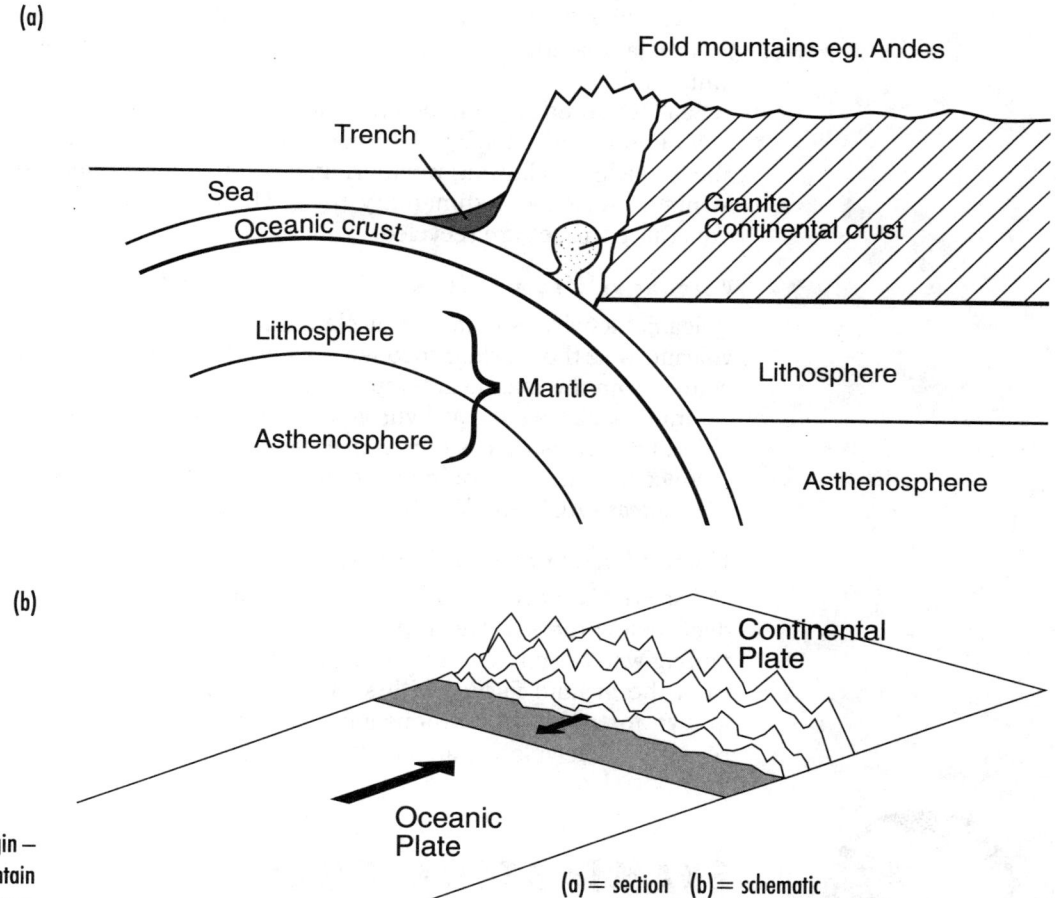

Fig. 16.11 Convergent margin – formation of the Andean mountain range and ocean

Sea floor spreading (divergent margin activity)

At divergent oceanic plate margins, the plates move apart. The crack produced by this movement is filled with molten material from the mantle which spews out and solidifies on contact with water, creating a new layer of crust between the old boundaries. This new crust can build up into high ridges. This has happened in the mid-atlantic where the ridge is up to 4 kilometres above the sea floor, breaking out above sea-level as Iceland. Over long periods of time, the original boundaries mover further and further apart and the ocean becomes wider – as is happening in the Atlantic Ocean (Fig. 16.10 above).

Earthquake areas not associated with mountain building (conservative margins)

The famous San Andreas fault is an example of a displacement of plate boundaries which neither create nor destroy crustal material. The Pacific plate is sliding past the North American plate and the motion causes earthquakes (Fig. 16.12)

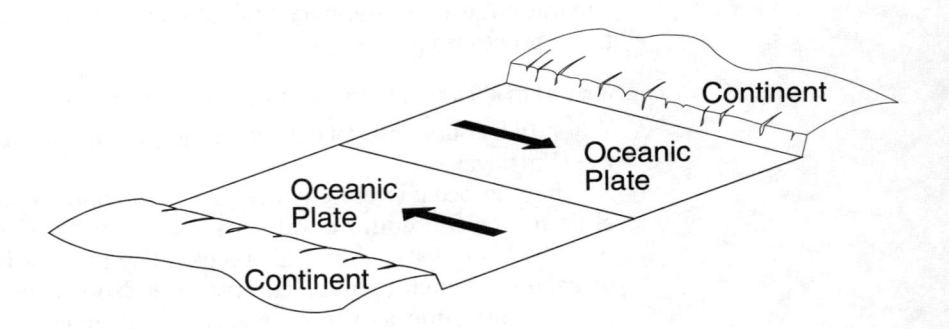

Fig. 16.12 A conservative (also called a transformfault) margin: schematic diagram.

Fold mountain formation (continental plates converging)

The Himalayas are relatively young mountains formed by collision of two continental plates. The folds are as deep as 300 km and are spread over a wide region.

It can be seen that plate collisions remove ocean crust for remelting (subduction). So crustal material becomes magma and can reform igneous rock (granite) at some future time.

Seafloor spreading, on the other hand, produces new oceanic crust and ridges.

Mountain building by plate collision throws up sedimentary material into folds above sea level, allowing weathering, erosion, transportation and deposition, being the formation of new sedimentary rock. Thus plate tectonics shows how the Earth's mineral resources are recycled.

Volcanoes (from *Vulcam* – Roman god of fire)

Volcanic activity is common at plate margins. There are currently about 500 active volcanoes in the world. Igneous rocks are formed from molten rock (magma) which comes from the mantle at temperatures around 1000°C. Volcanoes also give out large volumes of gases such as hydrogen sulphide, H_2S, sulphur dioxide, SO_2 and hydrogen chloride, HCl, as well as nitrogen, carbon dioxide and water vapour.

Volcanoes are the origin of two main types of igneous rock – extrusive and intrusive (see *igneous rocks* and Fig. 16.4 above).

Thermal springs and Geysers

These are sited over old volcanoes. An extinct volcano can take a million years to cool, deep below the surface. If ground water enters the fissures in the hot rock, nearly boiling water can rise to the surface. If steam is produced also, the hot water is ejected from the ground fissure with spectacular effect. Bath, in Somerset, has hot springs known for at least two thousand years. The Geysers of Iceland are located over a recently active volcanic area on the Mid-Atlantic Ridge.

EXAMINATION QUESTIONS

QUESTION 1

(a) Explain what is meant by the following terms:

   (i) igneous rock ....

   ....

   (ii) sedimentary rock ....

   ....

   (iii) metamorphic rock ....

   ....

(6)

(b) A student examined two samples of the same type of igneous rock using a microscope at the same magnification.
She made the drawing below.

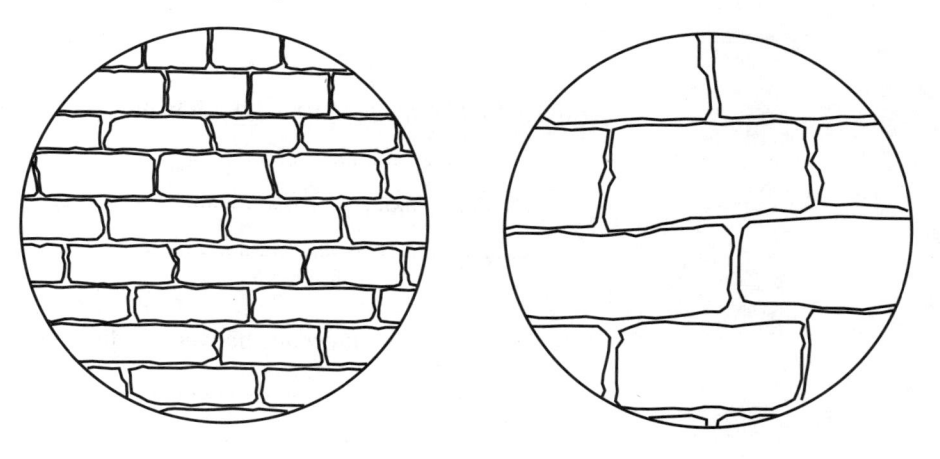

Fig. 16.13

Sample A   Sample B

What difference in the origin of the two samples is likely to have caused this difference in appearance?

....

....

(2)
(Total 8 marks)
(ULEAC)

QUESTION 2

(a) (i) What is rock type A?

....

(1 mark)

(ii) What changes take place to the magma to form rock type B?

....

(1 mark)

The diagram below shows part of the rock cycle

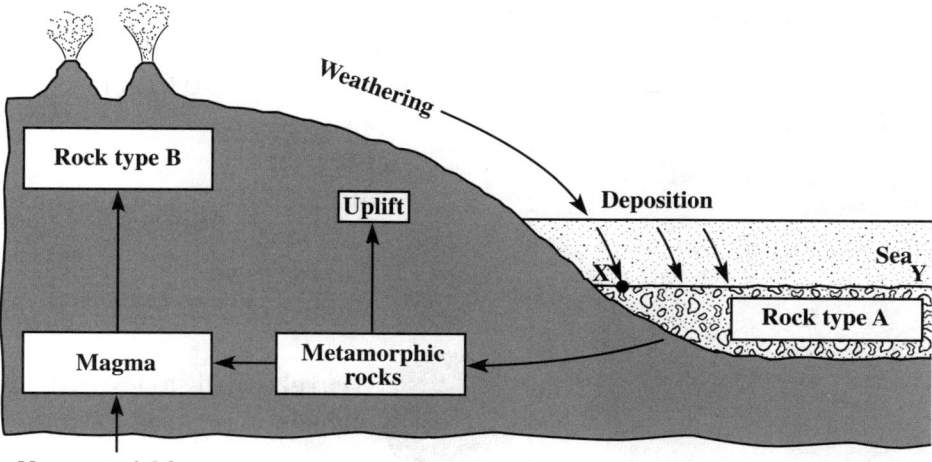

Fig. 16.14

(iii) Suggest **one** way that rain can act as a weathering agent on exposed rocks.

....

....

(1 mark)

(iv) What happens to rock type A while it is changing to metamorphic rock?

....

....

....

(2 marks)

(v) Suggest **one** difference between sediments found at X and Y on the diagram.

....

....

(1 mark)

(b) The diagram is a sketch map of a coastal area. The distance between Y and Z is about 300 metres.

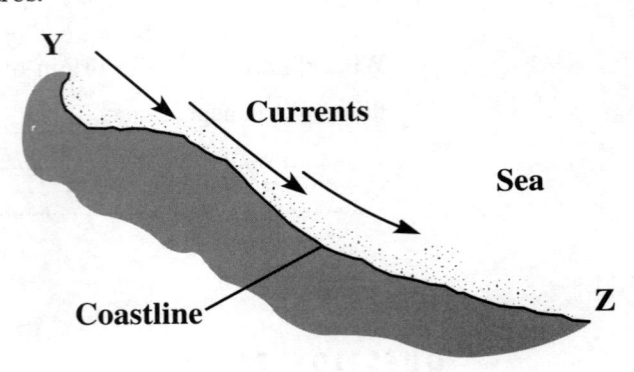

Fig. 16.15

Pebbles found on the beach at Z are more rounded than those at Y. Explain why the pebbles at Z are more rounded

(3 marks)

(c) The particle sizes of rocks found in sediments and soils are shown in this table.

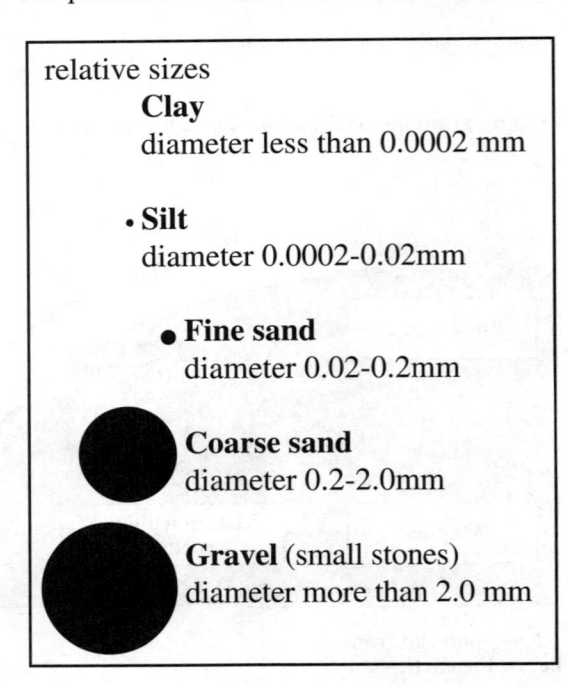

relative sizes

Clay
diameter less than 0.0002 mm

Silt
diameter 0.0002-0.02mm

Fine sand
diameter 0.02-0.2mm

Coarse sand
diameter 0.2-2.0mm

Gravel (small stones)
diameter more than 2.0 mm

(i) Write down **one** advantage of having clay particles in soils.

....

....

(1 mark)

(ii) Write down **one** advantage of having sand particles in soils.

....

....

(1 mark)

(iii) A sediment has particles with lots of different sizes. What else does it need to become a good soil for plants to grow in?

....

....

....

....

(2 marks)

(SEG)

QUESTION 3

The map below shows two of the continents bordering the Atlantic Ocean.

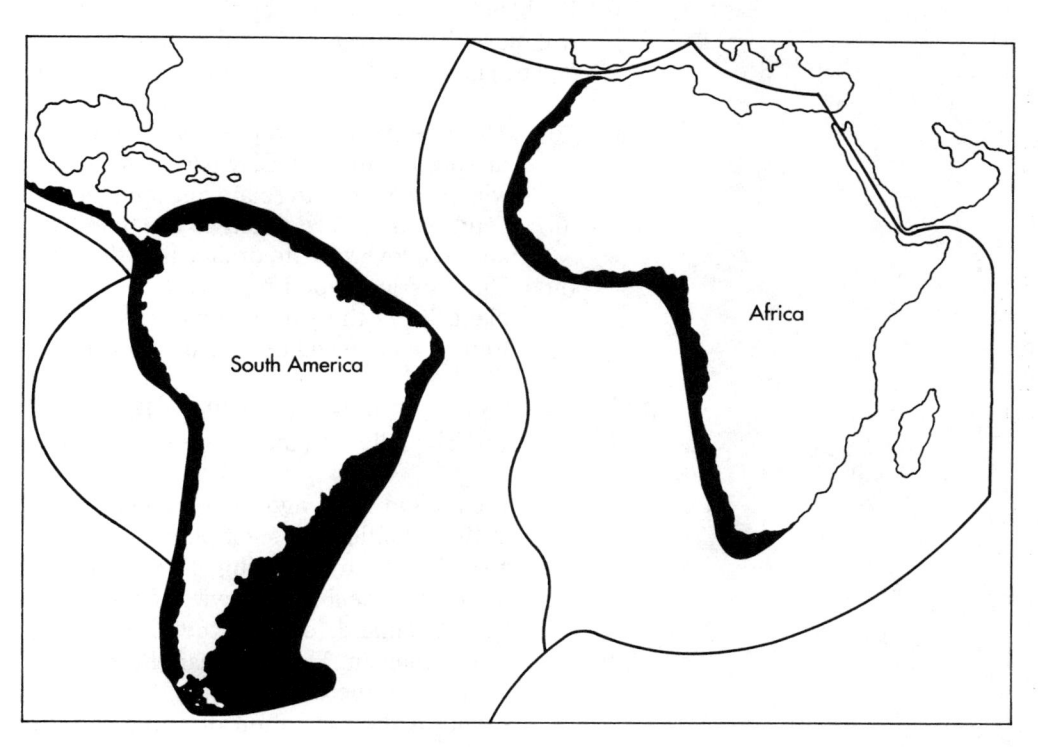

Fig. 16.16

KEY

———— = Plate Boundary

■ = Continental Shelf

It is believed that 150 million years ago these two continents were joined.
Use the theory of plate tectonics to explain how these continents could have moved apart to reach their present positions. You may use diagrams if you wish.

ANSWERS TO EXAMINATION QUESTIONS

1. (a) (i) Igneous rock is rock formed by crystallisation of magma from the mantle.
   (ii) Sedimentary rock is rock formed on the Earth's surface by the effect of pressure on the materials resulting from the breakdown of surface rock.
   (iii) Metamorphic rock is rock formed by the effect of heat and pressure on other types of rock – without melting. It forms beneath the crust.

   (b) Sample A has smaller crystals than sample B. Sample A has crystallised at a faster rate than B. Rapid cooling produces small crystals; slow cooling produces large crystals.

2. (a) (i) Rock type A is sedimentry.
   (ii) Rock type B is formed from magma on cooling as it moves to the Earth's surface.
   (iii) Rain contains dissolved carbon dioxide and reacts chemically with certain rock components, dissolving them. The material that does not react fragments.
   (iv) Rock types A is sedimentary. Under pressure and at high temperature it forms metamorphic rock.
   (v) Sediments carried by water to the sea are made up of particles with a range of sizes. On entering the sea the larger particles deposit on the bottom near the shore whilst the smaller particles travel further out. The difference is therefore in size or diameter.

   (b) Pebbles become rounded by the rolling action of sea-shore waves. The current will move the pebbles from Y along the shore to Z and in the process wear them down. The more they rool the more rounded they become.

   (c) (i) The fine particles trap water in the spaces between them and so retain dissolved nutrients. Clay particles absorb mineral ions from the soil water which also helps to retain nutrients in the soil.
   (ii) Sand particles are much larger than clay particles: they pack irregularly and so allow water to drain easily through the soil.
   (iii) Humous is needed to provide organic matter to encourage insect and plant life in the soil. Humous also provides nutrients because it results from decomposing plant and animal remains.

3. (i) Look back to Section 9, 'Plate Tectonics', and especially Fig. 16.8 (a) and (b). The following indicates some of the points you might make.

   150 million years ago the African and S. American continents were joined at their continental shelf boundaries. Since then they have been moving apart by ocean spreading. The plate boundary shown (also called a plate margin) is the line of activity of a divergent margin. Here magma wells up from the mantle causing the formation of new ocean crust on either side of the margin. Year by year the distance apart of the continental shelf boundaries increases as more magma emerges. The margin is also the scene of the formation of a mid-atlantic ridge and volcanic activity is evident. A diagram such as Fig. 16.10 (a) could also be used to illustrate this answer.

CHAPTER 16 **REVIEW SHEET** 347

REVIEW SHEET

- Name 4 different **layers** of the earth and describe their properties

    1. _____
    2. _____
    3. _____
    4. _____

- List the different gases in the atmosphere and give their approximate percentage of the total volume of gases

    1. _____
    2. _____
    3. _____
    4. _____

- How have earthquakes helped us understand more about the earth's structure?

    _____
    _____
    _____
    _____

- Describe two types of igneous rock, giving an example of each type.

    1. _____
    _____
    2. _____
    _____

- Describe **three** ways in which **sedimentary** rocks can be formed, giving examples of rocks formed in each way.

    1. _____
    _____
    2. _____
    _____
    3. _____
    _____

- How are **metamorphic** rocks formed?

    _____
    _____
    _____
    _____

CHAPTER 16 EARTH AND ITS ATMOSPHERE

- Complete the following tables.

Soil type	underlying rock	appearance	feel	characteristics
sandy soil				
loam (clay +sandy)				
clay soil				

- Outline some of the evidence in favour of the **continental drift** theory

    1. _____
       _____
    2. _____
       _____
    3. _____
       _____
    4. _____
       _____

- Explain the role of **plate margins** in each of the following

    1. **Mountain formation** _____
       _____
       _____

    2. **Sea Floor Spreading** _____
       _____
       _____

    3. **Earthquake areas** _____
       _____
       _____

    4. **Fold Mountain formations** _____
       _____
       _____

CHAPTER 17

GETTING STARTED

Many GCSE questions need data. This data is given either in the question or in the form of a booklet. In the remainder of this chapter there is some data that you will find useful and at the end of the chapter questions based on data interpretation.

DATA

REACTIVITY SERIES OF METALS

REACTIVITY SERIES FOR NON-METALS

COMMON IONS

ORGANIC COMPOUNDS

PROPERTIES OF ELEMENTS

PROPERTIES OF COMMON COMPOUNDS

PROPERTIES OF GASES

TESTING FOR GASES

OTHER USEFUL INFORMATION

ESSENTIAL PRINCIPLES

1. REACTIVITY SERIES OF METALS

The following list gives the order of **reactivity of metals** with the most reactive metal first and least reactive metal last.

> potassium   sodium   calcium   magnesium   aluminium   carbon
> zinc   iron   lead   hydrogen   copper   silver

More reactive metals can displace less reactive metals from their salts or their oxides. Thus iron will displace copper from copper(II) sulphate. Two non-metals, carbon and hydrogen, have been included in this list. It is important to realise that at high temperatures these non-metals would be higher in the list. Thus hydrogen will reduce zinc oxide at high temperatures.

2. REACTIVITY SERIES FOR NON-METALS

It is also possible to make a list of **reactivity for non-metals**. Again, the most reactive element is first.

> chlorine   bromine   oxygen   iodine   sulphur

A more reactive non-metal displaces a less reactive non-metal from a compound. Thus if chlorine is bubbled into potassium iodide, iodine is formed.

3. COMMON IONS

The symbols of the common ions are given in the list below. For **metal ions** it should be noted that the charge on the ion is **positive** and is equal to its **group number**. Hence sodium has a charge of +1, magnesium +2 and aluminium +3. For **non-metals** the charge is **negative** and is equal to eight (8) – (minus) the group number. The charge on the chloride ion is –1 (i.e. 8 – 7). For the oxide ion –2 (8 – 6) and the nitride ion –3 (8 – 5). The formulae of compounds can be worked out using these charges. A compound must be neutral and therefore the number of positive charges must be equal to the number of negative charges. The formula of copper(II) oxide is CuO (two positive charges on the copper ion and two negative charges on the oxide ion). The formula of magnesium chloride is $MgCl_2$. Magnesium has two positive charges and therefore two negative charges are needed to make the charges equal.

Positive ions		Negative ions	
Ag^+	silver	Br^-	bromide
Al^{3+}	aluminium	Cl^-	chloride
Ba^{2+}	barium	CO_3^{2-}	carbonate
Ca^{2+}	calcium	F^-	fluoride
Cu^{2+}	copper(II)	HCO_3^-	hydrogencarbonate
Fe^{2+}	iron(II)	HSO_4^-	hydrogensulphate
Fe^{3+}	iron(III)	I^-	iodide
H^+	hydrogen	N_3^-	nitride
K^+	potassium	NO_3^-	nitrate
Mg^{2+}	magnesium	O^{2-}	oxide
Na^+	sodium	OH^-	hydroxide
NH_4^+	ammonium	S^{2-}	sulphide
Pb^{2+}	lead(II)	SO_3^{2-}	sulphite
Zn^{2+}	zinc	SO_4^{2-}	sulphate

4. ORGANIC COMPOUNDS

Organic compounds are divided into homologous series. The names of the first few members in each series are given together with their melting points and boiling points.

Series	Name	Formula	M.p.°C	B.p.°C
Alkanes	methane	CH$_4$	−183	−162
	ethane	C$_2$H$_6$	−172	− 89
	propane	C$_3$H$_8$	−187	− 42
	butane	C$_4$H$_{10}$	−135	− 0.5
	pentane	C$_5$H$_{12}$	−130	36
Alkenes	ethene	C$_2$H$_4$	−169	−102
	propene	C$_3$H$_6$	−185	− 48
	butene	C$_4$H$_8$	−185	− 7
Alcohols	methanol	CH$_3$OH	− 97	65
	ethanol	C$_2$H$_5$OH	−114	78
	propanol	C$_3$H$_7$OH	−126	97
Acids	methanoic acid	HCO$_2$H	9	101
	ethanoic acid	CH$_3$CO$_2$H	17	118

(A) GAS

For a substance to be a gas, its melting point and boiling point must be below room temperature, say 20°C. Thus some gases in the above list are methane, ethene and butene.

(B) LIQUID

For a substance to be a liquid its melting point must be below room temperature and its boiling point above room temperature. Among the liquids in the above list are pentane, methanol and methanoic acid.

(C) SOLID

For a substance to be a solid its melting point and boiling point must be above room temperature. There are no solids in the above list, although if room temperature drops below 17°C, ethanoic acid becomes a solid.

5. PROPERTIES OF ELEMENTS

In this section the melting points and boiling points of the elements are listed together with their ability to conduct electricity. Only two elements are liquids at room temperature and pressure; they are bromine and mercury. You will also notice that all metals are good conductors of electricity:

Element	Relative Atomic Mass	Conductor of electricity	M.p.°C	B.p.°C
aluminium	27	yes	660	2450
argon	40	no	−189	−186
bromine	80	no	−7	−58
calcium	40	yes	845	1490
carbon	12			
diamond		no	–	–
graphite		yes	3500	3900
chlorine	35.5	no	−101	−34
copper	64	yes	1083	2600
helium	4	no	−270	−269
hydrogen	1	no	−259	−253
iodine	127	no	114	184
iron	56	yes	1540	2900
lead	207	yes	330	1750
magnesium	24	yes	650	1100
mercury	210	yes	−39	357
neon	20	no	−248	−246
nitrogen	14	no	−210	−196
oxygen	16	no	−218	−183
potassium	39	yes	63	760
silicon	28	yes	1410	2360
sodium	23	yes	98	880
sulphur	32	no	119	445
zinc	65	yes	419	907

6. PROPERTIES OF COMMON COMPOUNDS

In this section the melting points and boiling points of compounds are listed together with whether they conduct when molten. You will notice that all metal compounds conduct electricity when molten:

Compound	Relative Molecular Mass	Conduct when molten	M.p.°C	B.p.°C
ammonia	17	no	−78	−34
carbon dioxide	44	no	−111	−78
calcium carbonate	100	decomposes when heated		
calcium oxide	56	yes	2600	2850
copper(II) chloride	135	yes	620	990
copper(II) sulphate	160	decomposes when heated		
glucose	180	no	146	decomposes
hydrogen chloride	36.5	no	−114	−85
lead(II) chloride	278	yes	501	950
silicon dioxide	58.5	yes	801	1413
water	18	no	0	100

7 PROPERTIES OF GASES

The properties of gases can be studied using the mnemonic COWSLIPS – Colour; Odour; Weight; Solubility; Litmus; Inflammability; Poisonous; Support Burning.

> Substances that decompose easily do not have a melting point or a boiling point.

(A) COLOUR

The following gases are coloured:

chlorine	green
hydrogen chloride	colourless but fumes in moist air
iodine vapour	purple
nitrogen(IV) oxide	brown

(B) ODOUR (SMELL)

chlorine	pungent
sulphur dioxide	choking
ammonia	makes eyes water
hydrogen chloride	pungent, leaves a sour taste in mouth

(C) WEIGHT/DENSITY

To work out if a gas is denser or less dense than air calculate its relative molecular mass (M_r); if it is less than 30, it is less dense than air; if it is greater than 30 it is denser than air.

Hydrogen, methane and ammonia are less dense than air.
Nitrogen, oxygen and carbon monoxide have approximately the same density as air.
Carbon dioxide, chlorine and hydrogen chloride are denser than air.

(D) SOLUBILITY

Hydrogen chloride and ammonia are very soluble in water.
They both react with water, e.g.:

$$HCl + H_2O \rightarrow H_3O^+ + Cl^-,$$
$$NH_3 + H_2O \rightarrow NH_4^+ + OH^-.$$

> Acid solutions have an excess of H_3O^+ ions and alkaline solutions an excess of OH^- ions.

Chlorine and carbon dioxide are fairly soluble in water:

$$Cl_2 + H_2O \rightarrow HClO + HCl,$$
$$CO_2 + H_2O \rightarrow H_2CO_3.$$

Hydrogen, carbon monoxide, oxygen and nitrogen are 'insoluble' in water.

(E) LITMUS (OR UNIVERSAL INDICATOR PAPER)

All the gases that dissolve in water change the colour of damp litmus paper, and of universal indicator (UI) paper.

Those that form acids turn blue litmus and UI red, i.e. hydrogen chloride and sulphur dioxide.

> This is a good test for ammonia

Chlorine turns litmus and (UI) red, then bleaches it (also does this to U.I. paper).
Carbon dioxide only just changes the colour of litmus (turns U.I. paper orange).
Ammonia turns damp red litmus paper blue (turns U.I. paper blue/green).

(F) FLAMMABILITY

The following gases burn:

Hydrogen with a 'pop'.
Carbon monoxide with a blue flame.
Hydrocarbons: the higher the percentage of carbon in the hydrocarbon, the more yellow and smokier the flame.

(G) POISONOUS

All gases that smell are poisonous but not all poisonous gases smell! Carbon monoxide, for instance, has no smell, but it is very poisonous.

Thus chlorine, hydrogen chloride, ammonia, sulphur dioxide, hydrogen sulphide and carbon monoxide are poisonous.

(H) SUPPORTING BURNING

Only oxygen of the frequently met gases supports burning – the rest put out a burning splint.

8 TESTING FOR GASES

Before you start testing for gases, make sure that you have the following apparatus and chemicals at hand:

Bunsen (alight), splints, litmus or some other kind of indicator papers, delivery tube, lime-water, potassium dichromate(VI) paper, concentrated hydrochloric acid, silver nitrate solution, cobalt chloride paper.

The following tips will help:

(1) If you have added hydrochloric acid and a gas is *immediately given off*, you should test for **carbon dioxide**. If the powder looks metallic, test for **hydrogen**.
(2) If you have added **sodium hydroxide** or **sodium carbonate** and heated the solution, you should test for **ammonia** and not for acidic gases.
(3) You should *test in the order*: colour, smell, splint (glowing then burning), pH and then special tests (tests which identify a single gas).
(4) Some colours may be difficult to see, e.g. that of chlorine.
(5) If you cannot **smell** ammonia gas, it is not being given off.
(6) Make sure the litmus paper (or U.I. paper) is **damp**.
(7) All acidic gases give a white smoke with ammonia.
(8) All gases that **smell** are **poisonous**.
(9) If a **colourless liquid** forms near the top of the test tube, it is most likely to be **water**.

Colour	Smell	Splint	Litmus or U.I. paper	Special test	Gas
green/ yellow	pungent	put out	red then bleached		chlorine
colourless but fumes in moist air	pungent	put out	red	test with silver nitrate gives white precipitate	hydrogen chloride
colourless	choking	put out	red	turns potassium dichromate(VI) green	sulphur dioxide
colourless	none	burns with a 'pop'	none		hydrogen
colourless	none	burns with a blue flame	none	burnt gas turns lime-water milky	carbon monoxide
colourless	perhaps	burns with a blue/yellow flame	none	burnt gas turns lime-water milky	hydro- carbons

Colour	Smell	Splint	Litmus or U.I. paper	Special test	Gas
colourless	none	relights glowing splint	none		oxygen
colourless	none	put out	faint red	turns lime-water cloudy	carbon dioxide
colourless	pungent	put out	blue	white smoke with hydrogen chloride	ammonia
moist air (If you cannot smell ammonia, it is not present.)					
colourless liquid forms on cold part of test tube	none	put out	none	turns cobalt chloride pink	water vapour
colourless	none	put out	none	none	nitrogen

9 › OTHER USEFUL INFORMATION

Atomic mass — The number of protons and neutrons in the nucleus of an atom

Atomic number — The number of protons in the nucleus of an atom

Avogadro's constant — The number of particles in a mole. Its value is 6×10^{23} particles per mole

Faraday constant — The electrical charge on one mole of electrons. Its value is 96 500 coulombs per mole

Isomers — Compounds with the same molecular formula but different structural formulae

Isotopes — Atoms with the same atomic number but different mass numbers

Molar volume — The volume of one mole of gas at room temperature and pressure. Its value is 24 dm^3 (litres)

The mole — Number of moles = mass of element divided by relative atomic mass (A_r)

Relative atomic mass — The relative mass of an atom on a scale on which an atom of carbon-12 is 12.00

Relative molecular mass — The relative mass of a molecule on a scale on which an atom of carbon-12 is 12.00

QUESTIONS ON DATA

Use the data in Fig. 17.1 to help you to answer the following questions using the list A to D given below:

A : 1
B : 2
C : 3
D : 4

MULTIPLE CHOICE

QUESTION 1

The value of the positive charge on a calcium ion.

QUESTION 2

The number of atoms joined together to make a nitrate ion.

I	II											III	IV	V	VI	VII	O
1 H Hydrogen 1																	4 He Helium 2
7 Li Lithium 3	9 Be Beryllium 4											11 B Baron 5	12 C Carbon 6	14 N Nitrogen 7	16 O Oxygen 8	19 F Fluorine 9	20 Ne Neon 10
23 Na Sodium 11	24 Mg Magnesium 12											27 Al Aluminium 13	28 Si Silicon 14	31 P Phosphorus 15	32 S sulpher 16	35.5 Cl Chlorine 17	40 Ar Argon 18
39 K Potassium 19	40 Ca Calcium 20	45 Sc Scandium 21	48 Ti Titanium 22	51 V Vanadium 23	52 Cr Chromium 24	55 Mn Manganese 25	56 Fe Iron 26	59 Co Cobalt 27	59 Ni Nickle 28	63.5 Cu Copper 29	65 Zn Zinc 30	70 Ga Gallium 31	73 Ge Germanium 32	75 As Arsenic 33	79 Se Selenium 34	80 Br Bromine 35	84 Kr Krypton 36
85 Rb Rubidium 37	88 Sr Strontium 38	89 Y Yttrium 39	91 Zr Zirconium 40	93 Nb Niobium 41	96 Mo Molybdenum 42	Tc Technetium 43	101 Ru Ruthenium 44	103 Rh Rhodium 45	106 Pd Palladium 46	108 Ag Silver 47	112 Cd Cadmium 48	115 In Indium 49	119 Sn Tin 50	122 Sb Antimony 51	128 Te Tellurium 52	127 I Iodine 53	131 Xe Xenon 54
133 Cs Caesium 55	137 Ba Barium 56	139 La Lanthonum 57	178 Hf Halfnium 72	181 Ta Tantalum 73	184 W Tungsten 74	186 Re Rhenium 75	190 Os Osmium 76	192 Ir Iridium 77	195 Pt Platinium 78	197 Au Gold 79	201 Hg Mercury 80	204 Tl Thallium 81	207 Pb Lead 82	209 Bi Bismuth 83	Po Polonium 84	At Astotine 85	Rn Radon 86
Fr Francium 87	236 Ra Radium 88	227 Ac Actinium 89															

·58-57 Lanthanum series	140 Ce Cerium 58	141 Pr Praseodymium 59	144 Nd Neodymium 60	Pm Promethium 61	150 Sm Samarium 62	152 Eu Europium 63	157 Gd Gadolinium 64	159 Tb Terbium 65	162 Dy Dysprosium 66	165 Ho Holmium 67	167 Er Erbium 68	169 Tm Thulium 69	173 Yb Yiterbium 70	175 Lu Lutetium 34
†90-103 Actinium series	232 Th Thorium 90	Pa Protactinium 91	238 U Uranium 92	Np Neptunium 41	Pu Plutonium 94	Am Americium 95	Cm Curium 96	Bk Berkelium 97	Cf Californium 98	Es Einsteinium 99	Fm Fermium 100	Md Mendelevium 101	No Nobelium 102	Lr Lowrencium 103

Fig. 17.1 Periodic table of elements

QUESTION 3

The number of magnesium ions in the formula of magnesium hydrogencarbonate.

QUESTION 4

The number of sulphate ions in the formula of aluminium sulphate. (NEAB)

QUESTIONS 5–9

Select from the table the letter which represents the substance described in the question (Fig. 17.2).

Each letter may be used once, more than once, or not at all.

Substance	Melting point	Electrical conductivity		Result of heating in air or oxygen
		Solid	Molten	
A	770°C	Non-conductor	Good	No change
B	98°C	Good	Good	Burns forming a white solid
C	114°C	Non-conductor	Non-conductor	Burns forming a gas
D	31°C	Non-conductor	Non-conductor	Burns forming a gas and water
E	1080°C	Good	Good	Substance becomes coated with a black powder

Fig. 17.2

5 a non-metallic element;
6 a covalent compound;
7 an ionic compound;
8 a substance which could be copper;
9 a substance which could be a hydrocarbon.

	Density	Effect of a burning splint	Solubility in water
A	Less than air	Goes out immediately	Not soluble
B	Same as air	Goes out immediately	Slightly soluble
C	Less than air	Gas burns	Not soluble
D	Greater than air	Goes out immediately	Moderately soluble
E	Same as air	Splint burns more brightly	Slightly soluble

Fig. 17.3

QUESTIONS 10-12

Match the properties lettered A to E (Fig. 17.3) with the gases given in questions 10–12. Each letter may be used once, more than once, or not at all.
10   oxygen;
11   carbon dioxide;
12   hydrogen.

QUESTION 13

The table below (Fig. 17.4) contains information about five compounds, A, B, C, D, and E. From the compounds A to E select

(a) a liquid;
(b) a salt;
(c) an alkaline gas;
(d) a compound which could be formed by adding sodium to water;
(e) two compounds which would react with each other. *(5 marks)*

compound	A	B	C	D	E
melting point in °C	319	801	−115	−78	−117
boiling point in °C	1390	1413	−85	−33	78
pH of solution in water	14	7	1	11	7

Fig. 17.4

STRUCTURED QUESTIONS

QUESTION 14

(a) Using the table (Fig. 17.5) write the letter of:
   (i) a solid at room temperature (20 °C); .... *(1)*
   (ii) a gas at room temperature (20 °C); .... *(1)*
   (iii) a metal; .... *(1)*
   (iv) a covalent liquid; .... *(1)*
   (v) an ionic solid; .... *(1)*
   (vi) a liquid at room temperature which has the smallest temperature range between its melting point and boiling point; (1 line) *(1)*
(b) Substance E in the table was prepared by pupils in a school laboratory and the melting points of the samples were found to be between 88 and 90 °C. Give an explanation of this fact. (3 lines) *(1)*

CHAPTER 17 DATA

Substance	Melting point (°C)	Boiling point (°C)	Electrical conductivity of Pure solid	Electrical conductivity of Solution with water
A	−40	150	nil	insoluble
B	1083	2600	good	insoluble
C	−112	−84	nil	good
D	801	1450	nil	good
E	92	190	nil	insoluble
F	12	74	nil	nil

Fig. 17.5

QUESTION 15

Use the following data (Fig. 17.6) to answer the questions below:

Substance	Melting point (°C)	Boiling point (°C)
copper	1083	2582
copper(II) oxide	1328	over 3000
lead	330	1750
lead(II) oxide	886	1472
magnesium carbonate	–	–
sodium hydroxide	319	1390

Fig. 17.6

(a) If the highest temperature reached by a Bunsen burner flame is 850°C, which of the above substances could be melted by this flame? (1 line) (*1*)
(b) Suggest why the melting point of magnesium carbonate cannot be measured. (2 lines provided) (*1*)
(c) The apparatus below was used to investigate the reaction of hydrogen with copper(II) oxide and lead(II) oxide placed in a 'boat'. One of the reasons why lead(II) oxide is placed in a 'boat' is because it reacts with glass. Suggest another reason for placing lead(II) oxide in a 'boat' (Fig. 17.7). (2)

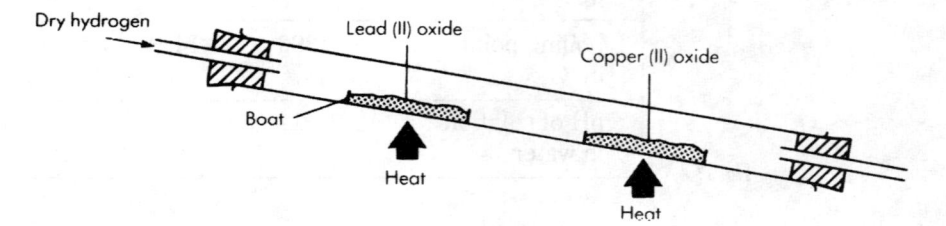

Fig. 17.7

OUTLINE ANSWERS

ANSWER 1

If you found the table in Section 3 you would have found the ions with their charges at the top right-hand side of each symbol. Answer to this questions is 2+, key B.

ANSWER 2

Nitrate ion has 1 nitrogen atom and 3 oxygen atoms hence the total number of atoms is 4, key D.

ANSWERS 3, 4

Answer 3, A; Answer 4, C.

For questions 5–9 you will need to remember that:
  (i) Non-metallic elements (except carbon in the form of graphite) do not conduct when solid or molten.
  (ii) Metallic elements conduct when solid and when molten.
  (iii) Ionic compounds do not conduct when solid but do conduct when molten.
  (iv) Covalent compounds do not conduct when solid or when molten.
  (v) Hydrocarbons burn to form carbon dioxide and water.

ANSWER 5

Key C – must be a non-metal; possibly sulphur.

ANSWER 6

Because it is a compound at least *two* substances must be formed when it is burnt. A covalent compound does not conduct electricity, hence key is D.

ANSWERS 7–9

See Section 6. Answer 7, A; Answer 8, E (black coating is copper(II) oxide); Answer 9, D (hydrocarbons contain hydrogen and carbon only and burn to form carbon dioxide and water).

ANSWER 10–12

You would find it helpful to refer to Section 7.
Answer 10, E; Answer 11, D; Answer 12, C.

ANSWER 13

(a) For a substance to be a liquid its boiling point must be above room temperature (20°C) and its melting point below room temperature. Hence the answer is E.

The answers to parts (b) to (e) are in Section 6, but the following tips will help you:

(b) a *salt* is usually neutral when dissolved in water and has a high melting point and boiling point. Answer, B.
(c) The melting point and boiling point of a gas are below room temperature. An alkaline solution has a pH greater than 7. Answer, D.
(d) Work out the compound formed. Is this a covalent or an ionic compound? Is this compound acid or alkaline? Answer, A.
(e) This is a difficult question! However, acids react with alkalis. Answer, C and D or C and A.

ANSWER 14

(a) (i) either B, D or E; (ii) C; (iii) B; (iv) A or F; (v) D; (vi) F.
(b) The sample was not pure. (Pure substances have a sharp melting point. If they contain impurities then melting points are lowered.)

ANSWER 15

(a) Lead and sodium hydroxide.
(b) Magnesium carbonate decomposes into magnesium oxide and carbon dioxide, hence its melting point cannot be measured.
(c) Lead would be formed and this would melt, run back down the tube and react with the copper(II) oxide. The lead might also block the exit tube and prevent hydrogen from escaping.

STUDENT'S ANSWERS – EXAMINER'S COMMENTS

In the table below are some data concerning a number of well-known elements and compounds. (The letters are not the symbols for these substances.)

Substance	A	B	C	D	E	F
Melting point/°C	98	685	1083	0	119	114
Boiling point/°C	890	1322	2600	100	444	183
Heat of vaporization kJ/mol	89		305	41		42
Electrical conductivity: when solid	Good	Nil	Good	Nil	Nil	Nil
when molten	Good	Good	Good	Poor	Nil	Nil
when in aqueous solution	Reacts with water	Good	Not soluble	Poor	Not soluble	Not soluble

(a) Which substance is water? **D**

State one piece of evidence you used in making this choice.

Melting point 0°C

(1 mark)

(b) State *two* pieces of evidence you would use to support the suggestion that substance C is a metal.

Good conductor of electricity and it does not dissolve in water

(1 mark)

❝ Many compounds do not dissolve. Very high melting point is the best answer. ❞

(c) Substance B is dissolved in water, and substance F is dissolved in sodium hydroxide solution. When both solutions are electrolysed in separate electrolysis cells, they form dark brown solutions at the anodes. On heating, both dark brown solutions give a purple vapour. Name the element which is common to B and F.

Iodine

(1 mark)

(d) One of the substances B and F readily changes to this purple vapour when heated. State which one is more likely to do this and write a brief explanation to support your choice.

B, because it conducts when it is molten

(1 mark)

❝ F is covalent (molecular) and would easily turn into a vapour. ❞

(e) The graph below shows the data for three elements. Add to this the values for A, D and F from the table of data, and use the graph to obtain an estimated value for the heat needed to vaporize one mole of substance E.

INDEX

1, 1, 1 - trichloroethane 284
1, 2 - methyl propane 283
Acetic acid 286
Acid rain 142, 242
Acidic oxides 81, 219
Acids 159, 160, 161, 162
    properties of 160, 163
    strong 159, 162
    testing for 160
    weak 159, 162
Activation energy 137
Addition polymerisation 297
Addition reaction 147, 283
    examples of 283
Adhesives 70, 300
Adipyl chloride 298
Agriculture 144, 228, 229
Air 221
    composition of 221
    uses of 221
Alcoholic drinks 285
Alcohols 285
Alkali metals 83
    properties of 83, 84
Alkaline earth metals 85
Alkalis 159, 160, 163
    weak 163
    strong 163
Alkanes 282
    uses of 283
Alkenes 283
Allotropes 259
Allotropy 260
Alloys 100, 181, 182
    uses of 182
Alpha particles 318
Alumina 104, 195
Aluminium 194, 195, 350
    chemical resistance 195
    manufacture of 104
    uses of 195
Aluminium hydroxide 164
Aluminium oxide 104, 195
Amalgam 106
Amide linkage 305
Amino acids 305
Ammeter 101
Ammonia 68
    analysis of 232
    manufacture of 230
    preparation of 230
    properties of 231
    siting of plant 233
    sources of 231
    uses in laboratory 234
    uses of 232
Ammonia scrubbing 23
Ammonium chloride 48
Ammonium compounds 232
Ammonium nitrate 23
Ammonium sulphate 23
Amphoteric oxides 81, 82, 219
Anhydrous 167
Anions 65, 101, 170
Anode 101
Anodising 107, 196
Araldite resin 300
Argon 90, 219

Aspirin 306
Atmosphere 325, 327
Atomic number 62
Atoms 61, 62
Attainment targets (AT's) 2
Avogadro's law 124
Avogadro's number (constant) 124

Bakelite 300
Barium 87, 350
Barium chloride 241
Barium sulphate 241
Bases 159, 161, 162, 163, 164
    testing for 161
    uses of 164
Basic oxides 81, 219
Battery 100, 108
Bauxite 194
Becquerel 317
Beer 285
Benedict's solution 304
Benezene-1, 4-dicarboxylic acid 298
Beta particles 318
Biodegradable 302
Biopol 301
Bitumen 281
Blast furnace 196
Bleach 253
Boiling 38, 49, 50
Boiling point 38, 49, 50, 351, 352
Bond breaking 138
Bond energies 138, 139
Bond making 138
Boyle's law 52
Brass 182
Bread 286
Brewing 285
Bromides 102
Bromine 87, 102, 103
Bronze 182
Brownian motion 50
Burning 220
Butane 147, 282, 351
Butanoic acid 286
Butanol 285
Butene 351

Caesium 83
Calcium 85, 86, 87
Calcium carbonate 164, 266
    uses of 264
Calcium hydrogencarbonate 264
Calcium hydroxide 86, 87
Calcium oxide 86, 266
    manufacture of 266
Calcium sulphate 23
Calorific value 220
Campden tablets 241
Carbohydrates 307
Carbon 70, 259
    properties of 261
Carbon containing compounds, test for 263, 303
Carbon cycle 266
Carbon dioxide 68, 262
    preparation of 262
    properties of 261
    structure of 263

    test for 263
    uses of 263
Carbon monoxide 261
    poisonous nature of 261
Carbonic acid 262
Carboxyhaemoglobin 261
Carboxylic acid 286
Cast iron 196
Castor oil 308
Catalyst 144
Cathode 101
Cations 65
Cell
    electrolysis 101
    rechargeable 109
    simple 107
Cells, fuel 109
Cellulose acetate 287
Centrifugation 36
Ceramics 183, 184
Charcoal 261
Charge on ions 64, 110, 350
Charles's law 52
Chernobyl disaster 317
Chemical industry and society 2
Choric (I) acid 253
Chlorides 249, 252
Chlorine 65, 87, 249, 251
    manufacture of 252
    preparation of 252
    properties of 252
    structure of 252
    test for 252
    uses of 253
Chloromethane 282
Chlorophyll 144, 267, 303
Chromatography 38, 304, 305
Chromium (III) oxide 188
Citric acid 163, 164
Clean Air Act 23
Coal 279
Coke 196
Collision theory 142
Combined gas laws 52
Combustion 141, 142, 220
Combustions reactions 141, 142, 220
Composites 183, 184
Compounds 32, 67, 100, 122, 352
    boiling point of 352
    formula of 122
    melting points of 352
    relative molecular mass 352
Condensation 145
Condensation polymerisation 298, 299
Conductors 100
Conservation
    energy 22
    materials 22
Contact process 238
Continental drift 338
Copper 105, 106, 107
Copper refining 106
Copper (II) ethanoate 287
Copper (II) sulphate 147, 212
Corrosive 160, 180
Coulomb 110
Coursework 14
Cracking 147, 284

Cross linking polymers 300
Crude oil 10, 31, 281
Cryolite 104
Crystallisation 36
Cupro-nickel 182

Data 349
Decane 285
Decantation 36
Dehydration 147, 167, 240
Denaturing 286
Density 50, 83
Depolymerisation 297, 305
Detergents, synthetic 297, 308
Deuterium 62
Diagrams, drawing 13
Diaminohexane 298
Diamond 260, 261
    properties of 260
    uses of 261
Diatomic 87
Dibromoethane 284
Dichlorodiphenyltrichlorophenol 307, 308
Diesel 281
Diffusion 48
    in gases 48
    in liquids 48
    in solids 48
Digestion 164
Direct current 100
Discharging of ions 101, 103
Displacement 189
Displacement reactions 147, 189
Distillation 36, 264
Domestos 253
Double bond 66
Dry cleaning 70
Duralumin 182
Dynamite 235

Earth
    atmosphere 327
    core 329
    crust 328
    mantle 328
    plate tectonics 338
    properties 326
    rocks 330, 331, 332, 333, 334, 335
    soil 336
    structure 328
Earthquakes 341
Electrical costs 111
Electrochemistry 99
Electrodes 100, 106
Electrolysis 100, 101, 104, 105, 126, 148
Electrolysis calculations 126
Electrolysis of aqueous solute 103
Electrolysis of molten compounds 102
Electrolysis, predicting products 103
Electrolyte 100, 102, 104, 105
Electron pairs 65
Electrons 63, 65
Electroplating 106
Elements 31, 32, 352
Empirical formula 125
Emulsification 308, 309
Endothermic 137, 148
Energetics of a reaction 138
Energy profile 140
Enzymes 144, 305

E-numbers 309
Equations
    ionic 123
    nuclear 318
    symbol 123
    word 122
Equilibrium 145, 148
Esters 306
Ethane 282, 351
    structure of 282
Ethane-1, 2-diol 298
Ethanoic acid 285, 286, 351
    preparation of 286
    uses of 286
Ethanol 285, 351
    manufacture of 285
    properties of 285, 351
    uses of 286
Ethene 283, 284, 285, 351
    preparation of 283
    properties of 283
    structure of 283
    uses of 285
Ethyl ethanoate 240
Ethylene glycol 298
Eutrophication 212
Evaporation 36, 145
Examinations, summary of 5
Excess reagent 125
Exothermic 137, 148
Extraction of metals 190, 193

Faraday 110
Fats 306
Fatty acids 306
Fehling's solution 304
Fermentation 148, 285
Fertilizers 229
    advantages of 229
    disadvantages of 229
Fibres 301
Filter 35
Filtrate 35
Filtration 35
Fire extinguishers 220, 263
Fixation 228
Flame tests 169
Fluorine 87, 89
Food 306
Food supply 229
Formic acid 164, 286
Fossil fuels 280
Fractional distillation 280, 286
Francium 83
Frasch process 236
Free radicals 147
Fuels 141, 220, 287
Functional groups 281

Galvanisation 221
Gamma rays 318
Gas Laws 51
Gases, properties of 351, 353
    testing for 354
Giant molecules 70, 71
    properties of 71
Glass 87
Glucose 305
Glycerine 306
Glyceryl tristearate 306
Gold 106, 181
Graphite 100, 260, 261
    properties of 260

Graphs, drawing 13
Grease 281
Greenhouse effect 262
Group 0 89
Group 1 83
Group 2 85
    reactions of 86
Group 7 64, 87
Group number 63, 64, 82, 83
Groups 63, 64, 82, 83
    trends down the 82

Haber process 230
Haematite 196
Half life 318
Halides
    tests for 169, 170
Halogens 87, 88, 89
    properties of 87, 88, 89
Hard water, advantages of 265
    disadvantages of 265
Hardness, permanent 264
    temporary 264
Health salts 163
Helium 62, 90
Hexane-1, 6-diamine 298
Hexanedioyl dichloride 298
Homologous series 281
Hydrated proton 161
Hydration 148, 167
Hydrochloric acid 251
    concentrated 251
    properties of 251
    uses of 251
Hydrogen 62, 91, 209, 210, 211
    manufacture of 210, 211
    uses of 211
Hydrogen chloride 249, 250
    preparation of 250
    properties of 250
    structure of 250
    test for 250
Hydrogen ions 103
Hydrogen peroxide 219
Hydrolysis 148, 304
Hydroxide ions 103
Hydroxyl ions 103, 219

Immiscible liquids 37
Indicators 160
Indigestion tables 164
    analysis of 164
Industrial sites, location of 20
Inert gases 90
Ink dyes 70
Insulators 99
Iodides 170
Iodine 87
    tincture of 286
Ion-exchange 264
Ionic bond 65
Ionic compounds, properties of 68, 69, 101
Ionic equations 123
Ions, charges on 64, 110, 350
Iron pyrites 196
Iron (II) sulphide 166
Iron (III) chloride 88, 165
Iron (III) oxide 123, 146, 196
Iron, manufacture of 196
    uses of 197
Isomers 283
Isotopes 62

Kerosene 281
Kettle fur 164
Kinetic theory 47, 49
Krypton 90, 91

Large molecules 71, 295
    properties of 71
Lead 198, 200
Lead-free petrol 142
Levels of attainment 2
Lime, uses of 266
Lime scrubbing 23
Limestone 266
Liquid 49, 351
Liquids, separation of 36
Lithium 83, 85
Lithium chloride 85
Lithium hydroxide 85
Lithium oxide 85
Lubricating oil 280, 281

Macromolecules 70, 295
    man-made 295
    natural 295
Magnesium 85
Magnesium carbonate 164
Magnesium hydrogencarbonate 264
Magnesium hydroxide 83, 164
Magnesium oxide 83
Maltose 305
Manganese (IV) oxide 188
Mantle 328
Manufacture of metals, cost of 193
Marble 142
Mass number 62
Mathematical requirements 11
Melamine 300
Melting 38
Melting point 38, 49, 50, 351, 352
    measurement of 38
Mendeleev 79
Mercury electrode 106
Metal chlorides 252
Metal compounds, stability of 187
Metal extraction, choice of method 193
Metal oxides 81
Metal resources, life span of 192
Metallic structures 72
Metalloids 80
Metals 79, 80, 86, 189
    extraction of 190
    properties of 184
    uses of 180
Metamorphic rock 333
Methane 65, 282
    properties of 282
    structure of 282
Methanoic acid 351
Methanol 285, 351
Methylpropane 282
Methylated spirits 286
Minerals and rocks 334
Mixtures 31, 32
Molar gas volume 124
Mole 110, 121, 124
Mole of electrons 110
Molecular compounds, properties of 67, 68
Molecular formula 125
Monomers 296
Mountain formation 341, 342

Nail varnish 70
Naphtha 230

National Curriculum 1–10
Neon 90
Neutralisation 148, 159
Neutrons 62
Nickel 91
Nitric acid 234
    manufacture of 234
    siting of plant 235
    uses of 235
Nitrification 228
Nitrogen, fixation 228
Nitrogen, manufacture of 227, 228
    uses of 227, 228
Nitrogen cycle 228, 229
Nitrogen oxide 24
Nitrogenous fertilisers 228
Noble gases 64, 65, 89, 90
    properties of 89
    uses of 90
Non-metal oxides 81
Non-metals 80, 81
North Sea Gas 141
Nuclear energy 318
Nuclear fission 318
Nuclear fusion 319
Nucleon number 62
Nylon 299
    properties of 299
    uses of 299

Octadecanoic acid 308
Organic compounds 279, 350
    naming of 279
Oxidation 148
Oxidation number 81
Oxides 81, 220
    neutral 221
Oxides of nitrogen 24, 142
Oxygen 218, 219, 221
    manufacture of 219
    properties of 219
    test for 219
    uses of 221
Oxyhaemoglobin 262

Paints 70
Particles 47
Penicillin 306
Pentane 351
Peptide linkage 304
Perchlorethene 70
Perfumes 70
Periods 63, 79, 80
    trends in a 80
Perspex 296
Petrol fumes 142
Petroleum 280, 281
    fractional distillation 280
pH 160
pH scale 160
Phosphate 239
Phosphatic fertilizer 239
Phosphoric acid 164
Phosphorus 197
Phosphorus oxide 197
Photography 144
Photosynthesis 144, 267, 303
Pickling 164
Pig iron 197
Pipe scale 164
Plastic, thermosetting 300
    thermosoftening 300
Plastics 300
    advantages of 301

    disadvantages of 301
    thermosets 300
    uses of 301
Plate margins 338, 339
Plate tectonics 340
Polar bonds 69
Pollution 22, 49, 142, 288, 302
Poly(ethene) 296
Poly(propene) 296
Poly(styrene) 296
Poly(vinyl chloride) (PVC) 296, 300
Polyamide 299
Polyester 299
Polymer 295, 296
Polymerisation 148, 297, 298
Polymers
    effect of heat on 300
    finding out composition of 303
    natural 303
    structure of 296
    synthetic 297
Polythene 300
    high density (HDP) 300
    low density (LDP) 300
Population of world 229
Potassium 83, 84, 85
Potassium chloride 84, 85
Potassium dichromate (VI) 147, 286
Potassium hydroxide 85
Potassium iodide 85, 147
Potassium manganate (VII) 48, 147, 251, 286
Precipitation 148, 166
Propane 351
Propanol 285, 351
Propanone 69
Propene 285, 296, 351
Proteins 305, 307
    breakdown of 305
Proton donor 163
Protons 62, 161, 318
Purity 38
Pyrolysis 303

Question papers, terms used 11
Questions
    essay 11
    matching pairs 10
    multiple choice 11
    objective 10
    structured 11

Radioactivity 317, 318
    uses of 319
Radioisotopes 318, 319
Radon 90
Reactant 144
Reaction, endothermic 137
Reaction, energetics of 138
Reaction, exothermic 137
Reaction, types 147, 148, 149
Reaction, speed of 142
Reaction techniques 38
Reactions, incomplete 125
    reversible 125, 137, 145
Reactivity and displacements 189
Reactivity series and cell emf's 108
Reactivity series for anions 103
Reactivity series for cations 103
Reactivity series for metals 184, 350
Reactivity series for non-metal 350
Recycling of metals 193
Redox 146, 147

Redox reactions, testing for 147
Reduction 103, 149, 188, 190, 192
Refineries, siting of 234
Relative atomic mass 63, 124
Relative molecular mass 124
Respiration 220
Residue 35, 166
Resistor 101
Resources, life span of 192
Reversible reactions 125, 137, 145, 149
Rock cycle 331
Rocks 330, 331, 332, 333, 334, 335
Rubidium 83
Rust, prevention of 198
Rusting 198, 221

Sacrificial protection 221
Saliva 304
Salts 159, 165
    analysis of 169
    preparation of 165
    uses of 168
Saponify 306
Saturated hydrocarbons 282
Sea of electrons 72, 100
Sedimentary rock 332
Sedimentation 212
Separation 35, 38
Semi-conductors 100
Semi-metals 80
Sharing of electrons 65, 66
Shellac 286
Shells of electrons 63, 64
Silicates 87
Silicon 70, 87
Silicon chip 70
Silicon dioxide 70, 71
Silver bromide 144
Silver chloride 169
Single bond 65
Slag 196
Soap, preparation of 308
    washing action of 308
Sodium 65, 83, 88, 105, 106
Sodium chlorate (I) 253
Sodium chlorate (V) 253
Sodium chloride 85, 88, 105, 106, 148
    bonding in 65
Sodium hydrogencarbonate 163, 164
Sodium hydroxide 83, 106
Sodium hypochlorite 253
Sodium nitrate 149
Sodium nitrite 149
Sodium oxide 84, 85
Sodium stearate 306
Sodium, manufacture of 105
Sodium tartrate 163
Soil 336, 337
Solder 182
Solid 49, 351
Solidifying 49, 351
Solvents 69
Sour gas 241
Spectator ions 123
Spelling, punctuation and Grammar (SPAG) 6
Starch 303
    breakdown of 304
    hydrolysis of 304
    test for 304
State symbols 123
States of matter 49, 351

Steel 182, 197
    high carbon 197
    medium carbon 197
    mild 197
Steels, manufacture of 197
Strands 2
Strontium 86, 319
Sub-atomic particles 62
Sublimation 260
Substitution reactions 282
Sugar 304
Sulphamic acid 164
Sulphates, testing for 241
Sulphur 235
Sulphur dioxide 227, 241
    properties of 241
Sulphur trioxide 238
Sulphur, allotropes of 235
    monoclinic 235
    rhombic 235
    sources of 235
    uses of 237
Sulphuric acid, manufacture of 237
    properties of 239
    siting of plant 239
Symbol 123
Syllabuses 5
Syndets 309
Synthesis 165
Synthetic polymers 297

Tartaric acid 163
Terephthalic acid 298
Terylene 299
    properties of 299
    uses of 299
Tetrachloromethane 67
Thermal decomposition 149
Thermal dissociation 149
Thermit process 188
Thermoplastic 300
Thermoplasticity 300
Three Mile Island disaster 317
Tippex 70
Titanium 192
Titration 167, 168
Transfer of electrons 65
Transition metals 91
    properties of 91
Trichloroethane 70
Trichloromethane 67
Tritium 62
Tungsten 180
Typical acids, properties of 160, 163

Universal indicator 160
Urea 233
Urea-formaldehyde resin 233

Valency 81, 91, 122
Vanadium (V) oxide 91
Variable resistor 101
Vinegar 163
Vitamins 307
Volcanoes 342
Vulcanising 237

Water as a solvent 69
Water of crystallisation 167
Water
    de-ionised 264
    detection of 212
    distilled 264

    hardness of 263, 265
    pollution of 212
    properties of 212, 265
    purification of 212
    rain 264
    soft 264
    structure of 212
    uses of 212
Wax 281
Weightings in examinations 6
Wine 286
Winemaking 286
World population 229
Writing equations 122, 123, 318
Wrought iron 197

Xenon 90, 91
Xylene 69

Yeast 286

Zinc 198
    extraction of 198
    uses of 199